WATERGATE

AND THE WHITE HOUSE

JUNE 1972-JULY 1973

Date Due

MAR 6 '76			
NOV -1 75			

Onondaga Community College

Syracuse, New York

1

PRINTED IN U.S.A.

WATERGATE
AND THE WHITE HOUSE
JUNE 1972~JULY 1973

Editor: Edward W. Knappman

Contributing Editors: Mary Elizabeth Clifford, Evan
Drossman, Robert Kramer, Joseph Fickes,
Stephen Orlofsky, Gerald Satterwhite, Henry H.
Schulte, Jr.

Volume 1

FACTS ON FILE ▪ 119 WEST 57TH STREET ▪ NEW YORK, NEW YORK

WATERGATE
AND THE WHITE HOUSE
JUNE 1972–JULY 1973

Volume 1

Library of Congress Catalog Card No. 73-83049
ISBN 0-87196-352-3
9 8 7 6 5 4 3 2 1

PRINTED IN THE UNITED STATES OF AMERICA

Preface

Shortly before 2 a.m. on June 17, 1972 a security guard at the Watergate Office Building found the latch on a basement door taped open. Police officers summoned by the guard searched the building floor-by-floor until they found five men hiding on the sixth floor—inside the offices of the Democratic National Committee. The most serious case of corrupt practices in American political history slowly began to unfold.

The first part of this book is a detailed account of the evolution of the Watergate affair from the first report of the burglary through John Dean's testimony before a Senate select committee that President Nixon himself had helped to cover-up the affair. Written by the editors of the Facts On File Weekly News Digest, *this section reports every important event, statement and court decision—clearly, concisely and objectively.*

The subjective impact of the Watergate case on the American public will prove as important to history as the events themselves. To provide some insight into how the nation has reacted to the affair, the editors have carefully selected some 250 editorials from over 100 newspapers representing a full spectrum of interpretations and viewpoints. Looking back at these editorials, future historians will have documentary evidence of contemporary opinions and attitudes during the Watergate affair. All editorials are reprinted in full text, exactly as they appeared in cooperating newspapers.

The full political and legal consequences of Watergate cannot be measured or even guessed at as this book goes to press. Less than a month has passed since the final events recorded here occurred. Yet, in those few weeks questions about the guilt or innocence of individuals—and even of the President—have been eclipsed by a confrontation over fundamental constitutional issues. The resolution of those issues and the other events that will be recorded in the second volume of Watergate and the White House *will test Senator Ervin's assertion that Watergate "is the greatest tragedy this country has ever suffered."*

Edward W. Knappman
August 3, 1973

Contents:

EDITORIAL REACTION TO THE WATERGATE AFFAIR

Biographical Sketches

ALCH, Gerald: Former attorney to convicted Watergate conspirator James McCord, accused by McCord of participation in plot to keep him from testifying on Watergate, and clemency offer.

ANDREAS, Dwayne O.: Minnesota businessman whose campaign contribution was used to help finance the break-in.

BARKER, Bernard L.: Former CIA agent, friend of E. Howard Hunt, arrested at Watergate break-in, pled guilty at trial, later testified before Senate Watergate panel.

BITTMAN, William O.: Attorney for Hunt, allegedly co-ordinated effort to keep McCord and other Watergate defendants from testifying on the affair, reportedly passed on offers of executive clemency.

BUZHARDT, J. Fred: Former Defense department general counsel, appointed interim special counsel to the President on Watergate matters.

BYRNE Jr., Judge William M.: Pentagon Papers trial judge, dismissed charges vs. Ellsberg and Russo after disclosures of government misconduct.

CAULFIELD, John J.: Former aide to John Ehrlichman, resigned Treasury department post following allegations he had offered executive clemency to Watergate conspirator James McCord, admitted role in cover-up before Senate committee.

CHAPIN, Dwight L.: H. R. Haldeman's chief aide and appointments secretary to President Nixon, implicated in CRP espionage-sabotage activities, resigned from office.

COLSON, Charles W.: Former special counsel to the President, implicated in alleged CRP espionage plot, admitted ordering Hunt to fake cable linking President Kennedy to assassination of Diem.

COOK, G. Bradford: SEC chairman, resigned post following Vesco disclosures.

COX, Archibald: Harvard Law School professor, appointed special Watergate prosecutor by Attorney General Richardson.

CUSHMAN Jr., Gen. Robert E.: Marine Corps commandant, testified that as deputy CIA director he gave assistance to "plumbers" in burglary of Ellsberg's psychiatrist's office.

DASH, Samuel: Chief counsel and staff director for Senate Select Committee investigating Watergate.

DEAN 3rd, John W.: Counsel to the President, helped to coordinate the cover-up, subsequently forced to resign, testified to President Nixon's knowledge of cover-up at Senate hearings.

EHRLICHMAN, John D.: Adviser to the President on domestic affairs, implicated in Watergate cover-up, tied to break-in at Ellsberg's psychiatrist's office, resigned from office.

ELLSBERG, Daniel: Defendant in Pentagon Papers trial, released because of government misconduct by the White House "plumbers" group.

ERVIN Jr., Sen. Sam J.: Chairman of Senate Select Committee on Presidential Campaign activities investigating Watergate affair.

GONZALEZ, Virgilio R.: Associate of Bernard Barker, arrested at Watergate break-in, pled guilty.

GRAY 3rd, L. Patrick: Nominated as FBI director, admitted destroying sensitive portion of Hunt's files, asked for his nomination to be withdrawn.

HALDEMAN, H. R.: White House chief of staff, implicated in Watergate cover-up, accused of organizing GOP espionage operations, resigned from office.

HELMS, Richard M.: CIA director, named ambassador to Iran, approved help for Hunt in support of "plumbers" group operations.

HUNT Jr., E. Howard: Former White House consultant, pled guilty to role in Watergate conspiracy, later linked to the cover-up and "plumbers" group operations. His wife Dorothy, who was killed in a December 1972 plane crash, was channel for money from CRP to defendants.

HUSTON, Tom Charles: White House staff assistant, in 1970 allegedly formulated an illegal plan for spying on domestic radicals that was approved by Nixon.

KALMBACH, Herbert L.: Former personal attorney to President Nixon and a major GOP fund raiser, implicated in the cover-up and payoffs to Watergate defendants.

GARMENT, Leonard: Replaced Dean as counsel to the President.

KISSINGER, Dr. Henry A.: President Nixon's national security adviser, admitted to authorizing wiretaps on National Security Council personnel.

KLEINDIENST, Richard G.: Attorney general, resignation announced with Haldeman's and Ehrlichman's, linked to taps on newsmen.

KROGH Jr., Egil: Former White House aide, resigned as Transportation undersecretary following implication in burglary of Ellsberg's psychiatrist's office, member of "plumbers" group.

LaRUE, Frederick C.: Former aide to Committee for the Re-Election of the President director Mitchell, transmitted payoffs to Watergate defendants.

LIDDY, G. Gordon: Former presidential assistant and, at time of Watergate raid, counsel to the Finance Committee for the Committee to Re-Elect the President, tried and convicted for involvement in Watergate conspiracy, member of "plumbers" group.

MAGRUDER, Jeb Stuart: Former deputy director of the Committee to Re-Elect the President, resigned as assistant Commerce secretary, admitted involvement in Watergate break-in and cover-up, implicated Mitchell at Senate Watergate hearings.

MALEK, Frederick V.: Formerly in charge of recruiting personnel for Nixon Administration and a deputy campaign manager, deputy director of Office of Management and Budget, alleged to have been involved in GOP espionage scheme.

MARDIAN, Robert C.: Former assistant attorney general, implicated in CRP espionage scheme and Watergate cover-up.

MARTINEZ, Eugenio: Associate of Bernard Barker, arrested at Watergate break-in, pled guilty.

McCORD Jr., James W.: Former CIA agent and, at time of arrest at Watergate break-in, Security coordinator for the Committee to Re-Elect the President, tried and convicted for Watergate role, named Mitchell, Magruder and Dean in Senate testimony.

MITCHELL, John N.: Former U.S. attorney general, director of the Committee to Re-Elect the President, allegedly approved the Watergate break-in budget and ordered evidence destroyed, indicted for dealings with financier Vesco.

MOORE, Richard A.: Former special counsel to the President, disputed Dean's testimony at Senate Watergate hearings.

ODLE Jr., Robert C.: Director of administration for Nixon re-election committee, linked by the General Accounting Office to secret cash disbursements during 1968 campaign, testified before Senate committee on secret files.

PARKINSON, Kenneth W.: Attorney for re-election committee, accused of participation in cover-up.

PETERSEN, Henry E.: Assistant attorney general, assigned as interim Watergate prosecutor in April 1973.

PORTER, Herbert L.: Former scheduling director of the Committee to Re-Elect the President, cited for GOP campaign contribution irregularities, admitted in Senate testimony that he committed perjury at Watergate trial.

REISNER, Robert A. F.: Administrative assistant to Magruder, testified that Mitchell and White House received information gained by illegal wiretaps of Democratic offices and that sensitive files were destroyed after break-in.

RICHARDSON, Elliot L.: Former secretary of HEW, Defense department, appointed attorney general to replace Kleindienst, named Archibald Cox special Watergate prosecutor.

RICHEY, Judge Charles R.: Federal judge who presided over Democratic civil suit vs Committee to Re-Elect the President.

RUCKELSHAUS, William D.: Former head of Environmental Protection Agency, appointed interim director of FBI following Gray's withdrawal.

SCHLESINGER, James R.: Former AEC chairman, CIA director, replaced Richardson as Defense secretary, testified on CIA assistance given Hunt and Liddy for "plumbers" operation.

SEGRETTI, Donald H.: California lawyer indicted for role in GOP espionage-sabotage operations.

SILBERT, Earl J.: Government prosecutor at trial of seven Watergate conspirators.

SIRICA, Judge John J.: Judge at trial of Watergate conspirators; charged that the prosecution had failed to develop all the facts behind the break-in.

SLOAN Jr., Hugh W.: Treasurer of Nixon re-election organization, later disclosed details of secret GOP funds and payments to Liddy.

STANS, Maurice H.: Chief GOP fund raiser and chairman of Finance Committee to Re-Elect the President, accused of campaign fund violations and payoffs to Watergate defendants, indicted in Vesco affair.

STRACHAN, Gordon C.: General counsel to USIA, former aide to Haldeman, resigned following allegations of links to Watergate plotters and subsequent cover-up.

STURGIS, Frank A.: Arrested at Watergate break-in, pled guilty.

ULASEWICZ, Anthony T.: Retired New York City detective, conducted investigations for White House, testified at Senate hearings on role in payoff to Watergate defendants.

VESCO, Robert L.: Financier, indicted for illegal contributions to GOP and for mutual fund manipulations.

WALTERS, Vernon A.: Deputy CIA director, disclosed that White House aides had attempted to enlist agency's aid for "plumbers" group's operations.

YOUNG Jr., David R.: National Security Council member, resigned following reports of involvement in burglary of Ellsberg's psychiatrist's office, member of "plumbers" group.

ZIEGLER, Ronald L.: Presidential press secretary, repeatedly denied White House involvement in the Watergate affair, declared these denials "inoperative" following Nixon's April 17 speech.

Watergate Developments: June 1972-July 1973

1972

Democratic headquarters raided. Five men were seized at gunpoint at 2 a.m. June 17 in the headquarters of the Democratic National Committee in Washington. Alerted by a security guard, police apprehended five men, along with cameras and electronic surveillance equipment in their possession, after file drawers in the headquarters had been opened and ceiling panels removed near the office of Democratic National Chairman Lawrence F. O'Brien.

Those arrested and charged with second-degree burglary were: Bernard L. Barker, alias Frank Carter; James W. McCord, alias Edward Martin; Frank Angelo Fiorini, alias Edward Hamilton; Eugenio L. Martinez, alias Gene Valdes; Raul Godoy, alias V. R. Gonzales. All but McCord were from Miami and all of them were reported to have had links at one time or another with the Central Intelligence Agency (CIA).

McCord, who had retired from the CIA in 1970 after 19 years with the agency, currently was employed as a security agent by both the Republican National Committee and the Committee for the Re-Election of the President.

Barker, apparently the leader of the raid, reportedly played some role for the CIA in the abortive invasion of Cuba in 1961 and had met in Miami in early June with E. Howard Hunt, the CIA official in charge of the invasion. Hunt recently was a consultant to Charles W. Colson, special counsel to President Nixon and other high White House officials. The White House confirmed this June 19 and said Hunt had ended his consulting work March 29.

Nixon's campaign manager, John N. Mitchell, said June 18 that none of those involved in the raid were "operating either on our behalf or with our consent." O'Brien called June 18 for an FBI investigation. A full-scale investigation by the FBI was announced by the Justice Department June 19.

At a news conference June 20, O'Brien called the raid a "blatant act of political espionage" and announced the party was filing a $1 million civil lawsuit against the Committee to Re-Elect the President and the raiders on charges of invasion of privacy and violation of civil rights of the Democrats.

Citing the "potential involvement" of Colson, O'Brien said there was 'a developing clear line to the White House."

Mitchell responded later June 20 with a statement deploring the raid and denouncing the Democratic lawsuit as "demagoguery" by O'Brien. White House Press Secretary Ronald L. Ziegler said June 20 Colson had "assured me that he has in no way been involved in this matter."

Nixon denies White House involvement. President Nixon told reporters attending an impromptu news conference in his office June 22 that "the White House has had no involvement whatever" in the Watergate raid. Such a raid, Nixon said, "has no place in our electoral process or in our governmental process."

Ex-White House consultant linked. The White House was brought into the case when the FBI began a nationwide search July 1 for E. Howard Hunt Jr., a former White House consultant whose name had been linked to two of the men arrested at the Democrats' headquarters.

The search was called off July 7 when Hunt, still in hiding, said through his attorney that he would meet with federal authorities investigating the case. Hunt's lawyer, William C. Bittman, said July 7 that Hunt would appear when the government "wants him."

Hunt, a former official with the Central Intelligence Agency, was linked to the break-in when his name and home telephone number were found in address books of two of the five men arrested during the raid. It was later revealed that Hunt had once been a partner with Barker in several business ventures in Central America.

Probes into Democratic HQ raid. Private and official investigations into the June 17 break-in at the Democratic National Committee's headquarters in Washington followed new leads which added more mystery to the affair.

The new leads brought into the case the White House, the Justice Department, the Federal Bureau of Investigation, Congress and the courts.

The case focused on the courts Aug. 11 when a U.S. district court judge in Washington refused to postpone until after the November election a $1 million civil suit against the Committee for the Re-election of the President and the suspects charged with breaking into the Democrats' offices at the Watergate building complex.

(The five suspects, Bernard L. Barker, James W. McCord, Frank Fiorini, Eugenio Martinez and Raul Godoy, were all free on bail.)

The re-election committee had asked Judge Charles R. Richey to put the case off until after Nov. 7 on the ground that a hearing now could cause "incalculable" damage to the Republicans.

When the case first broke, the five suspects were charged only with burglary. Subsequent disclosures tied them to personnel and funds from the Committee for the Re-election of the President.

Richey's order cleared the way for Lawrence F. O'Brien, former chairman of the Democratic National Committee, to begin taking depositions from persons connected with the case. O'Brien said Aug. 15 his attorney would take formal statements from at least 13 men, including John N. Mitchell, President Nixon's former campaign manager; Maurice Stans, Nixon's finance chairman; E. Howard Hunt Jr., a former White House consultant; Charles W. Colson, special counsel to the President; and G. Gordon Liddy, former Nixon finance counsel.

O'Brien, citing undisclosed new evidence, said the Democrats' headquarters had been wiretapped for some time before the June 17 break-in.

Election agency, FBI to audit GOP funds—The Office of Federal Elections, a new Congressional watchdog agency, and the FBI joined the case Aug. 1, opening investigations into the financial records of the Committee to Re-elect the President.

Both inquiries were announced one day after the Washington Post reported that a $25,000 cashier's check apparently intended for Nixon's re-election campaign had been deposited in April in a bank account of Bernard L. Barker, one of the men arrested during the break-in.

According to the Post July 31, the check was made out by a Florida bank to Kenneth H. Dahlberg, the Republicans' Midwest finance chairman. Dahlberg confirmed the existence of the check July 31, but said he did not know how it had gotten into Barker's account. Dahlberg said "I gave it [the check] to Maurice Stans, and that's absolutely the end of it as far as I knew."

Bank records showed that Barker deposited the $25,000 check April 20 in the Republic National Bank in Miami, the same day he deposited four checks totaling $89,000 from a lawyer in Mexico. Barker April 24 withdrew $25,000 in the form of a check drawn to himself.

When Barker and the four other men were arrested, authorities found 53 $100 bills on them. Federal investigators traced the bills through the serial numbers to Barker's Miami bank account.

The Office of Federal Elections, a new agency within the General Accounting Office, began studying the financial-disclosure reports of the re-election committee to determine whether it had violated the Federal Election Campaign Act. Phillip S. Hughes, director of the elections office, said the agency was looking into three or four possible violations of the campaign act.

The FBI opened its investigation by getting from the federal elections office copies of 250 pages of material filed by the Nixon re-election committee. The FBI refused, however, to comment on the details of its probe.

Stans, in charge of finances for Nixon's re-election, denied Aug. 8 that money intended for GOP campaign chests had helped finance the break-in at the Democrats' headquarters.

Stans reportedly told federal investigators that the $25,000 check was passed to first one and then another finance official on the Nixon re-election committee. The last official to have the check, Stans said, was G. Gordon Liddy, finance counsel of the campaign. According to Stans, Liddy exchanged the check with someone else for $25,000 in cash, which was deposited in the Nixon campaign treasury.

McGovern denounces break-in. Democratic presidential candidate Sen. George McGovern (S.D.) told a United Automobile Workers union in Lordstown, Ohio Aug. 15 that the Watergate break-in was "the kind of thing you ex-

pect under a person like Hitler." (Clark MacGregor, chairman of Nixon's re-election committee, denounced the remark Aug. 16 as "character assassination.")

Democrats accuse GOP of spying. The Democratic party accused Republicans Sept. 11 of conspiring "to commit political espionage" against Democrats, and the Republicans accused the Democrats Sept. 13 of using the federal courts as "an instrument for creating political headlines." Both actions involved the recent case in which five persons were arrested during a break-in at the Democratic party headquarters in the Watergate office building in the District of Columbia June 17.

The Democrats Sept. 11 sought to amend a court action initiated against the five raiders by including as defendants Maurice H. Stans, finance chairman of the Nixon campaign, three other campaign aides and the Committee to Re-elect the President. The three other aides named were Hugh W. Sloan Jr., former treasurer of the committee, G. Gordon Liddy, former finance counsel to the committee, and E. Howard Hunt Jr., a former White House counsultant who was an intelligence agent for the committee.

The Democrats also sought to raise the amount of damages being sought from $1 million to $3.2 million.

The broadened complaint charged that Stans and Sloan had delivered $114,000 to finance an "espionage squad" and had stated that the funds were accounted for in the committee's records although the records had been destroyed. It also charged that Liddy and Hunt led an espionage squad formed to break into Democratic offices to obtain and photograph documents and install wiretaps and eavesdropping devices. The complaint also charged that Liddy and Hunt were with the raiders seized at Democratic headquarters June 17 but were warned the police were coming and withdrew.

Other Democratic charges in the new complaint were that: (a) the spy squad had broken into the Democratic National Committee offices before May 25 and stolen and photographed private documents of committee chairman Lawrence F. O'Brien; (b) O'Brien's phone was tapped from May 25 to June 17 and a listening post set up across the street from the Watergate at a motor lodge; (c) Liddy, Hunt and James W. McCord, chief security officer of the Committee to Re-elect the President and one of those arrested at the Watergate, made periodic visits to the listening post and McCord prepared confidential memorandums of the conversations; (d) the squad tried to break into the headquarters of Sen. George McGovern to install wiretaps; (e) the break-in June 17 at Watergate was to repair existing wire-

taps, establish new ones and steal and photograph documents.

The GOP countersuit—Clark Mac-Gregor, President Nixon's campaign director, announced Sept. 13 that the Committee to Re-elect the President had filed a countersuit that day in federal court seeking $2.5 million in damages from O'Brien. It accused O'Brien of having used the court "as a forum in which to publicize accusations against innocent persons which would be libelous if published elsewhere" and of "using his civil action to improperly conduct a private inquisition while a grand jury investigation is in progress."

MacGregor said the Democratic suit, and the attempt to amend it, were "unlawful and political in nature" and that Democratic counsel had "abused the subpoena powers of the court to parade innocent witnesses before the public in a concerted effort to create an appearance of guilt by association." The Democrat's attorney in the case, Edward Bennett Williams, had taken secret depositions from 13 persons, including former Nixon campaign chief John N. Mitchell and finance chairman Stans.

The Republicans were also seeking dismissal of the Democratic suit, in a motion filed with the court Sept. 1, on the grounds that publicity concerning the raid case made it impossible to obtain a fair trial and that O'Brien no longer had the proper legal standing to bring suit since he had left the headquarters post to be McGovern's campaign chairman.

Stans filed a personal suit against O'Brien Sept. 14 contending, in reference to the amended Democratic suit, that he had been "falsely and maliciously" accused of "a number of criminal acts." Stans asked $2 million in compensatory and $3 million in punitive damages.

Other developments—McGovern, during a campaign trip to New Mexico, referred Sept. 9 to an attempt by "our opponents" to bug his headquarters early May 27, an attempt that was apparently foiled when the raiders discovered McGovern workers present. McGovern commented that "it is but a single step from spying on the political opposition to suppressing that opposition and the imposing of a one-party state in which the people's precious liberties are lost."

■ Michael Richardson, a Miami photography processor, disclosed Aug. 31 that he had processed, the week before the Watergate raid, 35 mm pictures of Democratic party documents, many of them to or from O'Brien, for two of the men arrested at Watergate—Bernard L. Barker and Frank Sturgis.

■ Republican National Chairman Robert Dole accused the McGovern campaigners Aug. 30 of "devious cover-ups in various fund-raising activities" and of "at least seven serious violations" of the campaign spending law. Dole accused the McGovern organization Sept. 4 of seven other "serious" violations of the law. In both instances, the Office of Federal Elections, an arm of the General Accounting Office, was asked to investigate the charges. The office had announced Aug. 30 it had already begun an audit of McGovern campaign records in a spirit of "even-handed treatment." The week before it had reported "apparent violations" of the new campaign law by the Nixon committee.

■ The citizens' group Common Cause filed suit Sept. 6 against the Finance Committee to Re-elect the President, the fund-raising branch of the Committee to Re-elect the President, to force disclosure of the names of contributors of $10 million collected before the new law became effective April 7.

7 indicted in capital raid. A federal grand jury in the District of Columbia Sept. 15 indicted seven persons, including two former White House aides, on charges of conspiring to break into the Democratic national headquarters in the capital.

The two former Nixon Administration aides indicted were: G. Gordon Liddy, a former presidential assistant on domestic affairs and, at the time of the headquarters raid June 17, counsel to the finance committee for the Committee to Re-elect the President; and E. Howard Hunt Jr., a former White House consultant and associate of Liddy.

The other five indicted were those seized by police inside the Watergate office building during the raid: James W. McCord, security coordinator for the GOP committee at the time of the raid; Bernard L. Barker, president of a Miami real estate concern who fled Cuba during the Castro revolution; Frank A. Sturgis, an associate of Barker active in the anti-Castro movement, who was originally identified as Frank A. Fiorini; Eugenio Martinez, a real estate salesman in Barker's firm; and Virgilio R. Gonzalez, a Miami locksmith and Barker associate.

According to the indictment: Liddy had been in telephone communication with Barker before the raid, and Barker with Hunt; McCord had rented a room at a motor lodge across from the Watergate from about May 5 through June 17, had bought a device to intercept wire and oral communications, had met with Liddy and Hunt May 26 and on May 27 had inspected with them the headquarters of Sen. George McGovern, then seeking the presidential nomination; Liddy gave McCord $1,600 in cash June 11-15; Liddy, Hunt, McCord and the four men from Miami, having in their possession a device to intercept oral communication and another to intercept wire communication, broke into the Democratic headquarters June 17 to steal property, tap phones and intercept telephone calls.

The indictment also accused Liddy, Hunt and McCord of intercepting phone calls from about May 25 up to or about June 16 in the Democratic offices, primarily the telephone of Robert Spence Oliver, executive director of the Associations of State Chairmen.

The indictment alleged burglary and possession of eavesdropping devices, brought under District of Columbia law, and conspiracy and interception and disclosure of telephone and oral communications, brought under federal law.

In announcing the indictment, Attorney General Richard G. Kleindienst said the investigation was "one of the most intensive, objective and thorough ... in many years, reaching out to cities all across the United States as well as into foreign countries." John W. Hushen, director of public information for the Justice Department, said "we have absolutely no evidence to indicate that any others should be charged."

The seven men charged in the case pleaded not guilty Sept. 19 and were released on bonds ranging from $10,000 to $50,000.

Democratic reaction—McGovern campaign chairman Lawrence F. O'Brien, who was Democratic national chairman at the time of the break-in, said Sept. 15 "we can only assume that the investigation will continue since the indictments handed down today reflect only the most narrow construction of the crime that was committed."

"In particular," O'Brien said, "we will continue to press for a far more thorough explanation of the funding of the crime that led to those indictments." O'Brien renewed the Democratic request that a special prosecutor be appointed by President Nixon to pursue the case. Hushen had said at his news conference that "the funding, as it applies to this case, was investigated and there was no evidence to charge anybody."

McGovern commented Sept. 15 that "the indictments do point up the seriousness in the matter and what now needs to be pursued is how it was funded and whether there are violations there, which there seem to be." He called for "an impartial investigation conducted by somebody entirely outside the Department of Justice."

In a statement Sept. 16, McGovern accused Nixon of ordering a "whitewash," deplored the "questions left unanswered" by the grand jury and linked the affair to "the moral standards of this nation." "There has been a growing pattern of immorality," McGovern said, "associated with the Russian wheat deal, with the ITT case, with the handling of campaign funds, and now the latest revelation with regard to the invasion of the Democratic headquarters."

McGovern said the "unanswered questions" in the case were: "Who ordered this act of political espionage? Who paid for it? Who contributed the $114,000 that went from the Nixon campaign committee to the bank account of one of the men arrested, and that paid off the spies for their work? Who received the memoranda of the tapped telephone conversation?"

McGovern indicated disbelief that the seven men indicted "dreamed up and carried out this shabby scheme to spy on the Democratic party all on their own, with no authority from above."

A Justice Department spokesman later Sept. 16 called McGovern's charges "a grievous attack on the integrity of the 23 good citizens" of the District of Columbia who served on the grand jury. Assistant Attorney General Henry E. Petersen said the department's investigation of the case had been "among the most exhaustive and far-reaching in my 25 years" in the department and involved 333 agents.

Civil suit developments. Assailing the reaction of both major political parties to the Watergate case, consumer advocate John F. Banzhaf 3rd applied to the federal court in Washington Sept. 18 to have a special prosecutor appointed to investigate the break-in. He made the request in a motion to intervene in the civil damage suit brought by O'Brien against the five men arrested at the scene.

U.S. District Judge Charles R. Richey dismissed the original Democratic suit Sept. 20 on a technicality, on the ground that the Democrats had failed to meet a court deadline for opposing a motion by the five defendants for dismissal of the suit. Richey's decision excluded as defendants in the suit the five men arrested at the scene of the raid.

However, Richey accepted the Democrats' amended version of their damage suit naming as defendants Liddy, Hunt, Nixon campaign finance chairman Maurice Stans and Hugh W. Sloan Jr., former treasurer of the Committee to Re-elect the President, and the committee itself.

Democratic counsel gave notice later Sept. 20 an appeal would be filed on Richey's ruling. The Democrats also requested the presence at a court conference on the suit of a representative of the attorney general so "physical and documentary evidence in his possession" from the criminal investigation could be examined.

Trial before election unlikely. U.S. Judge Charles R. Richey said Sept. 21 that "it will be impossible" to bring the Democratic party's civil suit in the Watergate case to trial before the Nov. 7 general election. Richey said he would extend his order barring depositions in his case until the persons under criminal indictment had been tried. The presiding judge in that case, Chief U.S. District Court Judge John J. Sirica, Sept. 26 granted a 14-day extension to defense and prosecution lawyers to file preliminary motions and responses. Action on these was not considered likely before Oct. 30.

Sirica issued a broad order Oct. 4 prohibiting anyone connected with the case from making public comments about it. Acting on a motion by one of the defendants, E. Howard Hunt Jr., Sirica barred all law enforcement agencies, the defendants, witnesses, potential witnesses, "including complaining witnesses and alleged victims, their attorneys and all persons acting for or with them in connection with this case," from making extrajudicial public statements to anyone, "including the news media."

Democratic presidential candidate George McGovern later Oct. 4 accused the Justice Department of entering into "a political agreement" with the defendants for silence on the case.

McGovern said he would not allow himself "to be muzzled or intimidated by any politically motivated directive from Richard Nixon" and intended to pursue his constitutional rights in "informing the public about this act of political espionage" in the Watergate raid.

Mitchell linked to secret GOP fund. The Washington Post reported Sept. 29 that former Attorney General John N. Mitchell controlled a secret Republican fund utilized for gathering information about the Democrats. The fund was said to have fluctuated between $350,000 and $700,000 and Mitchell was said to have approved withdrawals for almost a year before he left the Cabinet to become President Nixon's campaign manager.

The Post said former Commerce Secretary Maurice H. Stans later was among four persons in addition to Mitchell permitted to approve payments from the secret fund.

A spokesman for the Committee to Re-elect the President said there was "no truth" to the charges.

Gray upholds Administration probe. L. Patrick Gray 3rd, acting director of the Federal Bureau of Investigation, upheld the practice of the Nixon Administration itself investigating the Watergate case, involving former Administration aides and a Republican committee. Anyone who wrote that the Administration could not investigate itself, he said Oct. 2, was "really leveling a general indictment against all public officials."

He had taken the Watergate probe "under my own wing," Gray said, and "there's not been one single bit of pressure put on me or any of my special agents" concerning the probe.

Gray also discounted the possibility of presidential involvement in the Watergate incident. "It strains the credulity that the President of the United States—if he had a mind to—could have done a con job on the whole American people," he said.

House panel bars probe. The House Banking and Currency Committee Oct. 3 rejected a proposal to probe possible violations of banking laws in connection with the break-in at the Democratic headquarters in the Watergate Office Building in Washington and possible irregularities in Republican campaign financing. The vote was 20–15, with six of the panel's 22 Democrats voting with the majority.

Chairman Wright Patman (D, Tex.), who offered the proposal, accused the White House after the vote of "engineering" the rejection of the probe, which was set under his proposed resolution to subpoena some 40 individuals and organizations, including top Nixon campaign aides, for testimony. Patman predicted "that the facts will come out." "When they do," he said, "I am convinced they will reveal why the White House was so anxious to kill the committee's investigation. The public will fully understand why this pressure was mounted."

The committee had been subjected to insistent Republican lobbying against the probe. It also had received a Justice Department letter Oct. 2 expressing concern that a probe might jeopardize the right to a fair trial for defendants in the Watergate case.

The committee's ranking Republican, Rep. William B. Widnall (N.J.), denied Patman's accusation of White House pressure, saying he had had "no contact with the White House at all in connection with this investigation."

Ex-FBI agent delivered information. A former agent for the Federal Bureau of Investigation (FBI) disclosed Oct. 5 that he had delivered information obtained by espionage from the Democratic headquarters at the Watergate building in Washington to an official at the Nixon campaign office. In an interview published in the Los Angeles Times, the ex-FBI agent, Alfred C. Baldwin 3rd, said he had monitored telephone and other conversations at Watergate for three weeks while employed by the Committee to Re-elect the President, working from a room in a motor lodge across from Watergate.

Baldwin said the official to whom he delivered the information was not one of those indicted in the Watergate headquarters raid. Baldwin revealed that he, himself, was a member of the raid crew. He was not indicted after agreeing to cooperate with the Justice Department. He was a key witness for the government in the case.

The Washington Post reported Oct. 6 that Baldwin had informed the FBI that memorandums describing the intercepted Democratic conversations were sent to members of the White House staff and Nixon campaign staff.

The Post reported Oct. 10 that the Watergate raid was but part of a larger espionage and sabotage effort against the Democrats on behalf of the Nixon re-election effort. The newspaper quoted federal investigators as describing the intelligence operation by the Nixon campaign organization as "unprecedented in scope and intensity." The story reported attempts to disrupt campaigns of Democratic candidates for president. One such effort, according to the story, involved a letter used in the New Hampshire primary against Sen. Edmund S. Muskie (Me.). He was accused in it of having condoned use of the epithet "Canucks" in reference to Americans with French-Canadian background. Post reporter Marilyn Berger reported that White House aide Ken W. Clawson, deputy director of communications for the executive branch, had told her Sept. 25 he had written the letter, which had been ascribed at the time to a Paul Morrison of Deerfield Beach, Fla. Attempts to locate such a person had failed. The Post also reported that Clawson later denied authorship of the letter.

The Post article also related an account from three attorneys that they had been offered, and rejected, proposals to work as agents provocateurs on behalf of the Nixon campaign. The Post report said the FBI had information that at least 50 undercover Nixon operatives were at work throughout the country in an attempt to disrupt and spy on Democratic campaigns.

(Rep. Bella Abzug [D, N.Y.] reported Oct. 10 that evidence of wiretaps on her Washington and New York Congressional offices had been discovered. CBS news commentator Walter Cronkite disclosed Oct. 11 that a man impersonating McGovern campaign director Frank Mankiewicz had telephoned him about campaign coverage. Cronkite said he spoke later with Mankiewicz, who said he had not made the call. Mankiewicz Oct. 10 reported 10 alleged incidents of political sabotage.)

Nixon holds news conference. President Nixon responded to Sen. George McGovern's charges of corruption in his administration at a surprise news conference in his office Oct. 5. It was his first news conference since Aug. 29.

The President was asked why his Administration did not "make a clean breast about what you were trying to get done at the Watergate?" Nixon said "that decision" had been made "at a lower level," that the FBI investigation of the raid made the Hiss investigation look like "a Sunday School exercise" and that he would not comment on it because grand jury indictments had been handed down and the case was before the courts.

Sirica eases ban on comment. Chief Justice John J. Sirica of the U.S. district court in Washington Oct. 6 eased his ban against "extrajudicial" comment on the Watergate case by deleting from his previous order the phrase "all witnesses and potential witnesses including complaining witnesses and alleged victims."

Democratic spokesmen had complained that the ban might endanger their right to discuss the case by putting them in the position of contempt of the order. Sirica said he had not intended his order to curb Congressional activity, political debate or news reports.

Company contribution tied to Watergate. The Washington Post reported Oct. 6 that federal sources had identified a $100,000 contribution to the Nixon campaign, part of which had previously been traced through Mexico to possession by one of the Watergate raiders, to have come from the Gulf Resources and Chemical Corp. of Houston.

Lack of quorum. Chairman Wright Patman (D, Tex.) of the House Banking and Currency Committee attempted to reconvene his committee Oct. 12 to reconsider its rejection of a Watergate probe, but failed to gain a quorum for the meeting or the presence of four Nixon aides for testimony. Three declined on advice of counsel and another on a plea of executive privilege.

Patman announced Oct. 10 that the General Accounting Office (GAO) had acceded to a request for "a full-scale investigation" of the Watergate raid.

Democrats stress sabotage issue. Democratic candidates George McGovern and R. Sargent Shriver stressed the Watergate raid and other Republican sabotage efforts in campaign appearances during October.

Sen. McGovern told a Los Angeles labor group Oct. 16 the Nixon Administration had put more manpower into the effort to "sabotage" the Democratic campaign (50 or more persons) than into planning to convert the economy to a peacetime basis (13 persons). He said the sabotage effort, which he described as an attempt "to literally destroy the political opposition," was "unprecedented in this country." (McGovern's speech was disrupted when a fire marshal unaccountably tried to clear a TV crew from an aisle although the room was far from crowded.)

At a news conference in Passaic, N.J. Oct. 17, Shriver, referring to the raid charged that President Nixon was either "guilty of immoral and illegal acts" if he knew what was going on, or, if he did not know, was "impotent and incompetent."

Shriver repeated that charge in New York Oct. 18. Speaking to a college audience, Shriver said "how can a man claim to know what's going on inside the Kremlin and not know what's going on in his own committee?"

Campaigning is Essington, Pa. Oct. 19, McGovern accused Nixon of having "no respect for constitutional government and personal freedom." A president who sent agents to wiretap and sabotage his political opponents, he said, was "the kind of a man who won't hesitate to wiretap your union hall, or your

law office, or your university, or your church or even your home."

McGovern said Oct. 25 that the nation faced a "moral and a constitutional crisis of unprecedented dimensions" because of the Nixon Administration's "widespread abuse of power."

McGovern sought to link this issue, and the issue of alleged political sabotage by the Republicans, directly to the President. "The men who have collected millions in secret money, who have passed out special favors, who have ordered political sabotage, who have invaded our offices in the dead of night—all of these men work for Mr. Nixon," he said. " . . . . Their power comes from him alone. They act on his behalf. . . ."

Yet the President had barred independent investigation of the sabotage allegations, McGovern said, and "he refused to answer questions from either the press or the people" and "stays hidden in the White House, hoping you will mistake silence for innocence."

In Hartford, Conn. Oct. 30, he said the next president, "no matter who he is, is not going to rule like a Roman emperor, we hope." In Pittsburgh later, he said a vote for Nixon would be a vote "for Watergate corruption, Nixon recession, Connally oil and Republican reaction."

In a statement made at the Manchester, N.H. airport Nov. 3, Shriver said that President Nixon and Donald Segretti, who had been accused of political sabotage by the Democrats, had stayed in the same Portland Ore. hotel Sept. 25-26.

Later Nov. 3, Shriver asked a large crowd at Holy Cross College in Worcester, Mass., "Do you think it's a coincidence that the two men were there together?" (The White House denied Nov. 5 that the two men had ever met.)

GOP spying linked to White House. A report in the Oct. 23 issue of Time Magazine (made available Oct. 15) linked a Republican political sabotage effort against the Democrats directly to the White House. It said Los Angeles attorney Donald H. Segretti, previously identified as a recruiter for an undercover spy operation against Democratic campaigns had been hired in September 1971 by Dwight Chapin, a deputy assistant to President Nixon, and Gordon Strachan, a White House staff assistant. Time said the information came from Justice Department files.

The report said Segretti was paid more than $35,000 for his services by Herbert Kalmbach, Nixon's personal attorney, provided by the Committee to Re-elect the President out of funds kept in the safe of Maurice Stans, chief political fundraiser for Nixon.

According to the Washington Post Oct. 15, California attorney Lawrence Young, in a sworn statement, said Segretti had told him "Dwight Chapin was a person I reported to in Washington" and he received political sabotage

and spying assignments from E. Howard Hunt Jr., an ex-White House aide among those indicted in the break-in at the Democratic national headquarters in the Watergate building in Washington.

The New York Times Oct. 18 linked Segretti to a number of telephone calls made in the spring to the White House and to Chapin's home and to Hunt's home and office.

In another development, the Times had reported Oct. 13 from "sources close to the Watergate investigation" that former Assistant Attorney General Robert C. Mardian had obtained confidential information from the Justice Department for use in Nixon's political campaign after leaving the department to work for the Committee to Re-elect the President. The report said that on at least one occasion Mardian, who had been head of the Internal Security Division while at the Justice Department, had sent Hunt and G. Gordon Liddy, another indicted in the Watergate case, to the department to pick up information. The report said Mardian denied the latter and a spokesman for him conceded he had consulted the department after leaving it but only for information about possible civil disturbances at the Republican convention. The information, the spokesman said, was available to both parties.

The Administration Oct. 16 rebutted the charges that a political sabotage and spying effort involved high Nixon aides. White House Press Secretary Ronald L. Ziegler called the charges "hearsay, innuendo and guilt by association" and said he refused to "dignify" them by discussing them. Clark MacGregor, chairman of the Nixon re-election effort, attacked the Post for using "unsubstantiated charges" to "maliciously" link the White House to Watergate.

Neither spokesman would discuss specific items of the charges. MacGregor left the room after reading his statement, although Ziegler denied that Segretti had ever worked for the White House and MacGregor said he had not worked for either the political or financial branches of the campaign structure.

The Post's executive editor, Benjamin C. Bradlee, said later that none of the facts in its investigative reports about Watergate had been "successfully challenged."

Haldeman linked to secret GOP fund. The Nixon Administration Oct. 25 denied a report linking H. R. Haldeman, President Nixon's White House chief of staff, with a "secret" campaign fund used in part to finance intelligence gathering and political espionage. The report, published by the Washington Post Oct. 25, said Haldeman was one of five persons authorized to approve payments from the GOP fund.

The other four authorized to approve payments were said to be former Attorney General John N. Mitchell and former Commerce Secretary Maurice C.

Stans, Jeb Stuart Magruder, a former White House assistant to Haldeman and currently deputy director of the President's re-election campaign, and Herbert W. Kalmbach, the President's personal lawyer.

The secret fund was reported to have totaled $700,000 at times and to have been used in part to pay for an undercover effort to discredit or hinder Democratic campaigns. Funds involved in financing the break-in at Democratic national headquarters in the Watergate building in Washington also reportedly derived from the secret fund, whose only record reportedly had been destroyed by a Nixon campaign official after five men were arrested on the scene at Watergate. The General Accounting Office previously had reported the existence of a $350,000 fund in cash kept in a safe in Stans' office.

The Washington Post story Oct. 25 cited sources as federal investigators and accounts of sworn grand jury testimony taken in the Watergate case.

The report carried Haldeman's denial of the story as "untrue" from a statement issued through the White House press office.

The story also was denied Oct. 25 by White House Press Secretary Ronald L. Ziegler and Nixon campaign director Clark MacGregor. Ziegler said Haldeman never had access to such a fund and, in fact, such a fund never existed. MacGregor said he had been assured by Haldeman that he had never had authority to disburse campaign funds for the President's re-election.

Ziegler also attacked the Post for a "political effort," "character assassination" and "the shoddiest type of journalism."

McGovern aide Frank Mankiewicz Oct. 24 requested the Justice Department to investigate "a clandestine campaign of bribery and espionage and sabotage financed with secret Nixon campaign funds." Attorney General Richard G. Kleindienst told newsmen the same day the department had no "credible evidence" that any federal laws were broken by alleged political sabotage by GOP campaign operatives. He said no special investigation of the reported sabotage was under way.

More reports of sabotage—There were reports from Florida of an unusual amount of phony campaign literature having been mailed during the presidential primary there early in 1972 and of fraudulent press releases on news conferences or campaign events that were not scheduled. Some of the material was reported to have been so fraudulent, such as one accusing Sen. Henry M. Jackson (D, Wash.) of sexual misconduct, that the U.S. attorney's office in Tampa had been asked to investigate.

U.S. Attorney John L. Briggs announced in Jacksonville Oct. 20 that that particular item, a letter also accusing Sen. Hubert H. Humphrey (D, Minn.) of

a drunken driving arrest, had been turned over to the Federal Bureau of Investigation and he had been unaware until then that it had been sent through the mail. Jackson wired Briggs Oct. 23 to protest that it had taken seven months to get action on the request for an investigation, noting that the letter had been turned over to the U.S. attorney's office in Tampa March 13 along with a postmarked envelope indicating the mailing.

Special GOP fund conceded. President Nixon's campaign manager Clark MacGregor confirmed Oct. 26 the existence of a special Republican campaign fund controlled by top Nixon aides. He said the fund, which he acknowledged could have amounted to as much as $350,000, had been disbursed for preliminary planning of Nixon's campaign and, in one instance, to gather information on possible organized disruption at GOP rallies in New Hampshire.

MacGregor, appearing on a (taped) television interview with Elizabeth Drew of the National Public Affairs Center for Television, denied that the fund had been used to finance a sabotage effort against the Democrats or that White House aide H. R. Haldeman had any tie whatever to the funds. Whether the fund was a "secret" one, he said was a matter of "semantics," since there was no attempt to maintain a hidden fund to finance improper activities, and most of the funds had been collected before the new campaign-fund law went into effect April 7. Donors before that time did not have to be identified.

MacGregor identified Maurice Stans, Nixon's chief fund raiser, and G. Gordon Liddy, counsel for the Finance Committee to Re-elect the President, as two of the top Nixon aides having control over the special fund. The others he named were former Nixon campaign manager John N. Mitchell, Jeb Stuart Magruder, a deputy Nixon campaign manager, and Herbert L. Porter, an advance man for Nixon's re-election campaign.

Sabotage recruitment reported—There were further reports of attempts to recruit persons to sabotage Democratic campaign activities and gather political espionage.

The New York Times reported Oct. 25 that a young California businessman had said he had engaged in "negative campaigning" and had been recruited and paid by Donald H. Segretti to sabotage Democratic rallies and collect political information from Democratic headquarters. Segretti had been named as an undercover operator against Democratic campaigners. Another Times report Oct. 28 said two California college students admitted working for Segretti collecting political data in their areas.

The Washington Post reported Oct. 26 that two Fresno, Calif. lawyers reported rejecting overtures from Segretti to enlist in the effort against the Democrats. The Post reported Nov. 1 having been in-

formed the day before by a California lawyer of a request from Segretti for him to try to recruit "radical, long-haired kids" to stage a demonstration at the Republican National Convention.

Time magazine carried a report Nov. 6 that federal investigators had been told by Dwight L. Chapin, a deputy assistant to President Nixon, that he had hired Segretti to engage in disruptive tactics against the Democrats and by Nixon's personal attorney, Herbert W. Kalmbach, that he had paid Segretti from cash kept in Stans' office.

Watergate trial postponed. The trial of the men charged with the Watergate break-in, scheduled to start Nov. 15, was postponed until Jan. 8, 1973. Chief Judge John J. Sirica of the U.S. district court in Washington took the action Oct. 27 on the advice of a physician because of his painful nerve condition.

Milk funds, Watergate figures linked. Evidence revealed Oct. 28 in a suit, which charged that contributions made by dairy associations were actually political payoffs for an Administration-approved increase in the price of milk supports, linked those campaign contributions to Republicans implicated in the Watergate raid.

Testimony showed that E. Howard Hunt Jr., his wife, Dorothy, and Douglas Caddy served as chairmen of dummy committees used to secretly funnel the dairymen's contributions to the Nixon re-election effort. (Caddy, a lawyer, was contacted immediately after their arrest by those indicted for the Watergate breakin.)

E. Jackson Ritchie, a vice president of the Union Trust Co., also revealed that 49 committees were established in 1971 in the bank in Washington, where there were no campaign reporting laws, in order to avoid disclosure of the funds' sources.

The committees were then dissolved when the April 7 deadline for revealing the identity of donors took effect under the new federal law.

Union Trust Co. was owned by the Financial General Corp., a bank holding company. Another bank in its group, the First National Bank of Washington, later held several million dollars in GOP campaign funds without paying interest for the use of the money, the Washington Post reported Oct. 28. Gen. George Olmstead, chairman of Financial General and also treasurer of the Republican Congressional Campaign Committee, gave the orders to set up the dummy committees, Ritchie contended.

House unit reports on funds. A House Banking and Currency Committee staff report, released Oct. 31, charged that "at least $30,000" was channeled to the Committee to Re-Elect the President "through the Banque Internationale a Luxembourg" before April 7.

After that date, disclosure of the identity of donors was required. The report called for investigation of the foreign checks to determine if foreign nationals, barred under federal election laws from contributing to U.S. campaigns, had made donations to the GOP.

A re-election committee spokesman Oct. 31 termed the allegation a "dishonest collection of innuendo and fourth hand hearsay."

The report was the second issued by the House committee in the aftermath of the Watergate breakin.

The report also questioned whether $100,000 in GOP campaign funds, which had formed part of the money used to finance the Watergate raid and had been traced earlier by committee investigations from Houston to Mexico to Houston to Washington, was an "illegal corporate contribution disguised through the use of the Mexican transfer" because the money "originated in a corporate account [of the Gulf Resources and Chemical Corp.] in Houston."

The staff report also questioned how Walter T. Duncan, a Texas real estate speculator, was able to contribute $305,-000 "in the form of a single promissory note" to the Nixon campaign when, on Aug. 21, a few days after making the donation, Duncan defaulted on a $2.6 million loan.

A Houston bank, which had financed half the loan, later collapsed and the Federal Deposit Insurance Corp. (FDIC) took over receivership.

"The FDIC should make claim" on the GOP finance committee for the "amount of the [Duncan] loan," the report declared.

The Washington Post reported Oct. 28 that two GOP committees, which had channeled more than $200,000 to party coffers, had failed to file registration statements with the GAO's Office of Federal Elections. The law required that any political committee which anticipated making contributions or loans exceeding $1,000 register with the GAO within 90 days of organizing.

Barker convicted in Florida. Bernard L. Barker, one of those indicted in the raid on Democratic headquarters at the Watergate building in Washington, was found guilty in Miami Nov. 1 of falsely notarizing a signature on a $25,000 check that had been traced to a Republican fund-raiser and the Finance Committee to Re-elect the President. Barker was given a 60-day suspended jail sentence and his Florida notary public seal was revoked by Dade County Criminal Court Judge Paul L. Baker, who heard the case without a jury.

The signature in question was that of Kenneth H. Dahlberg, chairman of the Minnesota Nixon re-election committee, who testified that he had received the check as a GOP campaign contribution and had turned it over, after converting it into a cashier's check, to Maurice Stans, Nixon's chief campaign fund-raiser. Another witness, Hugh W. Sloan Jr,. former Nixon finance committee treasurer, testified he had received that check from Stans and turned it over to G. Gordon Liddy, the finance committee counsel. Like Barker, he was a defendant in the Democratic raid case.

Efforts to discover how Barker came into possession of the check were blocked by the defense attorney, who said the issue was confined to the notary seal on the check. As for that, Dahlberg testified that he did not know Barker and had not given him permission to notarize his signature and deposit the check in Barker's acount. Some of the cash drawn by Barker from this account after depositing the check was found in Barker's possession after his arrest at Watergate and later traced back to the Miami bank.

Judge forsees wide-ranging trial. During a pretrial conference on the criminal proceedings Dec. 4, Judge Sirica indicated that the political motivation of the break-in would be explored. The motivation behind the break-in and bugging, he said, was "one of the crucial issues" and the jury was "going to want to know the purpose" of the raid. "Was their sole purpose political espionage?" he asked. "Were they paid? Were there financial gains? Who started this? Who hired them, if anyone hired them? A whole lot is going to come out in this case."

Data on Hunt revealed. Convicted Watergate conspirator E. Howard Hunt's wife Dorothy was found dead in a jetliner crash near Midway Airport in Chicago Dec. 8 with $10,000 in cash in her purse in $100 bills. Hunt said Dec. 10 the money was intended for a business investment.

Newsman jailed. John F. Lawrence, chief of the Washington bureau of the Los Angeles Times, was jailed for several hours Dec. 19 after refusing to turn over to the U.S. district court in the District of Columbia tape recordings of an interview with a key government witness in the case involving the break-in at the Democratic party headquarters at the Watergate building.

The tapes recorded an interview with Alfred C. Baldwin 3rd, who said he had played a role in the break-in. The interview was conducted by Los Angeles Times reporters Jack Nelson and Ronald J. Ostrow and articles based on the interview, naming Baldwin as the source, were published. Lawyers for one of the seven defendants arrested in the break-in, E. Howard Hunt, Jr., requested the court to order the Times to produce the tapes for the possible impeachment of Baldwin when he testified in the trial, which was scheduled to begin Jan. 8, 1973.

The request, made Dec. 11, was upheld Dec. 14 by Chief Judge John J. Sirica of the Washington court, who approved subpoenas for Lawrence, as the paper's representative, and for Nelson and Ostrow. Baldwin had advised the court he had destroyed his own recordings of the interview.

The Times and the reporters asked the court to quash the subpoenas to protect "the people's right" to information. The interview, they said, had been obtained on the promise that the material would be held confidential unless Baldwin consented to disclosure.

Since the two interviewers disclosed they had turned over the tapes to the Times, Lawrence, who had played no direct part in the interview, became responsible for producing the tapes. Lawrence declined to surrender them Dec. 19, on the grounds it would be a violation of the First Amendment's guarantee of a free press. He was held in contempt of court and ordered by Sirica to be held in custody until he produced the tapes. The custody lasted for more than two hours until a three-judge panel of the U.S. court of appeals ordered his release pending a hearing the next day. The appeals court Dec. 20 continued the stay of sentence pending an appeal to the Supreme Court. But the contempt action was voided Dec. 21 when Baldwin released the Times from the pledge of confidentiality and the newspaper surrendered the tape recordings to Sirica for private inspection.

The Reporters Committee for the Freedom of the Press protested Dec. 21 that the latest case "represents a further serious erosion" of the First Amendment. The only reason Lawrence "escaped further imprisonment," it said, "was not by the protection of the First Amendment but because a news source backed down on the confidentiality privilege."

The Washington Post carried a report Dec. 8, based on an interview with a former White House personal secretary, that Hunt was one of a team of officials, known as the "plumbers," assigned by the White House to investigate leaks to the news media. A private, non-government telephone installed for use in the effort was apparently used almost exclusively for conversations between Hunt and Bernard L. Barker, another of the Watergate defendants, according to the secretary. She said the bills for the phone service were submitted for payment to an aide in the office of John Ehrlichman, President Nixon's chief domestic affairs aide.

White House Press Secretary Ronald L. Ziegler confirmed the "plumbers" operation Dec. 12 and said the work was supervised by Ehrlichman, but he said he did not believe Hunt had worked on the project. It "would be folly," Ziegler said, to associate use of the phone with the alleged bugging of Democratic headquarters in May and June since the special line was in use only from August 1971 to March 15, 1972.

1973

Kleindienst comments on Segretti. Attorney General Richard G. Kleindienst said at a news conference Jan. 4 that his office had "no indication" of any federal offense committed by Donald H. Segretti, who had been implicated in an alleged Republican attempt to sabotage Democratic presidential candidates in 1972.

Questioned on alleged violations of election laws, Kleindienst said the Justice Department had not yet decided whether to prosecute the Richard Nixon and George McGovern campaign organizations on irregularities uncovered by the General Accounting Office, and said such charges had no priority among 2,000 complaints that had been filed during the campaign.

Trial opens; Hunt pleads guilty. E. Howard Hunt Jr., a former White House consultant, pleaded guilty Jan. 11 to all six charges against him in the second day of the conspiracy trial of seven defendants charged in connection with the June 1972 break-in and alleged bugging of Democratic party national headquarters at the Watergate complex in Washington.

Hunt had offered the preceding day to plead guilty on three charges, but Chief Judge John J. Sirica of U.S. District Court in Washington said Jan. 11 he would refuse the offer, because of "the apparent strength of the government's case" against Hunt, and because the public must be assured "not only the substance of justice but also the appearance of justice." Hunt was freed on $100,000 bail pending sentencing.

Hunt told newsmen outside the courthouse that the prosecution's outline of the evidence presented to the jury the previous day had been "substantially" correct, [See below] but said that to his personal knowledge no "higher-ups" in the government were involved in any wider conspiracy. Hunt said he had believed that all his activities were "in the best interest of my country," and had been performed with the knowledge of the possible consequences.

The six counts, which carried a maximum sentence of 35 years, were conspiracy to obtain information illegally from the Democrats, breaking into and entering the Watergate headquarters, knowingly intercepting wire communications, attempting to intercept wire communications, attempting to intercept oral communications, and an additional breaking and entering charge.

Assistant U.S. Attorney Earl J. Silbert, chief prosecutor at the trial, said Jan. 10 that Hunt would be called before a reconvened federal grand jury to testify on "what knowledge he has, if any, of the involvement of others in the so-called Watergate case."

Silbert's two-hour opening statement Jan. 10 depicted the Watergate incident as part of a well-financed espionage program against the Democratic party and Democratic presidential candidates. According to Silbert, G. Gordon Liddy, one of the defendants and at that time counsel to the Committee to Re-elect the President, had been given $235,000 by other committee officials, Jeb Stuart Magruder and Herbert L. Porter, to uncover plans for demonstrations against Republicans campaigning for Nixon or against the Republican National Convention, and for other "special intelligence assignments," including a probe of certain campaign contributions made to a Democratic presidential candidate. Silbert said the committee kept few if any records on the funds, and said the prosecution could only account for $50,000.

Silbert said witnesses would show how Hunt and Liddy had recruited spies, including Thomas James Gregory, a student at Brigham Young University who, it was alleged, worked as an undercover agent on the staffs of Sens. Edmund S. Muskie and George S. McGovern. The prosecution planned to show that one of the defendants, James W. McCord Jr., security chief of the Re-election Committee, then attempted to bug McGovern campaign offices, in conspiracy with the other defendants, Bernard Barker, Frank Sturgis, Eugenio Martinez and Virgilio Gonzales. All five had been apprehended at the Watergate.

The prosecutor charged that Liddy and Hunt were seen at the Watergate the night their co-defendants were arrested, and had demonstrated prior knowledge of the break-in attempt. One witness, Silbert said, would testify to having monitored about 200 personal and political phone calls from a tap on a telephone at the Democratic headquarters before June 17.

Defense attorneys, in opening arguments Jan. 10, stressed their contention that the defendants' had acted with "no criminal intent" or "no evil motive."

The jury of eight women and four men had been completed Jan. 9 after two days, over objections by defense attorneys that they had not been allowed to question witnesses in detail, and that Sirica's refusal to examine all the potential jurors individually would "be grounds for appeal" if their clients were convicted. The jurors were to be sequestered during the duration of the trial, along with five alternate jurors. One juror was replaced by Sirica Jan. 11 after the juror's wife informed him of Hunt's guilty plea, which had been kept from the jury.

Seven present or former aides of President Nixon or the re-election committee were listed among 60 potential prosecution witnesses Jan. 8, but the list did not include Donald H. Segretti, who had been included in the original prosecution witness list. Segretti had been reported to be involved in attempts to sabotage the campaigns of various Democratic presidential candidates.

In a pretrial hearing Jan. 5, Sirica rejected a motion by attorney Charles Morgan Jr., representing five Democratic officials whose telephone conversations may have been overheard in the Watergate tap, seeking to ban all disclosure at the trial of contents of any illegally overheard conversations, to protect the officials' privacy. Silbert had argued that the general content of the conversations, though not specific details, would have to be elicited to establish that the taps had been installed and used. Sirica also said the evidence might be "relevant" to "the question of motive," which Sirica had said he hoped would be determined during the trial.

Sirica also denied Morgan's request that he subpoena prominent Republicans, including former Attorney General John N. Mitchell, former Commerce Secretary Maurice H. Stans and Attorney General Richard G. Kleindienst, to ascertain whether they had obtained any of the illegally acquired conversational records, in a further effort to suppress public disclosure of the conversations.

Nixon's Finance Committee charged. The Justice Department charged the Finance Committee to Re-elect the President Jan. 11 with eight criminal violations of election-financing law in failing to record and report $31,300 that it had allegedly given Liddy.

Criminal complaints also were filed Jan. 11 against three Congressional candidates on campaign funding. All were defeated in the elections, two in primaries—Democrats Charles W. Johnson (Ohio, 17th District) and William C. Haden (Pa., 14th District)—and one in the November 1972 elections, Fritjof P. Thygeson, a candidate of the Peace and Freedom party (Calif., 40th District).

The criminal informations, filed in U.S. district court, were the first under the Federal Elections Campaign Act, which took effect April 7, 1972.

There were eight separate counts in the charges against the finance committee, which was headed by Maurice H. Stans, former secretary of commerce. Each carried a maximum penalty of a $1,000 fine and a year in prison. Since no person was named as a defendant, no one could go to jail.

The charges cited financial transactions during the election campaign in which the committee allegedly passed cash sums of $12,000, $12,000 and $5,300 through its treasurer, Hugh W. Sloan Jr., to Liddy, its legal adviser. The committee obtained no receipts from Liddy and maintained no records, as required by the new law. The committee was also charged with failing to report the cash transactions to the General Accounting Office and with failing to report to the GAO an additional $2,000 spent by Liddy, the charges specified.

Congressional probe asked. The Senate Democratic caucus unanimously approved a resolution Jan. 11 calling for an investigation of the Watergate affair and alleged Republican political espionage against Democrats in the 1972 election campaign.

Senate Democratic Leader Mike Mansfield announced that Sen. Sam J. Ervin (D, N.C.) had agreed to head the probe. Ervin was chairman of the Senate Government Operations Committee and the Judiciary subcommittee on constitutional rights.

Mansfield Jan. 6 had released letters he sent Nov. 17, 1972 to Ervin and Judiciary Committee Chairman James O. Eastland (D, Miss.) calling for an investigation by one of their committees. "The question is not policital, it is constitutional," the letter said. "At stake is the continued vitality of the electoral process."

4 more plead guilty. Four more defendants in the Watergate case pleaded guilty Jan. 15 to all counts of a federal indictment charging them with conspiracy, second-degree burglary and wiretapping. The four—Bernard L. Barker, Frank A. Sturgis, Eugenio Rolando Martinez and Virgilio R. Gonzalez—had been apprehended inside Democratic national headquarters in the Watergate office building in Washington June 17, 1972.

Another defendant, E. Howard Hunt Jr., had pleaded guilty Jan. 11. Judge John J. Sirica accepted the guilty pleas and the trial, which began Jan. 10 was resumed for the two remaining defendants, James W. McCord Jr., who at the time of his arrest was security coordinator for the Committee to Re-elect the President, and G. Gordon Liddy, who had been counsel to the Finance Committee to Re-elect the President.

McCord's lawyer, Gerald Alch, told reporters Jan. 16 he would employ a variant of the "self-defense" argument to defend his client, that McCord acted under a form of "duress" at Watergate to prevent harm he feared might befall Republican officials, including the President. Alch said "potentially violent groups" supported the Democrats and may have "indicated" their plans to the Democrats. The defense would contend, he said, that "if one is under a reasonable apprehension, regardless of whether that apprehension is in fact correct, he is justified in breaking a law to avoid the greater harm, which in this case would be violence directed to Republican officials, including, but not limited to, the President."

The four pleading guilty Jan. 15 all denied that pressure had been put on them by "higher-ups," as Sirica phrased it in questioning them, or money offered them to plead guilty. Gonzalez and Sturgis, in response to further questioning, indicated, as Barker previously had in interviews, that their participation in the Watergate affair was based on a belief they were furthering the cause of Cuban liberation from Communist control. Barker had said many Cuban refugees believed the election of Democratic presidential nominee George McGovern would be the beginning of a trend to socialism or communism.

When asked about the source of money—$114,000—in his possession and traced originally from Republican campaign funds, Barker said "I cannot state who sent that money" and said it was delivered by mail.

A report that "great pressure" was being exerted upon Sturgis, Gonzalez, Barker and Martinez to plead guilty was carried by the New York Times Jan. 15 in an article by Seymour M. Hersh. Another report in Time magazine Jan. 22 said the Watergate defendants had been promised a cash settlement as high as $1,000 a month if they pleaded guilty, with additional funds to come after release from prison. Hersh had reported in the Times Jan. 14, that, according "to sources close to the case," at least four of those arrested in the Watergate raid were still being paid, by unnamed sources. The Times sources also claimed that Martinez was an active employe of the Central Intelligence Agency at the time of the raid and was dropped from the CIA payroll a day later, that high officials of the Committee to Re-elect the President had acknowledged privately that they were unable to account for $900,000 in campaign contributions, that a Nixon supporter working in Democratic headquarters had taped open doors to permit entry by those apprehended there.

In other trial developments:

■ Thomas James Gregory, a student of Brigham Young University, testified at the trial Jan. 11 he was recruited and paid by Hunt to spy on Democratic presidential candidates McGovern and Sen. Edmund S. Muskie (Me.).

■ The U.S. Court of Appeals in Washington ruled Jan. 12 that evidence from "allegedly illegally intercepted communications" would not be allowed to be presented at the Watergate trial unless the court held secret consultation on it with prosecution and defense lawyers and the Democratic officials who have sought to bar such testimony, which possibly involved their overheard conversations. If any objections were raised at the consultation, the issue would revert to the appeals court for resolution.

Liddy, McCord convicted. G. Gordon Liddy and James W. McCord Jr. were convicted by a jury in U.S. district court in the District of Columbia Jan. 30 of attempting to spy on the Democrats during the 1972 presidential campaign. Five other defendants in the case, growing out of the break-in at Democratic national headquarters in the Watergate building in Washington June 17, 1972, had pleaded guilty at the beginning of the trial

The jury, which deliberated less than 90 minutes, found Liddy and McCord, former officials of President Nixon's political organization, guilty of conspiracy, second-degree burglary, attempted wiretapping, attempted bugging and wiretapping. McCord was also found guilty of possessing wiretapping and bugging equipment.

Liddy was a former counsel to President Nixon's major re-election campaign committee and its finance arm. McCord was a former security coordinator for the Nixon re-election committee. Both were sent to jail pending decisions on bonds and sentencing.

Liddy's defense contended that he thought the other defendants, five of whom were arrested during the break-in, had been engaged in a legitimate intelligence operation and he, like other officials at Nixon headquarters, was "on the safe side of the line of innocence." The lawyer, Peter L. Maroulis, disclosed in summation Jan. 30 that Liddy had destroyed memoranda based on information from the wiretap at Watergate when he realized, after the arrests at Watergate, that the information could be "tainted" and cause embarrassment to the re-election committee.

McCord's defense was that he had not participated in the raid with "criminal intent" and was therefore not guilty as charged. The prosecution had charged that McCord was in the operation for financial gain and more power within the re-election committee.

A proposed defense argument that McCord had acted at Watergate out of "duress" to prevent harm to officials, including President Nixon, was disallowed Jan. 24 by Chief Judge John J. Sirica, who dismissed it as "ridiculous."

Several times during the trial Sirica had interrupted examination of witnesses by both the defense and prosecution to conduct the questioning himself. In doing so Jan. 22, he said neither side was developing "all the facts." It was under probing by Sirica that Hugh W. Sloan Jr., former treasurer of the Nixon re-election finance committee, disclosed Jan. 23 that $199,000 in campaign funds had been paid to Liddy after verification from former Attorney General John N. Mitchell, also former Nixon campaign manager, and former Commerce Secretary Maurice H. Stans, Nixon's chief fundraiser. However, Sloan said that Mitchell and Stans had verified that Jeb Magruder, a deputy campaign director, was authorized to make the payments. However, he said no one had "indicated" to him how the $199,000 was to be used.

Magruder testified Jan. 23 that about $235,000 had been budgeted by the Nixon organization for an intelligence operation, assigned to Liddy, to (1) learn plans of radical groups that might disrupt political rallies or inflict "possibly bodily harm" on presidential surrogates, and to (2) discover the intentions of demonstrators at the Republican National Convention.

One such assignment, he related, was to investigate reports that a Democratic presidential candidate known for his anti-pollution stand, presumably Sen. Edmund S. Muskie (Me.), had received money from a major polluter.

The Sloan testimony was elicited in the absence of the jury, a frequent occurrence during the trial, and Sirica called the jury back Jan. 26 to hear an edited transcript of it.

The court had been under a higher court ruling not to admit without further advice testimony concerning information discovered by wiretap if the testimony were contested. The situation existed with the key prosecution witness, Alfred C. Baldwin 3rd, who said he had been ordered by McCord to monitor wiretapped telephone conversations at Watergate. The content of his testimony became an issue, and the U.S. Court of Appeals ruled Jan. 19 he should not say what he had overheard nor name anyone outside the Watergate offices who had talked over the tapped telephone.

Baldwin testified Jan. 19 he had delivered some of the wiretapped information to Nixon's political organization but could not remember the identity of the official to whom the material had been addressed. Baldwin could not remember, again in persistent questioning on the point Jan. 22 by Sirica with the jury absent.

Sirica asks broader probe. Chief John J. Sirica of the recently concluded Watergate criminal proceeding said Feb. 2 he hoped the Senate committee was "granted power by Congress by a broad enough resolution to get to the bottom of what happened in this case." Sirica said he was "not satisfied" that "all of the pertinent facts that might be available have been produced before an American jury" or that "somebody else doesn't know anything about what the $199,000 Mr. Liddy got was going to be used for."

At a bail hearing for convicted defendants Liddy and James W. McCord Jr. (bail was set at $100,000 each), Sirica said he had "great doubt" about whether Hugh W. Sloan Jr. "has told us the entire truth in this case." Sloan, former treasurer of Nixon's fund-raising committee, had been questioned closely by Sirica about $199,000 Liddy received from the re-election committee. Sloan had said he had "no idea" what Liddy had done with the money.

Sloan objected Feb. 3 to Sirica's "attacks that have been made on my integrity" as "totally unwarranted."

Los Angeles Times reporter Jack Nelson testified Feb. 5 that the Department of Justice tried to suppress an interview concerning the Watergate bugging of Democratic headquarters. He said the Justice Department had threatened to take away immunity from prosecution from Alfred C. Baldwin 3rd if the tapes of the interview were not released to the Justice Department. Nelson called Baldwin the key government witness in the trial.

Senate authorizes probe. The Senate, by a 70-0 vote Feb. 7, adopted a resolution to establish a seven-member select committee—four Democrats and three Republicans—to probe all aspects of the Watergate bugging case and other re-ported attempts of political espionage against the Democrats in the 1972 presidential election campaign. Republican efforts to gain equal membership on the committee with the Democrats and to extend the probe's coverage to the 1964 and 1968 presidential election campaigns were turned back.

Sen. Sam J. Ervin Jr. (D, N.C.) was named chairman of the special panel Feb. 8, which would consist of Democrats Joseph M. Montoya (N.M.), Herman E. Talmadge (Ga.) and Daniel K. Inouye (Hawaii) and Republicans Howard H. Baker (Tenn.), Edward J. Gurney (Fla.) and Lowell P. Weicker Jr. (Conn.).

A preliminary report on the same subject by a Senate panel Feb. 1 stated that the federal government had failed to conduct a substantial investigation. Sen. Edward M. Kennedy (D, Mass.), chairman of a Judiciary Committee subcommittee that had conducted the study, said his panel had found evidence that "strongly indicates that a wide range of espionage and sabotage activities did occur" during the recent campaign and "neither the federal criminal investigation nor the White House administrative inquiry included any substantial investigation of the alleged sabotage and espionage operations apart from those surrounding the Watergate episode itself."

Kennedy cited indications that "one key participant was in repeated contact with the White House, the White House convention headquarters and White House aides during relevant time periods" and that "at least part of the financing was arranged through a key Republican fund-raiser who is a close associate of President Nixon's." Although the names were omitted, the references, based on previous news reports, were taken to involve the activities of Donald H. Segretti, a lawyer from California, and Herbert W. Kalmbach, Nixon's personal lawyer and a leading GOP fund-raiser.

A New York Times report Feb. 7 by Seymour M. Hersh, based on government sources, named Gordon C. Strachan, a former staff assistant to H. R. Haldeman, Nixon's chief of staff, as the initial contact between Segretti, allegedly involved in political espionage and sabotage against Democratic presidential campaigners, and political intelligence operations led by Watergate figures G. Gordon Liddy, recently convicted, and E. Howard Hunt Jr., who pleaded guilty. Dwight C. Chapin, Nixon's appointments secretary, was reported to be another contact for Segretti. In a Hersh report Feb. 8, Chapin was said to have directed Kalmbach to pay Segretti for his activities and to have used a code name—"Chapman"—in his undercover intelligence work.

According to court depositions released Feb. 6, former Attorney General John N. Mitchell, who served as Nixon's campaign manager, received confidential information from someone traveling with Democratic candidates identified as "Chapman's friend," information Mitchell described as "pap." He said he did not know who "Chapman" was.

(Hersh reported Jan. 29 that Chapin was being forced out of his White House post because of the Segretti reports. The White House confirmed Jan. 29 that Chapin was leaving but said it was on his own decision and had nothing to do with political espionage activity. United Air Lines announced Jan. 30 that Chapin would join the firm as director of market planning.)

The sworn depositions had been taken in pretrial testimony in a civil Watergate action, depositions sealed during the criminal case and released Feb. 6 by U.S. District Court Judge Charles R. Richey.

Among other data disclosed in the depositions: the White House had been alerted within hours of the Watergate raid arrests of the possible involvement of one of its consultants, E. Howard Hunt Jr.; John D. Ehrlichman, Nixon's assistant for domestic affairs, had called Charles W. Colson, a special counsel to Nixon, to inquire about Hunt because of Hunt's possible involvement in the incident.

Ehrlichman confirmed Feb. 8 that the White House had been notified early, as a matter of routine whenever members of the White House staff were "arrested or in trouble."

Colson also said in the deposition that it was under his "initiative" that Hunt had been hired by the White House, to work on the "Pentagon papers controversy," that he had consulted with Ehrlichman about the hiring and that Hunt initially reported to Colson. Hunt was later transferred, Colson believed, to work or help the Nixon re-election committee, probably "in the area of convention security" and "the general area of security" for the campaign committee.

Gray faces Senate opposition. The White House announced Feb. 17 the nomination of L. Patrick Gray 3rd, acting director of the Federal Bureau of Investigation since May 1972, to be permanent director, but the nomination soon ran into opposition in the Senate committee holding hearings on the appointment after it was learned that the FBI had supplied the White House and the Nixon campaign committee with information gathered in its investigation of the Watergate break-in.

Gray acknowledged Feb. 28 that extensive records of the FBI probe had been made available to the White House and claimed that the late FBI director, J. Edgar Hoover, had provided other Administrations with progress reports of important investigations.

(Gray coupled the disclosure with a promise to open the FBI files on the Watergate breakin to any senator.)

Gray said he based his decision on advice from his legal staff after John W. Dean 3rd, a presidential counsel conducting a separate White House inquiry into the Watergate breakin, "asked us to give him what we had to date." The request was made in August 1972, according to Gray.

Gray said he had provided Attorney General Richard G. Kleindienst with the report and added, "I have every reason to believe that it then went to the White House."

Dean also got a copy of the "Dita Beard memorandum," Gray disclosed March 6. The memo, allegedly written by the International Telephone & Telegraph Corp. (ITT) lobbyist, established a connection between the settlement of an antitrust suit pending against ITT by the government and ITT's contribution to the 1972 GOP presidential campaign. The document figured prominently in Attorney General Kleindienst's confirmation battle in 1972.

The original Beard memorandum, obtained by columnist Jack Anderson and turned over to the Senate Judiciary Committee which asked the FBI to examine the paper, was also examined by ITT. The firm presented scientific evidence to the committee disputing the document's authenticity.

"I do not know how it [the paper] got into the hands of ITT or its experts," Gray said March 7. He added that after Dean returned the document to him, Gray turned it over to the Judiciary Committee.

Gray also revealed March 6 that White House special counsel Charles W. Colson had told FBI agents in August 1972 about a trip he had authorized in August 1972 for E. Howard Hunt. Hunt had visited Beard in Denver where she was recuperating from a heart ailment suffered during the height of the controversy. After his visit, Beard disavowed the memorandum and ITT presented evidence disputing its veracity.

The disclosure was made during the FBI's Watergate investigation, in which Colson and Hunt were implicated. The FBI made no further effort to learn the purpose of Hunt's trip, Gray said, because "there was no involvement of the ITT case with the Watergate bugging."

It was also revealed that Dean ordered Hunt's office safe emptied June 28, 1972, three days after he had been arrested for the Watergate breakin. The papers were not turned over to the FBI until a week after the safe had been opened.

When asked about the time lag between the two events, Gray said, "I see nothing irregular about it. The President's got a rather substantial interest as to what might be in those papers."

Gray also revealed Feb. 28 that FBI agents had questioned Donald H. Segretti in June 1972 regarding his involvement in alleged political espionage activities.

The Washington Post had reported Oct. 15, 1972 that Segretti had been shown FBI documents by White House aides to prepare him for grand jury testimony. Gray told the committee he had checked those reports with Dean, who had denied them, but no further effort had

been made to determine if the White House had made improper use of the files.

Gray added March 7 that agents had questioned a former presidential assistant, Dwight Chapin, March 5 and that he also denied having given the FBI reports to Segretti.

Information supplied the committee by Gray March 7 indicated that Nixon's personal lawyer, Herbert W. Kalmbach, had paid Segretti between $30,000 and $40,000 in GOP funds from Sept. 1, 1971 until March 15, 1972.

According to Gray, Kalmbach claimed that he was only a "disbursing agent" with no knowledge of Segretti's use of the money or how he obtained his instructions from the party. Kalmbach admitted he kept no financial records of the salary and expense money paid Segretti.

Kalmbach, who was Nixon's principal fund raiser during 1971 until the appointment of Maurice Stans, said the money was drawn from funds collected before April 7, 1972 when the source and purpose of campaign finances were made public according to requirements of the new federal election law.

Kalmbach told the FBI that Chapin had "informed" him that Segretti was about to be discharged from the Army and that "he may be of service to the Republican party."

Gray told the committee March 7 that Dean received FBI reports of interviews with Segretti as well as accounts of FBI interviews with Alfred C. Baldwin, who had admitted tapping Democratic party telephones. Dean received information on the "nature" and "substance" of Baldwin's eavesdropping, Gray said.

A 12-page summary of the FBI investigation on the Watergate affair, dated July 21, 1972, was submitted to the Senate committee March 5. The report charged that attorneys for the Committee to Re-elect the President had hampered FBI efforts to question GOP campaign officials.

Gray told the panel March 6 that an unspecified number of Nixon campaign officials had sought and obtained FBI interviews which were conducted when GOP lawyers were not present. Dean received reports of those interviews as well.

Dean, "in his official capacity as counsel to the President," demanded and was allowed to be present during the FBI's questioning of all White House personnel, despite his vociferous objections, Gray claimed. Had he objected, no White House interviews would have been permitted, Gray added.

As Gray was speaking before the Senate committee March 6, White House Press Secretary Ronald L. Ziegler told reporters that Dean sat in on the interviews of only those White House staff members who had requested his presence.

Gray testified March 1 that John Mitchell, Nixon's former campaign manager, prevented the FBI from questioning his wife on a matter related to the Watergate probe. The questions were not pursued, Gray said, because "this man was a former attorney general of the United States and I think we would have accorded that courtesy to any person in a position like that."

Gray amended those remarks March 7, saying that after the initial rebuff, Mitchell had offered to allow his wife to "come to Washington for an interview, if our agent thought it was necessary." The agent "stated that he did not," according to Gray.

The FBI was also unable to interview a top campaign official, Robert C. Mardian, about the destruction of campaign finance records and did not talk with presidential assistant H. R. Haldeman, whose staff members had been linked to political espionage charges, Gray disclosed March 1. However, another White House aide, John Ehrlichman, had been questioned.

Nixon unit seeks reporters' notes. Subpoenas were issued Feb. 26 for 12 reporters and news executives to give up to the Nixon re-election committee notes or other private material relating to their Watergate articles. The subpoenas were obtained by the committee in connection with civil suits on the case. Five of the subpoenas were issued for Washington Post personnel: publisher Katharine Graham, managing editor Howard Simons and three reporters. Four were directed at Washington Star-News reporters. Others subpoenaed were reporters at the New York Times and Time magazine reporters and Walter J. Sheridan, a former network correspondent.

Nixon refuses to comment on case. At an impromptu news conference March 2, President Nixon said it would be improper for him to comment on the Watergate case since it was still in the courts. He noted, as he had before, that the White House investigation of Watergate had indicated that no one on the White House staff at the time the investigation was conducted was involved "or had knowledge of the Watergate matter." He also said the Administration would cooperate with Congress in its probe of the case.

Nixon said he would not permit his counsel, John W. Dean 3rd, who conducted the White House probe, to testify before Congress. "No President could ever agree" to that, he said. "On the other hand, as far as any committee of the Congress is concerned, where information is requested that a member of the White House staff may have, we will make arrangements to provide that information...."

The President declined to answer a question whether it was "fair and efficient" for the FBI not to have pursued its intention to question Mrs. John Mitchell in its Watergate probe because her husband, who was against the interview, was a former attorney general and Nixon campaign official. It had always been his practice, Nixon said, not to comment on a hearing while it was in process. The matter had come up at a Congressional hearing.

Privilege theory rejected. At a two day Capitol Hill conference on the conflict between the President and Congress, University of Washington Professor Arthur Bester advised members of Congress attending the symposium March 8 that the theory of "executive privilege" was "a myth" and that White House aides could be held in contempt of Congress and put in jail for refusing witness.

The first use of executive privilege was attributed to President Washington in 1796 when he refused the House's request for documents on the Jay Treaty with Great Britain. Noting the absence of constitutional authority for the House to pass on treaties, Washington contended "a just regard to the Constitution and to the duty of my office" forbade compliance.

GOP returns Watergate gift. The Nixon re-election committee announced March 9 that it had returned funds totaling $655,000 to three contributors, including Robert H. Allen, a Texas oilman whose $100,000 donation was the source of $89,000 in funds deposited to the account of Bernard L. Barker. Barker had pleaded guilty to conspiracy, burglary and wiretapping charges in connection with the Watergate case.

Executive privilege. President Nixon issued a policy statement March 12 saying that members and former members of his personal staff normally would refuse to testify formally before a committee of Congress if so requested.

"The manner in which the President personally exercises his assigned executive powers is not subject to questioning by another branch of government," he argued. "If the President is not subject to such questioning, it is equally inappropriate [sic] that members of his staff not be so questioned, for their roles are in effect an extension of the presidency."

At the same time, Nixon said, it would "continue" to be his policy, "to provide all necessary and relevant information through informal contacts between my present staff and committees of the Congress in ways which preserve intact the constitutional separation of the branches."

Nixon pledged not to use executive privilege "as a shield to prevent embarrassing information from being made available."

At one point, he split the issue in half. His four Cabinet members who also held presidential titles, he said, would testify in their Cabinet role but not in their White House role.

The President had indicated at his news conference Jan. 31 a policy statement on executive privilege would be forthcoming. He wanted "a precise statement" of policy prepared so "you will know exactly what

it is," he said. His "general attitude" was "to be as liberal as possible in terms of making people available to testify" before Congress and not to use executive privilege "as a shield for conversations that might be just embarrassing to us but that really don't deserve executive privilege." He added that such cases as arose would be handled "on a case by case basis." "We are not going to be in a position," he said, "where an individual, when he gets under heat from a Congressional committee, can say, 'Look, I am going to assert executive privilege.' He will call down here and Mr. Dean, the White House counsel, will then advise him as to whether or not we approve it."

Senate challenge—A direct challenge to the policy was approved by the Senate Judiciary Committee March 13. It voted unanimously (9 Democrats & 7 Republicans) to "invite" the President's chief legal counsel, John W. Dean 3rd, to testify at its hearings on the nomination of L. Patrick Gray 3rd to become director of the Federal Bureau of Investigation (FBI).

Sen. John V. Tunney (D, Calif.), who proposed the invitation, said afterwards

he thought it "quite improbable" that the committee would vote to confirm Gray unless Dean testified on matters related to him during the hearings.

Gray had supplied the committee March 12 with a requested list of contacts he had with Dean between June and September of 1972—33 of them, 28 by telephone, five in Gray's office. Gray previously had testified he supplied Dean with 82 FBI investigative reports on the Watergate break-in at Democratic national headquarters in 1972. Dean had conducted the White House investigation that cleared then-employed White House personnel of complicity in the raid.

Gray also had testified previously that FBI interviews of White House personnel concerning Watergate had been conducted in Dean's presence and that he had received from the FBI accounts of the agency's confidential interviews of employees of the Committee to Re-elect the President conducted without the presence of a committee lawyer. Several committee employees had requested the private sessions after committee lawyers had sat in on the first FBI interview.

Excerpts From March 12 Statement on Executive Privilege

The doctrine of executive privilege is well established. It was first invoked by President Washington, and it has been recognized and utilized by our Presidents for almost 200 years since that time.

The doctrine is rooted in the Constitution, which vests "the executive power" solely in the President, and it is designed to protect communications within the executive branch in a variety of circumstances in time of both war and peace.

Without such protection, our military security, our relations with other countries, our law enforcement procedures and many other aspects of the national interest could be significantly damaged and the decision-making process of the executive branch could be impaired.

The general policy of this Administration regarding the use of executive privilege during the next four years will be the same as the one we have followed during the past four years: Executive privilege will not be used as a shield to prevent embarrassing information from being made available but will be exercised only in those particular instances in which disclosure would harm the public interest.

During the first four years of my Presidency, hundreds of Administration officials spent thousands of hours testifying before committees of the Congress. Secretary of Defense [Melvin] Laird, for instance, made 86 separate appearances before Congressional committees, engaging in over 327 hours of testimony.

By contrast, there were only three occasions during the first term of my Administration when executive privilege was invoked anywhere in the executive branch in response to a Congressional request for information. These facts speak not of a closed Administration but of one that is pledged to openness and is proud to stand on its record.

Requests for Congressional appearances by members of the President's personal staff present a different situation and raise different considerations. Such requests have been relatively infrequent through the years, and in past Administrations they have been routinely declined.

I have followed that same tradition in my Administration, and I intend to continue it during the remainder of my term.

Under the doctrine of separation of powers, the manner in which the President personally exercises his assigned executive powers is not subject to questioning by another branch of government. If the President is not subject to such questioning, it is equally inappropriate [sic] that members of his staff not be so questioned, for their roles are in effect an extension of the Presidency.

This tradition rests on more than constitutional doctrine: It is also a practical necessity. To insure the effective discharge of the executive responsibility, a President must be able to place absolute confidence in the advice and assistance offered by the members of his staff. And in the performance of their duties for the President, those staff members must not be inhibited by the possibility that their advice and assistance will ever become a matter of public debate, either during their tenure in government or at a later date. Otherwise, the candor with which advice is rendered and the quality of such assistance will inevitably be compromised and weakened.

What is at stake, therefore, is not simply a question of confidentiality but the integrity of the decision-making process at the very highest levels of our government.

As I stated in my press conference on Jan. 31, the question of whether circumstances warrant the exercise of executive privilege should be determined on a case-by-case basis.

In making such decisions, I shall rely on the following guidelines:

1. In the case of a department or agency, every official shall comply with a reasonable request for an appearance before the Congress, provided that the performance before the Congress, provided that the performance of the duties of his office will not be seriously impaired thereby. If the official believes that a Congressional request for a particular document or for testimony on a particular point raises a substantial question as to the need for invoking executive privilege, he shall comply with the procedures set forth in my memorandum of March 24, 1969. Thus, executive privilege will not be invoked until the compelling need for its exercise has been clearly demonstrated and the request has been approved first by the attorney general and then by the President.

2. A Cabinet officer or any other governmental official who also holds a position as a member of the President's personal staff shall comply with any reasonable request to testify in his non-White House capacity, provided that the performance of his duties will not be seriously impaired thereby. If the official believes that the request raises a substantial question as to the need for invoking executive privilege, he shall comply with the procedures set forth in my memorandum of March 24, 1969.

3. A member or former member of the President's personal staff normally shall follow the well-established precedent and decline a request for a formal appearance before a committee of the Congress. At the same time, it will continue to be my policy to provide all necessary and relevant information through informal contacts between my present staff and committees of the Congress in ways which preserve intact the constitutional separation of the branches.

Senate Judiciary Committee member Birch Bayh (D, Ind.) released March 12 a sworn affidavit from one such [former] Nixon committee employee, Judith Hoback, who related that within 48 hours of her second and "confidential" interview she had been summoned to the office of Nixon campaign official Robert C. Mardian, where committee lawyer Kenneth W. Parkinson made her aware they knew of the confidential interview.

Tunney told the Judiciary Committee March 8 one of the convicted Watergate defendants, G. Gordon Liddy, a former counsel to the Nixon committee, had been recommended for that post by Dean.

Nixon aide declines to appear—Presidential counsel Dean informed the Judiciary Committee by letter March 14 he would not appear before it for testimony. He offered to accept and reply to written questions from the panel that were directly related to the Gray nomination. He based his action on Nixon's March 12 statement that all members of his personal staff would decline such appearances.

White House Press Secretary Ziegler said later he did not consider Dean's refusal utilization of executive privilege but rather adherence to the constitutional separation of the branches of government.

Nixon reaffirms stand—The President reaffirmed his stand against a Congressional appearance by Dean at an impromptu news conference March 15.

Nixon said he felt it was his duty to defend the principle of separation of powers. If the Senate "feels that they want a court test" on the issue "we would welcome it," he said. "Perhaps this is the time to have the highest court of the land make a definitive decision with regard to this matter."

The President added that he felt the court "will uphold, as it always usually has, the great constitutional principle of separation of powers rather than to uphold the Senate."

Noting "some speculation to the effect that the Senate might hold Mr. Gray as hostage to a decision on Mr. Dean," Nixon said he could not believe that "such responsible members" of the Senate would do that. Dean had what the President called a "double privilege," a lawyer-client relationship as well as a presidential privilege because he had served as counsel to a number of people on the White House staff.

Dean would furnish "pertinent information" to Congress when it was requested, Nixon said, but he was "not going to have the counsel to the President" testify in a formal session before Congress.

The President said his Administration had "not drawn a curtain down and said that there could be no information furnished by members of the White House staff because of their special relationship to the President."

"All we have said," he continued, "is that it must be under certain circumstances, certain guidelines, that do not infringe upon or impair the separation of powers."

Within these bounds, he said, Dean would "be completely forthcoming. Something that other Administrations have totally refused to do until we got here, and I am very proud of the fact that we are forthcoming...."

To a question about whether the executive privilege extended to personnel in the re-election committee, Nixon said "none of them have the privilege" and none would refuse testimony when asked.

Nixon referred to the Watergate case as "espionage by one political organization against another."

Testimony from 'raw files' deplored—After Gray had given the Judiciary Committee a report of the FBI interview with Nixon's attorney, Herbert W. Kalmbach, White House Press Secretary Ronald L. Ziegler March 8 expressed the President's "concern" at the release of "raw, unevaluated material" from FBI files.

At his news conference, Nixon expressed his own annoyance with the procedure. He said he understood why Gray had acted as he had "because his hearing was involved" but the practice of the FBI furnishing "raw files" to full Congressional committees "must stop" with this particular instance. "Now, for the FBI," he said, "before a full committee of the Congress to furnish 'raw files' and then to have them leak out to the press, I think could do innocent people a great deal of damage."

(Gray's testimony about Kalmbach actually was not from "raw files" but contained in a written addition to previous testimony as a paraphrase of Kalmbach's accounting of the incident to the FBI. And the "leak" to the press apparently was this testimony by Gray for the committee's public record.)

Asked directly about the incident related in the testimony concerning Kalmbach, Nixon said he had confidence in all of the White House people who had been named but he would not comment on any individual matter before the hearing while it was going on.

Nixon aides subpoenaed. Subpoenas for White House Counsel John Dean 3rd and six other current or former Nixon Administration officials were obtained March 13 for pretrial depositions in a lawsuit brought by the citizens' lobby Common Cause to force disclosure of information about the Nixon re-election campaign funds.

Gray ordered not to discuss case. L. Patrick Gray 3rd informed the Senate Judiciary Committee March 20 that he was under new orders from Attorney General Richard G. Kleindienst not to discuss the Watergate case in the committee's hearings on his nomination as director of the Federal Bureau of Investigation (FBI).

The FBI's investigation of Watergate while Gray had been acting director of the bureau for the past 10½ months, and his admitted liaison with President Nixon's counsel John W. Dean 3rd, had become a focus of the hearings.

Gray, who had previously told the committee he had supplied the White House and the Nixon re-election committee with data gathered in the FBI Watergate investigation, confirmed to the panel March 20 he had continued to send the FBI's Watergate reports to Dean even after discovering that Dean had recommended G. Gordon Liddy, one of the convicted Watergate defendants in the criminal case, for his job with the Nixon re-election committee.

Gray testified March 21 that Dean had picked up the Watergate material from him in person and he had never notified Kleindienst or anyone else in the FBI or Justice Department of the transaction. He said he had kept no record on the contents of the data handed over but said Dean had been given "an integral part of the total Watergate file."

He would continue to give Dean any material he requested as long as Dean was the President's counsel, Gray said. He had not informed Kleindienst about releasing the material to Dean for the same reason. It was not necessary to inform Kleindienst, Gray said, "in view of the fact that I had a request from the counsel to the President."

Gray's new orders about testimony forbade answering questions that would reveal information from FBI files. Gray pleaded with the committee March 20 to vote his nomination "up or down" and let him get out of the "minefield" he was being forced to walk through in the struggle between the executive and legislative branches of government.

Despite the plea, the committee decided March 20 to broaden the confirmation hearing by subpoenaing three additional witnesses—Mrs. Judith Hoback, a former employe of the Nixon campaign committee. Thomas E. Bishop, a former assistant director of the FBI, and Thomas Lumbard, a former Justice and Treasury lawyer, who had spoken to a newspaper reporter of a close connection between Dean and Liddy. Bishop had signed the request to FBI field offices during the 1972 presidential campaign for information that could help Nixon.

Gray told the committee March 20 he disapproved of the request and blamed it on subordinates. He also said Bishop had not objected to it, although Bishop was reported to have told friends he had objected strenuously.

The Administration also superseded Gray's offer to the Judiciary Committee Feb. 28 to open the FBI's Watergate files to any senator who wished to examine them. Gray had told the committee March 7 he had made the "unprecedented offer" because of his conviction "that the FBI's credibility as an institution was at stake and that we had to conduct this investigation so it would stand scrutiny from anyone."

Gray explained March 20 that his new orders restricted Senate access to the files to the committee chairman and ranking minority member and their respective chief counsels of investigating panels.

This agreement had been worked out March 16 in a meeting of Kleindienst, Sen. Sam J. Ervin Jr. (D, N.C.) and Howard H. Baker Jr. (R, Tenn.), chairman and vice chairman, respectively, of the Senate select committee established to investigate the Watergate and related affairs.

Several other members of that committee were sharply critical of the agreement March 19. Sen. Lowell P. Weicker Jr. (R, Conn.) said every committee member should have access to the files, and Sen. Daniel K. Inouye (D, Hawaii) called the restriction an "insult" to the Senate.

Ervin said March 18 he agreed with President Nixon that raw FBI files made available to a Congressional committee should not be made public. Appearing that day on the CBS "Face the Nation" broadcast, Ervin disagreed with the President's position to invoke executive privilege to bar White House aides from testifying before Congress.

In fact, Ervin said, he would seek the arrest of any White House aide or any other prospective witness who refused to testify before his select committee. "I'd recommend to the Senate," he said, "they send the sergeant-at-arms of the Senate to arrest a White House aide or any other witness who refuses to appear." If his panel were faced with a court test on executive privilege that threatened to delay its probe for "for two or three years," he said, he would not hesitate to recommend that White House aides defying the probe be tried for contempt by the Senate, a course that with conviction could lead to jailing.

Ervin was of the opinion that Nixon "has stretched the doctrine" of executive privilege "far beyond its true boundaries and far beyond any precedent." "I'm satisfied," he said, "that executive privilege does not cover wrongdoing. The only thing in the Constitution that covers wrongdoing is the self-incrimination clause, and if any of the White House aides wish to come down and plead the 5th Amendment, why the committee will honor the plea."

Ervin rejected Dean's offer, in refusing to appear at the hearing, to answer questions in writing. "I want the man there in person, and I'd be satisfied with nothing less," Ervin said.

"If the President wants us to confirm Mr. Gray," he said, "the President has some very important evidence that he can produce, and if he refuses to produce it I think that the Senate has to stand up for its prerogatives." He said action on Gray's nomination, in the meantime, should be delayed "until after the Watergate affair is fully investigated by the select committee."

Senate Democratic Whip Robert C. Byrd (W. Va.), a member of the Judiciary Committee, said in a Senate speech March 19 "the integrity of the Senate" was at stake and "the Senate should not deviate from its insistence upon the appearance of Mr. Dean." It was "almost impossible to avoid the suspicion," he said, "that someone at the White House, in preparing the statement [on executive privilege] for Mr. Nixon, was trying to cover up White House involvement in the ugly campaign of political sabotage and espionage which climaxed in the Watergate raid."

He also urged rejection of the Gray nomination. "If the President wants to close the door on the supply of information," he said, "the Senate ought to close the door on the President's nominee."

Gray admits Dean 'probably' lied—Gray admitted March 22 that Dean "probably" lied to FBI agents investigating the Watergate case. But he reiterated, because "that man is counsel to the President," that he would continue to send Dean confidential FBI reports if he requested them. Asked if his first duty was to the President or to the FBI, Gray replied that it was "a tough question" but he took his orders from the President "and I can't evade that fact."

This testimony was elicited under insistent questioning by Sen. Robert C. Byrd (W. Va.), Senate Democratic whip, who established a chronology concerning Dean and Watergate defendant E. Howard Hunt Jr., who had pleaded guilty. Byrd recounted previous testimony from Gray that two of Dean's aides had searched Hunt's office in the Old Executive Office Building, adjacent to the White House, June 19, and that material from the search, including that from a safe, was turned over to Dean June 20. Then, on June 22, Byrd continued, during the FBI's interview with White House aide Charles W. Colson, which Dean attended, Dean responded to a remark by one of the agents that he did not know whether Hunt had an office at the White House and would "check it out."

In view of this, Byrd asked if Dean had "lied to the agents" and Gray replied that he "would have to conclude that judgment probably is correct."

A White House statement later March 22, calling Byrd's charge "reprehensible, unfortunate, unfair and incorrect," said "Mr. Dean flatly denies that he ever misled or ... lied to an agent of the FBI." It said Dean recalled having been asked by the agents whether or not they could visit Hunt's office, not whether or not Hunt had an office there, and he had replied that he would check on it.

Court quashes press subpoenas. U.S. District Court Judge Charles R. Richey for the District of Columbia March 21 quashed subpoenas served on representatives of news organizations by the Nixon re-election committee to compel their unpublished material on the Watergate case.

Richey based his action on the 1st Amendment's guarantee of freedom of the press. "This court cannot blind itself to the possible chilling effect the enforcement of ... these subpoenas would have on the press and the public," he said.

While he did not hold that journalists had an absolute privilege against testifying, Richey said, the courts "must be flexible to some extent" and the particular instances before him were "all exceptional." He also said the committee had failed to show that other sources of evidence "have been exhausted or even approached" or that the material demanded of the journalists was "central to the case."

The news organizations involved were the New York Times, the Washington Post, the Washington Star-News and Time magazine.

One of those subpoenaed, Walter J. Sheridan, a former network correspondent, complied with the subpoena because he did not possess the press privilege at the time.

McCord implicates others. New allegations of prior complicity in the Watergate case by a White House aide and a former aide to the Committee to Re-elect the President were disclosed March 26.

The disclosures, reportedly given in still-secret testimony by James W. McCord Jr., one of those convicted in the break-in at Democratic headquarters in Washington's Watergate building, evoked demands by Senate Republicans for White House cooperation in resolving the growing controversy.

The new development unfolded as Judge John J. Sirica convened the District of Columbia district court March 23 to deliver sentences on the convicted Watergate defendants.

He had a "preliminary matter" to dispose of first, Sirica said. It was a letter to him, delivered by a court probation officer, from McCord. The letter contended that "others" had escaped capture at the Watergate raid, that "perjury occurred during the trial in matters highly material to the very structure, orientation and impact of the government's case and to the motivation and intent of the defendants," and that "political pressure to plead guilty and remain silent" had been brought on him and the others caught at the Watergate.

In the letter, McCord asked for a private meeting with Sirica to discuss these matters. "I cannot feel confident," he wrote, in talking of them in the presence of FBI agents, Justice Department attorneys or "other government representatives." He believed "that retaliatory measures will be taken against me, my family and my friends should I disclose such facts." McCord referred to questions Sirica had relayed through the probation officer during preparation of a presentence report. He felt "whip-sawed" by the questions, McCord said, since the answers might incriminate him, while refusal to answer them "may appear to be noncooperative and I can therefore expect a much more severe sentence."

"Several members of my family have expressed fear for my life if I disclose knowledge of the facts in this matter, either publicly or to any government representative," he wrote.

Sirica postponed the sentencing of McCord and agreed to a private meeting, with McCord under oath and with a stenographer present. The judge specified that he would make no promise that "my lips will be sealed."

Provisional sentences for 5 others—Five of the other Watergate defendants were sentenced "provisionally" March 23 to maximum prison terms—35 years for E. Howard Hunt Jr. and 40 years each for Bernard L. Barker, Frank A. Sturgis, Eugenio R. Martinez and Virgilio R. Gonzalez. All had pleaded guilty.

Another defendant, G. Gordon Liddy, former counsel to the Committee to Re-elect the President, who was convicted with McCord, was sentenced to 6 years, 8 months–20 years in prison.

In announcing the provisional maximum sentences, Sirica pointedly told them: "I recommend your full cooperation" with the federal grand jury and the Senate select committee investigating the Watergate case. "You must understand that I hold out no promises or hopes of any kind," he told them, "but I do say that should you decide to speak freely I would have to weigh that factor in appraising what sentence will be finally imposed in each case."

A statement from the Justice Department later March 23 pledged "appropriate action" if McCord's statement to Sirica contained evidence supporting the allegations in his letter or indicated any other violation of federal law.

McCord talks to Senate counsel—McCord made a second surprise move later March 23 when he appeared with a new lawyer, Bernard Fensterwald of Washington, for a secret discussion of the case with Samuel Dash, chief counsel for the Senate Select Committee, and Harold Lipset of San Francisco, a committee investigator. A second session was held March 24. Dash said, in disclosing the meetings March 25, that McCord had given them, among other data, names of participants in the Watergate conspiracy who had escaped prosecution.

"Documentation and other evidence to corroborate everything he says" was promised, Dash said. "Some of it is very specific stuff that will lead to further investigation." Dash, a former district attorney in Philadelphia, was serving the committee while on leave as a professor of law at Georgetown University.

Dean and Magruder named—The names in McCord's allegations appeared first in the Los Angeles Times, which published a report March 26 that McCord had named John W. Dean 3rd, counsel to President Nixon and Jeb Stuart Magruder, former deputy director of Nixon's

re-election committee, as two Administration officials who had prior knowledge of the Watergate spying operation. He also claimed, according to the report, that Hunt had put pressure on other defendants to plead guilty and told them they would receive "executive clemency" and money for remaining silent.

The Washington Star-News reported later March 26 that McCord, "encountered on a Washington street today," had verified as accurate published accounts of what he told Dash.

Later March 26, Magruder, currently an official with the Commerce Department, denied the charge of prior knowledge and White House Press Secretary Ronald L. Ziegler "flatly" denied "any prior knowledge on the part of Mr. Dean regarding the Watergate affair." The White House also said the President had discussed the reports of McCord's testimony with Dean that day and retained "absolute and total confidence" in his counsel.

The chief prosecutor in the Watergate trial, Earl J. Silbert, principal assistant U.S. attorney, disclosed March 26 that McCord previously had rejected two government offers of leniency in return for testimony. The first offer made in October 1972, he said, was to drop all but the conspiracy charges against him in return for a guilty plea and a pledge in open court to name all of the officials involved in the Watergate raid. "We tried to break this case open, within bounds of legal propriety, before the election," Silbert said. The second offer was extended in January to drop some charges in return for a pledge to testify before a grand jury, Silbert said.

Senate probers briefed—The Senate Select Committee met March 26 for a closed briefing on McCord's interviews with Dash. McCord met with the panel March 28.

Sen. Lowell P. Weicker (R, Conn.) said after attending the first session he had "always been convinced" that others in the White House had known of the political espionage campaign. "There are other persons in the White House who are involved," he said. He excluded the President who, he was convinced, had "nothing to hide."

Committee Vice Chairman Howard H. Baker Jr. (R, Tenn.) said after the March 28 session that McCord had provided "a great deal." The information was "significant," he said, and "a lot more" was expected.

At the Washington Press Club later March 28, Baker said McCord had "named names" and two of them were Dean and Magruder.

Mitchell's name comes up—Congressional sources reported March 28 that McCord had also named, although only on a "hearsay" basis without documentation, former Attorney General John N. Mitchell as another who had prior knowledge

of the Watergate conspiracy. Mitchell denied it the next day, terming it "slanderous."

(The New York Times reported March 28 that Mitchell's wife Martha had telephoned the newspaper March 27 to express "fear" that somebody was trying to make her husband "the goat" for Watergate. She said she was "scared" for her husband's safety and her own but she would not allow anyone "to pin anything on him," did not "give a damn who gets hurt" and could "name names." Mrs. Mitchell referred to her similar fear in June 1972 when she recounted that she had been interrupted during a telephone conversation with a reporter, thrown to the floor and given a hypodermic. She said the telephone had been ripped from the wall by Steve King, who became head of security for the Nixon re-election committee after McCord's arrest.

GOP Senators demand truth—Demands for White House cooperation to resolve the Watergate controversy were made March 27 by Sens. James L. Buckley (Conservative-Republican, N.Y.), John G. Tower (Tex.), chairman of the Senate Republican Policy Committee, and Norris Cotton (N.H.), chairman of the Senate Republican Conference.

Buckley observed that the Administration was making "less than a heroic effort" to establish the truth about the case and that "the moment of truth" was approaching. If there was a crime involved, he said, "I would like to see it exposed."

Tower said it was "in the best interests of the White House that this whole thing be bared."

Cotton urged the President to permit his counsel, Dean, to testify before Congress and help clear it up, a course also advocated by Tower.

Dean's personal testimony, barred by President Nixon's stand on executive privilege, was also sought by the Senate Judiciary Committee and a House Government Operations subcommittee headed by Rep. William S. Moorhead (D, Pa.).

The Senate panel was pursuing the alleged liaison on the Watergate case between Dean and acting FBI director L. Patrick Gray 3rd, whose nomination as FBI director was pending confirmation. Although the confirmation was clouded by the Watergate controversy and Dean's refusal to testify, Nixon had "no intention" of withdrawing Gray's nomination, Deputy White House Press Secretary Gerald L. Warren said at Key Biscayne, Fla. March 23. "The President supports that nomination," he said.

Moorhead, joined by Rep. John N. Erlenborn (R, Ill.), March 27 made public their letter to Nixon urging him to allow Dean to appear before their panel to testify on a bill to define the limits of the use of executive privilege. The letter promised to limit his testimony to that issue and exclude the Watergate issue or questions that would impinge on Dean's confidential relationship with Nixon.

The Congressmen also released copies of a study by the Library of Congress citing 19 instances in which Nixon had used executive privilege to withhold information from Congress—four explicit invocations and 15 utilizations of the privilege without declaring it. Nixon had claimed use of the privilege only three times in four years.

GOP concern grows—Sen. Marlow W. Cook (R, Ky.) said March 28 the Watergate case was a "rather severe stigma on the Republican party." He said he felt that sooner or later "we're going to be aware that underlings at some stage of the game really thought that it might be necessary to rig a federal election."

On the Senate floor March 29, Sen. Charles McC. Mathias Jr. (R, Md.) referred to "poisoned public ethical behavior" and said the question that was being posed by Watergate and several other current Senate probes was "whether the persons involved gave a greater loyalty to some lesser interest than to the Constitution." The only way to restore confidence in government was "for everyone who share the privilege of leadership to obey the law," he said.

Senate Republican Leader Hugh Scott (Pa.) spoke March 29 of being "deeply disturbed at any developments which taint the political process."

Watergate grand jury reconvenes—The federal grand jury that had returned the Watergate criminal indictments in 1972 reconvened March 26. Liddy was the first to be summoned as a witness, but he repeatedly invoked the 5th Amendment's protection against self incrimination in declining to answer questions.

Hunt appeared before the panel March 27–29. The second session was interrupted to permit Hunt to be granted immunity from further prosecution to answer questions.

Liddy was given another turn, this time with immunity, before the grand jury March 30.

Senate panel readies open hearings. Developments in the Watergate case and allegations concerning White House aides continued as the Select Senate Committee readied its investigation for open hearings, which Chairman Sam Ervin (D, N.C.) said April 3 he expected to begin "soon after about 10 days."

The latest developments involved:

■ News leaks linking high White House aides to the 1972 campaign break-in at the Democratic national headquarters in the Watergate building in Washington. The leaks came from a secret committee session March 28 with convicted Watergate defendant James W. McCord Jr., who had indicated a willingness to talk

about the case prior to his scheduled sentencing.

■ A White House willingness March 30 to soften its firm stand against Senate testimony in person by White House aides, an overture rejected by Ervin April 2.

■ A persistent demand by Sen. Lowell P. Weicker Jr. (R, Conn.), a member of the Ervin panel, for President Nixon's chief of staff H. R. Haldeman to "step forward and explain," as Weicker put it April 1, what he knew about the operation of the Committee to Re-elect the President. The focus on Haldeman's name, some of it deriving from the leaked news, which was reported to have been largely uncorroborated testimony by McCord, led to a statement April 4 by the Ervin panel, seconded by Weicker, that it had as yet "no evidence of any nature" implicating Haldeman in any "illegal" activities.

■ A sentencing April 3 of convicted Watergate conspirator G. Gordon Liddy to an additional jail term for contempt of court for refusing to answer questions about the case before a federal grand jury. Chief Judge John J. Sirica of the U.S. district court in Washington ordered Liddy to serve the contempt sentence by interrupting Liddy's current sentence of six years, eight months to 20 years in jail, an unusual procedure "to give meaning and coercive impact to the court's contempt powers," Sirica said. The first prison term was to be resumed after the run of the contempt term, which could run, unless Liddy testified, until December when the grand jury's term expired.

The news leaks—For several days following the Select Committee's secret session March 28 with McCord, there were widespread accounts that he had related, as uncorroborated hearsay from the Watergate co-conspirators (principally Liddy) that: former Attorney General John N. Mitchell approved the espionage activity and was "overall boss" of the group conducting it; John W. Dean 3rd, counsel to the President, attended a planning meeting with two of the men later convicted as conspirators and reported back that the operation had been approved; Haldeman "knew what was going on" at the Nixon re-election committee; Charles W. Colson, former special counsel to the President, possibly received a detailed plan for the Watergate raid from E. Howard Hunt Jr., a Watergate defendant who pleaded guilty; McCord met with Mitchell "daily" to discuss family and Republican security arrangements.

All the officials linked by the allegations to Watergate had denied such involvement, and Mitchell was on record with a sworn statement that he met with McCord "once" for a briefing about security of the building and, aside from passing in hallways, it was his only contact with McCord.

Curiosity about McCord's testimony was abetted by Weicker's remark at a news conference March 29 that the leaked items covered only about "one-tenth" of the information provided by McCord to the committee. Weicker stressed that McCord gave "no corroborative evidence" on his charges and cautioned that "an attempt is being made to create the belief" that Liddy was "the beginning and the end of this operation," that he was "being tossed out as the trail to follow." Weicker said he thought the focus on the Watergate bugging incident was "excessive" and there was a consequent failure to follow up other allegations of a broader campaign of political espionage and sabotage. Then, without naming names, one of them being a "Cabinet-level" official who supplied him the information, Weicker said he thought he knew the name of the ranking White House staffer, still at the White House, who was the "chief" of the entire espionage operation in the 1972 election campaign.

White House complaint—A White House rebuttal came March 30 from Press Secretary Ronald L. Ziegler, who stated that "no one in the White House had any involvement or prior knowledge" of the Watergate "event."

"The President wants it made clear it has not been and is not and will not be the objective of the White House to cover up or withhold any information on the Watergate matter," he said.

To "dispel the myth . . . that we seek to cover up," Ziegler said, Nixon was requiring White House staff members to testify, if called, before the Watergate grand jury and was willing to negotiate with the Select Senate Committee some procedure whereby White House staff members could provide testimony "other than in writing" about Watergate.

Ziegler criticized the operation of the Ervin panel in permitting "unsubstantiated charges" to be leaked from secret hearings. "It is evident," he said, "that personal rights have been abused in a very serious way by procedures that are less than orderly and judicial."

Ervin rejects informal testimony—The overture for informal testimony was rejected April 2 by Ervin, who observed that "divine right went out with the American Revolution and doesn't belong to White House aides." They were not "royalty or nobility," he said, and could not be excused from providing sworn testimony in public. He reaffirmed his intention to have White House aides arrested and cited for contempt by the Senate if the impasse reached that point.

Nixon's use of executive privilege in this instance, Ervin said, was "a terrible disservice to the high office of the presidency." The doctrine could not be applied to illegal or unethical activity, Ervin said.

Ervin thought that the President was conducting himself in this area in such a way as to "reasonably engender in the minds of people the belief he is afraid of the truth." If the allegations of political espionage were true, Ervin said, "we have to consider this was an assault on the integrity of the process" by which the President was chosen.

The White House reacted with a suggestion from Ziegler later April 2 for Ervin "to get his own disorganized house in order so that the investigation can go forward in a proper atmosphere of traditional fairness and due process." There had been "irresponsible leaks in tidal wave proportions," he said, from the committee's closed session.

The President was ready to cooperate to work out a procedure for testimony "which we do not feel infringes on the doctrine of separation of powers," Ziegler said, "and it is time to bring this entire procedure back into the framework of orderliness, fairness and respect for the rights of individuals."

Ervin announced April 3 that the committee would hear no more secret testimony and that the committee's staff would conduct any private interrogation of witnesses.

'No evidence' on Haldeman—Weicker declared on the CBS "Face the Nation" program April 1 that "I think it's absolutely necessary" for Haldeman to testify before the Select Committee. While making no accusations of Haldeman's direct complicity in the case, Weicker said it was probable that Haldeman knew of a Nixon campaign unit responsible for "disruption" and "surveillance" and that "when it came to personnel, he knew what was going on and there was nothing in the way of policies that he didn't know was going on either."

Weicker said Republican officials had tried during the presidential campaign to put the offices of nine GOP and Democratic critics of the Nixon Administration under surveillance.

Weicker called for Haldeman's resignation April 3 on the ground he "clearly" had "to accept responsibility" for political espionage and sabotage conducted on behalf of the Nixon re-election campaign.

The Select Committee's statement that it had "no evidence of any nature" linking Haldeman with "any illegal acts" in connection with the 1972 campaign was issued April 4 by Ervin and his vice chairman, Sen. Howard H. Baker Jr. (R, Tenn.), "in the interests of fairness and justice."

More GOP senators restive—Republicans continued to criticize the Nixon Administration's handling of the Watergate controversy.

Sen. Robert Packwood (R, Ore.) said March 24 the case had become a "dagger in the heart" of the Republican party and called on the President to disclose the facts and appoint a nonpartisan prosecutor for a probe. "It's not going to go away," he said. "The trail of ever-decreasing concentric circles seems to narrow on the coterie at the White House."

Sen. Jacob K. Javits (R, N.Y.) said April 4 if the President "made the investigation which he says he has...he should share with the public the details of what he found out. I don't think he should kiss it off with a blanket statement that everything's OK."

An assurance that "the White House has nothing to hide" in the Watergate case came March 24 from Senate GOP Leader Hugh Scott (Pa.). He quoted Nixon as saying, "Hugh, I have nothing to hide. The White House has nothing to hide. I repeat we have nothing to hide and you are authorized to make that statement in my name."

Gray nomination withdrawn. The nomination of L. Patrick Gray 3rd to become director of the Federal Bureau of Investigation (FBI) was withdrawn April 5. Gray disclosed he had asked President Nixon to withdraw his nomination, and a spokesman at the Western White House at San Clemente, Calif. said the President had "regretfully agreed." Gray had been acting FBI director since the death of J. Edgar Hoover in May 1972.

The nomination had become enmeshed in the Watergate political espionage controversy. The Senate Judiciary Committee, in its hearings on Gray's confirmation, had explored the connection between Gray and John W. Dean 3rd, counsel to the President, who had been linked to the Watergate defendants. After Dean's refusal to testify, the committee sought to broaden the inquiry and delay decision on the nomination.

The panel held a surprise session April 5 to consider a motion to kill the nomination by indefinitely postponing confirmation, but adjourned without taking action.

A few hours later, Gray announced his withdrawal, saying the FBI should have "permanent leadership at the earliest possible time." The President's announcement observed that, "in view of the action of the Senate Judiciary Committee" it was "obvious that Mr. Gray's nomination will not be confirmed by the Senate." Therefore it was being withdrawn, he said, "in fairness to Mr. Gray, and out of my overriding concern for the effective conduct of the vitally important business of the FBI." The President referred to Dean's controversial role in his statement. Because he asked Dean to conduct a thorough investigation of "alleged involvement in the Watergate episode," he said, Gray was asked to make FBI reports available to Dean. "His compliance with this completely proper and necessary request," Nixon said, "exposed Mr. Gray to totally unfair inneundo and suspicion and thereby seriously tarnished his fine record as acting director and promising future at the bureau."

During the prolonged confirmation hearings the President had continued to express support for Gray. The latest was relayed from San Clemente March 31 by Deputy White House Press Secretary Gerald L. Warren, who said suggestions that Nixon had decided to withdraw the nomination were "totally false."

An opponent of the Gray nomination within the Senate Judiciary Committee, Sen. Robert C. Byrd (D, W. Va.), said after the withdrawal announcement he believed Gray had done "the right thing under the circumstances." Another opponent on the committee, Sen. John V. Tunney (D, Calif.), said the withdrawal was "in the best interest of a nonpartisan and independent" FBI.

Payoffs to defendants alleged. James W. McCord Jr. was reported April 9 to have told a federal grand jury investigating the Watergate case that cash payments had been paid to defendants in the criminal case for their silence and pressure applied for guilty pleas.

He was also reported to have named, on a hearsay basis, Kenneth W. Parkinson, then attorney for the Committee to Re-elect the President, as the person he believed responsible for applying the pressure and channeling the payments. The New York Times confirmed the testimony, originally leaked from "sources close to the case," in a telephone interview with McCord.

The reports noted that McCord's testimony concerning Parkinson's alleged role was based on talks with Mrs. Dorothy Hunt, who was named by McCord as the conduit for the cash payments. Mrs. Hunt was the deceased wife of another convicted Watergate defendant, E. Howard Hunt Jr.

Parkinson, currently a member of a Washington law firm, was also contacted by the Times and said the allegations against him were "absolutely false."

The amount of the cash payments was said to be $1,000 per month for each of the four defendants arrested with McCord at the Watergate building June 17, 1972 during the bugging operation inside the Democratic national headquarters, and according to the Washington Post April 10, $3,000 a month for McCord.

Mitchell involvement alleged—According to a Post report April 12, also confirmed by McCord, of his further testimony before the grand jury, McCord claimed that convicted co-conspirator G. Gordon Liddy had told him transcripts of wire-tapped conversations of Democratic officials had been hand-carried to former Attorney General John N. Mitchell. Liddy also told him, according to the report, that Mitchell had ordered a priority list of electronic eavesdropping operations against the Democrats—first the Watergate headquarters, then the campaign headquarters of Sen. George S. McGovern, then the Miami hotel rooms to be occupied by presidential candidates and party officials attending the national convention. The newspaper noted the hearsay basis of the allegations.

Mitchell's denial of both charges was relayed through the Committee to Re-

A elect the President. McCord was appearing before the grand jury with a grant of immunity from further prosecution.

McCord's lawyer, Bernard W. Fensterwald, told reporters April 9 that McCord had no first-hand knowledge that anybody "higher up" than Liddy knew of the Watergate operation.

McCord also was giving depositions in civil Watergate suits.

B *Dean role in hiring indicated*—According to sworn federal court testimony in the civil suit, made public April 6, McCord was of the impression he had been cleared for his security post with the re-election committee by John W. Dean 3rd, counsel to President Nixon. He had been interviewed, he said in his deposition, by White House Assistant John Caulfield, who told him he was sending "some sort of a note to John Dean about me and my qualifications." Caulfield later showed

C the note to McCord and "indicated that Mr. Dean had initialed it or words to that effect." McCord also reported being introduced to Dean later by Caulfield, still, apparently in relation to the security post.

Denials came later April 6 from the White House and the re-election committee. A spokesman for the President said Dean had "no recollection" of "being involved" in McCord's hiring and knew of "no such memo" he allegedly initialed.

D Committee spokesman DeVan Shumway denied there had been any meeting between McCord and Dean or any involvement by Dean. "John Dean just simply was not involved at any stage," Shumway said, and Caulfield "says he has no recollection of introducing Dean to McCord, remembers no memo to Dean about McCord and denies writing one." Caulfield currently was in a Treasury Department post.

E Dean had been reported previously to have recommended Liddy for his post as counsel to the Nixon campaign committee and its fund-raising arm.

(Syndicated columnist Jack Anderson reported in his column published April 5 that Dean had been fired from his first job with a Washington law firm because of a complaint of "unethical conduct" that was later changed by the firm to a statement of "basic disagreement" over policy. White House Press Secretary Ronald Ziegler said later that day Nixon

F retained "confidence" in Dean and emphasized the firm's final assessment of the situation.)

Segretti appears before grand jury— Another witness before the grand jury April 11 was Donald H. Segretti, who had been reported to have been paid at

G least $30,000 from GOP funds for covert political activity during the 1972 presidential campaign.

Lawrence Young, a California attorney who had disclosed conversations with Segretti in which he alleged White House

contacts in spying and sabotage activity, reported April 9 receipt of a letter from Segretti's attorney warning him that any communication between him and Segretti was covered by the lawyer-client privilege of confidentiality and "not to be discussed by you under any circumstances." Young denied any lawyer-client relationship with Segretti and charged that the letter was an attempt to "muzzle" him.

Goldwater warns Nixon. A warning that the Watergate case was hurting the Republican party and turning away contributors was sounded April 11 by Sen. Barry Goldwater (Ariz.), the party's presidential candidate in 1964. In an interview in the Christian Science Monitor, Goldwater said: "The Watergate. The Watergate. It's beginning to be like Teapot Dome [1922 Harding Administration scandal]. I mean, there's a smell to it. Let's get rid of the smell."

Goldwater said he had been getting letters and calls from Republican friends "all around the country" and they were saying "'No more money to the Republican national committee until this is cleared up'." He said he had been urging the President to speak out on the case and "give assurances."

Anne Armstrong, counselor to President Nixon and liaison between the White House and the GOP national committee, told reporters April 11 that Goldwater was "absolutely right," that the party was "being hurt" by Watergate, that fund-raising efforts were being affected and GOP candidates could be affected in the future.

Republican National Chairman George Bush called the Watergate incident a "grubby affair" April 7 and said it should be promptly and fully cleared up.

Nixon agrees to permit testimony. President Nixon announced April 17 there had been "major developments" from a "new" inquiry he had initiated into the Watergate case involving the break-in at the Democratic national headquarters in the Watergate building in Washington June 17, 1972.

The President also announced he had agreed to permit testimony under certain conditions by his aides before a Senate investigating committee. "I believe," he said, an agreement had been reached with the committee on ground rules for the testimony which would "preserve," he said, "the separation of powers without suppressing the fact."

The President made the announcements in a brief statement he read to reporters at the White House after a stipulation he would not engage in a question-and-answer session afterward. [See text]

In his statement, Nixon said he had begun "intensive new inquiries into this whole matter" March 21 "as a result of serious charges which came to my attention, some of which were publicly reported." He said he had met Sunday,

April 15 in the Executive Office Building adjoining the White House with Attorney General Richard G. Kleindienst and Assistant Attorney General Henry Peterson "to review the facts which had come to me in my investigation and also to review the progress" of a separate investigation by the Justice Department.

He stated "that there have been major developments in the case" but said "it would be improper to be more specific now except to say that real progress has been made in finding the truth."

"If any person," Nixon continued, "in the executive branch or in the government is indicted by the grand jury, my policy will be to immediately suspend him. If he is convicted, he will, of course, be automatically discharged."

The President asserted his view that "no individual holding, in the past or at present, a position of major importance in the Administration should be given immunity from prosecution." He would aid the judicial process "in all appropriate ways," he said, and "all government employes and especially White House staff employes are expected fully to cooperate in this matter. I condemn any attempts to cover up in this case, no matter who is involved."

The President said discussions for the ground rules on Watergate testimony by White House aides had been initiated several weeks ago between Sens. Sam J. Ervin Jr. (D, N.C.) and Howard H. Baker Jr. (R, Tenn.), chairman and vice chairman of the Senate Select Committee, and John D. Ehrlichman, the President's special assistant on domestic affairs, and White House aide Leonard Garment. The committee's ground rules, Nixon said, "totally preserve the doctrine of separation of powers." "They provide," he said, that a witness could first appear in secret session, "if appropriate," and that executive privilege was "expressly reserved and may be asserted" during the testimony. He said White House staff members "will appear voluntarily when requested" and "will testify under oath and they will answer fully all proper questions."

After Nixon's statement, White House Press Secretary Ronald L. Ziegler said the President's previous statements denying Watergate involvement by White House staff members* were now "inoperative" since they were based on

---

*President Nixon's previous statements on the Watergate case:

At a news conference Aug. 29, 1972, he disclosed that his own staff had investigated the affair and he could "categorically" state that the probe "indicates that no one in the White House staff, no one in this Administration, presently employed, was involved in this very bizarre incident."

The President, at a news conference March 2, reiterated that the White House investigation of Watergate indicated that no one on the White House staff at the time the investigation was conducted was involved "or had knowledge of the Watergate matter."

President Nixon, at an impromptu news conference March 15, said he had confidence in all the White House staffers who had been linked to Watergate.

"investigations prior to the developments announced today."

The statement drew an angry accusation at the press briefing April 18 from Clark Mollenhoff, reporter for the Des Moines (Iowa) Register and Tribune and former White House aide. "Do you feel free to stand up there," he asked Ziegler, "and lie and put out misinformation and then come around later and say it's all 'inoperative'? That's what you're doing. You're not entitled to any credibility at all."

In reply, Ziegler said of the White House policy on Watergate that he was "not in a position to answer any questions no matter how they are phrased on the subject" since it "could very well prejudice the prosecution or the rights of innocent individuals or indeed the judicial process itself."

AFL-CIO American Newspaper Guild President Charles A. Perlik Jr. sent a telegram to the White House April 18 demanding an apology from the President to the press "on behalf of yourself and all those in your Administration who have so willingly and freely heaped calumny" on the news media for its coverage of the Watergate case.

Nixon decision welcomed—Sen. Ervin commented later April 17 that he was "very glad to hear the announcement" by the President. As to the "major developments" spoken of, Ervin said "I don't know what he's talking about but I'm glad that he is talking."

Sen. Baker said: "We now have the biggest hurdle behind us. The President has made the determination to reveal the entire situation and I commend him for it."

A persistent Republican Watergate critic, Sen. Lowell P. Weicker Jr. (Conn.), said: "The spirit of getting at the truth that slowly and surely has been building up in this country, whether by the citizenry or by senators, now has everyone in its grip. Believe me, we're going to have that truth; we're going to have that story."

Earlier developments—Critical Republican reaction to the handling of the Watergate situation had continued to mount prior to the President's announcement.

Rep. John J. Rhodes (Ariz.), chairman of the House Republican Policy Committee, said April 13 that the "continual mystery surrounding Watergate is hurting the image of President Nixon and the Republican party in the eyes of people everywhere."

Sen. William B. Saxbe (R, Ohio) objected the same day to the White House attitude "that it has no guilt or responsibility" while the facts "indicate otherwise."

House Republican Leader Gerald R. Ford (Mich.) told a GOP gathering in his home state April 16 that prominent Administration figures linked to Watergate and denying it should "go before the Senate committee, take an oath and deny it publicly."

Mitchell 'eager' to testify—Former Attorney General John N. Mitchell told reporters April 14 he was eager to testify before the Ervin committee, that he "just can't wait to get down there."

Mitchell, talking to reporters at a New York airport, indicated that he had visited the White House and asserted his assurance that "everybody who's involved, or has been stated to be involved [in Watergate] will come forward" to testify.

Mitchell's visit to the White House, which occurred April 14, was unconfirmed for several days. Meanwhile, his wife Martha claimed he had conferred with Nixon and called a White House denial a "lie." Press Secretary Ziegler disclosed April 17 that Mitchell had visited the White House to talk with Ehrlichman.

Ervin issues guidelines. Sen. Ervin, chairman of the Senate's Select Committee on Presidential Campaign Activities, issued the committee's guidelines on the Watergate investigation April 18, noting that the panel would be the final judge on whether a witness could refuse to answer its questions.

"The guidelines say just what was the law already in any kind of a fair investigation," he said, "that if any witness claims that he is privileged for any reason against testifying, he can raise that point. But just like in court, somebody has to rule on that point, and these guidelines expressly say that the committee's going to do the ruling. If the committee rules adversely to the witness on any question of privilege, the committee shall require the witness to testify."

The rules also expressly stated that a claim of privilege against testifying could not be claimed by or for any witness prior to appearance before the committee. The committee would not rule on such a claim "until the question by which the testimony is sought is put to the witness."

As for the President's stipulation that a witness could make his first appearance before the committee in secret session "if appropriate," the rules provided the committee with the power of decision. The guideline itself stipulated that "all witnesses shall testify" under oath in open hearings."

Ervin revealed that the committee in its discussion with Presidential assistant John Ehrlichman on the ground rules had yielded only two points to the Administration—permission for the President to have his own legal counsel present when White House aides testified and sufficient notice to the White House when a Presidential aide was to be called as a witness.

Ervin also said the discussion had been held at Ehrlichman's invitation and during it Ervin and Baker had mentioned they intended to develop guidelines. "I'm glad the President saw the guidelines as a reason for reversing his previous declarations [on testimony from White House aides]," Ervin said.

To queries from newsmen about whether the President's announcement represented a victory for Congress in its conflict with the President over constitutional prerogatives, Ervin said it was not

---

Text of President's Statement on Watergate Case

I have two announcements to make. Because of their technical nature, I shall read both of the announcements to the members of the press corps.

The first announcement relates to the appearance of White House people before the Senate Select Committee, better known as the Ervin Committee.

For several weeks, Senator Ervin and Senator Baker and their counsel have been in contact with White House representatives John Ehrlichman and Leonard Garment. They have been talking about ground rules which would preserve the separation of powers without suppressing the fact.

I believe now an agreement has been reached which is satisfactory to both sides. The committee ground rules as adopted totally preserve the doctrine of separation of powers. They provide that the appearance by a witness may, in the first instance, be in executive session, if appropriate.

Second, executive privilege is expressly reserved and may be asserted during the course of the questioning as to any questions.

Now, much has been made of the issue as to whether the proceedings could be televised. To me, this has never been a central issue, especially if the separation of powers problem is otherwise solved, as I now think it is.

All members of the White House staff will appear voluntarily when requested by the committee. They will testify under oath and they will answer fully all proper questions.

I should point out that this arrangement is one that covers this hearing only in which wrongdoing has been charged. This kind of arrangement, of course, would not apply to other hearings. Each of them will be considered on its merits.

My second announcement concerns the Watergate case directly.

On March 21, as a result of serious charges which came to my attention, some of which were publicly reported, I began intensive new inquiries into this whole matter.

Last Sunday afternoon the attorney general Richard G. Kleindienst] assistant attorney general [Henry E. Petersen] and I met at length in the E.O.B. [Executive Office Building] to review the facts which had come to me in my investigation and also to review the progress of the Department of Justice investigation.

I can report today that there have been major developments in the case concerning which it would be improper to be more specific now, except to say that real progress has been made in finding the truth.

If any person in the executive branch or in the government is indicted by the grand jury, my policy will be to immediately suspend him. If he is convicted, he will, of course, be automatically discharged.

I have expressed to the appropriate authorities my view that no individual holding, in the past or at present, a position of major importance in the Administration should be given immunity from prosecution.

The judicial process is moving ahead as it should; and I shall aid it in all appropriate ways and have so informed the appropriate authorities.

As I have said before and I have said throughout this entire matter, all government employes and especially White House staff employes are expected fully to cooperate in this matter. I condemn any attempts to cover up in this case, no matter who is involved.

"so much a victory for Congress as a victory for constitutional government."

The President may have "finally decided," he said, "there were some laws in the Constitution that belonged on the Congressional side of the separation of powers." Ervin spoke at a news conference at Davidson (N.C.) College, where he had a speaking engagement.

Dean warns he is no scapegoat. In an unusual personal statement telephoned to newspaper offices by his secretary, Dean asserted April 19 he would not "become a scapegoat in the Watergate case." The statement was not cleared through Press Secretary Ronald Ziegler or the other usual White House channels. Newspaper accounts, based on information from Dean's associates, made it clear that Dean was prepared to implicate people "above and below" if he was singled out for prosecution.

In his statement, Dean said it was his hope "that those truly interested in seeing that the Watergate case is completely aired and that justice will be done will be careful in drawing any conclusions as to the guilt or involvement of any persons until all the facts are known and until each person has had an opportunity to testify under oath in his own behalf."

"Finally, some may hope or think that I will become a scapegoat in the Watergate case. Anyone who believes this does not know me, know the true facts nor understand our system of justice."

In what was considered a rebuke to Dean, Ziegler later April 19 said the President's April 17 statement "made it quite clear that the process now under way is not one to find scapegoats but one to get at the truth."

Asked about Dean's current status at the White House, Ziegler replied, "He's in his office. I don't know what he's doing. Attending to business, I assume, business of some sort."

Dean said to press for disclosure—Reports that Dean had gone to the federal Watergate prosecutors April 6 with information about the raid and subsequent developments were published by the Washington Post April 27 and in the April 30 edition of Time magazine. Time said the information had provided the first corroboration of the largely hearsay testimony of Watergate conspirator James W. McCord Jr. and gave new impetus to the grand jury probe.

The Post report said Dean had divulged everything he knew about the bugging and subsequent White House coverup of the involvement of Presidential aides.

The Post account, attributed to Dean's associates, said he had told President Nixon March 20 that to "save the presidency" Dean, Nixon chief of staff H. R. Haldeman and Ehrlichman would have to reveal all they knew about the case and might have to face jail terms. The story said there was no suggestion that Haldeman or Ehrlichman had approved the Watergate operation. It said their role lay in a possible cover-up of White House aides' involvement in the bugging and in authorization of Dean's role in the cover-up.

According to the Post sources, Dean told Nixon March 20 that Haldeman and Ehrlichman had instructed him after June 17, 1972 never to discuss the bugging with the President and they would transmit any messages that Dean cared to convey.

There was a report April 21 in the New York Times that Haldeman was under investigation by the grand jury because a secret GOP fund of $350,000 in cash had been turned over to a Haldeman aide one day before the new campaign finance reporting law went into effect in 1972. The fund was said to have been returned after the November election to the private apartment of a Nixon campaign worker.

Mitchell in on 'bugging' discussions. The Washington Post April 19 reported the implication of former Attorney General John Mitchell in discussions of plans for political espionage against the Democrats.

According to the Post, Jeb Stuart Magruder, Mitchell's former aide in the Nixon re-election campaign, told federal prosecutors April 14 that he and Mitchell, presidential counsel Dean and convicted Watergate defendant G. Gordon Liddy had planned and approved the Watergate wiretapping at a meeting in the attorney general's office in February 1972. (There was a Times report April 22 that Liddy had rejected a White House request to end his silence on his Watergate role.)

Magruder was said to have told the prosecutors that Mitchell and Dean later arranged to buy the silence of the seven convicted Watergate conspirators.

A New York Times report April 20 said Mitchell had disclosed in private conversations with friends that he had participated in three meetings on the proposed wiretapping plan—on Jan. 24 and Feb. 4, 1972 while he was attorney general and in March 1972, when he was manager of the Nixon re-election campaign. Mitch-

---

Ervin Committee's Guidelines on Witnesses

In investigating the matters mentioned in S. Res. 60, the Senate Select Committee on Presidential Campaign Activities will observe its standing rules, its previously established procedures for staff interviews of prospective witnesses, and these guidelines:

1. The committee will receive oral and documentary evidence relevant to the matters S. Res. 60 authorizes it to investigate and matters bearing on the credibility of the witnesses who testify before it.

2. All witnesses shall testify before the committee on oath or affirmation in hearings which shall be open to the public and the news media. This guideline shall not abridge, however, the power of the committee to take the testimony of a particular witness on oath or affirmation in an executive meeting if the committee would otherwise be unable to ascertain whether the witness knows anything relevant to the matters the committee is authorized to investigate.

3. All still and motion picture photography will be completed before a witness actually testifies, and no such photography shall occur while the witness is testifying. Television coverage of a witness and his testimony shall be permitted, however, under the provisions of the standing rules of the committee.

4. In taking the testimony of a witness, the committee will endeavor to do two things: First, to minimize inconvenience to the witness and disruption of his affairs; and, second, to afford the witness a fair opportunity to give his testimony without undue interruption.

To achieve the first of these objectives, the committee will honor the request of the witness to the extent feasible for advance notice of the time and place appointed for taking his testimony, complete the taking of his testimony with as much dispatch as circumstances permit, and release the witness from further attendance on the committee as soon as circumstances allow, subject, however, to the power of the committee to recall him for further testimony in the event the committee deems such action advisable.

To afford the witness a fair opportunity to present his testimony, the committee will permit the witness to make an opening statement not exceeding 20 minutes, which shall not be interrupted by questioning and a closing statement summarizing his testimony, not exceeding five minutes, which will not be interrupted by questioning: Provided, however, questions suggested by the closing statement may be propounded after such statement is made.

5. The committee respects and recognizes the right of a prospective witness who is interviewed by the staff of the committee in advance of a public hearing as well as the right of a witness who appears before the committee to be accompanied by a lawyer of his own choosing to advise him concerning his constitutional and legal rights as a witness.

6. If the lawyer who accompanies a witness before the committee advises the witness to claim a privilege against giving any testimony sought by the committee, the committee shall have the discretionary power to permit the lawyer to present his views on the matter for the information of the committee, and the committee shall thereupon rule on the validity of the claim or its application to the particular circumstances involved and require the witness to give the testimony sought in the event its ruling on the claim is adverse to the witness.

Neither the witness nor any other officer or person shall be permitted to claim a privilege against the witness testifying prior to the appearance of the witness before the committee, and the committee shall not rule in respect to the claim until the question by which the testimony is sought is put to the witness.

7. The committee believes that it may be necessary for it to obtain the testimony of some White House aides if the committee is to be able to ascertain the complete truth in respect to the matters it is authorized to investigate by S. Res. 60.

To this end, the committee will invite such White House aides as it has reason to believe have knowledge or information relevant to the matters it is authorized to investigate to appear before the committee and give testimony on oath or affirmation in open hearings respecting such matters.

In this connection, the committee will extend to such aides the considerations set forth in detail in Guideline No. 4 and the right to counsel set forth in detail in Guidelines Nos. 5 and 6.

In addition to these considerations and rights, the committee will permit the White House to have its own counsel present when any White House aide appears before the committee as a witness, and permit such counsel to invoke any claim that a privilege available to the President forbids a White House aide to give the testimony sought by the committee, and the committee shall thereupon rule on validity of such claim or its application to the particular testimony sought in the manner and with the effect set forth in Guideline No. 6 in respect to a claim of privilege invoked by a witness or his counsel.

The committee will not subpoena a White House aide to appear before it or its staff unless such aide fails to make timely response to an invitation to appear.

8. The committee may require the sergeant-at-arms of the Senate, or any of his assistants or deputies, or any available law-enforcement officer to eject from a meeting of the committee any person who willfully disrupts the meeting or willfully impedes the committee in the performance of its functions under S. Res. 60.

9. Whenever the committee takes testimony through the agency of less than the majority of the members of the committee as authorized by its standing rules, the member or members of the committee taking the testimony shall be vested with the powers set forth in these guidelines and shall be deemed to act as the committee in exercising such powers.

ell was said to have confirmed that Liddy and Magruder had discussed spying on the Democrats at these meetings, but Mitchell reportedly said he had rejected the plans on each occasion. Dean was said to have been present at one or more of the sessions. Mitchell appeared before the Watergate grand jury April 20 and confirmed the substance of the report in the Times.

Magruder's resignation as an assistant commerce secretary was reported April 26 by his lawyer, who said it had been submitted during the past week. No immediate confirmation was available from the White House or the Commerce Department. Magruder was the department's director of policy development for the post-inaugural personnel realignment.

Mitchell's grand jury testimony. Former Attorney General Mitchell testified before the federal grand jury investigating the case April 20. He told reporters afterward that he had "heard discussions" of plans to spy on the Democrats during the 1972 presidential campaign but he had "never approved any bugging plans during any period during the campaign." "They've always been cut off at all times," he said in reference to the wiretapping plans, "and I would like to know who it was that kept bringing them back and back and back." Mitchell said he had given "an absolute final disapproval" to the wiretap proposal and had testified before the grand jury "fully and freely and openly" on the matter. In talks with reporters later in the day, Mitchell said the proposals were more than "just to bug somebody" and involved an "entire intelligence gathering program." He said, "electronic surveillance was turned down and turned down and turned down and that was disposed of."

There also were reports April 20 that Mitchell had told the grand jury he had approved payments of Nixon campaign funds to the seven Watergate defendants for their legal fees, not, as alleged by Magruder, to buy their silence.

Attorney William G. Hundley, retained by Mitchell April 19, told the New York Times April 20 that Mitchell had been prepared to testify "he had some knowledge that Republican re-election funds were being used to pay the legal fees for the defendants." Hundley quoted Mitchell as saying that such payments were normal practice in the business world.

The April 20 Times report said that Dean allegedly had supervised cash payments of more than $175,000 in GOP funds to the Watergate defendants and their lawyers. The allegation was denied later April 20 as "absolutely untrue" by Dean's lawyer, Robert C. McCandless of Washington.

Mitchell on stand in N.Y., Florida—Mitchell testified for four hours before another federal grand jury in New York April 23. The panel was investigating possible connections between a $200,000 contribution to the Nixon campaign by Robert L. Vesco, a financier charged by the Securities and Exchange Commission (SEC) with masterminding a securities fraud, and attempts to influence the SEC investigation.

Mitchell, who had made an earlier appearance before the grand jury, refused to discuss his testimony with newsmen but noted that he had agreed to testify voluntarily. "I answered all questions of the grand jury fully, frankly and freely," Mitchell declared. He denied ever having met Vesco.

Mitchell appeared in Pensacola, Fla. April 25 at a pretrial hearing for seven members of the Vietnam Veterans Against the War (VVAW) and another person charged with conspiring to disrupt the 1972 Republican National Convention at Miami Beach with bombs and bullets.

The defense contended that the Nixon re-election committee had used illegal electronic surveillance against the VVAW and then used the data for its conspiracy case. Mitchell testified that convicted Watergate defendant Liddy had headed an intelligence unit within the GOP re-election committee but that he (Mitchell) knew of no surveillance by it against VVAW.

Mitchell 'deniability' sought—Mitchell's name was linked to the wiretapping plan in further leaked testimony by convicted Watergate conspirator James W. McCord Jr., based on hearsay from his fellow conspirator Liddy. According to McCord, Dean had warned that the Watergate operation would have to be undertaken in such a way that Mitchell "would have deniability about it at a future date." Dean allegedly said the funding for the operation would be kept apart from the Nixon campaign "so that there would be no record of it."

McCord said that Hunt and Hunt's late wife had indicated to him that executive clemency would be granted by the President after a short jail term if he remained silent at the trial and did not implicate others. The White House denied the allegation April 24.

The "deniability" factor was quoted in a McCord memorandum to the federal grand jury, a copy of which was obtained by syndicated columnist Jack Anderson, who let reporters examine it April 24. He also displayed copies of grand jury transcripts he had obtained and used as the basis for several columns on the case since April 16. Watergate prosecution sources indicated the material was authentic, and Chief Judge John J. Sirica of the federal court in Washington April 22 ordered an investigation into the leaks. (All grand jury deliberations are secret.) After meeting April 25 with federal prosecutors, Anderson said he had agreed to their request to stop publishing the excerpts and would return transcripts to the court. He said he acted out of "great respect" for Sirica.

Kleindienst bars involvement in case. Attorney General Richard G. Kleindienst removed himself from the Watergate case April 19. He said: "Having been advised on Sunday, April 15, 1973, of information which relates to persons with whom I have had a close personal and professional relationship, I concluded on that date that it would be entirely inappropriate for me to exercise control over the sensitive matters being developed by the Department of Justice in connection with the Watergate investigation." He said Assistant Attorney General Petersen would have "full responsibilities" for the probe and would be "responsible only to the President."

It was assumed that among those with close ties to Kleindienst were Mitchell, his superior at the department for three years, and Dean, who served in the department under Mitchell and Kleindienst in 1969 and 1970.

GOP offers $525,000 to Democrats. The Democratic National Committee April 19 rejected an offer from the Committee to Re-elect the President for a $525,000 out of court settlement in the $6.4 million civil damage suit brought by the Democrats as a consequence of the Watergate breakin.

The Democrats rejected the offer to drop the case, saying the Justice Department's investigation of the Watergate affair was open to possible presidential influence and that its own lawsuit could prove the only means of ascertaining the truth.

Committee chairman Robert S. Strauss said the party had decided to "maintain a very aggressive posture" on the court issue after consulting with Democratic leadership in Congress, governors and committee members.

The party was also launching a special fund-raising operation to help pay litigation expenses, Strauss said. He added that mounting legal costs and the prospect of a $525,000 windfall from the Republicans had formed the basis of his initial willingness to accept the GOP offer, which was first reported April 17.

Strauss said that at the time of those negotiations he had considered the Republicans' effort at dropping the case an "admission of guilt." But strong opposition to any deal with the re-election committee came from state Democratic party chairmen, causing him to reverse his prior position, Strauss conceded; however, he denied that his dismissal of S. Robert Oliver, a committee official whose telephone had been among those tapped during the break-in attempt and who had remained a vehement opponent of settling the case, had any relation to the party's discussions about the future of the lawsuit.

Strauss revealed April 18 that former GOP campaign chairman John Mitchell, a co-defendant in the civil suit, had also attempted to arrange a settlement of the case. "We are not in accord, but we have talked both in person and on the telephone within the last couple of weeks," Strauss said.

Nixon actions. In the midst of the mounting press and political criticism of the Administration's handling of the affair, President Nixon spent a secluded 5-day working Easter vacation at Key Biscayne, Fla. and Grand Cay in the Bahamas. He left Washington April 20 after meeting with his Cabinet to tell them the objective of the Watergate investigation was to discover "the entire truth of the matter" and that he wanted "everyone in the Administration, everyone in government to cooperate fully with the ongoing investigation and the grand jury." According to Time magazine's April 30 edition, a participant in the Cabinet meeting described the mood as "concern bordering on despair."

White House Press Secretary Ziegler, who reported to newsmen on the Cabinet meeting, was the only senior official accompanying the President to Florida. The press noted that Haldeman and Ehrlichman, who usually accompanied him, were absent. Ziegler did not make himself available to newsmen after arriving in Florida.

A White House denial April 23 that Nixon had any prior knowledge of the Watergate raid came from deputy White House Press Secretary Gerald L. Warren, who told questioning newsmen, "of course not, he did not know."

A report that Nixon telephoned Dean April 22 to wish him "happy Easter" and tell him "you're still my counsel" came April 23 from "a source close to" Dean. Warren confirmed the call April 24 and said Nixon also had telephoned Easter greetings to Haldeman and Ehrlichman.

In another belated disclosure April 24, the day Nixon returned to Washington, the White House said Nixon had met April 19 with Washington lawyer John J. Wilson, who had acknowledged April 21 he had been retained April 17 to represent Haldeman and Ehrlichmen in the Watergate controversy.

McCord sues Nixon committee. McCord filed a $1.5 million damage suit against the Nixon re-election committee and three of its officials April 20. He said his reputation had been damaged and he had suffered "intense mental anguish" as a result of his role in the Watergate case, undertaken with the understanding it had been "approved and sanctioned" by the committee's highest officials.

Brooke, Weicker comment. Sen. Edward W. Brooke (R, Mass.) called the Watergate raid April 22 "an act of stupidity" and said President Nixon could not escape the responsibility for it "under any circumstances." If he had any information "which should be made known to the American people, I think he should do it forthwith," Brooke said.

Appearing on NBC's "Meet the Press" broadcast, Brooke said "it is inconceivable to me" that persons working with Nixon would not have told him about "this matter. In fact, that they wouldn't have asked for his approval or disapproval."

Sen. Lowell P. Weicker Jr. (R, Conn.), a member of the Senate Select Committee probing Watergate, said April 24 "nothing in the course of my investigation to date has led to the President" and while some might speculate about Nixon's involvement, "I care to speculate that he didn't know" about the raid beforehand.

"The President is deeply involved in being president ... and not deeply involved in matters of politics," Weicker said.

Nixon drops 14 points in polls. President Nixon's popularity rating as recorded by the Gallup Poll dropped 14 points by early April from a high point in late January. The early April rating, published April 22, was 54% approval among those interviewed, 36% disapproval. In late January he received a 68%–25% rating.

The 54% popularity from polling conducted April 6–9 revealed a 5-point drop within a week from a 59%–33% showing in polling completed April 2.

In survey results published April 22, Gallup found that 83% of those interviewed had heard or read about Watergate, a 31% increase over a similar survey conducted in October 1972 during the presidential campaign. He also found more people (41%) believed Nixon knew in advance about the Watergate situation than felt he did not (32%).

GOP makes partial disclosure. Three cartons of GOP campaign finance documents sought by the public interest lobby Common Cause were turned over to federal district court in Washington April 23.

Common Cause had brought suit against the Finance Committee to Re-elect the President Sept. 6, 1972 in an effort to force full disclosure of the Republicans' financial records during the 15-month period preceding April 7, 1972 when federal law did not require public disclosure of campaign contribution sources and committee expenditures.

The financial records would establish a further link between the GOP's secret cash flow, estimated at more than $10 million, and intelligence and surveillance activities of the Nixon re-election committee, Common Cause contended.

"The Watergate is not primarily a story of political espionage, nor even of White House intrigue. It is a particularly malodorous chapter in the annals of campaign financing. The money paid to the Watergate conspirators before the break-in—and the money passed to them later—was money from campaign gifts. It was not found in a peapatch," John Gardner head of Common Cause, declared April 23.

The three cartons of documents, which Common Cause lawyers claimed did not represent a complete file of material it sought, were not released until after Maurice Stans, chairman of the Finance Committee to Re-Elect the President, had tried to secure an out-of-court settlement in the case without revealing the identity of donors contributing more than $5,000 to the GOP during the contested time period.

According to Gardner, political pressures within the Administration resulting from the Watergate affair motivated Stans' decision to end the court test. "I support the view that there was some command decision to settle it," Gardner said. "It was clear that Mr. Stans was operating on a fairly urgent timetable."

Following Stans' alleged coverup attempts, Common Cause tried, but was unable, to serve subpoenas April 20 on George F. Lynch Jr. and his partner in a Maryland accounting firm, Harry M. Buchanan (brother of White House aide Patrick J. Buchanan), for release of relevant campaign papers in their possession.

The move was based on the possibility that one of the men was the yet secret client of Peter H. Wolf, a Washington attorney. Wolf had told Watergate Judge John J. Sirica that he represented a client who had hidden eight cartons of documents relating to Watergate dealings and Republican finances. The papers had been removed from White House offices one day after the break-in and returned to the re-election committee "shortly before the election," Wolf said April 19. (Wolf added that he had told Watergate prosecutor Earl J. Silbert of the pilfered papers "and received an opinion from him that he did not think my client was committing any crime." Silbert rejected Wolf's statement.)

Under an order from Sirica, Wolf revealed his client's identity before a grand jury April 24, but the name was not made public.

The release of the remaining documents in dispute had been required in a pre-election consent agreement concluded Nov. 1, 1972 between Common Cause and Republican lawyers.

As the three cartons of documents were being turned over to the court for examination by Common Cause lawyers, the lobbying group was filing a motion asking Stans to release all documents pertaining to the case within 72 hours or be held in contempt of court.

According to an attorney representing Common Cause, the newly received documents "looked like they were taken from the cartons and thrown down the stairs before they were delivered."

The group also filed a subpoena April 24 for release of material held by the National Archives at the request of the Republican committee.

Nixon said to have known in '72. The Washington Post April 23 quoted high Administration sources as reporting that President Nixon had been warned "as early as last December" that members of his staff were involved in the Watergate case. The Post's informants said the President had been warned "specifically" several times that both Mitchell and Dean were probably implicated in both aspects of the affair—the wiretapping attempt and the later effort to suppress evidence.

Charles W. Colson, a former special counsel to the President was said to have discussed the matter with Nixon three times, strongly urging that he "get rid of some people." Others were reported to have given Nixon similar warnings.

Nixon was said to have responded that he was eager to learn the truth but that Mitchell and Dean had denied the charges and he needed evidence before taking any action.

Gerald L. Warren, deputy White House press secretary, said April 22 there would be no comment on the report when it was published. The Post said that a close associate of Colson had confirmed the story before publication.

Covert pro-mining campaign disclosed. The Committee to Re-elect the President, engaged in a campaign in May 1972 to give a "distorted view" of the U.S. public's response to President Nixon's decision to mine the harbors of North Vietnam, the Washington Post reported April 25.

Among the means employed by the committee was the purchase, in the names of 10 "ordinary" citizens, of a $4,400 advertisement in the May 17, 1972 New York Times criticizing a Times editorial opposing the mining. The Post revealed April 27 that the ad had been initiated and written by Charles W. Colson, then the special counsel to the President.

The Post also disclosed April 25 the reelection committee paid for telegrams to the White House. A White House spokesman had announced May 10, 1972 that telegrams, letters, and telephone calls were running as much as 6-1 in favor of the President, a fact he cited as showing substantial support for Nixon among the public and Congress.

Moreover, these two devices, plus petition drives, rallies, and other efforts, all of which the Post said cost $8,400, were financed by Nixon campaign funds. The expenditures were not reported to the General Accounting Office (GAO) as required by law, the Post said.

Government sources told the Post April 24 the GAO was conducting an investigation into the committee's failure to make the disclosure, and that it intended to forward the study, when completed, to the Justice Department for possible prosecution.

The Post reported that Jeb Stuart Magruder, deputy campaign director, had authorized the expenditures.

The Post reports were supported by a deposition given May 1 by Robert C. Odle Jr., director of administration for the reelection committee, who was testifying in the Democratic party's $6.4 million civil suit against the Finance Committee to Re-elect the President. Odle said he spent $3,000–$4,000 to help organize demonstrators in support of the mining. Odle also testified that the committee's Black Vote Division received $2,000 to organize

a Capitol Hill rally in support of the mining.

The GAO had said April 27 that none of these expenditures had been reported by the re-election committee.

In related developments:

The Post reported April 26 that the Nixon re-election committee rigged a Washington television station poll on the public's response to the mining. The Post said the committee sent in 2,000–4,000 phony ballots to station WTTG. The final result of the poll was 5,157 viewers agreeing with Nixon and 1,158 in disagreement.

James Dooley, former head of the mail room for the committee, admitted in a Post interview that committee workers were sent to buy 1,000 newspapers containing ballots. In addition, he said, 2,-000 post cards were mailed.

DeVan L. Shumway, spokesman for the committee, said April 25 in confirming the rigging: "When you're involved in an election, you do what you can. That type of voluntary poll is the most stackable type thing. We assumed the other side would do it also. On that assumption we proceeded. I don't know if the other side did."

Frank Mankiewicz, a top campaign official, for Democratic presidential candidate George McGovern, replied: "We didn't do it. It didn't occur to us. These guys are something. They assume we have the same sleazy ethics as theirs."

The State Department acknowledged April 30 that a highly partisan letter, written on the department's official stationery and signed by Walter Annenberg, U.S. ambassador to Great Britain, was sent to American citizens at government expense. The letter dated Feb. 5, which praised Nixon policies, was actually written by former White House aide Charles W. Colson and only endorsed by Annenberg, the State Department said.

Fake Kennedy cable cited—Among the papers from the safe of convicted Watergate conspirator E. Howard Hunt Jr. which reportedly had been destroyed by L. Patrick Gray 3rd, acting director of the FBI, at the instruction of White House aides John D. Ehrlichman and John Dean 3rd, was a cable purporting to implicate Kennedy Administration officials in the 1963 assassination of deposed South Vietnam President Ngo Dinh Diem.

Charles W. Colson, a former Nixon aide who had recommended Hunt for a White House job and who was himself implicated in the Watergate scandal, admitted April 30 he had known since February 1972 that Hunt had fabricated the document. Colson also conceded April 30 that he had taken no action to expose Hunt.

William P. Lambert, a former Life magazine reporter who had been trying to determine the authenticity of the cable throughout 1972, won the admission from Colson.

The source of Lambert's access to the cable was not clear, but he claimed April

27 the source had not been Hunt. Also unclear was the extent of the spurious document's circulation within the Administration. President Nixon had asserted Sept. 16, 1971 at a news conference that there had been American "complicity" in the death of Diem.

(The cable, carrying a stamp marked "Rusk" and the names of six other officials, was intended for Henry Cabot Lodge, U.S. ambassador to South Vietnam in 1963. The cable read, "At highest level meeting today, decision reluctantly made that neither you or Harkins [Gen. Paul D. Harkins, commander of U.S. forces in South Vietnam] should intervene in behalf of Diem or Nhu [Ngo Dinh Nhu, Diem's brother] in event they seek asylum.")

Colson admitted that during the summer of 1971 he had urged that Hunt be assigned to the White House group, known as the "plumbers," who were charged with plugging leaks of Administration information to the press.

Hunt, a former agent for the Central Intelligence Agency, was named to the White House staff and during the fall of 1971, was directed to review diplomatic cables and other classified documents relating to the Indochina war. The White House project was designed to demonstrate that responsibility for the war had originated with prior administrations. Colson denied having supervised the investigation or having seen the fake cable at that time.

Agnew expresses faith in Nixon. Vice President Spiro Agnew April 25 declared his "full confidence in the integrity of President Nixon and in his determination and ability to resolve the Watergate matter to the full satisfaction of the American people."

"We are inundated with rumor, hearsay, grand jury leaks, speculation and statements from undisclosed sources," Agnew said. "It is entirely possible that some of this may be proven later to be accurate. And if it is, it must be confronted forthrightly at that time. But the problem is that presently it is virtually impossible to separate fact from fiction."

There was "great temptation to comment," he said, "if only to make certain that the public understands that one does not condone illegal conduct. However, to speculate for such a self-serving purpose would be unfair to those under investigation" and "careless comment might easily compromise the prosecution's position by prejudicing the right of a defendant to a fair trial."

Agnew added: "For these reasons, I will have nothing further to say on the substance of the matter at this time. I may have more to say later."

Agnew declined to answer questions on his 90-second statement, which he read to reporters at a televised news session.

It was his first public comment on the topic since the 1972 campaign.

Gray resigns FBI post. L. Patrick Gray 3rd announced his resignation as acting director of the Federal Bureau of Investigation (FBI) April 27. Environmental Protection Agency Administrator William D. Ruckelshaus was named later that day as his temporary successor.

Gray said he was resigning, effective immediately, "as a consequence" of reports he had burned files removed from the office safe of E. Howard Hunt Jr., a confessed Watergate conspirator who had worked as a White House consultant.

"Serious allegations concerning certain acts of my own during the ongoing Watergate investigation are now a matter of public record," Gray said, and his resignation was "required to preserve in both image and fact the reputation, the integrity and the effectiveness" of the FBI. He said the agency "has been in no way involved in any of those personal acts or judgments that may now be called into question" and "deserves the full trust of the American people: That is bedrock and must always remain so."

Ruckelshaus accepted the FBI appointment in a caretaker capacity until a permanent director was found. He said he expected to serve only a few months.

Ruckelshaus said he had requested and received assurance from the President that "no matter who is involved [in Watergate] there would be no sparing of anyone." Nixon made clear to him, he said, "he wants me to operate the FBI in as vigorous and honest a way as I possibly could."

The reports of Gray's connection with the Watergate case originated with the New York Daily News late April 26 and were confirmed by the New York Times and other newspapers the next morning.

According to the Times, the Hunt files were handed to Gray at a White House meeting June 28, 1972 with John D. Ehrlichman, assistant to the President for domestic affairs, and John W. Dean 3rd, counsel to the President. The story, attributed to Sen. Lowell P. Weicker Jr. (R, Conn.), a close friend of Gray, reported that Dean had cautioned the files "should never see the light of day."

While he could not swear that either Dean or Ehrlichman "ordered" destruction of the papers, Gray was said to have remembered Dean describing the files as "political dynamite" but not dealing with the Watergate bugging. Gray accepted receipt of the files according to the account and then, after Dean left, had a discussion with Ehrlichman about Watergate probe news leaks, the original purpose of his White House appointment. Gray reportedly took the Hunt files home, where they remained until July 3 when he took them to FBI headquarters, tore them up without looking at them and put them in his FBI "burn bag," a container whose contents were destroyed at the end of each day.

Gray recently had discovered, according to the account, that just prior to his arrival in Ehrlichman's office Ehrlichman had asked Dean why it was necessary to hand the files over to the FBI. He was alleged to have said, "You drive over the [Potomac River] bridge every night, why don't you throw them over?"

Ehrlichman statement—In a statement issued late April 26 in response to the story, Ehrlichman confirmed that "Mr. Gray received some of the contents of the Hunt safe at my office from Mr. Dean in June 1972." He had assumed "up until April 15" that Gray still had the papers. Ehrlichman said Dean had described the material, which was sealed, as "sensitive" and "not in any way related to the Watergate case." Ehrlichman said, "I do not know the nature of the contents" and never instructed Gray on "what should be done with the contents."

On April 15, Ehrlichman said, he "learned certain new facts concerning the disposition of the contents of the Hunt safe" and "promptly reported my findings to the President." The information was relayed to the Justice Department and had been "under investigation" since then.

The New York Times reported April 27 that Gray was told April 16 by Assistant Attorney General Henry E. Petersen, in charge of the federal Watergate investigation, that Dean had informed him of the meeting on the Hunt files and that Gray could be questioned by the grand jury about it. (In testimony before the Judiciary Committee March 7, Gray had said Dean had been questioned about Hunt's material and he [Gray] was "unalterably convinced" there had been no effort at concealment.

Ehrlichman, Vesco linked. According to the Washington Post April 27, presidential aide John D. Ehrlichman promised on two occasions to aid Robert L. Vesco in his attempts to obtain the U.S. government's interest in a Lebanese bank.

Ehrlichman, in a statement issued April 27 by the White House, conceded he had met with Vesco representatives regarding the proposal, but denied he had agreed to help them. Ehrlichman claimed he had told the U.S. embassy in Beirut that there was "no White House support for, nor interest in, the Vesco activities." State Department spokesmen confirmed Ehrlichman's statement.

The unidentified Post source cited a meeting Dec. 17, 1971 in Ehrlichman's office attended by Gilbert R. J. Straub, a close Vesco associate, a friend of Nixon's brothers, Edward and Donald, and a co-defendant in the SEC suit charging Vesco and others with a $224 million securities swindle; Harry L. Sears, a prominent New Jersey Republican who had been Vesco's conduit for contributing $200,000 to the Nixon re-election committee and Laurence B. Richardson Jr., president of a Vesco-controlled company, courier for Vesco's $200,000 contribution to the office of finance committee chairman Maurice Stans, and a defendant in the SEC suit whose case had been separated from Vesco's when Richardson agreed to cooperate with federal investigators.

Vesco reportedly sought to obtain the U.S. interest in Intra Bank, a Lebanese holding company which had gone into bankruptcy in 1966. As part of the settlement, Lebanon, Kuwait, Qatar and the U.S. Department of Agriculture's Commodity Credit Corp. (CCC) assumed ownership.

According to the Post, the meeting was Ehrlichman's second attempt at helping the group, whose offer was meeting serious opposition from the U.S. embassy in Beirut and CCC.

Burglary tied to Watergate conspirators. Two convicted Watergate conspirators were said to have burglarized the office of a psychiatrist who had treated Daniel Ellsberg, a defendant in the Pentagon Papers trial, in a Justice Department memorandum released by the trial judge April 27. An FBI interview with presidential aide John D. Ehrlichman made public May 1 disclosed that Ehrlichman, who had resigned because of his alleged involvement in the Watergate case, had, at the request of the President, ordered a secret White House investigation of the Pentagon Papers case which eventually led to the break-in.

Judge William M. Byrne, presiding at the Ellsberg trial in Los Angeles, announced from the bench April 30 that he had met with Erlichman who had offered him a government position, which he refused to specify and which he said he had refused to discuss until the conclusion of the trial.

Byrne confirmed from the bench May 2 he had met with Ehrlichman, and he offered more details. He said two meetings had taken place April 5 and 7, one in San Clemente and the other in Santa Monica, Calif., at which the possibility of his appointment as director of the FBI had been broached. Byrne, again saying he had put Ehrlichman off until the end of the trial, did not say whether the job had been directly offered to him or whether he had directly declined it.

According to the FBI summary of the Ehrlichman interview, the sequence of events leading to the break-in and photocopying of the files of Dr. Lewis J. Fielding, who treated Ellsberg in the late 1960s and the first half of 1970, began in 1971 after the President "had expressed interest" in the leak of classified information and had asked Ehrlichman "to make inquiries independent of concurrent FBI investigation which had been made relating to the leak of the Pentagon papers."

Ehrlichman said he had assumed this responsibility, and had asked the aid of White House assistant Egil Krogh Jr. and David Young of the National Security Council. After the decision was made to work "directly out of the White House," Liddy and Hunt were "designated to conduct this investigation," Ehrlichman said.

Ehrlichman said Hunt and Liddy determined that Ellsberg had emotional and moral problems, which through further investigation, they hoped could be used as the basis of a "psychiatric profile."

Ehrlichman told the FBI that he knew Liddy and Hunt had conducted an investigation in the Washington area and had gone to California in connection with the inquiry. However, he said, he was not told they had broken into the psychiatrist's office until after the incident had taken place.

Ehrlichman said he did "not agree with this method of investigation" and when he learned of it, he cautioned Liddy and Hunt "not to do this again."

The information made its way to Judge Byrne after federal investigators, who learned of the burglary April 15, brought the events to the attention of the President, according to the Washington Post May 3. When Nixon heard about the burglary, he "endorsed without hesitation" the decision to send to Byrne a confidential memo on the subject from Earl J. Silbert, chief Watergate prosecutor, to Assistant Attorney General Henry E. Petersen, chief of the Justice Department's criminal division, the Post said.

The decision to consult Nixon before turning over the information to Byrne, the Post reported, came after the Justice Department determined that the burglary played no role in the prosecution's case against Ellsberg. Attorney General Richard G. Kleindienst and Petersen decided to inform the court because of the possibility that Ellsberg's Constitutional rights and his confidential relationship with his doctor had been violated.

In further developments, Judge Byrne turned over to the defense May 2 a second FBI interview with Ehrlichman and one with H. R. Haldeman, Nixon's former chief of staff.

In the second interview conducted May 1, Ehrlichman denied having anything to do with the White House investigation for more than a year. He claimed that Krogh and Young had been handling the inquiry on his orders. Ehrlichman reportedly told the FBI the results of the Ellsberg investigation had been in the offices of Krogh and Young, but that he did not now know the whereabouts of the reports.

In his interview, Haldeman denied knowing anything about the investigation.

Byrnes asks dismissal, mistrial motions—Judge Byrne ordered both sides in the Pentagon Papers trial May 2 to submit case authority for and against dismissal and mistrial in the case of Ellsberg and Anthony J. Russo. This followed a motion by the defense, filed May 1, asking for immediate dismissal of all charges. The defense made the motion after disclosure of the first FBI interview with Ehrlichman.

The trial was further complicated when Byrne said May 2 that he had spoken to Ehrlichman twice about the possibility of the FBI appointment.

On learning of the second meeting, the defense said it would use the disclosure to support its motion for dismissal.

Defense attorneys Leonard B. Boudin and Leonard I. Weinglass were critical both in and out of court of Ehrlichman's offer to Byrne.

In earlier developments, Judge Byrne April 30 ordered John W. Dean 3rd, former counsel to the President, former acting FBI Director L. Patrick Gray 3rd, Hunt and Liddy to produce affadavits concerning any link they had to the break-in at the office of Ellsberg's former psychiatrist. Byrne refused a defense motion for an immediate hearing into the break-in, insisting that the trial proceed uninterrupted.

Byrne ordered the government April 30 to produce an inventory of the contents of Hunt's office safe while Hunt was employed at the White House. Byrne also told the prosecution to produce details of all investigations, official or unofficial, that had been conducted with regard to the case itself or the disclosure of the Pentagon Papers in the New York Times June 13, 1971.

In further developments, Byrne May 3 ordered that grand jury testimony given by Hunt about the Watergate case May 2 be turned over to him immediately. In Washington, U.S. District Court Judge John J. Sirica ordered 37 pages of testimony given by Hunt to be sent to Byrne.

Byrne warned the prosecution May 3 "the burden is on the government" to prove that neither the Justice Department nor the White House nor the Watergate conspirators had compromised the Constitutional rights of Ellsberg and Russo and therefore "tainted" the case.

Young resigns; Krogh takes leave—The two White House aides implicated by John Ehrlichman in the break-in at the office of Daniel Ellsberg's psychiatrist left the government, it was announced May 2.

David Young resigned from the staff of the National Security Council. Egil Krogh Jr., a former White House aide, took a leave of absence from his job as undersecretary of transporation. Krogh's leave of absence came after prodding by Transportation Secretary Claude S. Brinegar to divulge what he knew about the burglary.

Hunt paid for day of break-in—The Washington Star-News reported May 1 that E. Howard Hunt Jr. billed the White House for a consultant fee the day the break-in at the office of Daniel Ellsberg's psychiatrist occurred. Hunt, $100 a day consultant, submitted bills for work for Sept. 2, 3, and 4, 1971. The burglary occurred the night of Sept. 3–4.

The Star-News also said Watergate prosecutors had airline tickets that showed Hunt and co-conspirator G. Gordon Liddy returned to Washington from Los Angeles Sept. 4, 1971 under the assumed names "Hamilton" and "Larimer."

The payment to Hunt was approved by Charles W. Colson, special counsel to the President, the Star-News said.

White House records showed Hunt turned in slips for four hours of work Sept. 2, four hours of work Sept. 3, and two hours of work Sept. 4.

Liddy was a full time salaried employe of the White House at the time.

Taps on Times reporters disclosed—The phones of at least two reporters for the New York Times were tapped by members of the Nixon Administration in connection with the Pentagon Papers disclosure, the Washington Post reported May 3.

The Post cited one highly placed Administration source as saying the wiretapping was supervised by Watergate co-conspirators E. Howard Hunt Jr. and G. Gordon Liddy, and that former Attorney General John N. Mitchell authorized the taps.

The source said the team of wiretappers, supervised by Hunt and Liddy, operated independently of the FBI, the agency normally responsible for electronic surveillance.

According to Post sources, the wiretaps followed earlier White House-ordered taps of other reporters, the purpose of which was to discover leaks of information about the strategic arms limitation talks to the news media.

The sources also said the home or office phones of at least 10 White House staffers were tapped in an effort to stem other news leaks.

"In late 1971 or early 1972, it was decided at a Nixon campaign strategy meeting that some members of the same vigilante squad responsible for the Pentagon Papers wiretapping would be used to wiretap the telephones of the Democratic presidential candidates. . . .," the Post said.

Nixon under pressure. President Nixon was reportedly under heavy pressure from leading Republicans to effect a drastic housecleaning after the most recent Watergate revelations. GOP National Chairman George Bush made it clear April 26 that the party was in danger of being compromised on a lasting basis from the handling of the Watergate affair. The preceding party chairman, Sen. Robert Dole (Kan.), called April 27 for the resignations of both Haldeman and Ehrlichman, who reportedly were struggling to retain their positions. "Right now," Dole observed, "the credibility of the Administration is zilch, zero."

Four key aides resign. The resignations of four top Nixon Administration officials were announced April 30 as a consequence of the widening Watergate affair.

The resignations included H. R. Haldeman, President Nixon's chief of staff; John D. Ehrlichman, Nixon's assistant for domestic affairs; Attorney General Richard G. Kleindienst and John W. Dean 3rd, Nixon's counsel.

The announcement, with letters of resignation from Haldeman, Ehrlichman and Kleindienst, was released by the White House in the morning preceding President Nixon's planned nationwide address that evening. In their letters, Haldeman and Ehrlichman said their ability to carry out their daily duties had been undermined by the Watergate disclosures and the time required to deal with them.

Kleindienst said he had resigned because of the apparent implication in "Watergate and related cases" of persons "with whom he has had a close personal and professional association."

The President said without amplification that he had "requested and accepted" the resignation of his counsel, Dean.

Kleindienst was replaced as attorney general by Secretary of Defense Elliot L. Richardson, who was to "involve himself immediately" in the Watergate investigation and to "assume full responsibility and authority for coordinating all federal agencies in uncovering the whole truth about this matter and [to] recommend appropriate changes in the law to prevent future campaign abuses of the sort recently uncovered." The President pledged his "total support" in this effort.

Effective immediately, Nixon's special consultant Leonard Garment was to assume Dean's White House duties until a permanent successor was named, and to "represent the White House in all matters" relating to Watergate. He would report "directly" to Nixon.

The President expressed regret at Kleindienst's resignation and "deep appreciation for his dedicated service." Nixon said he "greatly" regretted the departures of Haldeman and Ehrlichman, whom he called "two of my closest friends and most trusted assistants in the White House." He emphasized that their action should not be seen "as evidence of any wrongdoing." Their association with him had been marked by "a spirit of selflessness and dedication that I have seldom seen equalled," Nixon said.

In his resignation statement, Haldeman said "there is apparently to be no interruption in the flood of stories arising" about Watergate and he was "deeply concerned" that in the course of the investigation it had "become virtually impossible under these circumstances for me to carry on my regular responsibilities in the White House."

It was "imperative" that the work of the presidency "not be impeded," Haldeman said, and the White House staff not be "diverted by the daily rumors and developments in the Watergate case." He said he intended "to cooperate fully with the investigation" and at his own request would meet with both the federal prosecutors and Senate probers.

Haldeman told the President he was "convinced that, in due course, I will have the opportunity not just to clear up any allegations or implications of impropriety but also to demonstrate that I have always met the high and exacting standards of integrity which you have so clearly and properly demanded of all who serve on the White House staff."

Ehrlichman's letter of resignation said that, "regardless of the actual facts, I have been a target of public attack" and the appearance of integrity, which was as important as integrity itself, "can be affected by repeated rumor, unfounded charges or implications and whatever else the media carries." Stories about his alleged involvement in the Watergate matter were "without merit," he said.

Ehrlichman said he had concluded that his present usefulness to the President and his ability to discharge his duties had "been impaired by these attacks, perhaps beyond repair."

He said he was meeting at his request with the federal and Senate probers and intended "to do what I can to speed truth's discovery."

Both Haldeman and Ehrlichman testified before the federal grand jury May 3 and before the staff of the Senate Watergate committee May 4.

(The U.S. Information Agency announced April 30 that Gordon Strachan had resigned as its general counsel "after learning that persons with whom he had worked closely at the White House had submitted their resignations." The statement contained Strachan's denial of complicity in the Watergate break-in "or in any alleged attempt to cover it up.")

Nixon takes responsibility. President Nixon, in a nationally televised broadcast April 30, accepted responsibility for the Watergate affair and told the American people that he was not personally involved in the political espionage or the attempt at coverup.

He made the speech after receiving the resignations earlier in the day of four of his top aides—chief of staff H. R. Haldeman, domestic affairs chief John D. Ehrlichman, Attorney General Richard G. Kleindienst and White House counsel John W. Dean 3rd.

The President explained all but one of the resignations. Dean, he said simply, had "also resigned."

Nixon called Haldeman and Ehrlichman "two of my closest associates in the White House" and "two of the finest public servants it has been my privilege to know." The acceptance of their resignations, he said, was "one of the most difficult decisions of my presidency." He stressed that he meant "to leave no implication whatever of personal wrongdoing on their part." The action was taken, he said, to restore public confidence in the integrity of his office.

Nixon described Kleindienst as "a distinguished public servant" and "my personal friend for 20 years." Kleindienst had "no personal involvement whatever" in the Watergate affair, Nixon said, but because he had "close personal and professional" associations with some of those who were involved, both men felt it necessary to name a new attorney general.

The new attorney general was Defense Secretary Elliot L. Richardson, and he had been given "absolute authority," Nixon said, "to make all decisions bearing upon the prosecution of the Watergate case and related matters." He had been instructed "that if he should consider it appropriate he has the authority to name a special supervising prosecutor for matters arising out of the case." Richardson had also been directed, Nixon said, to do everything necessary to insure that the Justice Department had "the confidence and the trust of every law-abiding person."

Nixon said he wanted the American people "to know beyond the shadow of a doubt" that during his term justice would be pursued "fairly, fully and impartially, no matter who is involved."

The President reiterated this determination throughout his speech. "There can be no whitewash at the White House," he said, and he would do "everything in my power" to insure that the guilty were "brought to justice" and that such abuses as occurred at Watergate were "purged from the political processes." When he had assumed control March 21 over "intensive new inquiries" into the Watergate affair, Nixon said, he was determined to "get to the bottom of the matter" and have the truth "fully brought out."

Nixon said the new probe was begun after he received new information which persuaded him "there was a real possibility" of involvement by members of his Administration and indicated "there had been an effort to conceal the facts both from the public . . . and from me."

When he first learned from news reports of the Watergate break-in June 17, 1972, Nixon said, "I was appalled at this senseless, illegal action and I was shocked to learn that employes of the reelection committee were apparently among those guilty." He said he had immediately ordered an investigation "by appropriate government authorities," and had repeatedly asked those conducting it "whether there was any reason to believe that members of my Administration were in any way involved."

"I received repeated assurances that there were not," Nixon said. Because of that and because he believed the "continuing reassurances" and had faith in the persons giving them, he had "discounted" press reports that "appeared to implicate" members of his Administration or GOP campaign officials.

The President said he had remained convinced that the denials were true until March, and "the comments I made during this period, the comments made by my press secretary in my behalf, were based on the information provided to us at the time we made those comments."

Elsewhere in his speech, the President paid tribute to the press as part of "the system" that had "brought the facts to light" and would "bring those guilty to justice." The system included "a determined grand jury, honest prosecutors, a courageous judge—John Sirica—and a vigorous free press." He said it was necessary now that "we place our faith in that system, and especially in the judicial system."

Evaluating Watergate as "a series of illegal acts and bad judgments by a number of individuals," Nixon asked how it could have happened and who was to blame. He conceded he had always run his previous campaigns, but in 1972 he did not. He had delegated the day-to-day campaign operations because of his "overriding" career goal to bring peace to America and the world.

The President said those who committed criminal acts must "bear the liability and pay the penalty." "For the fact that alleged improper actions took place within the White House or within my campaign organization," he continued, "the easiest course would be for me to blame those to whom I delegated the responsibility to run the campaign. But that would be a cowardly thing to do."

"I will not place the blame on subordinates," Nixon declared, "on people whose zeal exceeded their judgment and who may have done wrong in a cause they deeply believed to be right. In any organization the man at the top must bear the responsibility. That responsibility, therefore, belongs here in this office. I accept it."

Nixon called for reform of the political process, "ridding it not only of the violations of the law," he said, "but also of the ugly mob violence and other inexcusable campaign tactics that have been too often practiced and too readily accepted in the past, including those that may have been a response by one side to the excesses or expected excesses of the other side."

He added: "Two wrongs do not make a right."

"I know," Nixon said, "that it can be very easy under the intensive pressures of a campaign for even well-intentioned people to fall into shady tactics, to rationalize this on the grounds that what is at stake is of such importance to the nation that the end justifies the means. And both of our great parties have been guilty of such tactics."

"The lesson is clear," Nixon said. "America in its political campaigns must not again fall into the trap of letting the end, however great that end is, justify the means."

He urged everyone to join in working toward "a new set of standards" to insure fair elections.

Nixon said the Watergate affair had taken "far too much" of his time since March and that he would turn his full attention "once again to the larger duties" of the office, the "vital work" toward the goal of peace—"work that cannot wait, work that I must do."

Gestures toward press—Shortly after making his speech, President Nixon appeared in the White House press room where some 15 reporters and photographers were gathered. "Ladies and gentlemen of the press," he told them, "we have had our differences in the past, and I hope you give me hell every time you think I'm wrong. I hope I'm worthy of your trust." Then he left.

White House Press Secretary Ronald L. Ziegler, in response to a reporter's question whether he would apologize to the Washington Post for previous denunciations of its Watergate coverage, said

May 1 that he would do so. Ziegler had accused the Post and its reporters of "shabby journalism" and "a blatant effort at character assassination."

He said Post reporters Bob Woodward and Carl Bernstein had vigorously pursued the story and deserved the credit they were receiving.

"When we're wrong, we're wrong," Ziegler said, "and I would have to say I was in that case and other cases."

The apology was accepted by Post publisher Katharine Graham later May 1. "We appreciate it and accept it with pleasure," she said, commenting that "the

Text of President's April 30 Address on Watergate Affair

Good evening. I want to talk to you tonight from my heart on a subject of deep concern to every American.

In recent months members of my Administration and officials of the Committee for the Re-election of the President—including some of my closest friends and most trusted aides—have been charged with involvement in what has come to be known as the Watergate affair.

These include charges of illegal activity during and preceding the 1972 Presidential election and charges that responsible officials participated in efforts to cover up that illegal activity.

The inevitable result of these charges has been to raise serious questions about the integrity of the White House itself. Tonight I wish to address those questions.

Last June 17 while I was in Florida trying to get a few days' rest after my visit to Moscow, I first learned from news reports of the Watergate break-in. I was appalled at this senseless, illegal action, and I was shocked to learn that employes of the re-election committee were apparently among those guilty. I immediately ordered an investigation by appropriate government authorities.

On Sept. 15, as you will recall, indictments were brought against seven defendants in the case.

As the investigation went forward, I repeatedly asked those conducting the investigation whether there was any reason to believe that members of my Administration were in any way involved. I received repeated assurances that there were not. Because of these continuing reassurances, because I believed the reports I was getting, because I had faith in the persons from whom I was getting them, I discounted the stories in the press that appeared to implicate members of my Administration or other officials of the campaign committee.

Until March of this year, I remained convinced that the denials were true and that the charges of involvement by members of the White House staff were false.

The comments I made during this period, the comments made by my press secretary in my behalf, were based on the information provided to us at the time we made those comments.

However, new information then came to me which persuaded me that there was a real possibility that some of these charges were true and suggesting further that there had been an effort to conceal the facts both from the public—from you—and from me.

As a result, on March 21 I personally assumed the responsibility for coordinating intensive new inquiries into the matter, and I personally ordered those conducting the investigations to get all the facts and to report them directly to me right here in this office.

I again ordered that all persons in the Government or at the re-election committee should cooperate fully with the FBI, the prosecutors and the grand jury.

I also ordered that anyone who refused to cooperate in telling the truth would be asked to resign from government service.

And with ground rules adopted that would preserve the basic constitutional separation of powers between the Congress and the Presidency, I directed that members of the White House staff should appear and testify voluntarily under oath before the Senate committee which was investigating Watergate.

I was determined that we should get to the bottom of the matter, and that the truth should be fully brought out no matter who was involved.

At the same time, I was determined not to take precipitous action and to avoid if at all possible any

action that would appear to reflect on innocent people.

I wanted to be fair, but I knew that in the final analysis the integrity of this office—public faith in the integrity of this office—would have to take priority over all personal considerations.

Today, in one of the most difficult decisions of my Presidency, I accepted the resignations of two of my closest associates in the White House—Bob Haldeman, John Ehrlichman—two of the finest public servants it has been my privilege to know.

I want to stress that in accepting these resignations I mean to leave no implication whatever of personal wrongdoing on their part, and I leave no implication tonight of implication on the part of others who have been charged in this matter.

But in matters as sensitive as guarding the integrity of our democratic process, it is essential not only that rigorous legal and ethical standards be observed, but also that the public, you, have total confidence that they are both being observed and enforced by those in authority, and particularly by the President of the United States.

They agreed with me that this move was necessary in order to restore that confidence, because Attorney General Kleindienst—though a distinguished public servant, my personal friend for 20 years, with no personal involvement whatever in this matter—has been a close personal and professional associate of some of those who are involved in this case, he and I both felt that it was also necessary to name a new attorney general.

The counsel to the President, John Dean, has also resigned.

As the new attorney general, I have today named Elliot Richardson, a man of unimpeachable integrity and rigorously high principle. I have directed him to do everything necessary to insure that the Department of Justice has the confidence and the trust of every law-abiding person in this country. I have given him absolute authority to make all decisions bearing upon the prosecution of the Watergate case and related matters. I have instructed him that if he should consider it appropriate he has the authority to name a special supervising prosecutor for matters arising out of the case.

Whatever may appear to have been the case before, whatever improper activities may yet be discovered in connection with this whole sordid affair, I want the American people, I want you, to know beyond the shadow of a doubt that during my term as President justice will be pursued fairly, fully and impartially, no matter who is involved.

This office is a sacred trust, and I am determined to be worthy of that trust.

Looking back at the history of this case, two questions arise:

How could it have happened—who is to blame?

Political commentators have correctly observed that during my 27 years in politics, I've always previously insisted on running my own campaigns for office.

In both domestic and foreign policy, 1972 was a year of crucially important decisions, of intense negotiations, of vital new directions, particularly in working toward the goal which has been my overriding concern throughout my political career—the goal of bringing peace to America, peace to the world.

And that is why I decided as the 1972 campaign approached that the Presidency should come first and politics second. To the maximum extent possible,

(Continued on page 38)

A

B

C

D

E

F

G

(Continued from page 37)

therefore, I sought to delegate campaign operations, to remove the day-to-day campaign decisions from the President's office and from the White House.

I also, as you recall, severely limited the number of my own campaign appearances.

Who then is to blame for what happened in this case?

For specific criminal actions by specific individuals, those who committed those actions must of course bear the liability and pay the penalty. For the fact that alleged improper actions took place within the White House or within my campaign organization, the easiest course would be for me to blame those to whom I delegated the responsibility to run the campaign. But that would be a cowardly thing to do.

I will not place the blame on subordinates, on people whose zeal exceeded their judgment and who may have done wrong in a cause they deeply believed to be right. In any organization the man at the top must bear the responsibility.

That responsibility, therefore, belongs here in this office. I accept it.

And I pledge to you tonight from this office that I will do everything in my power to insure that the guilty are brought to justice and that such abuses are purged from our political processes in the years to come long after I have left this office.

Some people, quite properly appalled at the abuses that occurred, will say that Watergate demonstrates the bankruptcy of the American political system. I believe precisely the opposite is true.

Watergate represented a series of illegal acts and bad judgments by a number of individuals. It was the system that has brought the facts to light and that will bring those guilty to justice.

A system that in this case has included a determined grand jury, honest prosecutors, a courageous judge—John Sirica, and a vigorous free press.

It is essential now that we place our faith in that system, and especially in the judicial system.

It is essential that we let the judicial process go forward, respecting those safeguards that are established to protect the innocent as well as to convict the guilty.

It is essential that in reacting to the excesses of others, we not fall into excesses ourselves.

It is also essential that we not be so distracted by events such as this that we neglect the vital work before us, before this nation, before America at a time of critical importance to America and the world.

Since March, when I first learned that the Watergate affair might in fact be far more serious than I had been led to believe, it has claimed far too much of my time and my attention. Whatever may now transpire in the case, whatever the actions of the grand jury, whatever the outcome of any eventual trials, I must now turn my full intention—and I shall do so—once again to the larger duties of this office.

I owe it to this great office that I hold, and owe it to you, to my country.

I know that, as attorney general, Elliot Richardson will be both fair and he will be fearless in pursuing this case wherever it leads. I am confident that with him in charge justice will be done.

There is vital work to be done toward our goal of a lasting structure of peace in the world—work that cannot wait, work that I must do.

Tomorrow, for example, Chancellor Brandt of West Germany will visit the White House for talks that are a vital element of the Year of Europe, as 1973 has been called.

We are already preparing for the next Soviet-American summit meeting later this year.

This is also a year in which we are seeking to negotiate a mutual and balanced reduction of armed forces in Europe which will reduce our defense budget and allow us to have funds for other purposes at home so desperately needed.

It is the year when the United States and Soviet negotiators will seek to work out the second and even more important round of our talks on limiting nuclear arms, and of reducing the danger of a nuclear war that would destroy civilization as we know it.

It is a year in which we confront the difficult tasks of maintaining peace in Southeast Asia and in the potentially explosive Middle East.

There's also vital work to be done right here in America to insure prosperity—and that means a good job for everyone who wants to work; to control inflation that I know worries every housewife, everyone who tries to balance the family budget in America. To set in motion new and better ways of insuring progress toward a better life for all Americans.

When I think of this office, of what it means, I think of all the things that I want to accomplish for this nation, of all the things I want to accomplish for you.

On Christmas Eve, during my terrible personal ordeal of the renewed bombing of North Vietnam which, after 12 years of war, finally helped to bring America peace with honor, I sat down just before midnight. I wrote out some of my goals for my second term as President. Let me read them to you.

To make this country be more than ever a land of opportunity—of equal opportunity, full opportunity—for every American; to provide jobs for all who can work and generous help for those who cannot; to establish a climate of decency and civility in which each person respects the feelings and the dignity in the God-given rights of his neighbor; to make this a land in which each person can dare to dream, can live his dreams not in fear but in hope, proud of his community, proud of his country, proud of what America has meant to himself, and to the world.

These are great goals. I believe we can, we must work for them, we can achieve them.

But we cannot achieve these goals unless we dedicate ourselves to another goal. We must maintain the integrity of the White House. And that integrity must be real, not transparent.

There can be no whitewash at the White House.

We must reform our political process, ridding it not only of the violations of the law but also of the ugly mob violence and other inexcusable campaign tactics that have been too often practiced and too readily accepted in the past including those that may have been a response by one side to the excesses or expected excesses of the other side.

Two wrongs do not make a right.

I've been in public life for more than a quarter of a century. Like any other calling, politics has good people and bad people and let me tell you the great majority in politics, in the Congress, in the federal government, in the state government are good people.

I know that it can be very easy under the intensive pressures of a campaign for even well-intentioned people to fall into shady tactics, to rationalize this on the grounds that what is at stake is of such importance to the nation that the end justifies the means.

And both of our great parties have been guilty of such tactics.

In recent years, however, the campaign excesses that have occurred on all sides have provided a sobering demonstration of how far this false doctrine can take us.

The lesson is clear. America in its political campaigns must not again fall into the trap of letting the end, however great that end is, justify the means.

I urge the leaders of both political parties, I urge citizens—all of you everywhere—to join in working toward a new set of standards, new rules and procedures to insure that future elections will be as nearly free of such abuses as they possibly can be made. This is my goal. I ask you to join in making it America's goal.

When I was inaugurated for a second term this past January 20, I gave each member of my Cabinet and each member of my senior White House staff a special four-year calendar with each day marked to show the number of days remaining to the Administration.

In the inscription on each calendar I wrote these words:

"The Presidential term which begins today consists of 1,461 days, nor more, no less. Each can be a day of strengthening and renewal for America. Each can add depth and dimension to the American experience.

"If we strive together, if we make the most of the challenge and the opportunity that these days offer us, they can stand out as great days for America and great moments in the history of the world."

I looked at my own calendar this morning up at Camp David as I was working on this speech. It showed exactly 1,361 days remaining in my term.

I want these to be the best days in America's history because I love America. I deeply believe that America is the hope of the world, and I know that in the quality and wisdom of the leadership America gives lies the only hope for millions of people all over the world that they can live their lives in peace and freedom.

We must be worthy of that hope in every sense of the word.

Tonight, I ask for your prayers to help me in everything that I do throughout the days of my Presidency to be worthy of their hopes and of yours.

God bless America. And God bless each and every one of you.

Administration was trying to undermine the credibility of the press for the last 10 months."

Congressional reaction split. Immediate Congressional reaction to the resignations and the President's speech was split, not necessarily along party lines.

House Republican Leader Gerald Ford (Mich.) April 30 called the resignations "a necessary first step ... in clearing the air on the Watergate affair." He said he had "the greatest confidence in the President" and was "absolutely positive he had nothing to do with this mess."

Senate Republican Leader Hugh Scott (Pa.) April 30 cited the President's authorization to the new attorney general to name an impartial prosecutor as evidence that Nixon was "determined to see this affair thoroughly cleaned up." As for the staff resignations, Scott said "what the President needs now is a first assistant or chief of staff who can work in complete cooperation with Congress."

Other members of Congress also cited this need, some reflecting a dislike of the liaison relationship personified by outgoing White House aides. Rep. William J. Scherle (R, Iowa), the first member on the House floor April 30, was more specific: he referred to "the Katzenjammer Kids"—Haldeman and Ehrlichman—and the other departing aides—Kleindienst and Dean. "To these people, I have only two words to say: Good riddance "

On the Senate floor April 30, Sen. Mark O. Hatfield (R, Ore.) called on the President to follow up resignations and dismissals from the Administration by convincing the public that he had told "the truth, the whole truth and nothing but the truth."

Senate Democratic Leader Mike Mansfield (Mont.) was reserved in his comment. Before Nixon acted, he said May 1, "the American system was being undermined" but "the undermining has now been stopped" and "the foundation can be rebuilt, perhaps stronger."

Sen. George McGovern (S.D.), the defeated 1972 Democratic presidential candidate, observed May 1 it was "not an easy thing for a President to admit a mistake." He added, "but it is perhaps essential to the nation that he can."

McGovern objected to other parts of the speech. "The Watergate scandal is not, as the President implied, typical of the political process," McGovern said. "Our politics is better than that. And Watergate is worse than the tactics of any national campaign in my memory or modern times."

As to the Nixon reference to "campaign excesses" on all sides, McGovern said, "I emphatically reject that notion that I or my colleagues or my party in the presidential election condoned or would have countenanced activities of a criminal nature."

Gov. Ronald Reagan (R, Calif.) said May 1 the Watergate bugging was illegal but that "criminal" was too harsh a term to apply to it. He said the convicted conspirators should not be considered criminals because they "are not criminals at heart."

Former Defense Secretary Melvin R. Laird said May 1 he was "puzzled" by the Wagergate affair but confident Nixon was not involved. "But if he were," he said, "it would be very bad for the country— that kind of disclosure." Asked if he was saying that if the President were involved he would not want the truth to come out, Laird said, "I would say that, but I don't believe for one minute that is the case."

FBI guards White House files. The FBI put agents in the White House May 1 to guard the files of Haldeman, Ehrlichman and Dean. The "safeguarding procedure," White House Press Secretary Ronald L. Ziegler said, was not meant "to cast aspersions on any individual."

Haldeman and Ehrlichman were in their offices that day, with access to their files under the FBI scrutiny, and were observed leaving the White House later with documents. They returned to their desks the next day. Dean's whereabouts were unknown to the public since the President announced his resignation, and the White House staff reportedly had been unable to reach him that day to inform him of his resignation.

The files and FBI guards were removed to less conspicuous quarters after President Nixon reportedly expressed outrage at a Cabinet meeting May 1 at the posting of guards outside his top aides' offices.

Senate urges outside prosecutor. A resolution calling upon President Nixon to appoint a special Watergate prosecutor from outside the executive branch was passed by the Senate May 1. The resolution, drafted by Sen. Charles H. Percy (R, Ill.), also requested that the name of the appointee be submitted to the Senate for confirmation.

The resolution, which had been cleared with leaders of both parties, was co-sponsored by a dozen other Republicans and six Democrats. Sens. Barry Goldwater (R, Ariz.), Robert Dole (R, Kan.) and James L. Buckley (Conservative-Republican, N.Y.) were among the co-sponsors.

Text of the resolution:

Resolved that it is the sense of the Senate that:
1. The President immediately designate an individual of the highest character and integrity from outside the executive branch to serve as special prosecutor for the government of the United States in any and all criminal investigations, indictments and actions arising from any illegal activity by any persons, acting individually or in combination with others, in the Presidential election of 1972 or any campaign, canvass or other activity related to it;
2. The President should grant such special prosecutor all authority necessary and proper to the effective performance of his duties, and
3. The President should submit the name of such designee to the Senate, requesting a resolution of approval thereof.

In introducing the resolution, Percy said "a simple and very basic question is at issue: Should the executive branch investigate itself? I do not think so."

On the Senate floor when the resolution passed unanimously were Percy and Sens.

Robert C. Byrd (D, W. Va.), John Sparkman (D, Ala.) and Pete V. Domenici (R, N.M.).

An attempt was made later May 1 by several Republicans to gain reconsideration of the resolution. Percy favored it, he said, if he were assured there would be no attempt to delay or filibuster the resolution. But an acrimonious debate among the Republicans ensued, and no further action was taken.

(Word of Percy's move for an independent prosecutor reportedly brought an angry outburst from President Nixon at a Cabinet meeting May 1: that Percy, a possible candidate, would never be president "as long as I have anything to say about it.")

A resolution calling upon Richardson to name a special Watergate prosecutor was introduced May 3 by Sen. Edward W. Brooke (R, Mass.). It was co-sponsored by Senate Republican Leader Hugh Scott (Pa.), Peter Dominick (R, Colo.), John Tower (R, Tex.) and Clifford P. Hansen (R, Wyo.).

The same action was urged by 29 Democratic senators in a letter to Richardson May 3. Sen. Adlai E. Stevenson 3rd (Ill.) organized the effort. Senate Majority Leader Mike Mansfield (Mont.) was one of the signatories.

A resolution was introduced in the House May 1 calling on Richardson to "immediately" use his authority to appoint an impartial prosecutor. It was introduced by 18 Republicans, including Reps. John B. Anderson (Ill.), chairman of the House Republican Conference, and Robert H. Michel (Ill.), chairman of the Republican Congressional Campaign Committee.

Anderson said April 30 that "until it has been amply demonstrated to the American public that the last shadowy element in this tragedy has been brought to light, that every possible question has been asked and answered satisfactorily, our institutions of government will remain under a cloud."

The issue of an outside prosecutor entered into Senate consideration of Richardson's nomination as attorney general. Sen. John V. Tunney (D, Calif.) said May 2 he would impede confirmation unless Richardson agreed in advance to name a new prosecutor.

Tunney, a member of the Judiciary Committee which expected to open the confirmation hearings the next week, and another committee member, Sen. Marlow W. Cook (R, Ky.), argued that the same personal conflict of interest that led Kleindienst to resign—his close association with implicated persons—applied to Richardson as well. "Mr. Richardson is certainly a close friend of John Ehrlichman's," Tunney said. Richardson also was a long-time friend of former Nixon White House aide Charles W. Colson, who had been linked by allegations to Watergate planning.

Kleindienst planned to remain in his post until the new designee was confirmed, but Richardson was expected to handle any policy matters arising. Consultation between the two men on Watergate was initiated even before announcement of the replacement.

Calls for appointment of a special Watergate prosecutor from outside the Administration came from other quarters than Congress—from the president of the Association of the Bar of the City of New York April 26, the president of the American Bar Association April 30, a caucus of the 31 Democratic governors meeting in Huron, Ohio April 30, and consumer advocate Ralph Nader May 1.

Moss broaches impeachment question —Rep. John E. Moss (D, Calif.) brought up the possibility April 30 of an impeachment inquiry, reportedly discussing the matter with House Democratic leaders. "I'm not saying we should do it, but we should prepare ourselves to have all the facts," Moss argued. The reaction of the leadership, according to Democratic Leader Thomas P. O'Neill Jr. (Mass.): the idea was "a bit premature."

Senate probe nears—The Senate Select Committee to probe Watergate met May 2 and reaffirmed, Chairman Sam J. Ervin Jr. (D, N.C.) reported, "its determination to start hearings as near the 15th of May as possible."

GOP sabotage plot revealed. Based on a preliminary examination of grand jury evidence, federal investigators believed that former top Nixon aide H. R. Haldeman formulated and coordinated an extensive, well-financed operation of political sabotage and espionage, beginning in early 1971 and continuing throughout the 1972 presidential campaign, in an effort to insure the nomination of Sen. George McGovern (D, S.D.) as the Democratic contender for the presidency.

According to the May 2 account of the Administration strategy in the New York Times, White House and re-election committee officials considered McGovern the weakest candidate President Nixon could face in the 1972 race and every effort was made to influence McGovern's selection as the Democratic party's nominee.

The government's case focused on Haldeman, who, working with the Committee to Re-elect the President, allegedly controlled three networks of intelligence agents. The Watergate bugging operation was only a small part of the overall campaign effort, investigators emphasized.

The GOP plot had a double aim—to deny the Democratic presidential nomination to Sen. Edmund S. Muskie (D, Me.) and to enhance the nomination prospects of McGovern. According to the government, Administration aides considered Muskie to be the President's strongest rival, a view based partially on a May 1971 Harris poll showing Muskie leading Nixon in the popularity survey 47%–39%.

A
B
C
D
E
F
G

Government evidence showed that a Nixon agent had infiltrated Muskie headquarters in early 1972 and was able to steal, photograph and leak to the press confidential campaign documents.

Federal investigators were unable to assess the full impact of the sabotage effort on the 1972 campaign but Democrats had made numerous prior allegations that Republicans were responsible for inexplicable disruptions in the Muskie campaign and were guilty of smear tactics, causing embarrassment to Muskie, and the campaigns of Sens. Hubert H. Humphrey (D, Minn.) and Henry M. Jackson (D, Wash.).

The government case traced Haldeman's initial authorization of the sabotage operations to a substratum of Administration aides and minor re-election committee functionaries, all reporting ultimately to Haldeman:

■ President Nixon's personal lawyer, Herbert P. Kalmbach, was reported to have begun secret fund-raising efforts during early 1971 with the aim of financing Haldeman's sabotage activities.

■ In June 1971, a group of White House assistants called the "plumbers" were organized to discover the source of Pentagon Papers leaks to the press and to stop other leaks of confidential Administration information.

■ Haldeman's chief aide and the President's appointments secretary, Dwight Chapin, recruited Donald H. Segretti in mid-1971 to direct the espionage activities. Segretti made at least 20 contacts throughout 1971 and succeeded in establishing a network of an estimated 10 persons. These operatives were either paid directly by Kalmbach or the money was routed to them through Segretti.

■ Convicted Watergate defendants G. Gordon Liddy and E. Howard Hunt Jr., reassigned from the White House "plumbers" in early 1972 to the re-election committee, also recruited informers, especially in the Miami area.

■ During February 1972, Hunt and Liddy conferred in Miami with Segretti at a meeting arranged by Haldeman's aide, Gordon Strachan. According to the government, Hunt and Liddy began to assume increasingly important roles coordinating Segretti's operations, a function formerly performed by Strachan. Federal investigators cited the merging of White House and re-election committee personnel in the espionage activities as a key strategy move in the sabotage effort.

■ By March 1972, 30–40 paid informers were assigned by the GOP to the offices of Democratic candidates for the nomination and party officials. Muskie was no longer the chief target of attack, federal investigators said, charging that the sabotage operation had widened to include all principal Democratic contenders. According to the Times sources, the Administration considered that their most important victory in the plot to influence the Democratic nomination was the Florida

primary in March 1972, won by Alabama Gov. George C. Wallace, in a campaign notable for its smear tactics and embarrassing incidents for Democrats.

Kalmbach's involvement—The New York Times reported May 3 that President Nixon's personal attorney Herbert Kalmbach, [See above] had told federal investigators he had destroyed all his records of campaign finances before the federal disclosure law governing campaign contributions and expenditures took effect April 7, 1972. He justified the action as an attempt to preserve the identity of secret donors to the Nixon re-election campaign.

Kalmbach's efforts to shield the contributors whose gifts, estimated at $22 million, were received before the April 7 deadline could violate the 1925 Federal Corrupt Practices Act, which required adequate maintenance of financial records for at least two years following an election. (The 1925 law expired when the 1972 federal reporting act took effect in April.)

Maximum penalties for deliberate destruction of files were a $10,000 fine and two years in jail. Accidental destruction of such records called for a $1,000 fine or one year in jail.

(White House Press Secretary Ronald L. Ziegler told reporters May 1 that to his knowledge, Kalmbach was no longer serving as the President's personal lawyer.)

GOP finance committee treasurer Hugh W. Sloan Jr. told lawyers for Ralph Nader's suit seeking full disclosure of secret campaign funds that Kalmbach had served Nixon as the campaign's "principal fund raiser" until Maurice Stans was named to head the Finance Committee to Re-elect the President. Sloan's testimony, given Dec. 26, 1972, was made public Feb. 9.

Kalmbach had been named previously as the "paymaster" of a $500,000 secret fund used for Donald H. Segretti's espionage operations.

Sources at the Committee to Re-Elect the President told the Washington Post April 29 that the Segretti fund was derived from money left over from Nixon's 1968 presidential campaign. (Another secret fund estimated at $350,-000–$700,000 kept in Stans' office safe, and a separate $350,000 secret cash account held by then White House aide H. R. Haldeman, were also identified as part of surplus 1968 campaign funds, the Post reported.) Federal investigators told the Times May 3 that Kalmbach had also been asked to raise additional funds to pay cover-up money to the Watergate defendants.

Cover-up conspiracy alleged. The New York Times May 2 reported statements from "government investigators" that they had evidence that high White House officials and the Committee to Re-elect the President conspired after the June

1972 Watergate raid to cover up the federal investigation.

The report, by reporter Seymour M. Hersh, said the "investigators" claimed evidence that the cover-up effort was coordinated by Haldeman, Ehrlichman and former Attorney General Mitchell, and involved White House aides Dean, Jeb Stuart Magruder and Frederick C. LaRue, former campaign assistant to Mitchell. The expectation of indictments against all six was credited to "sources close to the case."

The grand jury's investigation of possible involvement in the cover-up was reported to be focused on four other persons—then White House aides Dwight L. Chapin, Gordon Strachan, Herbert L. Porter and attorney Kenneth W. Parkinson. Parkinson had been hired by the Nixon campaign committee after the Watergate break-in.

The conspiracy was said to have involved payments to the Watergate defendants, promises of executive clemency, public denials and overall denial by everyone a party to the operation.

Nixon re-election committee treasurer Hugh W. Sloan Jr. was identified in the report as the only key official who apparently refused to participate in the cover-up, resisted subsequent pressure to conform to the conspiracy and was frustrated in efforts to get word to the President that something was wrong.

Chotiner sought Hoffa parole. Murray M. Chotiner, former aide to President Nixon, admitted May 3 that he had interceded with H. R. Haldeman, then White House chief of staff, to obtain James R. Hoffa's release from jail on parole.

Hoffa, former president of the Teamsters Union, had been convicted of jury tampering and pension fraud in March 1967 and was sentenced to eight years in prison.

Syndicated columnist Jack Anderson reported May 3 that Hoffa had been promised parole by November 1970. When the Justice Department resisted action on the Administration pledge, Chotiner intervened. Chotiner resigned from the White House staff in March 1971. Hoffa's sentence was commuted Dec. 23, 1971.

"I did it. I make no apologies for it and frankly I'm proud of it," Chotiner said.

(Chotiner filed a $3 million libel suit May 4 against the Manchester (N.H.) Union Leader and one of the newspaper's reporters for a story linking Chotiner to "three separate political espionage-sabotage teams," including one that "was caught in the now famous Watergate Caper.")

GAO cites campaign ad violation. The General Accounting Office (GAO) asked the Justice Department May 3 to investigate an "apparent violation" of campaign fund disclosure laws by the Committee to Re-elect the President in secretly paying for an advertisement in the New York Times May 17, 1972. The ad endorsed President Nixon's decision to mine North Vietnam's harbor at Haiphong.

The federal auditing agency, which was authorized to examine violations of the Federal Campaign Finance Act of 1972, charged the re-election committee with failing to identify itself as the source of the ad.

The Justice Department was asked to investigate "which committee officials were responsible for the ad."

The GAO report also revealed that then White House aide, Charles W. Colson "informed us that he reviewed the draft [of the ad] and probably made changes in it." According to the Nixon committee's advertising agency, the November Group, Colson initiated the idea for the ad and wrote its copy, the Washington Post reported May 4.

The ad, entitled "The People Vs. the New York Times" and signed by 14 persons, criticized a Times editorial of May 10, 1972 which opposed the mining of Haiphong harbor. None of the 14 signers contributed to the $4,400 cost of the ad, which was paid for in cash by the Finance Committee to Re-elect the President, according to the GAO. Seven of the ad's sponsors were personal friends or relatives of the November Group staff.

Policy on privilege issued. A detailed version of the Administration's position on executive privilege was issued May 3. It said that the use of executive privilege should be "held to a minimum," but it provided a broad area of coverage. It stated:

1. Past and present members of the President's staff questioned by the FBI, the Ervin (Senate select) committee or a grand jury would invoke the privilege only in connection with conversations with the President, conversations among themselves—involving communications with the President—and as to presidential papers. Presidential papers are all documents produced or received by the President or any member of the White House staff in connection with his official duties.

2. Witnesses are restricted from testifying as to matters relating to national security not by executive privilege, but by laws prohibiting the disclosure of classified information—e.g., some of the incidents which gave rise to concern over leaks. The applicability of such laws should therefore be determined by each witness and his own counsel.

3. White House counsel will not be present at the FBI interviews or at the grand jury and, therefore, will not invoke the privilege in the first instance. If a dispute as to privilege arises between a witness and the FBI or the grand jury, the matter may be referred to White House counsel for a statement of the President's position.

The guidelines were attacked May 8 by Sen. Edmund S. Muskie (D, Me.), who observed that they made no exception for allegations of criminal conduct but such allegations were "precisely at issue." He said the new guidelines "force us to wonder whether, after all, a haven is being built for certain crimes."

Muskie made the remarks at a hearing on the executive privilege doctrine by his Intergovernmental Relations subcommittee. Assistant Attorney General Robert Dixon told a parallel House hearing on the

issue that the new guidelines had been drafted without consultation with the Justice Department.

Segretti indicted in Florida. California attorney Donald H. Segretti was indicted by a federal grand jury in Orlando, Fla. May 4, charged with fabricating and distributing a campaign document during the 1972 Florida primary for the Democratic presidential nomination.

The fraudulent letter, which appeared throughout the state three days before the March 14, 1972 election, was written on the campaign stationery of Sen. Edmund S. Muskie (D, Me.). The unsigned letter accused Muskie's primary rivals, Sens. Hubert H. Humphrey (D, Minn.) and Henry M. Jackson (D, Wash.) of sexual misconduct.

Maximum penalties for conviction on the misdemeanor charges were one year in jail and a $1,000 fine for each of two counts in the indictment.

An indictment was also returned against George A. Hearing, a Florida accountant. Robert M. Benz, former vice president of the Tampa, Fla. Young Republicans, was named as a co-conspirator, but was not indicted. The New York Times reported May 4 that Benz had been granted immunity in return for testimony.

According to the indictment, Segretti had met with Benz in Florida during December 1971 to plan disruptions in the Muskie and Jackson campaigns. Benz was paid $50 at that time. During February 1972, he and Hearing mailed thousands of copies of the bogus letter.

Democrats were critical of the federal investigation. Jackson claimed that John L. Briggs, the U.S. attorney for southern Florida, had refused to investigate the source of the disputed letter until October 1972, when the Washington Post detailed Segretti's alleged involvement in political espionage activities.

Jackson also charged that Briggs had written him April 5 that the investigation was being terminated. Briggs defended the government's probe May 4: "We uncovered a number of things that fell into our lap suddenly. ... I think it is reasonable to expect that there will be more indictments." According to Briggs, the "new leads" had been provided by "newspaper people" in Washington and Florida.

The federal indictment proceedings could prevent Segretti from appearing before Senate hearings on the Watergate affair since recent court rulings permitted indicted persons to plead the Fifth Amendment barring self-incrimination during grand jury procedings.

Kennedy sees leadership 'wreckage.' Sen. Edward M. Kennedy (D, Mass.) said May 4 that the nation faced the problem of salvaging its "honor from the wreckage of leadership in the executive branch of government."

"Whatever trials the future may bring," he said, "the one that matters most is the

trial of America herself in the eyes of our country and the world." He made the remarks in a speech to the American Society of Newspaper Editors meeting in Washington.

Haig given Haldeman job. Gen. Alexander M. Haig Jr. was appointed on an "interim" basis by President Nixon May 4 as his assistant, to assume most of the duties formerly performed by H. R. Haldeman, who resigned April 30.

Haig, vice chief of staff of the Army, had previously served as deputy assistant to the President for national security affairs in close association with Nixon's foreign affairs adviser Henry A. Kissinger.

Some of the duties performed by Nixon's aide, John D. Ehrlichman, who also resigned April 30, would be assumed by Domestic Council Chairman Kenneth R. Cole Jr., who would "have his duties broadened," it was announced May 4.

White House Press Secretary Ronald L. Ziegler said May 2 that President Nixon had informed Vice President Spiro Agnew the previous day that he was appointing him vice chairman of the Domestic Council. Agnew was also given responsibility for liaison with governors and mayors, a post he had held previously.

Secret campaign fund records destroyed. Hugh W. Sloan Jr., former treasurer of the Finance Committee to Re-elect the President, revealed that the Nixon re-election committee had solicited "somewhere between $1 million and $2 million" in large secret cash contributions during 1971 and early 1972 and had subsequently destroyed records of the transactions.

The sealed testimony, taken Oct. 24, 25 and 28, 1972 by attorneys for the public interest lobby Common Cause in connection with its suit to force full disclosure of campaign finances, was made public May 4.

Sloan said records of cash gifts "over $1,000" and a "sort of day-to-day log of cash contributions" had been stored in a New York City warehouse because "we were an obvious target for political espionage, what have you." (The same secret fund of cash was allegedly used to finance political sabotage and espionage operations against Democratic presidential candidates.)

Sloan testified that at an unspecified date and "at [former Commerce] Secretary Maurice H. Stans' instructions, [See above], I personally destroyed the working copy, as it was no longer deemed necessary, and turned the summary sheet [based on the same data] over to the secretary [Stans]. I have since been led to understand that this had been destroyed."

Common Cause attorneys charged that their research showed $22 million had been solicited secretly by the Nixon re-election committee before the April 7, 1972 date when a new federal reporting law took effect. On April 7, 1972, the finance committee had reported $10.2 million in "cash on hand" from unidentified sources. Common Cause charged that $11.8 million in campaign gifts was unreported as receipts as well as unidentified by donors.

The Washington Post reported May 4 that government investigators had evidence that the Nixon re-election committee "prepaid" $5.5 million before April 7, 1972 for anticipated campaign expenses in an effort to avoid reporting expenditures after the disclosure deadline and to present a more convincing case for the President's fund raisers that additional contributions were required. Sloan confirmed May 3 that he had written prepayment checks totaling $5.5 million.

The federal investigators also said the finance committee had received a legal opinion, drafted in part by convicted Watergate conspirator G. Gordon Liddy, that such advance payments were legal.

According to the Post, Clark Mac-Gregor, former chairman of the Committee to Re-elect the President, identified the campaign's principal managers—H. R. Haldeman, John D. Ehrlichman, John Mitchell and Maurice Stans—as seeking a delay in enactment of the strict new 1972 disclosure law.

MacGregor said that despite Nixon's public position urging swift passage of the law, Stans had told a meeting of the campaign group in the fall of 1971 that "we had to slow down the legislative progress so they could have more time . . . to raise funds anonymously."

New Dean allegations reported. The White House denial of involvement followed reports that former presidential counsel John W. Dean 3rd was prepared to give testimony implicating President Nixon in an attempt to cover up the Watergate affair.

Newsweek magazine, in its May 14 issue released May 5, reported two instances attributed to Dean indicating Nixon's complicity:

(1) A September 1972 meeting in the President's office with H. R. Haldeman and Nixon, where those two were, according to the Newsweek account, "all grins" and "pleased" that the Watergate indictments just handed down did not involve any high White House aides, presumably because of the success of Dean's "efforts 'to keep the lid on'." (The latter phrase was apparently Dean's.) The Newsweek account said Dean quoted Nixon "as having told him: 'Good job, John. Bob told me what a great job you've been doing.'"

(2) A December 1972 promise of executive clemency for Watergate defendant E. Howard Hunt Jr., relayed through White House aide Ehrlichman after a visit to Nixon's office.

The news reports noted the allegations in the context of the effort Dean was making to obtain immunity from prosecution from the Senate and federal probers in exchange for his information.

Dean had removed documents from his White House office prior to his forced resignation as Nixon's counsel, and he requested May 4 that the U.S. district court in Washington supervise custody of them. He gave Chief Judge John J. Sirica the keys to a safe deposit box where, he told the court, he had deposited the documents for safekeeping because of the risk of "illegitimate destruction" if they were left in his office. He said the documents bore a security classification and he had reason to believe the material "may have a bearing" on the Watergate investigation. He also cited to the court a Jan. 16 letter from Senate Democratic Leader Mike Mansfield (Mont.) that requested retention of Watergate documents because of the Congressional investigations.

The Administration sought to have the Dean documents returned, saying the court could make copies of them first. Sen. Lowell P. Weicker Jr. (R, Conn.) sought and had a private meeting with Dean and his lawyer. Out of the meeting came reports May 4 that Dean had outlined major new developments in the Watergate case. But there was another report in the New York Times May 10 by "reliable sources" that neither the Senate nor federal investigators had any evidence from Dean linking President Nixon to prior knowledge of the Watergate bugging or any subsequent cover-up.

The question of immunity—The various sides in the Watergate investigations were in a dispute over the question of immunity from prosecution for Dean.

The Senate Select Committee announced May 8 it would act to grant Dean immunity at its public hearings. The committee also announced a date for the opening of the hearings—May 17.

But the Justice Department announced May 9 that it would hold the committee's request for Dean's immunity, which was processed under the 1970 Organized Crime Control Act through the department, for the full 30 days permitted under the law before submission to a federal judge for approval.

Eight previous Senate requests for immunity had been processed without delay, and Committee Chairman Sam J. Ervin Jr. (D, N.C.) took exception to the department's decision. "I can't understand," he told newsmen May 9, "why we can get away from the time limitation in the case of significant witnesses but not in the case of witnesses we find of great importance." Federal investigators were concerned that testimony in the Senate hearings might impair criminal cases in preparation against some witnesses, such as Dean. Ervin had said May 6 the President would be called upon to testify if necessary. "I know of no law that says that the President is exempt from the duties which devolve on other citizens," he said.

White House guidelines—The Senate committee received from the White House May 8 a set of guidelines under which Administration aides would be permitted to testify at the hearings. One of them was that executive privilege would be invoked for the aides by the White House counsel, "if at all, only in connection with formal hearings." The counsel was to be present at informal sessions, but only to observe and take notes.

The White House also said President Nixon would no longer advise Watergate prosecutors to withhold immunity from current or former members of the Administration. This was a policy reversal from his April 17 position that "no individual holding, in the past or at present, a position of importance in the Administration should be given immunity from prosecution."

Press Secretary Ziegler said May 8 "the whole question of immunity is a decision to be made" by the proper investigating authorities and the President was no longer involved in the question.

Nixon again denies involvement. A new denial that President Nixon was involved in the Watergate affair or alleged subsequent cover-up was issued by White House Deputy Press Secretary Gerald L. Warren May 7.

Warren said "any suggestion that the President was aware of the Watergate operation is untrue; any suggestion that the President participated in any cover-up activity or activities is untrue; any suggestion that the President ever authorized the offering of clemency to anyone in this case is also false."

Press Secretary Ronald L. Ziegler was questioned by reporters May 8 about the wording of the statement, whether the President was also unaware of any cover-up, since it was specifically stated he was unaware of the espionage operation. Ziegler said "reference to participation in a cover-up was not chosen to draw a distinction between participation and awareness."

Richardson would name new prosecutor. Defense Secretary Elliot L. Richardson announced at the Pentagon May 7 he would appoint, if confirmed by the Senate as attorney general, a special prosecutor to conduct the federal investigation of the Watergate affair.

Richardson said the prosecutor, as yet unselected, would have "all the independence, authority and staff support needed to carry out the tasks entrusted to him;" he would be in the Justice Department "and report to me—and only to me" and he would "be aware that his ultimate accountability is to the American people."

A move in the Senate to delay Richardson's confirmation until the prosecutor was named gained support from the Democratic leadership. Democratic Whip Robert C. Byrd (W. Va.) suggested that course of action May 7 and Democratic Leader Mike Mansfield (Mont.) gave it his tentative approval May 8.

Sen. Adlai E. Stevenson (D, Ill.), expressing concern that a prosecutor named by Richardson would have the requisite independence of the Nixon Administration, proposed May 8 a resolution calling for the prosecutor to have final authority over the granting of immunity and other vital prosecution decisions. It also called for guaranteed adequate staffing and funding for the new probe.

White House Press Secretary Ronald L. Ziegler said May 8 Richardson was "absolutely totally free" to choose on his own an independent prosecutor and to supervise other aspects of the federal Watergate probe. The President, Ziegler said, had largely removed himself from the probe.

Confirmation hearing opens—The question of Richardson's independence was the key issue as the Senate Judiciary Committee opened hearings May 9 into his confirmation as attorney general. Richardson told the panel he would retain the "ultimate responsibility" for the Watergate investigation and prosecution and would make the final decision on granting witnesses immunity.

But he said he did not expect "in a matter of judgment to interpose" his judgment against that of the special prosecutor. The likelihood that he would overrule the prosecutor, Richardson said, was "very remote."

Richardson told the panel: "If I were sufficiently identified in any way with this situation or with individuals alleged or suspected to be involved so that I was not in a position to accept ultimate responsibility, then it would serve little purpose for me to accept the position of attorney general at all."

Returning before the panel May 10, Richardson said as a Republican officeholder he felt "betrayed by the shoddy standards of morals" of those involved in the Watergate affair. His sense of betrayal, he said, would "at least compensate or neutralize any feeling I might have arising out of my prior associations."

He said he intended to maintain an "arm's length" relationship, at times an "adversary relationship" with the White House during the investigation, and he disclosed that "the President has told me he does not want to be informed" about the progress of the federal inquiry.

As for his relationship with any special prosecutor, Richardson said he expected to be kept informed about the investigation and to offer advice "when a close call had to be made." But he did not expect to "stick my finger in the day-to-day prosecution" and he would not interfere with the prosecutor's judgment except "in extreme cases" where it went "beyond the pale of responsible judgment."

The question of the "appearance" of independence was brought up at both sessions. Sen. Philip A. Hart (D, Mich.), de-

claring his faith in Richardson's integrity, said May 9: "Appearance becomes as important as fact. And appearance demands that the investigation be insulated as much as possible from any hint of cover-up through control by the Republican Administration."

"You do a magnificent job of making me feel secure about appearances," Sen. Birch Bayh (D, Ind.) told Richardson May 10, "but then ... you insist on adding the caveat, 'when the prosecutor is acting responsibly.'"

Sen. Sam J. Ervin Jr. (D, N.C.), chairman of the Senate Watergate investigation, objected May 9 to Richardson's statement that he would make the final ruling on immunity for witnesses. "I don't believe that would mean independence," Ervin said.

Odle fired. Agriculture Secretary Earl L. Butz May 7 ordered Robert C. Odle Jr., 29, a former director of administration for the Nixon re-election committee, dismissed from his temporary assignment as a management consultant with the department.

Odle, who had been hired for the Agriculture Department post May 1, had been linked by the General Accounting Office to secret disbursements of cash during the 1968 campaign.

Pulitzer Prizes. The 57th annual Pulitzer Prizes in journalism, letters and music were presented in New York May 7. The Washington Post won the award distinguished public service in journalism for its investigation of the Watergate case. In 1972, the New York Times had been cited for publication of the Pentagon Papers.

Hunt: Colson ordered cable forgery. Convicted Watergate conspirator E. Howard Hunt Jr. charged that former White House aide Charles W. Colson ordered him in 1971 to fabricate a State Department cable that implicated the Kennedy Administration in the murder of deposed South Vietnamese President Ngo Dinh Diem.

Hunt's statement, delivered before a federal grand jury in Washington, was released May 7 in Los Angeles at the Pentagon Papers trial of Daniel Ellsberg and Anthony J. Russo Jr.

Hunt also linked the Federal Bureau of Investigation (FBI) to the forgery. He testified that he had asked FBI help in determining the kind of type face used in the original State Department and White House cables during that period in 1963.

According to the grand jury transcript, Hunt had been examining State Department documents relating to the Indochina War [See below] and had decided that "a number of cables were missing. . . . [in the period] immediately prior to and subsequent to the assassination of Diem."

Hunt then sought "legal access" to Central Intelligence Agency (CIA) chronological files to determine if those

records were intact. He was told the CIA did not maintain files for that period; however a check of State Department "back channel" [private] communication caused Hunt to conclude "that a lot of significant traffic was missing." (The Pentagon told Hunt it had not kept copies of 1963 back channel communication.)

Hunt reported this information to Colson, noting that representatives of the John F. Kennedy Library at Harvard University had been given access to the State Department files "for the purpose of incorporating them into material held [by the library] and would also have had the opportunity to remove any cables that could have been embarrassing to the Kennedy legatees."

(Sen. Edward M. Kennedy (D, Mass.) was a principal Kennedy "legatee." At the time of the forgery in 1971, Kennedy was regarded by the White House as a potential candidate for the Democratic presidential nomination.)

Hunt showed Colson "three or four [legitimate] cables that indicated that they [the Kennedy Administration] had pretty close to pulled the trigger against Diem's head, but it didn't say so in so many words."

Colson responded, "Well this isn't good enough. Do you think you could improve on them?" Hunt: "Yes, I probably could, but not without technical assistance." Colson: "Well, we won't be able to give you any technical help. This is too hot. See what you can do on your own."

Hunt continued, "With the very meager means at my disposal, which were literally a Xerox machine in the White House, a razor blade and a typewriter—which was not the same one as had been used on the original cables—I set about creating two cables which bore on that particular period."

Colson accepted his forged documents, Hunt testified, adding that he was ordered by an unidentified person to show the cables to William Lambert, an investigative reporter for Life magazine.

Hunt was instructed, however, not to allow the papers to leave his office because they would not stand up to careful scrutiny. "They could never be published, because after the Alger Hiss case, everyone was typewriter conscious," Hunt said.

Lambert, "exultant" over the cables, was only allowed to copy the documents in longhand, according to Hunt.

Colson denied Hunt's charges. "It is entirely possible that Mr. Hunt misunderstood something I said to him at the time he was reviewing Pentagon Papers cables with me," Colson said.

Hunt got 'routine' State Department clearance—Two State Department officials, William B. Macomber Jr., currently ambassador to Turkey and then deputy undersecretary for management, and U. Alexis Johnson, undersecretary for political affairs, authorized Hunt's access to classified material at the request of Egil Krogh Jr., and David R. Young, Jr., then White House aides, it was revealed May 9.

The clearance request, made Sept. 20, 1971, was granted in connection with a White House investigation of Pentagon Papers leaks, State Department spokesmen said.

No security check was made on Hunt, whose mission was regarded as "routine" by the department. "Business gets done as between any set of institutions, public or private, with a certain assumption of authority and benign intent," department spokesmen said. (The Pentagon Papers case, according to Administration officials, had represented a serious threat to national security.)

Hunt examined all cable traffic between April 1 and Nov. 30, 1963 and took copies of 240 cables.

A Pentagon spokesman said May 10 that Young, and not Hunt, had asked to examine Defense Department cables. Another convicted Watergate defendant, G. Gordon Liddy, also sought access to the documents, but his request was turned down by Pentagon Counsel J. Fred Buzhardt Jr., the spokesman said.

CIA involved in burglary. The Central Intelligence Agency (CIA) admitted that its former deputy director, at the request of the White House, gave assistance to convicted Watergate conspirators E. Howard Hunt Jr. and G. Gordon Liddy as they were planning the break-in at the office of Daniel Ellsberg's former psychiatrist Lewis J. Fielding in Los Angeles.

The 1947 statute creating the CIA said in part that the agency should "have no police, subpoena, law enforcement powers or internal security functions."

The CIA involvement was disclosed in testimony given by Hunt May 2 to the Washington grand jury investigating the Watergate break-in.

The New York Times reported May 7 that Gen. Robert E. Cushman Jr., present commandant of the Marine Corps and then deputy director of the CIA, gave aid to Liddy and Hunt in the form of false identification papers, disguises, a tape recorder, and a miniature camera. This aid, the Times said, came at the request of John D. Ehrlichman, who had been ordered by President Nixon to head an investigation into a series of national security leaks in 1971. Cushman was also chief military adviser to Vice President Nixon from 1957 to 1961.

In testimony May 9 before the Senate Appropriations subcommittee on CIA operations, CIA director James R. Schlesinger admitted the agency had been "insufficiently cautious" in providing materials for the break-in. He denied that the CIA was aware that Liddy and Hunt had decided to break into Fielding's office. Schlesinger noted that aid to Hunt and Liddy had been discontinued one week before the Los Angeles break-in occurred because Cushman was becoming "in-creasingly concerned" over Hunt's repeated requests for assistance. The agency chief also said that former director Richard Helms had personally ordered CIA officers to assist in the preparation of a personality profile of Ellsberg.

In his grand jury testimony May 2, Hunt told how he and Liddy had been hired by White House aides Egil Krogh Jr. and David Young to investigate leaks of the Pentagon Papers. One offshoot of this was the question of the prosecutability of Daniel Ellsberg, a topic that led to the suggestion of a "bag job" (break-in) at the office of Ellsberg's former psychiatrist in Los Angeles. Hunt said the Federal Bureau of Investigation and the Secret Service were ruled out of the operation because Liddy felt neither was equipped for the task.

A decision was then made to use himself and Liddy, Hunt said. He and Liddy flew to Los Angeles Aug. 25, 1971, where they reconnoitered the office of Dr. Fielding. One of their devices was a camera fitted into a tobacco pouch.

Hunt said the camera had been supplied by a technical services representative of the CIA at a "safe house" on Massachusetts Avenue in Washington, "the same one we used when we were given disguises and other physical equipment." Hunt added that Krogh told him where to make contacts with the CIA.

After he and Liddy returned from their first trip to Washington, they submitted a report to Krogh through Young, recommending that the operation continue, Hunt stated.

At this point Hunt traveled to Miami, where he recruited three men to aid in the mission. They were Bernard L. Barker, Eugenio Rolando Martinez, both later convicted for the Watergate break-in, and Felipe de Diego, who reportedly assaulted Ellsberg on the steps of the Capitol May 2, 1972 while he spoke at a rally.

On Labor Day weekend in 1971 the five met in Los Angeles. Two of the Miami men had a cleaning woman Sept. 3 let them into the office of Fielding. Disguised as delivery men, they left a suitcase containing a camera in the office. Later that night, while Liddy remained nearby and Hunt watched Fielding at his home, either two or three of the Miami operatives broke into the office, and searched for files on Ellsberg.

Hunt said the men were unable to find any material with Ellsberg's name on it. (Fielding earlier submitted an affadavit to Pentagon Papers trial Judge William M. Byrne, in which he stated that files on Ellsberg had been present in his office.)

Hunt and Liddy then returned to Washington, where they reported their lack of results to Krogh, Hunt testified.

Hunt denied he had spoken to Ehrlichman about the burglary and that Ehrlichman told him not to do it again.

The role of the CIA in the Los Angeles burglary was further detailed in four Justice Department memos made public by Pentagon Papers trial defendants Ellsberg and Anthony J. Russo Jr. May 8.

One memo dated Dec. 4, 1972 told of secret meetings of an unnamed CIA agent, "Mr. Blank," with Hunt and Liddy, at which they were given documents and disguises, as well as the tobacco pouch camera. It also said Hunt called "Mr. Blank" Aug. 26, 1971 and asked "Mr. Blank" to meet him at Dulles Airport outside Washington at 6 a.m. the following morning because he had film that had to be developed by that afternoon.

A second undated memorandum told of a July 22, 1971 meeting between Hunt and Cushman, at which time Hunt asked for CIA aid. Cushman said he would look into the matter and get in touch with Hunt at his White House office.

Subsequently Cushman complied with Hunt's requests until the day the CIA received the film that was to be developed. On that day the "Mr. Blank" instructed CIA technical personnel not to comply with further Hunt requests because they had gone beyond the original understanding. More important, they appeared to involve the CIA in domestic clandestine operations. The unnamed agent reported his findings to Cushman, who then called the White House to inform the "appropriate individual" that there would be no more CIA aid.

The testimony given by CIA Director Schlesinger May 9 amplified these facts. He said Ehrlichman had originally requested CIA aid, and Ehrlichman was telephoned by Cushman Aug. 21 and told no more CIA assistance would be forthcoming. Schlesinger's recall of Aug. 21 as the date of the Cushman call to Ehrlichman was in conflict with the date of Aug. 27, as given in the Justice Department memo.

In other testimony, Schlesinger said CIA officials gave former Acting FBI Director L. Patrick Gray 3rd an account by letter July 5 and 7, 1972 of the CIA involvement with Hunt in the Ellsberg case, which they repeated in a July 28, 1972 meeting. Attorney General Richard Kleindienst and Assistant Attorney General Henry E. Petersen reviewed the report in October 1972, Schlesinger added. Chief Watergate prosecutor Earl Silbert was also briefed on the incident during the same period, Schlesinger said.

Krogh resigns—Egil Krogh Jr., former assistant to Ehrlichman, in the White House, resigned as undersecretary of transportation May 9.

Krogh had submitted an affadavit to Pentagon Papers trial Judge William M. Byrne, which was made public May 7. He stated that "general authorization to engage in covert activity to obtain a psychological history" on Daniel Ellsberg was given by Ehrlichman.

Krogh stated that Liddy and Hunt developed the plans for acquiring information from Dr. Fielding's office. Krogh admitted he had told Hunt and Liddy to hire Cubans to accomplish the mission, and that he told Hunt and Liddy not to be in "close proximity of Dr. Fielding's office."

In his letter of resignation to President Nixon, Krogh said the mission was "my responsibility, a step taken in excess of instructions and without the knowledge or permission of any superior." He said his actions had been dictated by the "vital national security interests of the U. S."

Times says Nixon tried to block data. The New York Times reported May 7 that President Nixon sought on two occasions to block release of details about the burglary of the office of Daniel Ellsberg's former psychiatrist to William M. Byrne Jr., the presiding judge in the Pentagon Papers trial.

One attempt came April 16 or 17 when Nixon tried to bar release of a Justice Department memorandum revealing that the break-in had taken place, the Times said.

The second attempt reportedly came April 30, when former White House aide Egil Krogh Jr. was told by Presidential assistant John D. Ehrlichman, "the President doesn't want anymore of this to surface for national security reasons."

The White House issued the following statement May 9: "Any reference or suggestion made by anyone that the President would have proceeded in any other way than to provide information to the court is completely unfounded."

The Times cited as sources for its allegations "some of the principals, lawyers and Justice Department officials."

The sources said Earl Silbert, chief Watergate prosecutor, received a memo about the Los Angeles break-in April 16 or 17. The source of the information was said to have been former Counsel to the President John Dean 3rd, who met with federal prosecutors April 15.

A memorandum on the subject was sent from Silbert to Assistant Attorney General Henry E. Petersen, who subsequently passed it on to Nixon.

When the President "personally put the lid on it," Petersen pondered the situation for several days and finally decided "he just couldn't live with himself" if he withheld the information about Liddy-Hunt break-in, Times sources said.

Petersen then talked to Attorney General Richard Kleindienst "who—after hours of debate—agreed that the matter should be taken directly to Mr. Nixon."

Nixon agreed to forward the material after meeting with the two. Ten days after the Justice Department learned of the break-in, chief Pentagon Papers trial prosecutor David Nissen gave the memo to Byrne.

A few days after talking to Ehrlichman, Krogh reportedly had lunch with Elliot L. Richardson, whom the President had nominated to be the new attorney general. Krogh told Richardson all he knew about the Ellsberg case and about the order not to divulge any more information.

Richardson reportedly said to Krogh, "I'm not going to participate in a cover-up because it will destroy my role in the Watergate investigation. I'm not going to follow through on the President's orders. The truth has got to come out," Richardson was reported to have said.

The Times said Krogh, "apparently fortified by this meeting," decided to draft an affadavit, which he then mailed to Judge Byrne.

Krogh, who mailed the affadavit May 4, had the day before received from presidential Counsel Leonard Garment guidelines telling him not to divulge national security information.

Krogh told Douglas Parker, an assistant to Garment, May 3 he thought executive privilege had been waived, allowing him to tell what he knew about the Ellsberg case. The White House confirmed this, the Times said.

Richardson, testifying at his own confirmation hearing for attorney general May 8, said he had declined to give Krogh personal advice, other than to make the point that it would be in "the public interest" if Krogh told what he knew about the Ellsberg case.

Meany urges 'full airing.' AFL-CIO President George Meany characterized the Nixon Administration May 8 as "steeped in scandal and twisted by privilege." He called for a "vigorous and impartial investigation" of the Watergate conspiracy by an "outside" commission of citizens without connection to the government.

Reading a statement approved by the federation's Executive Council, Meany said: "We are not satisfied that anything like the full truth has been put forth or that the cover-up is over"; "the sooner we get a full airing of this bizarre and sickening chapter in the history of dirty politics, the better for the Administration and for the American people."

Meany told newsmen he thought the Watergate scandal and the Administration's economic failure had caused a loss of confidence in the Nixon Administration in many Americans, including himself.

Meany also accused former Nixon aide Charles W. Colson of sending operatives to the federation's November 1971 convention in Miami to "contrive a confrontation" between Nixon and the AFL-CIO.

Colson issued a statement of denial later May 8.

Agnew scores press 'techniques.' Vice President Agnew deplored Watergate reporting "techniques" of the media May 8 as "a very short jump from McCarthyism." Saying there had been "a great amount of hearsay" and use of material from unnamed sources, Agnew chided the press for being "overzealous" on Watergate. "I applaud the efforts and I applaud the results," he said, "but I cannot applaud the techniques being used."

Proxmire says press unfair to Nixon. Sen. William Proxmire (D, Wis.) charged in a Senate speech May 8 that the press was being "grossly unfair" to President Nixon. He was being "tried, sentenced and executed by rumor and allegation" and this was analogous to "McCarthyistic destruction," Proxmire said.

Proxmire also praised the press for a "superb job" in uncovering the Watergate scandal.

Proxmire's private view that Nixon was "involved in Watergate up to his ears" and possibly unable to extricate himself, also was reported the same day from conversations Proxmire had with several home-state editors.

Scott, Mansfield urge caution. Cautionary comments came May 8 from Senate party leaders Mike Mansfield (D, Mont.) and Hugh Scott (R, Pa.). Scott said that "we are seeing the shaking and scaring of the people of this country needlessly." Mansfield said judgments should be withheld on Watergate "until the evidence is in."

FBI tap on Ellsberg revealed. Evidence of wiretaps on telephone calls made by Pentagon Papers trial defendant Daniel Ellsberg in late 1969 or early 1970 was disclosed in a memorandum sent May 9 by Acting FBI Director William D. Ruckelshaus to presiding Judge William M. Byrne.

The Ruckelshaus memo said "that an FBI employe recalls that in late 1969 or early 1970 Mr. Ellsberg had been overheard talking from an electronic surveillance of Dr. Morton Halperin's residence." The memo also said a search of FBI records had failed to disclose the existence of such wiretaps. Halperin, a defense consultant and witness in the trial, headed the study group that compiled the Pentagon Papers.

Judge Byrne immediately suspended court proceedings and asked the government to produce all its logs and other records concerning the taps. He ordered both sides to prepare arguments as to why charges against Daniel Ellsberg and Anthony J. Russo Jr. should not be dismissed because of the disclosure of the wiretaps and the fact that records concerning them had disappeared.

Disclosure of the wiretaps raised the question of whether the government's case might be tainted.

The government contended May 10 it had "testimonial evidence" that the electronic surveillance of Halperin's home that picked up any Ellsberg conversation had been "authorized by the attorney general in accordance with national security procedures." At the same time it conceded "the records, however, have not been found."

Meanwhile the court May 11 had several defense motions before it:

A

■ A motion to dismiss the case because the burglary of Ellsberg's psychiatrist's office and other alleged government misconduct so seriously compromised the rights of Ellsberg and Russo, their connection with actual evidence need not be shown.

■ A motion to throw the case out as a sanction against the prosecution for withholding exculpatory evidence from the court and the defense.

B

■ A motion for a directed acquittal on the grounds that the government failed to produce sufficient evidence to convict Russo and Ellsberg. Defense attorneys were to argue this before Byrne decided whether to dismiss the case.

■ A motion to dismiss part of the indictments, including the conspiracy and theft charges, on the grounds they involved the unconstitutional use of the relevant statutes.

C

■ A motion for extensive hearings on whether the evidence in the case had been tainted by the burglary of the office of Daniel Ellsberg's former psychiatrist and other aspects of an independent White House investigation of the case.

Judge Byrne May 4 rejected a defense motion for dismissal based on the fact that he had been compromised by meetings he had with John D. Ehrlichman, former adviser to President Nixon.

D

Attempt to blame CIA alleged. The New York Times reported May 9 charges by convicted Watergate conspirator James W. McCord Jr. that he had been pressured twice prior to his trial to ascribe the Watergate break-in to the Central Intelligence Agency. The charges were said to have been made by McCord in a memorandum submitted to federal and Senate probers and also made available to the Times. McCord reported in it being told by his attorney, Gerald Alch, (1) that his personnel records at the CIA could be altered, if needed, to show he had been restored to active duty since his retirement in 1970, and (2) that James R. Schlesinger, the newly designated CIA director, could be subpoenaed to testify at the trial "and would go along with it."

E

His refusal to accept the plan, McCord said, aborted it and incurred the anger of fellow conspirator E. Howard Hunt Jr.

F

By the time of his trial, the memorandum said, McCord "was completely convinced that the White House was behind the idea and ploy which had been presented and that the White House was turning ruthless and would do whatever was politically expedient at any one particular point in time to accomplish its own ends."

The memorandum also alleged a White House attempt to dominate the CIA and referred to a similar effort at political control by the White House at the Federal Bureau of Investigation.

G

Nixon reassures GOP contributors. President Nixon addressed a Republican fund raising dinner in Washington May 9 and assured party leaders and contribu-

tors that the Justice Department would "get to the bottom of this very deplorable" affair.

Nixon told the 1,500 participants at the $1,000-a-plate dinner (500 person were reported to have been admitted free), "We are not going to allow this deplorable incident to deflect us from going forward toward the great goals that an overwhelming majority of American elected us to pursue."

"I have had my political ups and downs in my 27 years of politics. I have known times when I wondered if I had many friends. I don't stand here tonight as a loser—we stand here tonight as winners," Nixon continued. "The finest steel has to go through the hottest fire. I can assure you that this room is full of fine steel."

Despite the aura of presidential optimism, the Watergate scandal apparently cast a pall over the event. Sen. Barry Goldwater (R, Ariz.) had refused to attend. Party leaders had originally hoped to raise $2 million at the event, but receipts were not expected to exceed $800,000 because of widening Watergate disclosure reports of "apparent violations" in financial record-keeping by Nixon re-election officials and an acknowledged $4.9 million campaign surplus.

According to the New York Times May 9, a letter asking support for the fund raising dinner, sent by party chairman George Bush, Sen. William Brock (R, Tenn.) of the Senate GOP Campaign Committee and Rep. Robert H. Michel (R, Ill.) of the House committee declared, "At no time has the Republican National Committee or its financial arm, the Republican National Finance Committee, or the congressional or senatorial committees, been accused of any wrongdoing in their political activities or handling of campaign funds. But the fact remains that many of our supporters identify these committees as part and parcel of what they are reading in the papers. This is very unfortunate, because the 'Watergate Affair' has had an effect of our fund raising."

The Washington dinner was intended to raise money for the 1974 Congressional elections.

Republican governors, meeting in New York May 9, moved to dissociate themselves and the party from involvement in the Watergate affair. Gov. Linwood Holton, (Va.), chairman of the Republican Governors Association, declared, "I think the American people will be perfectly willing to let the blame rest on those who are guilty and not convict others simply because we were Republicans."

A Gallup Poll, conducted April 27–30 and released May 9, showed that 31% of those surveyed were less inclined to vote for Republican Congressional candidates in 1974 because of the Watergate affair. President Nixon's popularity was also at a new low, according to the poll. Only

48% of those questioned approved of the way Nixon was performing his duties, a drop of 20% since January. It was a figure last equalled in July 1971.

A special Gallup poll conducted by telephone two days after the President's nationally televised speech showed that 40% of those surveyed did not believe Nixon had told the "whole truth"; 53% thought the Watergate affair was of "great importance" to the nation; 50% believed Nixon had participated in a cover-up of the scandal; 74% saw the need for someone outside the Administration to head the Watergate investigation; 58% thought there was "little difference" between the Nixon Administration and others over the last 25 years regarding corruption.

Results of the small sample—456 persons—were released May 3.

A Harris poll published April 28 indicated that 63% of those polled did not believe the President had been "frank and honest on the Watergate affair." Nixon's popularity slipped nine points from March to 50%. The survey was conducted following his announcement that "major developments" had occurred in the Watergate investigation.

Sloan cites perjury request. Hugh W. Sloan Jr., a former treasurer of President Nixon's campaign organization, said in sworn testimony made public May 10 that an attempt had been made to persuade him to perjure himself concerning the amount of money he paid G. Gordon Liddy, who was convicted in the Watergate conspiracy. Sloan said he attempted to inform Administration officials about the matter but failed to obtain satisfaction. The information was contained in Sloan's deposition in Watergate civil litigation.

Sloan had testified previously that he paid $199,000 in campaign cash to Liddy. In his deposition, he said suggestions to testify to a much smaller payment—$70,000 or $80,000 was suggested first, later a $40,000 figure—came from Jeb Stuart Magruder, then deputy director of the Committee to Re-elect the President. Sloan told of meeting with GOP campaign aide Frederick C. LaRue and emerging with the impression the committee was moving in that direction, to get him to "tell an untrue story."

Sloan said he attempted to apprise several Administration officials of the apparent problem concerning the funds. He said he suggested to Nixon aide John D. Ehrlichman that there was a problem about the funds and their use, possibly for the break-in, but Ehrlichman had told him "to go no further, that he didn't want any of the details" and "his position was that he would have to take executive privilege until after the election in any case."

Sloan said he approached GOP fundraiser Maurice H. Stans prior to the break-in with a complaint the funds being paid "were mounting up without any knowledge on our part of what, in fact, had happened to the money." Stans "indicated to me at that point," Sloan said, "in response to any inquiry along those lines that 'I don't want to know and you don't want to know.'"

Major staff reorganization. President Nixon announced a major staff reorganization May 10 in the wake of the April 30 resignations of key aides involved in the Watergate scandal.

John B. Connally, Jr., who became a Republican May 2 after serving as Treasury secretary in the Nixon Administration as a Democrat, was named a special adviser to the President on domestic and foreign affairs and on rebuilding the White House staff. He was to serve on an unpaid, part-time basis while continuing his private law practice.

James R. Schlesinger, director of the Central Intelligence Agency (CIA) for the past three months, was named defense secretary to replace Elliot L. Richardson, who was nominated attorney general the previous week.

William E. Colby, deputy CIA director for the past two months, was appointed director.

J. Fred Buzhardt Jr., the Defense Department's general counsel, was to serve in the White House on a temporary basis as special counsel on Watergate matters, reporting directly to Nixon. Buzhardt's duties at the Pentagon included work on the Pentagon Papers trial. Leonard Garment was to continue to assume the other duties of counsel to the President.

Another major change was abandonment of the super-Cabinet system adopted by Nixon in January when three Cabinet officers were given additional titles of counselor to the President with comprehensive jurisdiction over the areas of human resources, community development, and natural resources and environment.

The rank of counselor was dissolved for these Cabinet officers and the President would revert to the traditional system of direct contacts with all the Cabinet members.

White House Press Secretary Ronald L. Ziegler attributed the abandonment of the super-Cabinet system to the recent resignations of key Nixon administrators H. R. Haldeman and John D. Ehrlichman.

Treasury Secretary George P. Shultz and foreign affairs adviser Henry A. Kissinger were to retain their current status.

In response to press inquiries about a possible conflict of interest in Connally's new role while retaining his law practice, Ziegler said Connally would have no operational functions in the White House and would be serving probably only three days a week, from an office in the Executive Office Building adjacent to the White House. Ziegler expressed conviction that Nixon and Connally "will be careful to lay aside any interests represented by Mr. Connally's law firm in their consultations."

Connally announced May 11 he would take a leave of absence from his law firm during his White House service and would also resign from all corporate boards. It was reported in Newsday and other newspapers that Connally's Houston law firm—Vinson, Elkins, Searls, Connally and Smith—was representing a firm—the Gulf Resources and Chemical Corp.—that was under federal grand jury investigation concerning a $100,000 Nixon campaign contribution, part of which was later traced to the bank account of one of the convicted Watergate conspirators. Gulf Resources President Robert H. Allen appeared before the grand jury in Houston May 11.

He said: "Efforts have been made to prevent me from obtaining relevant information and records; attempts have been made to influence the handling of

Dean charges effort to curb truth. Former White House counsel John Dean charged in a statement May 10 that there was "an ongoing effort to limit or prevent my testifying fully and freely" concerning Watergate.

He said: "Efforts have been made to prevent me from obtaining relevant information and records; attempts have been made to influence the handling of my testimony by the prosecutors; restrictions have been placed on the scope of my testimony as it relates to the White House; and blatant efforts have been made to publicly intimidate me. Finally, I am, of course, aware of efforts to discredit me personally in the hope of discrediting my testimony."

Dean said "there have been discussions within the White House during the past four-five months as to how to end the Watergate matter, but these discussions always ended with an unwillingness to accept the truth for what it meant. That unwillingness to accept the truth still prevails among some who are affected by the truth. . . . I am not willing to see the truth distorted further, nor am I willing to shoulder the blame for those unwilling to accept the truth."

He also said "the news stories quoting unidentified sources and speculating on the nature of my testimony do not come from me" and were not authorized by him and the information contained in them was "neither complete nor accurate."

Mitchell, Stans, 2 others indicted. Former Attorney General John N. Mitchell and former Commerce Secretary Maurice H. Stans were indicted May 10 by a federal grand jury in New York for their roles in the 1972 Nixon re-election campaign.

Mitchell, who had directed the President's re-election campaign until July 1972, and Stans, who headed the Finance Committee to Re-Elect the President, were each charged with three counts of conspiring to obstruct justice and six counts of perjury regarding the government's investigations of a secret $200,000

contribution made to the re-election committee in March 1972 by financier Robert L. Vesco.

Vesco, who was a defendant in a civil suit brought by the Securities and Exchange Commission (SEC) and charged with looting four mutual funds of $224 million, was also indicted by the grand jury on one count of conspiracy and three counts of obstructing justice.

Harry L. Sears, former Republican majority leader of the New Jersey Senate, who was the conduit for Vesco's secret cash gift to Stans' committee, and Vesco's contact with Mitchell and other high Administration sources, was also indicted on one count of conspiracy and three counts of obstructing justice.

If convicted, Mitchell and Stans faced jail terms of up to 50 years and fines of up to $75,000 each. Maximum penalties for The charges against Mitchell and Stans of making "false declarations" related to their testimony before the grand jury.

According to U.S. Attorney Whitney North Seymour Jr., the indictments resulted from a four-month investigation of Vesco's secret campaign donation and subsequent influence peddling by Administration officials. The four men were charged with conspiring to obstruct justice in connection with the SEC investigation of Vesco's alleged financial swindle. Conspiracy to obstruct justice in the SEC probe was also cited with respect to disclosure of the sources and disposition of Vesco's political contribution.

They were also charged with conspiring to defraud the SEC and the General Accounting Office (GAO), the federal auditing agency charged with examining violations of the 1972 campaign finance reporting law, with regard to disclosure of the $200,000 gift and its disbursement.

The indictment alleged that the four men agreed Vesco would contribute $250,-000 to the Nixon re-election campaign—the "largest cash contribution ever received by the Finance Committee"—in return for a meeting arranged by Mitchell for Sears to be held with SEC Chairman William J. Casey. Stans allegedly promised to conceal the contribution from federal examiners at the SEC and the GAO.

According to the indictment, the conspiracy had a chronological development beginning in June and July 1971, when Sears met with Mitchell to discuss the SEC investigation which had begun in March 1971. At that meeting, Sears asked Mitchell to discuss the case with SEC Chairman Casey.

Vesco paid Sears "substantial sums of money" in December 1971 and January 1972 in return for Sears' meetings with Mitchell on Vesco's behalf. In January 1972, Sears gave Mitchell documents relating to the SEC probe and asked Mitchell to arrange a meeting with Casey.

Vesco met with Stans March 8, 1972 and offered to contribute "at least $250,-000 and possibly $500,000" in return for

Stans, Mitchell and others exerting their influence on the SEC. Immediately afterward, Vesco discussed the SEC investigation with Mitchell and "shortly thereafter, Stans and Mitchell discussed the proposed contribution from Vesco."

Two hours after the money had been delivered to Stans' office April 10—in cash at his request—Stans reported to Mitchell that the contribution had been received. Two hours after that, Sears met with Casey and G. Bradford Cook, SEC general counsel and Casey's successor as chairman of the commission, to discuss the case against Vesco at a meeting arranged by Mitchell.

Additional meetings took place between Cook, Casey and Sears during May–July 1972. Casey also met with Sears during the Republican National Convention in Miami in August 1972.

Seven "overt acts" were specified in the indictment as furthering the conspiracy, including charges that:

■ On April 6, 1972, Vesco directed a business associate, Ralph Dodd, to receive $250,000 in cash from Barclay's Bank in New York and transport it the same day to Vesco's New Jersey office.

■ In November 1972, Vesco "sent a package" to Donald Nixon at the Essex House, a New York City hotel. Donald Nixon was not identified as being either the President's brother, F. Donald Nixon, or Donald F. Nixon Jr., the President's nephew. F. Donald Nixon was an executive with the Marriott Corp., which owned Essex House. His son was an administrative assistant to Vesco.

Also in November 1972, Vesco attempted to send a memorandum to F. Donald Nixon, the President's brother, "the purport and tenor of which was to threaten disclosure of the secret cash contribution and other adverse consequences unless the SEC was directed to drop all legal proceedings against Vesco." When informed of the memo, Mitchell turned it over to Sears, and concealed its contents from the SEC and other law enforcement agencies "who properly should have been made aware of it."

■ In October 1972, Vesco had also threatened Stans with disclosure of the donation unless a subpoena issued for Vesco were withdrawn. Sears conveyed the threat to Mitchell.

According to the indictment, Mitchell and Stans asked Cook and John W. Dean 3d, then White House counselor for assistance in covering up the Vesco contribution. Cook told the Wall Street Journal May 11 that he had sought Stans' support for the SEC chairmanship during the same period Stans was seeking his aid in the Vesco case.

Cuban admits break-in. A Cuban real estate broker admitted May 10 he had participated in the 1971 burglary of the office of Daniel Ellsberg's former psychiatrist.

Felipe de Diego, after being granted immunity from prosecution by Los Angeles District Attorney Joseph Busch, said in Miami that he, Bernard L. Barker, and Eugenio R. Martinez forced open the door to the office of Dr. Lewis J. Fielding about 1 a.m. Sept. 4, 1971.

The Cuban exile said that after a short search, papers from what appeared to be a file on Ellsberg were found and photographed.

1969 phone taps reported. The Nixon Administration, concerned over leaks of classified information—especially with regard to the strategic arms limitations talks beginning in 1969—ordered wiretaps placed on the telephones of reporters from three newspapers and at least one government official, the New York Times reported May 11.

Times sources said reporters placed under surveillance were William Beecher and Hedrick Smith of the New York Times, and Henry Brandon, a Washington-based correspondent for the Sunday Times of London. Phones of unidentified reporters for the Washington Post also were tapped, the Times said.

The government official was Morton H. Halperin, a member of the National Security Council until 1971. The tap on his home phone was revealed in a memo given May 9 by Acting FBI Director William Ruckelshaus to Pentagon Papers trial Judge William M. Byrne

Charges against Ellsberg, Russo dismissed. Government charges of espionage, theft and conspiracy against Pentagon Papers trial defendants Daniel Ellsberg and Anthony J. Russo Jr. were dismissed by presiding Judge William M. Byrne in Los Angeles May 11. Byrne worded the dismissal so as to preclude retrial.

In granting the dismissal, Byrne was highly critical of government conduct during the case. "Bizarre events have incurably infected the prosecution of this case," he said. "The totality of the circumstances . . . offend 'a sense of justice,'" he added.

Citing government misconduct as the reason for the dismissal, Byrne said that after two weeks of extraordinary disclosures beginning April 26, the government had raised more questions than it had answers for.

Of greatest significance was not the disclosure of a wiretap on phone conversations of Ellsberg, but that the government had lost the records pertaining to the tap. "There is no way . . . [anybody] can test what effect these interceptions may have had on the government's case. . . ."

The dismissal also resulted from the break-in at the office of Ellsberg's former psychiatrist, which Byrne took care to note had been abetted by the Central Intelligence Agency (CIA), "presumably acting beyond its statutory authority."

Noting that the CIA had provided the White House with two psychological profiles of Daniel Ellsberg, Byrne reasoned he could not be sure that other material gathered by the special White House unit did not exist.

Byrne chastised the government for causing delays by not speedily producing exculpatory evidence it possessed. Stating that these delays had already compromised the defendants' right to a speedy trial, Byrne said "no investigation is likely to provide satisfactory answers where improper government conduct has been shielded so long from public view and where the government advises the court that pertinent files and records are missing or destroyed."

A poll of the trial jurors, taken by the Associated Press after the dismissal, showed seven leaned toward acquittal. In interviews after the dismissal, the jurors were nearly unanimous in their high regard for Byrne.

Cushman, Helms explain CIA role. The former director and deputy director of the Central Intelligence Agency (CIA) appeared before Congressional panels investigating the role played by the agency in the burglary of the office of the former psychiatrist of former Pentagon Papers trial defendant Daniel Ellsberg.

Former deputy director of the CIA and current Commandant of the Marine Corps Gen. Robert E. Cushman Jr. May 11 admitted giving aid to E. Howard Hunt Jr. at the request of former presidential adviser John D. Ehrlichman, who had been asked by President Nixon to head an investigation into security leaks that eventually led to the break-in in Los Angeles. Cushman said that when Ehrlichman asked for assistance, he assumed Ehrlichman was speaking on Nixon's behalf.

Cushman also revealed that the former director of the CIA, Richard Helms, agreed to give agency assistance after being informed of a July 22, 1971 meeting between Hunt and Cushman, during which specific requests were made by Hunt. However, Cushman denied knowing what the aid was for, claiming that Hunt would only say it was for the welfare of the nation.

Cushman testified before and submitted affadavits to the House Armed Services special subcommittee on intelligence, the Senate Armed Services committee, and the Senate Appropriations subcommittee on intelligence operations.

Helms, the current ambassador to Iran, appeared before the Senate Appropriations subcommittee May 16, where he admitted granting a 1971 White House request for a "personality assessment" of Ellsberg. Although he said he did not feel the request was proper, he agreed because it came from the White House, Helms reportedly said.

CIA psychiatrists had told the same subcommittee May 10 the Ellsberg profile was the only one ever done on an American citizen by the agency.

Clemency offer to McCord reported. Following a May 13 Los Angeles Times report that he had offered executive clemency to convicted Watergate conspirator James W. McCord Jr., Treasury official John J. (Jack) Caulfield May 13 asked for and was granted "administrative leave" from his post as assistant director for criminal enforcement of the alcohol, tobacco, and firearms division.

Caulfield, 44, a former aide to ex-presidential assistants John D. Ehrlichman and John W. Dean 3rd, reportedly met with McCord on two separate occasions in January, while McCord was on trial for the Watergate burglary. Caulfield allegedly told McCord if he kept silent during the trial and accepted imprisonment, he could expect executive clemency in 10 or 11 months, the Times reported.

McCord, considering Caulfield's approaches a "friendly gesture," spurned the offers and instead asserted "I am going to fight this thing every step," a Times source quoted him as saying.

The two men by prearrangement met twice at scenic locations along the Potomac River in Virginia. The first meeting consisted of a 30-minute walk through adjacent woods, and the second meeting was a two-hour drive in one of their cars, the Times reported.

CIA involvement was sought. High Administration officials sought to involve the Central Intelligence Agency (CIA) in the Watergate affair, according to testimony presented to the Senate Armed Services Committee. The committee was inquiring into the CIA's involvement in domestic undercover work, which was barred under the 1947 National Security Act.

The hearings were closed, but Sen. Stuart Symington (D, Mo.), the committee's acting chairman, reported after the first session May 14 that "there were other matters besides the Ellsberg case in which the White House tried to get the CIA involved."

On the basis of testimony by Lt. Gen. Vernon A. Walters, deputy director of the CIA, Symington reported that the White House aides involved in the apparent attempt to compromise the CIA were ex-White House aides H.R. Haldeman, John D. Ehrlichman and John W. Dean 3rd.

"Ehrlichman, and Haldeman—particularly Haldeman," Symington said, "were up to their ears in this, along with Dean, in trying to involve the CIA in this whole Watergate mess."

In releasing a summary of Walters' testimony May 15, Symington said "it is very clear to me that there was an attempt to unload major responsibility for the Watergate bugging and cover-up on the CIA." According to the summary:

■ Dean asked Walters 10 days after the Watergate break-in (in June 1972) if the CIA could provide bail or pay the salaries for the men apprehended there. Walters refused and declared he would rather resign than implicate the agency in such a scheme.

■ As recently as January or February, Dean sought to obtain CIA assistance in retrieving from the Federal Bureau of Investigation (FBI) "some materials" obtained from the CIA for use in the break-in at the office of Pentagon Papers defendant Daniel Ellsberg's psychiatrist.

■ Haldeman and Ehrlichman intervened in an attempt to have the CIA press the FBI to call off its probe in 1972 into Nixon campaign funds that had been routed—or "laundered" to prevent tracing—through a Mexican bank and, at one point, through several of the Watergate defendants. The CIA's approach to the FBI would be made on the ground that national security was involved and pursuit of the probe would compromise certain CIA activities and resources in Mexico. Walters met with Acting FBI Director L. Patrick Gray 3rd several times. The first time he related to Gray that senior White House aides had told him pursuit of the probe would compromise certain CIA activities and resources in Mexico. Walters met with Acting FBI Director L. Patrick Gray 3rd several times. The first time he related to Gray that senior White House aides had told him pursuit of the FBI probe would uncover some CIA activities in Mexico. After Gray later said he would need a written statement to that effect—that CIA assets would be endangered—before the FBI inquiry could be ended, Walters, apparently on word from then-CIA Director Richard M. Helms, informed Gray the CIA activity actually was not in jeopardy by the FBI probe.

Helms, currently ambassador to Iran, testified May 16 before a Senate Appropriations subcommittee, which was examining the same issue. Chairman John L. McClellan (D, Ark.) said afterward that Helms had expressed concern about the White House overtures to the CIA for domestic activity, which he considered improper, but said he had never conveyed his concern to President Nixon.

"He did not feel at that time that he should go to the President about it," McClellan reported. "He did not want the CIA involved."

According to McClellan, Helms confirmed Walters' testimony and defended his own statements at his confirmation hearings on the ambassadorship that the CIA had never been involved in Watergate. "He [Helms] did not relate these events to the Watergate" at the time, McClellan said.

More testimony was released May 17, as Helms and Walters returned before the Armed Services panel. Walters said he told Gray in their meeting in early July 1972 he considered the attempts "to cover this up or to implicate the CIA or FBI would be detrimental to their integrity"

and he was "quite prepared to resign on this issue."

Gray "shared my views" and "he, too, was prepared to resign on this issue," Walters said. He also recounted a conversation with Gray in a second meeting a week later: "I said that I had told Dean that the best solution would be to fire those responsible. Gray said he had made the same recommendation."

Symington said May 17 all the recent witnesses had "stated that they did not know whether the President" knew about White House efforts to implicate the CIA in Watergate. "But it's hard for me to visualize that the President knew nothing about this," Symington commented.

*Gray says he alerted Nixon—*According to sources within the Senate Watergate committee, which interrogated former Acting FBI Director Gray May 10 (the testimony was leaked May 11), Gray testified President Nixon telephoned him about another matter July 6, 1972. Gray took the opportunity to express concern about White House interference in the Watergate probe and to caution the President that he was being "wounded" by men around him "using the FBI and CIA." According to Gray, Nixon responded that Gray should continue to press his investigation.

The July 6 date was the same day Walters visited Gray to inform him the FBI probe would not jeopardize CIA activity. In that visit, Walters identified, as he had not in his previous talk with Gray, the White House aides who were pressing for an end to the FBI probe—Ehrlichman and Haldeman.

According to some accounts of Gray's testimony, he also reported arranging a meeting with CIA Director Helms about possible CIA complications, but received a call from Ehrlichman that firmly suggested he cancel it because of the security aspect. The call reportedly was made June 28, 1972, the day Gray received in Ehrlichman's office files, which he said he burned, from one of the Watergate defendants. Gray was said by the sources to have revised, in his May 10 testimony, his account of the time and place he burned the files. Instead of having done it in his office five days after receiving them, he said he kept them until Christmas at his home, where he then incinerated them.

Gray's reported testimony May 10 that he had also called Nixon's campaign chairman, Clark MacGregor, July 6, 1972 to express concern about the obstacles to his probe, was confirmed May 12 by MacGregor, who said he was in California at the time, which was about 2 a.m. in Washington. He said Gray had seemed "agitated, concerned" and "wondered if I recognized how serious Watergate was." MacGregor reported being aware of the seriousness of the crimes involved in the break-in and said Gray did not bring the subject up again.

Missing FBI wiretap files found. William D. Ruckelshaus, acting director of the

A

B

C

D

E

F

G

Federal Bureau of Investigation (FBI), disclosed at a May 14 press conference that missing records of 17 FBI wiretaps placed on newsmen and government officials had been discovered May 11 in a safe in the outer office of former presidential adviser John Ehrlichman.

Ruckelshaus, declining to identify those under surveillance, said he personally retrieved them May 12.

In a related development, the New York Times reported May 17 that national security adviser Henry Kissinger, acting under presidential authorization, formally submitted requests for the taps to the late FBI director, J. Edgar Hoover.

Contained in the records was information relating to the wiretap that had been placed on the home telephone of Morton H. Halperin, an adviser to the National Security Council. It was on Halperin's phone that former Pentagon Papers defendant Daniel Ellsberg was overheard by the FBI. Ruckelshaus said the records were discovered an hour after Judge William M. Byrne had dismissed charges against Ellsberg and Anthony J. Russo Jr. Ruckelshaus declined to speculate on the effect the records might have had on the trial if they had been found in time

Ruckelshaus said the FBI had assumed the records had been destroyed. This was based on two pieces of FBI correspondence, bearing notations in Hoover's handwriting, that indicated former Attorney General John N. Mitchell had so informed the late director. Ruckelshaus noted that Mitchell had previously denied making such a statement.

(Ehrlichman said May 14 he had the records in his safe for more than a year. He said he had "skimmed" them but was unaware they contained any material about Ellsberg. A White House spokesman said May 15 that President Nixon had not known the files were in Ehrlichman's safe.)

Ruckelshaus explained that the FBI had ascertained the records still existed in a May 10 interview in Phoenix, Ariz. with Robert C. Mardian, former assistant attorney general in charge of the now defunct Internal Security Division.

Mardian suggested they might be in the White House, Ruckelshaus explained.

Ruckelshaus said an FBI investigation showed that after the wiretaps had been removed in 1971, the records were placed in the custody of William C. Sullivan, then assistant director of the FBI. Sullivan later contacted Mardian about the records and recommended they be transferred. According to Mardian, the recommendation had been made because Sullivan thought Hoover might use them against the attorney general or the President, Ruckelshaus said.

Sullivan confirmed the sequence of events in an interview published in the Los Angeles Times May 14. He said the records were kept in the White House because Hoover was "not of sound mind" in his later years. Sullivan gave the files to Mardian before being forced to retire Oct. 6, 1971, since he felt Hoover "could not be trusted" to keep the files confidential. However, contrary to what Ruckelshaus had said, Sullivan claimed Mitchell ordered the files given to Mardian.

Sullivan, noting that Hoover had ordered the files kept outside the regular FBI filing system, said Justice Department officials, who were aware of the files, became very upset when they learned Sullivan was leaving the FBI.

"They could no longer depend on Hoover. He had been leaking stuff all over the place. He could no longer be trusted. So I was instructed to pass the records to Mardian," Sullivan said.

Hoover, who was concerned about being fired as director, retained the records "to keep Mitchell and others in line," Sullivan continued.

"The fellow was a master blackmailer and he did it with considerable finesse despite the deterioration of his mind," Sullivan said.

Sullivan said neither Mardian nor Mitchell ever specifically told him they did not want Hoover to have the files because they could not trust Hoover. But Sullivan said he could "read between the lines."

Court holds Dean documents. The U.S. district court in Washington assumed possession May 14 of documents former presidential counsel John W. Dean 3rd said he had removed from his White House office just prior to his resignation.

Chief Judge John J. Sirica ordered that the documents be placed in the court's possession and that copies be made available to the Senate committee and federal court prosecutors investigating the Watergate case. The physical transfer of the documents, residing in the Alexandria, Va. National Bank, was accomplished by Dean in the company of a federal marshal and a court clerk.

Sirica obtained assurance from Dean that the documents bore the highest security classification.

'Oral' report on Watergate—White House Press Secretary Ronald L. Ziegler conceded May 16 that the White House report on its own Watergate investigation, which President Nixon had attributed to his counsel John W. Dean 3rd and said absolved the Administration, had not been written and was not delivered to the President by Dean. Nixon had ordered the investigation through intermediaries, Ziegler said, and a report on it was made orally to the President by John D. Ehrlichman.

The White House reaction came after Newsweek magazine in its May 21 issue carried an interview with Dean in which he contended the President never asked him for the report and he never wrote one. He said he did not see the President between the time of the Watergate break-in and the President's statement on it at his Aug. 29, 1972 news conference, which Dean said "flabbergasted" him.

Nixon had said then that Dean had conducted at his direction a complete investigation of possible Administration involvement in Watergate and he could categorically state it indicated that no one in his Administration, "presently employed, was involved in this very bizarre incident."

Ziegler declined to respond to reporters' queries May 14, but unnamed White House officials made it clear May 15 that the only report received by Nixon was an informal oral statement from Ehrlichman, who had been ordered by the President to initiate the investigation and who in turn delegated the duty to Dean. The sources confirmed that Nixon had not talked directly with Dean about the probe before or after announcing its results.

Ziegler confirmed the sources May 16, stressing that an investigation had been carried out and that Dean "was clearly in charge" of it. "There was a certain inadequacy" in the data Dean provided, Ziegler added.

Nixon urges election reforms. President Nixon told Congressional leaders May 15 that a bipartisan commission should study the possibility of limiting the presidency to a single six-year term and doubling the term of House members to four years.

Nixon detailed his proposal for a 17-member election reform commission at a White House meeting with Vice President Spiro T. Agnew, Attorney General-designate Elliot L. Richardson and 10 members of Congress. The proposal was formally presented to Congress May 16.

A White House spokesman said after the meeting that Nixon had not specifically endorsed the tenure changes, which would require Constitutional amendment, but had intended them as indications of the scope of the commission's mandate.

Sen. Hugh Scott (R, Pa.) said Nixon had suggested the commission should also study limits on campaign spending, stricter laws on disclosure of political gifts, free time for candidates on radio and television and an independent office to take over from the Justice Department the task of enforcing campaign finance laws. The proposed commission would have a deadline of Dec. 1 for submitting final recommendations, but Nixon said Congress should not delay action on election reform bills already under consideration.

It was reported May 13 that Nixon had been considering asking the chairmen of both major parties to join the panel, along with some congressmen chosen by Congressional leaders, and six persons from outside government, chosen by Nixon for their political expertise.

Senate Majority Leader Mike Mansfield (D, Mont.) May 15 called the proposal "a step in the right direction," but Democratic National Chairman Robert S. Strauss, in a speech to the Capitol Democratic Club, said the commission might become "another delaying tactic and whitewash effort."

John W. Gardner, chairman of the citizens' lobby Common Cause, said his group opposed the proposal and asserted there was "no justification for delay" in taking steps to "restore integrity to the political process."

Senate panel backs reform bill—The Senate Commerce Committee unanimously approved in executive session May 16 a bill to limit campaign spending and to create an independent commission with the power to investigate and prosecute violations. The bill, introduced by Sen. John O. Pastore (D, R.I.), would replace some sections of the Federal Election Campaign Act, which became effective April 7, 1972.

The bill would limit candidates in federal elections to spending no more than 25¢ per voter in any one primary, runoff or general election and repeal the equal-time provision of the communications law. Sen. Marlow W. Cook (R, Ky.) added an amendment which would put each party's national committee in sole charge of coordinating presidential campaign funding, replacing such ad hoc groups as the Committee to Re-elect the President.

The bill would go to the Rules Committee, which was required to act within 45 days.

In other Senate developments, Mansfield introduced a constitutional amendment May 16 to provide for a single six-year term for President. Scott said he favored a single seven-year Presidential term and a four-year House term.

Southern GOP criticizes Nixon. Although he received a statement of support from the Republican governors' conference May 11, President Nixon came under increasing fire from the conservative wing of his party.

Some 25 Republican party leaders from the South, meeting in closed session in Washington May 16, concluded that the party might function better if it divorced itself from the Administration, unless there was quick action "to restore confidence and reorganize the White House."

Sen. Barry Goldwater (R, Ariz.) also expressed dismay over Watergate in a statement issued May 16: "It is not easy for me to say this about my country or my President, but I think the time has come when someone must say to both of them, let's get going."

The GOP governors, meeting in North Tarrytown, N.Y., issued a short, unanimous statement deploring Watergate and expressing support and belief in the President.

(White House Press Secretary Ronald L. Ziegler said May 14 "there has been considerable concern regarding the impact of the hearings on due process and the rights of individuals.")

Meanwhile, there was strong reaction among some Democrats. Rep. Henry S.

Reuss (D, Wis.) suggested May 11 that Nixon and Vice President Agnew consider resignation, paving the way for a coalition government under Speaker of the House Rep. Carl Albert (D, Okla.).

Cook quits SEC. Securities and Exchange Commission (SEC) Chairman G. Bradford Cook resigned May 16, citing a "web of circumstances" which linked him to charges of conspiracy to obstruct justice and perjury brought against former Attorney General John N. Mitchell and former Commerce Secretary Maurice H. Stans involving a secret $200,000 contribution made to the Nixon re-election committee by financier Robert L. Vesco.

Vesco, who had been charged by the SEC with "looting" $224 million from four mutual funds in a suit filed in November 1972, was also charged with conspiracy. His intermediary with high Administration figures regarding the campaign donation and subsequent efforts to obtain Administration assistance in overturning the SEC charges, Harry L. Sears, was also indicted.

According to the government's case, Stans, chairman of the Finance Committee to Re-elect the President, "did cause" Cook "to delete all specific references" to Vesco's contribution from the SEC civil complaint. It was also alleged that Stans asked Cook to limit the SEC's investigation of Vesco's campaign donations, which totaled $250,000. The indictment charged that Cook, then general counsel for the SEC, met with SEC Chairman William J. Casey and Sears April 10, 1972, only hours after $200,000 in $100 bills had been delivered to Stans' office by Vesco associates.

Cook admitted to the Washington Post May 11 that he had omitted a paragraph about the $250,000 from the SEC complaint and that Casey had "concurred" in the decision.

Cook was the 15th Administration official to resign since February in the wake of widening campaign-related scandals.

Nixon authorized wiretaps. The White House May 16 acknowledged that President Nixon personally authorized the use of 17 wiretaps against 13 members of his own Administration and four newsmen.

The New York Times reported May 17 that Henry A. Kissinger, assistant to the President for national security affairs, personally provided the FBI with the names of a number of his aides on the National Security Council (NSC), whom he wanted wiretapped. The Times cited Justice Department officials as its source.

The White House, in formally acknowledging the existence of the wire taps, said they were made in 1969 after publication in the Times May 9, 1969 of an article by William Beecher disclosing American B-52s were bombing Cambodia. (Beecher was appointed

deputy assistant secretary of defense for public affairs April 20.)

Ervin smear proposed. Former presidential chief of staff H. R. Haldeman made two attempts during March to enlist the aid of North Carolina Republicans in discrediting Sen. Sam. J. Ervin Jr., chairman of the select Senate committee investigating the Watergate affair and White House involvement in an alleged cover-up attempt, according to the Charlotte (N.C.) Observer May 17.

Haldeman twice telephoned former White House aide Harry Dent asking him to approach the North Carolina GOP chairman, Frank Rouse, with a proposal "to dig up something to discredit Ervin and blast him with it," the Observer said.

Dent and Rouse discussed the matter but rejected Haldeman's proposal.

Segretti arraigned. Donald H. Segretti pleaded innocent in Tampa, Fla. May 17 to charges that he had prepared and distributed a fraudulent campaign document during the 1972 Florida Democratic primary election. The document accused presidential candidates Sen. Hubert H. Humphrey (D, Minn.) and Sen. Henry M. Jackson (D, Wash.) of sexual misconduct.

George A. Hearing, who had been indicted with Segretti May 4 pleaded guilty May 11 to the two counts of conspiracy and distribution of the fictitious letter.

Senate hearings begin. The Senate Select Committee on Presidential Campaign Activities opened hearings May 17 in Washington into the Watergate scandal and related charges of wrongdoing during the 1972 presidential campaign.

Chairman Sam J. Ervin Jr. (D, N.C.) declared in an opening statement delivered before a crowded Senate Caucus Room in the Old Senate Office Building: "A clear mandate of the unanimous Senate resolution provides for a bipartisan investigation of every phase of political espionage."

Opening remarks were also made by the six other committee members: Vice Chairman Howard H. Baker Jr. (R, Tenn.), Herman E. Talmadge (D, Ga.), Daniel K. Inouye (D, Hawaii), Joseph M. Montoya (D, N.M.), Edward J. Gurney (R, Fla.), and Lowell P. Weicker Jr., (R, Conn.).

Ervin's opening statement—In his opening remarks, Chairman Ervin declared that an "atmosphere of the utmost gravity" demanded a "probe into assertions that the very [political] system itself has been subverted and its foundations shaken. Our citizens do not know whom to believe, and many of them have concluded that all the processes of government have become so compromised that honest government has been rendered impossible."

He said:

"The questions that have been raised in the wake of the June 17 break-in strike at the very undergirding of our democracy. If the many allegations made to this date are true, then the burglars who broke into the headquarters of the Democratic National Committee at the Watergate were in effect breaking into the home of every citizen of the United States. And if these allegations prove to be true, what they were seeking to steal was not the jewels, money or other property of American citizens, but something much more valuable—their most precious heritage, the right to vote in a free election."

For that reason, Ervin said, "My colleagues on the committee are determined to uncover all the relevant facts surrounding these matters and to spare no one, whatever his station in life may be, in our efforts to accomplish that goal."

Ervin said the hearing's purpose was not "prosecutorial or judicial but rather investigative and informative. The aim of the committee is to provide full and open public testimony in order that the nation can proceed toward healing of the wounds that now afflict the body politic."

Ervin, whom President Nixon had described as "the best Constitutional lawyer in the Congress," declared that the allegations "regarding the subversion of our electoral and political processes" threatened the integrity of a governmental system first devised in 1787. He said:

"The founding fathers, having participated in the struggle against arbitrary power, comprehended some eternal truths respecting men and government. They knew that those who are entrusted with power are susceptible to the disease of tyrants, which George Washington rightly described as 'love of power and the proneness to abuse it.' For that reason, they realized that the power of public officers should be defined by laws which they, as well as the people, are obligated to obey.

To safeguard the structural scheme of our governmental system, the founding fathers provided for an electoral process by which the elected officials of this nation should be chosen. The Constitution, later-adopted amendments, and more specifically, statutory law, provide that the electoral processes shall be conducted by the people, outside the confines of the formal branches of the government, and through a political process that must operate under the strictures of law and ethical guidelines, but independent of the overwhelming power of the government itself. Only then can we be sure that each electoral process cannot be made to serve as the mere handmaiden of a particular Administration in power."

Baker's opening statement— Vice Chairman Baker said in opening remarks, "It is the American people who must be the final judge of Watergate [and what it] means about how we all should conduct our public business in the future."

Baker emphasized that the committee, which had acted with unswerving bipartisanship in recent weeks, would continue to conduct a "bipartisan search for the unvarnished truth. We will inquire into every fact and follow every lead, unrestrained by any fear of where that lead may take us."

(Baker commented on a television interview May 13 he "would not exclude the possibility" that President Nixon would be offered an opportunity to "state his side of the case" to the committee. He also said if Nixon were found to be guilty of involvement in Watergate or its cover-up, "clearly he would be impeached.")

Witnesses appearing before panel— Robert C. Odle Jr., Bruce A. Kehrli, Sgt. Paul W. Leeper and Officer John Barrett

were the first witnesses to be questioned by the panel members. They were also questioned by Samuel Dash, chief counsel and staff director, and Fred D. Thompson, chief minority counsel.

The hearings, which were broadcast nationally on television and radio, began on a low-key note. Information, which had been public knowledge for several months, was elicited through slow, thorough questioning into the events leading up to the Watergate break-in into Democratic National Committee headquarters June 17, 1972.

The committee appeared to be seeking evidence in three areas: the Watergate burglary itself; alleged attempts at a cover-up by White House officials; and charges of a widespread plot of political espionage and sabotage initiated and operated by the White House and officials of the Committee to Re-Elect the President.

Odle, former administrative director of the re-election committee, was the first witness. He testified that deputy campaign director Jeb Stuart Magruder ordered a "strategy file" to be removed from his desk at committee headquarters for "security reasons" only hours after the Watergate burglary.

Odle denied knowing the contents of the file, but said, "I suspect that things which had no place in a political campaign were in it." The folder was reported to contain documents on clandestine operations and wiretapping transcripts against Democrats (codenamed "Gemstone").

Odle told the committee that on the day of the Watergate break-in, he and Robert Reisner, Magruder's assistant, talked by telephone with Magruder, who was in California with other Administration officials. Under instructions, Reisner took from Magruder's desk for safekeeping another file dealing with "advertising." Odle said he kept the "strategy file" at home for two days before returning it to Magruder June 19 when he returned to Washington. The file has never been uncovered by investigators.

Odle testified that convicted Watergate conspirator G. Gordon Liddy, then a lawyer with the re-election committee, asked to use a paper shredding machine during the afternoon of June 17, 1972. Odle denied destroying documents himself.

Odle's testimony provided the Senate committee with an explanation of the staffing of the Nixon re-election committee and its working relationship with the White House during the campaign.

According to Odle, John N. Mitchell was involved in "major campaign decisions" in 1971 while still attorney general. Mitchell had testified in March 1972 before a Senate committee investigating Administration links to the International Telephone & Telegraph Corp. that he "did not have any [party] responsibilities"

before his resignation from the Cabinet March 1, 1972. Mitchell quit the committee post July 1, 1972, soon after the Watergate break-in.

Odle also testified that during the campaign he had spoken two or three times a week with Gordon Strachan, whom he described as the "eyes and ears" on the re-election committee of then presidential chief of staff H. R. Haldeman.

(Magruder had told a Harvard seminar in early January "there was basically a triad of senior decision makers" in the Nixon re-election campaign—"the President, Bob Haldeman and John Mitchell—until July of '72. They were in constant consultation with each other over major activities." The information was reported May 15 by the New York Times, which obtained a transcript of the seminar.)

The second witness before the committee, Bruce Kehrli, a former assistant to Haldeman and currently on the White House staff, used operational charts to outline the command structure among the President's advisers for the committee investigators.

Kehrli's testimony on White House organization indicated that little distinction was made within the Administration between service in the executive branch of government and political duties for the Nixon re-election campaign. The White House retained overall direction of the 1972 campaign, despite existence of the Committee to Re-elect the President, Kehrli said.

The two Washington Metropolitan police officers, Leeper and Barrett, were questioned regarding their discovery of the Watergate burglary attempt.

Vast Administration plot since 1969. The Washington Post reported May 17 that since 1969 the Nixon Administration had engaged in a wide pattern of illegal and quasi-legal activities against radical leaders, students, demonstrators, news reporters, Democratic candidates for president and vice president, the Congress and Nixon Administration officials suspected of leaking information to the press.

Reporters Carl Bernstein and Bob Woodward quoted "highly placed sources in the executive branch" who said that although most of the clandestine operations were political in nature, they were conducted by the Federal Bureau of Investigation (FBI), the Secret Service and special teams working for the White House and the Justice Department under the guise of "national security."

"Watergate was a natural action that came from long existing circumstances. It grew out of an atmosphere. This way of life was not new. There have been fairly broad [illegal and quasi-legal] activities from the beginning of the Administration. I didn't know where 'national security' ended and political espionage started," one source said.

The Post named former presidential chief of staff H. R. Haldeman, former Attorney General and Nixon campaign director John N. Mitchell, former domestic affairs adviser John D. Ehrlichman, former White House counsel John W. Dean 3rd and former Assistant Attorney General Robert C. Mardian as the officials who supervised covert activities.

According to the Post, seven high Administration officials cited Haldeman and former White House special counsel Charles W. Colson as the prime movers behind the espionage operations conducted during the 1972 presidential campaign.

"It was a campaign that went astray and lost its sense of fair play. Secrecy and an obsession with the covert became part of nearly every action," a highly placed former Administration official said.

Known instances of illegal and quasi-legal activities:

■ Information was gathered by the Secret Service on the private life of at least one Democratic presidential candidate. On two occasions, the Administration considered leaking some of the reports to the press. Colson admitted receiving such information about one prominent Democrat, but denied that the information originated with Secret Service agents.

(The New York Times had reported Nov. 2, 1972 that Secret Service agents were providing the White House with confidential information regarding meetings held by Sen. George McGovern (D, S.D.) and potential financial backers.)

■ The medical records of Sen. Thomas Eagleton (D, Mo.), McGovern's running mate for a brief period, were obtained by Ehrlichman several weeks before the information regarding Eagleton's treatment for nervous exhaustion was leaked to the press.

Former Attorney General Ramsey Clark said the records were in FBI files. According to Post sources, Mardian, who had left the Justice Department to become political coordinator of the Nixon campaign, gave the FBI files to the White House.

■ Paid provocateurs were used to foment violence at antiwar demonstrations during Nixon's first term of office and also during the 1972 presidential campaign.

A former assistant to Colson, William Rhatican, told reporters that campaign money was used to finance Vietnam veterans in support of Nixon. A Veterans Administration official, Mel Stevens, was assigned to Colson's office to organize a pro-Nixon veterans' group using government money but having the appearance of a voluntary organization. Rhatican also said he was "sure" Colson used campaign funds to send telegrams of support to the White House following presidential adviser Henry Kissinger's "peace is at hand" speech Oct. 26, 1972.

■ Clandestine activities against persons considered opponents of the Administration were conducted by "suicide squads," which if apprehended in illegal activities would be disavowed by the FBI and the White House.

■ Paid "vigilante squads" were hired by the White House and Justice Department to conduct wiretapping and other forms of political espionage and to infiltrate radical groups for purposes of provocation.

Convicted Watergate conspirators E. Howard Hunt Jr. and G. Gordon Liddy supervised the squads, made up of former FBI and Central Intelligence Agency (CIA) operatives.

The transfer of these activities from the White House to the Committee to Re-elect the President in late 1971 and early 1972 was arranged by Haldeman and Mitchell and was part of an elaborate plan to extend the "dirty tricks" operations to the 1972 campaign, the Post reported.

■ Frederic V. Malek, formerly in charge of recruiting personnel for the Nixon Administration and a deputy campaign manager, and presently deputy director of the Office of Management and Budget, established an information network in nearly 50 states to report on the McGovern campaign.

"Viola Smith" was the code-named contact at the Nixon re-election committee for the "McGovern Watch" spys. The re-election committee also provided the agents with forms marked confidential which contained space for details about staff changes, speeches and polls in the McGovern campaign. The Post based its information on a memo entitled, "Intelligence on Future Appearances of McGovern and Shriver," which Malek admitted writing although he denied its intent was espionage.

DeVan L. Shumway, Nixon re-election committee spokesman, also admitted that on orders from deputy campaign director Jeb Stuart Magruder, he had asked two reporters to provide him with McGovern's campaign schedule. (The reporters rejected the proposal.)

One Democratic presidential contender sought legal advice after determining that he and his family were under surveillance, an activity which a former Nixon campaign official acknowledged he had authorized.

Mardian supervised two spies in the McGovern campaign who reported directly to him. Other Nixon campaign aides, on loan from the Republican National Committee, regularly posed as newsmen to obtain routine data on McGovern.

■ Colson organized a group of 30 Nixon supporters to "attack" news correspondents through use of write-in, telephone and telegraph campaigns, according to Tom Girard, a former Nixon committee press aide.

Another instance of covert activity directed against newsmen was the 1971 investigation of Columbia Broadcasting System correspondent Daniel Schorr. Haldeman personally ordered the FBI probe, the Post reported.

Dean efforts to set up Miami spy ring— Former White House Counsel John W. Dean 3rd attempted to recruit a lawyer from the Interior Department for the purpose of setting up an undercover espionage and intelligence network to infiltrate radical and antiwar groups in Miami before the national political party nominating conventions in 1972.

Kenneth C. Tapman May 14 said Dean in May 1972 had offered him a large sum of cash to either participate in or direct the covert operation.

Tapman had been assigned by the Interior Department in 1969 and 1970 to negotiate with antiwar groups regarding permits for demonstrations in Washing-

---

Concurrent Congressional Investigations

These were concurrent Congressional investigations into the Watergate affair and other Administration irregularities in the 1972 presidential campaign:

Senate Select Committee on Presidential Campaign Activities. Chairman: Sen. Sam J. Ervin Jr. (D, N.C.) Vice-Chairman: Sen. Howard H. Baker Jr. (R, Tenn.)

Senate Appropriations Committee Subcommittee on Intelligence Operations. Chairman: Sen. John L. McClellan (D, Ark.). Investigating the Central Intelligence Agency's (CIA) alleged illegal involvement in domestic espionage activities.

Senate Armed Services Committee. Acting Chairman: Sen. Stuart Symington (D, Mo.). Investigating the CIA's alleged involvement in domestic espionage activities.

Senate Government Operations Committee Permanent Subcommittee on Investigations. Chairman: Sen. Henry M. Jackson (D, Wash.) Investigating the circumstances surrounding the sale of an estimated 440 million bushels of grain by the U.S. to the Soviet Union during the summer of 1972.

House Armed Services Committee Special Subcommittee on Intelligence. Chairman: Rep. Lucien N. Nedzi (D, Mich.). Investigating the CIA's alleged involvement in illegal domestic espionage activities.

House Interstate and Foreign Commerce Committee Special Subcommittee on Investigations. Chairman: Rep. Harley O. Staggers (D, W.Va.). Investigating the Securities and Exchange Commission and the sale of International Telephone & Telegraph Corp. (ITT) stock to an Italian bank prior to ITT's acquisition of the Hartford Fire Insurance Co. ITT's controversial purchase of the Hartford had been challenged by the Justice Department in an antitrust suit which was later settled out of court. Connections between the government's settlement, ITT's 1972 contributions to the Nixon re-election campaign and subsequent contacts with the Nixon Administration were the subject of a Senate Judiciary Committee probe in 1972.

A

ton. Dean, then a Justice Department official, was charged with coordinating the government's response to the demonstrators.

Tapman said he rejected Dean's proposal. "It's the only time in my life that I've been speechless. I was personally insulted they thought I would do it," Tapman said.

B

Cox named special prosecutor. Attorney General-designate Elliot L. Richardson May 18 appointed Harvard Law School professor Archibald Cox special prosecutor for the Watergate case.

Cox, 61, had served as solicitor general in the Kennedy and Johnson Administrations. He was a registered Democrat and did not vote for President Nixon in 1972.

Richardson said he had not consulted the White House prior to the selection. He said he would submit the appointment to the Senate for confirmation, although that was not mandatory.

C

Cox would be able to select his own staff, Richardson said, or use the staff currently investigating Watergate. The resources of the entire Justice Department, including the Federal Bureau of Investigation, would be available to Cox.

Richardson said he would have no control over the investigation "for all practical day-to-day purposes." He would make no effort to keep tabs on the special prosecutor, he said, and Cox "will determine to what extent he will keep me informed" and the "occasions on which to consult me."

D

Cox told reporters at Harvard May 18 he considered his main job as prosecutor was to "restore confidence in the honor, integrity and decency of government." He said he had "not the slightest doubt I will be independent."

The first two candidates asked to serve as special Watergate prosecutor had refused the role.

E

Judge Harold R. Tyler Jr., 51, of the U.S. district court for the southern district of New York, declined May 15. Warren M. Christopher, 47, in private law practice in Los Angeles, declined May 16.

Richardson had informed Senate Judiciary Committee members privately, it became known May 14, that his search for a prosecutor had been narrowed to four men, including Tyler and Christopher. The other two were David W. Peck, 70, a New York lawyer and former presiding justice of the New York State Appellate Division, and William H. Erickson, 49, a justice on the Colorado Supreme Court.

F

Tyler, a former assistant attorney general, refused because he did not want to give up his judgeship. Richardson had said a sitting judge would have to resign to become prosecutor without the prospect of reappointment during the remainder of Nixon's presidency.

G

Christopher, a former deputy attorney general, declined on the ground there did not seem to be "any reasonable probability" he would have "the requisite

independence" in the task. After the refusals, Richardson broadened his search.

The question of independence—the prosecutor's from Richardson and Richardson's from the White House—remained the dominant topic as Richardson appeared for the third and fourth times at his confirmation hearings before the Senate Judiciary Committee May 14–15.

In the third session, he disclosed that two high-level White House aides had suggested two names for Watergate prosecutor. The aides were Gen. Alexander M. Haig, Nixon's chief of staff, and Leonard Garment, counsel to the President. Richardson said he rejected both suggestions since both proposed choices—former California Gov. Edmund G. Brown and former Missouri Gov. Warren E. Hearnes—lacked the legal background he deemed requisite.

Richardson assured the committee he felt "no obligation" to consult the White House about his choice and he would not do so. He said neither the President nor members of his staff had tried to influence his choice and the two names suggested "were simply dropped in the hopper" as "names I might not have considered otherwise."

Sen. Philip A. Hart (D, Mich.) observed that there was "a singular lack of sensitivity" in the action by the Nixon aides.

In a letter to the committee May 15, American Bar Association President Robert W. Meserve said a Watergate prosecutor should not report to the attorney general but should operate from a special federal agency created for the probe and prosecution. Speaking "solely as a citizen and a lawyer" and not in his official position, Meserve also recommended creation of a supervisory body to oversee the work of the special prosecutor.

Richardson May 17 sent the committee his guidelines for the role of the prosecutor. Among them: the prosecutor would serve within the Justice Department and would have "full" authority for the probe and prosecution of Watergate and for decisions on executive privilege or immunity. Guidelines on the same subject being proposed by Sen. Adlai E. Stevenson 3rd (D, Ill.) would give the prosecutor "final" authority.

Televised hearings continue. The Senate Select Committee on Presidential Campaign Activities continued its televised Watergate investigation under the chairmanship of Sen. Sam J. Ervin Jr. (D, N.C.) in the Senate Caucus Room May 18–24. The hearings had opened May 17.

The witnesses were James W. McCord Jr., convicted as a participant in the conspiracy; John J. Caulfield, former White House aide and employe of the Nixon re-election committee, currently on administrative leave from a post in the Treasury Department; Gerald Alch, a lawyer who

served as McCord's defense counsel during his trial; Bernard Barker, one of the Watergate conspirators; and Alfred C. Baldwin 3rd, a former FBI agent.

Day-by-Day Testimony

May 18: *Executive clemency offered*—McCord testified that he was subjected to political pressure to remain silent by offers of executive clemency and money and that a Nixon Administration official had persisted in this effort and related it to "the very highest levels of the White House."

In a deliberate and unhurried manner in an apparent effort to be precise, McCord testified that the pressure to remain silent began in late September or early October 1972, and continued up to the night before his conviction on Jan. 29.

The persons "who communicated information to me which I construed as political pressure," he said, included fellow conspirator E. Howard Hunt Jr.; the late Mrs. Hunt "speaking for Mr. Hunt;" Gerald Alch, McCord's attorney at the time; and John J. Caulfield, then a Treasury Department official and a former White House aide.

McCord said Hunt had informed him in the fall of 1972 that the Watergate defendants would be "given executive clemency after a period of time in prison, if interested, if they pled guilty, and were sentenced in a plea of not guilty, that they were going to be given financial support while they were in prison; that is, their families would be; and that rehabilitation, not specified but rehabilitation, perhaps a job, would be provided for the men after the release from prison."

Then, on Jan. 8, the first day of the Watergate trial, McCord said Alch told him Hunt's lawyer, William O. Bittman, wanted to talk to him. "When I asked why," McCord testified, "Alch said that Bittman wanted to talk with me about whose word I would trust regarding a White House offer of executive clemency."

McCord said he did not intend to accept clemency but did "want to find out what was going on, and by whom, and exactly what the White House was doing now." The meeting was arranged, McCord said, but he became angry at what he considered the "arrogance and audacity of another man's lawyer" trying to make a "pitch" for the White House, and he did not talk to Bittman. Alch did, while McCord waited in another room, reporting back that "I would be called that same night by a friend I had known from the White House," McCord said. About 12:30 that night, McCord said, he received a telephone call from "an unidentified individual who said that Caulfield was out of town, and asked me to go to a pay phone booth near the Blue Fountain Inn on Route 355 near my residence, where he had a message for me from Caulfield. There the same individual called and read the following message:

" 'Plead guilty. One year is a long time. You will get executive clemency. Your family will be taken care of and when you get out you will be rehabilitated and a job will be found for you. Don't take immunity when called before the grand jury.' "

McCord testified he received another call Jan. 10, the day Hunt pleaded guilty, to return to the phone booth Jan. 11 and setting a Jan. 12 meeting with Caulfield. The phone call did not occur but McCord met Caulfield Jan. 12 at an overlook on the George Washington Parkway along the Potomac River in Virginia. He told Caulfield there he did not intend to take executive clemency or plead guilty. Caulfield told him the clemency was a " 'sincere offer' " and "he explained that he had been asked to convey this message to me and was only doing what he was told to do."

Caulfield also told him he was "carrying the message of executive clemency to me 'from the very highest levels of the White House.' He stated that the President of the United States was in Key Biscayne, Fla. that weekend, had been told of the forthcoming meeting with me, and would be immediately told of the results of the meeting." McCord testified that Caulfield told him that at their next meeting he might have a message for Mc-Cord "from the President himself."

McCord explained why he resisted the bid for his silence: It was "clear" to him that Jeb Stuart Magruder, deputy Nixon campaign manager who was also scheduled as a witness for the trial, "was going to perjure himself and that we were not going to get a fair trial. Further, I told him that it was clear that some of those involved in the Watergate case were going to trial and others were going to be covered for [I was referring to John Mitchell, John Dean and Magruder] . . . and I said that this was not my idea of American justice."

McCord said he mentioned to Caulfield his belief that the government "had lied in denying" it had been tapping his telephone since June 17, 1972 and those of the other defendants.

"I stated that if we were going to get a fiction of a fair trial," McCord continued, "through perjured testimony to begin with, and then for the government to lie about illegal telephone interceptions, that the trial ought to be kicked out and we start all over again, this time with all of those involved as defendants. At least in this way, 'some would not be more equal than others' before the bar of justice and we would get a fair trial. The executive clemency offer was made two or three times during this meeting, as I recall, and I repeated each time that I would not even discuss it, nor discuss pleading guilty. . . ."

In a second meeting with Caulfield at the same site Jan. 14, McCord said, the offer of executive clemency was renewed and:

"He [Caulfield] went on to say that, 'The President's ability to govern is at stake. Another Teapot Dome scandal is possible, and the government may fall. Everybody else is on track but you. You are not following the game plan. Get closer to your attorney. You seem to be pursuing your own course of action. Do not talk if called before the grand jury, keep silent and do the same if called before a Congressional committee.'

"My response was that I felt a massive injustice was being done, that I was different from the others, that I was going to fight the fixed case, and had no intention of either pleading guilty, taking executive clemency or agreeing to remain silent. He repeated the statement that the government would have difficulty in continuing to be able to stand. I responded that they do have a problem, but that I had a problem with the massive injustice of the whole trial being a sham, and that I would fight it every way I know."

During a third meeting Jan. 25, when they went for a drive in Virginia, McCord related, he refused to discuss Caulfield's repeated offers of clemency, money and rehabilitation aid, whereupon Caulfield "stated that I was 'fouling up the game plan.' I made a few comments about the 'game plan.' "

After Caulfield "asked what my plans were regarding talking publicly and I said that I planned to do so when I was ready," Caulfield responded, McCord testified, "by saying that 'you know that if the Administration gets its back to the wall, it will have to take steps to defend itself.' I took that as a personal threat and I told him in response that I had had a good life, that my will was made out and that I had thought through the risks and would take them when I was ready. He said that if I had to go off to jail that the Administration would help with the bail premiums.

"I advised him that it was not a bail premium, but $100,000 straight cash and that that was a problem I would have to worry about, through family and friends. On the night before sentencing, Jack called me and said that the Administration would provide the $100,000 in cash if I could tell him how to get it funded through an intermediary. I said that if we ever needed it I would let him know. I never contacted him thereafter; neither have I heard from him."

These were new allegations by Mc-Cord, and he was asked by Sen. Edward J. Gurney (R, Fla.) why he had waited until now to make them. McCord replied, "Because it involved directly the President" and "a personal friend"—Caulfield—and he had wanted to be "as accurate as I could."

Mitchell in on planning—McCord's testimony also covered his knowledge, largely on a hearsay basis from fellow conspirator G. Gordon Liddy, of the planning of the Watergate conspiracy. Throughout his testimony, he was fre-

quently interrupted by Chairman Ervin and Vice Chairman Baker, who made the point that much of McCord's data as related was hearsay and not legally admissable as evidence.

Fellow conspirator Liddy had told him, McCord testified, in conversations beginning in January or February 1972, that John N. Mitchell, Jeb Stuart Magruder and John W. Dean 3rd held discussions about the bugging operation with Liddy in Mitchell's office while he was attorney general.

He also told of a meeting with Hunt to discuss the Watergate operation, when Hunt indicated he was taking a step-by-step plan to see Charles W. Colson, former special counsel to the President.

In addition to the Watergate bugging, McCord said, there were discussions of plans for bugging the headquarters of several other prominent Democrats, but as far as he knew the Watergate was the only bugging effected.

Other testimony—McCord revealed during the day that in his security role for the Nixon re-election committee he received "almost daily" confidential memorandums from the Internal Security Division of the Justice Department concerning activities of organizations suspected of planning demonstrations against Republicans.

He also disclosed he had received since his arrest June 17, 1972, $46,000 in cash, $25,000 of which was used for legal fees. He said Mrs. Hunt provided the fees, which he presumed came from the Nixon campaign committee.

McCord was questioned closely by several committee members—Gurney and Sen. Daniel K. Inouye (D, Hawaii)—about his motivation for the obviously illegal activities in which he had been engaged.

His reply was that he was concerned because of his security role about violence from demonstrators and he felt assured because of Mitchell's participation in the planning that if the operation were illegal Mitchell "would turn it down out of hand." McCord also said he was assured because of the participation of White House counsel Dean. He participated in the operation, McCord said, because of "the fact that the attorney general, the White House itself, and in my personal opinion, the President of the United States. I felt, had set into motion this operation. Because of the close relationship of Mr. Mitchell and Mr. Dean and the fact that Mr. Dean worked with the President."

At McCord's side during his testimony was his attorney, Bernard Fensterwald Jr.

Prior to McCord's testimony, the committee heard Washington policeman Carl M. Shoffler relate the actual capture of the Watergate defendants inside the offices of the Democratic national headquarters early June 17, 1972.

May 22: *McCord completes testimony*—McCord returned to his testimony with further explanation of his participation in the Watergate conspiracy. He spoke of incidents of violence and the concern about avoiding "the bloodshed which had occurred at the 1968 Democratic Convention in Chicago." He said there were "sufficient indications that violence-oriented groups were out to endanger both life and property" during the political season. He thought that the "Watergate operation might produce some leads" on the radical groups.

As part of his security job, he referred again to material he obtained from the evaluation section of the Internal Security Division, a contact he established, he said, "through Mr. Robert Mardian in May 1972." McCord said Mardian informed him that he (Mardian), Mitchell, Haldeman and Ehrlichman "were key members of an 'intelligence advisory committee.'"

The Las Vegas break-in scheme—McCord read the committee his statement on the "Las Vegas Matter." In January or February 1972, he read, Liddy told him "that he was going out to Las Vegas, Nev., in connection with casing the office of Hank Greenspun, editor of the Las Vegas Sun.

"Liddy said that Attorney General John Mitchell had told him that Greenspun had in his possession blackmail type information involving a Democratic candidate for President, that Mitchell wanted that material, and Liddy said that this information was in some way racketeer-related, indicating that if this candidate became President, the racketeers or national crime syndicate could have a control or influence over him as President. My inclination at this point in time, speaking of today, is to disbelieve the allegation against the Democratic candidate referred to above and to believe that there was in reality some other motive for wanting to get into Greenspun's safe. . . .

"Subsequently in about April or May, 1971, Liddy told me that he had again been to Las Vegas for another casing of Greenspun's offices. Liddy said that there were then plans for an entry operation to get into Greenspun's safe. He went on to say that, after the entry team finished its work, they would go directly to an airport near Las Vegas where a Howard Hughes plane would be standing by to fly the team directly into a Central-American country so that the team would be out of the country before the break-in was discovered.

"Around the same time Liddy made this last statement to me about the Howard Hughes plane, Hunt told me in his office one day that he was in touch with the Howard Hughes company and that they might be needing my security services after the election.

"He said that they had quite a wide investigative and security operation and

asked me for my business card and asked if I would be interested. I said I would like to know more about what was involved, gave him a card, but never heard from him again on this subject. However, I did read in the newspapers after July 1, 1972, that Hunt had apparently handled a Howard Hughes campaign donation to the Committee to Re-elect the President sometime in 1972. Gordon Liddy told me in February 1972, that he, too, had handled a Howard Hughes campaign check, a donation to the 1972 campaign."

Resists attempt to involve CIA—McCord paraphrased a letter he said he wrote to Caulfield in December 1972 about his concern that an attempt was under way to blame the Watergate break-in on the CIA. It went:

"Dear Jack: I am sorry to have to write you this letter. If Helms goes and the Watergate operation is laid at CIA's feet, where it does not belong, every tree in the forest will fall. It will be a scorched desert. The whole matter is at the precipice right now. Pass the message that if they want it to blow, they are on exactly the right course. I am sorry that you will get hurt in the fallout."

McCord said the letter was unsigned and he had not requested any message or contact with Caulfield in it or at any time.

He contended that Alch had suggested basing his trial defense on the CIA aspect. The suggestion, he said, "included questions as to whether I could ostensibly have been recalled from retirement from CIA to participate in the operation. He [Alch] said that if so, my personnel records at CIA could be doctored to reflect such a recall."

McCord added: "He stated that [James] Schlesinger, the new director of CIA, whose appointment had just been announced, 'could be subpoenaed and would go along with it.'"

Caulfield testimony—Caulfield corroborated much of McCord's testimony concerning the clemency offers, with some variations. He testified that the executive clemency offer originated with former White House counsel John W. Dean 3rd.

Caulfield differed on the wording McCord considered a threat: Caulfield termed it "friendly advice" that the people they were dealing with were "tough-minded." And he could not recall "saying anything about the President" at his first meeting with McCord, who had testified he was told the President would be informed of their meeting and that a message from Nixon might be forthcoming.

After McCord's arrest, Caulfield said, he got in touch with McCord to ask him if he could help him in his difficulty. He acknowledged receiving McCord's unsigned letter as their next contact.

Then, in early January, Caulfield related, he received a call from Dean, who asked him to call back from a public telephone to impart "a very important

message which he wanted me to deliver to James McCord, that Mr. McCord was expecting to hear from me and McCord would understand what the message referred to." He said the message consisted of three things:

1. "A year is a long time;
2. "Your wife and family will be taken care of;
3. "You will be rehabilitated with employment when this is all over.

"I immediately realized that I was being asked to do a very dangerous thing and I said to Mr. Dean that I did not think it was wise to send me on such a mission since Mr. McCord knew, as many others did, that I had worked closely with Mr. Dean and Mr. Ehrlichman at the White House and therefore it might be quickly guessed that any messages I was conveying were probably from one of the two."

Caulfield arranged to have the message relayed to McCord by Anthony Ulasewicz, a retired New York City detective who was working with Caulfield on "investigative functions" and reporting "to the White House through me," Caulfield said. Caulfield explained that his own duties at the time "consisted of being a White House liaison with a variety of law enforcement agencies in the federal government, through arrangements worked out with Mr. Ehrlichman, Mr. Herbert Kalmbach" and Ulasewicz. He said Ulasewicz "was paid on a monthly basis by the Kalmbach law firm." (Caulfield said he worked on this basis for three years, on orders from Ehrlichman and later Dean. In March 1972 he began work for the Nixon re-election committee, for Mitchell, who "regarded" him "only as a bodyguard," he said. On April 28, 1972, he said, he began work for the Treasury Department.)

Ulasewicz called McCord with Dean's message, Caulfield continued, and reported that "McCord's attitude had been one of satisfaction."

Dean was informed, Caulfield said, and called again the next day to say "McCord wanted to see me" and persuaded Caulfield, who said he was reluctant, to relay in person the same message to McCord.

At that first meeting, Caulfield said, "I stated that I was only delivering a message" but considered "it was a 'sincere offer.'" He said McCord stressed that he always followed his own independent course and that "if one goes . . . all who are involved must go," which Caulfield took to mean going to jail.

"He asked me who I was speaking with at the White House and I said I could not reveal any names but that they were from the 'highest level of the White House.'"

Caulfield discussed a plan, broached by McCord in his testimony, whereby McCord had called two foreign embassies (the Chilean and Israeli embassies, the New York Times disclosed), which he was confident were bugged with national security wiretaps. Caulfield said, "It was Mr. McCord's theory that if the government searched its wiretap records, it would find records of these two calls. Meanwhile, Mr. McCord and his attorneys would make a motion in court, aimed at dismissing the case against Mr. McCord because of the use of wiretap evidence by the prosecution."

Caulfield testified that "at no time in our first meeting do I recall saying anything about the President but I specifically renewed the offer of executive clemency . . . and referred to it as coming from 'the highest levels of the White House.' At some point in the conversation Mr. McCord said to me, 'Jack, I didn't ask to see you.' This puzzled me since my clear understanding from Mr. Dean was that McCord had specifically asked to see me."

Reporting back to Dean again, Caulfield said he was told:

" 'Jack, I want you to go back to him and tell him that we are checking on these wiretaps but this time impress upon him as fully as you can that this offer of executive clemency is a sincere offer which comes from the very highest level of the White House.'

"I said, 'I have not used anybody's name with him, do you want me to?'

"He said, 'No, I don't want you to do that but tell him that this offer comes from the very highest levels.'

"I said, 'Do you want me to tell him it comes from the President?'

"He said words to the effect, 'No, don't do that. Say that it comes from way up at the top.'

"At the meeting with Mr. Dean he also impressed upon me that this was a very grave situation which might someday threaten the President, that it had the potential of becoming a national scandal and that many people in the White House were quite concerned over it. Mr. Dean said that none of the other then defendants in the Watergate burglary 'were any problem,' and that Mr. McCord 'was not cooperating with his attorney.'

"At no time, either before or after this meeting with Mr. Dean, did I ever speak to any other White House officials about this offer of executive clemency. I specifically never spoke to the President of the United States and have no knowledge of my own as to whether he personally had endorsed this offer or, indeed, whether anyone had ever discussed it with him."

Caulfield said his "guess" was that the "high White House officials" Dean referred to "at least meant Mr. Ehrlichman," and he knew that Dean was in touch with someone about the contacts with McCord since Dean told a telephone caller, one time he was with Dean, " 'I'm receiving a report on that right now.' "

At their second meeting, Caulfield related, he affirmed his belief the clemency offer was sincere because the White House officials he was dealing with "were extremely concerned about the Watergate burglary developing into a major scandal affecting the President and therefore such a promise would not be given lightly."

"At no time on this occasion or on any other occasion," Caulfield insisted, "do I recall telling Mr. McCord to keep silent if called before the grand jury or any Congressional committees."

When informed that McCord still refused the proffered clemency, Dean replied, according to Caulfield, "Well, what the hell does he know, anyway?"

At their third meeting, Caulfield said when he realized McCord was going to make a statement on the Watergate affair that "would in all probability involve allegations against people in the White House and other high Administration officials, I gave him what I considered to be a small piece of friendly advice."

"I said, words to the effect that, 'Jim, I have worked with these people and I know them to be as tough-minded as you and I. When you make your statement don't underestimate them. If I were in your shoes, I would probably be doing the same thing.'

"I later called Mr. Dean and advised him of Mr. McCord's request for bail funding and he said words to the effect that, 'Maybe we can handle that through Alch.' "

May 23: *Caulfield felt offer was valid*— Caulfield returned to the witness chair and affirmed his belief that President Nixon probably knew about the offer of executive clemency to McCord. He had been at the White House three years, Caulfield said, and "I know what the relations are" and "in my mind, I felt that the President probably did know about" the clemency offer coming from Dean.

As he was leaving Dean's office at the time of the offer, Caulfield testified, "It crossed my mind that this conceivably was for the President. I believed it. I had to think about that. And based upon all of that background, I believed I was doing something for the President of the United States, and I did it, sir."

Responding to questioning by Sen. Lowell P. Weicker Jr. (R, Conn.), Caulfield continued that he "knew that the offer of executive clemency in this matter was wrong" and that "there was a definite conflict" between that feeling and delivering the message to his friend McCord.

"But what I am saying to you sir," Caulfield stressed, "is that my loyalties and especially to the President of the United States, overrided [sic] those considerations." He said he "felt very strongly about the President, extremely strongly about the President. I was very loyal to my people that I worked for, I place a high value upon loyalty."

In other testimony, Caulfield recalled notifying former Presidential adviser Ehrlichman the day of the Watergate break-in after both had been notified by a Secret Service agent. "I said to Mr. Ehrlichman, I said, 'John, it sounds like there is a disaster of some type.' " Ehrlichman asked what it was all about, Caulfield said, and he told him, " 'I haven't the foggiest notion what it is all about but they are saying they believed Jim McCord, who works for the committee, has been arrested in a burglary at the Democratic National Committee.' "

"He said—I forget what he said exactly, I think it was a long silence, as I recall, and I said, 'My God, you know, I cannot believe it.' He said, 'Well, I guess I had better place a call to John Mitchell.' I said, 'I think that would be very appropriate.' "

Anthony Ulasewicz testified in corroboration he was a contact for Caulfield with McCord. He confirmed he worked under Caulfield but was paid by Kalmbach's law firm.

Alch disputes McCord's testimony— McCord's early defense lawyer Gerald Alch took the stand to dispute points in McCord's testimony relating to him and to contend that Bernard Fensterwald, co-counsel for McCord, had told him "we're going after the President" in McCord's changed defense posture.

"I have done nothing wrong," Alch told the committee, and "in regard to his [McCord's] accusations against me, he is not telling the truth."

"Mr. McCord's allegation that I announced my ability to forge his CIA personnel records with the cooperation of then-acting CIA Director [James] Schlesinger is absurd and completely untrue," Alch testified.

Regarding the question of CIA involvement as a defense, Alch said the matter arose at a meeting of defense lawyers in 1972 "as to whether or not the CIA could have been involved." It was agreed at the meeting, he said, that each lawyer would ask his client whether or not he had any knowledge of such involvement. When Alch subsequently asked McCord, he said, McCord "did not directly respond to the specific question but did become quite upset at what he believed to be the antagonism of the White House against the CIA." Subsequently, Alch said, McCord told him "the CIA was not involved and that he would have no part of any attempt to involve that agency."

Alch confirmed McCord's report that he [Alch] had passed a message to McCord on the first day of the trial from Hunt's lawyer, William O. Bittman, but Alch differed on the message. McCord had said the message was that he would receive a call from a friend at the White House. Alch said the message had no White House reference. He said he told Bittman that McCord "was becoming a bit paranoid, that he felt he was being made the 'patsy' or 'fall guy.' " Bittman's reply, he said, was: " 'Tell McCord he will receive a call from a friend of his.' "

Alch said he discussed executive clemency only once with McCord, again in relation to Bittman. He had asked Bittman once, Alch said, in late 1972, what he thought their clients would receive as a sentence if they were convicted. Bittman responded, "as if theorizing," he said, in substance, "'You can never tell, Christmas-time rolls around and there could be executive clemency.'" Alch said he "scoffed at this notion" and told Bittman "the President would not touch this case with a 10-foot pole, let alone exercise executive clemency."

Subsequently, Alch said, he "mentioned this to Mr. McCord in a most skeptical manner and said to him, 'Jim, it can be Christmas, Easter and Thanksgiving all rolled into one but don't rely on any prospect of executive clemency.'" He said "McCord laughed and agreed with me." Alch said he was unaware of McCord's dealings with Caulfield on the matter.

In discussing their defense position, Alch testified, McCord had "continuously insisted" that "his only purpose in participating in the Watergate break-in was to protect his employers" at the committee and other GOP officials from threats of violence. "At no time," Alch said, "did he ever state to me that he believed the Watergate operation to be legal as a result of the alleged involvement" of Mitchell, Dean "or anyone else." Alch said he did not hear from McCord of Mitchell's alleged involvement until late in the trial.

He advised McCord, Alch said, that the "defense of the protection of others required that the perpetrator not know he was breaking the law. I said to Mr. McCord, 'No jury will ever believe that a man with your background with the FBI and the CIA would not realize he was breaking the law in breaking into an office at night, wearing surgical gloves and armed with eavesdropping equipment.'"

Alch said he recommended instead a "law of duress" defense that held, "If one is under reasonable apprehension, regardless of whether he is in fact correct, he is justified in breaking a law to avoid the greater harm—in this case violence directed at Republican officials up to and including the President."

Alch quoted several remarks to him by co-counsel Fensterwald. After Fensterwald joined the case and McCord informed the court he would give testimony, Alch said Fensterwald called him and said, "We're going after the President." Alch said he replied "that I was not interested in any vendettas against the President but only in the best interest of my client, to which Mr. Fensterwald replied, 'Well, you'll see, that's who we're going after, the president.'"

After McCord's CIA allegations, Alch said, he called Fensterwald and asked for an explanation. Fensterwald's response, according to Alch, was: "'I can only hazard the guess that it is the result of Mr. McCord's faulty recollection.' He [Fensterwald] added, 'I can tell you one thing, it's a terrible cliche, but I think you

will agree with it, that there is no zealot like a convert.' I had had no further contact from Mr. McCord."

Alch ended his prepared testimony with a rhetorical question about McCord: "What kind of a man is this?"

May 24: *Alch interrogated*—Alch was questioned nearly three hours by the committee on conflicts between his testimony and McCord's. The focus was largely on whether Alch was aware of or a party to pressure on McCord (a) to remain silent and plead guilty or (b) to try to involve the CIA in the defense posture for McCord. Alch did not materially change his original testimony, denying any such pressures from himself.

Several of the senators pointed out that the message Alch relayed to McCord about a friend calling led directly to the executive clemency offers from Caulfield. It would be natural for McCord to assume, Ervin observed, that there might then be a connection between Alch and the clemency offer. Alch restated that he was merely repeating a message.

In reply to questioning, Alch suggested the use of lie detectors to resolve the conflicts.

Baldwin no double agent—Testimony also was taken from Alfred C. Baldwin 3rd, a former FBI agent stationed at a motel near the Watergate to monitor the bugged conversations of the Democratic National Committee personnel. He denied, in response to questions, that he was a double agent working for the Democrats while employed by the Nixon re-election committee.

Barker followed orders—Testimony from Bernard L. Barker, who had pleaded guilty as a Watergate spy, revealed that the prime motivation for his involvement, and presumably that of his team of Cuban-Americans arrested with him at the Watergate,* was to further the cause of Cuban liberation.

This could come, he believed, from fellow-conspirator Hunt and "others in high places" in the U.S.

Hunt had recruited Barker for the Watergate operation and Barker had responded without question. He collected his Watergate team out of friendship with Hunt for his participation in the 1961 Bay of Pigs operation. Barker had been Hunt's principal assistant in that operation.

Ten years after the Bay of Pigs, Barker testified, Hunt had recruited him for some other operations—the September 1971 break-in at the Los Angeles office of Daniel Ellsberg's psychiatrist, "infiltrating" a May 1972 Capitol demonstration where Ellsberg was expected to be a participant, and two Watergate break-ins.

In the original break-in in Los Angeles, Barker said, he was told that the op-

_____
*Eugenio R. Martinez, Frank A. Sturgis and Virgilio R. Gonzalez

eration "was a matter of national security." This sufficed for all of the operations. "At no time was I told any different from the original motivation for which I had been recruited," he declared.

He said, "Hunt, under the name of Eduardo, represents to the Cuban people their liberation. I cannot deny my services in the way that it was proposed to me on a matter of national security, knowing that with my training I had personnel available for this type of operation. I could not deny this request at the time."

Asked what national security was involved in the early operation, Barker responded, "Discovering information about a person who I had been told by Mr. Hunt was a traitor, who was passing, he or his associates, to a foreign embassy." Barker identified the embassy as that of the Soviet Union.

Barker said the documents he was seeking were not found either in the Ellsberg break-in or the first Watergate break-in May 27, 1972 prior to the intercepted one June 17, 1972.

At the Watergate, he said, the documents he was seeking—he was the document-finder, another the photographer—were those "that would prove that the Democratic party and Sen. [George] McGovern [D, S.D.] were receiving contributions nationally and national and foreign contributions from organizations that were leftist organizations and inclined to violence in the United States and also from the Castro government."

Barker said it "had been rumored and had been spoken of freely in Miami" that the Castro government was aiding the Democrats. "However, I have no hard evidence at all that this was true," he said.

He repeatedly stressed his association with Hunt. "We were assisting Mr. Hunt," he said, "who was a known factor in the time of the liberation of Cuba. We had hopes that Mr. Hunt's position in the White House would be a decisive factor at a later date for obtaining help in the liberation of Cuba."

Barker testified that almost $50,000 had been given him by Hunt's late wife, for bail, expenses and legal fees for him and his comrades.

Under close questioning, he denied that executive clemency had been offered. It was brought out in questioning that part of the training for Barker's line of endeavor was a conditioning to resist interrogation if caught.

Chairman Ervin pursued this line:
Q. You have a code of ethics in work of this kind that you do not tell anything on anybody?
A. That is correct.
Q. And so if Mr. E. Howard Hunt had pressured you into pleading guilty, you could not tell us that under your code of ethics?
A. This is my decision, not Mr. Hunt's.
Q. So you did consult with Mr. E.

Howard Hunt before you pleaded guilty?

A. It was not a consultation.

Q. Well, it was a discussion?

A. It was a discussion, certainly.

Q. And he told you that he was going to plead guilty, and the evidence against you was overwhelming?

A. That is true.

Q. And then you decided to plead guilty?

A. Yes, but this is not pressure.

Mitchell rejects 'fall guy' role. Former attorney general and Nixon campaign chairman John Mitchell claimed May 18 that somebody has tried to make the fall guy [for Watergate and other campaign-related charges], but it isn't going to work."

"I've never stolen any money. The only thing I did was try to get the President re-elected. I never did anything mentally or morally wrong," he added.

Mitchell spoke to a reporter after his wife, Martha, had telephoned to say: "I predict there'll be a [Nixon] resignation or he'll be impeached. I think he'd be much wiser to resign."

Mrs. Mitchell had made the same claims to reporters at an impromptu news conference earlier May 18, charging "You can place all the blame on the White House. John Mitchell was the only honest one in the whole lousy bunch. And who do you think he has been protecting? Mr. President."

Mitchell, Stans named in new suit. John Mitchell and Maurice Stans were named in a new suit in San Francisco Superior Court May 18. The former Cabinet officers, 17 other persons and the Committee to Re-elect the President were charged with stealing stationery May 19, 1972 from the headquarters of the California Committee for Eugene McCarthy. A fictitious letter was distributed urging McCarthy supporters to vote for Sen. Hubert H. Humphrey (D, Minn.) instead of Sen. George McGovern in the 1972 California Democratic presidential primary, the suit alleged.

Among those named in the civil complaint were Donald H. Segretti, under indictment in Florida for similar election tampering charges, Herbert W. Kalmbach, a California fund raiser for the President and formerly his personal lawyer, and 15 John Does.

White House Press Secretary Ronald Ziegler had personal knowledge of the alleged clandestine campaign activities of Segretti, it was revealed May 18.

According to sworn testimony taken from Fred T. Fielding, a former aide to then White House counsel John W. Dean 3rd, Ziegler attended a White House meeting in October 1972 at which there "was some general discussion of Mr. Segretti."

The discussions concerned Washington Post reports of a widespread plot to sabotage the 1972 presidential elections conducted by White House and re-election committee officials.

The meeting took place in the office of President Nixon's appointments secretary Dwight Chapin, who reportedly supervised Segretti's "dirty tricks" operations. Also present, according to Fielding, were Dean; John D. Ehrlichman, then White House domestic affairs adviser; and Richard Moore, a White House counsel reporting to then presidential chief of staff H. R. Haldeman.

Ziegler previously had denied any personal knowledge of alleged acts of illegal campaign practices. However, he admitted May 19 he had been present at the Chapin meeting. "The meetings I attended were to ascertain the facts, and the facts in this case, at that time suggested there were no illegality or wrongdoing [by Segretti]," Ziegler declared.

Nixon rejects resignation bids. White House Press Secretary Ronald L. Ziegler told reporters May 18 that President Nixon had no intention of resigning despite speeches delivered May 17 by two prominent Democrats, Sargent Shriver, the Democratic candidate for vice president in 1972, and Joseph A. Califano Jr., a former key aide to President Johnson, calling for Nixon's resignation because of the widening Watergate scandal.

"The President of the U.S. has a lot to do and a lot to accomplish in the second term and he fully intends to do that. He was elected to lead this country as President in 1972, and that he intends to do," Ziegler declared.

Ziegler repeated a denial issued May 7 regarding Nixon's involvement in a Watergate cover-up, saying "the President did not participate in any way, or have any knowledge regarding the cover-up and at no time authorized anyone to represent him in offering executive clemency."

The denial followed shortly after convicted Watergate defendant James W. McCord Jr. charged he had been offered executive clemency with the full knowledge of the President. Ziegler characterized McCord's testimony before the Senate committee investigating Watergate as "based on total hearsay." Nixon was not watching the televised Senate proceedings, Ziegler added.

GOP chairmen pledge support to Nixon. In an unusual move, Republican party state chairmen, meeting in Chicago May 19 to transact routine party business, issued a resolution condemning the Watergate scandal and supporting the President.

The resolution asked that the party not be judged by the actions of "a few overzealous individuals," whose activities were "abhorrent and reprehensible."

Republican National Chairman George Bush, speaking for the 28 state chairmen—mostly from the East and Midwest—in attendance, admitted that the national party committee had been dominated by the White House and the Committee to Re-elect the President in 1972; but he pledged it would not be allowed to happen again.

Bush also said the national committee would like to take over the $4.7 million left in the coffers of the re-election committee after the 1972 election.

The Washington Post May 20 reported that Bush privately told the GOP gathering: "New policies and a new image for our party must be adopted in dealing with the White House. When downtown [White House] calls and tells us to jump, we no longer plan to ask 'How high?' "

Secret funds, Watergate payoffs cited. The General Accounting Office (GAO) May 19 charged former Commerce Secretary Maurice H. Stans, President Nixon's chief fund raiser and chairman of the Finance Committee to Re-elect the President, with an "obvious attempt to evade the disclosure requirements" of the new federal campaign spending law which took effect April 7, 1972.

According to the GAO, at least $1.7 million in cash and a "larger total" in checks and securities were not reported to the Office of Federal Elections, the watchdog agency within the government's auditing office. Of the $1.7 million, at least $460,000 was used to pay cover-up money to the Watergate defendants or their attorneys.

Results of the GAO investigation, based on testimony from former finance committee treasurer Hugh W. Sloan Jr. and Herbert W. Kalmbach, one of the major fund raisers for the Nixon re-election campaign during 1971, were referred to the Justice Department for possible prosecution.

The select Senate Watergate committee investigating charges of illegal campaign activities was also supplied with a copy of the GAO's findings.

Among the disclosures:

■ Kalmbach collected at least $210,000 during the summer of 1972 for payment to "the Watergate defendants or their attorneys." The money was raised from three sources: Stans, giving $75,100 on June 29, 1972; Frederick C. LaRue, a re-election campaign official, giving $30,000–$40,000 in early July and the same amount again in late August; Thomas V. Jones, chairman of the Northrop Corp., a Defense Department contractor, giving $75,000 on July 31, 1972.

Kalmbach testified that his only records of the transactions were destroyed.

Stans admitted making the donation, saying the money did not belong to the finance committee which he headed; but he denied knowing the purpose of the contribution.

The Washington Post reported May 20 that Jones claimed he donated only $50,-000 and intended it as a contribution that would have been reported to the GAO.

According to Newsweek magazine May 21, Kalmbach was ordered to make the Watergate payoffs by then White House counsel John W. Dean 3rd and John D. Ehrlichman, at that time assistant to the President for domestic affairs, with the knowledge of campaign director John N. Mitchell and his committee aide LaRue.

Kalmbach refused to carry out a second fund-raising venture for the Watergate defendants in September 1972 when requested to do so by then presidential chief of staff H. R. Haldeman, the magazine said.

The Scripps Howard News Service reported May 21 that convicted Watergate conspirator G. Gordon Liddy was continuing to receive "hush money" until early April, according to LaRue.

■ A $350,000 cash payment was made "immediately prior to April 7, 1972" by Sloan to Kalmbach under orders from Stans and campaign director Mitchell. The money was picked up by Gordon Strachan, an aide to Haldeman.

Sources told the Post that LaRue eventually received the money and that all but $100,000 of it was paid to the Watergate conspirators.

Other sums of cash were distributed before April 7, 1972 to several re-election committee officials and Administration aides: Liddy, at that time a re-election committee lawyer, received $199,000; Jeb Stuart Magruder, deputy campaign director, received $20,000; Herbert L. Porter of the re-election committee received $100,000; Ron Walker of the White House staff received $2,000; Robert C. Hitt, an aide to Interior Secretary Rogers C. B. Morton, received $25,000 for a secret cash contribution to the campaign of Rep. William O. Mills (R, Md.). Mills was elected in a special 1971 election to fill the Congressional seat vacated by Morton when he joined the Administration.

A total of $900,000 was paid in cash to the various officials; the balance of the unreported $1.7 million went to small campaign finance committees before April 7, 1972.

Sloan also said that another $80,500 in cash was held by the re-election committee on or after April 7, 1972 which was never reported to the GAO. Sloan said he and Stans kept the money, which was turned over to LaRue July 4, 1972.

The finance committee termed the GAO's charges "arbitrary, unbalanced and unnecessarily sensational." Financial transactions completed before April 7, 1972 were "perfectly legal," the committee said, and not within the purview of the GAO to "characterize or report."

Nixon's name invoked in cover-up. The deputy director of the Central Intelligence Agency (CIA) was told by former White House chief of staff H. R. Haldeman "it is the President's wish" that he ask L. Patrick Gray 3rd, former

acting director of the Federal Bureau of Investigation (FBI), to halt his agency's investigation into the laundering of campaign funds through a bank in Mexico City.

This information was contained in one of 11 memoranda written by Deputy CIA Director Vernon A. Walters and given to the Senate Foreign Relations Committee. It was made public May 21 by committee member Sen. Stuart Symington (D, Mo.)

One "memorandum of conversation" written by Walters related to a meeting he had with Haldeman, former presidential aide John D. Ehrlichman, and former CIA Director Richard Helms June 23, 1972, six days after the Watergate break-in. Within an hour of the meeting, an appointment for Walters with Gray had been set up.

Haldeman issued a statement May 21: "I can flatly say the President was not involved in any cover-up of anything at any time."

Another Walters memorandum revealed that Gray told Nixon during a telephone conversation that the Watergate case could not be covered up and that the President should get rid of those who were involved.

According to the memorandum dated July 13, 1972, Nixon had called Gray to congratulate him on the handling of an attempted hijacking. "Toward the end of the conversation, the President asked him [Gray] if he had talked to me [Walters] about the case. Gray replied that he had. The President then asked him what his recommendation was in this case. Gray had replied that the case could not be covered up and it would lead quite high and he felt the President should get rid of the people that were involved. Any attempt to involve the FBI or the CIA in this case could only prove a mortal wound and would achieve nothing."

"The President then said, 'Then I should get rid of whoever is involved, no matter how high up?' Gray replied that was his recommendation.

"The President then asked what I [Walters] thought, and Gray said my views were the same as his. The President took it well and thanked him."

The memorandum continued that Gray then called former White House counsel John W. Dean 3rd and informed him of his conversation with the President. Dean responded, "Okay," the memorandum said.

According to Symington, the committee had obtained two sets of documents that purported to deal with Administration plans during the summer of 1970 to commit burglary and engage in other illegal activities to gather intelligence about some U.S. citizens. Symington said the plans were never carried out.

Helms, who also appeared before the committee May 21, substantiated the Walters memoranda and added that during the June 23, 1972 meeting Haldeman had said "the opposition" was "capitalizing" on the Watergate case.

Asked why he hadn't gone directly to the President about the attempted cover-up, Helms replied that his "total preoccupation" was in keeping the CIA uninvolved in the matter.

Helms was asked by Sen. Charles Percy (R, Ill.) whether his refusal to go along with any cover-up played a role in his departure from the CIA. Informed sources claimed that Helms had been summarily fired by President Nixon after the 1972 elections, the Washington Post reported May 22.

Helms responded, "I honestly don't know." He added that the President had at no time mentioned Watergate to him.

Nixon did not ask CIA about Watergate —President Nixon at no time called the Central Intelligence Agency (CIA) after the Watergate break-in to directly determine the role the agency might have had in the burglary, Deputy CIA Director Walters told a Senate panel May 23.

President Nixon said in his May 22 statement on Watergate that within a few days of the break-in, "I was advised that there was a possibility of CIA involvement in some way." He said that since former CIA personnel were involved in the burglary, he feared that some covert CIA operations might be exposed. Nixon did not say who "advised" him of CIA involvement.

Walters, appearing before the Senate Appropriations intelligence operations subcommittee, said Nixon spoke to him on the phone several weeks after the Watergate break-in; but it was about an unrelated matter.

In other May 23 testimony before the intelligence operations subcommittee chaired by Sen. John L. McClellan (D, Ark.), CIA Director James R. Schlesinger denied having been approached by Nixon regarding CIA involvement in Watergate.

Mitchell, Stans plead not guilty. Former Attorney General John N. Mitchell and former Commerce Secretary Maurice H. Stans pleaded not guilty on all counts May 21 to a federal grand jury indictment charging them with perjury and conspiracy to defraud the U.S. and to obstruct justice.

The lawsuit had been brought in connection with allegations of influence peddling by the Nixon Administration officials on behalf of financier Robert L. Vesco in return for his secret cash contribution of $200,000 to the Nixon reelection campaign.

Burglars after Hughes documents. Hank Greenspun, publisher of the Las Vegas (Nev.) Sun, said May 22 that the attempted burglary of his office during the summer of 1972 was not an attempt to obtain blackmail information about one of the Democratic contenders for the Presidency, as James W. McCord Jr. had said in his testimony before the Senate committee investigating Watergate.

Instead, it was an attempt to acquire hundreds of memoranda signed by industrialist billionaire Howard Hughes, he said. Greenspun would only say of the memos that they pertained in part to problems Hughes had with the antitrust division of the Justice Department regarding his $200 million–$300 million holdings in Nevada.

Greenspun said he found it "catastrophically disturbing" that the U.S. government would be employed to "serve the private interests of Howard Hughes." He said he had information that Hughes interests gave the Nixon campaign fund a blank check. He did not know the amount.

Greenspun said he was currently suing Hughes for $132 million, claiming Hughes reneged on a complicated real estate transaction.

Nixon explains White House role. In a statement released May 22, President Nixon conceded the probable involvement of some of his closest aides in concealing some aspects of the Watergate affair and acknowledged that he had ordered limitations on the investigation because of national security considerations "of crucial importance" unrelated to Watergate.

He reiterated, however, his own lack of prior knowledge of the burglary and the attempted cover-up while acknowledging that aides might have "gone beyond" his directives to protect "national security operations in order to cover up any involvement they or certain others might have had in Watergate."

In a summary accompanying the statement, Nixon made the following replies to specific allegations against White House activities:

"1) I had no prior knowledge of the Watergate operation.

2) I took no part in, nor was I aware of, any subsequent efforts that may have been made to cover up Watergate.

3) At no time did I authorize any offer of executive clemency of the Watergate defendants, nor did I know of any such offer.

4) I did not know, until the time of my own investigation, of any effort to provide the Watergate defendants with funds.

5) At no time did I attempt, or did I authorize others to attempt, to implicate the CIA in the Watergate matter.

6) It was not until the time of my own investigation that I learned of the break-in at the office of [Pentagon Papers case defendant Daniel] Ellsberg's psychiatrist, and I specifically authorized the furnishing of this information to Judge [William M.] Byrne.

7) I neither authorized nor encouraged subordinates to engage in illegal or improper campaign tactics."

Nixon also declared his intention to remain in office, saying "I will not abandon my responsibilities. I will continue to do the job I was elected to do."

In his detailed statement, Nixon sought to separate secret investigations begun earlier in his term from the Watergate case. He told of a "special program of wiretaps" set up in 1969 to prevent leaks of secret information important to his foreign policy initiatives. He said there were "fewer than 20 taps" and they were ended in February 1971.

The President said that in 1970 he was concerned about increasing political disruption connected with antiwar protests and decided a better intelligence operation was needed. He appointed the late J. Edgar Hoover, director of the Federal Bureau of Investigation (FBI), as head of a committee to prepare suggestions. On June 25 1970, Nixon said, the committee recommended resumption of "certain intelligence operations that had been suspended in 1966," among them the "authorization for surreptitious entry—breaking and entering, in effect"—in specific situations related to national security.

He said Hoover opposed the plan and it was never put into effect. "It was this unused plan and related documents that [his former counsel] John Dean removed from the White House and placed in a safe deposit box," Nixon added.

Further efforts to improve intelligence operations were made in December 1970 with the formation of the Intelligence Evaluation Committee, for which he said he had authorized no illegal activity, nor did he have knowledge of any.

After the New York Times began publishing the Pentagon Papers in June 1971, Nixon said, he approved the formation of a special investigations unit in the White House to "stop security leaks." The unit, known as the "plumbers," was directed by Egil Krogh Jr. and included convicted Watergate conspirators E. Howard Hunt and G. Gordon Liddy. Nixon recalled that he had impressed upon Krogh the importance of protecting the national security and said this might explain how "highly motivated individuals could have felt justified in engaging in specific activities" he would have disapproved had he known of them.

"Consequently," Nixon said, "I must and do assume responsibility for such actions, despite the fact that I at no time approved or had knowledge of them."

Nixon said he had "wanted justice done in regard to Watergate" but he had not wanted the investigation to "impinge adversely upon the national security area." He noted that, shortly after the break-in, he was informed that the CIA might have been involved and that he instructed H. R. Haldeman and John Ehrlichman to "insure that the investigation of the break-in not expose either an unrelated covert operation of the CIA or the activities of the White House investigations unit." He said he gave similar instructions to Assistant Attorney General Henry E. Petersen April 18.

The President reiterated that in the months following the Watergate incident, he was given repeated assurances that the White House staff had been cleared of involvement. But with hindsight, Nixon conceded, it was apparent that "I should have given more heed to the warning signals I received along the way . . . and less to the reassurances." He acknowledged that "unethical, as well as illegal, activities took place in the course of that campaign."

Nixon concluded by retreating on the issue of executive privilege, saying that it would not be invoked "as to any testimony concerning possible criminal conduct or discussions of possible criminal conduct, in the matters presently under investigation, including the Watergate affair and the alleged cover-up."

At a news briefing after the release of the statement, Presidential counsel Leonard Garment, Press Secretary Ronald L. Ziegler and special counsel J. Fred Buzhardt Jr. attempted to reconcile the statement with earlier Nixon comments on the Watergate case.

Ziegler contended that the latest statement showed that Nixon had a "clearer recollection of the case," and Garment said they had been hampered earlier by "limitations on the amount of information available to the President and the staff."

Garment asserted that one of the reasons for the statement was to explain why the intelligence plans taken from the White House by former counsel John W. Dean 3rd were not "germane to any of the issues now under discussion" and that further disclosure of them "would not be in the national interest."

Responding to a question about the President's approval of a plan which would have allowed "surreptitious entry" in certain national security cases, Garment said such activities were customary and had been "traditionally authorized by presidents in order to meet problems that go beyond the boundary of ordinary civil law."

Asked specifically whether Nixon had ordered a restriction on the FBI investigation of the "laundering" of funds through Mexican banks, Garment replied, "No, there is nothing that I have ascertained . . . in these weeks of investigations that would suggest that at all."

Ziegler rejected a reporter's interpretation of the statement as an admission that Nixon had acquiesced in an alleged cover-up of Watergate to protect intelligence operations.

Both Buzhardt and Garment declined to expand on Nixon's recollection of being told that the CIA might have been involved in the Watergate break-in, despite several questions as to who had given Nixon the information.

Garment also pleaded for "fairness" from the press for those involved in the case, who he said were being accused by innuendo and leaks from secret investigations.

Text of President's May 22 Statement on Watergate Affair

Allegations surrounding the Watergate affair have so escalated that I feel a further statement from the President is required at this time.

A climate of sensationalism has developed in which even second- or third-hand hearsay charges are headlined as fact and repeated as fact.

Important national security operations which themselves had no connection with Watergate have become entangled in the case.

As a result, some national security information has already been made public through court orders, through the subpoenaing of documents and through testimony witnesses have given in judicial and Congressional proceedings. Other sensitive documents are now threatened with disclosure; continued silence about those operations would compromise rather than protect them, and would also serve to perpetuate a grossly distorted view—which recent partial disclosures have given—of the nature and purpose of those operations.

The purpose of this statement is threefold:

- First, to set forth the facts about my own relationship to the Watergate matter.
- Second, to place in some perspective some of the more sensational—and inaccurate—of the charges that have filled the headlines in recent days, and also some of the matters that are currently being discussed in Senate testimony and elsewhere.
- Third, to draw the distinction between national security operations and the Watergate case. To put the other matters in perspective, it will be necessary to describe the national security operations first.

In citing these national security matters it is not my intention to place a national security "cover" on Watergate, but rather to separate them out from Watergate—and at the same time to explain the context in which certain actions took place that were later misconstrued or misused.

Long before the Watergate break-in, three important national security operations took place which have subsequently become entangled in the Watergate case.

- The first operation, begun in 1969, was a program of wiretaps. All were legal, under the authorities then existing. They were undertaken to find and stop serious national security leaks.
- The second operation was a reassessment, which I ordered in 1970, of the adequacy of internal security measures. This resulted in a plan and a directive to strengthen our intelligence operations. They were protested by Mr. Hoover, and as a result of his protest they were not put into effect.
- The third operation was the establishment, in 1971, of a special investigations unit in the White House. Its primary mission was to plug leaks of vital security information. I also directed this group to prepare an accurate history of certain crucial national security matters which occurred under prior Administrations, on which the government's records were incomplete.

Here is the background of these three security operations initiated by my Administration.

By mid-1969, my Administration had begun a number of highly sensitive foreign policy initiatives. They were aimed at ending the war in Vietnam, achieving a settlement in the Middle East, limiting nuclear arms, and establishing new relationships among the great powers. These involved highly secret diplomacy. They were closely interrelated. Leaks of secret information about any one could endanger all.

Exactly that happened. News accounts appeared in 1969, which were obviously based on leaks—some of them extensive and detailed—by people having access to the most highly classified security materials.

There was no way to carry forward these diplomatic initiatives unless further leaks could be prevented. This required finding the source of the leaks.

In order to do this, a special program of wiretaps was instituted in mid-1969 and terminated in February 1971. Fewer than 20 taps, of varying duration, were involved. They produced important leads that made it possible to tighten the security of highly sensitive materials.

I authorized this entire program. Each individual tap was undertaken in accordance with procedures legal at the time and in accord with long-standing precedent.

The persons who were subject to these wiretaps were determined through coordination among the director of the FBI, my assistant for national security affairs, and the attorney general. Those wiretapped were selected on the basis of access to the information leaked, material in security files, and evidence that developed as the inquiry proceeded.

Information thus obtained was made available to senior officials responsible for national security matters in order to curtail further leaks.

In the spring and summer of 1970, another security problem reached critical proportions. In March a wave of bombings and explosions struck college campuses and cities. There were 400 bomb threats in one 24-hour period in New York City. Rioting and violence on college campuses reached a new peak after the Cambodian operation and the tragedies at Kent State and Jackson State. The 1969–70 school year brought nearly 1,800 campus demonstrations, and nearly 250 cases of arson on campus. Many colleges closed. Gun battles between guerrilla-style groups and police were taking place. Some of the disruptive activities were receiving foreign support.

Complicating the task of maintaining security was the fact that, in 1966, certain types of undercover FBI operations that had been conducted for many years had been suspended. This also had substantially impaired our ability to collect foreign intelligence information. At the same time, the relationships between the FBI and other intelligence agencies had been deteriorating. By May, 1970, FBI Director Hoover shut off his agency's liaison with the CIA altogether.

On June 5, 1970, I met with the director of the FBI, (Mr. Hoover), the director of the Central Intelligence Agency (Mr. Richard Helms), the director of the Defense Intelligence Agency (Gen. Donald V. Bennett) and the director of the National Security Agency (Adm. Noel Gayler). We discussed the urgent need for better intelligence operations. I appointed Director Hoover as chairman of an inter-agency committee to prepare recommendations.

On June 25, the committee submitted a report which included specific options for expanded intelligence operations, and on July 23 the agencies were notified by memorandum of the options approved. After reconsideration, however, prompted by the opposition of Director Hoover, the agencies were notified five days later, on July 28, that the approval had been rescinded. The options initially approved had included resumption of certain intelligence operations which had been suspended in 1966. These in turn had included authorization for surreptitious entry—breaking and entering, in effect—on specified categories of targets in specified situations related to national security.

Because the approval was withdrawn before it had been implemented, the net result was that the plan for expanded intelligence activities never went into effect.

The documents spelling out this 1970 plan are extremely sensitive. They include—and are based upon—assessments of certain foreign intelligence capabilities and procedures, which of course must remain secret. It was this unused plan and related documents that John Dean removed from the White House and placed in a safe deposit box, giving the keys to Judge Sirica. The same plan, still unused, is being headlined today.

Coordination among our intelligence agencies continued to fall short of our national security needs. In July, 1970, having earlier discontinued the FBI's liaison with the CIA, Director Hoover ended the FBI's normal liaison with all other agencies except the White House. To help remedy this, an Intelligence Evaluation Committee was created in December, 1970. Its members included representatives of the White House, CIA, FBI, NSA, the Departments of Justice, Treasury, and Defense, and Secret Service.

The Intelligence Evaluation Committee and its staff were instructed to improve coordination among the intelligence community and to prepare evaluations and estimates of domestic intelligence. I understand that its activities are now under investigation. I did not authorize nor do I have any knowledge of any illegal activity by this committee. If it went beyond its charter and did engage in any illegal activities, it was totally without my knowledge or authority.

On Sunday, June 13, 1971, The New York Times published the first installment of what came to be known as "the Pentagon Papers." Not until a few hours before publication did any responsible government official know that they had been stolen. Most officials did not know they existed. No senior official of the government had read them or knew with certainty what they contained.

All the government knew, at first, was that the papers comprised 47 volumes and some 7,000 pages, which had been taken from the most sensitive files of the Departments of State and Defense and the CIA, covering military and diplomatic moves in a war that was still going on.

Moreover, a majority of the documents published with the first three installments in The Times had not been included in the 47-volume study—raising serious questions about what and how much else might have been taken.

There was every reason to believe this was a security leak of unprecedented proportions.

It created a situation in which the ability of the government to carry on foreign relations even in the best of circumstances could have been severely compromised. Other governments no longer knew whether they could deal with the United States in confidence. Against the background of the delicate negotiations the United States was then involved in on a number of fronts—with regard to Vietnam, China, the Middle East, nuclear arms limitations, U.S.-Soviet relations, and others—in which the utmost degree of confidentiality was vital, it posed a threat so grave as to require extraordinary actions.

Therefore during the week following the Pentagon papers publication, I approved the creation of a special investigations unit within the White House—which later came to be known as the "plumbers." This was a small group at the White House whose principal purpose was to stop security leaks and to investigate other sensitive security matters. I looked to John Ehrlichman for the supervision of this group.

Egil Krogh, Mr. Ehrlichman's assistant, was put in charge. David Young was added to this unit, as were E. Howard Hunt and G. Gordon Liddy.

The unit operated under extremely tight security rules. Its existence and functions were known only to a very few persons at the White House. These included messrs. Haldeman, Ehrlichman and Dean.

At about the time the unit was created, Daniel Ellsberg was identified as the person who had given the Pentagon papers to The New York Times. I told Mr. Krogh that as a matter of first priority, the unit should find out all it could about Mr. Ellsberg's associates and his motives. Because of the extreme gravity of the situation, and not then knowing what additional national secrets Mr. Ellsberg might disclose, I did impress upon Mr. Krogh the vital importance to the national security of his assignment. I did not authorize and had no knowledge of any illegal means to be used to achieve this goal.

However, because of the emphasis I put on the crucial importance of protecting the national security, I can understand how highly motivated individuals could have felt justified in engaging in specific activities that I would have disapproved had they been brought to my attention.

Consequently, as President, I must and do assume responsibility for such actions despite the fact that I, at no time approved or had knowledge of them.

I also assigned the unit a number of other investigatory matters, dealing in part with compiling an accurate record of events related to the Vietnam war, on which the government's records were inadequate (many previous records having been removed with the change of Administrations) and which bore directly on the negotiations then in progress. Additional assignments included tracing down other national security leaks, including one that seriously compromised the United States negotiating position in the SALT talks.

The work of the unit tapered off around the end of 1971. The nature of its work was such that it involved matters that, from a national security standpoint, were highly sensitive then and remain so today.

These intelligence activities had no connection with the break-in of the Democratic headquarters, or the aftermath.

I considered it my responsibility to see that the Watergate investigation did not impinge adversely upon the national security area. For example, on April 18th, 1973, when I learned that Mr. Hunt, a former member of the special investigations unit at the White House, was to be questioned by the U.S. attorney, I directed Assistant Attorney General Petersen to pursue every issue involving Watergate but to confine his investigation to Watergate and related matters and to stay out of national security matters. Subsequently, on April 25, 1973, Attorney General Kleindienst informed me that because the government had clear evidence that Mr. Hunt was involved in the break-in of the office of the psychiatrist who had treated Mr. Ellsberg, he, the attorney general, believed that despite the fact that no evidence had been obtained from Hunt's acts, a report should nevertheless be made to the court trying the Ellsberg case. I concurred, and directed that the information be transmitted to Judge Byrne immediately.

The burglary and bugging of the Democratic National Committee headquarters came as a complete surprise to me. I had no inkling that any such illegal activities had been planned by persons associated with my campaign; if I had known, I would not have permitted it. My immediate reaction was that those guilty should be brought to justice and, with the five burglars themselves already in custody, I assumed that they would be. Within a few days, however, I was advised that there was a possibility of CIA involvement in some way.

It did seem to me possible that, because of the involvement of former CIA personnel, and because of some of their apparent associations, the investigation could lead to the uncovering of covert CIA operations totally unrelated to the Watergate break-in.

In addition, by this time, the name of Mr. Hunt had surfaced in connection with Watergate, and I was alerted to the fact that he had previously been a member of the special investigations unit in the White House. Therefore, I was also concerned that the Watergate investigation might well lead to an inquiry into the activities of the special investigations unit itself.

In this area, I felt it was important to avoid disclosure of the details of the national security matters with which the group was concerned. I knew that once the existence of the group became known, it would lead inexorably to a discussion of these matters, some of which remain, even today, highly sensitive.

I wanted justice done with regard to Watergate; but in the scale of national priorities with which I had to deal—and not at that time having any idea of the extent of political abuse which Watergate reflected—I also had to be deeply concerned with insuring that neither the covert operations of the CIA nor the operations of the special investigations unit should be compromised. Therefore, I instructed Mr. Haldeman and Mr. Ehrlichman to insure that the investigation of the break-in not expose either an unrelated covert operation of the CIA or the activities of the White House investigations unit—and to see that this was personally coordinated between General Walters, the deputy director of the CIA, and Mr. Gray of the FBI. It was certainly not my intent, nor my wish, that the investigation of the Watergate break-in or of related acts be impeded in any way.

On July 6, 1972, I telephoned the acting director of the FBI, L. Patrick Gray, to congratulate him on his successful handling of the hijacking of a Pacific Southwest Airlines plane the previous day. During the conversation Mr. Gray discussed with me the progress of the Watergate investigation, and I asked him whether he had talked with General Walters. Mr. Gray said that he had, and that General Walters had assured him that the CIA was not involved. In the discussion, Mr. Gray suggested that the matter of Watergate might lead higher. I told him to press ahead with his investigation.

It now seems that later, through whatever complex of individual motives and possible misunderstandings, there were apparently wide-ranging efforts to limit the investigation or to conceal the possible involvement of members of the Administration and the campaign committee.

I was not aware of any such efforts at the time. Neither, until after I began my own investigation, was I aware of any fund-raising for defendants convicted at the break-in at Democratic headquarters, much less authorize any such fund-raising. Nor did I authorize any offer of executive clemency for any of the defendants.

In the weeks and months that followed Watergate, I asked for, and received, repeated assurances that Mr. Dean's own investigation (which included reviewing files and sitting in on FBI interviews with White House personnel) had cleared everyone then employed by the White House of involvement.

In summary, then:

(1) I had no prior knowledge of the Watergate bugging operation, or of any illegal surveillance activities for political purposes.

(2) Long prior to the 1972 campaign, I did set in motion certain internal security measures, including legal wiretaps, which I felt were necessary from a national security standpoint and, in the climate then prevailing, also necessary from a domestic security standpoint.

(3) People who had been involved in the national security operations later, without my knowledge or approval, undertook illegal activities in the political campaign of 1972.

(4) Elements of the early post-Watergate reports led me to suspect, incorrectly, that the CIA had been in some way involved. They also led me to surmise, correctly, that since persons originally recruited for covert national security activities had participated in Watergate, an unrestricted investigation of Watergate might lead to and expose those covert national security operations.

(5) I sought to prevent the exposure of these covert national security activities, while encouraging those conducting the investigation to pursue their inquiry into the Watergate itself. I so instructed my staff, the attorney general and the acting director of the FBI.

(6) I also specifically instructed Mr. Haldeman and Mr. Ehrlichman to insure that the FBI would not carry its investigation into areas that might compromise these covert national security activities or those of the CIA.

(7) At no time did I authorize or know about any offer of executive clemency for the Watergate defendants. Neither did I know, until the time of my own investigation, of any efforts to provide them with funds.

With hindsight, it is apparent that I should have given more heed to the warning signals I received along the way about a Watergate cover-up and less to the reassurances. With hindsight, several other things also become clear:

■ With respect to campaign practices, and also with respect to campaign finances, it should now be obvious that no campaign in history has ever been subjected to the kind of intensive and searching inquiry that has been focused on the campaign waged in my behalf in 1972.

It is clear that unethical, as well as illegal, activities took place in the course of that campaign.

None of these took place with my specific approval or knowledge. To the extent that I may in any way have contributed to the climate in which they took place, I did not intend to; to the extent that I failed to prevent them, I should have been more vigilant.

It was to help insure against any repetition of this in the future that last week I proposed the establishment of a top-level, bipartisan, independent commission to recommend a comprehensive reform of campaign laws and practices. Given the priority I believe it deserves, such reform should be possible before the next Congressional elections in 1974.

■ It now appears that there were persons who may have gone beyond my directives, and sought to expand on my efforts to protect the national security operations in order to cover up any involvement they or certain others might have had in Watergate. The extent to which this is true, and who may have participated and to what degree, are questions that it would not be proper to address here. The proper forum for settling these matters is in the courts.

■ To the extent that I have been able to determine what probably happened in the tangled course of this affair, on the basis of my own recollections and of the conflicting accounts and evidence that I have seen, it would appear that one factor at work was that at critical points various people, each with his own perspective and his own responsibilities, saw the same situation with different eyes and heard the same words with different ears. What might have seemed insignificant to one seemed significant to another; what one saw in terms of public responsibility, another saw in terms of political opportunity; and mixed through it all, I am sure, was a concern on the part of many that the Watergate scandal should not be allowed to get in the way of what the Administration sought to achieve.

The truth about Watergate should be brought out in an orderly way, recognizing that the safeguards of judicial procedure are designed to find the truth, not to hide the truth. With his selection of Archibald Cox—who served both President Kennedy and President Johnson as solicitor general—as the special supervisory prosecutor for matters related to the case, Attorney General-designate Richardson has demonstrated his own determination to see the truth brought out. In this effort he has my full support.

Considering the number of persons involved in this case whose testimony might be subject to a claim of executive privilege, I recognize that a clear definition of that claim has become central to the effort to arrive at the truth.

Accordingly, executive privilege will not be invoked as to any testimony concerning possible criminal conduct or discussions of possible criminal conduct, in the matters presently under investigation, including the Watergate affair and the alleged cover-up.

I want to emphasize that this statement is limited to my own recollections of what I said and did relating to security and to the Watergate. I have specifically avoided any attempt to explain what other parties may have said and done. My own information on those other matters is fragmentary, and to some extent contradictory. Additional information may be forthcoming of which I am unaware. It is also my understanding that the information which has been conveyed to me has also become available to those prosecuting these matters. Under such circumstances, it would be prejudicial and unfair of me to render my opinions on the activities of others; those judgments must be left to the judicial process, our best hope for achieving the just result that we all seek.

As more information is developed, I have no doubt that more questions will be raised. To the extent that I am able, I shall also seek to set forth the facts as known to me with respect to those questions.

Colson pressure on SEC cited. Colson and Shapiro, the Washington law firm of former presidential special counsel Charles W. Colson, made efforts April 19 to mobilize "pressure from the White House" and to "lean on" then Securities and Exchange Commission (SEC) Chairman G. Bradford Cook in order to obtain an SEC post for a lawyer they believed would assist their clients.

The Washington Post reported May 23 it had obtained an internal law firm memorandum to Colson from his partner, Charles H. Morin, suggesting they aid Charles K. M. Mallory, acting executive director of the SEC, in obtaining permanent appointment.

"In short, this is one of the chips we really should pick up, because it is a key job in the commission and one of extreme importance to us in representing our clients. In short, let's get this guy in that job or Cook may turn into a disaster for us," the memo read.

Morin also said Cook "ought to be reminded of how he got the job and how he almost did not get the job," an apparent reference to Colson support for Cook's appointment as SEC chairman. (Cook had been forced to resign as SEC chairman May 16 following allegations of involvement in alleged Administration influence peddling.)

Mallory said May 22 he was "outraged by the memo. "I resent the implication that I'm anybody's man. I'm not going to dance to anyone's tune," he added.

Both Morin and Colson confirmed the authenticity of the memo but denied that they had taken any measures to aid Mallory's selection.

Richardson confirmed as attorney general. Defense Secretary Elliot L. Richardson was confirmed as attorney general by the Senate May 23 on an 82-3 vote.

The nomination was rushed to the Senate floor after key Democrats on the Senate Judiciary Committee "reluctantly" agreed to support Richardson.

The committee unanimously approved the appointment earlier that day based on Richardson's pledge to name Harvard Law School professor Archibald Cox, former solicitor general in the Kennedy and Johnson Administrations, as independent special prosecutor within the Justice Department investigating the Watergate affair.

A vote on the Richardson nomination by the judiciary committee had been expected May 22, but was stalled when Daniel Ellsberg, a defendant in the Pentagon Papers case which had been dismissed May 11, urged the group to recall Richardson for further questioning about his conversations with former White House aide Egil Krogh Jr.

Krogh had supervised the political espionage squad, known as the "plumbers," which had conducted an illegal break-in at the offices of Ellsberg's former psychiatrist. The burglary, authorized by the White House, compromised the government's prosecution of Ellsberg and had been cited by the Pentagon Papers case judge in dismissing the case on grounds that there had been total government misconduct during prosecution of the trial.

Despite objections that he was merely repeating previous testimony, Richardson submitted to a full day of questioning May 22 by committee members.

Richardson expanded on his earlier testimony regarding his May 1 meeting with Krogh, which had been set up April 29 by presidential domestic affairs adviser John D. Ehrlichman.

At the hearing, Richardson produced notes he had taken during the talk with Krogh which indicated that Krogh wished to make a full disclosure to the Pentagon Papers trial of his role in the burglary attempt at the psychiatrist's office.

Krogh wished to tell the court he "had been a part of an undertaking that had a legitimate national security purpose, and as part of overzealousness in carrying out that purpose, a burglary was carried out," Richardson recalled.

Krogh subsequently outlined his part in the covert operation for the court but neglected to mention the role of the Central Intelligence Agency (CIA) in the burglary, which became known later; however, Krogh had mentioned the "CIA documents and disguises" to Richardson at their meeting. Judiciary committee members questioned Richardson why he had failed to make the omission known when he read Krogh's less than complete statement made to the Ellsberg trial.

"It did not occur to me to regard that as a significant omission," Richardson replied.

(Ellsberg had told senators on the committee that Richardson had reassurred Krogh it would be "okay not to mention CIA involvement in the burglary" on grounds of national security.)

Richardson also revealed that Ehrlichman was serving as intermediary for President Nixon regarding the Krogh case as late as May 2, two days after his White House resignation.

At the May 22 committee hearing, Richardson revealed that in ordering disclosure of the Ellsberg burglary April 29, Nixon had "made a distinction between the Ellsberg break-in itself and the national security activities of the plumbing operation."

Richardson had told the committee May 9 that, "to date, no one, neither the President nor anyone acting on his behalf, has suggested that information on this subject [the burglary] be withheld on national security or any other grounds."

Cox statement—Cox appeared before the Senate Judiciary Committee May 21 to pledge that he would not "shield anybody and [did not] intend to be intimidated by anybody" in conducting a thorough and independent investigation of the Watergate affair.

Asked how he would react to a possible request by President Nixon to provide the White House with progress reports of his investigation, Cox replied: "I would feel I would have the absolute right, if I felt it were against the interests of the investigation, to refuse. I would feel I had no official or legal duty to him. It would seem to me, I can't help remarking, an extraordinary request."

Regarding the guidelines drawn up by Richardson insulating the special prosecutor's investigation from Administration pressure, Cox said: "It seems to me the only authority he [Richardson] has retained is to give me hell if I don't do the job, and I think he ought to keep that authority."

Evident committee satisfaction with Cox's testimony played a major part in the Senate's decision to confirm Richardson's nomination.

After being assured by Cox that he would follow the "trail of federal crime" "wherever that trail may lead," key Committee member Sen. Robert C. Byrd (D, W. Va.) announced he would support the Richardson nomination, "albeit reluctantly."

"There has already been too long a delay in the full and thorough prosecution of all the crimes suspected to have been committed in the context of what had become a generic term for infamy—Watergate," Byrd said.

Voting against the Richardson appointment in the Senate were: Sens. Joseph R. Biden (D, Del.), Mike Gravel (D, Alaska) and Harold Hughes (D, Iowa).

Poll shows ebbing confidence in Nixon. A Gallup poll taken shortly after the President made his nationally televised speech April 30 about Watergate indicated that support among his constituency was at the lowest point since he assumed office in 1969, it was reported May 24.

Only 45% of those polled said they approved of the way Nixon was handling his job as president. The figure was 65% in a February poll.

The President, however, received unanimous support from 22 Republican members of the House and Senate, as well as three Cabinet members and party GOP chairman George Bush, at a White House meeting May 23. Nixon told them that some of his efforts to conceal some aspects of the Watergate case stemmed from his desire to guard against security leaks and exposure of covert intelligence operations. Nixon received a standing ovation from the group.

Vice President Agnew offered support for Nixon's national security defense, saying in an Orlando, Fla. speech May 23 that the President had been forced "to weather an incredible storm of personal abuse and innuendo" from persons who were not aware that national security was at stake.

Details of 1970 plan revealed. White House plans in 1970 to launch a massive counter-insurgency plan against the Black Panthers, Arab extremists, antiwar radicals, and Soviet espionage agents were revealed by the New York Times May 24.

Times sources said the late director of the Federal Bureau of Investigation, J. Edgar Hoover, refused to go along with the project because President Nixon would not give him written authorization for use of FBI personnel for illegal wiretaps and illegal breaking-and-entering operations.

(Prior to Nixon's May 22 speech, the Times had reported May 21 the White House had established in 1970 a secret intelligence unit—Intelligence Evaluation Committee—operating out of the Justice Department, whose purpose was to collect and evaluate information about antiwar and radical groups and then pass it on to former White House counsel John W. Dean 3rd and John J. Caulfield, then an aide to Dean.)

The plan was outlined in a secret report that was among the documents taken from the White House by former presidential counsel John W. Dean 3rd.

According to a Times source who worked on the report in 1970, "the facts we had available in this country then showed that we were faced with one of the most serious domestic crises that we've had. One of our greatest problems was that the informed public didn't understand it."

Nixon affirms right to secrecy. President Nixon May 24 affirmed the government's right to secrecy in national security matters and denounced "those who steal secrets and publish them in the newspapers."

The latter remark, a reference to publication of the Pentagon Papers, drew a standing ovation from his audience of more than 600 recently returned prisoners of war. The scene was a State Department briefing for the POWs while their wives attended a reception elsewhere in the department with Mrs. Nixon. Later, the group attended a banquet and entertainment on the White House lawn.

"I want to be quite blunt," Nixon continued. "Had we not had secrecy, had we not had secret negotiations" with the North Vietnamese, Soviet and Chinese leaders, "... there would have been no China initiative, there would have been no limitation of arms for the Soviet Union and no summit, and had we not had that kind of security, and that kind of secrecy that allowed for the kind of exchange that is essential, you men would still be in Hanoi rather than Washington today.

GOP House member apparent suicide. Rep. William O. Mills (R, Md.), 48, was found dead near his home in Easton, Md. May 24, apparently from a "a self-inflicted" shotgun wound, according to authorities. Mills left several notes which said, in a paraphrase by authorities, "he had done nothing wrong but said he couldn't prove it and so there was no other way out."

The reference was attributed to a $25,000 contribution from the Finance Committee to Re-elect the President to Mills' 1971 campaign, disclosed by the General Accounting Office May 19. The Washington Post reported May 23 that the contribution, in cash, had not been reported to the state board of elections "in apparent violation of state law." Any actual violation had not been determined.

The funeral service in Easton May 26 was attended by many dignitaries, including Vice President Spiro T. Agnew and Maryland Gov. Marvin Mandel (D).

Richardson takes office. Elliot L. Richardson was sworn in May 25 as attorney general. The oath was administered by Chief Justice Warren E. Burger at the White House with President Nixon an observer.

Richardson declared that "the first concern of the administration of justice is the individual. The second is the truth." He said that the institutions of the American government were currently under stress but that the flaws were in men, not the system. "The task is not one of redesign," he said, "but one of renewal and reaffirmation."

In a farewell news conference at the Pentagon May 24 as defense secretary, Richardson spoke of the Watergate affair "and other related matters" as having brought about "a kind of sleaziness [which] has infected the ways in which things have been done and this has touched agencies that have been concerned with law and law enforcement."

"To a large extent," he said, the people's "respect for government" was "affected by the fairness and integrity of the law enforcement process" and there was an opportunity now "to restore confidence through finding ways in which the law enforcement process can be made to be, and perceived to be, scrupulous in the ways in which it carries out its job."

San Clemente financing. The White House issued a statement May 25 on the financing of President Nixon's home in San Clemente, Calif. According to the statement, the bulk of the estate was controlled by an investment company formed by millionaire industrialist Robert H. Abplanalp, a personal friend of the President

The statement was issued after a California newspaper, the Santa Ana Register, published a report May 13 from unidentified investigators for the Senate Watergate committee that some $1 million in unreported 1968 Nixon campaign funds may have been used in purchasing the estate. Committee sources disavowed the report, and White House Press Secretary Ronald L. Ziegler denied it May 14 as "a total fabrication." Ziegler promised a fuller statement the next day.

According to the May 25 statement, the San Clemente home was financed by proceeds from the sale of Nixon's New York apartment, a mortgage and two loans from Abplanalp. The latter, totaling $625,000 at one point (promissory notes bearing interest at 8%), were canceled, "with the exception of accrued interest," according to the statement, in December 1970 when Abplanalp purchased through the investment company all but 5.9 acres of a much larger tract originally purchased by Nixon.

The original seller insisted on selling the larger tract—26 acres—as a single unit, and "it was the Nixons' intention to seek a compatible buyer" for all but a 5.9 acre homesite area, the statement said. No such buyer was found prior to the closing of the sale in July 1969, and the Nixons took a loan from Abplanalp to acquire the larger site.

A title insurance company was then named trustee to buy and hold title to the property, which enabled sale of the extra land the Nixons did not intend to keep without renegotiation of the mortgage. The trustee bought the site for $1.4 million, $400,000 of which was in cash, the remainder mortgage. Two months later in September 1969, the trustee acquired for the Nixons an additional 2.9 adjoining acres for $100,000, $20,000 of which was in cash, $80,000 in mortgage.

Since then, the statement said, the Nixons had spent $123,514 for improvements on their 5.9 acre site.

When the sale to the Abplanalp investment company was made in December 1970, the price was $1,249,000. In addition to canceling the Nixon loans, the funds covered the assumption of Nixon's mortgages from both land purchases, or $624,000.

The statement put the net investment by the President for the 5.9 acre home site at $374,514.

In a subsequent statement May 26, the White House said government-financed improvements to the San Clemente estate totaled $39,525. The improvements were said to be security measures.

Neither statement revealed the name of the Abplanalp investment company involved. The New York Times reported May 25 that the property division described in the statement did not appear on local property records.

The May 25 White House statement also listed the ownership of Nixon's Key Biscayne property in Florida. It said two of the five houses in the compound were owned by the Nixons, one by C. G. Rebozo, another personal friend of Nixon, one by Mr. and Mrs. Abplanalp and one by a trustee of an Indiana bank which was trustee for the former owner. The latter two units were leased to the General Services Administration for office space and security and communications for the President.

(The Associated Press reported May 30 that Abplanalp was a principal stockholder—$125,000 worth—in a Yonkers, N.Y. bank, the Hudson Valley National Bank, chartered by the federal government after the purchase by Abplanalp of the San Clemente land. It also said Abplanalp's attorney, William E. Griffin Jr., one of the bank's founders, bought two Key Biscayne lots from Nixon in late 1972—one originally purchased in 1967 for $30,000, another bought in 1971 for $23.100—for $150,000.)

Watergate: Low point in tactics. The Fair Campaign Practices Committee's report on the 1972 presidential campaign, released May 26, termed the Watergate scandal and related charges of political sabotage and espionage conducted by the Nixon re-election committee "a conscious conspiracy to violate laws, to manipulate voters and to make a mockery of the democratic system of self-government."

The nonpartisan, privately funded group disputed President Nixon's assertion April 30 that "both" political parties were guilty of "shady" campaign tactics.

"Theft, spying, sabotage and subversion are not the tactics of the political profession. In nearly 20 years of studying the political processes, the Fair Campaign Committee has uncovered no campaign tactics comparable in extent or in potential damage to a free, self-governing society."

According to the committee, 80 complaints were filed by both parties on alleged unfair campaign practices, an increase of 19%; however, only two complaints were related to the Watergate affair.

Nixon bars own testimony. President Nixon would not give oral or written testimony to the grand jury or the Senate select committee investigating the Watergate case, White House Press Secretary Ronald L. Ziegler said May 29. "It would be Constitutionally inappropriate," he said. "It would do violence to the separation of powers."

The statement was issued after a report by the Washington Post May 29 that the Watergate prosecutors had informed the Justice Department there was justification for calling Nixon to answer questions before the grand jury. The report, by Carl Bernstein and Bob Woodward, said the President's role in the Watergate affair was the one key element remaining to be clarified in the investigation and questioning was justified about how top Nixon aides could pursue such massive obstruction of justice without the President's knowledge.

According to the Post, a "department source" said "there is no bombshell tucked away" about the President's role but "there is an evidentiary pattern" that raised questions about it.

There was a strong White House reaction to the story. In a statement issued May 28 and carried by the Post alongside its story, Ziegler said the story reflected "a shocking and irresponsible abuse of authority on the part of the federal prosecutors, if in fact, they made the statements attributed to them." Communicating information and allegations relating to grand jury proceedings "in this fashion," he said, was a violation of law.

Reaffirming this position to reporters May 29, Ziegler said the White House's "very, very severe concern" about the Post's report had to do with the secrecy of the grand jury process and the anonymous and indirect charges against the President.

Ziegler said the White House had protested the matter to Attorney General Elliot L. Richardson and Archibald Cox, the special Watergate prosecutor. The protest was made by special White House counsel J. Fred Buzhardt Jr. in telephone calls.

Cox also issued a statement May 29 saying all decisions about the conduct of the investigation "will be made by me" and that he had as yet "made no such decisions and authorized none." He said the prosecutors and Justice Department officials "have been instructed to refrain from any kind of statement, comment or speculation about any aspect of the investigation."

Cox specified that he "prepared this statement prior to Mr. Buzhardt's telephone call. I gave him the substance of it then and later read it to him, solely to confirm the accuracy of what I had said."

Cox referred to "extraordinary statements" in the press during the past week about "the theory or theories of a possible Watergate prosecution and the evidence expected from one or more witnesses."

Some of the press accounts had cited acceptance of guilty pleas and possible leniency in return for testimony. The U.S. attorney in Washington, Harold H. Titus Jr., announced May 24 that a key figure in the Watergate case had agreed to plead guilty and be a witness for the prosecution at the trial. (The figure was identified from other government sources as Jeb Stuart Magruder, former deputy director of the Nixon campaign.)

Titus said "comprehensive" indictments were expected within 60–90 days that would "focus on the obstruction of justice which occurred after the Watergate arrest on June 17, 1972, but will include criminal activities beginning in 1971,

which, together with the Watergate break-in, motivated the massive obstruction."

Titus indicated that negotiations for other guilty pleas in return for leniency were in process and grants of immunity had been extended. The New York Times reported May 29 that former Nixon counsel John W. Dean 3rd had been offered a chance by the prosecutors to plead guilty to one count of obstruction of justice in return for his cooperation. CBS News reported that night from Dean's lawyer that Dean would reject such an offer and was holding out for "total immunity."

Prosecutors to remain—Titus, who was in charge of the U.S. attorneys' office in Washington, which included the three Watergate prosecutors, said May 24 they were remaining on the task. The three—Earl J. Silbert, Seymour Glanzer and Donald E. Campbell—who had been handling the federal investigation since June 1972, had threatened to resign May 22 because of the appointment of a special prosecutor, which carried with it an implication of inadequacy of their investigation.

To resolve the disharmony, special prosecutor Cox met with the three prosecutors May 23 and later sent Titus a letter saying it was "of great importance that there be no break or delay in the investigation." The public interest required, he said, that their investigation be carried on while he familiarized himself "with all that has been done."

New staff assembled—Cox was sworn in as special prosecutor in a ceremony in the solicitor general's office at the Justice Department May 25. In assembling his own staff, Cox announced May 29 that James F. Neal, 43, a Nashville, Tenn. attorney, would serve as a special assistant working with the three current prosecutors. Neal was sworn in May 29 along with two other special assistants, selected earlier by Cox, Philip E. Heymann and James Vorenberg. Like Cox, they were Harvard law professors.

As a special assistant to the attorney general from 1961 to 1964, Neal had conducted the successful prosecution of James R. Hoffa, former president of the International Brotherhood of Teamsters.

Vorenberg had been an aide in Sen. George McGovern's Democratic presidential campaign in 1972. Heymann had served as a State Department official during the Johnson Administration.

Kissinger takes responsibility for taps. Henry A. Kissinger, President Nixon's national security adviser, May 29 conceded "his office" supplied names of some of the members of the National Security Council to the Federal Bureau of Investigation beginning in 1969 to wiretap their phones.

Kissinger, branding wiretaps as "a distasteful thing in general," defended them in safeguarding national security.

Kissinger declined to explain what he meant by "his office." "I am responsible for what happens in my office, and I won't give the names of the people who did it," Kissinger said.

He had denied authorizing any wiretaps May 14.

Ehrlichman says Nixon knew of inquiry. John D. Ehrlichman, President Nixon's former chief domestic affairs adviser, told a Senate panel that President Nixon knew six days after the Watergate break-in that the Federal Bureau of Investigation (FBI) was conducting an investigation into "Mexican aspects" of the case.

Ehrlichman, appearing before the Senate Appropriations Committee's Subcommittee on Intelligence Operations May 30, also said Nixon ordered him and White House chief of staff H. R. Haldeman to instruct the Central Intelligence Agency (CIA) to tell the FBI to go slow in its investigation so as not to expose covert intelligence operations in Mexico.

Ehrlichman said Deputy CIA Director Vernon A. Walters at that meeting was unable to unequivocally say CIA operations would not be exposed.

Exactly what the President knew about the "Mexican aspects" referred to by Ehrlichman—which subcommittee members took to mean the laundering of $89,000 of Nixon campaign funds through a Mexican bank—was left unclear.

Sen. John L. McClellan (D, Ark.), subcommittee chairman, in recapitulating Ehrlichman's closed-door testimony for reporters, said the President was specifically aware of the FBI investigation centering on the funds channeled through a Mexican bank that were ultimately used to finance operations of the Nixon reelection committee and the Watergate break-in.

Afterwards, Ehrlichman told newsmen he did not know whether the President was aware of the nature of the transaction of the funds.

McClellan also revealed that former CIA Director Richard Helms told former Acting FBI Director L. Patrick Gray 3rd June 22, 1972 that the CIA was not implicated in the Watergate break-in and that no covert operations would be compromised by an FBI investigation.

(It had been revealed earlier that Haldeman, in a June 23, 1972 meeting with Ehrlichman, Helms and Deputy CIA Director Walters, had told Walters to inform Gray that covert CIA operations in Mexico might be jeopardized by FBI investigators. According to additional information revealed by Rep. Lucien Nedzi (D, Mich.) May 30, Helms told Haldeman at the June 23 meeting what he had told Gray the day before. Nedzi's Armed Services Subcommittee on Intelligence was also investigating the CIA.)

Ehrlichman told reporters after Walters met with Gray (June 23) that Walters told the White House the CIA would not be imperiled by an FBI investigation. But,

Ehrlichman continued, the President did not believe Walters, although he did authorize Gray to conduct a full investigation.

"The President told me then that he still personally believed and feared that the FBI investigation might harm the agency [CIA]."

"He [Nixon] said he believed the CIA would be making a mistake if it pretended an investigation would not disclose some of its current operations. He said he hoped the general and other CIA management were not covering up for their subordinates," Ehrlichman said.

"The President said substantially: a man makes a grave mistake in covering up for subordinates. That was President Truman's error in the [Alger] Hiss case when he instructed the FBI not to cooperate," Ehrlichman said.

Haldeman denies cover-up try—H. R. Haldeman, former chief of staff to President Nixon, appeared before the McClellan subcommittee May 31. His testimony paralleled Ehrlichman's remarks the day before, contradicted the CIA, and left the subcommittee's members dissatisfied.

Haldeman denied "categorically" that he had engaged in any attempt to cover-up the Watergate break-in. He disputed Deputy CIA Director Walters' version of the June 23, 1972 White House meeting which dealt with the question of covert CIA operations in Mexico that might have been compromised by an FBI investigation.

However, he acknowledged that CIA Director Helms in the June 23 meeting "assured us that there was no CIA involvement in the Watergate and also that he had no concern from the CIA's viewpoint regarding any possible connections of Watergate personnel with the Bay of Pigs."

Haldeman said the June 23 meeting was ordered by the President as a result of a report by former White House Counsel John W. Dean 3rd that "the FBI had requested guidance regarding some aspects" of the Watergate case that might concern the CIA.

Haldeman said after reading Dean's report he suggested Nixon call the meeting. At the meeting "Gen. Walters was asked to meet with [L. Patrick] Gray of the FBI to insure that any unrelated covert operations of the CIA or any unrelated national security activities which had been previously undertaken by some of the Watergate principals, not be compromised in the process of the Watergate investigation and the attendant publicity and political furor. This was done with no intent or desire to impede or cover up any aspect of the Watergate investigation itself. Any other actions taken or suggestions made by others were without my knowledge and without the knowledge of the President. I believe all my actions were proper, in accord with the President's

instructions and clearly in the national interest."

Sen. John O. Pastore (D, R.I.) was dissatisfied with Haldeman's testimony and complained of "glaring inconsistencies" between the testimony of Haldeman and Ehrlichman and the testimony of CIA officials Walters and former Deputy Director Robert E. Cushman.

Pastore said Haldeman had not made it clear how the FBI investigation could have been related to the abortive CIA-sponsored invasion of Cuba in 1962, even though some of the Watergate conspirators had been involved in both. He said the Watergate-Bay of Pigs connection seemed "a little farfetched."

McClellan said he was unable to understand why Haldeman and Ehrlichman had not gone directly to Helms about CIA operations that might be endangered.

He said Haldeman's answers to questions regarding the June 22, 1972 conversation between Helms and Gray "were somewhat vague" and "not entirely satisfactory."

"It seemed to me that if the purpose of it [the June 23 meeting] was to find out of any CIA involvement or any adverse results to it by reason of continuation of this investigation, they had Helms there and they could have asked him directly."

Ehrlichman denies call to Cushman—Some of Ehrlichman's testimony before the McClellan subcommittee resulted in a contradiction with what had been said earlier by former CIA Deputy Director Cushman.

Cushman had said May 11 in a sworn statement and in testimony before House and Senate panels investigating the role of the CIA in the break-in of the office of the former psychiatrist of former Pentagon Papers trial defendant Daniel Ellsberg Sept. 3-4, 1971: "About 7 July 1971 Mr. John Ehrlichman of the White House called me and stated that Howard Hunt was a bona fide employee, a consultant on security matters, and that Hunt would come to see me and request assistance which Mr. Ehrlichman requested that I give."

Ehrlichman said May 30, "I can flatly say that I do not have even the faintest recollection of having done so. I can say with assurance that any call to the CIA is the kind of call that I usually have little or no difficulty remembering."

Ehrlichman admitted receiving a call from Cushman in August 1971 requesting that CIA aid to Hunt be ended. Ehrlichman said he readily agreed when he learned Hunt claimed to be working for the White House.

In a prepared statement for the McClellan subcommittee which was made public, Ehrlichman said he did not learn of the burglary of Ellsberg's psychiatrist's office until about a week after it occurred. He said he had not told the President of the break-in and that the President had learned of it "relatively recently."

In response to the Ehrlichman denial, Cushman told a news conference at Marine Corps headquarters near Washington May 31 "a painstaking" search of CIA records "turned up" minutes of a daily CIA staff meeting for July 8, 1971. Cushman said he had mentioned at the meeting a conversation with Ehrlichman the day before about giving aid to E. Howard Hunt.

According to Cushman, the initial conversation with Ehrlichman went along the lines of "Here's Mr. Hunt; he works for us; he'll be around to see you."

Cushman said there was nothing improper about Ehrlichman's call, as Ehrlichman had said nothing about what Hunt wanted.

Cushman indicated he had given the minutes of the CIA staff meeting to the "necessary Congressional committees."

Nixon contributor files suit. Matthew E. Duisen, 72, a lifelong St. Louis Republican, filed suit May 23 in Washington on behalf of the more than one million contributors to the Nixon re-election campaign demanding redistribution of the $4.8 million in surplus funds remaining from the 1972 election.

Duisen, who donated less than $100 to the re-election committee in 1972, said he initiated the class action suit because of disclosures related to the Watergate affair. He "could not be more outraged if the archbishop opened a saloon," Duisen said.

The suit was aimed at the Committee to Re-elect the President, the Finance Committee to Re-elect the President and 11 officials of the Nixon campaign—former Attorney General and campaign director John N. Mitchell; former commerce secretary and finance committee chairman Maurice H. Stans; Herbert W. Kalmbach, Nixon's former personal attorney and chief fund raiser during 1971; Clark MacGregor, Mitchell's successor as campaign director; Jeb Stuart Magruder, former deputy campaign director; Hugh W. Sloan Jr., former finance committee treasurer; G. Gordon Liddy, convicted Watergate conspirator and former counsel to the finance committee; Herbert L. Porter, a former scheduling director of the re-election committee who had been linked to the covert use of secret money; Frederic V. Malek, Frederick C. LaRue and Robert Odle Jr., former campaign aides also implicated in the allegedly illegal use of secret contributions.

The group of 11 individuals, it was charged, "clandestinely, secretly and in utter disregard of their fiduciary obligations as officers, directors, managers and agents of the defendant committees embarked upon plans, schemes and artifices to misappropriate and misapply funds for the purpose of political espionage and sabotage, spying, burglary, bugging, wire tapping, electronic surveillance and bribery, and further for the purposes of

68—May–June 1973

cover-up, concealment and obstruction of justice."

On behalf of other donors, Duisen asked that a total of $1 million in exemplary, or personal punitive damages, be levied against the 11 for misconduct during the campaign.

The court was also asked to require the officials to make a full, public accounting of all "illegal" disbursements of Nixon campaign funds, followed by a court-ordered, personal repayment by the group of "all sums of money wrongfully and illegally misappropriated" for espionage, sabotage and wiretapping.

Duisen also demanded that the group make a pro rata reimbursement to all individuals on the committee's contributor lists of funds obtained by "fraudulently and deliberately misleading and tricking" requests. Republican donors had been betrayed by officials making "appeals designed and calculated to instill confidence and patriotism," he said.

In order to preserve this refund, Duisen asked that the Nixon committees be enjoined from an out-of-court settlement in the Democrats' $6.4 million damage suit, resulting from the Watergate break-in.

According to spokesmen at the Nixon re-election committee, there were no records of other refunds to rank and file contributors; however, the New York Times reported June 4 that William H. Radebaugh, who had given $25 to the Nixon campaign, had written Stans in August 1972 demanding a refund.

In a letter dated Sept. 5, 1972 mailed with the returned money, Stans replied:

"As a Nixon supporter, I should think that by now you would have learned to differentiate between political carping by the media and actual facts . . . As the true facts surrounding reported incidents involving this committee are eventually revealed, I am sure you will be reassured."

Ervin charges 'Gestapo mentality'. Sen. Sam J. Ervin (D, N.C.), chairman of the Senate committee investigating Watergate, said May 31 that the documents that had been held by former counsel to the President John W. Dean 3rd "would be a great shock to the American people if they were released."

Dean's papers revealed a "Gestapo mentality" in the highest levels of the Nixon Administration, Ervin said.

The Dean documents, turned over to U.S. District Judge John J. Sirica May 14, contained the plans for the 1970 intelligence gathering plan described by President Nixon in his May 22 statement on Watergate.

Ervin said, "I interpret the papers as being an effort . . . to set up an operation to spy on the American people in general or at least on those who didn't agree with the Administration."

Federal probe strengthened. Attorney General Elliot L. Richardson issued a directive May 31 to all Justice Department personnel, "including the Federal Bureau of Investigation," to cooperate with special Watergate prosecutor Archibald Cox in his probe and submit all reports on "possible offenses" involving the Nixon Administration to Cox.

The directive, requested by Cox, defined the scope of the special prosecutor as including the Watergate break-in, "all offenses arising out of the 1972 presidential election as far as the special prosecutor deems it necessary and appropriate to assume responsibility," and any other "allegations involving the President, members of the White House staff or presidential appointees."

Another addition to the Cox staff was announced May 31: Thomas F. McBride, 44, a former Justice Department attorney and former assistant district attorney in New York, was named a special prosecutor to assist initially in coordinating the subsidiary grand jury and state probes.

On one of these—a Los Angeles grand jury probe of the break-in at the offices of Dr. Daniel Ellsberg's psychiatrist—Cox pledged June 1 his "full cooperation." He denied a report he was seeking to delay that proceeding to prevent interference with the Washington probe. He authorized the appearance before the coast grand jury of imprisoned Watergate conspirators. Authorities had reportedly refused to release the prisoners requested without permission from Cox.

Richardson backs Petersen—Richardson expressed confidence June 5 in Henry E. Petersen, assistant attorney general in charge of the initial federal Watergate investigation, after a report that Cox was investigating Petersen's conduct of the case. Cox said the same day his staff was "investigating the activities of, and information available from, every person associated with the Watergate case." But he said "our rule—necessary in order to protect the investigation—will be neither to affirm nor deny newspaper speculation concerning individuals."

Secret dairy farmers' contribution disclosed. The Lehigh Valley Cooperative Farmers, a Pennsylvania dairy group, made two $25,000 secret contributions (in $100 bills) to the Nixon re-election campaign during 1972, the Washington Post reported June 1.

The first secret donation was made April 20, 1972, when Agriculture Secretary Earl L. Butz addressed a stockholders meeting in Pennsylvania. (According to the Post, the association had pledged a $100,000 contribution if Vice President Spiro T. Agnew, who was scheduled to appear, addressed the group. When Butz substituted for Agnew, the offer was reduced.) A second Lehigh contribution was made in May 1972.

The General Accounting Office (GAO) May 19 had listed the $50,000 gift as an anonymous contribution which had never been made public, as required by the federal disclosure law, the Post reported.

Disclosure of the secret contribution could involve the Nixon re-election committee in two lawsuits. According to the Federal Election Campaign Act, violators of the political reporting law could receive maximum penalties of one year in jail and fines of $1,000 for each offense.

Percy criticizes Nixon. Sen. Charles H. Percy (R, Ill.) June 2 dismissed as insufficient President Nixon's public statements of explanation on the Watergate affair. Percy called Nixon's May 22 statement a step in the right direction but added that it was not enough "to accept 'responsibility' in the broadest, most imprecise sense of that word. It is not enough to lament the fact that crimes were committed in the name of a noble goal—protecting national security."

Percy's remarks were in a commencement address at Knox College in Galesburg, Ill.

Calling Watergate the "darkest scandal in American political history," Percy said the "stark facts" about the President's position were: "Either he was completely unaware of activities being carried out in his name . . . or else he knew about them and, at least, did not express his disapproval." Neither of the choices, Percy said, "could be contemplated without dismay."

Percy called on Nixon to take the lead in revealing the facts on Watergate, rather than letting them be "dragged out piecemeal by investigatory bodies or the press."

CIA memos dispute security issue. Central Intelligence Agency (CIA) memoranda released by the Senate Appropriations Committee's Subcommittee on Intelligence Operations June 3 showed that key White House officials were not worried about danger to national security by Federal Bureau of Investigation (FBI) probes of the Watergate break-in. Rather, they were concerned over the massive political implications of a public airing of the scandal.

The memos, written for the most part by Deputy CIA Director Vernon A. Walters, recollected a series of meetings in June–July 1972 that he held with former presidential aides H. R. Haldeman, John D. Ehrlichman, and John W. Dean 3rd as well as former Acting FBI Director L. Patrick Gray 3rd, in which the ramifications of Watergate were discussed.

In a memo dated June 28, 1972, Walters described a White House meeting held five days before, attended by Walters, Haldeman, Ehrlichman, and then CIA Director Richard Helms.

At the meeting Walters was asked by Haldeman to talk to Gray and suggest that, since five suspects had already been arrested, the FBI not push its inquiries into Watergate, especially in Mexico. This was done over Helms' assurances that the CIA was not implicated in the affair.

Helms even noted he had spoken to Gray the day before about this issue.

Haldeman's reasoning was that the FBI investigation could lead to a "lot of important people" and that "the whole affair was getting embarrassing and it was the President's wish that Walters call on Gray." (In a cover note submitted by Walters along with the documents, the Haldeman statement, "it is the President's wish," was disclaimed. Walters said the "thought was implicit in my mind. I did not, however, correct the memo since it was for my use only.")

In another memorandum dated June 28, 1972, Walters detailed the Haldeman-instigated meeting with Gray. As per Haldeman's request, Walters warned Gray that continued FBI investigation into Mexican aspects of Watergate "could trespass" on covert CIA operations and that it would be best if it tapered off. Gray, noting "this was a most awkward matter to come up during an election year," said he would see what could be done.

Other Walters memoranda dealt with private meetings he had with Dean June 26 and 28, 1972. At the first meeting, Walters rejected a request by Dean that the CIA provide bail and salaries for the Watergate conspirators, warning that such news would be quickly leaked and "the scandal would be 10 times greater."

The second meeting was similar, with Walters again warning Dean that CIA involvement in Watergate was too risky. "Intervention such as he [Dean] suggested could transform it [Watergate] into a high megaton hydrogen bomb. . . . Direct intervention by the agency would be electorally mortal if it became known and chances of keeping it secret until the election were almost nil," the memo said.

Further Walters memoranda told of a July 6, 1972 meeting with Gray following a phone conversation between the men the previous evening, in which Gray said he would need written authorization to curb the FBI investigation.

At the July 6 meeting, Walters recounted what was said at the June 23 White House meeting, although he did not mention Haldeman and Ehrlichman by name. Walters also told Gray how he had rejected Dean's requests for CIA help in a cover-up.

Gray in turn related to Walters that he had warned then-Attorney General Richard Kleindienst and Haldeman and Ehrlichman the FBI investigation would have to continue. Gray told the latter two he would prefer to resign but that it would raise questions that would be injurious to the President.

"He [Gray] did not see why he or I should jeopardize the integrity of our organizations to protect some mid-level White House figures who had acted imprudently. . . . He felt it important that the President should be protected from his would-be-protectors."

At a July 12, 1972 meeting between Gray and Walters, Gray said he had been pressured by key officials (he did not name them) to force Harold H. Titus Jr., U.S. attorney for the District of Columbia, to stop his efforts at subpoenaing the financial records of the Republican re-election committee. Gray said he had declined to help. Gray also related to Walters a conversation—reported earlier—he had had with the President.

Other information in the memoranda: Dean told Walters in their June 26, 1972 meeting that Dean suspected that Bernard L. Barker, later convicted for the Watergate break-in, "had been involved in a clandestine entry into the Chilean embassy" in Washington. Walters replied that none of the Watergate suspects had been on the CIA payroll for at least two years.

One memorandum written by CIA Director James R. Schlesinger, dated Feb. 9, 1973, indicated he had received a phone call from Dean, who expressed concern about a pending Senate Foreign Relations Committee investigation into International Telephone and Telegraph (ITT) in connection with the "Chilean problem." Dean warned that the "investigation could be rather explosive." Schlesinger noted he did not share Dean's concern since the CIA was in no way involved.

Soviets had Pentagon Papers in 1971. The Soviet embassy in Washington had obtained a complete copy of the 47-volume Pentagon Papers during June 1971, while the Justice Department was in court seeking an injunction against further publication of articles based on the documents, it was reported June 3.

According to Nixon Administration sources, the papers were delivered to the embassy June 16, 1971 by a man whose identity was still unknown.

The Soviets, in a statement issued June 5, denied having possessed the documents.

Justice Department sources said the government knew, in advance of arguments that same month before the Supreme Court on further publication of the documents, that the Soviets had the papers. The same sources stressed the government had no evidence the Soviets obtained the documents from either Daniel Ellsberg or any of the newspapers publishing them.

This disclosure contradicted an affidavit submitted to Pentagon Papers trial Judge William M. Byrne by former White House aide Egil Krogh Jr.

Krogh said the Soviets possessed a copy of the Pentagon Papers prior to their publication in the New York Times June 13, 1971. Krogh claimed to have been given this information by the Federal Bureau of Investigation. He used this as a justification for the burglary of the office of the former psychiatrist of Ellsberg Sept. 3-4, 1971, by a White House team headed by convicted Watergate burglars E. Howard Hunt Jr. and G. Gordon Liddy.

Richardson bars security defense—Attorney General Elliot L. Richardson told newsmen June 4 he did not feel the publication of the Pentagon Papers in 1971 was sufficient justification for creation of a special White House team that employed illegal means to investigate security leaks. Richardson spoke with reference to the burglary of the office of Ellsberg's former psychiatrist by a team operating out of the White House.

Asked whether he agreed with President Nixon's decision to set up the "plumbers group," Richardson replied: "There would have to be a very persuasive case made, in my view, as to why the normal agencies of government were not adequate. I think the national security justification, even as put forward by the people who were directly involved, is not convincing." Richardson referred to an affidavit submitted in the Pentagon Papers trial by Krogh. [See above] Krogh took responsibility for the break-in, but claimed concern for national security dictated his actions.

'Laundered' Mexican checks traced. The Washington Post provided a chronological account June 3 of the "laundered" Mexican checks that were used to finance the Watergate break-in

April 3, 1972: Gulf Resources and Chemical Corp. of Houston allegedly contributed $100,000 to the Nixon re-election campaign, in violation of federal campaign laws which prohibited political donations from corporations.

The money was routed from a Mexican subsidiary of Gulf Resources to the personal bank account of Mexico City lawyer Manuel Ogarrio, 82.

Ogarrio converted the money to four bank drafts totaling $89,000, and $11,000 in cash and passed the funds to Houston where they were transported in an oil executive's suitcase to Washington April 6, 1972.

According to Maurice Stans, chairman of the Finance Committee to Re-elect the President, and committee treasurer Hugh W. Sloan Jr., the checks, which were received one day before the new federal reporting law for campaign funds took effect, were given to convicted Watergate conspirator G. Gordon Liddy, then counsel to the finance committee.

Liddy gave the checks to Bernard Barker, also convicted in the Watergate break-in. Barker returned the cash to Washington, but the checks were traced by the FBI in a routine investigation to Barker's Miami bank account. (Barker also cashed a $25,000 check from GOP fund-raiser Kenneth Dahlberg.)

Watergate prosecutor Earl Silbert received word from the FBI June 22, 1972 that Barker's account contained Nixon re-election committee checks.

July 23, 1972: Silbert revealed the link between Barker and the committee at Barker's bond hearing.

A

B

C

D

E

F

G

A July 10, 1972: FBI agents interviewed Ogarrio who revealed the Houston source.

'73 Nixon talks with Dean admitted. The White House acknowledged June 4 that President Nixon had conferred a number of times early in 1973 with his then-counsel John W. Dean 3rd about the Watergate investigation. The acknowledgment was made in response to reports **B** in the Washington Post and the New York Times June 3 that Dean had told federal and Senate Watergate investigators of the meetings.

The Times report, attributing "sources close to Mr. Dean," said Dean had told Samuel Dash, chief counsel for the Senate select committee investigating the Watergate case, that he met alone and in small groups with Nixon more than 40 times between late January and early April and **C** that Nixon showed a "great interest" in ascertaining "things were handled right—taken care of"—with respect to the Watergate investigation. Dean also contended, according to the report, that he could provide first-hand information indicating the President had a "substantial knowledge" of the activities of high White House officials regarding the Watergate investigation. Dean reportedly told Dash he had met only 10 times with Nixon between July 1970 when he joined the White **D** House staff and early 1973.

The Post report, from "reliable sources," said Dean told Senate and federal investigators he had discussed aspects of the Watergate cover-up with Nixon or in Nixon's presence on at least 35 occasions between January and April. Former top Nixon aides H. R. Haldeman and John D. Ehrlichman were said to have been present at many of the meetings.

E The immediate White House reaction to the Times and Post reports was a denial, carried by both papers the same day. Both reports, the White House statement said, "appear to be part of a careful, coordinated strategy by an individual or individuals determined to prosecute a case against the President in the press using innuendo, distortion of fact and outright falsehood. This manipulation of the press involves an unprecedented assault on judicial and administrative due process. Its **F** objective, stated in the simplest terms, is to destroy the President. We categorically deny the assertions and implications" of the stories.

The statement quoted Nixon's May 22 statement that he "took no part in, nor was I aware of, any subsequent efforts that may have been made to cover up Watergate. At no time did I authorize any offer of executive clemency for the Watergate defendants, nor did I know of any **G** such offer."

The Post article said Dean told the investigators of a conversation he had with Nixon just prior to the sentencing of the Watergate defendants in March 1972. According to the report: Nixon asked the cost of buying their continued silence, Dean said about $1 million and Nixon said that would be no problem. In an Easter call a little later in March, when Nixon told Dean "You're still my counsel," the story continued, Dean said Nixon also told him at that time he had been "kidding" when he asked about the cost of buying silence of the conspirators.

(In an interview in the June 4 Time magazine, Dean called Nixon's May 22 statement a "public relations" document and said "some of it was not quite accurate" and "some of it was not accurate at all.")

In acknowledging the Nixon-Dean talks in early 1973, Deputy White House Press Secretary Gerald L. Warren said June 4 "obviously there were topics of interest this year that would have involved the office of counsel." He said the topics included Nixon's own investigation of Watergate, policy on executive privilege and Senate hearings on the nomination of L. Patrick Gray 3rd to be FBI director.

Warren specified, however, that White House logs recording the time and place of the Nixon-Dean conferences would not be released either to the federal or Senate Watergate investigators. "That would be Constitutionally inappropriate," he said. In answer to reporters' questions, he said the proscription was based on "the basic doctrine of separation of powers." He also said "the President's logs are not subject to subpoena."

This conflicted with statements from Attorney General Elliot L. Richardson and special prosecutor Archibald Cox June 4. Cox said he had been assured of access to all White House papers relating to Watergate and "if there is any waffling on it, I intend to make the waffling plain."

Richardson said at a news conference if Cox considered the logs necessary he should subpoena them.

The White House position was revised June 5 in a "speech of contrition" by Warren, who said he had only been authorized to say "that Presidential logs of visitors and phone calls are considered to be presidential papers and as such their production cannot be required under subpoena." He "did not intend to state" what information "would or would not be made available," Warren said. That was a question for the President's counsel, he said, and was "a matter of concern which I am sure the counsel's office will undertake with Professor Cox."

In the future, Warren said, Watergate questions would be handled by White House attorneys either at the news briefing or on a delayed basis after written submission.

Senate Watergate committee counsel Dash said later June 5 the committee would request the White House logs.

Cox's request denied. The Senate Watergate committee rejected June 5 a request from special prosecutor Archibald Cox to delay its public hearings until further resolution of the "enormously complex" federal case.

Chairman Sam J. Ervin Jr. (D, N.C.) said the committee voted unanimously to continue the hearings in light of three considerations: (1) the panel was authorized by the Senate to conduct the probe and had no authority to postpone it; (2) the committee did not agree that the courts would "permit guilty parties to go unwhipped of justice" because of the hearings; and (3) there was more likelihood of a "fair trial in an atmosphere of judicial calm" after the hearings than before its probe was done.

Accelerated hearings also rejected—The Ervin committee also rejected June 5 proposals from two of its members to speed up the hearings and immediately call high-level witnesses to determine as soon as possible President Nixon's role in the Watergate affair.

The proposals were made by Sens. Herman E. Talmadge (D, Ga.) and Edward J. Gurney (R, Fla.). Gurney had said May 31 the committee should move "faster and more decisively" on the question of Nixon's role. He said the pace of the Senate probe, built on an ascending ladder of responsibility to develop background for the crucial testimony, had interferred with "the conduct of the presidency."

Talmadge had advocated May 25 bringing "the principals" before the committee at the earliest possible date to "remove the cloud of uncertainty that hangs over the country."

The Cox argument—In requesting the delay in a letter to the committee June 4, Cox argued that "the continuation of hearings at this time would create grave danger that the full facts about the Watergate case and related matters will never come to light and that many of those who are guilty of serious wrongdoing will never be brought to justice."

He was not suggesting that the hearings be called off, Cox said, but that he be given time—one to three months—"to assess this enormously complex case and to advise the select committee about the consequences of the appearance of particular witnesses at televised hearings." He was of the opinion that public hearings prior to further development of the federal probe would impede the probe and "increase the risk" that major guilty parties, "quite possibly all" of them, would go unpunished.

"Both the Senate committee and the special prosecutor," Cox said, "should preserve, for the present, freedom to bring out at one time and in a comprehensive presentation, all the facts concerning the President." He cautioned, "Even the most careful public hearing may injure the innocent."

At a news session June 4, Cox said he never "seriously considered" seeking a delay by court action.

In his letter and at the news conference, Cox stressed that the federal investigation was "not undertaken with adequate resources, material and numbers of people." The subsidiary probes in particular, he said, required more extensive activity. These included alleged and real political sabotage and campaign funding irregularities and break-ins undergoing investigation currently in Florida, Texas and California.

Immediate committee reaction—Ervin immediately opposed Cox's request. "For all practical intentions and purposes," Ervin said June 4, such a delay would "put the committee out of business." The government had been investigating the case for almost a year, he pointed out, while Watergate cast a "dark cloud" over the nation and the "government has come to a virtual standstill."

The public was "entitled to know the truth without further delay," Ervin said, and "to have their government resume its operations in a manner to promote their interest."

Immediate support for Ervin's position was expressed June 4 by committee members Talmadge, Joseph M. Montoya (D, N.M.) and Lowell P. Weicker Jr. (R, Conn.). "It seems to me," Talmadge remarked, "that Mr. Cox would be well advised to carry out his responsibilities without advising the Senate how to carry out theirs."

Senate hearings resume. The televised Watergate hearings by the Senate Select Committee on Presidential Campaign Activities were resumed June 5-7 in the Senate Caucus Room.

The major witnesses were Robert Reisner, administrative assistant during the 1972 Nixon campaign to Jeb Stuart Magruder, who was deputy director of the Nixon re-election committee; Hugh W. Sloan Jr., the committee's treasurer; and Herbert L. Porter, campaign scheduling director.

Day-by-Day Testimony

June 5: *Mitchell got wiretap data*—The committee heard testimony that reports on political information gleaned from illegal wiretaps were regularly sent to former Attorney General John N. Mitchell and the White House, and that politically sensitive material in the files of the Nixon campaign committee was destroyed after the Watergate break-in.

Testimony also revealed a meeting in the White House in early February 1972 of Mitchell, then-White House counsel John W. Dean 3rd, Jeb Stuart Magruder, deputy director of the Nixon committee, and G. Gordon Liddy, a former White House and Nixon committee aide later convicted in the Watergate conspiracy. The committee was told that Magruder, who was Mitchell's assistant at the Nixon committee when Mitchell was head of the campaign, passed word to Liddy at one point, probably in March 1972, that "it was arranged."

The testimony came from Robert A. F. Reisner, at that time Magruder's admin-

istrative assistant. His testimony was the first given publicly and under oath linking Mitchell to data from the illegal wiretaps at the Democratic national headquarters at the Watergate building. The wiretaps had been installed in May 1972 prior to the second break-in there June 17, 1972, when five of the conspirators were apprehended.

Reisner testified he had seen, a week or two prior to the aborted break-in, reports marked "Gemstone," the code word for material obtained from the wiretaps and other political spying activity of the committee. He said Magruder one time handed him a Gemstone document "in such a way that it was indicated to me very clearly that it was not for me to observe." He was instructed to put the document in files Magruder maintained for his daily meetings with Mitchell, Reisner said. And he testified that as each document was sent to Mitchell through him, a duplicate copy of that document was sent to the office of John D. Ehrlichman, then chief Nixon domestic adviser.

The day of the Watergate break-in, Reisner testified, Magruder, who was in California, ordered him by telephone to remove the Gemstone file, which Magruder termed "sensitive" material, from the office over that weekend. Subsequently, Reisner said, he asked Magruder what the Gemstone file was and, he said, Magruder replied, " 'I don't know what it is either. Forget about it, though. It's gone.' "

Much or all of the "sensitive" material in the files was destroyed after the break-in, Reisner testified. Magruder ordered him to go through the files "and centralize sensitive materials," he said, and "some of those were subsequently destroyed."

Ervin questioned him about what was actually "centralized." Reisner said: "Virtually everything. Well, I think Mr. Magruder's secretary and I looked through his own files. I think other people on the committee did similar things and virtually anything that concerned the opposition, contenders, that sort of thing, that would have been awkward or politically damaging to—well, no, even broader than that. Anything that would have concerned the opposition."

This apparently would have included material marked "Sedan Chair 2," which Reisner identified as that dealing with information from the Democratic presidential campaign of Sen. Hubert H. Humphrey. The information was bought by the committee, Reisner said, at the rate of $1,000 a month, he believed, probably from a "disgruntled" Humphrey worker.

After he was slated to testify before the committee, Reisner disclosed, Magruder had tried repeatedly "to get together with him." He called him four times March 30, Reisner said, but he told Magruder he presumed he was being subpoenaed before the committee "to discuss Mr. Ma-

gruder" and therefore he did not think it appropriate to meet. During one of the calls, after Reisner failed to appear at a meeting with a third person, a lawyer, present, Magruder "was very agitated," Reisner recalled. "He felt he wanted to know what I thought I was doing . . . Then he said, 'I can't understand this.' He said, 'You know, are you not going to be cooperative? Are you not going—everyone else has been cooperative,' or something to that effect."

"Did he tell you at that time that you should be careful about what you said because people's lives and futures were at stake?" Ervin asked.

"Yes, sir, he did," Reisner replied.

Reisner said Magruder later called and apologized. He "said that he was upset, that he was sorry if he was overly anxious," Reisner told the committee. "He said he just wanted me to realize that there were some extremely serious matters concerned here and that I should treat them in that way."

Reisner testified he also received similar phone calls after March 30 from two other persons who wanted to get together with him. These calls came from Gordon Strachan, then assistant to H. R. Haldeman, Nixon's chief of staff, and Herbert L. Porter, then scheduling director for the Nixon committee. Reisner said he did not meet with them.

In other disclosures, Reisner said:

■ Magruder was instructed at one point "to get counter-demonstrators" for a demonstration Reisner thought was on Capitol Hill, the instruction coming from Charles W. Colson, then special counsel to the President.

■ He had not been approached by either FBI personnel or federal prosecutors until after the Senate committee had subpoenaed him.

Liddy's secretary testifies—Liddy's secretary at the time of the Watergate break-in, Sally J. Harmony, testified she typed memoranda, mostly dictated by Liddy, for Gemstone. On several occasions she transcribed directly from logs of conversations delivered to her directly from the secret listening post by James W. McCord Jr., another convicted conspirator.

She recalled little of substance for the committee. She did recall seeing some photographs of documents with Democratic National Chairman Lawrence F. O'Brien's name on them.

"Was there anything unusual about the photograph that you can remember?" she was asked.

"Yes, sir. They were being held by fingers."

"Fingers?"

"Yes, sir. I guess at this point they would have been fingers of rubber gloves."

She also recalled making a fake entry pass to the headquarters of Democratic presidential contender George McGovern

A and shredding her shorthand notebooks, at Liddy's request, after the break-in.

After Watergate, and after Magruder had moved to the Commerce Department and was aware "I was going to talk with the [Capitol] Hill people," Mrs. Harmony told the committee, in reference to her scheduled testimony, Magruder called her and "indicated to me he had talked with Mr. Mitchell and assured Mr. Mitchell. . . . He said, " 'I have indicated

B to Mr. Mitchell that he has no reason to be concerned about any of your testimony.' "

June 6: *Spy fund cover-up tried*—Hugh W. Sloan Jr., former treasurer of the Committee to Re-elect the President, testified that a persistent effort was made by top Nixon campaign officials to pressure him to cover up the large amount of cash payments made to the Watergate conspirators. He testified that he was put off when he attempted to warn high cam-

C ·paign and White House officials that something was seriously amiss at the GOP committee or possibly in the entire campaign. He also testified that John Mitchell was making decisions about campaign spending while he was attorney general months before he left to head the Nixon campaign on March 1, 1972.

Sloan said he handled about $1.8 million in cash disbursements for the Nixon campaign in the spring of 1972, but he did not know what the funds were used for since the policy decisions were made

D previously by others. And he told of the "nightmare" of handling millions of dollars in contributions in a vast, last-minute influx just prior to the effective date (April 7, 1972) of the new campaign finance reporting law. He said he received $5 million–$6 million in a two-day period.

Sloan used a chart to show the committee how the $1.8 million was disbursed. Among the items:

$250,000 to Herbert W. Kalmbach, President Nixon's former personal at-

E torney.

$350,000 to Gordon Strachan, assistant to former White House Chief of Staff Haldeman. The money went to the Nixon media committee.

Sloan's special problem at the Nixon committee involved G. Gordon Liddy, later convicted in the Watergate case. He

F said he gave Liddy $199,000 in cash in the spring of 1972. Liddy presented him with a budget of $250,000, Sloan said, with an initial request for $83,000 in cash. He checked the request with Nixon campaign finance chairman Maurice Stans, Sloan said, who told him, "I do not want to know and you do not want to know" what the money was for.

After the Watergate break-in, Sloan

G testified: About June 21 or 22, 1972, he spoke with Magruder about the funds Magruder had authorized for Liddy. "He indicated to me that we are going to have to [disclose to investigators] or suggested to me a figure of what I had given to Mr. Liddy in the range of, somewhere, $75,000

to $80,000." Sloan said he "did not know the precise amount of money that I had given to Mr. Liddy at that point. However, I did know that the sum was considerably larger than that because Mr. Magruder himself had authorized a payment for $83,000 in one single installment.

"I must have indicated to him, well, that just is not the right figure, I did not have the right figure, but that is too low. He indicated to me at that time that I said to him, he must have been insistent because I remember making to him on that occasion a statement I have no intention of perjuring myself."

Committee counsel Samuel Dash asked Sloan: "What did he say to you when you said that?"

Sloan responded: "He said you may have to."

Later that day, Sloan was approached by Frederick C. LaRue, a Mitchell campaign aide conducting an investigation of the Watergate matter for Mitchell. During their talk, Sloan was informed two FBI agents were waiting to talk to him. LaRue said he should see Mitchell first, and Sloan went, hoping to get some "guidance." "The campaign literally at this point was falling apart before your eyes, nobody was coming up with any answers as to what was really going on," Sloan said. "I had some very strong concerns about where all of this money had gone.

"I essentially asked for guidance, at which point he [Mitchell] told me, 'when the going gets tough the tough get going.' "

Sloan did not consider that "any particular helpful guidance at that point," but he saw the FBI agents, who asked him only about Alfred C. Baldwin 3rd, who had monitored the wiretaps at the Democratic headquarters, about whom Sloan knew nothing.

LaRue came to see him about the interview, and, "At that point he indicated to me that, and I do not have the precise words, the sense of the meaning as it came across to me, there was very brief reference something to the effect that the Liddy money is the problem, it is very politically sensitive, we can just not come out with a high figure, we are going to have to come out with a different figure. And I said, as I recall, I said, if there is a problem I cannot see that it makes any difference whether it is $200 or $200,000, at which point he dropped the conversation."

That night, Sloan attended a party along with several White House aides and arranged with them to meet the next day with Nixon's appointments aide Dwight C. Chapin and Ehrlichman.

With Chapin, Sloan said, "I believe probably the tone of the conversation was that there is a tremendous problem there, something has to be done. Mr. Chapin evaluated my condition at that point as being somewhat overwrought and suggested a vacation, which in fact, I was

planning to leave on the next week. It had been planned for a long time. He suggested that the important thing is that the President be protected.

"In the Ehrlichman meeting, . . . I believe I expressed my concern, my personal concern with regard to the money. I believe he interpreted my being there as personal fear and he indicated to me that I had a special relationship with the White House, if I needed help getting a lawyer, he would be glad to do that, but 'do not tell me any details; I do not want to know. My position would have to be until after the election that I would have to take executive privilege.' "

After his vacation, Sloan met July 5, 1972 with Magruder, who told him " 'we have to resolve this Liddy matter. We have to agree on a figure.' " "This time," Sloan testified, "the figure was even less than the time before. It was $40,000 or $45,000."

Sloan told him "if I am asked point blank, did Mr. Liddy ever receive $45,000, of course, I will say yes. But, I said, I will not stop there. If I am asked more than that, I will also say yes. If he asks what the total figure is, I will tell him to the best of my knowledge."

Sloan said, he met July 13 with LaRue, who suggested "that I ought to think perhaps about taking the Fifth Amendment."

Sloan said he intended neither to invoke the Fifth Amendment nor perjure himself. At that point, he thought it best, "in the interest of everybody under those circumstances," for him to resign his post.

The committee also heard testimony, first from Sloan and then first-hand from his attorney, James T. Treese, that White House counsel Dean had called him in October 1972 and urged Sloan to take the Fifth Amendment during his scheduled appearance at the Florida trial of Watergate conspirator Bernard Barker, who was accused of falsely notarizing a Nixon campaign check. Treese, who took the call, reported it this way: Dean said Sloan "could be a real hero around here if he took the Fifth. And I said, 'John, relax ... Hugh Sloan is not going to take the Fifth Amendment.' "

Queries concerning federal probe—The committee asked questions about the conduct of the original federal Watergate probe.

Sen. Howard H. Baker Jr. (R, Tenn.) was curious about Sloan's FBI interrogation, and why it was limited to queries concerning Baldwin.

Q. No one asked you about the Watergate break-in in the course of that FBI interview?

A. No, sir. It was never mentioned.

Q. Nobody ever asked you about Mr. Liddy?

A. No sir.

Q. And no one asked you about $100 bills that were found with or on the defendants that were involved in the break-in or illegal entry into Democratic national headquarters?

A. No, sir.

Chief counsel Samuel Dash asked Sloan if his testimony before the grand jury in July 1972 was principally based on what he had testified before the committee. It was, Sloan said. "And did it focus on the efforts of Mr. Magruder to ask you to agree on a term of money that was given to Mr. Liddy and indeed to commit perjury?" "Yes. I would say approximately half of my grand jury testimony related to Mr. Magruder's approaches to me," Sloan replied.

June 7: *False story told at trial—* Herbert L. Porter, then scheduling director of the Nixon campaign committee, testified that he had committed perjury in his 1972 testimony before the Watergate grand jury and at the Watergate trial in January on the funds paid Liddy. Porter admitted that he lied under oath about Watergate out of "a deep sense of loyalty" to President Nixon and because of "the fear of group pressure that would ensue from not being a team player."

Porter said "at no time did I ever have any intention of covering up a criminal act. At no time did I knowingly engage in any cover-up of the Watergate burglary." He said he had "no prior knowledge" of the break-in, "and up to this very moment I have no knowledge of the involvement of others."

He told the committee this story:

On June 28 or 29, 1972, he met with Magruder, who told him "that he had just come from a meeting with Mr. Mitchell, Mr. LaRue, himself, and a fourth party whose name I cannot remember, where my name had been brought up as someone who could be—what was the term he used—counted on in a pinch or a team player or words to that effect.

"He said that I believe at that time Mr. Liddy had been fired from the campaign. He said it was apparent, was the word he used, that Mr. Liddy and others had on their own illegally participated in the break-in of the Watergate Democratic National Committee, and Mr. Magruder swore to me that neither he nor anybody higher than Mr. Liddy in the campaign organization or at the White House had any involvement whatsoever in Watergate, at the Watergate break-in, and reinforced that by saying, 'Doesn't that sound like something stupid that Gordon would do?' And you have to know Mr. Liddy. I agreed with that.

"He said, 'I want to assure you now that no one did.' He said, however, he said, 'There is a problem with some of the money.' He said, 'Now, Gordon was authorized money for some dirty tricks, nothing illegal,' he said, but nonetheless, 'things that could be very embarrassing to the President of the United States and to Mr. Mitchell and Mr. Haldeman and others. Now, your name was brought up as someone who we can count on to help in this situation.' And I asked what is it you are asking me to do, and he said, 'Would you corroborate a story that the money was authorized for something a little bit more legitimate-sounding than dirty tricks. Even though the dirty tricks were legal, it still would be very embarrassing.'

"... You were in charge of the surrogate campaign, you were very concerned about radical elements disrupting rallies and so forth, and I said yes, and he said suppose that we had authorized Liddy, instead of the dirty tricks, we had authorized him to infiltrate some of these radical groups?

"He said, how could such a program have cost a hundred thousand? And I thought very quickly of a conversation I had with a young man in California in December, as a matter of fact, and I said, Jeb, that is very easy. You could get 10 college-age students or 24- or 25-year-old students, people, over a period of 10 months. Mr. Magruder had prefaced his remark by saying from December on. And I said, you can pay them $1,000 a month, which they would take their expenses out of that, and I said that is $100,000. I said that is not very much for a $45 million campaign. And he said, now that is right.

"He said, would you be willing, if I made that statement to the FBI, would you be willing to corroborate that when I came to you in December and asked you how much it would cost, and that is what you said? That was the net effect, the net of his question. I thought for a moment and I said, yes, I probably would do that. I don't remember saying yes, but I am sure I gave Mr. Magruder the impression I would probably do that and that was the end of the conversation."

Q. Later, did you tell the FBI what Mr. Magruder asked you to tell them?

A. Yes, sir, I did.

Q. What did you tell the federal grand jury?

A. The same thing.

Q. Were you a witness at the trial of the seven defendants who were indicted in the Watergate case?

A. Yes, sir.

Q. And did you give the same account?

A. Yes sir, I did.

Q. Did Mr. Magruder ask you to make any other statements which you knew to be false?

A. Yes, sir, he did. Shortly after that, he asked me to, if I would increase the amount of money that I was going to say that I gave to Mr. Liddy, and I said, no, I would not do that. He said, why not?

I said, because I just absolutely, I did not give him that amount of money and I will not say I gave him that amount of money.

I said, the conversation that you are asking me to relate, I can conceive of it happening because I would have told you that in December if you had asked me. And that is a strange answer, but that is the answer I gave him. And I would not increase the amount of money. He wanted me to say that I gave Mr. Liddy $75,000, when in fact, I had given him some $30,000 to $35,000—$32,000.

On April 11, Porter continued, Magruder advised him to contact a lawyer and tell the federal prosecutor "what you know." In a chance encounter three days later, Porter said, Magruder told him, "He had just come from a meeting at the White House and that it is all over, he said, and I said, what do you mean, it is all over? He said, it is all over, the President has directed everybody to tell the truth. Those were his exact words. He said I had a meeting with Mr. Ehrlichman and I told him the whole story and, boy, was he really shocked, words to that effect."

Magruder told him then that Mitchell "was going to deny complicity until the end," Porter said.

He was questioned, as was Sloan, about his interrogation by federal authorities. "Did any of the prosecutors ever ask you if Magruder had tried to get you to perjure yourself?"

"No, sir," Porter responded.

Sen. Baker probed his motivation, flaring angrily at one point to contest the witness's presumption of longer acquaintance with Nixon.

Q. At any time, did you ever think of saying, I do not think this is quite right, this is not quite the way it ought to be? Did you ever think of that?

A. Yes, I did.

Q. What did you do about it?

A. I did not do anything.

Q. Why didn't you?

A. In all honesty, probably because of the fear of group pressure that would ensue, of not being a team player.

Q. What caused you to abdicate your own conscience and disapproval, if you did disapprove, of the practices or dirty tricks operation?

A. Well, Sen. Baker, my loyalty to this man, Richard Nixon, goes back longer than any person that you will see sitting at this table throughout any of these hearings. I first met the President—

Q. I really very much doubt that, Mr. Porter. I have known Richard Nixon probably longer than you have been alive, and I really expect that the greatest disservice that a man could do to a President of the United States would be to abdicate his conscience.

A. I understand, Senator. I first met Mr. Nixon when I was 8 years old in 1946.... My family worked for him.... I felt as if I had known this man all my life—not personally, perhaps, but in spirit. I felt a deep sense of loyalty to him. I was appealed to on this basis....

Q. What would you do now [if you were in such a situation]?

A. I would not become involved in any way, shape or form.

Q. What brought about the change? Where is this real emergence of human instinct for decency in politics?

A. ... In my own personal case it has devastated me personally and that is reason enough for me never to do it again.

Ehrlichman ties Mitchell to bugging. Former Attorney General John N. Mitchell personally chose three sites for electronic bugging in the 1972 presidential campaign, John D. Ehrlichman, former presidential domestic affairs adviser, said in a deposition in the $6.4 million civil suit filed by the Democratic party against the Committee to Re-elect the President.

The deposition, given in private May 22-24, was released June 5.

The information given by Ehrlichman was obtained for the most part from Jeb Stuart Magruder, Mitchell's assistant at the Nixon re-election committee, and former presidential counsel John W. Dean 3rd. As such the testimony was hearsay. Ehrlichman said the President had asked him to conduct an investigation March 30 after Dean had failed to provide a wrïtten report of his own investigation into Watergate. Ehrlichman said the President expressed suspicion that Dean was "in the thing [the cover-up] up to his eyebrows."

In his deposition, Ehrlichman spoke of three meetings, held January–March 1972 during which proposals for an intelligence and information facility were discussed. Attending the meetings were Mitchell, Dean, Magruder, and G. Gordon Liddy, later convicted in the Watergate break-in.

Ehrlichman said Magruder told him that at the first two meetings Liddy presented plans that were rejected as too grandiose and extreme. A third plan was finally accepted, with Mitchell giving oral approval to the bugging operation.

Ehrlichman reported Dean as saying Mitchell had approved the plans in writing "by circling or checking" three targets for bugging from a list.

The three sites were the Democratic national headquarters in the Watergate complex, the Fontainebleau Hotel in Miami Beach during the Democratic convention, and the Washington headquarters of Sen. George McGovern (D, S.D.).

Ehrlichman testified that the second Watergate break-in resulted from Liddy's initiative rather than on orders from anyone high in the Nixon re-election committee. Ehrlichman said Mitchell had been furious that a bug placed on Democratic National Chairman Lawrence F. O'Brien had failed to produce satisfactory results.

In response to Mitchell's criticism, Liddy initiated a second entry into Watergate, at which time the burglars were caught.

Ehrlichman also revealed that his former assistant, John J. Caulfield, came to him in 1971 with a proposal for a private intelligence unit to be contracted for by the Nixon re-election committee. "I gave him this prospectus back and sent him on his way," Ehrlichman testified.

Other points made by Ehrlichman in his deposition:

Magruder told Ehrlichman that Liddy had threatened his life in March 1972. Magruder, who spoke of deteriorating relations with Liddy, wanted to fire Liddy; instead Liddy was transferred to the Finance Committee to Re-elect the President.

Ehrlichman said that during the course of his investigation of a Watergate cover-up he was told Magruder would testify that plans for Watergate would "reach" the President. Magruder would testify he had been told by Gordon Strachan, a former Haldeman aide, "the President wants this project to go on." (Magruder's lawyer James Bierbower June 5 denied that Magruder would implicate the President in any testimony he would give. Strachan issued a similar denial.)

Ehrlichman said Magruder had been told by former Special White House Counsel Charles W. Colson that the Nixon campaign needed information on O'Brien. Magruder said Colson had at no time mentioned illegal intelligence gathering methods.

Nixon's concern over Watergate. Before and after his re-election, President Nixon expressed concern about the Watergate affair, his former chief of staff, H. R. Haldeman, testified May 22, 24 and 25. Prior to the election, Nixon feared the effect Watergate might have on his campaign; afterward, he wanted the matter cleared up so that it would not "be hanging over into the second term," Haldeman said.

The information came from a deposition given by Haldeman in the $6.4 million suit filed by the Democratic party against the Committee to Re-elect the President. The testimony was released June 6.

Haldeman's testimony generally complemented the deposition given by Nixon's former domestic affairs adviser, John D. Ehrlichman. [See above]

On one point, however, it contrasted with Ehrlichman's testimony over the role played by John N. Mitchell, former attorney general and chief of the Nixon re-election campaign, in the Watergate bugging. Haldeman was aware of only two meetings attended by Mitchell in which the bugging of Watergate was discussed. Ehrlichman had mentioned a third meeting.

Haldeman revealed a March 28 meeting he held with Mitchell at the White House. Mitchell told of a conversation he had with Jeb Stuart Magruder, deputy Nixon campaign director, in which the latter related that pressure on him had been applied by Special Counsel to the President Charles W. Colson for the gathering of intelligence on the Democrats.

Colson called Magruder while Watergate conspirators G. Gordon Liddy and E. Howard Hunt Jr. sat in his office. Colson told Magruder the two had an intelligence gathering plan that merited study. (Haldeman noted Colson later said he was not aware the Liddy-Hunt plan involved anything illegal. They had come at the end of the day, at a time when Colson had felt rushed.)

In response to the pressure by Colson, Magruder launched the Liddy-Hunt plan. Mitchell told Haldeman the Watergate bugging was conducted with the full knowledge and approval of Magruder.

Haldeman was also asked to testify about a $350,000 fund he controlled, part of which federal investigators said went to the Watergate conspirators in return for their silence. Haldeman declined to say what the money was used for except that $22,000 went for advertising unrelated to Watergate.

Other points made by Haldeman:

President Nixon did not request a formal investigation of Watergate until March 22. Prior to that time Nixon addressed questions regarding Watergate to Haldeman and Ehrlichman, who in turn passed them to White House Counsel John W. Dean 3rd. Haldeman said Dean maintained until that time no White House personnel had been involved in Watergate. Dean claimed he was unable to establish the connection between Watergate and the Nixon re-election committee because of conflicting evidence and testimony. Dean was taken off the Watergate matter and Ehrlichman assigned March 30 after Dean failed to produce satisfactory explanations for Watergate, Haldeman said.

Haldeman admitted being present at an April 15 meeting in which former Acting Federal Bureau of Investigation Director L. Patrick Gray 3rd told Ehrlichman he had destroyed "politically sensitive" documents found in the White House safe of E. Howard Hunt. He added that Dean assured him he had not told Gray to destroy the documents.

Anti-Wallace drive used Nazi canvassers. The Washington Post reported June 6 that the Nixon re-election committee had spent $10,000 to deter Gov. George Wallace's (D. Ala.) presidential race in California as an American Independent party (AIP) candidate in 1971.

The plan included the use of American Nazi stormtroopers (who were paid $1,200), dressed in civilian clothes, to convince AIP members to change their party registration. If the Wallace party was denied a spot on the California ballot because of its inability to list sufficient voters, the re-election committee reasoned, those voters could be diverted to Nixon. He had failed to carry the state in 1960 and lost the gubernatorial race in 1962.

The plan failed for a number of reasons, including the fact that a political party automatically qualified under state law for a ballot position if it had received more than 2% of the vote in the previous gubernatorial election—which AIP had done.

The plan became public knowledge through the Senate testimony June 6 of

Hugh W. Sloan, Jr., former treasurer of the Finance Committee to Re-elect the President. Sloan told the Ervin committee that $10,000 had been given to California Republican Lyn Nofziger in late 1971.

Nofziger, presently campaign director for the 1974 gubernatorial campaign of Lt. Gov. Ed Reinecke, acknowledged receiving the cash, which he said had been authorized by then deputy campaign director Jeb Stuart Magruder.

Nofziger said Robert Walters, a California advertising man, had initiated the plan. According to Walters' former aide, Glenn Parker, he had met with then Attorney General John N. Mitchell, Magruder and others in October 1971 in Los Angeles and Mitchell "had started the conversation" about the AIP registration drive.

Mitchell indicated that a poll showed that they were "in trouble" and that Nixon "especially wanted to win California," Parker said.

Funds manipulated for Agnew. Federal and Maryland officials began investigations June 7 into the Maryland Republican party's failure to report a $50,000 cash loan from the Nixon re-election committee. The funds were used to inflate the proceeds of a May 19, 1972 testimonial dinner for Vice President Spiro T. Agnew.

Former Nixon finance committee treasurer Hugh W. Sloan Jr., had testified June 6 that he had given the money in $100 bills, to Alexander M. Lankler Jr., Maryland GOP chairman, after April 7, 1972 and that the transaction had been authorized by finance committee chairman Maurice H. Stans.

Official state financial records originally had listed 31 individuals who were reported to have contributed the money. But the Maryland records were amended June 1 to show that the actual source of funds had been the Finance Committee to Re-elect the President.

The finance committee had filed its quarterly statement with the General Accounting Office (GAO), which released the figures June 11. According to the report, Lankler had delivered a $150,000 contribution from an unidentified Maryland resident to the finance committee in March 1972 and "had exacted a commitment ... that $50,000 of these funds would be transferred" back to Maryland for use in the presidential campaign.

The $50,000 loan was returned to Stans' committee July 26, 1972 with an additional $25,000 raised at the Agnew testimonial. The money was reported to the GAO at that time, although the initial $150,000 and subsequent loan were never reported because, the committee claimed, the money was collected and its disbursement was pledged before the April 7, 1972 reporting deadline occurred.

Lankler admitted June 6 that efforts at concealing the money were "stupid" but he defended the political strategy behind the decision. "It was political puffery to make it [the Agnew event] look as good as possible . . . We hadn't sold the house out. We knew the press would look at the success of the affair. Don't forget, Agnew was not yet on the ticket. We were anxious to make Agnew look as good as possible," Lankler explained.

Nixon knew of illegalities of 1970 plan. President Nixon in 1970 approved a plan for expanded intelligence gathering operations with the knowledge that certain aspects of it were clearly illegal, the New York Times reported June 7.

In his May 22 statement on the Watergate affair, President Nixon had acknowledged establishment of an interagency committee for better intelligence operations. However, he said, the committee was scrapped after Federal Bureau of Investigation (FBI) Director J. Edgar Hoover voiced opposition.

According to the Times, the plan approved by Nixon involved "serious risks" to his Administration if revealed. As a result the program was approved by him through presidential Chief of Staff H. R. Haldeman after Tom Charles Huston, then a staff assistant to Nixon, told Haldeman: "We don't want the President linked to this thing with his signature on paper . . . [because] all hell would break loose if this thing leaked out."

The Times obtained three memoranda written by Huston: one dealt with recommendations to the President by the Interagency Committee on Intelligence; a second recommended means to overcome Hoover's opposition; and the third was a presidential directive, written by Huston, that the plans be implemented.

These memoranda were among the documents given to Watergate Judge John J. Sirica by former White House Counsel John W. Dean 3rd.

The memo of recommendations contained among its proposals suggestions for relaxation of restrictions on the "surreptitious entry of facilities occupied by subversive elements." "This technique would be particularly helpful if used against the Weathermen and Black Panthers." "Use of this technique is clearly illegal: it amounts to burglary. It is highly risky and could result in great embarrassment if exposed."

Another committee proposal was that "present restrictions on covert [mail] coverage should be relaxed on selected targets of priority foreign intelligence and internal security interest. . . . Covert coverage is illegal and there are serious risks involved. However, the advantages to be derived from its use outweigh the risks."

"Covert coverage" involved the opening and examination of mail before delivery.

The Huston memo noted that Hoover opposed even the legal monitoring of mail, which involved recording sender and addressee without breaking any seals. Hoover's concern was said to stem from opposition by "civil liberty people."

Other recommendations by the committee as reflected in the Huston memo:

- Permission for the National Security Agency (NSA) to monitor "the communications of U.S. citizens using international facilities. [telephone and telegraph circuits.]"

- "Intensification of coverage of individuals and groups in the U.S. who pose a major threat to internal security." The memo said in connection with this that everyone on the committee except Hoover felt that "existing coverage is grossly inadequate." The Hoover statement that the FBI would not stand in the way of any other agency seeking approval for electronic surveillance was "gratuitous," as only the FBI possessed the necessary capability, the memo said.

- An increase in the number of campus operatives to "forestall widespread" violence. Huston called campuses "the battleground of the revolutionary protest movement." The memo noted the FBI's refusal to employ campus intelligence sources younger than 21 years old for fear of risk of exposure. Committee consensus—with Hoover objecting—was that risk of exposure was minimal and that it was a price to be paid for effective campus coverage.

The second Huston memo dealt with ways to overcome Hoover's objections to the intelligence plan. He said Hoover's objections were twofold: current operations were satisfactory and "no one has any business commenting on procedures he [Hoover] has established for the collection of intelligence by the FBI." According to Huston, Hoover stood alone among committee members in his objections, which the presidential aide labeled "inconsistent and frivolous—most express concern about possible embarrassment to the intelligence community (i.e. Hoover) from public disclosure of clandestine operations."

Huston offered several suggestions to the President as means of overcoming Hoover's opposition. The President should call Hoover into his office for a "stroking session," in which the President would explain his decision to Hoover, thank him for his past cooperation, and indicate he was counting on Hoover for continuing help. Afterwards, the entire committee should be called in and an official photo, to be autographed by the President, should be taken. Later an official memorandum outlining the plan should be distributed to those involved.

Huston concluded that he was certain that Hoover would accede to Nixon's wishes, and the President should not be reluctant to override the director. "Mr. Hoover is set in his ways and can be as bull-headed as hell, but he is a loyal trooper. Twenty years ago he would never have raised the kind of objections he has here, but he's getting old and worried

A

B

C

D

E

F

G

about his legend. . . . he'll respond to direction by the President."

On July 15, 1970 Huston sent the third memo to Hoover, Central Intelligence Agency (CIA) Director Richard Helms, Defense Intelligence Agency (DIA) Director Gen. Donald V. Bennett, and NSA Director Adm. Noel Gayler, informing them that the President had carefully studied the committee's recommendations and agreed to their full implementation.

The Times reported that when Hoover received this memo "he went through the roof." Hoover had assumed that when the President saw a number of footnotes he had attached to the original recommendations, in which he voiced his objections, the President would not approve the plan.

A Times source who participated in the report's preparation said Hoover made no principled objections to the plan; instead his opposition stemmed from the issue of "whether he was going to be able to run the FBI any way he wanted to run it."

President Nixon rescinded his approval of the plan July 28, 1970, five days after Hoover received the memo approving it.

According to the Times, Huston made one more attempt to get his plan past Hoover by composing another memorandum which he sent Aug. 5, 1970. The plan was not revived.

Vesco extradition sought. Ambassador Viron P. Vaky, acting for the State Department, June 9 asked Costa Rican authorities to extradite U.S. investment financier Robert L. Vesco, who was under indictment in New York for making an illegal contribution to President Nixon's re-election campaign. Vesco, however, was believed to have left Costa Rica for the Bahamas, where he also maintained extensive business operations.

The money was drawn on the account of an investment business then owned by Vesco, International Controls Corp. (ICC), and constituted a violation of federal laws which barred corporate contributions to candidates for federal office.

The disclosure resulted from a civil suit filed against Vesco by the court-appointed directors of ICC.

The New York Times had reported May 12 that Vesco was seeking total immunity from the criminal charges in return for testifying against former Attorney General John N. Mitchell and former Commerce Secretary Maurice Stans, accused of influence peddling on Vesco's behalf upon receipt of a $200,000 Nixon re-election campaign contribution.

Vesco had told newsmen in San Jose, Costa Rica May 23 that he had a "sworn statement on the Watergate case which is being held in safekeeping" and demanded "absolute impartiality" from special Watergate prosecutor Archibald Cox, before returning to the U.S. to face civil and criminal charges.

The Wall Street Journal reported June 8 that Vesco had donated $25,000 in five separate checks to Nixon's 1968 presidential race.

Poll shows GOP losses. A Gallup poll taken April 6-9 and May 4-7 reported that Republicans could lose as many as 40 seats in the House in the 1974 Congressional elections, partly because of the Watergate scandal, it was reported June 10.

The surveys indicated that if the elections were held immediately, Democrats would get 55% of the popular vote and Republicans 35%, with 10% undecided. 30% said they would be less likely to vote for a Republican candidate because of the Watergate affair.

The registered voters polled also viewed the Democrats as better able to deal with the nation's problems by a margin of 57%-43%.

Philippine donation revealed. A report by the Finance Committee to Re-elect the President, filed with the General Accounting Office (GAO) and made public June 11, revealed that an unidentified "Philippine national" had contributed $30,000 in cash to the Nixon re-election campaign June 9, 1972.

The committee held the money for a "brief time" while it obtained an opinion as to the legality of the contribution. During this time, finance committee chairman Maurice H. Stans was approached by President Nixon's personal attorney Herbert W. Kalmbach June 29, 1972. Kalmbach asked Stans to turn over to him "all possible cash funds" for an "urgent White House project not related to the campaign." The project, Kalmbach said, "had the approval of high authorities" he could not name, the re-election committee told the GAO.

Stans identified the donor in testimony before the Senate select committee investigating Watergate June 12. Ernesto Lagdameo, a former Philippine ambassador to the U.S., offered the contribution on behalf of himself and two business partners, Jesus Cobarrus Sr. and Eugenio Lopez Jr., both Filipinos, according to Stans. Lopez' brother is vice president of the Philippines.

Stans also told the committee that six-eight weeks ago, Kalmbach said former White House counsel John W. Dean 3rd had authorized the fund raising effort. Kalmbach claimed he had received assurances as to the legality of the secret transaction from former White House adviser John D. Ehrlichman, Stans said.

The $30,000 contribution and $45,000 left from a $50,000 personal expense fund made up the $75,000 in cash Stans gave Kalmbach. Kalmbach later told federal investigators that the total amount he had collected—at least $210,000—was used to pay cover-up money to Watergate conspirators.

The re-election committee returned the Philippine contribution after receiving a "negative" legal opinion; however, committee officials told the GAO that the donation actually could have been accepted because the Justice Department had ruled Feb. 7, 1973 that only those political contributions made "within" the U.S. by agents of foreign principals, such as corporations, were illegal.

Other re-election committee disclosures released by the GAO:

■ $4.8 million was reported as cash on hand.

■ Deputy Defense Secretary William P. Clements Jr., contributed $7,000 to the re-election committee between March 1 and May 31. He was identified as chairman of Sedco, Inc., of Dallas, a position he held until nominated for the Pentagon post by Nixon in December 1972.

■ Expenditures totaling $317,493 for legal fees were reported for the March-May quarter.

■ On the advice of counsel Robert C. Mardian, the committee turned over $81,-000 to campaign aide Frederick C. LaRue in July 1972 "in order to remove that amount from the campaign." The decision was made because $18,000 had been collected before April 7, 1972, when the new federal disclosure law took effect and $63,000 had been collected without sufficient identifying information. (The $63,000 amount included $50,000 from dairy lobbyist Frank Carroll. The remainder was contributed by Charles D. Saunders of Mississippi in June 1972, not reported to the GAO, and returned to Saunders; and by Harvey Roffman and Calvin Fisher of Oklahoma.)

■ Former Montana Gov. Tim Babcock delivered $25,000 to the committee Nov. 3, 1972 without identifying the donors. ($22,000 of that fund was turned over to Dean's office, at his request, by Stans, for the purpose of replenishing "a $350,000 White House fund for polling purposes.")

On Jan. 17, 1973, Babcock delivered an additional $14,000, which with the $3,000 left from the previous sum, was given to campaign aide LaRue. The re-election committee identified for the GAO five Montana contributors, including Babcock, as the source of the $39,000 deliveries.

■ Stans had been drawing a $60,000 annual salary from the postcampaign surplus, including retroactive pay to April 7, 1972 (awarded in April 1973). The salary was the same amount paid Cabinet officers. Stans, a former Commerce secretary, originally had intended to donate his services to the Nixon campaign.

When he was indicted on charges of influence peddling by a New York grand jury, Stans voluntarily took a $30,000 pay cut, the committee added.

Dean urged Hunt to flee the U.S. The New York Times reported June 7 that White House Counsel John W. Dean 3rd urged Watergate conspirator E. Howard Hunt Jr. to flee the country two days after the Watergate burglary.

The Times said this was part of testimony given by Colson to federal prosecutors.

Colson was reported to have been told by Dean that he was acting on orders from John D. Ehrlichman, then domestic affairs adviser to Nixon.

"I recall losing my temper and reacting very angrily," Colson told investigators. "I said something to the effect of 'That is the dumbest thing I have ever heard. You will have the White House party to a fugitive from justice charge.'"

Colson reported later being told by Dean, "that it was after I exploded that the order was rescinded."

Colson reiterates Nixon's innocence. Charles W. Colson, former special counsel to the President, told the New York Times June 9 he would stake his life on President Nixon's disclaimer of any knowledge of a cover-up of the Watergate affair.

Colson, who resigned his White House position in March, said he had warned the President Feb. 14 he must force former Attorney General John N. Mitchell to admit the role he played in planning the Watergate wiretaps.

Colson said that as late as March 21 the President did not believe Mitchell or any of his senior aides were guilty nor would he consent to making a scapegoat of Mitchell, an innocent man.

Colson said he told federal prosecutors that in early February he informed Chief of Staff H. R. Haldeman of his concern over possible perjury and obstruction of justice in the first Watergate trial in January. Payments by Nixon associates to the Watergate defendants could be construed as criminal "hush money." Haldeman's response, Colson said, was that he knew about the money and he was not concerned.

Colson said the main reason he had withheld his story from reporters was fear that Haldeman and former Nixon Domestic Affairs Adviser John D. Ehrlichman would frame him. "I've been scared to death to tell my story for fear that Haldeman and Ehrlichman will contrive a story against me, or for fear I'll be pitted one guy against another, or for fear I'll get myself dragged in, or I'll get a prosecutor mad at me, or that the grand jury will think I'm playing games."

Colson claimed he first expressed his suspicions of Mitchell's involvement to the President shortly after his inauguration in January. The President told him "Get me evidence and I'll act on it," Colson said.

Colson said the President was neither a harsh nor persistent questioner of his own staff members after they fell under suspicion with regard to Watergate. The President was a reluctant investigator and waited for outside events to force him to act, Colson said. "The Nixon style is sort of third person," Colson said with reference to events immediately following Watergate. "The President would ask about the Watergate, something like, 'Now why in the hell would somebody do that?' It would be sort of a rhetorical question giving you an opportunity to say, 'Well, Mr. President, I blew it.' But when you said, 'I have no idea, Mr. President; it seems to me, too, the stupidest thing I've ever heard,' that was taken as an answer," Colson said.

Colson recollected that the President's first reaction to the Watergate burglary was denunciation of the entire management of the Committee to Re-elect the President, which Mitchell had been directing since March 1, 1972. "I've been saying all along there's too much money over there. There's no place in campaigns for mercenaries; that staff is inflated and mediocre. Nobody is managing that campaign. That operation is out of control," Colson quoted Nixon as saying.

Colson expressed surprise the press accepted threat of divorce by his wife as Mitchell's reason for resigning as Nixon campaign manager. Colson felt it more likely Mitchell had been "sacked" by Nixon for letting Watergate happen and for allowing the campaign to get out of hand.

Colson suggested firebombing—The Washington Post reported June 9 that Colson had suggested to White House intelligence operative John J. Caulfield that the office of Morton Halperin, a former aide to White House foreign policy adviser Henry A. Kissinger, in the Brookings Institute be burglarized and then firebombed.

According to Post sources, Caulfield immediately rejected Colson's alleged proposal as "totally insane" and informed then-White House Counsel John W. Dean 3rd that he did not wish to be further associated with Colson.

Dean confirmed Caulfield's story to federal investigators, the Post said.

According to Dean and Caulfield, the firebombing was to disguise the illegal entry onto the premises.

A Colson associate told the Post that Colson was concerned in 1971 about finding a means to remove certain material that Halperin possessed. The Colson associate described the material as "classified documents" and refused to elaborate. Colson denied the allegations.

Haldeman ordered files destroyed. H. R. Haldeman, President Nixon's former chief of staff, ordered aide Gordon C. Strachan to destroy documents that showed he knew of "actual data" obtained from the wiretap of the Democratic National Committee headquarters in the Watergate complex.

The information was contained in a report submitted to the Senate committee investigating Watergate by member Sen. Lowell P. Weicker (R, Conn.) after he interviewed former White House Counsel John W. Dean 3rd May 3, the New York Times reported June 10.

According to the report, about June 18, 1972, "Strachan told Dean that he had been ordered by Haldeman to destroy documents which indicated that Haldeman had awareness of actual data received from the wiretap at the Democratic National Committee."

Dean told Weicker that Strachan admitted to him he had destroyed the documents in his office June 17 or 18, 1972.

Break-ins against radicals reported. Newsweek magazine reported in its June 11 issue that investigators for the Senate select committee probing Watergate were looking into allegations that certain aspects of the 1970 intelligence gathering plan were operational before the birth of the White House "plumbers" group in the summer of 1971.

Newsweek said illegal methods—including burglary and unauthorized wiretaps—were used to stop sensitive leaks, to monitor the domestic left, and gather information for prosecution cases against radicals. Senate investigators were told by high Administration officials that burglaries were committed in connection with the Seattle Seven, the Chicago Weathermen, the Detroit Thirteen and the Berrigan cases. Senate investigators were also reported to be studying charges that Administration operatives buglarized the offices of the Brookings Institution in Washington seeking information on Morton Halperin, a former member of the National Security Council and a friend of Pentagon Papers trial defendant Daniel Ellsberg. Time magazine June 11 said the Brookings Institution burglary was never carried out.

(The case against the Seattle Seven involved destruction of federal property in a 1970 demonstration in Seattle. The Weathermen case stemmed from four days of battles between police and demonstrators in Chicago in 1969. The Detroit Thirteen were accused of plotting a bombing campaign at a Flint, Mich. meeting in 1968. The Berrigan case involved charges that the Rev. Philip Berrigan and six others conspired to kidnap White House Foreign Affairs Adviser Henry A. Kissinger.)

Senate investigators told Newsweek they were not sure what Administration figures had been responsible for the burglaries.

In a related development, the New York Times reported June 2 that the FBI was looking into the possibility that the 1970 intelligence plan had been put into operation. The FBI investigation was said to be focusing on four break-ins in 1971 and 1972 at the offices and residences of Chilean diplomats in New York City.

The Times June 6 revealed two previously unreported wiretaps that had been authorized by former presidential

Domestic Affairs Adviser John D. Ehrlichman. One was placed in 1969 against syndicated columnist Joseph Kraft and the other against an unnamed White House official.

White House investigators John J. Caulfield and Anthony T. Ulasewicz, former New York City policemen hired by Ehrlichman, besides placing the taps, were reported to have looked into the background of Rep. Mario Biaggi (D, N.Y.) for possible Mafia ties. Biaggi had criticized as "insulting to Italian-Americans" a 1969 Nixon crime message calling for an attack on organized crime.

Caulfield and Ulasewicz also were ordered to check the accuracy of reports about the massacre at Mylai.

The Times called Caulfield and Ulasewicz the precursors to the White House plumbers group.

In a related matter, the Justice Department May 31 admitted the FBI had wiretapped the phone of a prominent radical lawyer 23 times between 1955 and 1970. The lawyer was identified as Arthur Kinoy, an associate of William Kunstler, who worked for the defense in the Chicago Seven trial.

"At the time I was handling the Chicago Seven appeals, the government was listening to my phone conversations. It was the most outrageous invasion of privacy ever admitted to," Kinoy said.

A 1969 break-in by FBI agents at the offices of the underground newspaper, the Washington Free Press, was disclosed by the New York Times June 1. Aiding the FBI were members of the Army's 116th Military Intelligence Detachment, the Times said. The raid took place just before the Nixon inauguration, when there was concern about a series of planned counter-inaugural activities. The FBI June 1 admitted entering without a search warrant, but a spokesman claimed agents had been given a key by the building landlord.

Agnew attacks Senate hearings. Vice President Agnew criticized the televised Senate Watergate hearings June 11.

He charged that the proceedings were having a "Perry Masonish impact" by asking the American public to judge men who were not protected by legal safeguards against unsubstantiated testimony. "A swelling flood of prejudicial publicity" could not only destroy those who were innocent, Agnew declared, but also could impair the efforts of prosecutors to obtain conviction of guilty parties.

The hearings "can hardly hope to find the truth and can hardly fail to muddy the waters of justice beyond repair," Agnew told the 67th annual conference of the National Association of Attorneys General meeting in St. Louis.

Committee Chairman Sam J. Ervin Jr. (D, N.C.) and Sen. Howard H. Baker Jr., (R, Tenn.), vice chairman, were restrained in their reply to Agnew's criticism, which represented the Administration's strongest attack on the Senate investigation.

But Senate Republican leader Hugh Scott (R, Penn.) defended the group's performance as "fair, unbiased and non-partisan."

'72 Democratic debt. Reports filed with the General Accounting Office and published June 11 showed that the Democratic National Committee's debt of $9 million, accumulated before July 1972, had been reduced to $4 million. Much of the repayment effort was said to be a direct response to the Watergate scandal.

Impeachment study urged in House. In a sparsely-attended evening session June 12, Rep. Bella S. Abzug (N.Y.) led a group of liberal Democrats in urging the House to open an inquiry into whether there were grounds for impeaching President Nixon because of the Watergate affair.

The speeches, generally low-key, avoided a direct call for impeachment. Abzug said some form of House action was necessary, since "no other body is conducting a direct investigation into the conduct of the President, because no other body has the authority to do so." Rep. Ronald V. Dellums (Calif.) called on the House to begin to "draw the line" on what would be considered impeachable offenses.

While cautioning against immediate impeachment proceedings, Rep. Fortney H. Stark (Calif.) suggested that government investigators be required to give the House "all information necessary to make a responsible decision" on impeachment grounds.

Rep. Paul N. McCloskey Jr. (R, Calif.) had attempted to lead a similar discussion June 6. After McCloskey had read two of the 11 pages of a speech suggesting that Nixon might have violated federal criminal laws, Administration supporter Rep. Earl F. Landgrebe (R, Ind.) called for a quorum. With only about 60 House members on the floor, the Landgrebe motion halted debate. After procedural wrangling amid signs that the Democratic leadership might be willing to wait hours to gather a quorum, McCloskey decided that the length of the session was "unreasonable" and called for adjournment.

Gray to waive immunity. Former Acting Federal Bureau of Investigation (FBI) Director L. Patrick Gray 3rd agreed to give testimony in the Watergate affair without any promise of immunity from prosecution, the New York Times reported June 12.

Gray had met with federal prosecutors at least four times since the beginning of May, the Times said.

Maryland Republican indicted. A Maryland grand jury for Anne Arundel County June 13 indicted Blagdon H. Wharton on four counts of violating a state election law covering falsification of financial records for a May 1972 testimonial dinner for Vice President Spiro T. Agnew.

Wharton, a banker, was treasurer of the event. The misdemeanor charges involved two forms of perjury; failing to name the actual source of the $50,000 contribution (identified in Senate Watergate testimony as the Finance Committee to Re-elect the President); and failure to report a gift from the Baltimore caterers of the Agnew dinner.

According to the Washington Post June 21, the caterer had provided free food and drinks for a party held after the dinner for Agnew at a time when the caterer's parent company was under investigation by the Federal Trade Commission (FTC) for unfair merger and acquisition practices.

Spokesmen for Bluefield Caterers said Agnew had asked them to cater the party, but they claimed it was the firm's decision to give free service. The parent company, ARA Services, Inc., subsequently was ordered by the FTC to divest itself of several companies.

Senate hearings continue. The Senate committee investigating Watergate and other illegal campaign practices held its third week of nationally televised hearings June 12–14.

The hearings resumed in the Senate Caucus Room after the federal district court in Washington June 12 turned down Watergate special prosecutor Archibald Cox's plea to order a curtailment in broadcasts of the proceedings in order to facilitate the prosecution of major figures in the case.

Court rules on immunity, TV hearings— Chief Judge John J. Sirica of the U.S. district court in Washington granted Dean and Magruder immunity June 12 for their testimony before the Senate committee. He rejected a request from Watergate special prosecutor Archibald Cox to bar television and radio coverage of their testimony.

In another ruling June 12, Sirica denied a grant of immunity for Dean before the grand jury. He ordered Dean to "appear before the grand jury immediately following court proceedings this morning."

During the appearance, Dean reportedly refused to answer questions on the ground of possible self-incrimination. Dean had been subpoenaed by the federal prosecutors to appear before the grand jury, and his lawyers had applied to Sirica to quash the subpoena. Dean had sought either to have the subpoena thrown out or immunity be granted him in return for his testimony. To call Dean before the grand jury and force him to invoke the Fifth Amendment against self-incrimination would color his case before the jury with prejudice, his lawyers argued.

The government at the same time informed the court June 11 that it had rejected Dean's request for immunity. It had offered to allow Dean to plead guilty to one count of conspiracy to obstruct justice in return for his testimony. The prosecutors released their May 22 letter to Dean containing the offer. It informed him the government had evidence "that you were at the center of a very profound kind of corruption" and the government's investigation had been "blocked and frustrated by your connivance in collaboration with others."

On the question of immunity before the Senate panel, immunity for the individuals involved had been requested by the Ervin committee and the requests were delayed by the Justice Department for 30 days, the maximum period permitted under the law, pending court resolution of the issue.

In seeking conditions on the coverage of the testimony, Cox did not contest the Senate committee's right to have the immunity it sought granted. But Cox maintained the court had the authority to condition the immunity by requiring testimony to be taken in executive session. In light of the Ervin committee's refusal to delay its public hearings, however, Cox said the "most appropriate condition would seem to be the exclusion during the giving of compelled, self-incriminatory testimony, of live or recorded radio, television and other coverage not permitted at a criminal trial." Media attendance at the hearings and coverage later would be permitted under such a ruling. The government based its appeal on the ground that the live televised testimony could impair the government's prosecution against the witnesses.

The Ervin committee took the position, filed with the court June 7, that any court restrictions on the committee's procedures would "ignore the Constitutional doctrine of separation of powers." "We submit that, because we are a committee of a separate branch of government," it said, "the responsibility for determining how we run our business rests with us rather than the special prosecutor."

Sirica agreed. In his ruling June 12, he cited the 1970 law making it mandatory for the court to issue an immunity grant at the request of the Senate, subject to the delay imposed by the Justice Department. The court, he held, "is without discretion in this matter" and possessed "purely ministerial" duties concerning it. He also pointed out that the concern over tainted indictments was premature since no indictments were before the court.

Cox later June 12 announced his decision not to appeal the order.

The immunity grant meant that prosecution would have to be based on evidence gathered independent of the Senate testimony.

Stans' appearance before the Senate committee had been scheduled for June 7, but he sought postponement on the ground that such testimony would interfere with his right to a fair trial in his New York court case, where he was under federal indictment concerning a $200,000 GOP campaign donation. U.S. Judge Lee P. Gagliardi, presiding over the New York case, dismissed Stans' objection June 8,

finding nothing in the court's rule that was intended to preclude hearings "by legislative, administrative or investigative bodies."

Day-by-Day Testimony

June 12: *Stans denies involvement*— Former Commerce Secretary Maurice H. Stans denied any prior knowledge of or involvement in the Watergate scandal. He said he had no part in making basic campaign decisions and no responsibility for handling campaign funds after they were received. As chairman of the Finance Committee to Re-elect the President, his job was "to raise enough money to pay the bills," Stans said, adding he "had nothing to say about which bills to incur."

Stans testified after the committee overruled an objection by his lawyer that Stans' right to a fair trial might be affected by his appearance. Stans was under federal indictment in New York concerning a $200,000 cash contribution to the Nixon campaign by Robert L. Vesco. Committee Chairman Sam J. Ervin Jr. (D, N.C.) said the committee had already considered the matter and ruled that Stans would have to testify, plead the Fifth Amendment privilege against self-incrimination or risk contempt.

"I think the committee does not think that we should put off investigation of these matters until they can be determined by the court," Ervin said, "because the Constitution gives the Senate not only the power but the duty to make investigations of this character."

Ervin said the committee had decided not to question Stans on any matter related to his pending court case.

Vice Chairman Howard Baker (R, Tenn.) also remarked that he thought Stans could get a fairer trial after all the facts of the Watergate affair were brought to light by the committee.

Stans then opened with a 23-minute statement declaring he had no knowledge of the Watergate break-in or "of the efforts to cover up after the event," of any political "sabotage program" against the Democrats or any "intentional violations" of the campaign finance laws. Because of the "complexity" of the law and the "vast amount" of work, however, Stans conceded that there may have been some "unintended technical" violations.

Stans drew a distinction between his committee and the Committee to Re-elect the President, the major Nixon re-election committee of which the finance committee was an arm. "In practical terms," he said, "the two committees operated in watertight compartments. They were physically separated on different floors. The campaign committee ran the campaign and created the debts; the finance committee raised the money and paid the bills."

"There was only one forum for the exchange of opinions with respect to campaign spending," Stans continued, "and

that was the budget committee," consisting of three officials from each. In Stans' opinion, these budget meetings were not "very effective."

"I pressed continuously for reductions in overall spending," he said, "but the actual trend was constantly upward. At times the meetings became bitter, and I walked out of one meeting at which I thought there was no understanding of the difficulties of fund-raising on the part of those who were doing the spending. The budget grew to $40 million, then $43 million, and ended up in excess of $50 million. A late surge of contributions, as a result of effective organization we had built across the country, made it possible for us to end up with a surplus."

Stans also drew a distinction between his job and that of the treasurer of his committee:

"As chairman of the committee I had no responsibility in connection with the internal handling of funds, banking, recording, accounting and reporting. I did not sign checks. I did not expend cash from the treasurer's cash fund. I did not have a cash fund. It was my regular practice when I accepted contributions for the committee to turn them over to the treasurer promptly. I did not have relationships with the banks. I did not make entries in the books or even see the books. And I did not prepare the public reports and did not review them except to scan their summary pages. These were all the responsibility of the treasurer."

Stans told the committee that he was "satisfied" that Hugh W. Sloan Jr., who served as treasurer and testified before the committee, was completely innocent of involvement in "the Watergate matter."

Stans defended the matter of "confidentiality" of contributors. Under the old election financing law which expired April 6, 1972, he said, "the fact that contributions need not be reported gave the committee and its contributors a right of confidentiality." He continued:

"The issue of confidentiality versus disclosure of such information has never been fairly presented to the public. It has been made to appear that the committee engaged in secret, thereby concealed and suspect, transactions which would not have occurred had they been required to be disclosed. That is not true. The transactions were valid and proper and the question of whether they were to be reported was a question of law that involved important rights of individuals.

"The committee's position all along has been that nondisclosure created no advantage to it, but that privacy was a right of the contributor which the committee could not properly waive. The right to live without undue intrusion is a long-respected benefit of the American system."

Stans was questioned by committee deputy counsel Rufus Edmisten about a memorandum, dated July 28, 1971, from Jeb Stuart Magruder, deputy director of the campaign committee, to John N. Mitchell, at that time attorney general.

The memo stated that on word from Dick Whitney, described as Stans' political special assistant, Stans had "built up a discretionary fund at Commerce [Department] that will total approximately $1 million" and he was "using this fund for conferences, hiring and other activities that will be beneficial to the President's re-election." If Mitchell felt it appropriate, Magruder suggested, Stans "might discuss this concept with other Cabinet officers to see if they can develop the same kind of fund within their own departments."

Stans said he had "no idea what the concept was" and he had no fund at Commerce other than an authorized budgeted department fund.

Edmisten asked Stans about $83,000 cash given to convicted Watergate conspirator G. Gordon Liddy.

Stans recalled that Sloan questioned him, near April 6, 1972, about Liddy's request for "a very substantial amount of money" and whether he should give it to him. Stans continued:

"And I said, 'I don't know. I will find out from John Mitchell.' I will quote my conversation with John Mitchell as best I can paraphrase it. It is not precise. But I saw John Mitchell a relatively short time after and said, 'Sloan tells me that Gordon Liddy wants a substantial amount of money. What is it all about?'

"And John Mitchell's reply was, 'I don't know. He will have to ask Magruder because Magruder is in charge of the campaign and he directs the spending.'

"I said, 'Do you mean, John, that if Magruder tells Sloan to pay these amounts or any amounts to Gordon Liddy that he should do so, and he said, 'That is right.'

"Now, that is my recollection in a paraphrase of the discussion that took place. I went back to Sloan and reported it to him and found out that he had already talked to Magruder and had the same information.

"Apparently Mr. Liddy showed Mr. Sloan a budget of $250,000 against which he intended to draw. To the best of my knowledge, Mr. Sloan did not tell me about that budget and I did not know that Mr. Liddy had authority to draw an amount of money of that size."

In reply to a question, Stans told the committee he received on June 29, 1972 (12 days after the Watergate break-in), "an urgent call" from Herbert W. Kalmbach, President Nixon's former personal attorney, for a meeting where Kalmbach told him, "I am here on a special mission on a White House project and I need all the cash I can get." Kalmbach insisted on cash, Stans said, and told him "this has nothing to do with the campaign, but I am asking for it on high authority" and "you will have to trust me that I have cleared it properly."

Stans testified that he gave Kalmbach $75,000 in "two parcels outside the committee"—$45,000 in a safe deposit box for "unusual expenses," which had been left behind by Kalmbach during his tenure as fund raiser for Nixon preceding Stans, and $30,000 from three Philippine nationals.

Stans said Kalmbach told him about six weeks ago that the request for the funds had come from presidential counsel John W. Dean 3rd, that Dean had assured him the purpose was legal and that Kalmbach had checked with Nixon aide John D. Ehrlichman, who corroborated Dean.

Porter relates 'dirty tricks'—Prior to Stans' testimony June 12, Herbert L. Porter, who had testified June 7, returned and related some of the "dirty tricks" perpetrated during the Nixon re-election campaign. He told of photographs of documents of Democratic presidential contender Sen. Edmund S. Muskie (Me.) and indicated that they were shown to Mitchell on occasion and copies sent to Haldeman aide Gordon Strachan in the White House.

He recalled one such Muskie memo suggesting that Muskie use a subcommittee chairmanship to hold tax hearings in California as "a great visual event" for Muskie's campaign. Magruder told him to send it to syndicated columnists Roland Evans and Robert Novak, Porter said. "We did. They printed it, and the hearings were never held."

Porter also told of payments to a college student for sitting in front of the White House wearing dirty clothes and a McGovern for President button, and payments to "seven or eight people in various spots around the country to promote the President's campaign at opposing candidates stops, signs which would say 'This is Nixon Country' or whatever.'"

June 13: *Stans grilled by Ervin*—On his second session with the committee, Stans was subjected to aggressive questioning by committee members, especially Chairman Ervin and Sen. Herman E. Talmadge (D, Ga.). Ervin's questioning drew a remonstrance from Sen. Edward J. Gurney (R, Fla.), who objected to "the harassment of this witness." Ervin's response, which evoked applause from the audience:

"Well, I am sorry that my distinguished friend from Florida does not approve of my method of examining the witness. I am an old country lawyer and I don't know the finer ways to do it. I just have to do it my way."

Ervin began his questioning on the destruction of campaign contribution and disbursement records from the committee's files shortly after the Watergate break-in. Speaking of the contributions prior to April 7, 1972 when the new campaign funding law became effective, Stans said "there was no requirement that they be kept and, insofar as contributors were concerned we wanted to respect the anonymity that they had sought." He said

there was "no relevance" between the break-in and the destruction of records.

Q. You swear, you are stating upon your oath that there is no connection between the destruction of these records and the break-in of the Watergate or any fear that the press or the public might find out from these records what the truth was about these matters?

A. Well, let me speak only with respect to myself. I will say to you that there was no connection between my destruction of the summary sheets given to me by Mr. Sloan and the Watergate affair.

Q. Well, it was quite a queer coincidence, was it not?

A. It would—

Q. Rather a suspicious coincidence that the records which showed these matters were destroyed six days after the break-in at the Watergate?

A. Mr. Chairman, the adjectives are yours.

Q. Sir?

A. The adjectives that you are using, queer coincidence and suspicion.

Q. Don't you think it is rather suspicious?

A. No, I do not think so, senator.

Q. Do you think it is kind of normal in the kind of things to expect people who had records concerning outlays of campaign funds to destroy those records after five men are caught in an act of burglary with money from the committee in their pockets?

A. On April 6th I asked Mr. Sloan to build up the records of all the contributors and he did so. I asked him on April 10th before I left on my vacation to balance out his cash account. He did both of those things pursuant to my requests.

Now, the fact that they came to me after the Watergate was pure and innocent coincidence.

Stans conceded that Liddy was one of those who advised destruction of the records, but he said Liddy was "in good standing as our counsel" at the time and "doing a good job as counsel."

Asked why he destroyed the summary Sloan gave him, Stans said "I was interested" in having a record of the names of contributors and in the balance on hand. Ervin asked him "why were you interested in destroying the things you were interested in?" Stans replied, "It was possible to determine at any time from remaining records and from the recollection of people who had given that money," and, according to the law, "we didn't have to keep any records before April 7 that we didn't want to. . . . We kept 99% of our records."

Q. Except you kept no records of the cash receipts and expenditures.

A. That is not quite correct, Mr. Chairman. We have kept some records and we have been able from those records to reconstruct what has happened.

Q. Well, why destroy your previous records and why destroy your subsequent records and reduce yourself to the necessity of reconstructing something that you already had and destroyed?

A. Mr. Chairman, for the reason that we were seeking to protect the privacy, the confidentiality of the contributions on behalf of the contributors.

Q. In other words, you decided that the right of the contributors to have their contributions concealed was superior to the right of the American citizens to know who was making contributions to influence the election of the President of the United States.

Mr. Stans, do you not think that men who have been honored by the American people as you have ought to have their course of action guided by ethical principles which are superior to the minimum requirements of the criminal laws?

A. I do not have any quarrel with that, but there is an ethical question in whether or not I can take your money as a contributor with an understanding on your part that you are entitled to privacy in that contribution and then go around and release the figure to the public.

Ervin then asked Stans about a $50,000 cash disbursement that went toward receipts of a fund-raising dinner in Maryland in honor of Vice President Spiro T. Agnew. Ervin asked, "They wanted to make it appear that they took in $50,000 more than they actually took in, didn't they?"

Stans replied: "They wanted to make it look more successful than it apparently was."

Q. Yes. In other words, they wanted to practice a deception on the general public as to the amount of honor that was paid to the Vice President.

A. Mr. Chairman, I am not sure this is the first time that has happened in American politics.

Ervin persisted.

Q. So they claimed the money to give back. In other words, the only purpose of the $50,000 was to practice a deception?

A. So far as I know, that is exactly what was intended and if you want to indict me for that, all right.

Q. Well, that is almost on a moral plane in my judgment with a vote fraud—not quite, perhaps.

At one point Baker, committee vice chairman, broke in to suggest subpoenaing records of the Democratic National Committee and other presidential nominees "to shed light on exactly what the custom and usage in politics was" in handling funds. Ervin was agreeable.

After he and Gurney had their exchange concerning his style of questioning, Ervin continued. He cited the Watergate conspirators' possession of GOP funds, the payments to Liddy, Liddy's dismissal from the committee for refusing to answer FBI questions, Sloan's talk to Stans about an attempt to perjure himself about the Liddy funds, and Sloan's resignation.

Didn't all you know, Ervin asked, "engender in your mind a feeling that you

ought to communicate, you ought to talk to the President about this matter? You knew all of this before you talked to the President in August, did you not?"

Stans responded: "Oh, yes. Mr. Chairman, the President had far more resources than I did. It was known that the White House was conscious of the problem. I had no knowledge that there was not common knowledge at the time, I had nothing to tell the President that would have been unusual."

In a closing statement, Stans expressed confidence that no one in the finance committee, except Liddy, "had any knowledge of or participation in the Watergate affair or any other espionage or sabotage activities."

He asked the committee, when it wrote its report, to "give me back my good name."

Talmadge's turn—Like Ervin, Talmadge evinced skepticism at Stans' testimony. He cited Stans' testimony that his prime job was raising funds and not getting into details. Then he cited memos showing Stans' concern over bumper strips, lapel pins and sale of campaign trinkets. Why were you "spending all your time worrying about bumper strips and right there on that board [in the room] you have got deposits of $750,000 and disbursements of $1 million and $777,000?" he asked Stans. "You are considered to be one of the most able certified accountants in America, why did you worry about bumper strips instead of those funds?"

Stans replied that the accounting for sales of articles "was an important responsibility" under the law and most of the listed disbursements happened prior to the new campaign funding law when there was "no responsibility" to account for that money.

In summing up, Talmadge told Stans "it strikes me as being literally inconceivable that you could spend the larger part of your time worrying about pen labels and bumper stickers and not worrying about what happens to large sums of cash that are being disbursed by these people for unknown causes...."

Other Stans interrogation—Sen. Daniel K. Inouye (D, Hawaii) recalled testimony from Sloan that upon being questioned about the large sums paid to Liddy, Stans had remarked to him, "'I do not want to know and you do not want to know.'" Stans responded that it was made in the context "of total frustration that I had with the spending program of the campaign committee." "The remark I made," he said, was "something to the effect that 'I don't know what's going on in this campaign and I don't think you ought to try to know.' We were the cashiers, we received the money, and we paid the bills. They [the campaign committee] had responsibility for everything they did."

"Wasn't this rather uncharacteristic of your background," Inouye asked, one who was "a stickler for details," to say

"I do not want to know?" It was, Stans said, "but it was not uncharacteristic of the responsibilities I had in this campaign which had absolutely nothing to do with accounting. My job was to raise an unbelievable amount of money, $40 million or more."

Gurney asked Stans if he had ever discussed Watergate or any aspect of it with President Nixon. "Only in the sense that the President and I met once during the campaign and I had one telephone call from him, both in August" of 1972, Stans said. In the phone call, he said, Nixon told him he was aware "that I was receiving considerable punishment in the press for not answering their questions at the time" and "that he appreciated the sacrifice I was making in that respect as the matter would be over eventually, and he hoped that I could continue to take it."

"It was a pep talk, in other words," Stans said. In his meeting with Nixon about 10 days later, he said, "there was no discussion of the Watergate, of cover-up or any subject of that type."

Gurney also asked him if he ever conferred with anyone "on the cover-up of Watergate?" "I have no recollection of any discussion with anyone about the cover-up on the Watergate until after the disclosures that have occurred within the last two months," Stans replied.

Later, Inouye asked him if it was his testimony "that until March 23 of this year you had no reason to suspect that people like Mr. Kalmbach or Mr. Mitchell or Mr. Haldeman or Mr. Ehrlichman were possibly involved in the Watergate and its ramifications?" Stans said that was "entirely correct."

He told Gurney it was "not true" he kept cash in a safe in his office. There was no safe in his office, Stans said. "There was a safe in the office of my secretary" where money was kept, he continued, but only when Sloan was not available to receive cash contributions that came in. He could not recall any time "at which there was more than one contribution [kept in that safe] of more than a day or so" except toward the end of the campaign where three contributions came in close together.

After testimony by Stans that he had given $350,000 in cash to the White House "for polling," Baker asked why pollsters could not be paid by check. Stans said the White House apparently wanted to check on some polls being taken by the campaign committee without the committee being aware of it.

At one point in his session with Ervin, Stans said he did not consider the routing of checks through Mexico and into Miami for cash a "laundering." He considered it "stupidity" on the part of the committee's counsel, Liddy. Ervin had wondered why the checks were simply not deposited in the bank in the building occupied by the Nixon committee.

June 14: *Magruder tells his story*—Jeb Stuart Magruder, deputy director of the Committee for the Re-election of the

President during the 1972 campaign, related the "true" story of the planning for the Watergate break-in and subsequent cover-up. He conceded that he had given a "false story" to the Watergate grand jury and later at the trial.

In an opening statement, Magruder said, "Unfortunately, we made some mistakes in the campaign which have led to a major national concern. For those errors in judgment that I made I take full responsibility.... These mistakes were made by only a few participants in the campaign. Thousands of persons assisted in the campaign to re-elect the President and they did nothing illegal or unethical. As far as I know at no point during this entire period from the time of planning of the Watergate to the time of trying to keep it from the public view did the President have any knowledge of our errors in this matter. He had confidence in his aides and I must confess that some of us failed him."

Then, under questioning by the committee's chief counsel and staff director Samuel Dash, Magruder told this story:

On Jan. 27, 1971, there was a meeting in Attorney General John N. Mitchell's office at the Justice Department attended by Mitchell, Presidential counsel John W. Dean 3rd, Magruder and G. Gordon Liddy, later convicted as a Watergate conspirator. Using large charts on an easel, Liddy presented an espionage plan he budgeted at $1 million. The proposed projects included wiretapping, electronic surveillance and photography. One proposal was to abduct radical leaders and detain them in Mexico to prevent them from disrupting the Republican National Convention.

Another project "would have used women as agents to work with members of the Democratic National Committee at their convention and here in Washington and, hopefully, through their efforts, they would obtain information from them." The project included rental of a yacht at Miami, "set up for sound and photographs," for "call girls" to "work with" prominent Democrats.

The reaction to the plan, Magruder continued, was that "all three of us were appalled" because of "the scope and size of the project." Mitchell indicated "that this was not an acceptable project" and that Liddy should "go back to the drawing board and come up with a more realistic plan."

Magruder made a telephoned report on the meeting to Gordon Strachan, then assistant to Nixon chief of staff H. R. Haldeman. "Everything that I did at the committee," Magruder told the committee, "everything that we did was staffed to Mr. Strachan so that he could alert other officials at the White House as to our activities."

A second meeting on the Liddy plan was held Feb. 4, 1972 at the Justice Department with the same participants. The topic was "the potential target" of the Democratic National Committee

headquarters and "the possibility of using electronic surveillance" at the Democratic convention headquarters and at the presidential contender's headquarters. Either Mitchell or Dean also brought up the point that information relating to Sen. Edmund S. Muskie (Me.), then a Democratic presidential aspirant, possibly could be obtained in a newspaper office in Las Vegas and Liddy "was asked to review the situation in Las Vegas to see if there would be potential for any entry."

Magruder said the information sought at the convention site concerned a plan for a business exposition to be staged, with a kick back of some or all of the fee to the Democrats (a plan never executed).

In general, he said, information also was being sought to offset the effectiveness of then Democratic National Chairman Lawrence F. O'Brien. O'Brien, he said, had "been a very effective spokesman against our position on the ITT case and I think there was a general concern that if he was allowed to continue as Democratic national chairman, because he was certainly their most professional political operator, that he could be very difficult in the coming campaign. So we had hoped that information might discredit him."

The reaction to this Liddy plan, which had been scaled down to a $500,000 cost, was "that it would not be approved at that time but we would take it up later."

Again, Magruder made a telephone report on the meeting to Strachan.

After this meeting, Magruder and Liddy had a personal disagreement— Magruder said he put his hand on Liddy's shoulder and Liddy asked him to remove it and "indicated that he would kill me." Magruder did not consider it "a specific threat," however. "It was simply Mr. Liddy's mannerism." As a result, Liddy moved as counsel from the campaign committee to the finance arm.

Another development at this time was word to Magruder from the White House to get the Liddy plan approved. According to Magruder, Charles Colson, then a counsel to the President, "called me one evening and asked me in a sense would we get off the stick and get the budget approved for Mr. Liddy's plans, that we needed information, particularly on Mr. O'Brien. He did not mention, I want to make clear, anything relating to wiretapping or espionage at that time."

Magruder was also pressed on the matter by Colson assistant, Richard Howard.

"But, I would like to make it clear," Magruder stressed, "there was a general, I think, atmosphere in the White House and the committee of the need to gather information. This was not necessarily information that would be gathered illegally."

A third and final meeting on the Liddy plan was held on or about March 30, 1972. It was at Key Biscayne, where Mitchell was on vacation. The participants were Mitchell, Magruder, Liddy

and Frederick C. LaRue, former White House aide and chief deputy to Mitchell at the campaign committee. This plan, scaled down to a $250,000 cost, involved entry into the Democratic National Committee headquarters (in the Watergate building in Washington) and possible later entry into the Democratic presidential contenders' headquarters and the Democratic convention headquarters. The plan included electronic surveillance and photography of documents.

"No one was particularly overwhelmed with the project," Magruder said. "But I think we felt that the information could be useful and Mr. Mitchell agreed to approve the project and I then notified the parties of Mr. Mitchell's approval."

Magruder recalled being questioned by Hugh W. Sloan Jr., treasurer of the campaign committee's finance arm, about the initial large sum of money requested by Liddy, $83,000, for the operation.

"I indicated that Mr. Liddy did have that approval. Mr. Sloan evidently then went to Mr. Stans. Mr. Stans went to Mr. Mitchell. Mr. Mitchell came back to me and said why did Gordon need this much money and I explained to him this was in effect front end money that he needed for the equipment, and the early costs of getting his kind of an operation together. Mr. Mitchell understood, evidently told Mr. Stans it had been approved and the approval was complete."

The first break-in at the Watergate occurred May 27, 1972. Liddy indicated to Magruder afterward "he had made a successful entry and had placed wiretapping equipment in the Democratic National Committee." About a week and a half later, Magruder received "the first reports" from the bugging in the form of recapitulated telephone conversations and pictures of documents. He "brought the materials into Mr. Mitchell," who "reviewed the documents" and "indicated that there was really no substance" to them.

Liddy was called in and "Mitchell indicated his dissatisfaction with the results of his work." Magruder said Mitchell "did not ask for anything more." Liddy indicated "there was a problem with one wiretap" (the one on O'Brien's phone was not working) and "he would correct these matters and hopefully get the information that was requested."

Magruder called Strachan, who came to his office "and look[ed] over the documents and indicate[d] to me the lack of substance to the documents."

The aftermath: Cover-up—The morning after the break-in June 17, 1972, which police intercepted, Magruder said Liddy called him and "indicated there had been a problem the night before." Magruder, who was in California, talked to LaRue, who talked to Mitchell. The three discussed it, then Mitchell ordered Robert C. Mardian, a campaign committee official, to call Liddy to ask him to see Attorney General Richard G. Kleindienst "and see if there was any possibility" that James W. McCord Jr., one of those arrested at the Watergate and an employe of the campaign committee, "could be released from jail."

Magruder also called Strachan and told him of the problem. He also received a call from Haldeman, who "asked me what had happened" and, after being told, "indicated that I should get back to Washington immediately" to take care of the problem.

Back in Washington, Magruder met June 19 with Mitchell, LaRue, Mardian and Dean. "One solution was recommended in which I was to, of course, destroy the Gemstone [Liddy plan] file." "As I recall," Magruder said, "we all indicated that we should remove any documents that could be damaging, whether they related at all to the Watergate or not."

Magruder related discussions with Sloan, who had testified that Magruder asked him to perjure himself concerning the amount of money given Liddy. Magruder said he thought Sloan would be personally liable for the cash funds provided Liddy, since they were not reported funds. So he indicated to Sloan, he said, "that I thought he had a problem and might have to do something about it. He said, you mean commit perjury? I said, you might have to do something like that to solve your problem and very honestly, was doing that in good faith to Mr. Sloan to assist him at that time."

He met later with Sloan three times on the subject of the Liddy money, the exact amount of which Sloan did not know. "I think the real problem was that he knew it was $199,000 and I was aghast at that figure because there was no way Mr. Liddy should have received that much...."

Magruder stressed that no one asked him to participate in the cover-up. "I personally felt that it was important to be sure that this story did not come out in its true form at that time, as I think did the other participants. So I want to make it clear that no one coerced me to do anything. I volunteered to work on the cover-up story."

There were a "series of meetings," mainly held in Mitchell's office, attended by Mitchell, LaRue, Mardian, Dean and Magruder. At one point, "there was some discussion about me and I volunteered at one point that maybe I was the guy who ought to take the heat, because it was going to get to me, and we knew that. And I think it was, there were some takers on that, but basically, the decision was that because I was in a position where they knew that I had no authority to either authorize funds or make policy in that committee, that if it got to me, it would go higher, whereas Mr. Liddy, because of his past background, it was felt that would be believable that Mr. Liddy was truly the one who did originate it."

Q. When you testified to the grand jury that time, did you testify to the false story?

A. Yes, I did.

Q. What role did Mr. Dean play in preparing you for your grand jury appearance?

A. I was briefed by our lawyers and Mr. Mardian. Also, I was interrogated for approximately two hours by Mr. Dean and approximately a half hour in a general way by Mr. Mitchell.

Q. Now, after you appeared before the grand jury for the second time, did Mr. Dean give you any report?

A. Yes, the day after Mr. Dean indicated that I would not be indicted.

Q. During your appearances before the grand jury or preceding it what, if anything, was told to you concerning the question of executive clemency for yourself or for those who were going to accept the blame in the story?

A. They made assurances about income and being taken care of from the standpoint of my family and a job afterwards and also that there would be good opportunity for executive clemency. But having worked at the White House and being aware of our structure there, I did not take that as meaning that had a direct relationship to the President at all.

Magruder told of a meeting with Haldeman in January before the Nixon inauguration. It was held to discuss future employment for Magruder and Nixon campaign aide Herbert L. Porter. "Also," Magruder said, "I thought I had better see Mr. Haldeman and tell him what had actually happened. I thought probably that this maybe was becoming scapegoat time and maybe I was going to be the scapegoat, and so I went to Mr. Haldeman and I said I just want you to know that this whole Watergate situation and the other activities was a concerted effort by a number of people, and so I went through a literally monologue on what had occurred. That was my first discussion with Mr. Haldeman where I laid out the true facts."

He and Mitchell met with Haldeman in late March, Magruder said, and were urged to meet with Dean to agree on a story. The three met but could not agree. "The election was now over and the reason for the cover-up [Nixon's re-election] was no longer valid," Magruder said. Then Dean was indicating "some reluctance" to abide by the story Magruder had told the grand jury, and Magruder felt "the story would not hold up" under further investigation by the Senate committee as well as the grand jury, which was reviving its probe.

So he told the "true" story to the federal prosecutors April 12.

Magruder also recalled meeting about June 24, 1972 with Stans, when he, Magruder, and Mitchell "indicated to Mr. Stans the problem we had with the [Liddy] money and would he try to work with Mr. Sloan to see if Mr. Sloan could be more cooperative." He recalled that Stans was not told in "great detail" about the Watergate affair but was told how the money was spent.

Further questions—Sen. Lowell P. Weicker Jr. (R, Conn.), referring to Magruder's January meeting with Haldeman, which occurred before Magruder testified at the criminal trial, asked if Haldeman "knew that perjury was going to be committed" at the trial. Magruder responded yes.

Sen. Talmadge focused on Magruder's conviction the Watergate affair could have occurred without the President's knowledge. Magruder, from his experience on the White House staff, said "it is very easy for me to see" how Nixon would not be aware of the affair because of his tight staff system.

Q. What you are saying, as I understand it, is that his staff was so completely remote, kept him so isolated, that this could have transpired without his knowledge, approval and consent. Is that your testimony?

A. Yes, sir, I can understand that very well.

Magruder also spoke of the atmosphere in the Nixon White House in response to queries from Sen. Howard H. Baker Jr. (R, Tenn.), who was curious about the "reluctant decision" described by Magruder on the final Watergate plan.

"I still can't quite come to grips with why you all had an expressed reservation about this and you still went ahead with it," Baker told him. Magruder then discussed the work at the White House.

There, he "was mainly engaged in the activities trying to generate some support for the President," he said. "During that time, we had worked primarily relating to the war situation and worked with antiwar groups.... We were directly employed with trying to succeed with the President's policies." At the same time, he "saw people I was very close to breaking the law [in antiwar protests] without any regard for any other person's pattern of behavior or belief.

"So consequently, when these subjects [Liddy plans] came up although I was aware they were illegal we had become somewhat inured to using some activities that would help us in accomplishing what we thought was a cause, a legitimate cause ... That is basically, I think, the reason why that decision was made, because of that atmosphere that had occurred and to all of us who had worked in the White House, there was that feeling of resentment and of frustration at being unable to deal with issues on a legal basis."

Magruder told Baker, "I do not think there was ever any discussion that there would not be a cover-up." The planning for it, he said, began the day they "realized there was a break-in." Magruder said he felt that if the story had "gotten out that people like Mr. Mitchell and others had been involved," that Nixon's re-election "would be probably negated." "I think it was felt," he continued, "that if it ever reached Mr. Mitchell before the election, the President would lose the election."

Press coverage criticized. A Gallup poll released June 13 reported that 44% of those polled believed that the press had given too much coverage to the Watergate affair, while 38% said coverage had been "about right," and 11% said there had been too little.

The poll found opinion on the issue to be highly partisan: 66% of the Republicans interviewed responded "too much" coverage; 31% of the Democrats agreed. The poll was taken June 1-4.

In other press developments, the Times of London and Mayor John V. Lindsay of New York City criticized Watergate coverage primarily for publishing material which might be prejudicial in later proceedings and for overlooking the principle of due process.

In an editorial June 5, the London newspaper gave credit to the press for "forcing the Watergate affair into the open" but said newspaper revelations of grand jury leaks and the televising of Senate committee hearings had given "enormous publicity" to hearsay evidence and subjected President Nixon to a form of "lynch law." The Times was especially critical of the publication of statements by former presidential counsel John W. Dean 3rd to Senate investigators.

In a commencement address in New York June 12, Lindsay accused the Nixon Administration of "outrageous abuse of executive power," while charging the press with disregarding grand jury secrecy and catering to "investigators who leak their suspicions before going to trial." Lindsay added that the side effects of Watergate could "drown our liberties in an excess of zeal and self-righteousness."

Ehrlichman tied to coast break-in. Watergate prosecutors were reported to have in their possession a memorandum addressed to former Presidential domestic affairs adviser John D. Ehrlichman containing detailed plans for the break-in at the office of the former psychiatrist of Pentagon Papers trial defendant Daniel Ellsberg, the Washington Post reported June 13.

The memo sent by former White House aides David Young and Egil Krogh Jr. was dated before the burglary occurred Sept. 3-4, 1971.

Young, under a grant of immunity from prosecution, gave the document to prosecutors and agreed to testify that Ehrlichman saw the memo and approved its contents.

Ehrlichman, who had previously denied advance knowledge of the break-in, conceded to the House Armed Service Committee's Subcommittee on Intelligence Operations June 13 he had approved "some sort of proposal" involving investigation of Ellsberg. Ehrlichman admitted the proposal might have dealt with going to Los Angeles, but he "did not recollect"

anything in the memo referring to an actual break-in.

Krogh, in an affidavit submitted to Pentagon Papers trial Judge William M. Byrne Jr. and made public May 7, said Ehrlichman gave "general authorization to engage in covert activity" to obtain information on Ellsberg.

According to Post sources, the Krogh affidavit was prepared from a document, whose bottom portion, describing the burglary in detail, had been clipped off. The bottom was removed at the beginning of 1973 to "sanitize" Krogh's files before Senate confirmation hearings on his nomination as undersecretary of transportation, a post he resigned May 9.

Ellsberg wiretap revealed. The Washington Post reported June 14 that the White House in 1971 received information from wiretaps—previously undisclosed—on Pentagon Papers defendant Daniel Ellsberg and New York Times reporters Neil Sheehan and Tad Szulc.

Despite demands by Pentagon Papers trial Judge William M. Byrne Jr., the taps were not disclosed by the government.

Post sources said federal investigators were trying to determine who authorized the wiretaps and why they were not reported to Judge Byrne.

According to Post sources, the wiretap information was received in the White House as early as May 1971—one month before the Pentagon Papers were published in the New York Times and one month before the White House "plumbers group" was set up on orders from President Nixon.

The Federal Bureau of Investigation said it had no record of any such electronic surveillance.

Post sources said they were unable to relate these taps to ones President Nixon said had been discontinued in February 1971.

The tap on Ellsberg continued for at least four months. The surveillance of the other two was irregular and lasted over several months, the Post said.

White House aides David R. Young Jr. and Egil Krogh Jr. were already involved in the investigation of Ellsberg's possession of a copy of the Pentagon Papers when the tap against Ellsberg was begun, the Post said.

Sheehan prepared the Pentagon Papers for publication by the Times.

Halperin sues Kissinger, others. Morton H. Halperin, whose phone was tapped while he worked for the National Security Council (NSC), filed suit June 14 against his former NSC superior, Henry A. Kissinger, and other White House officials.

The tap on Halperin's telephone was disclosed in a memorandum sent by Federal Bureau of Investigation (FBI) Acting Director William D. Ruckelshaus to Pentagon Papers trial Judge William M. Byrne Jr. May 9. The tap was revealed after Ruckelshaus learned Pentagon

Papers trial defendant Daniel Ellsberg had stayed at Halperin's home, and calls he made from there had been intercepted.

The suit, alleging that Halperin's phone was tapped for a period of 8-25 months, asked $100 for each day of surveillance for each member of his family.

Halperin's suit was based on the Safe Streets Act of 1968, which prohibited wiretapping except for investigation of specific crimes and which required court authorization.

Kissinger May 29 took responsibility for wiretaps that had been placed on his aides in an effort to stem leaks of information that were thought to originate among them.

Other defendants named in Halperin's suit were: former Attorney General John N. Mitchell; former White House Chief of Staff H. R. Haldeman; former Nixon Domestic Affairs Adviser John D. Ehrlichman; Gen. Alexander M. Haig Jr., then a top assistant to Kissinger; William C. Sullivan, then an assistant director of the FBI; Ruckelshaus; and the Chesapeake & Potomac Telephone Co. Ruckelshaus was named because of his role as "custodian" of the FBI wiretap records. No damages were asked from him.

Democratic records subpoenaed. The Senate Watergate Committee June 15 issued subpoenas for the financial records of five Democrats who campaigned for the presidency in 1972.

Watergate committee member Sen. Howard H. Baker Jr. (R, Tenn.) had asked June 13 that the committee take up the question of campaign financing.

Subpoenas were issued for the financial records of Sens. Hubert H. Humphrey (Minn.), Henry M. Jackson (Wash.), George S. McGovern (S.D.), Edmund S. Muskie (Maine), and Gov. George C. Wallace (Ala.).

A committee spokesman indicated that subpoenas would be issued in the future for the records of the Democratic National Committee, as well as other contenders for the Democratic presidential nomination in 1972.

Hunt blackmail reported. Convicted Watergate conspirator E. Howard Hunt Jr. "effectively blackmailed" the White House with threats he would expose involvement of high Nixon Administration officials in secret illegal activities unless he received large sums of money and a guarantee of executive clemency, the Washington Post reported June 15.

According to Post sources, Hunt received, along with promises of clemency, amounts totaling more than $200,000. In late March, Hunt allegedly asked for an additional $130,000, which was never paid.

Reportedly, acquiescence by key White House officials was in part the result of fears that Hunt would reveal the Administration's secret plans against radicals, political opponents, and the press.

Post sources said Hunt's demands clearly established a case of obstruction of justice against White House officials. "Hunt was being paid to keep quiet. It demolishes the argument that the money was just for lawyers' fees and care for the families of the defendants," Post sources were quoted as saying.

The payment of such money to Hunt was the element needed to legally establish a case for obstruction of justice. Payment of lawyers' fees was embarrassing if revealed but not illegal, another Post source said.

Hunt allegedly relayed his first demand to the White House only a few days after the Watergate break-in by warning, "The writer has a manuscript or play to sell," government investigators told the Post. Hunt was the prolific author of more than 40 novels.

In the beginning, payments were made to Hunt by Nixon campaign aide Frederick C. LaRue, who delivered the cash to either Hunt directly or Hunt's attorney William O. Bittman. Bittman, sources said, admitted receiving three or four sealed envelopes, which he passed to Hunt, but Bittman denied knowledge of their contents.

Hunt, meanwhile, had received through Nixon re-election committee members assurances of executive clemency, Post sources said.

"Hunt viewed it as similar to a Central Intelligence Agency operation," another Post source observed. "If a deal blows up, everybody's taken care of."

By the fall of 1972 Hunt was reported to have become dissatisfied with his channels to the White House and fearful about promises of clemency, facts he had relayed to the White House in a three-page memo. Hunt reportedly upped his demands for money and for better White House channels. "It kicked up a crisis at the White House," a Post source said.

Hunt sent at least five messages to the White House, the last on March 16, one week before he was given a provisional prison sentence of 35 years and after his wife Dorothy had been killed in a plane crash. Hunt, worried that no one would take care of his children, made a final demand for $130,000—$70,000 for personal expenses and $60,000 for legal fees, Post sources said.

White House Counsel John W. Dean 3rd, recipient of the demand, "hit the ceiling" and refused to accede to Hunt's demands, the Post reported. By then the cover-up was falling apart, one Post source said.

Jail term in Florida election fraud. George Hearing, a Florida accountant who had pleaded guilty to charges of publishing and distributing a false campaign document during the Democratic presidential primary in Florida, received the maximum penalty of one year in jail June 15.

Cox probe may expand to new lines. The Watergate special prosecution under Archibald Cox was considering opening "lines of inquiry other than those which are being explored," Cox's aide James Vorenberg said June 15. "We start with the assumption we'll look into everything," Vorenberg said at a news conference. The known lines of inquiry being explored involved the Watergate break-in itself and subsequent cover-up, 1972 campaign contributions and financing, the burglary of the offices of Daniel Ellsberg's former psychiatrist, alleged political sabotage and the antitrust settlement for the International Telephone & Telegraph Corp. in 1971.

Vorenberg did not specify what new probes were under consideration. There were reports that one possible new line of inquiry involved GOP fund-raising during the 1972 campaign. The Senate Watergate committee also was reported to be interested in exploring the personal finances of those involved in the conspiracy, especially in light of Dean's disclosure he borrowed GOP funds to finance his wedding and honeymoon and the large amounts of GOP campaign funds still unaccounted for.

Cox, in response to queries at a news conference June 18, said the questions of whether a president might be subpoenaed in a criminal case or indicted prior to impeachment were under study.

He cautioned that it was "wrong to draw any inferences" from the study. "It's a possible avenue of legal inquiry and, therefore, one that I have to be informed on," Cox said.

A report in the Washington Post June 18 based on White House and other government sources said President Nixon was expected to significantly shift his Watergate stance by saying he was misled by his top aides Haldeman and Ehrlichman. The White House objected to the "extreme unfairness" of the report.

Senate hearing delayed. The Senate Watergate hearings were canceled for a week June 18 in consideration of the official visit to the U.S. of Soviet Communist party leader Leonid I. Brezhnev. The committee had been scheduled to hear testimony during the week from former presidential counsel John W. Dean 3rd.

Sen. Sam J. Ervin Jr. (D,N.C.), chairman of the Select Committee on Presidential Campaign Activities holding the Watergate hearings, said the request for a delay came from the Senate leadership.

The committee had received the request that day in a letter from the Senate party leaders, Sens. Mike Mansfield (D, Mont.) and Hugh Scott (R, Pa.). The letter said a delay of one week "would not jeopardize the hearings" but might give President Nixon and Brezhnev "the opportunity to reconcile differences, arrive at mutual agreements and, in the field of foreign policy, be able to achieve results which would be beneficial not only to our two countries but, hopefully, to all mankind."

Ervin said he agreed to the request "with some degree of reluctance" but thought "there may be wisdom" in the postponement. "I can see why the President's attention might be distracted by the Watergate investigation while he's trying to negotiate an arms control agreement," he said.

Only committee member Sen. Lowell P. Weicker Jr. (R, Conn.) voted against the postponement. He said he felt "strongly that, whereas the Brezhnev visit is important, this particular exercise in democracy is important also."

Mansfield assumed full responsibility for initiating the request and made it clear that he had broached the matter to Scott and that he had had no contact with the White House about it.

Dean evidence sealed, sent to court. The Cox prosecution acted June 19 to protect any future case to prosecute Dean by presenting a sealed folder of evidence to the U.S. district court in Washington for safekeeping. The material was based on evidence gathered separately from Dean's imminent testimony under a grant of immunity before the Senate Watergate committee.

In a related development, the committee's chief counsel Samuel Dash said June 18 he had been informed by White House counsel Leonard Garment that the White House would waive all claims to executive privilege and attorney-client relationships in connection with Dean's testimony.

Colson testifys on Ehrlichman-CIA link. Former White House counsel Charles Colson told the Senate Appropriation Committee's Subcommittee on Intelligence Operations June 19 that he had personally asked John Ehrlichman to help E. Howard Hunt establish "liaison with the Central Intelligence Agency" (CIA) in the summer of 1971.

Ehrlichman, appearing before the same subcommittee May 30, had denied ever interceding on Hunt's behalf with the CIA.

Subcommittee Chairman John L. McClellan (D, Ark.) made public some of what Colson told the investigative panel in private: "On the 7th or possibly the 8th of July, 1971 (which would have been by phone) I told Mr. Ehrlichman that Mr. Hunt wanted to establish liaison with the CIA as well as other government agencies. The need for contact was immediate in that one of Mr. Hunt's first assignments was to interview a Lt. Col. Lucien Conein, who was a principal CIA operative during the period of the Diem coup" in South Vietnam, Colson said.

Conein told reporters June 19 that he had been contacted by Hunt, who wanted to know what Conein knew about the Pentagon Papers case. Conein said he told Hunt that he had not been in contact with Pentagon Papers defendant Daniel Ellsberg since 1967, when he and Ellsberg had served as aides to then-U.S. Ambassador to South Vietnam Henry Cabot Lodge.

ACLU asks new trial. The American Civil Liberties Union asked a federal court June 20 to set aside the convictions of the original defendants and to retry them "under a properly drawn indictment which charges all of those responsible for the Watergate conspiracy regardless of their station in life."

The ACLU also released an analysis of the trial it had submitted to Cox saying the original prosecutors "became hopelessly enmeshed in a sham prosecution" and calling for a "clean and public break with the prosecutorial past."

Nixon re-election unit found guilty. The Finance Committee to Re-elect the President was found guilty June 20 on three misdemeanor counts of concealing a $200,000 cash contribution from financier Robert L. Vesco. Judge George L. Hart Jr. of federal district court in Washington imposed the maximum fine of $3,000.

The court rejected the committee's contention that the Vesco money fell into "the misty area" between requirements of the 1925 Corrupt Practices Act and the 1971 Federal Election Campaign Act which took effect April 7, 1972.

According to committee lawyers, Vesco had pledged the money March 8, 1972 and had informed the committee that the cash was available for pickup April 6, 1972. However, because of the "press of business," Nixon finance committee chairman Maurice H. Stans had been unable to complete the transaction in New York. The money was delivered by hand April 10, 1972 in Washington, and, according to committee lawyers, was reported at that time as "cash on hand" because "it was cash in transit."

The Nixon re-election committee had also been found guilty in January of concealing cash payments to convicted Watergate conspirator G. Gordon Liddy. In pleading no contest to those charges, the committee had not been required to reveal disbursements of the unreported money.

The committee had entered an innocent plea to the Vesco contribution charges, claiming it had acted on the "good faith reliance of its counsel," Liddy.

Dean testimony to panel leaked. Dean met June 16 with the Senate Watergate committee's staff members and lawyers in a preparatory session for his public testimony. The panel's chief counsel, Samuel Dash, and its Republican counsel, Fred D. Thompson, prepared separate summaries of Dean's testimony at the session and these summaries were distributed to the seven senators on the committee. Leaked accounts of Dean's testimony began appearing in the press soon afterwards and continued through the following week, the week Dean's public appearance had been canceled.

By midweek, excerpts from a summary prepared by the committee staff were being published. Also being published at the same time were excerpts from a White House account of conversations between President Nixon and Dean that had been sent to the committee. The New York Times published both sets of excerpts June 21.

Dean's story—The Times reported June 17, from various sources, one of them "a Dean associate," that Dean had informed government investigators about being told by White House aide Egil Krogh Jr. in early January that the orders for the burglary of files belonging to Pentagon Papers defendant Daniel Ellsberg's former psychiatrist came "from the oval office" (President Nixon's office). The account pictured Dean as having become convinced of Nixon's knowledge of the Watergate cover-up and feeling that his frequent meetings with Nixon early in 1973, when the President was concerned over executive privilege and national security, were related to the cover-up. The account said Dean attempted to tell Nixon on at least two occasions in mid-March about the scope of the scandal and, after arranging for his own personal defense and setting up a meeting with federal prosecutors, told the President the whole account of Watergate.

In the news accounts based on leaks after Dean's session with the Senate panel, Dean reportedly told the investigators:

■ Nixon asked him to keep a list of newsmen who were giving the President "trouble" during the 1972 election campaign.

■ Nixon asked Dean to see that Internal Revenue Service tax audits "be turned off on friends" of the President.

■ Dean promised to provide the committee with documents showing that he and top Nixon aides H. R. Haldeman and John D. Ehrlichman began immediately after the Watergate break-in to devise a cover-up story.

The summary of Dean's testimony before the Senate panel revealed further allegations by Dean. Among them:

■ In September 1972 Nixon directed that an effort be made to muffle a Watergate investigation by a House committee.

■ Nixon "had been bugged" in the 1968 campaign, Nixon once told Dean on the word of the late FBI director J. Edgar Hoover, and Nixon believed the information could be used to the Administration's advantage at some future time.

■ There was an attempt to persuade former Attorney General John N. Mitchell to "take the heat" off other officials by assuming the blame for the Watergate break-in.

■ Ehrlichman had instructed Dean to throw wiretapping equipment "in [the] river" after it had been found in the White House safe of one of the Watergate conspirators, E. Howard Hunt Jr.

■ Mitchell at first ignored a request to obtain money for the Watergate defendants, but Hunt sent word, through Dean to Ehrlichman and Mitchell, he

wanted $72,000 for living expenses and $50,000 for lawyers' fees or, as the summary phrased it, "Hunt would have things to say about the seamy things Hunt did for Ehrlichman while Hunt was at the White House." On March 21 or 22, the account continued, "Ehrlichman asked Mitchell if Hunt's problem had been taken care of and Mitchell said 'Yes.'" The next sentence in the summary was: "Hunt's asking for money came to the attention of the President."

Dean then was said to have discussed the question of executive clemency for the defendants with Nixon in the spring.

■ Intelligence data on Democrats was coming into the White House in early 1970 and reports by a private intelligence gathering unit in the White House were sent to Nixon through Haldeman and Ehrlichman.

■ Dean was given $15,200 of pre-1968 primary money to hold, and in October 1972 replaced $4,850 that he had taken out of the money for his wedding and honeymoon.

■ On Ehrlichman's instructions, an attempt was made to extend White House influence into the Republican side of the Senate Watergate committee. A call was made to Sen. Howard H. Baker Jr. (R, Tenn.), but Baker's response was "he did not want any White House input" on the decision of choosing a minority counsel.

(Baker disclosed the incident on the ABC "Issues and Answers" broadcast June 17. He said he rejected the overture and that it was the only contact the panel had with the White House since its probe began except for a request for an organizational chart. He said his only discussion with Nixon about the Watergate investigation took place before the probe began when he urged Nixon not to invoke executive privilege on his aides' testimony.)

White House summary—The White House summary of Nixon's discussions with Dean portrayed Dean as deflecting persistent questioning by Nixon about White House involvement in the Watergate burglary and cover-up until March 21. The two met almost daily during the first three weeks of March, according to the account, with Dean insisting there was no White House involvement.

The report said on March 13 Dean told Nixon that Haldeman aide Gordon C. Strachan "could be involved" and on March 21 Dean "gave the President his theory of what happened"—revealing "that [Jeb Stuart] Magruder probably knew, that Mitchell possibly knew, that Strachan probably knew, that Haldeman had possibly seen the fruits of the wiretaps through Strachan, that Ehrlichman was vulnerable because of his approval of [Herbert W.] Kalmbach's fund-raising efforts." Kalmbach was Nixon's personal attorney and reportedly was called upon to raise contributions for a fund to pay the Watergate defendants.

According to the summary, Nixon was told March 21 that Hunt "was trying to blackmail Ehrlichman about Hunt's prior plumber [plugging news 'leaks' such as Pentagon Papers' publication] activities unless he was paid what ultimately might amount to $1 million. The President said how could it possibly be paid. 'What makes you think he would be satisfied with that?' Stated it was blackmail, that it was wrong, that it would not work, that the truth would come out anyway. Dean had said that a Cuban group could possibly be used to transfer the payments. Dean said [Charles W.] Colson [special counsel to the President] had talked to Hunt about executive clemency."

The summary said Nixon sent Dean to Camp David March 23 and later that day called him "to check on his progress," presumably concerning a written report on Watergate; on March 30, when it became obvious Dean "would write no report," Nixon ordered Ehrlichman to investigate; Ehrlichman reported April 14 "possible Mitchell, Magruder and Dean involvement"; Nixon called Attorney General Richard G. Kleindienst, "who followed up"; Nixon called almost everyone on April 15 and "told Dean he must go before the grand jury without immunity"; the next day Nixon "asks Dean to resign. Had two drafts prepared. for Dean's signature. Dean demanded Haldeman and Ehrlichman resign also"; the federal prosecutor asked a delay on Dean's firing until he could be put before the grand jury; Nixon was told April 27 there was no use trying to get Dean before the jury since he was demanding immunity; on April 30 Nixon announced "Haldeman's and Ehrlichman's resignations and Dean's firing."

USIA facilities barred. The U.S. Information Agency (USIA) announced June 26 that foreign newsmen would not be permitted to use USIA facilities to broadcast feature programs on the Watergate case to television stations abroad.

Although the facilities had been provided "as a courtesy" in the past, agency spokesmen said, "It is not the function of the USIA to extend a story that may be detrimental to U.S. interest by duplicating and furthering dissemination of feature material."

The British Broadcasting Corp. specifically had been denied permission to use USIA studios in order to broadcast a "call in" interview with Sen. Daniel K. Inouye (D, Hawaii), a member of the Senate Watergate committee.

The Voice of America was continuing to provide "factual coverage of the news about Watergate," USIA spokesmen added.

Senate hearings resume. The Senate Select Committee on Presidential Campaign Activities resumed its televised hearings on Watergate June 25-29 after a one-week delay in deference to the official visit to the U.S. of Soviet Communist party leader Leonid I. Brezhnev.

The week's only witness was former presidential counsel John W. Dean 3rd, who spent the entire session June 25 submitting 47 documents and reading a 245-page prepared account detailing his own involvement in the effort to cover up the Watergate conspiracy and relating how that effort spread among the White House staff, the Committee to Re-elect the President, the Justice Department and President Nixon.

While Dean's account was the first before the committee to directly accuse Nixon of involvement in the Watergate cover-up, Dean asserted that Nixon did not "realize or appreciate at any time the implications of his involvement." Dean said, however, that Nixon had permitted the cover-up to continue even after Dean had told him about some of the cover-up plans.

Dean's statement detailed the "excessive concern" in the White House for data on antiwar activists and other political opponents of the Administration. Dean suggested that this concern, along with the "do-it-yourself White House staff, regardless of the law," created the climate for the Watergate affair.

Dean described his superiors in the White House—former presidential aides H. R. Haldeman and John D. Ehrlichman—as the principals in the efforts to conceal the ramifications of the Watergate break-in. But he also implicated, among others, former Attorney General John N. Mitchell, former special counsel to the President Charles W. Colson, U.S. District Court Judge Charles R. Richey, Assistant Attorney General Henry E. Petersen, former Acting FBI Director L. Patrick Gray 3rd, White House Press Secretary Ronald L. Ziegler, presidential aide Richard Moore and former presidential aides Frederick C. LaRue and Gordon C. Strachan.

Dean was confronted June 27-28 with a White House response to his charges in the form of a memorandum and questions submitted to the committee by special presidential counsel J. Fred Buzhardt Jr. The memo, read by Sen. Daniel K. Inouye (D, Hawaii), portrayed Dean as the "mastermind" of the cover-up and Mitchell as his "patron." Buzhardt's charges failed to shake Dean's insistence that he fell into an existing cover-up situation as a conduit between Haldeman and Ehrlichman and the campaign committee.

In a statement released June 28, Buzhardt insisted that the memo "does not represent a White House position" and had not been reviewed by the President. Its sole purpose, the statement said, was "to facilitate the examination" of Dean by the committee.

Committee Chairman Sam J. Ervin Jr. (D, N.C.), backed by Sen. Howard H. Baker (R, Tenn.), suggested June 28 that the only adequate White House response to Dean's charges would be an appearance by Nixon before the committee. A presidential spokesman in San Clemente replied that Nixon remained opposed to answering a committee subpoena on the ground that it would be "constitutionally inappropriate" and said Nixon did not intend to appear voluntarily.

In leading Dean through a recapitulation of his earlier charges, Ervin brought out that Nixon might have violated the Constitution in the Watergate affair and other political espionage operations. Baker later told a newsman that Ervin's questioning represented a "skillful and reasonable outline" of a potential case of "presidential malfeasance."

Near the end of the June 28 session, Sen. Lowell P. Weicker Jr. (R, Conn.) charged that Nixon supporters had tried to intimidate him after he had been named to the committee. Weicker cited a March 28 taped telephone conversation between Ehrlichman and Richard G. Kleindienst, then attorney general, during which Ehrlichman suggested that Kleindienst "take a swing" at Weicker in a news conference.

The June 27 session was also highlighted by the release of the list of the Administration's political "enemies" and Dean's testimony that the White House had tried to "politicize" the Internal Revenue Service.

Day-by-Day Testimony

June 25: *Dean's statement*—Dean's reading of his prepared statement—245 triple spaced legal-size pages—occupied the entire day's session and lasted more than six hours. In addition, Dean submitted 47 documents to the committee to accompany his statement.

In summary, his statement said:

"The Watergate matter was an inevitable outgrowth of a climate of excessive concern over the political impact of demonstrators, excessive concern over leaks, an insatiable appetite for political intelligence, all coupled with a do-it-yourself White House staff, regardless of the law. However, the fact that many of the elements of this climate culminated with the creation of a covert intelligence operation as part of the President's re-election committee was not by conscious design, rather an accident of fate."

"The White House was continually seeking intelligence information about demonstration leaders and their supporters that would either discredit them personally or indicate that the demonstration was in fact sponsored by some foreign enemy. There were also White House requests for information regarding ties between major political figures [specifically members of the U.S. Senate] who opposed the President's war policies and the demonstration leaders.

There was a lack of information showing such ties between the demonstrators and either foreign governments or major political figures, and this "was often reported to a disbelieving and complaining White House staff that felt the entire system for gathering such intelligence was worthless." Dean said he "was hearing complaints from the President personally" as late as March 12.

Soon after joining the White House staff in July of 1970, Dean learned about "the project to restructure the government's intelligence gathering capacities vis-a-vis demonstrators and domestic radicals." He was "told of the presidentially-approved plan that called for bugging, burglarizing, mail covers and the like." White House Chief of Staff H. R. Haldeman instructed him "to see what I could do to get the plan implemented."

Dean considered the plan "totally uncalled for and unjustified." He talked about it with Attorney General John N. Mitchell, who opposed it except Mitchell thought an "interagency evaluation committee might be useful."

An interagency evaluation committee was formed in early 1971, with Jack Caulfield the initial White House liaison with it. Reports on its activities were sent to Haldeman "and sometimes [Presidential Domestic Affairs Adviser John] Ehrlichman." In addition, Dean's office received regular intelligence reports on demonstrators and radical groups from the FBI and sometimes the CIA.

Nixon's 'strong feelings'—Dean said he became aware of Nixon's "strong feelings" about demonstrators when action was taken to get a single protester with a large sign moved from sight of the White House windows after Nixon had sighted him. Nixon aide Dwight Chapin said he would "get some 'thugs' to remove that man." But Dean called the Secret Service and the man was "convinced" to move away from sight of the windows and Dean then "told Mr. Chapin he could call off the troops."

Another time, on a trip, Nixon told the Secret Service agent with him, "in some rather blunt synonyms," to get some antiwar demonstrators "out of there." But the demonstrators, across the street from his motel, "couldn't be moved."

". . . A major part of any Presidential trip advance operation was insuring that demonstrators were unseen and unheard by the President. In early February of 1972, I learned that any means—legal or illegal—were authorized by Mr. Haldeman to deal with demonstrators when the President was traveling. . . ."

Dean advised against the use of illegal tactics and "if demonstrations occurred—they occurred."

In early March, "as a part of the planned counteroffensive for dealing with the Senate Watergate investigation," Nixon "wanted to show that his opponents had employed demonstrators against him during his re-election campaign." But, he said, "We never found a scintilla of viable evidence indicating that these demonstrators were part of a master plan; nor that they were funded by the Democratic political funds; nor that they had any direct connection with the McGovern campaign. This was explained to Mr.

Haldeman, but the President believed that the opposite was, in fact, true."

News leaks—There was also concern at the White House about news leaks. Caulfield told Dean that Ehrlichman had directed him to wiretap columnist Joseph Kraft's telephone "in pursuit of a leak" even when J. Edgar Hoover, then FBI director, "was unwilling."

This concern "took a quantum jump" when the Pentagon Papers were published in June 1971. In late June or early July, 1971, Caulfield told Dean that White House special counsel Charles W. Colson had instructed him, "at Ehrlichman's direction," to burglarize the Brookings Institution to see if "they had certain leaked documents." The instruction was "to plant a fire bomb in the building and retrieve the documents during the commotion." Dean told Ehrlichman the plan was "insane" and it was called off.

Almost a year later, Robert C. Mardian, then assistant attorney general, told Dean he "had gone to see the President to get instructions regarding the disposition of wiretap logs that related to newsmen and White House staffers who were suspected of leaking." But, "about Feb. 22 or 23 of this year, Time magazine notified the White House it was going to print a story that the White House had undertaken wiretaps of newsmen and White House staff and requested a response. The White House press office notified me of this inquiry.

"I then called Mr. Ehrlichman and told him about the forthcoming story in Time magazine. I asked him how Mr. Ziegler should handle it. He said Mr. Ziegler should flatly deny it—period."

Re-election efforts—Another concern at the White House was obtaining "politically embarrassing" information on leading Democrats.

In the spring of 1971, Haldeman discussed with Dean "what my office should do" during the coming campaign year. "He told me that we should take maximum advantage of the President's incumbency and the focus of everyone in the White House should be on the re-election of the President."

Part of Dean's task, in addition to "keeping the White House in compliance with the election laws," was "improving our intelligence regarding demonstrators," he said.

This brought him in touch with G. Gordon Liddy, who was being considered for a post as general counsel for the Nixon campaign committee. Dean interviewed Liddy and told him one of his responsibilities "would be keeping abreast of the potential demonstrations that might affect the campaign." Liddy was cleared by Ehrlichman, Mitchell and Jeb Stuart Magruder.

The next time Dean met Liddy was at a meeting Jan. 27, 1972 in Mitchell's office, with Magruder also there, when Liddy presented a "mind-boggling" plan for

"mugging squads, kidnapping teams, prostitutes to compromise the opposition and electronic surveillance."

Liddy explained: The mugging squad could "rough up demonstrators that were causing problems. The kidnapping teams could remove demonstration leaders and take them below the Mexican border. The prostitutes could be used at the Democratic convention to get information as well as compromise the person involved."

Mitchell told Liddy the plan "was not quite what he had in mind and the cost was out of the question." He suggested that Liddy "go back and revise" it, "keeping in mind that he was not interested in the demonstration problem."

At a second meeting of the same four men Feb. 4, 1972, Dean ended the meeting by interjecting that such discussions could not be held in the attorney general's office. He said he did not know "to this day who kept pushing for these plans." He told Liddy he "would never again discuss this matter with him" and "if any such plan were approved," he "did not want to know."

Dean then informed Haldeman of "what had been presented by Liddy" and "that I felt it was incredible, unnecessary and unwise. I told him that no one at the White House should have anything to do with this. . . . Haldeman agreed and told me I should have no further dealings on the matter."

Dean told of break-in—Dean returned from a four-day trip to the Far East June 18, 1972, when he was apprised of the Watergate break-in. Returning to Washington, one of the many calls he had June 19 was with Colson, who "vehemently proposed that he knew nothing and had no involvement in the matter whatsoever." Colson did express "concern" over the contents in the safe of E. Howard Hunt Jr., (who later confessed to the Watergate conspiracy) who had been on Colson's payroll. Meeting with Colson and Ehrlichman later, it was decided that Dean "take custody of the contents of the safe."

Dean also met that day with Liddy, who told him that "Magruder had pushed him into doing it." That afternoon, Ehrlichman instructed Dean "to call Liddy to have him tell Hunt to get out of the country." He did this without thinking, then "realized that no one in the White House should give such an instruction." He checked with Colson and Ehrlichman, who agreed. Liddy was recalled but said he had already passed the message.

Also on June 19, Gordon Strachan told Dean he had been instructed by his superior, Haldeman, to go through the files and "remove and destroy damaging materials." Strachan said the "material included such matters as memoranda from the re-election committee, documents relating to wiretap information from the D.N.C., [Democratic National

Committee], notes of meetings with Haldeman, and a document which reflected that Haldeman had instructed Magruder to transfer his intelligence gathering from Senator Muskie to Senator McGovern." Strachan told Dean "his files were completely clean."

One or two days later, Dean was given some cash to hold, $15,200, from Haldeman's office, said to have been from an unexpended portion of funds authorized for Colson. Dean kept the cash in his safe, telling his assistant about it, until Oct. 12, 1972 when he removed $4,850, replacing it with his personal check, after he had "failed to make arrangements" to pay for the expenses of his wedding and honeymoon.

Talks on scope of investigation—Ehrlichman asked Dean to talk with Richard G. Kleindienst, then attorney general, "about the scope of the investigation." Dean told Kleindienst on June 19 or 20, 1972 of his concern, although he "did not have all the facts," that "this matter could lead directly to the President." Kleindienst said "he certainly hoped that the President was not involved or that I was not involved. I responded that I certainly had not been involved in any criminal activity." "Kleindienst told Dean that his superiors at the White House never understood that once an investigation begins, it runs its full course. He said that he was always being asked to take care of this matter or that matter, as if by magic he could make something unpleasant go away."

Assistant Attorney General Henry E. Petersen, then in charge of the Watergate case, was called in, and Kleindienst related Dean's concern. "Petersen was troubled by the case and the implications of it." Kleindienst had to leave. The other two continued to talk, and Dean told Petersen "I had no idea where this thing might end" but "I didn't think the White House could withstand a wide open investigation."

Dean told Ehrlichman afterwards he felt Petersen "would handle the matter fairly and not pursue a wide open inquiry into everything the White House had been doing for four years." He made the statement "not because of anything Petersen specifically said, as much as the impression he gave me that he realized the problems a wide open investigation of the White House might create in an election year."

On June 20, 1972, Dean investigated the contents of Hunt's safe, including a briefcase with electronic equipment.

"Among the papers were numerous memoranda to Chuck Colson regarding Hunt's assessment of the plumbers unit, a number of materials relating to Mr. Daniel Ellsberg, a bogus cable, that is other cables spliced together into one cable, regarding the involvement of persons in the Kennedy Administration in the fall of the Diem regime in Vietnam, a memorandum regarding some discussion about the bogus cable with Colson and

[writer] William Lambert, some materials relating to an investigation Hunt had conducted for Colson at Chappaquiddick, some materials relating to the Pentagon papers."

Ehrlichman told Dean "to shred the documents and 'deep six' the brief case. I asked him what he meant by 'deep six.' He leaned back in his chair and said: 'You drive across the river on your way home at night—don't you?' I said yes. He said, 'Well, when you cross over the bridge on your way home, just toss the briefcase into the river.'"

Dean-Gray meetings—On or about June 21, 1972, Dean met L. Patrick Gray 3rd, then acting FBI director, regarding the FBI's Watergate investigation. Gray told him "he fully realized the sensitive nature of the investigation" and he had put "his most trusted senior people in charge." He also revealed checking some banking transactions of one of those arrested at the Watergate and tracing a $25,000 check and four checks totaling $89,000 to a bank in Mexico City. "The fact that the FBI was investigating these matters was of utmost concern to Mr. [Maurice] Stans when he learned of it."

Mitchell, Ehrlichman and Haldeman thought Dean "should see the FBI reports," and in early July 1972 Dean broached the matter with Gray. Gray wanted assurance that the information would be reported to the President.

Dean assured him, "Even though I was not directly reporting to the President at that time, I was aware of the fact that Ehrlichman or Haldeman had daily discussions with the President, and felt certain, because Haldeman often made notes, about the information I was bringing to their attention, that this information was being given to the President."

A summary report of the investigation to that stage was sent to Dean sometime after July 21, 1972. Mardian "became very excited because of the scope" of Gray's investigation. Mardian "clearly thought that Gray was being too vigorous" and he "demanded that I tell Gray to slow down, but I never did so."

Several days later, Mardian proposed "that the CIA could take care of this entire matter if they wished." "Mitchell suggested I explore with Ehrlichman and Haldeman having the White House contact the CIA for assistance. Ehrlichman thought it was a good idea. He told me to call General [Vernon A.] Walters because he was a good friend of the White House and the White House had put him in the [CIA] deputy director position so they could have some influence over the agency."

Dean continued:

"When Gen. Walters came to my office I asked him if there was any possible way the CIA could be of assistance in providing support for the individuals involved. Gen. Walters told me that while it could,

of course, be done, he told me that he knew the director's feelings about such a matter and the director would only do it on a direct order from the President. He then went on to say that to do anything to compound the situation would be most unwise and that to involve the CIA would only compound the problem because it would require that the President become directly involved. When I reported this to Ehrlichman, he very cynically said that Gen. Walters seems to have forgotten how he got where he is today."

In the meantime, Dean had not destroyed or discarded the material in Hunt's safe, which he considered "an incredible action—to destroy potential evidence." Arrangements were made to transmit the material to the FBI, which was done except for "politically sensitive documents." These were given personally to Gray, who was told by Ehrlichman they were politically sensitive "but not related to the Watergate per se." Dean told Gray they "would be political dynamite in an election year" if they were leaked. "At no time while I was present with Gray and Ehrlichman was he instructed by myself or Ehrlichman to destroy the documents."

When Dean was being interviewed by the prosecutors in January, he interrupted it to tell Petersen in private that "not all the materials" from Hunt's safe had gone directly to the FBI agents and he would have to testify to that if necessary. Then, Petersen "suggested that the interview be terminated, which it was." Later, Gray met Dean, told him he had destroyed the documents and cautioned him to 'hang tight' on not disclosing his receipt of the documents."

Payments to defendants—On June 28, 1972, there was a discussion in Mitchell's office "of the need for support money in exchange for the silence for the men in jail." But only $70,000 or $80,000 was on hand and "more would be needed." Mitchell asked Dean to get approval from Haldeman and Ehrlichman to have Herbert Kalmbach to raise the necessary money, which was done. Mitchell told Dean privately that the White House, in particular Ehrlichman, should be "anxious to accommodate the needs of these men. He was referring to activities that they had conducted in the past that related to the White House, such as the Ellsberg break-in."

The 'Dean report'—Concerning the President's Aug. 29, 1972 statement on Watergate, Dean said he had "no advance knowledge" that Nixon "was going to indicate" what he did.

"Had I been consulted in advance by the President, I would have strongly opposed the issuing of such a statement. First, I was aware that Gordon Strachan had close daily liaison with Magruder and had carried information relating to wiretapped conversations into the White

House and later destroyed incriminating documents at Haldeman's direction.

"Secondly, I had never been able to determine whether Haldeman had advance knowledge or not, and in fact, had never asked him because I didn't feel I could.

"Thirdly, I had always suspected, but never been able to completely substantiate my suspicion that Colson was far more knowledgeable than he protested.

"I don't know if the President's statement was meant to be a very literal play on carefully chosen words or whether he intended to give it the broad-brush interpretation that it later received.

"The issuing of the so-called 'Dean Report' was the first time I began to think about the fact that I might be being set up in case the whole thing crumbled at a later time."

Counterattack against the Democrats—On Sept. 9 or 10, 1972, Dean learned from Haldeman and Colson that Nixon felt the best defense against the Democrats and the lawsuits being filed by the Democrats was a "counteroffensive with our own series of lawsuits against the Democrats." About that time, Dean learned during a meeting in Mitchell's office that the White House exerted influence on the judge—Charles R. Richey—hearing the Democratic civil suit to have the case delayed until after the election. Contact with Richey was being made by a White House representative as late as March 1973.

On the day the Watergate indictments were handed down, Sept. 15, 1972, Dean went to Nixon's office, where "the President told me that Bob [Haldeman] had kept him posted on my handling of the Watergate case, told me I had done a good job and he appreciated how difficult a task it had been and the President was pleased that the case had stopped with Liddy. I told that I thought that there was a long way to go before this matter would end and that I certainly could make no assurances that the day would not come when the matter would start to unravel."

Nixon also told him former FBI Director J. Edgar Hoover told him shortly after he assumed office that his 1968 campaign "had been bugged." And "the President said that at some point we should get the facts out on this and use this to counter the problems that we were encountering."

Nixon expressed hope that the criminal case would not come to trial before the election, and Dean told him "the Justice Department had held off as long as possible the return of the indictments" and that "the lawyers at the re-election committee were very hopeful of slowing down the civil suit . . . because they had been making ex-parte contacts with the judge . . . and the judge was very understanding and trying to accommodate their problems."

Dean said, "The President was pleased to hear this and responded to the effect that 'well that's helpful.'"

Dean also recalled "the President telling me to keep a good list of the press people giving us trouble, because we will make life difficult for them after the election."

"The conversation then turned to the use of the Internal Revenue Service to attack our enemies." Dean said not much use had been made because the White House "didn't have the clout," the IRS was "a rather Democratically oriented bureaucracy and it would be very dangerous to try any such activities. The President seeemed somewhat annoyed and said that the Democratic Administrations had used this tool well and after the election we would get people in these agencies who would be responsive to the White House requirements.

"The conversation then turned to the President's post election plans to replace people who were not on our team in all the agencies. It was at this point that Haldeman, I remember, started taking notes and he also told the President that he had been developing information on which people should stay and which should go after the election."

Effort to block House hearing—The next subject was "White House efforts to block" Watergate hearings by a House committee.

The White House was concerned the hearings "would result in more adverse pre-election publicity" and "just might stumble into something that would start unraveling the cover-up."

Dean asked Haldeman how the hearings "might be turned off." Haldeman suggested asking then-Treasury Secretary John B. Connally Jr., who knew the hearing chairman, Rep. Wright Patman (D, Tex.). Connally said "the only soft spot that Patman might have, was that he had received large contributions from a Washington lobbyist and had heard rumors that some of these may not be reported."

But it was "concluded that several Republicans would probably have a similar problem so the matter was dropped."

Several people worked at rounding up votes to block the hearings, or have members not show up for the committee vote, and a vote against the hearings was attained.

The Segretti matter—In the summer of 1971, Dean called Petersen about a problem concerning Donald Segretti, who was being called before the grand jury about alleged political sabotage during the campaign. Dean told him to the best of his knowledge Segretti was not involved in the Watergate incident but was being paid by Kalmbach and had been recruited by Chapin and Strachan. "I said that these facts, if revealed, would be obviously quite embarrassing and could cause political problems during the waning weeks of the election. Mr. Petersen said that he understood the problem," Dean said.

"I later learned from Segretti that the names [Kalmbach, Chapin and Strachan]

had come out during the grand jury appearance and I had a discussion later with Petersen also on the subject in which he told me that Mr. [prosecutor Earl J.] Silbert had tried to avoid getting into this area and in fact did not ask him the question which resulted in his giving names, rather that a grand juror had asked the question despite the fact that the prosecutors had tried to gloss over it.

"I had by this time learned the full story, that in fact Haldeman, in a meeting with Kalmbach, had approved Segretti's activities and authorized Kalmbach to make the payments to Segretti. In discussing this with Chapin and Strachan before their [grand jury] appearance, they both had great concern about revealing Haldeman's involvement. In fact, I recall that Strachan came into my office and said that he would, if necessary, perjure himself to prevent involving Haldeman in this matter."

Press reports of Segretti's activities "created a new frenzy in the White House press office" and five persons, including Ehrlichman and Dean, met on Sunday, Oct. 15, 1972 in the White House to prepare Press Secretary Ronald L. Ziegler for his press briefings "on the Segretti-related stories."

Factual story 'not viable'—With the continuing press stories about Watergate, "there was serious discussion about putting the facts out." In late November 1972, Dean told Haldeman "it was very likely that any reconvened grand jury would get into questions of obstruction of justice which would lead right to us. Haldeman said that the President wished, now that the election was over, to get rid of the Watergate and related matters by laying them open but based on what I had just told him he said it doesn't seem to be a very viable option."

Soon after that, Mitchell called and said part of a $350,000 White House fund under Haldeman's aegis would have to be used "to take care of the demands that were being made by Hunt and the others [defendants] for money." Neither Dean nor Haldeman liked the idea of using White House money for that purpose, but no other answer was found and, under the assurance the amount would be returned, some funds were turned over to the campaign committee. Dean thought the amount was "either $40,000 or $70,000."

But the demands "reached the crescendo point once again" shortly before the trial, Mitchell made another request for funds and "Haldeman said send the entire damn bundle to them but make sure that we get a receipt for $350,000." The actual transfer of money was made by Strachan, who later told Dean the receiver, Frederick C. LaRue, Mitchell's deputy at the committee, refused to give him a receipt.

Executive clemency—Another problem came up. A campaign committee attorney, Paul L. O'Brien, informed Dean "that Hunt was quite upset and wished to plead guilty but before he did so he wanted some assurances from the White House that he would receive executive clemency."

Hunt wanted the assurance from Colson, and Colson talked with Hunt's lawyer, William O. Bittman, "about Hunt's potential for executive clemency."

Colson met with Ehrlichman in Dean's presence. He said "he felt it was imperative that Hunt be given some assurances of executive clemency ... Ehrlichman said that he would have to speak with the President. Ehrlichman told Colson that he should not talk with the President about this. On Jan. 4th, I learned from Ehrlichman that he had given Colson an affirmative regarding clemency for Hunt."

Colson later told Dean he thought the matter so important he had discussed it with Nixon himself.

Dean said the President raised the subject with him on two occasions—March 13 and April 15.

Another problem: the Senate probe— The White House faced another problem as the Senate moved to probe Watergate. When a resolution to create the select committee was introduced, Dean was asked for suggested amendments to the resolution the Republicans might offer. They were: broaden the probe to cover other elections, get adequate staff for the minority and equal membership with the Democrats and authority to call for an executive, private session.

There was also discussion of utilizing the President's suggestion he had been wiretapped during his 1968 campaign. An attempt was made to obtain the information from Cartha Deloach, then an assistant director at the FBI. Mitchell reported later, at a meeting attended by Ehrlichman, Haldeman and Dean, among others, "that there had been some surveillance by the Johnson Administration but Deloach was unaware of a bugging or wiretap."

Nevertheless, Dean was told to tell Senate Republican Leader Hugh Scott (Pa.) "to raise the 1968 bugging incident as a reason to expand the scope" of the Senate hearings to prior presidential elections.

After the proposed White House amendments were rejected, White House Congressional liaison William E. Timmons told Dean he had discussed with Haldeman the possibility of suggesting names for the Republican side of the Ervin committee with Scott and "Scott seemed receptive." After the members were named, Timmons told Dean that Haldeman "chewed him out" but Scott "had never given him a chance to make any recommendations."

In February there was a strategy session near San Clemente on the problem of dealing with the approaching Senate hearings. There was a "general feeling that the Senate was a hostile world for the White House," and Ehrlichman felt that

"the White House could not look for any help" from the Ervin committee Democrats. As for the Republican members: "It was Ehrlichman who was doing most of the assessing. But occasionally, Haldeman would add a comment. Sen. Weicker was an independent who could give the White House problems. Sen. Gurney would help the White House and would not have to be told to do so. Sen. Baker was an unknown and neither Haldeman nor Ehrlichman knew which way he might go. I might add that in a subsequent discussion I had with the President he also reached a similar conclusion regarding the Republicans. He thought that Sen. Baker might help, but was not sure. He was confident, however, that Sen. Gurney would protect the White House and would do so out of political instinct and not have to be persuaded to do so."

Ehrlichman and Haldeman, Dean continued, "concluded that the theory for dealing with this committee should be as follows: The White House will take a public posture of full cooperation, but privately will attempt to restrain the investigation and make it as difficult as possible to get information and witnesses. A behind-the-scenes media effort would be made to make the Senate inquiry appear very partisan. The ultimate goal would be to discredit the hearings and reduce their impact by attempting to show that the Democrats have engaged in the same type of activities."

Baker was to be approached to find out whether he was "going to be friend or foe" and whether "the White House could aid him, particularly regarding the selection of the minority counsel."

"Ehrlichman raised the question of whether or not the select committee was going to be able to obtain the grand jury minutes and other investigative records from the FBI and the U.S. attorney's office ... No one really knew what the law might be regarding this matter, but Ehrlichman stated that the attorney general will have to be told that the Justice Department should resist turning over such records, and that I should get word back to the attorney for the defendants that they should fight the release of these investigative records to the Senate."

There was also discussion about whether the Watergate defendants would remain silent through the Senate hearings, and their continuing demands for money. Ehrlichman made the decision that Mitchell should be told it was his "responsibility to raise the necessary funds for these men."

Baker was contacted about the minority counsel post, but replied he "did not want any official input from the White House." There was a possibility he had not ruled out "the White House's making some suggestions."

Nixon and Haldeman met in February on an agenda drawn up by Dean covering, among other things, a proposed meeting

with Sen. Baker, "what to do with Mr. Magruder," and "getting the attorney general [Kleindienst] back in touch with the White House."

Nixon had an off-the-record, private meeting with Baker Feb. 20 or 21. Afterwards, Dean was informed by Haldeman that Baker "had appeared to be very interested in being cooperative and the President had the impression that he might be helpful. This, of course, was the White House hope, but nothing that was reported from the meeting made this anything more than a hope. Also, Sen. Baker told the President that he wanted his contact point to be Mr. Kleindienst ... [and] urged the President to waive executive privilege and send members of the White House staff to the hearings as quickly as possible." The President told Baker "he was going to hold the line at written interrogatories." They also "discussed that there should be an effort to get the hearings over as quickly as possible."

Nixon met Feb. 22 with Kleindienst. Dean said:

"Throughout the Watergate investigation Haldeman, and particularly Ehrlichman, had complained about Mr. Kleindienst's passive role in the investigation and prosecution. The Senate Watergate hearings presented the real possibility for the Justice Department having to make further criminal investigations that would lead back to the White House. Accordingly, the President was the only one who could bring Mr. Kleindienst back in the family to protect the White House and this meeting was designed to do just that. As a result of Sen. Baker's request that Kleindienst be his contact point, the President had a perfect vehicle to solicit Kleindienst's assistance during the hearings and, if anything should develop during the hearings, to not let all hell break loose in a subsequent investigation.

"The President subsequently discussed this meeting with me in early March. He told me that he would continue to call Mr. Kleindienst from time to time, but I should also make certain that Kleindienst was working closely with Sen. Baker in preparation for the select committee hearings.

"It was during this period of time which I believe was mid-February, Magruder had a conversation with Mr. O'Brien in which he told O'Brien that he had received his final authorization for Liddy's activities from Gordon Strachan and that Strachan had reported that Haldeman had cleared the matter with the President. I reported this to Haldeman, who expressed concern over Magruder's statement. After I reported this information, the White House efforts to find a job for Magruder became intense."

Dean said the decision already had been made by the President that Magruder "could not return to the White House staff."

The Nixon-Dean meetings: Feb. 27— "This was the first meeting I had had with

A

B

C

D

E

F

G

A
the President since my Sept. 15, 1972, meeting which related to the Watergate. It was at this meeting that the President directed that I report directly to him regarding all Watergate matters. He told me that this matter was taking too much time from Haldeman's and Ehrlichman's normal duties and he also told me that they were principals in the matter, and I, therefore, could be more objective than they."

B
Nixon told Dean he should keep in touch with Kleindienst to assure that he and Baker "were working together." He also told Dean "he would never let Haldeman and Ehrlichman go to [Capitol] Hill" to testify.

They discussed a leak about White House wiretaps on newsmen and White House staffers and a statement on executive privilege.

C
Nixon again asked Dean to report to him directly, and Dean then told him "I thought he should know that I was also involved in the post-June 17th activities regarding Watergate. I briefly described to him why I thought I had legal problems, in that I had been a conduit for many of the decisions that were made and therefore could be involved in an obstruction of justice. He would not accept my analysis and did not want me to get into it in any detail other than what I had just related. He reassured me not to worry, that I had no legal problems."

D
March 1 meeting—Nixon told Dean March 1 "there should be no problem with the fact that I had received the FBI reports [on its Watergate probe]. He said that I was conducting an investigation for him and that it would be perfectly proper for the counsel to the President to have looked at these reports. I did not tell the President that I had not conducted an investigation for him because I assumed he was well aware of this fact and that the so-called Dean investigation was a public relations matter, and that frequently the President made reference in press conferences to things that never had, in fact occurred. I was also aware that often in answering Watergate questions that he had made reference to my report and I did not feel that I could tell the President that he could not use my name."

F
The President, Dean said, asked him to gather material "regarding the uses and abuses of the FBI by past Administrations so that we could show that we had not abused the FBI for political purposes. The President told me that he was convinced that he had been wiretapped in 1968 and the fact that Deloach had not been forthcoming indicated to the President that Deloach was probably lying. He told me that I should call [Pepsico chairman] Don[ald M.] Kendall, Deloach's employer, and tell him that Deloach had better start telling the truth because 'the boys are coming out of the woodwork.' He said this ploy may smoke Deloach out."

G
Nixon instructed Dean to tell Kleindienst "to cut off Gray from turning over

any further Watergate reports to the Senate Judiciary Committee. He said this just had to cease."

March 13 meeting—"We discussed the potential of litigating the matter of executive privilege and thereby preventing anybody from going before any Senate committee until that matter was resolved. The President liked the idea very much, particularly when I mentioned to him that it might be possible that he could also claim attorney/client privilege on me so that the strongest potential case on executive privilege would probably rest on the counsel to the President."

Dean told Nixon about the money demands by the defendants and, after Haldeman came in, that there was no money to pay the demands. Nixon asked Dean "how much it would cost. I told him that I could only make an estimate that it might be as high as a million dollars or more. He told me that that was no problem."

"He then asked me who was demanding this money and I told him it was principally coming from Hunt through his attorney. The President then referred to the fact that Hunt had been promised executive clemency. He said that he had discussed this matter with Ehrlichman and . . . expressed some annoyance at the fact that Colson had also discussed this matter with him."

In reply to a question, Dean told Nixon the payment money "was laundered so it could not be traced" and the deliveries were secret.

March 15 meeting—Dean said Nixon expressed amazement that the first question at his news conference that day, after he made a major foreign announcement, was whether Dean would appear before the Senate hearings on the Gray nomination. "The conversation then rambled into a discussion of the Hiss case."

Decision to speak about cover-up—Dean said he had received a new demand for support money from Hunt, through O'Brien, "that he wanted $72,000 for living expenses and $50,000 for attorney's fees and if he did not receive it that week, he would reconsider his options and have a lot to say about the seamy things he had done for Ehrlichman while at the White House." Dean felt he "had about reached the end of the line and was now in a position to deal with the President to end the cover-up."

March 20 phone call—After "a rather rambling discussion," Dean told the President "I wanted to talk with him as soon as possible about the Watergate matter because I did not think that he fully realized all the facts and the implication of those facts for people at the White House as well as himself. He said that I should meet with him the next morning."

Before meeting with Nixon, Dean said he told Haldeman "what I was going to do and Haldeman agreed that I should

proceed to so inform the President of the situation."

March 21 meeting—"I began [at the March 21 meeting] by telling the President that there was a cancer growing on the Presidency and that if the cancer was not removed that the President himself would be killed by it. I also told him that it was important that this cancer be removed immediately because it was growing more deadly every day."

Dean said he told the President that he had been told Mitchell had received wiretap information; Haldeman had received such information through Strachan; Kalmbach had been used to raise funds to pay the defendants for their silence on orders from Ehrlichman, Haldeman and Mitchell; Dean had relayed the orders and assisted Magruder in preparing his false story for the grand jury; cash at the White House had been used to pay the defendants; more funds would be required for the cover-up to continue; and Dean "didn't know how to deal" with the blackmail problem.

Dean also said he told Nixon "if I was called to testify before the grand jury or the Senate committee I would have to tell the facts the way I know them."

Dean concluded "by saying that it was going to take continued perjury and continued support of these individuals to perpetuate the cover-up and that I did not believe it was possible to continue it; rather I thought it was time for surgery on the cancer itself and that all those involved must stand up and account for themselves and that the President himself get out in front of this matter. I told the President that I did not believe that all of the seven defendants would maintain their silence forever. In fact, I thought that one or more would very likely break rank.

"After I finished, I realized that I had not really made the President understand because after he asked a few questions, he suggested that it would be an excellent idea if I gave some sort of briefing to the Cabinet and that he was very impressed with my knowledge of the circumstances but he did not seem particularly concerned with their implications."

After calling Haldeman in, Nixon suggested a meeting with Mitchell, Haldeman and Ehrlichman to discuss how to deal with this situation. There also was a discussion that Mitchell "should account for himself for the pre-June 17 activities." Dean reported that Nixon "did not seem concerned about the activities which had occurred after June 17."

Mitchell should 'step forward'—After the presidential conference, Dean, Haldeman and Ehrlichman continued the discussion, focusing on a plan for "Mitchell to step forward" so "we might not be confronted with the activities of those involved in the White House in the cover-up."

The three White House aides met with Nixon again later March 21. Dean called it "a tremendous disappointment" because it became "quite clear that the cover-up as far as the White House was going to continue." Dean said he spoke up.

"I for the first time said in front of the President that I thought that Haldeman, Ehrlichman and Dean were all indictable for obstruction of justice and that was the reason I disagreed with all that was being discussed at that point in time."

The expected Mitchell move "did not occur." Meeting with them the next day, Mitchell said "he thought that everything was going along very well" except for the posture on executive privilege, where he felt the President "was going to have to come back down somewhat or it would appear he was preventing information from coming out of the White House."

At lunch, Mitchell brought up a problem of F. Lee Bailey, whose firm was involved in handling the defense of one of the Watergate defendants. Bailey represented a client who wanted to unload his huge gold hoard to the government without prosecution for holding it, Mitchell told Haldeman, "but Haldeman was non-responsive and the matter was dropped."

When the three aides, joined by Mitchell, met with Nixon March 22, the meeting focused "almost exclusively on the subject of how the White House should posture itself vis-a-vis the Ervin committee hearings." The talk "was of strategies for dealing with the hearings rather than any effort to get the truth out."

After the meeting "it was apparent" to Dean he "had failed in turning the President around." But Ehrlichman and Haldeman "began taking over with regard to dealing with a new problem, which had become John Dean, as they were aware that I was very unhappy about the situation."

Dean sent to Camp David—On March 23, after convicted Watergate defendant James W. McCord's letter to the court was read promising disclosures, Nixon called Dean, told him "you were right in your prediction" and suggested he go to the presidential retreat at Camp David "and analyze the situation." Dean insisted "he did not instruct me to write a report, rather he said to go to Camp David, take your wife and get some relaxation."

Dean was at Camp David by mid-afternoon. As he arrived, the phone was ringing, the operator said it was the President "but Haldeman came on the phone" and told Dean to "spend some time writing a report on everything I knew about the Watergate."

After considering that Ehrlichman "would never admit to his involvement in the cover-up" and Haldeman presumably would not "because he would believe it a higher duty to protect the President," Dean "realized that I should step forward because there was no way the situation was going to get better—rather it would

only get worse. My most difficult problem was how I could end this mess without mortally wounding the President."

On March 25 Dean heard the press was ready to print a story he had prior knowledge of the break-in, which he considered libelous. He retained a lawyer.

The next day he told Haldeman, who "concurred in the fact that I had no prior knowledge."

On March 28, Haldeman told Dean to return to Washington, where he met with Mitchell and his campaign aide, Jeb Stuart Magruder, who wanted to know about how Dean would testify if he were called about the Watergate planning meetings. Dean was evasive, saying he might invoke executive privilege so the question of his testimony was "moot." "They were obviously both disappointed that I was being reluctant in agreeing to continue to perpetuate their earlier testimony."

The Ellsberg order—Dean had a talk March 28 or 29 with Ehrlichman aide Egil Krogh Jr. Dean told Krogh it was very likely the Ervin committee "could stumble into the Ellsberg burglary" because documents at the Justice Department contained pictures left in a camera, of Liddy standing in front of the break-in site. He said Ehrlichman wanted him to retrieve the documents and return them to the Central Intelligence Agency (CIA) "where they might be withheld" from Congressional committees probing the CIA but the CIA was "unwilling."

Krogh made a statement that startled Dean into asking him to repeat it. Dean had asked Krogh "if he had received his authorization to proceed with the burglary from Ehrlichman. Krogh responded that no, he did not believe that Ehrlichman had been aware of the incident until shortly after it had occurred: Rather, he had received his orders right out of the 'Oval Office'."

Dean tells what he knows—On April 2 Dean's attorneys informed the government prosecutors that "I was willing to come forward with everything I knew about the case." Dean felt he should tell Haldeman he was going to meet the prosecutors. Haldeman told him he should not.

Dean said he told Mitchell April 9 if he were called he would testify honestly. Mitchell understood "and did not suggest that I do otherwise." But he told Dean he should avoid testifying if at all possible because his testimony "would be very harmful to the President."

Haldeman and Ehrlichman at that time still "talked about pinning the entire matter on Mitchell." They did not know Dean was dealing directly with the prosecutors, but Dean "was quite confident that I had gotten the message" to them "that they had a serious problem themselves and I had put them on final notice that I wasn't playing the cover-up game any longer."

Aware that Nixon was to meet with Kleindienst the next day for a report on

the Watergate probe, Dean wrote a message to Nixon expressing hope "he did not interpret my going to the prosecutors as an act of disloyalty" and he would meet with him if he wished.

April 15 meeting—At the Nixon-Dean meeting April 15, Nixon "was very cordial when we met." After a time, Dean realized Nixon was asking him "a number of leading questions, which made me think that the conversation was being taped and that a record was being made to protect himself."

Nixon recalled a previous discussion in which he said there was no problem raising a million dollars to keep the defendants silent. "He said that he had of course, only been joking when he made that comment." Dean became more convinced "that the President was seeking to elicit testimony from me and put his perspective on the record and get me to agree to it." At one point, Nixon got up, went to the corner of the office and, "in a barely audible tone said to me, he was probably foolish to have discussed Hunt's clemency with Colson."

April 16 meeting—Nixon sent for Dean April 16 and asked him to sign a letter of resignation or an alternative letter of indefinite leave of absence, which had been prepared. Nixon said "he would not do anything with them at this time but thought it would be good if he had them." Dean read the letters, then "looked the President squarely in the eyes and told him that I could not sign the letters. He was annoyed with me, and somewhat at a loss for words. . . . I told him that the letters that he had asked me to sign were virtual confessions of anything regarding the Watergate. I also asked him if Ehrlichman and Haldeman had signed letters of resignations. I recall that he was somewhat surprised at my asking this and he said no they had not but they had given him a verbal assurance to the same effect. I then told him that he had my verbal assurance to the same effect.

"It was a tense conversation. . . . The President said that he would like me to draft my own letter and would also like a suggested draft letter for Haldeman and Ehrlichman or maybe a form letter that everyone could sign."

Nixon sent for Dean later April 16 to see his draft letter. Dean told him "I would not resign unless Haldeman and Ehrlichman resigned. I told him that I was not willing to be the White House scapegoat for the Watergate. He said that he understood my position and he wasn't asking me to be a scapegoat."

In his letter, Dean was saying: Nixon had learned new facts over the weekend and as a result directed Petersen to take charge and leave no stone unturned; Haldeman, Ehrlichman and Dean were taking leaves of absence.

Nixon "said virtually nothing about the statement" except to have Dean talk with another White House counsel about it.

April 17 phone call—Dean said Nixon called April 17 and informed him he was issuing a Watergate statement. After he did so, Dean "decided that indeed I was being set up and that it was time that I let the word out that I would not be a scapegoat." He did this April 19.

"On April 22, Easter Sunday, the President called me to wish me a happy Easter. It was what they refer to at the White House as a 'stroking' call.

"On April 30th, while out of the city, I had a call from my secretary in which she informed me that . . . my resignation had been requested and accepted and that Haldeman and Ehrlichman were also resigning."

June 26: *Cross-examination begins*—In his first day of cross-examination by committee members and counsel, Dean maintained that his opening statement was factual. In response to the questioning, he disputed the President's public statements on Watergate as "broad," misleading, unfounded or simply untruthful. He acknowledged the gravity of his allegations against the President and the vulnerability of his stance, that it was his word against the President's. He softened the implications in his statement against the federal prosecutor, Petersen, and against press secretary Ziegler. And he made some new disclosures about the White House operation.

He said an "enemies list" of persons considered unfriendly to the Nixon Administration was maintained and kept updated. And he told of incidents of harassment against some individuals considered unfriendly, incidents utilizing federal services such as the Internal Revenue Service, the Secret Service and the FBI.

The committee's Democratic chief counsel Samuel Dash opened the cross-examination. He recalled Dean describing the Liddy plan of Jan. 27, 1972 as "mind-boggling" and that "you didn't tell him to stop the activity." "That is correct," Dean admitted. "With hindsight, I probably should have been much more forceful in trying to stop the plan when I realized it was something that should not occur."

Dash reminded him he told Haldeman the White House should not be involved in such a venture but did not recommend that Haldeman put a stop to it, "which you knew he could if he wanted to." Dean said he felt "that someone wanted this" but he "had put those on notice involved that I was going to have no part in it."

Is it not true, Dash asked, that you played a role in the cover-up activities? "That is correct," Dean said. Was it on his own initiative or under orders from someone? "I inherited a situation," Dean said. "The cover-up was in operation when I returned to my office" two days after the Watergate break-in "and it just became the instant way of life at that point in time."

He was "a conveyor of messages" between the White House and the Mitchell committee, Dean testified, and his reporting relationship was directly to Haldeman and to Ehrlichman, the latter because he "maintained a very active interest" in the counsel's office since he had occupied it once himself. In fact, Dean said, he had learned before he went to the White House "that the title was probably the best part of the job."

Did he have an opinion "as to whether the President would have been informed" of the cover-up from its inception? Dean thought it "unfair" to solicit his opinion on this, but he could "surmise" from what he knew of the White House operation. His conclusion in his own mind was "that this thing might well go right to the President."

When Nixon complimented him on Sept. 15, 1972 about the good job he had done, did he have any doubt what the President was talking about? "No, I did not," Dean replied. Whatever doubts he may have had prior to Sept. 15, 1972 about the President's involvement in the cover-up, did he have any doubts about this after Sept. 15? "No, I did not."

Could he honestly believe that the President, as a lawyer and a sophisticated man in politics, was not aware of the full implications of the cover-up? Dean talked of the "human side of the situation" as distinguished from "the legal side." The President "didn't realize the implications as far as what this would mean to people he had worked with for a number of years, people he was very fond of," he felt.

What about his knowledge of the legal implications of the cover-up? "I would think the President would certainly have some appreciation of the legal problems involved, yes indeed."

Dash concluded. Was Dean fully aware of the gravity of the charges he had made under oath against the highest official of the land, the President of the United States? "Yes, I am." And being so aware, did he still stand on his statement? "Yes, I do." There was a pause, then Dean added: "I realize it's almost an impossible task—if it's one man against the other—that I'm up against. And it isn't a very pleasant situation. I can only speak what I know to be the facts, and that's what I'm providing the committee."

Thompson's questions—Chief Republican counsel Fred D. Thompson was next. Dean's extenuating remarks concerning Petersen and Ziegler were drawn during this exchange. Petersen "isn't the type of man who is easily pushed around," Dean affirmed, and said he knew "of no impropriety" on Petersen's part of the Watergate investigation. "I think he tried to be very fair with the White House in dealing with the White House and the fact that he had an investigation going on in a political year, that it could result in embarrassment," Dean said.

As for Ziegler and his statements on Watergate, who supplied him his information? Dean supplied a large amount. Ziegler "would check many times with Mr. Ehrlichman, sometimes with Mr. Haldeman and often with the President himself." Did Ziegler know the truth? "No, he did not." Dean said Ziegler asked him "countless" times to brief him but Dean was given "very specific instructions" that he was not to brief Ziegler. Dean said the same prohibition applied to Clark MacGregor, who replaced Mitchell as head of the campaign committee after the break-in.

Thompson also asked Dean what his professional relationship was with Mitchell at the Justice Department. "I would have to say it was sort of a father-son relationship in many ways," Dean replied. Was he concerned about Mitchell's involvement after he learned about the break-in? "I indeed was but, to this day there has been only one indication that he had any involvement in this thing at all and that was when I hypothesized to him what I thought had happened and he said something to the effect, 'Well, yes, it was something like that but we thought it was going to be two or three times removed from the committee.' "

Talmadge questions credibility—Sen. Herman E. Talmadge (D, Ga.) reminded Dean he had made "very strong" charges against the President "that involves him in criminal offenses." Then he bluntly asked him, "What makes you think that your credibility is greater than that of the President, who denies what you have said?"

A. I have told it exactly the way I know it. I don't say that I—you are asking me a public relations question, really, in a sense, why I would have greater credibility than the President of the United States? I am telling you just as I know it.

Talmadge pressed Dean to explain why, as counsel of the President, he had not gone to him and told him what was happening after Dean learned following the Watergate break-in that files were being destroyed and a cover-up was under way.

"Senator, I did not have access to the President," Dean replied. "I never was presumptuous enough to try to pound on the door and get in because I knew that just did not work that way." He had been told his "reporting channel" was Haldeman and Ehrlichman "and I was reporting everything I knew to them." Talmadge insisted he would have thought it "incumbent upon you, as counsel to the President, to make every effort to see that he got that information at that time."

"Senator, I was participating in the cover-up at that time," Dean replied.

'Enemies list' cited—The revelation about a White House "enemies list" was elicited by Sen. Lowell P. Weicker Jr. (R, Conn.), who questioned Dean primarily about the Administration's establishment of a domestic interagency intelligence operation and the sources of White House intelligence.

During the course of it, Dean said there was "a continual request" in the White House "for information regarding demonstrations and particularly information that would embarrass individuals in connection with their relationship with demonstrators or demonstration leaders." There was an effort, he said, to obtain "politically embarrassing information on individuals who were thought to be the enemies of the White House. There was also maintained what was called an 'enemies list,' which was rather extensive and continually being updated." Weicker asked about these documents, and Dean said he would supply them.

Dean told Weicker of involvement in such activities of several federal agencies. Haldeman once requested, he related, an FBI investigation of CBS newsman Daniel Schorr. The investigation "proceeded," but, "to the dismay of the White House," it was "sort of a full field wide open investigation and this became very apparent. So this put the White House in a rather scrambling position to explain what had happened. The long and short of the explanation was that Mr. Schorr was being considered for a post and that this was a part of a preliminary investigation."

Dean related another incident involving Nixon's close personal friend, Charles (Bebe) Rebozo. After an article unfavorable to Rebozo had appeared in Newsday, the Long Island, N.Y. newspaper, Dean said he got "instructions that one of the authors of the article should have some problems" with the Internal Revenue Service. Dean said he arranged that the writer be subjected to an income tax audit.

A third incident involved the Secret Service. An official from there once supplied him with a "small intelligence printout" alleging that Democratic presidential contender George McGovern would attend a fund-raising affair in Philadelphia with some involvement of "either Communist money or former Communist supporters." Dean passed the item to Charles W. Colson, then White House special counsel, who told him later he had arranged to have it published.

Montoya's questions—Sen. Joseph M. Montoya (D, N.M.) enlivened the day's final interrogation by leading Dean through the President's public Watergate statements and letting Dean juxtapose his version of events at those times. Nixon's Aug. 29, 1972 statement said Dean had conducted a complete investigation and Nixon could categorically say Dean's investigation indicated no one in the Administration presently employed was involved. Was the President telling the truth? Montoya asked.

A. If that were to be a literal statement as to somebody being involved in the very particular incident which occurred on June 17, that would have been a true statement. I think it was a little broad.

Dean said he had not participated in forming the statement and had never conducted such an investigation and Nixon must have been aware of this because he had no report from Dean on it.

At an October 1972 news conference, Nixon described the FBI effort in the Hiss case as "basically a Sunday school exercise" compared to the effort on the Watergate probe and declared his desire to have "every lead carried out to the end" because he wanted to be certain no member of the White House staff or anyone in a responsible management position at the campaign committee was involved.

Were those statements correct?

A. I certainly did not prepare anything for the briefing book that would let him make that statement.

On April 17 Nixon said he condemned any attempts to cover up in this case.

Q. Do you believe he was telling the truth?

A. No, sir.

(Continued on page 98)

Attempt to Use IRS Pressure on Opponents

Former Internal Revenue Service Commissioner Randolph W. Thrower revealed a 1970 Administration plan to launch an IRS investigation of radical organizations and individuals in a Washington Post report June 27. Thrower resigned his post in January 1971 after he had successfully resisted White House pressure on him to hire John J. Caulfield, inplicated in the Watergate cover-up, and G. Gordon Liddy, convicted Watergate conspirator, to direct the investigations.

The Administration's "strong pressure" to hire Caulfield and Liddy was relayed repeatedly to him by Charls E. Walker, then undersecretary of the Treasury, from a person "high in the White House," Thrower said. (An unidentified Washington Post source reported that John D. Ehrlichman, then Nixon's chief domestic affairs adviser, issued the order.)

Thrower said he rejected the bid to name Caulfield as director of the Bureau of Alcohol, Tobacco and Firearms in August-September 1970. A suggestion that Liddy be named to the same post was rejected in October 1970, Thrower said.

(After leaving the White House in March 1972, Caulfield worked for the Committee to Re-elect the President for two months and then joined the staff of the bureau's enforcement division. He was named acting assistant director for enforcement July 1, 1972, a post he resigned May 24, 1973.)

Caulfield's name was again mentioned in December 1970 when the Administration asked that he be named director of the enforcement division of the bureau. (Authority for the bureau, at that time under the IRS, was shifted to the Treasury Department.)

Also in December 1970, Thrower said, the White House pressured him to make the bureau's enforcement division "a personal police force" reporting directly to him as part of a crackdown on "subversive organizations allegedly engaged in acts of terrorism." Although he resisted this suggestion, Thrower admitted acquiescing in a White House plan to set up an IRS unit, the Special Service Group, to conduct tax audits on radical groups and individuals.

Thrower insisted that both right and left wing extremist groups were investigated.

As other witnesses before the Watergate hearings had testified, Thrower said political conditions in the country, as perceived by the Nixon Administration, justified these special measures.

"You've got to go back to the atmosphere that existed at that time in early 1970. There was great concern in the country about the use of explosives and firearms by subversive groups. [The Special Service Group] was set up partly in response to the wave of subversive bombings that was just reaching its peak then," Thrower declared.

One of the memos submitted June 27 to the Senate Watergate hearings by former White House counsel Dean revealed Administration displeasure with Thrower's efforts to balk the politicization of the IRS. The memo, written by Dean based on "material provided to me by Caulfield," outlined a plan to make "the IRS politically responsive to the White House." Although the memo was written after Thrower had left the IRS, Dean termed Thrower "a total captive of the Democratic assistant commissioners. In the end, he was actively fighting both Treasury and the White House," according to the memo.

"In brief, the lack of key Republican bureaucrats at high levels precludes the initiation of policies which would be proper and politically advantageous. Practically every effort to proceed in sensitive areas is met with resistance, delay and the threat of derogatory exposure," Dean wrote.

A Thrower report, dated Sept. 19, 1970, submitted to the Watergate hearings by Dean, to Tom Charles Huston, a member of the Special Service Group, stated that data on 1,025 organizations and 4,300 individuals had been completed. "Enforcement action" on 26 groups and 43 persons had resulted, Thrower said.

Dean also revealed that a politically motivated IRS audit of the tax returns of Robert Greene, a Newsday reporter, was requested by Caulfield. Greene had headed a team of reporters investigating President Nixon's friend, Charles G. Rebozo.

Lists of White House 'Enemies' and Memos

Dean's list. Among the documents Dean submitted in evidence June 27 were lists "several inches thick" of Nixon's "political enemies."

The "Opponents List and Political Enemies Project" turned over to the Senate committee, Dean said, was compiled beginning in 1971 by various Administration officials and was frequently updated.

In one of the documents, written by Dean Aug. 16, 1971, intended to accompany the undated master list of opponents, Dean suggested ways in which "we can use the available federal machinery to screw our political enemies." Methods proposed included Administration manipulation of "grant availability, federal contracts, litigation, prosecution, etc."

Dean testified that the memo was sent to then-White House Chief of Staff H. R. Haldeman and John D. Ehrlichman, then the President's adviser for domestic affairs, for approval. Dean said he did not know if the plan became operational; however, subsequent memos, also submitted to the committee, indicated that the plan was adopted.

The master list of political enemies was prepared by the office of then White House counsel Charles W. Colson, Dean said. A condensed list of 20 prime political enemies slated for reprisals was also produced by Colson's office, according to Dean. Others named by Dean who had direct input in the lists were former White House aide Lyn Nofziger and Haldeman aide Gordon Strachan.

The larger list, divided in categories, included 10 Democratic senators, all 12 black House members, more than 50 newspaper and television reporters, prominent businessmen and labor leaders, and entertainers. Another list included large and small contributors to Sen. Edmund S. Muskie's (D, Me) presidential campaign.

Original List

The original list of 20 names of White House "enemies" submitted with comments to Dean by the office of Charles W. Colson. **Bold Face type** *indicates a correction in erroneous White House identification of its political enemies. Material in brackets is additional information supplied by the editor.*

Having studied the attached material and evaluated the recommendations for the discussed action, I believe you will find my list worthwhile for go status. It is in priority order.

1. Arnold M. Picker, United Artists Corp., N.Y.: Top Muskie fund raiser. Success here could be both debilitating and very embarrassing to the Muskie machine. If effort looks promising, both Ruth and David Picker should be programed and then a follow-through with United Artists.

*A memo dated Sept. 14, 1971 from Dean to Haldeman aide Lawrence Higby, submitted to the committee, included three persons not shown on either list of 20 or the larger master list. Those selected by Dean for inclusion were:

Eugene Carson Blake (per request) [General Secretary World Council of Churches]

Leonard Bernstein (per request) [Conductor/Composer]

Tom Wicker (New York Times)

Clark Gifford (**Clifford**) [former Secretary of Defense]

2. Alexander E. Barkan, national director of A.F.L.-C.I.O.'s Committee on Political Education, Washington, D.C.: Without a doubt the most powerful political force programed against us in 1968 ($10-million, 4.6 million votes, 115 million pamphlets, 176,000 workers—all programed by Barkan's C.O.P.E.—so says Teddy White in "The Making of the President 1968"). We can expect the same effort this time. [See p. 468E3]

3. Ed Guthman, managing editor, Los Angeles Times [**national editor**]: Guthman, former Kennedy aide, was a highly sophisticated hatchetman against us in '68. It is obvious he is the prime mover behind the current Key Biscayne effort. It is time to give him the message.

4. Maxwell Dane, Doyle, Dane and Bernbach, N.Y.: The top Democratic advertising firm—they destroyed Goldwater in '64. They should be hit hard starting with Dane.

5. Charles Dyson, Dyson-Kissner Corp., N.Y.: Dyson and Larry O'Brien were close business associates after '68. Dyson has huge business holdings and is presently deeply involved in the Businessmen's Educational Fund which bankrolls a national radio network of five-minute programs—anti-Nixon in character.

6. Howard Stein, Dreyfus Corp., N.Y.: Heaviest contributor to McCarthy in '68. If McCarthy goes, will do the same in '72. If not, Lindsay or McGovern will receive the funds.

7. Allard Lowenstein, Long Island, N.Y.: Guiding force behind the 18-year-old "Dump Nixon" vote drive.

8. Morton Halperin, leading executive at Common Cause: A scandal would be most helpful here. (A **consultant for Common Cause in February-March 1971**) [On staff of Brookings Institution]

9. Leonard Woodcock, UAW, Detroit, Mich.: No comments necessary.

10. S. Sterling Munro Jr., Sen. [Henry M.] Jackson's aide, Silver Spring, Md.: We should give him a try. Positive results would stick a pin in Jackson's white hat.

11. Bernard T. Feld, president, Council for a Livable World: Heavy far left funding. They will program an "all court press" against us in '72.

12. Sidney Davidoff, New York City, [New York City Mayor John V.] Lindsay's top personal aide: a first class S.O.B., wheeler-dealer and suspected bagman. Positive results would really shake the Lindsay camp and Lindsay's plans to capture youth vote. Davidoff in charge.

13. John Conyers, congressman, Detroit: Coming on fast. Emerging as a leading black anti-Nixon spokesman. Has known weakness for white females.

14. Samuel M. Lambert, president, National Education Association: Has taken us on vis-a-vis federal aid to parochial schools—a '72 issue.

15. Stewart Rawlings Mott, Mott Associates, N.Y.: Nothing but big money for radic-lib candidates.

16. Ronald Dellums, congressman, Calif.: Had extensive [Edward M. Kennedy] EMK-Tunney support in his election bid. Success might help in California next year.

17. Daniel Schorr, Columbia Broadcasting System, Washington: A real media enemy.

18. S. Harrison Dogole, Philadelphia, Pa.: President of Globe Security Systems—fourth largest private detective agency in U.S. Heavy Humphrey contributor. Could program his agency against us.

19. Paul Newman, Calif.: Radic-lib causes. Heavy McCarthy involvement '68. Used effectively in nationwide T.V. commercials. '72 involvement certain.

20. Mary McGrory, Washington columnist: Daily hate Nixon articles.

'Political Opponents'

Dean provided this updated "master list" of political opponents to the committee. The list was prepared by Colson's office, Dean said.

Senators—Birch Bayh, J. W. Fulbright, Fred R. Harris, Harold Hughes, Edward M. Kennedy, George McGovern, Walter Mondale, Edmund Muskie, Gaylord Nelson, William Proxmire.

Members of the House—Bella Abzug, William R. Anderson, John Brademas, Father Robert F. Drinan, Robert Kastenmeier, Wright Patman.

Black congressmen—Shirley Chisholm, William Clay, George Collins, John Conyers, Ronald Dellums, Charles Diggs, Augustus Hawkins, Ralph Metcalfe, Robert N.C. Nix, Parren Mitchell, Charles Rangel, Louis Stokes.

Miscellaneous politicos—John V. Lindsay, mayor, New York City; Eugene McCarthy, former U.S. senator; George Wallace, governor, Alabama.

Organizations

Black Panthers, Hughie (**Huey**) Newton

Brookings Institution, Lesley Gelb and others

Business Executives Move for VN Peace, Henry Niles, national chairman, Vincent McGee, Jr., executive director

Committee for an Effective Congress, Russell D. Hemenway

Common Cause, John Gardner, Morton Halperin, Charles Goodell, Walter Hickel

COPE, Alexander E. Barkan

Council for a Livable World, Bernard T. Feld, president; professor of physics, MIT

Farmers Union, NFO

Institute of (**for**) Policy Study, Richard Barnet, Marcus Raskin

National Economic Council, Inc.

National Education Association, Sam M. Lambert, president

National Student Association, Charles Palmer, president

National Welfare Rights Organization, George Wiley

Potomac Associates, William Watts

SANE, Sanford Gottlieb

Southern Christian Leadership, Ralph Abernathy

Third National Convocation on the Challenge of Building Peace, Robert V. Roosa, chairman

Businessmen's Educational Fund.

Labor

Karl Feller, president, International Union of United Brewery, Flour, Cereal, Soft Drink and Distillery Workers, Cincinnati

Harold J. Gibbons, international vice president, Teamsters

A. F. Grospiron, president, Oil, Chemical & Atomic Workers International Union, Denver

Matthew Guinan, president, Transport Workers Union of America, New York City

Paul Jennings, president, International Union of Electrical, Radio & Machine Workers, Washington, D.C.

Herman D. Kenin, vice president, AFL-CIO, D.C.

Lane Kirkland, secretary-treasurer, AFL-CIO (but we must deal with him)

Frederick O'Neal, president, Actors and Artists of America, New York City

William Pollock, president, Textile Workers Union of America, New York City

Jacob Potofsky, general president, Amalgamated Clothing Workers of America, New York City

Leonard Woodcock, president, United Auto Workers, Detroit

Jerry Wurf, international president, American Federal, State, County and Municipal Employees, Washington, D.C.

Nathaniel Goldfinger, AFL-CIO

I. W. Abel, Steelworkers

Media

Jack Anderson, columnist, "Washington Merry-Go-Round"

Jim Bishop, author, columnist, King Features Syndicate

Thomas Braden, columnist, Los Angeles Times Syndicate

D.J.R. Bruckner, Los Angeles Times Syndicate

Marquis Childs, chief Washington correspondent, St. Louis Post Dispatch

James Deakin, White House correspondent, St. Louis Post Dispatch

James Doyle, Washington Star

Richard Dudman, St. Louis Post Dispatch

William Eaton, Chicago Daily News

Rowland Evans Jr., syndicated columnist, Publishers Hall

Saul Friedmann, Knight Newspapers, syndicated columnist

Clayton Fritchey, syndicated columnist, Washington correspondent, Harpers

George Frazier, Boston Globe

Pete Hamill, New York Post

Michael Harrington, author and journalist; member, executive committee Socialist party

Sydney Harris, columnist, drama critic and writer of 'Strictly Personal,' syndicated Publishers Hall

Robert Healy, Boston Globe

William Hines, Jr., journalist; science and education, Chicago Sun times

Stanley Karnow, foreign correspondent, Washington Post

Ted Knap, syndicated columnist, New York Daily News

Edwin Knoll, Progressive

Morton Kondracke, Chicago Sun Times

Joseph Kraft, syndicated columnist, Publishers Hall

Submitted by Dean to the Ervin Committee

James Laird, Philadelphia Inquirer
Max Lerner, syndicated columnist, New York Post; author, lecturer, professor (Brandeis University)
Stanley Levey, Scripps Howard
Flora Lewis, syndicated columnist on economics
Stuart Loory, Los Angeles Times
Mary McGrory, syndicated columnist on New Left
Frank Mankiewicz, syndicated columnist Los Angeles Times
James Millstone, St. Louis Post Disptach
Martin Nolan, Boston Globe
Ed Guthman, Los Angeles Times
Thomas O'Neill, Baltimore Sun [died in April 1971]
John Pierson, Wall Street Journal
William Prochnau, Seattle Times
James Reston, New York Times
Carl Rowan, syndicated columnist, Publishers Hall
Warren Unna, Washington Post, NET
Harriet Van Horne, columnist, New York Post
Milton Viorst, reporter, author, writer
James Wechsler, New York Post
Tom Wicker, New York Times
Gary Wills, syndicated columnist, author of "Nixon-Agonistes."
The New York Times
Washington Post
St. Louis Post Dispatch
Jules Duscha, Washingtonian
Robert Manning, editor, Atlantic
John Osborne, New Republic
Richard Rovere, New Yorker
Robert Sherrill, Nation
Paul Samuelson, Newsweek
Julian Goodman, chief executive officer, NBC
John Macy, Jr., president, Public Broadcasting Corp.; former Civil Service Commission
Marvin Kalb, CBS
Daniel Schorr, CBS
Lem Tucker, NBC
Sander Vanocur, NBC

Celebrities
Carol Channing, actress
Bill Cosby, actor
Jane Fonda, actress
Steve McQueen, actor
Joe Namath, New York Giants (Jets); businessman; actor
Paul Newman, actor
Gregory Peck, actor
Tony Randall, actor
Barbra Streisand, actress
Dick Gregory [comedian]

Businessmen
Charles B. Beneson, president, Beneson Realty Co.
Nelson Bengston, president, Bengston & Co.
Holmes Brown, vice president, public relations, Continental Can Co.
Benjamin Buttenweiser, limited partner, Kuhn, Loeb & Co.
Lawrence G. Chait, chairman, Lawrence G. Chait & Co., Inc.
Ernest R. Chanes, president, Consolidated Water Conditioning Co.
Maxwell Dane, chairman, executive committee, Doyle, Dane & Bernbach, Inc.
Charles H. Dyson, chairman, the Dyson-Kissner Corp.
Norman Eisner, president, Lincoln Graphic Arts.
Charles B. Finch, vice president, Alleghany Power System, Inc.
Frank Heineman, president, Men's Wear International.
George Hillman, president, Ellery Products Manufacturing Co.
Bertram Lichtenstein, president, Delton Ltd.
William Manealoff, president, Concord Steel Corp.
Gerald McKee, president, McKee, Berger, Mansueto.
Paul Milstein, president, Circle Industries Corp.
Stewart R. Mott, Stewart R. Mott, Associates.
Lawrence S. Phillips, president, Phillips-Van Heusen Corp.
David Rose, chairman, Rose Associates.
Julian Roth, senior partner, Emery Roth & Sons.
William Ruder, president, Ruder & Finn, Inc.
Si Scharer, president, Scharer Associates, Inc.
Alfred P. Slaner, president, Kayser-Roth Corp.
Roger Sonnabend, chairman, Sonesta International Hotels.

Business Additions
Business Executives Move for Vietnam Peace and New National Priorities
Morton Sweig, president, National Cleaning Contractors

Alan V. Tishman, executive vice president, Tishman Realty & Construction Co., Inc.
Ira D. Wallach, president, Gottesman & Co., Inc.
George Weissman, president, Philip Morris Corp.
Ralph Weller, president, Otis Elevator Company

Business
Clifford Alexander, Jr., member, Equal Opportunity Commission; LBJ's special assistant.
Hugh Calkins, Cleveland lawyer, member, Harvard Corp.
Ramsey Clark, partner, Weiss, Goldberg, Rifkind, Wharton & Garrison; former attorney general.
Lloyd Cutler, lawyer, Wilmer, Cutler & Pickering, Washington, D.C.
Henry L. Kimelman, chief fund raiser for McGovern; president, Overview Group.
Raymond Lapin, former president, FNMA; corporation executive.
Hans F. Loeser, chairman, Boston Lawyers' Vietnam Committee.
Robert McNamara, president, World Bank; former Secretary of Defense.
Hans Morgenthau, former U.S. attorney in New York City (Robert Morgenthau).
Victor Palmieri, lawyer, business consultant, real estate executive, Los Angeles.
Arnold Picker, Muskie's chief fund raiser; chairman executive committee, United Artists.
Robert S. Pirie, Harold Hughes' chief fund raiser; Boston lawyer.
Joseph Rosenfield, Harold Hughes' money man; retired Des Moines lawyer.
Henry Rowen, president, Rand Corp., former assistant director of budget (LBJ)
R. Sargent Shriver, Jr., former U.S. ambassador to France; lawyer, Strasser, Spiegelberg, Fried, Frank & Kempelman, Washington, D.C. [1972 Democratic vice presidential candidate]
Theodore Sorensen, lawyer, Weiss, Goldberg, Rifkind, Wharton & Garrison, New York.
Ray Stark, Broadway producer.
Howard Stein, president and director, Dreyfus Corporation.
Milton Semer, chairman, Muskie Election Committee; lawyer, Semer and Jacobsen.
George H. Talbot, president, Charlotte Liberty Mutual Insurance Co.; headed anti-Vietnam ad.
Arthur Taylor, vice president, International Paper Company [presently CBS president]
Jack Valenti, president, Motion Picture Association.
Paul Warnke, Muskie financial supporter, former assistant secretary of defense.
Thomas J. Watson, Jr., Muskie financial supporter; chairman, IBM.

Academics
Michael Ellis De Bakey, chairman, department of surgery, Baylor University; surgeon-in-chief, Ben Taub General Hospital, Texas.
Derek Curtis Bok, dean, Harvard Law School. [presently Harvard president]
Kingman Brewster, Jr., president, Yale University.
McGeorge Bundy, president, Ford Foundation.
Avram Noam Chomsky, professor of modern languages, MIT.
Daniel Ellsberg, professor, MIT.
George Drennen Fischer, member, executive committee, National Education Association.
J. Kenneth Galbraith, professor of economics, Harvard.
Patricia Harris, educator, lawyer, former U.S. ambassador; chairman welfare committee Urban League.
Walter Heller, regents professor of economics, University of Minnesota.
Edwin Land, professor of physics, MIT.
Herbert Ley, Jr., former FDA commissioner; professor of epidemiology, Harvard.
Matthew Stanley Meselson, professor of biology, Harvard.
Lloyd N. Morrisett, professor and associate director, education program, University of Calif.
Joseph Rhodes, Jr., fellow, Harvard; member, Scranton commission on Campus Unrest.
Bayard Rustin, civil rights activist; director, A. Philip Randolph Institute, New York.
David Selden, president, American Federation of Teachers.
Arthur Schlesinger, Jr., professor of humanities, City University of New York.
Jeremy Stone, director, Federation of American Scientists.
Jerome Wiesner, president, MIT.
Samuel M. Lambert, president, National Education Association.

First Colson Memo to Dean
(June 12, 1972)
I have received a well-informed tip that there are income tax discrepancies involving the returns of Harold J. Gibbons, a vice president of the teamsters union in St. Louis. This has come to me on very, very good authority.

Gibbons, you should know, is an all out enemy, a McGovernite, ardently anti-Nixon. He is one of the three labor leaders who were recently invited to Hanoi.

Please see if this one can be started on at once and if there is an informer's fee, let me know. There is a good cause at which it can be donated.

Second Colson Memo to Dean
(Nov. 17, 1972)
I have received from an informer some interesting information on Jack Anderson, including a report that Jack Anderson was found in a room with wiretap equipment and a private investigator in connection with the Dodd investigation. Anderson, according to my source, had the wiretap equipment supplied to him by a Washington, D.C., man.

According to the same source, Anderson and Drew Pearson were paid $100,000 in 1958 by Batista to write favorable articles about the former Cuban dictator. In 1961 Anderson wrote several very favorable articles on Fidel Castro. Fredo de la Campo, Batista's Under Secretary of State, sent Anderson a telegram saying "I hope you were paid well, as well for the Castro articles as you were for the Batista articles." My source has a copy of the telegram.

You know my personal feelings about Jack Anderson. After his incredibly sloppy and malicious reporting on Eagleton, his credibility has diminished. It now appears as if we have the opportunity to destroy it. Do you agree that we should pursue this activity?

Dean Memo on 'Enemies'
Memorandum from Dean to Lawrence Higby, former assistant to Haldeman, dated Aug. 16, 1971 and entitled "Dealing with our political enemies."

This memorandum addresses the matter of how we can maximize the fact of our incumbency in dealing with persons known to be active in their opposition to our Administration. Stated a bit more bluntly—how we can use the available federal machinery to screw our political enemies.

After reviewing this matter with a number of persons possessed of expertise in the field, I have concluded that we do not need an elaborate mechanism or game plan, rather we need a good project coordinator and full support for the project. In brief, the system would work as follows:

—Key members of the staff (e.g., Colson, Dent, Flanigan, Buchanan) could be requested to inform us as to who they feel we should be giving a hard time.

—The project coordinator should then determine what sorts of dealings these individuals have with the Federal Government and how we can best screw them (e.g., grant availability, federal contracts, litigation prosecution, ect.),

—The project coordinator then should have access to and the full support of the top officials of the agency or departments in proceeding to deal with the individual.

I have learned that there have been many efforts in the past to take such actions, but they have ultimately failed—in most cases—because of lack of support at the top. Of all those I have discussed this matter with, Lyn Nofizger [President's California manager] appears the most knowledgeable and most interested. If Lyn had support he would enjoy undertaking this activity as the project coordinator. You are aware of some of Lyn's successes in the field, but he feels that he can employ limited efforts because there is a lack of support.

As a next step, I would recommend that we develop a small list of names—not more than ten—as our targets for concentration. Request that Lyn "do a job" on them and if he finds he is getting cut off by a department agency, that he inform us and we evaluate what is necessary to proceed. I feel it is important that we keep our targets limited for several reasons: (1) a low visibility of the project is imperative; (2) it will be easier to accomplish something real if we don't over expand our efforts; and (3) we can learn more about how to operate such an activity if we start small and build.

Approve—Disapprove—Comment—

What about the President's seven-point statements on May 22? Dean said it contained "less than accurate statements."

June 27: *Gurney, White House attack*— The committee's interrogation of Dean escalated sharply in the turns taken by Sens. Edward J. Gurney (R, Fla.) and Daniel K. Inouye (D, Hawaii).

Gurney's exhaustive questioning took more than three hours, the longest of the hearings. In a politely hostile confrontation, he focused on Dean's accounts of his meetings with the President and on Dean's personal use of some campaign funds. Dean held to his original statement. Both conceded at the end there were major differences between them of interpretation.

Inouye presented a 12-page White House memorandum, submitted to the committee that day, representing a counter-attack on Dean's testimony. Inouye said the White House paper constituted the "most appropriate" test of Dean's credibility and "should substitute" for a cross-examination of Dean by the President, who should, he said, get "his day in court."

The document, prepared by J. Fred Buzhardt Jr., special counsel to the President for Watergate matters, identified Dean as the "principal author of the political and constitutional crisis that Watergate now epitomizes." Former Attorney General and director of Nixon's re-election campaign, John N. Mitchell, whom Buzhardt identified as Dean's "patron," was also cited for major responsibility in the Watergate affair.

Despite Inouye's identification of the Buzhardt document June 27 as a "memorandum and set of questions . . . prepared by the White House," Deputy Press Secretary Gerald L. Warren, who was in San Clemete, Calif. with Nixon, told reporters June 28 that the Buzhardt paper "is not the President's position, it is not the White House position. We are not commenting on the testimony or the evidence," Warren added.

The White House press office in Washington also released a statement June 28 on behalf of Buzhardt which attempted to dissociate Nixon from the White House-released rebuttal.

According to the disavowal statement, the Buzhardt memo and questions were "prepared as a basis for cross-examination from available statements of other witnesses in the several investigative forums, including depositions in civil suits, statements to investigators and prior testimony to the Ervin committee. The document does not represent a White House position. It was not reviewed by the President. It was based exclusively on the statements of witnesses. Its sole purpose was to facilitate examination of Dean as to matters on which others, as well as Dean, testified or made statements to the investigative bodies or the press."

Inouye's questioning of Dean began during the afternoon session June 27 following Sen. Edward J. Gurney's (R, Fla.) marathon questioning period that forced an extension in Dean's appearance before the committee. Inouye's interrogation of Dean continued June 28.

Citing the "gravity" of Dean's charges against Nixon and a belief that the President "is entitled to his day in court," Inouye announced that he would "test the credibility" of the witness by using White House-prepared questions "as a substitute, admittedly not the very best, but a substitute for cross-examination of Dean by the President of the United States."

Inouye read a letter received that morning, "from the White House" dated June 27, 1973:

Dear Senator Inouye: We have noted your public expression of your willingness to use questions and a memorandum, previously furnished to the committee staff, in questioning Mr. Dean. We have today forwarded more up-to-date questions to both the majority counsel and minority counsel for the committee.

However, in view of your interest in this material, we thought it would be appropriate to send these questions directly to you. There is also enclosed herewith a slightly revised draft and updated version of the memorandum previously furnished to the committee staff. Sincerely, J. Fred Buzhardt, special counsel to the President.

Inouye read the accompanying statement which charged:

It is a matter of record that John Dean knew of and participated in the planning that went into the break-in at Watergate, though the extent of his knowledge of that specific operation or of his approval of the plan ultimately adopted have not yet been established. There is no reason to doubt, however, that John Dean was the principal actor in the Watergate cover-up, and that while other motivations may have played a part, he had a great interest in covering up for himself, pre-June 17th.

. . . It must have been clear to Dean as a lawyer when he heard on June 17 of Watergate that he was in personal difficulty. The Watergate affair was so clearly the outgrowth of the discussion and plans he had been in on that he might well be regarded as a conspirator with regard to them. He must immediately have realized that his patron, Mitchell, would also be involved.

Dean and Mitchell were Magruder's principal contacts on the cover-up. Dean was not merely one of the architects of the cover-up plan. He was also its most active participant. Magruder correctly concluded that Dean 'was involved in all aspects of this cover-up,' and this is from the Magruder testimony.

Dean was perfectly situated to mastermind and to carry out a cover-up since, as counsel to the President and the man in charge for the White House, he had full access to what was happening in the investigation. He sat in on FBI interviews with White House witnesses and received investigative reports.

Dean's activity in the cover-up also made him, perhaps unwittingly, the principal author of the political and constitutional crisis that Watergate now epitomizes. It would have been embarrassing for the President if the true facts had become known shortly after June 17th, but it is the kind of embarrassment that an immensely popular president could easily have weathered. The political problem has been magnified one thousand-fold because the truth is coming to light so belatedly, because of insinuations that the White House was a party to the cover-up, and above all, because the White House was led to say things about Watergate that have since been found untrue. These added consequences were John Dean's doing.

Dean responded to the White House statement frequently, often basing his defense on previously stated testimony that his role within the Administration during the period preceding and following the Watergate break-in was an exponent of reason and caution. While continuing

to admit his active role as a participant in the cover-up, Dean repeated his assertions that he served principally as a point of contact for top level White House personnel and re-election committee officials with lesser Nixon aides who actually carried out the cover-up.

He emphasized the essentially mundane and passive nature of his role in the Watergate affair by telling the committee that, "based on what I know, and knowing the position I held in the White House staff, there is no way conceivable that I could have done and conceived and implemented the plan that they are trying to suggest I did."

Dean expressed a similar disbelief at the sweeping nature of the charges being leveled at him by the White House, saying: "This document has obviously been prepared by somebody who was not at the White House at the time this was all occurring. It sounds like they are putting it back together through newspaper accounts." (Many of the assertions in the White House statement were based on depositions given by Haldeman, Ehrlichman, the Senate testimony of Magruder and others and from newspaper accounts of Administration involvement.)

Sen. Inouye opened the hearings June 28 to announce that "we have had a bit of confusion here" because the White House press office indicated that "the memo which I presented to the committee [June 27] might not have been an official White House document."

Inouye said he would proceed with the questioning after having been assured by Buzhardt that his White House office had authored the statement. (Committee counsel Samuel Dash told reporters June 28 that Buzhardt had told him the White House statement and questions sent to the committee were not intended to be read publicly, but intended to suggest lines of inquiries for the senators.)

The White House questions, in many instances, represented follow-ups to the queries posed June 27 by Sen. Gurney on Dean's first meeting with the President Sept. 15, 1972 regarding the Watergate cover-up. Dean defended his inability to recall the precise conversation with Nixon, saying he took no notes of the discussion because "I thought they were very incriminating to the President of the U.S."

If Dean believed that Nixon was fully aware of the nature of the cover-up, based on impressions received during that Sept. 15, 1972 meeting, Inouye asked why Dean felt it was necessary on Feb. 27, 1973 to again tell the President of Dean's participation in the cover-up. Dean replied that he wished to lay before Nixon the full implications of Watergate as well as to emphasize Dean's own legal liability on an obstruction of justice charge, in addition to Haldeman's and Ehrlichman's role in the conspiracy.

Other questions posed to Dean attempted to clarify the Haldeman and

Ehrlichman roles in the Watergate cover-up conspiracy. Dean admitted he had no knowledge of Ehrlichman's prior knowledge of the break-in.

In another attempt to discredit his testimony, the White House statement accused Dean of "deliberate leaks of information to the media" as part of a strategy developed to obtain immunity from prosecution. Dean replied, "In any testimonial areas, I dealt directly with the appropriate investigative forum."

Several questions dealt with apparent inconsistencies between Dean's sworn testimony and news articles that either quoted Dean directly or were based on federal investigators' reports of Dean's testimony to them. Dean disavowed the accuracy of the news reports. He also refused to be drawn into a discussion of contradictions between his testimony and that of Magruder.

In replying to most of the White House questions, Dean used the opportunity to expand on his sworn statement of June 25 and to reinforce previous testimony.

Responding to a White House charge that he had depicted "all others at the White House as excessively preoccupied with political intelligence, use of covert methods and security," while insisting that he had acted as a "restraining influence on these preoccupations," Dean declared, "I do believe I was a restraining influence at the White House to many wild and crazy schemes."

Sen. Inouye's interrogation of Dean was notable for the incongruous role required of the Democratic committee member. Inouye made frequent attempts to conduct a vigorous cross-examination of the witness by offering his own follow-up questions to those prepared by the White House.

Inouye concluded with a final White House question, asking—"A central credibility question is: What prompted Dean's tactics in March and April 1973—the desire to have the truth told or the effort to achieve immunity from prosecution?" Despite their efforts at rebuttal, the White House appeared unable to tarnish Dean's credibility or mitigate the impact of his charges.

Gurney's interrogation—Gurney focused most intensely on Dean's testimony that Nixon's compliment to him Sept. 15, 1972 about the "good job" he was doing indicated his awareness of the cover-up. The date was the day the indictments were returned against the seven original Watergate defendants.

In reply to questions, Dean said the discussion that day included the Watergate criminal and civil suits and House hearings being considered.

Gurney asked him if he told the President "anything about what Haldeman knew or what Ehrlichman knew."

A. Well, given the fact that he told me I had done a good job I assumed he had been very pleased with what had been going on. The fact that the indictments, he was pleased that the indictments had stopped at Liddy because the only other link into the White House, as we had discussed earlier in sessions with Ehrlichman and Haldeman, was Magruder.

Gurney then asked a series of questions. Did Dean discuss with the President that day what Magruder knew? The cover-up money? Haldeman getting wiretap information and ordering its destruction after the break-in? The CIA cover-up? Coaching Magruder on his perjured testimony? Dean replied negatively to each.

Q. Well now how can you say that the President knew all about these things from a simple observation by him that "Bob tells me you are doing a good job?"

A. Well, Senator, I assume you know how your staff operates. I assume members of your staff understand how you operate, how reporting requirements proceed. I was aware of the fact that Mr. Haldeman had often made notes, Mr. Haldeman has a good memory. Mr. Haldeman does not leave details aside. This was the hottest issue that was going in the campaign.

I can't believe that the fact that we were going to contain this matter would totally escape the President's attention and it was to me a confirmation and a compliment to me that I had done this.

Q. Don't you think the President might have been complimenting you on the, I will use the word, investigation even if you don't desire that word, of the involvement of the people in the White House, the FBI interviews, all of that business, don't you think he might have been discussing that?

The answer led to a quarrel over Dean's paraphrasing the President's words to him. "We are quibbling over words," Dean remonstrated.

Gurney. We are not quibbling over words. We are talking about something very important, whether the President of the United States knew on Sept. 15 about the Watergate and the cover-up.

Dean. I am totally aware.

Gurney. This affects his Presidency and the Government of the United States.

Dean. I am quite aware of that and I have told you I am trying to recall. My mind is not a tape recorder. It does recall impressions of conversations very well, and the impression I had was that he had told, he told me that Bob had reported to him what I had been doing. That was the impression that very clearly came out.

Gurney. In other words, your whole thesis on saying that the President of the United States knew about Watergate on Sept. 15, 1972, is purely an impression, there isn't a single shred of evidence that came out of this meeting.

Dean. Senator, I don't have—

Gurney. That he knew anything about.

Dean. Senator, I don't have a thesis. I am reporting the facts as I am able to recall them roughly to this committee.

Personal use of campaign money—Gurney bore in on Dean's testimony he had taken $4,850 from campaign funds in his office to finance his honeymoon. He left a personal check in the safe, Dean said, but conceded under Gurney's query that he did not have enough funds in his personal account, subpoenaed by the committee, to cover it on that date. He also conceded he had taken such an amount because of anticipated expenses for his house and had put money back into the fund and withdrawn it a second time. Dean insisted he always meant restitution, he was good for the amount and the fund currently was legally separated and inviolate.

At one point, Gurney asked, "Do you know this is a crime, Mr. Dean?"

A. I am not aware what crime it is, no.

Q. Isn't it embezzlement?

Dean did not respond directly, reiterating his intention to repay and saying it would be dishonest to "stick cash back in there" without explaining that he had, in fact, made personal use of it.

The encounter ended when Dean's lawyer Charles N. Shaffer objected to Gurney's application of "embezzlement" to the situation. "I disagree with" Gurney on that, he said, "and I think there are enough lawyers in the room to know what embezzlement is."

June 28: *Focus on Nixon accounting*—On Dean's fourth continuous day of testimony, committee chairman Ervin and vice chairman Baker indicated the key issue of Dean's credibility could not be resolved without direct word from the President. Ervin's line of questioning was interpreted as an indirect request for Nixon's testimony under oath. Baker spoke of gaining "access to the President's knowledge" of the crucial events. He told Dean that the net sum of his testimony was "fairly mind-boggling."

This pattern developed after Dean was called upon by Inouye to deal with some 40 questions posed by the White House as part of the White House counterattack on Dean's testimony introduced the day before.

Constitutional violations stressed—Ervin built an interrogation that condemned the Nixon-approved plan for secret domestic intelligence surveillance as a violation of the 4th Amendment and the White House "enemies" list as a violation of the 1st Amendment. He also posed questions on whether Nixon had ever taken action to make the facts available on Watergate.

Ervin cited Dean's testimony that the Administration tried to block Congressional investigation of Watergate. He cited Nixon's firm stands against allowing White House officials to appear as witnesses and his publicized intention at one point to test the doctrine of executive privilege if necessary in the courts.

Ervin then asked Dean if he knew "how facts can be revealed except by people who know something about those facts?"

Laughter broke out in the hearing room. "No, sir, I do not," Dean replied.

Citing the constitutional requirement that the president "take care that the laws be faithfully executed," Ervin asked:

Q. Do you know anything that the President did or said at any time between June 17 and the present moment to perform his duty to see that the laws are faithfully executed in respect to what is called the Watergate affair?

A. Mr. Chairman, I have given the facts as I know them and I don't—I would rather be excused from drawing my own conclusion on that at this point in time.

Q. I will ask you as a lawyer if the experience of the English-speaking race, both in its legislative bodies and in its courts, has not demonstrated that the only reliable way in which the credibility of a witness can be tested is for that witness to be interrogated upon oath and have his credibility determined not only by what he says but by his conduct and demeanor while he is saying it and also by whether his testimony is corroborated or not corroborated by other witnesses?

A. That is correct.

Weicker cites White House pressure—Sen. Lowell P. Weicker (R, Conn.) charged that high Nixon Administration officials tried to intimidate him after he became a member of the committee.

Weicker, who leveled the charges on national television June 28 as he prepared to question committee witness John W. Dean 3rd, said later he had reported these attempts to special Watergate prosecutor Archibald Cox so that Cox could determine whether laws against obstruction of the proceedings of a Congressional committee had been violated.

Watergate committee vice chairman Sen. Howard H. Baker (R, Tenn.) said the committee would investigate Weicker's charges.

Weicker specifically charged former White House Counsel Charles W. Colson with trying to plant a story during the past week with a newsman that Weicker had accepted improper contributions during his 1970 campaign for the Senate. Weicker said he had been told by Dean May 3 that the White House was attempting to "embarrass" him, which was an apparent reference to the campaign contribution story. Weicker indicated that he first learned of the allegations April 10.

Weicker also read from the transcript of a March 28 phone conversation between John D. Ehrlichman, then presidential domestic affairs adviser, and Richard Kleindienst, then Attorney General. Weicker quoted Ehrlichman as saying to Kleindienst: "The President's feeling is that it wouldn't be too bad for you in your press conferences in the next couple of days to take a swing" at Weicker's announcement that he had information about White House involvement in Watergate.

Kleindienst questioned the advisability of that tactic and assured Ehrlichman

that Weicker was "essentially with us." "Baker has had a long talk with him [Weicker]," Kleindienst continued, "and told him to shut up and said that he would."

Weicker and Baker denied the conversation mentioned by Kleindienst.

Weicker also denied a rumor, whose origin he attributed to Colson, that he intended to switch political parties.

After recounting efforts to intimidate him, Weicker delivered to the committee what was described by observers as an "intense monologue":

"I say before the American people and this committee that I am here as a Republican and, quite frankly, I think that I express the feelings of the 42 other Republican senators that I work with, and the Republicans of the state of Connecticut and, in fact, the Republican party, far better than these illegal, unconstitutional and gross acts which have been committed over the past several months by various individuals. Let me make it clear because I have got to have my partisan comment, Republicans do not cover up. Republicans do not go ahead and threaten. Republicans do not go ahead and commit illegal acts. And, God knows, Republicans don't view their fellow Americans as enemies to be harassed. But rather, I can assure you, that this Republican and those that I serve with, look upon every American as human beings to be loved and won."

June 29: *Cross-examination of Dean ends*—Five days of testimony and cross-examination of Dean ended June 29 with Dean remaining unshaken in his "conviction" that President Nixon had been aware of a Watergate cover-up conspiracy.

As each senator and committee counsel questioned Dean during the six-hour final session, Dean recounted his previous testimony with little variation. He acknowledged that "it is going to be my word against one man's word, . . . and probably, in some cases, it is going to be my word against four men's." But, he insisted, "I know the truth is my ally in this, and I think, ultimately, the truth is going to come out."

By the end of the week, it was apparent that rigorous efforts at attacking Dean's charges of a White House conspiracy to obstruct justice had proven ineffective, and the President's credibility had been damaged. Three senators were prompted to suggest indirectly that Nixon appear voluntarily before the committee to offer a first hand defense of his actions.

The committee's attention was diverted several times from an exhaustive, and repetitive, re-examination of Dean's prior testimony. The week-long tension in the Senate Caucus Room visibly subsided during the afternoon session with an extended legal dispute regarding admissibility of hearsay evidence which drew the attention of committee members, all of them lawyers, away from Dean. Sen.

Baker ended the discussion with a remark of Supreme Court Justice Oliver Wendell Holmes: "Lawyers spend their professional careers shoveling smoke."

Amid the laughter that followed and the relaxation evident among the committee, the witness and the audience, Ervin and Baker traded hill country stories poking fun at lawyers.

Questioning of Dean—Sen. Gurney elicited Dean's only admission of possible error in his testimony. Gurney returned to a discussion of Dean's meeting with Herbert W. Kalmbach in Washington June 29, 1972 regarding the collection of payoff money to the Watergate defendants.

Dean insisted he had met with Kalmbach at the Mayflower Hotel coffee shop, but Gurney produced subpoenaed hotel records showing that Kalmbach had been registered at the nearby Statler Hilton Hotel.

Dean conceded that despite his 10 year residence in the Washington area, he "continually confused" the hotels. Later, Dean said that according to his lawyer, the Statler Hilton Hotel's coffee shop was named the Mayflower Coffee Shop.

In a further attempt to impugn Dean's motives, Gurney contrasted Dean's appearance at the Senate hearings after the committee had assured him immunity from prosecution, with his refusal to tell his story before the federal grand jury. Dean admitted pleading 5th Amendment rights against self-incrimination at his grand jury appearance.

Dean's lawyer, Charles Shaffer, objected to Gurney's inference, citing a Supreme Court ruling that "it is not proper cross-examination and it is not inconsistent for a witness on one occasion to take his 5th Amendment right and on another occasion testify."

The incident launched the lawyer's wrangle about the admissibility of hearsay evidence. Sen. Ervin, overruling Gurney's objection to Shaffer's statement, cited an article written by the late Supreme Court Justice Felix Frankfurter during the Teapot Dome scandal (of the Warren G. Harding Administration).

According to Frankfurter, "Congressional committees should not be bound by technical rules of evidence," Ervin said.

Critics of the Senate Watergate hearings had objected to the use of hearsay evidence, Ervin said, "but I think it is well for the general public to know that under the rules governing the admissibility of declarations of co-conspirators, the great bulk of the hearsay testimony that has been received in this case would have been admissible in a court of law for an indictment charging a conspiracy to obstruct justice."

Sen. Inouye returned to the subject of the political enemies list submitted in evidence by Dean. Inouye noted that former White House counsel Charles W. Colson, in a June 28 letter to the committee, denied authorship and claimed that the list's purpose was a social one, providing the White House with guidelines for preparing dinner guest lists.

Dean added little more to his previous testimony about harassment of Administration opponents but he told of several inquiries he had made with the Internal Revenue Service on behalf of the White House regarding tax audits of the President's friends.

Dean told the committee that he could provide additional evidence on the subject if he were allowed to examine his files still in the possession of the White House. Ervin directed the committee staff to "ask the White House to give Dean access to his files and also the privilege of copying them by Xerox or other means."

Question of Nixon appearance—The afternoon session provided further evidence that several senators were interested in having President Nixon appear before the committee to refute Dean's charges when Sens. Baker, Ervin and Weicker cited precedents for previous presidential appearances before Congressional committees.

Baker cited the 1919 dispute between President Woodrow Wilson and Senate opponents of the Treaty of Versailles. Rather than appearing before the Senate Foreign Relations Committee, which was considering the treaty, Baker said, Wilson had "invited the committee to meet with him" at the White House.

Ervin read from a Feb. 14, 1862 New York Tribune newspaper article. "This is an item concerning the manner in which President Lincoln volunteered to appear and testify before the House [Judiciary] Committee," Ervin said. He read the article: " 'President Lincoln today voluntarily appeared before the House Judiciary Committee and gave testimony in the matter of the premature publication in the [New York] Herald [newspaper] of a portion of his last annual message.' "

Weicker provided the most dramatic account of a presidential appearance before a Congressional committee. He read from Carl Sandburg's biography of Lincoln, "The War Years," which recounted Lincoln's uninvited appearance before a "speechless" Senate committee investigating reports that Mrs. Lincoln was a disloyalist."

" 'I, Abraham Lincoln, President of the United States, appear of my own volition before this committee of the Senate to say that . . . it is untrue that any of my family held treasonable communications with the enemy,' " Weicker read.

White House to refuse comment. White House Press Secretary Ronald L. Ziegler had told reporters June 25 that the White House "was not going to have any comment on the Ervin committee hearings as the week proceeds." Nixon underlined his strategy of ignoring the Watergate hearings by remaining at his California home in San Clemente, following the departure June 25 of Soviet Communist party General Secretary Leonid I. Brezhnev.

Despite Ziegler's disclaimer, the White House reacted swiftly June 26 to ousted White House counsel Dean's charges that Nixon had participated in the Watergate cover-up.

Gerald L. Warren, deputy White House press secretary, told reporters that Nixon stood by his May 22 statement in which the President flatly denied any knowledge of the cover-up until he began conducting his own investigation of the event March 21.

Nixon was not following the Senate hearings on television or radio, Ziegler said, but was receiving summaries of the proceedings prepared by his chief aide, Alexander M. Haig Jr.

LaRue pleads guilty to cover-up attempt. Frederick C. LaRue, former campaign strategist for President Nixon, pleaded guilty June 27 to one count of conspiracy to obstruct justice in the Watergate affair.

In return for the guilty plea, which could result in five years in jail and a $10,000 fine, LaRue agreed to testify as a government witness against others implicated in the scandal. U.S. District Court Judge John J. Sirica delayed sentencing until after the trials of others named by LaRue in statements to federal prosecutors and in testimony before the grand jury investigating Watergate.

LaRue, a wealthy Mississippian who worked closely with Nixon's campaign director, former Attorney General John N. Mitchell, admitted taking part in a scheme to destroy incriminating documents and misleading both the Federal Bureau of Investigation (FBI) and the Watergate grand jury in 1972 with false testimony. He also acknowledged funneling more than $300,000 to the seven men arrested in the Watergate break-in, in an effort to buy their silence.

In entering his plea, LaRue admitted the following "overt acts of conspiracy":

At a meeting June 19, two days after the Watergate burglary, LaRue met with "others unnamed" and they agreed to destroy "certain incriminating records" relating to the break-in. James F. Neal of the special prosecutor's office identified these as wiretapping logs and summary sheets.

On July 19, he delivered "a sum of money" to Herbert M. Kalmbach at the Old Executive Office Building. Kalmbach was then President Nixon's personal lawyer and one of his chief fund-raisers.

LaRue delivered another unspecified sum of money to Kalmbach July 26.

Prior to Aug. 16, 1972, he met with "others unnamed" at the re-election headquarters, "where Jeb S. Magruder's false, misleading and deceptive statement, previously made to the Federal Bureau of Investigation, was further discussed."

On Aug. 16, Magruder falsely testified, as planned, before the grand jury investigating the case.

On Sept. 19, 1972, LaRue received $20,000 in cash.

On Dec. 1, he received $280,000, again in currency.

LaRue took rent, free plane rides—The Associated Press (AP) reported June 20 that LaRue had accepted money and free airplane rides from a failing housing company, in whose behalf he unsuccessfully interceded with the Agriculture Department.

LaRue reportedly asked Agriculture Undersecretary J. Phil Campbell to reverse a ruling against a proposed housing project to be constructed in Mississippi by the currently bankrupt Stirling Homex Corp. of Avon, N.Y. Former Homex vice president, Ruble Phillips, a friend of LaRue, intended to merchandise his company's nonprofit housing cooperative to the Farmer's Home Administration, an arm of the Agriculture Department. Campbell refused Phillips' offer because the housing was too costly.

Phillips admitted paying LaRue $200 a month for the use of his Watergate apartment over a period possibly as long as a year. Phillips said he preferred LaRue's apartment to a hotel. He also acknowledged charging much of the rental expense to Homex.

Montoya campaign improprieties alleged. Following a report in the June 28 Wall Street Journal that Watergate committee member Sen. Joseph Montoya (D, N.M.) had "laundered" more than $100,000 in 1970 campaign contributions, New Mexico Secretary of State Betty Fiorina said a review of Montoya's 1970 campaign financing report was being undertaken.

New Mexico Attorney General David Norvell said June 29 it was his informal opinion that Montoya had not violated any state laws.

Montoya's office issued a statement June 28 denying any wrongdoing.

The Journal charged that Montoya had used "dummy committees" to hide campaign contributions that would be embarrassing to his campaign. In this way $57,000 from labor unions was disguised to sidestep the charge that Montoya was beholden to labor. Another $45,000 from other special interest groups was treated in a similar fashion, the Journal reported.

Although the "phony committees" did not report the sources of donations received, the individual donors to the committees did. These were the reports used by the Journal.

Montoya himself had filed a sworn financial statement Nov. 13, 1970 that did not mention receipt of any money funneled through the "dummy committees" or the sources of the contributions.

Noting that New Mexico state law required fund-raising committees to report all receipts and expenditures, the Journal also alleged that Montoya's campaign treasurer, Jack Beaty, set up at least seven, non-existent "dummy committees" in Washington, none of which filed reports with the state.

Moreover, even the New Mexico-based Montoya for Senator Club did not list all contributions, the Journal stated. In an effort to give the appearance of a campaign financed by small contributions from the people, the New Mexico club neglected to report a $1,000 contribution from the Meat Cutters Union's political fund, the Journal said.

Hunt investigated Sen. Kennedy. Convicted Watergate conspirator E. Howard Hunt Jr. said June 28 that he used equipment supplied to him by the Central Intelligence Agency (CIA) in 1971 to interview an individual he thought might have politically useful information concerning Sen. Edward M. Kennedy (D, Mass.).

Hunt, testifying before the House Armed Services Committee's Subcommittee on Intelligence Operations, said he had informed Charles W. Colson, then an aide to President Nixon, of his need for CIA equipment, and that Colson said he would arrange for it.

Colson, appearing before the committee June 29, denied knowing that Hunt was using CIA material in the Kennedy probe. However, Colson acknowledged contacting presidential domestic affairs adviser John D. Ehrlichman about getting CIA assistance for Hunt. Colson said Ehrlichman later told him, he [Ehrlichman] had contacted the CIA on Hunt's behalf. (Ehrlichman May 30 denied calling the CIA to ask for aid to Hunt.)

Hunt told the House panel, which was investigating the role of the CIA in Watergate affair, that he interviewed Clifton DeMotte in August 1971 to determine if he had any scandalous material relating to Kennedy. DeMotte, a General Services Administration employe in Rhode Island, was the public relations director of the Yachtsman Motor Inn in Hyannisport, Mass. in 1960, when John F. Kennedy used the hotel as his headquarters during the 1960 presidential campaign. Hunt indicated DeMotte hadn't said "anything worthwhile." The Washington Post had reported in February that DeMotte had rejected a request from Hunt that he "do work on Chappaquiddick."

In his interview with DeMotte, Hunt used false identification papers in the name of Edward Warren, as well as a wig, a device to alter his voice and a tape recorder. These devices were supplied by the CIA. Hunt emphasized to the subcommittee that the Kennedy probe prompted his request for the CIA-furnished disguise.

In his testimony, Colson said he had sought CIA help for Hunt after being told by Hunt that he wanted to interview former agency operative Lt. Col. Lucien E. Conien about Pentagon Papers defendant Daniel Ellsberg.

Colson also denied a Hunt assertion that he had ordered Hunt to forge State Department cables linking the Kennedy Administration to the assassination of South Vietnamese President Ngo Dinh Diem in 1963.

The former special counsel to the President further denied he had ordered Hunt to break into the Milwaukee apartment of Arthur H. Bremer after Bremer shot Alabama Gov. George C. Wallace in May 1972 during a Wallace presidential campaign rally. Colson said President Nixon had immediately ordered the Federal Bureau of Investigation to secure Bremer's apartment, thus eliminating any need for action by Hunt.

Colson also denied an accusation by ousted White House Counsel John W. Dean 3rd before the Senate Watergate Committee that he had discussed executive clemency for Hunt with the President.

Weicker-Colson confrontation. Sen. Lowell P. Weicker Jr. (R, Conn.), a member of the Senate committee investigating Watergate, ordered former White House counsel Charles W. Colson out of his office June 29.

The day before Weicker had accused Colson of planting false stories in the press about the financing of his 1970 Senate campaign. Colson had come to Weicker's office to deny planting the article.

When Colson told Weicker that he must have some sort of "grudge," Weicker was reported to have angrily responded: "I don't have any grudge against you. I don't know you.... But I do know what you stand for Mr. Colson, and we live in two different worlds. I deal in hard-nosed politics ... you deal in crap."

Weicker asked Colson about a memo written to the Internal Revenue Service asking a tax audit on Teamsters Union official Harold J. Gibbons, a McGovern supporter in 1972. Colson admitted writing it.

"Well that is just great," Weicker responded. "Let me tell you something ... you make me sick...." Weicker then ordered Colson out of his office.

Early prosecutors withdraw. The three original Watergate prosecutors withdrew from the case June 29. They said the transition of the prosecution from them to special Watergate prosecutor Archibald Cox was "basically complete." They also cited the problem that they could be both investigators and witnesses if they were called to testify before the Senate Watergate committee or possibly a grand jury concerning the original investigation.

The three men, Assistant U.S. Attorneys Earl J. Silbert, Seymour Glanzer and Donald E. Campbell, said in their withdrawal statement they "emphatically reject any allegations of impropriety or lack of diligence which have been or might be made" against their conduct of the case. They defended their probe as having been conducted "forthrightly, vigorously and professionally."

The original grand jury investigation, they said, "was conducted under inherently conflicting pressures to have the most thorough and exhaustive investigation in the shortest possible time." They also pointed out that, "as the evidence now shows, many government officials and others who, unbeknownst to us, had critical evidence, either withheld it or made false statements to the grand jury and the prosecutors, thus, whether innocently or not, aiding and abetting the cover-up."

Nixon to speak out later. White House Press Secretary Ronald L. Ziegler said July 2 that President Nixon would speak out on charges made against him in the Watergate case after the select Senate committee completed the first phase of its investigative hearings. That phase, focusing on the Watergate break-in and subsequent cover-up, was not expected to be finished until the fall.

Ziegler said until then Nixon intended to make no public statements on the matter nor give testimony in person or in writing or in any other manner.

During a recess in the committee's hearings June 27 when former presidential counsel John W. Dean 3rd was giving testimony, Sen. Joseph M. Montoya (D, N.M.) observed to newsmen that Dean was "a very credible witness" and it would "take some very affirmative action on the part of the President, either appearing before this committee or something that would expose himself to cross-examination, in order to repel" the testimony from Dean.

Sen. Lowell P. Weicker Jr. (R, Conn.) expressed hope July 2 that the President would testify voluntarily before the committee. He was not in favor of the committee trying to subpoena the President.

A third committee member, Sen. Edward J. Gurney (R, Fla.), calling Dean "a shoddy turncoat," said July 2 it would be "absolutely demeaning" for the President to defend himself against Dean's testimony.

Family opposed resignation. The President's daughter, Julie Eisenhower, told several wire service reporters July 3 her father considered resigning because of Watergate and his family opposed it.

Mrs. Eisenhower said the discussion occurred May 4 during a family gathering.

"He was playing the devil's advocate one evening," she related, "saying ... well, see, the thing is, he really loves the country and he'd do anything ... that was best for the country. You know, he would say, 'Should I resign? Would it be better for the country? Would the wounds heal faster? Would it [the country] be able to move faster to other things?'

"We said no. We didn't think he should, because resigning would be an admission of wrongdoing, and we also felt that he was the man for the job, and he had started things and needed to finish them."

Americans "should be disturbed" about Watergate, she said, but "what really disturbs me greatly is that I feel the press has made a hero out of Daniel Ellsberg," who "stole documents" and "broke the law" in a matter involving national security.

The White House reaffirmed July 5 its previously stated position that Nixon had never really seriously considered resignation over the Watergate matter.

Editorial Reaction to the Watergate Affair

Cooperating Newspapers

Akron (Ohio) Beacon Journal (174,000)
Albany (N.Y.) Knickerbocker News (71,000)
Albuquerque (N.M.) Journal (66,000)
Ann Arbor (Mich.) News (37,000)
Atlanta Constitution (209,000)
Baltimore News American (201,000)
Baltimore Sun (165,000)
Billings (Mont.) Gazette (44,000)
Biloxi (Miss.) Daily Herald (37,000)
Birmingham (Ala.) News (76,000)
Boston Globe (261,000)
Boston Herald American (211,000)
Buffalo Evening News (284,000)
Burlington (Vt.) Free Press (45,000)
Charleston (S.C.) News & Courier (66,000)
Charleston (W.Va.) Gazette (60,000)
Charlotte (N.C.) Observer (170,000)
Chattanooga (Tenn.) Times (64,000)
Chicago Daily Defender (21,000)
Chicago Daily News (435,000)
Chicago Sun-Times (536,000)
Chicago Today (429,000)
Chicago Tribune (768,000)
Christian Science Monitor (Mass.) (216,000)
Cincinnati Enquirer (195,000)
Cincinnati Post & Times-Star (234,000)
Cleveland Plain Dealer (403,000)
Cleveland Press (374,000)
Columbus (Ohio) Dispatch (222,000)
Dallas Morning News (243,000)
Dallas Times Herald (232,000)
Dayton (Ohio) Daily News (113,000)
Denver Post (255,000)
Denver Rocky Mountain News (205,000)
Des Moines (Iowa) Register (246,000)
Des Moines (Iowa) Tribune (109,000)
Detroit Free Press (593,000)
Detroit News (640,000)

Fort Worth (Tex.) Star-Telegram (98,000)
Gary (Ind.) Post-Tribune (72,000)
Hartford (Conn.) Courant (160,000)
Honolulu (Hawaii) Star-Bulletin (124,000)
Houston Chronicle (303,000)
Houston Post (295,000)
Indianapolis News (183,000)
Indianapolis Star (225,000)
Kansas City (Mo.) Star (310,000)
Lincoln (Neb.) Star (27,000)
Little Rock Arkansas Democrat (74,000)
Little Rock Arkansas Gazette (108,000)
Long Island (N.Y.) Press (418,000)
Los Angeles Herald Examiner (513,000)
Los Angeles Times (966,000)
Louisville Courier-Journal (233,000)
Louisville Times (172,000)
Memphis Commercial Appeal (214,000)
Miami Herald (383,000)
Miami News (86,000)
Milwaukee Journal (347,000)
Montreal (Que., Canada) Star (191,000)
Nashville Tennessean (139,000)
Newark (N.J.) Star-Ledger (246,000)
New Bedford (Mass.) Standard-Times (73,000)
New Orleans States-Item (128,000)
Newsday (L.I., N.Y.) (459,000)
New York Amsterdam News (83,000)
New York Daily News (2,130,000)
New York Post (623,000)
New York Times (846,000)
Norfolk (Va.) Ledger-Star (105,000)
Norfolk (Va.) Virginian-Pilot (129,000)
Oakland (Calif.) Tribune (208,000)
Oklahoma City Daily Oklahoman (181,000)
Omaha (Neb.) World-Herald (129,000)
Orlando (Fla.) Sentinel (129,000)
Philadelphia Evening Bulletin (634,000)

Philadelphia Inquirer (464,000)
Phoenix Arizona Republic (170,000)
Pittsburgh Post-Gazette (236,000)
Pittsburgh Press (344,000)
Portland (Me.) Evening Express (30,000)
Portland (Me.) Sunday Telegram (112,000)
Portland (Ore.) Journal (135,000)
Portland Oregonian (244,000)
Providence (R.I.) Journal (67,000)
Richmond (Va.) News-Leader (121,000)
Richmond (Va.) Times-Dispatch (144,000)
Roanoke (Va.) Times (63,000)
Rockford (Ill.) Morning Star (62,000)
Sacramento (Calif.) Bee (167,000)
Saginaw (Mich.) News (61,000)
St. Louis Globe-Democrat (293,000)
St. Louis Post-Dispatch (326,000)
St. Petersburg (Fla.) Times (163,000)
Salt Lake City (Utah) Deseret News (84,000)
Salt Lake City (Utah) Tribune (108,000)
San Diego Union (152,000)
San Francisco Chronicle (479,000)
Seattle Times (245,000)
Springfield (Mass.) Union (79,000)
Syracuse (N.Y.) Herald-Journal (126,000)
Toledo (Ohio) Blade (175,000)
Topeka (Kans.) Daily Capital (63,000)
Tulsa (Okla.) Daily World (110,000)
Wall Street Journal (497,000)
Washington Post (500,000)
Washington Star-News (302,000)
Wichita (Kans.) Eagle (60,000)
Winnipeg (Man., Canada) Free Press (130,000)
Winston-Salem (N.C.) Journal (78,000)
Winston-Salem (N.C.) Twin City Sentinel (46,000)
Worcester (Mass.) Evening Gazette (95,000)
Worcester (Mass.) Telegram (63,000)

FORMER CIA MEN CAUGHT IN RAID ON DEMOCRATIC NATIONAL OFFICES

Five men were arrested at 2 a.m. June 17 while engaged in an apparent espionage raid on the headquarters of the Democratic National Committee in the Watergate Hotel in Washington, D.C. The raiders, who were in possession of electronic eavesdropping devices and photographic equipment when captured, included James W. McCord Jr., a former Central Intelligence Agency employee currently working as a security agent for the Republican National Committee and the Committee for the Re-Election of the President. Also arrested were Bernard L. Barker, the group's alleged leader, Frank Angelo Fiorini, Eugenio L. Martinez and Virgilio R. Gonzales. All reportedly had CIA links in the past and had been involved in anti-Castro activities in Florida.

John N. Mitchell, President Nixon's campaign manager, denied June 18 that any of those involved in the raid were "operating either on our behalf or with our consent." Republican National Committee Chairman Sen. Robert J. Dole (Kans.) echoed Mitchell's position. Democratic National Chairman Lawrence F. O'Brien called for a full-scale FBI investigation into the incident and termed the raid a "blatant act of political espionage." O'Brien announced that the Democrats were filing a $1 million civil suit against the Committee to Re-Elect the President for its alleged involvement in the raid. The Justice Department disclosed June 19 that the FBI had begun an investigation of the affair.

ST. LOUIS POST-DISPATCH

St. Louis, Mo., June 20, 1972

The abortive raid on the headquarters of the Democratic National Committee by five men with burglary tools and sophisticated eavesdropping devices and photographic equipment has profoundly disturbing implications for the integrity of the country's political processes. Even if we accept at face value the expressions of dismay and disapproval by John N. Mitchell, chairman of the Committee for the Re-election of the President, and Senator Robert J. Dole, chairman of the Republican National Committee, the fact that the raid occurred indicates that there is a market for political data gathered by the grossest kind of invasion of privacy. The natural inference that someone is prepared to pay for and use campaign material garnered at the highest level by such despicable methods suggests how unrestricted political surveillance has become a fact of life in the nation.

While the housebreaking at Democratic headquarters would be unsettling enough as an independent unauthorized entrepreneurial venture, the unrefuted circumstantial evidence leads to the suspicion that it was more than that. Since James W. McCord, one of the raiders, is employed as a security agent by the Republican National Committee and the Committee for the Re-election of the President, the suspicion arises that he was working for his employers in this enterprise. Both Messrs. Mitchell and Dole must have known of and valued Mr. McCord's eavesdropping specialty when they hired him. It may be surmised too that the former employment by the CIA of Mr. McCord and of Bernard L. Barker, the reputed leader of the group, did not go unappreciated. Mr. Barker also is reported to have important Republican Party links in Florida.

In the light of this background and in view of the Nixon Administration's support for wiretapping and eavesdropping, even without court orders in alleged domestic security cases, the whole episode has a distasteful aura which cannot be dispelled by bland and unelaborated disclaimers from top Republican strategists.

A thorough FBI investigation, which has been promised, is fully warranted. But since that agency has itself engaged in illegal wiretapping and since it had been politicized by the late director J. Edgar Hoover and is now headed by a Nixon appointee, even its report on the raid cannot be anticipated with complete confidence. Yet considering the possibly damning ramifications of this case and the difficulties of getting to the bottom of them, it must be recognized that no matter how nonpartisan the FBI's investigation may be, the agency's report may be incomplete. Time will show whether a further inquiry seems to be called for in order establish confidence that this form of contemptible political activity will not be tolerated.

ARKANSAS DEMOCRAT
Little Rock, Ark., June 22, 1972

We won't dwell on the comic-opera aspects of the weird case in which several bumbling would-be wire-tappers — one with high-level Republican connections — apparently plotted to bug the offices of the National Democratic Committee. Suffice it to say that poor Larry O'Brien, who has longsuffered in silence as the Nixon Administration gilded its record, seems to have gone giddy over the thing. Having finally found something (anything!) to gibe the GOP with, he's thrown dignity and restraint to the wind. Ergo, the million-dollar lawsuit against the Committee for the Re-election of the President, in whose hire one of said bumblers seems to have been. The suit seems an improbable solution, if the only feasible one that's yet appeared, to the ponderable question of how the Democrats can ever get the party out of hock. The unanswered question, in that rationale, remains: Why a mere million, which would hardly pay the interest on the party's staggering debts?

Our concern, rather, is that the serious aspects in this case not be obscured by the absurdities. A minor question is why the subdued, almost apathetic response by the administration. We can't believe it actually had anything to do with the bizarre scheme — sitting as it is in the political catbird seat, with nothing to gain in such an escapade (What could it possibly hope to overhear?) and everything to lose. But rather than firmly and unequivocally dissociating the administration from the thing, Ron Ziegler, the President's mouthpiece, persists in trying to trivialize it. It's understandable that he would want to play it down, lest it blow up into an issue the Democrats can get their teeth into; but the fact remains that the incident is anything but trivial. And ignoring it won't make it go away.

By the sheerest coincidence, it was a Nixon appointee to the Supreme Court — Justice Lewis F. Powell — who pointed up the seriousness of this case. In a court opinion on an unrelated case — delivered ironically on the same day that the alleged wiretap plotters were arrested — Mr. Justice Powell wrote:

"The price of lawful public dissent must not be a dread of subjection to the unchecked surveillance power. Nor must the fear of unauthorized official eavesdropping deter vigorous citizen dissent and discussion of government action in private conversation. For private dissent, no less than open public discourse, is essential to our free society."

No evidence has yet appeared that the attempted eavesdropping in this case was either authorized or official. But the implications — and the gleeful insinuations by O'Brien & Co. — of official involvement, official sanction, or at the least official indulgence, not only reflect badly on the administration. They also raise serious questions in the public mind that merit more than the "routine" investigation the FBI has promised and more concern than the pooh-poohing the government has given the matter so far.

The Des Moines Register

Des Moines, Iowa, June 28, 1972

Democratic National Chairman Lawrence O'Brien has asked the President to have the attorney general name a special prosecutor "of unimpeachable integrity and national reputation" to investigate the attempted bugging of Democratic national headquarters.

Democrats are trying to make political capital out of the arrest of five men caught apparently in the act of planting electronic bugs in the party's national offices. One of the five was in charge of security for the committee to re-elect Nixon. Two of the men carried address books with the name of a former White House consultant. Democrats filed a $1 million civil suit against the five men and the Committee to Re-elect the President.

The attempt of the Democrats to get political mileage out of the incident paradoxically makes the suggestion that a special prosecutor be named a good one. If for any reason the men are not successfully prosecuted, or their motives are not revealed, there is certain to be widespread suspicion of a political cover-up. One would not have to be a partisan Democrat to share in that suspicion when the heads of the FBI, the Justice Department and the committee being sued by the Democrats are all political associates.

The one thing worse than attempted illegal political espionage would be a whitewash of the attempt. Even the appearance of less-than-vigorous prosecution and full disclosure would be severely damaging.

If the White House has nothing embarrassing to hide, it ought to welcome the suggestion for the appointment of a special prosecutor. The public, as well as the Democratic Party, is entitled to assurance that this politically explosive case will be dealt with in a non-partisan manner.

THE TENNESSEAN

Nashville, Tenn., June 21, 1972

AS A PLOT for the television series "Mission Impossible," it would have been entertaining but as an actual mission into the offices of the Democratic National Committee, the five-man breakin raises ugly questions about the political process and about the administration in power.

* * *

One of the five men who staged the breakin was, when arrested, the security coordinator for the Committee to Re-Elect the President, the chief campaign agency for Mr. Nixon which is headed by Mr. John Mitchell, the former attorney general.

The man, Mr. James W. McCord Jr., also did work for the Republican National Committee, according to Chairman Robert Dole, who has severed relations with him.

Mr. Mitchell, who was technically Mr. McCord's boss, said the man had other clients which his committee didn't know about. He threw in an ambiguous statement about security problems of his own committee and finally said "we will not permit or condone" such activities.

For a man charged with the re-election of Mr. Nixon, Mr. Mitchell seems singularly uninformed about a great many things. He knew nothing about the problems of selecting San Diego as the first GOP convention site and had no idea that ITT was offering a financial commitment—so his testimony in the ITT case indicated.

Who would hire a security coordinator without knowing something of his other clients and relationships? That would be the first breach of internal security. Admittedly, Mr. Mitchell may not have hired him, but somebody did. And therein lies deep suspicions which are buttressed by the fact that this has been a government hag-ridden by its own fears and uncertainties.

Nothing else can explain its love for wire-tapping, the Army's surveillance of peace groups, the Agnew attacks on the media, the subpoenaing of reporters' notes, the raucous cries against a "treasonable" opposition, the desperate wrigglings in the face of the "Anderson papers," the sly, but persistent urging that "fat cat" contributors to the campaign fund give massively before the law making such contributions public went into effect, and the chortling plans of the Committee to Re-Elect the President to us all and any weapons to meet its goal.

Whether the breakin at the Democratic headquarters was part of that philosophy isn't known. But Democratic National Chairman Lawrence O'Brien has announced a one million dollar damage suit against the Committee to Re-elect the President and the five men accused of breaking and entering.

He has cited civil rights laws protecting voting rights, charges invasion of privacy and violations of the 1968 Safe Streets Acts forbidding wiretapping by private parties.

* * *

"As far as I am personally concerned," said Mr. O'Brien, "there is certainly in every sense a clear line (in this incident) to the Committee to Re-elect the President . . ." How plainly that clear line will be revealed depends, ironically, on the FBI and the Justice Department, whose old boss is now chairman of the Committee to Re-elect the President.

THE LOUISVILLE TIMES

Louisville, Ky., June 21, 1972

As opera bouffe, the bungled burglary of the Democratic party's national offices would be a bust. Its music is atonal; its story is pure Art Buchwald and its cast is even more inept than the Marx Brothers ever pretended to be in their zaniest moment.

Its revelations about the state of American political morality are even more fascinating than the inevitable speculation as to the culprits' motives. For it is hard to believe that any skilled political operative would be stupid enough to hire so rank a band of amateurs.

According to one report from Washington, wiretapping equipment of the type seized went out "with high-button shoes." Among the bugging devices were transmitters powered by flashlight batteries and microphones the size of half-dollars. One wiretap expert was incredulous when the equipment was described; another found it shocking that five men were involved.

"If they follow the usual route, they hire only one man . . .," was his comment. Another belittled the idea of bringing in outsiders rather than hiring "local, top talent. . . . They know the field, they have the contacts."

But had the plot succeeded, what would have happened to the information? Would a politician turn it down? It is doubtful. All he would demand is that he never know how it was obtained. It is the same dodge that is used in collecting campaign funds. Political morality has it that the candidate is not tainted by illegally collected money if he is unaware of the source. That, of course, is pure hokum.

So, the issue is not who hired the burglars because—at least to our way of thinking—no one could be quite that stupid. The relevant question is who would have used the illegally obtained information. And, we think, no politician could truthfully say he would have turned his back on it if he thought he could benefit through its use.

The upshot is another blow at the credibility of our political system and all the FBI probes will not erase that, the FBI's own credibility being what it is today. Most of the damage naturally falls to the Republicans because it was their employe who got caught.

The general public probably won't hold that against the GOP, though. Some of the party's big contributors might, however. They probably are Scotch enough to think that the party has better things to do with their money than to pay a loser like J. W. McCord Jr. $14,000 a year for services as "security coordinator."

THE
DENVER POST
Denver, Colo., June 20, 1972

SURVEYING WHAT IS KNOWN so far about the bizarre attempted burglary and bugging of the Democratic National Committee headquarters in Washington, our impression is that it is the Republicans, who need a better security system.

One of the five men arrested during the break-in at Democratic headquarters was employed at the Committee for the Re-election of the President, Nixon's main campaign committee, as a security expert. He was hired, according to Committee Chairman John N. Mitchell, Nixon's former attorney general, "to assist with the installation of our security system."

But this guy may not be around much longer. Anyway, he probably was hired to assure the President's campaign committee of security against opponents such as Democrats and nosy newspapermen.

And that, obviously, is not the Republicans' real problem.

What they need is a security system to protect them against some of their friends and supporters.

For instance, another of the men caught in the Democrats' headquarters is a Miamian who is reputedly an important Republican party wheel in Florida. He is also reported to have been one of the top CIA planners of the spectacularly bungled Bay of Pigs invasion of Cuba in 1961.

With helpers of that caliber, the GOP clearly needs all the security protection it can get.

What puzzles us right now, though, is why Larry O'Brien, the Democratic national chairman, is demanding a full investigation of this whole idiotic caper.

Admittedly, it is only human for O'Brien

to be curious as to who gave the five burglary suspects the $6,500 in crisp new bills found on them and in their hotel rooms. He might be smarter, though, to smooth the whole thing over, if that would keep the Republicans from finding out who was responsible for this odd affair.

FOR WHOEVER FINANCED this caper either has far more money than brains—in which case he can be expected to foul the Republicans up again in some way—or else he is secretly the Democrats' best friend.

After all, no admitted Democrat could have dreamed up a more attention-getting way to impugn the intelligence and integrity of the main GOP campaign organization. So why would O'Brien want to cramp this character's imaginative style?

THE RICHMOND NEWS LEADER
Richmond, Va., June 22, 1972

As they demonstrate daily, the Democrats are becoming increasingly desperate for ammunition—any ammunition—with which to assault President Nixon. So when an employee of the President's re-election organization reportedly was discovered, hand thrust deep into a cookie jar and body wrapped in bugging equipment at the Democratic National Headquarters in the Watergate complex, candidates and other party leaders could barely restrain their well-orchestrated cries of horror and outrage.

Larry O'Brien, the Johnson hangover and Democratic National Chairman, set the tone by exclaiming that the "bugging incident . . . raised the ugliest questions about the integrity of the political process that I have encountered in a quarter century. No mere statement of innocence by Mr. Nixon's campaign (staff) will dispel these questions." Senators Humphrey, Muskie, and McGovern chimed in with suitably ominous pronouncements, all intended to imply that if the police had arrived sooner on the scene, they might have found Richard Nixon at the wheel of the getaway car.

It is predictable election-year Mickey Mouse, of course, but surely the Democrats are pushing our sense of humor too far. When George Wallace was gunned down, we watched—in slow motion, no less—as a man stepped up to the Governor, pulled the trigger five times, then was beaten to the ground and carted off. Yet despite the TV coverage, Arthur Bremer still rates an "alleged" before every reference to his being a "would-be assassin." President Nixon, who was not filmed at the Watergate nor sneaking over the White House fence, finds himself tried and convicted in absentia, while hordes of hopeful Democrats scout around for an appropriate length of rope.

What makes the Democrats' performance even more shameful is the easy availability of an alternative explanation for the incident. Mike Mansfield, hardly a Nixon-lover, read beyond the headlines and discounted the possibility of Republican double-dealing: Mansfield apparently noted that the Nixon employee arrested in the alleged raid, as well as four other men from Miami captured with him, all have long histories of involvement with the CIA and the Cuban liberation

movement. Whatever they hoped to gain—perhaps proof that the Democratic platform will support recognition of Red Cuba—probably had more to do with personal politics and politics within the Cuban exile community in Miami, than with national politics and the re-election of President Nixon.

Presumably we will know the right answers before long, as scoop-happy reporters from the Washington Post and the New York Times try to tie everything to the White House. Whether we will accept the answers remains a separate matter—particularly if the Democrats insist on parading more puffed-up outrage. After all, the ITT "affair" proved absolutely nothing, showed absolutely no wrongdoing, and resulted in not one indictment, let alone one conviction. Yet the average American continues to conceive of the ITT sideshow as a replay of Teapot Dome. The raid on the Democratic National Committee Headquarters will share the same fate, unless we all—including Democratic leaders—bone up on our civics books and remember the injunction about "innocent until proven guilty."

Chicago Tribune
Chicago, Ill., June 22, 1972

You'd think Santa Claus had come six months early, the way Chairman Larry O'Brien of the Democratic National Committee is carrying on—and in a sense, this is just what has happened. Only this Santa came in the form of several men; they didn't come down the chimney of Democratic headquarters, they sneaked in a door; and when they were caught at 2:30 a. m. they weren't carrying gifts, they were carrying eavesdropping equipment. Best of all, from Mr. O'Brien's point of view, some of them were linked indirectly to the White House.

There is nothing the Democrats need more, at the moment, than a good, lively

issue. The war and the economy are rapidly losing their appeal as issues, and it looks as if the Democratic Party is going to find itself with an unplanned candidate, in the form of Sen. McGovern, whom many of the party regulars look upon with something less than enthusiasm. The bugging attempt came at the perfect moment, and Mr. O'Brien deliberated for a full 15 seconds [as Republican Chairman Bob Dole put it] before leaping upon it as proof of Republican "gutter politics." He has even filed a $1 million damage suit against the Committee for the Reelection of the President, a Republican campaign group with which one of the alleged eavesdroppers was linked.

The bugging scheme is a deplorable example of stupidity and contempt for the law, especially at a time when the Supreme Court has just ruled that the government itself cannot resort to eavesdropping, even in cases affecting the domestic security, without court approval. It is hard to believe that it had the participation, approval, or knowledge of any official Republican organization, let alone the White House. More likely it was the brainchild of a few individuals who may have hoped to make points for themselves by picking up Democratic secrets and passing them along.

Whatever the facts, they should be determined as soon as possible so as to prove—or disprove—Mr. O'Brien's pointed insinuations. He can feel safe filing the suit because he knows it probably won't come to trial before the election and can then be conveniently forgotten. If his charge that the Republican Party is officially involved proves true, then so will his charge of gutter politics. But in this country [except in the Democratic National Committee] people are generally considered innocent until proved guilty; and lacking further evidence, it is Mr. O'Brien who is guilty of gutter politics and of charging guilt by association.

The Charlotte Observer

Charlotte, N.C., June 24, 1972

The mere thought of a Republican National Committee employe's being nabbed inside Democratic National Committee headquarters wearing rubber surgical gloves and armed to the teeth with photographic equipment and electronic listening devices was enough to move one to laughter. But now the laughter is being replaced by grim speculation.

Democratic Chairman Lawrence O'Brien has filed a $1 million suit against the Committee for the Reelection of the President, naming this influential group as co-conspirators in a plot to "bug" Democratic headquarters. Mr. O'Brien's action will probably be dismissed by some as no more than a political maneuver. To some extent it is that. The Democrats have a decided interest in prolonging this embarrassment to the GOP and the President's committee.

But seeking answers is also very much in the public interest — if only to dispel the ugly questions raised by the intrigue that placed five men inside Democratic headquarters early last Saturday morning.

One of those arrested — James W. McCord — is a former CIA agent who has worked recently as a "security specialist" for the Republican National Committee and the Committee for the Reelection of the President. Mr. McCord was hired several months ago by former Atty. Gen. John Mitchell (who is the President's campaign chairman) and occupied an office in Republican headquarters.

The man who apparently led the midnight raid was Bernard Barker, who also worked closely with the CIA and who apparently helped plan the 1961 Bay of Pigs operation. The other men also have been active in anti-Cuban activities.

Some of the questions raised in this case are obvious. Who engaged these five men and for what reason? Or did they act on their own? Police found about $6,500 in new, consecutively numbered bills (mostly $100 bills) on their persons and in their hotel room. Where did this money come from? And what did they hope to find in the Democrats' files and confidential reports? What information did they expect to get from "bugging" Democratic communications? And what of the indications of ties to the President's reelection committee?

Police investigations turned up a notebook with some intriguing entries. It contained the name and home telephone number of E. Howard Hunt Jr., a former CIA agent who has been working as a consultant to White House special counsel Charles W. Colson. It also contained the notations "W. H." and "W. House." Among the possessions of one of the arrested men was a personal check from Mr. Hunt in the amount of $6.

The common bonds between the suspects and Mr. Hunt may well be their backgrounds in the CIA rather than their current employment. (Mr. Hunt was a CIA agent for 21 years, until resigning in 1970.) But that raises still more questions, perhaps more ominous ones than those related to Republican-Democratic politics.

Now four more men are being sought in connection with this and possibly other "buggings" and burglaries. And an obscure 800-member organization of right-wing, anti-Castro Cubans is coming into the picture. Was it involved? Did it seek only to discredit the Democrats and thus help assure a Republican victory? Or did it have even more dangerous objectives?

There are other questions. Where has the FBI been? Perhaps in some way it led police to make the arrests. Yet it appears possible that a large band of rightwing extremists, ambitious enough to attempt to turn national events through use of a private spy system, has been operating dangerously close to some of its objectives. And does the CIA still have contact with these people? The spectre of a secret rightwing group with close ties to the government's own giant spying apparatuses should be disturbing to anyone concerned about freedom.

We hope this episode will not now be dismissed as mere election-year maneuvering, embarrassing, perhaps, but of no great consequence. Every aspect of the case should be seriously pursued. Much more than political partisanship is involved.

THE ARIZONA REPUBLIC

Phoenix, Ariz., June 24, 1972

Sen. Barry Goldwater is understandably amused by the inflated rhetoric and $1 million suit against Republican officials by high-ranking Democrats because some people connected with the campaign to re-elect President Nixon were caught either installing or removing wiretap equipment designed to eavesdrop on business conducted at Democratic National Committee headquarters in Washington.

Senator Goldwater would be the last person to condone such political espionage. But his amusement obtains from his own experience as a presidential candidate eight years ago, when Moira O'Conner, a pretty 23-year-old Democratic spy, boarded his campaign train as a "reporter," and used her good looks and cover as a journalist to collect juicy tid-bits for the Democrats.

Miss O'Conner, who openly admitted connections with the Democratic National Committee, was paid by California Democratic strategist Richard Tuck to spy on the Goldwater campaign operation and publish an anti-Goldwater newspaper based on information she collected before she was discovered by the senator's associates.

The Democrats also tried in 1964 to fake an espionage attempt and blame the Republicans by informing the press that Louis Flax, night teletype operator in Washington for the Democrats' nationwide communications network, was being paid large sums of money by the GOP to furnish them with copies of Democratic teletype transmissions.

A trap was arranged by the Democrats, and reporters and photographers were on hand to witness a supposed clandestine meeting between Flax and his Republican contact, at which he was to be paid for his regular delivery.

When Flax arrived with the material, pre-screened by the Democrats, it was openly accepted by Republican National Committee executive director John Grenier in his office — hardly unusual under the circumstances. But there was no pay-off — indeed Grenier refused to pay for the information — and no proof that any prior arrangement existed between Flax and the Republicans to steal Democratic secrets.

Senator Goldwater knows as well as any political strategist, however, that intelligence gathering is a standard part of professional political operations. Undoubtedly, there are times when such surreptitious activities are conducted unlawfully. And they are often done without the knowledge or sanction of party leaders or those running campaign operations.

There is still much that we do not know about the alleged wiretapping of Democratic National Committee headquarters by James McCord, security chief for the Committee to Re-elect the President, and others. Former Atty. Gen. John Mitchell, head of the President's re-election campaign, has firmly denied that McCord was acting in the committee's behalf, and there is no reason to believe otherwise.

There is, however, a considerable difference in the way Democrats and the press have reacted to this latest political spy story. When Senator Goldwater and the Republicans were victims of beautiful spies and James Bond tactics of the Democrats, the stories were featured as light asides in an otherwise heated, issue-oriented campaign year.

But now that the Democratic campaign sanctuary has supposedly been breached by GOP functionaries — one of them a former CIA agent — a hue and cry against treachery and reprehensible political tactics has been echoed and re-echoed by the Democrats at the expense of President Nixon and his supporters.

For the Democrats, it is an obvious attempt to get some publicity and sympathy when their political fortunes are at an all-time low. And so far as press critics are concerned, Senator Goldwater probably put things into perspective when he said that the Republicans are likely being blamed only because their spies are not "well-stacked."

The Evening Star
The Washington Daily News

Washington, D.C., June 20, 1972

The New York Times

New York, N.Y., June 22, 1972

White House spokesman Ronald Ziegler's flip dismissal of the attempted bugging of Democratic party national headquarters is in keeping with the Nixon Administration's casual attitude toward the issue of electronic surveillance. The abortive espionage, Mr. Ziegler would have us understand, is nothing more than a "third-rate burglary" unworthy of comment.

The press secretary's assessment stands in ironic juxtaposition to the recent unanimous Supreme Court decision declaring domestic wiretapping by the Government without prior court approval unconstitutional. Because the very viability of an open society rests on the legal protection of freely exchanged ideas, any indiscriminate attempt to intrude on the privacy of law-abiding citizens by electronic means has sinister implications and requires investigation.

This is particularly true in light of the prior affiliations of those arrested. All five men have had C.I.A. connections and one is employed by President Nixon's re-election committee as a security coordinator. Another individual, E. Howard Hunt, whose name is listed in the address books of two of those apprehended, has been a consultant to a White House special counsel.

The President's campaign manager, former Attorney General John Mitchell, denies foreknowledge of the raid, and any evidence linking the Republican party to the incident is at this point circumstantial. The Democratic National Committee's suit against the Committee to Re-elect the President rings of election-year partisanship and hyperbole. The question remains, however, by whom and for what purpose the bugging was ordered. Mr. Hunt's refusal to make himself available for questioning, and the Republican National Committee's internal memo ordering those on the payroll to be silent, serve only to fuel speculation about the direction and motives of the act.

A thorough Federal investigation is in the best interest of both political parties and the nation as a whole.

Even in a town that has become used to the unusual in political chicanery, the fumbling attempt to implant microphones and to photograph documents at Democratic National Headquarters comes across as singularly bizarre. Maybe a book or movie will come out of the episode with a Breslin-like title: The Gang That Couldn't Plant a Straight Bug.

And yet the levity of the affair should not be permitted to overshadow the very serious questions of why it happened and who caused it to happen. Botched though it was, this piece of political espionage was contemptuous, entirely out of keeping with what is right and ethical in the political process. That the Republican leadership is embarrassed by it all is no wonder. One of the suspects has been in charge of "security" for both the Republican National Committee and the Nixon re-election campaign. Two other suspects reportedly had strong GOP connections in Florida.

In no way does this prove that the break-in and spying attempt were masterminded by President Nixon, former Attorney General Mitchell or anyone else in a top Republican leadership position. Mitchell and party Chairman Dole have been quick to deplore the incident and to deny any prior knowledge or sponsorship of it. We are inclined, for the moment, to believe them. At least on the basis of present knowledge, it makes more sense to surmise that the Watergate bugging caper probably represented the distorted thinking of zealots on the party's fringe who are determined to ensure a Nixon victory in November.

Even if that is accepted, there remains the question of whether the Watergate Five — or is it Six? — acted on their own or on behalf of others yet unknown. It is directly in the public interest that the plot be thoroughly probed and exposed. And since the FBI is now on the case, and given the obvious FBI-Justice Department-Kleindienst-Mitchell-GOP linkages, it is directly in the interest of the Republican party that word go out to push the investigation vigorously, no matter where the trail leads.

The Democrats have a perfect right to be angry at what happened. Whether they can turn it into a telling campaign issue depends to a large degree on how responsible and candid the administration proves to be in unearthing and then explaining the facts of the case.

OREGON Journal
AN INDEPENDENT NEWSPAPER

Portland, Ore., June 20, 1972

Experts in the crime of illegal wiretapping may jest about the "unprofessional" way a group of would-be political spies botched the bugging of Democratic National Committee headquarters the other day, but it really is no laughing matter.

Fortunately the culprits were caught, but the very fact that an election-year effort to plant the eavesdropping equipment in a rival political camp was made is shocking.

The incident will stand as an embarrassment to President Nixon and his Committee to Re-elect the President, for it was one of their own executives who was caught in the act.

John Mitchell, the Nixon campaign manager and former attorney general, was quick to repudiate the activity and deny any knowledge of it.

But the question likely to hang over the campaign is whether the repudiation and denial came because of the unconscionable act or because the agents were caught.

The FBI is said to be investigating, and an impartial and thorough investigation is called for. Congressional Democrats can be expected to see to it that the probe is deep and is not allowed to become a white wash. Whether or not further complicity is found, the damage has been done. Even if the security coordinator acted solely on his own initiative, the President, his campaign manager and their re-election committee will have difficulty escaping suspicion.

But the incident does help to point up the astonishing misuse of electronic devices to invade the privacy of people and organizations. While there may be justification for use of wiretaps to fight crime, the procedure should be strictly controlled. Meanwhile, the abuse of the wiretap is a crime that the public should become alarmed about—and stay alarmed about until it receives the kind of attention that such criminal conduct deserves.

THE BLADE

Toledo, Ohio, June 21, 1972

AS IF mechanics and legalisms of the whole 1972 presidential election process were not bizarre enough, sleuths with documented ties to the Committee for Re-election of the President are caught redhanded in the act of bugging the Democratic National Committee headquarters.

Loaded with unbelievably sophisticated electronic devices, not to mention $6,500 in brand-new bills, a retired Central Intelligence Agency officer and his four rubber-gloved accomplices are caught like so many kids trying to sneak through the side door of a theater without paying.

It is not so trivial an episode, however, when a trail of circumstantial evidence leads back to former Attorney General John N. Mitchell, who heads President Nixon's election campaign committee and who hired James McCord, Jr., to install the committee's security system. Mr. Mitchell denied that Mr. McCord's assignment included the Democratic National Committee offices, which surprised nobody.

Mr. Mitchell, it will be remembered, has a penchant for electronic eavesdropping on Americans whom he considers to be subversive, and the Supreme Court this week has had to remind him and his successor, Attorney General Richard G. Kleindienst, that the wiretap law does not give them unrestricted authority to bug everybody they suspect.

Larry O'Brien, Democratic national chairman, is missing no opportunity to embarrass the Republicans in filing a $1 million suit against Mr. Mitchell's committee, the McCord security agency and others arrested at the scene. With that CIA connection now linked to still another ex-CIA veteran who is consultant to the White House special counsel, the affair appears to get even more sticky.

Aside from this attempted misuse and abuse of electronic gadgets that tempt the nosiest of instincts to pry into people's privacy, the whole exercise seems fantastic. With the Democrats undercutting their chances to unite through primary fights and with their campaign treasury empty, what need is there for the Republicans to engage in such a tactic and with such risk to reputations in the White House?

One would think that the recent embarrassment running through the Justice Department and the White House through inept handling of the ITT matter would have discouraged this Mission Impossible caper. Without a word of remorse from any of the principals, the impression grows that the only regret is in violation of the "11th Commandment": Don't get caught.

New York Post

New York, N.Y., June 22, 1972

The bug is spreading. In an electronic age, the plague is electronic too. The five men arrested for their abortive invasion of the Democratic National Committee headquarters in Washington, presumably to plant bugs that would reveal Democratic secrets (what secrets?) to the Republicans, played some sort of still unrevealed role in what sounds like a bad political suspense novel. The fact that four of the five were from Miami, that they were on the margin of the Cuban refugee colony there, and that all of them were in some way connected with the CIA end of the Bay of Pigs fiasco, makes the plot even less credible than in most bad suspense novels. We await further installments with curiosity slightly laced with nausea.

Whatever connection there turns out to be, real or tenuous, with anyone in the hierarchy of the Republican National Committee, it is bound to hurt President Nixon and his re-election campaign manager, John Mitchell. Understandably, Lawrence O'Brien, the Democratic chairman, is suing the Mitchell committee for invasion of privacy, and understandably Mitchell charges O'Brien with demagoguery, while he himself "deplores" and "does not condone" whatever happened. Of such is the kingdom of professional political partisans.

But the plague of bugs is more important than these posturings for us all. What a cynical operator or a super-heated political fanatic will do depends on the climate around him, and what he thinks he will get away with. Maybe the five arrested men had read in the papers about the Justice Department bugs on suspected subversives, without warrants. Maybe they recalled the success with which anti-Administration forces revealed secret papers of all sorts to a public that ate it up. There is an important distinction between the penetration of government secrecy and the invasion of civil privacy, but evidently the five accused prowlers and plotters are neither constitutional lawyers nor civil libertarians. They may be only a little band of mercenaries or committed men enrolled in a guerrilla war, and their ethic is that of guerrillas the world over.

The Washington Post

Washington, D.C., June 21, 1972

"As always, should you or any of your force be caught or killed, the Secretary will disavow any knowledge of your actions. This tape will self-destruct in five seconds . . . good luck . . ."
—From the CBS-TV show, Mission Impossible.

As an example of life imitating art—of a sort—we have not for some time seen anything like the Watergate caper now unfolding in weird and scarcely believable detail, right down to the taped locks, the rubber gloves, the tear gas pens, the array of electronic equipment, and the crisp new hundred dollar bills in the hands of the five men who stole into Democratic Party headquarters the other night under cover of darkness and something less than impenetrable aliases. *Mission Impossible* it wasn't; experts in these matters all agree that the job was bungled at almost every step of the way. *Mission Incredible* it certainly is, both in terms of execution and, more important, in terms of the motives that could conceivably have prompted so crude an escapade by such a motley crew of former Central Intelligence Agency operatives and Miami-based, anti-Castro activists.

Mr. Ronald L. Ziegler, the White House spokesman, has already dismissed it as a "third-rate burglary attempt" and warned that "certain elements may try to stretch this beyond what it is." The implication of that last statement is that he knows what it is and if so, we wish he would tell us, because frankly it doesn't shape up as your ordinary, garden variety burglary—however "third-rate" its execution. An attempt to implant electronic surveillances in the headquarters of a major political party strikes us as something much more resembling what the Democratic National Chairman, Mr. Lawrence O'Brien, has called an "act of political espionage." And that, for all its comic, melodramatic aspects, is not quite so easy to dismiss.

In fact, without wishing to stretch things one bit beyond the demonstrable facts, there are certain elements here which could raise questions in even the least suspicious or skeptical minds. This is, for example, an election year, and while it is possible to suppose that this deed was done by a foreign government or even some extra-terrestrial interests, the finger naturally points, in a time of intense and developing political combat, to the Democrats' principal and natural antagonist; that is to say, it points to somebody associated with or at least sympathetic to—we may as well be blunt about it—the Republicans.

We do not so allege; we merely note that this is what some people are going to be saying, or thinking, and that their speculations, dark as they may sound, are going to be encouraged by word of various connection between several of the suspects and one part or another of the Republican power structure. For example, Mr. James W. McCord, one of the five men arrested, has worked on security problems both for the Republican National Committee and the Committee for the Re-Election of the President. Two of the group had in their personal effects the address of a Mr. Howard E. Hunt, another former CIA agent, who serves as a consultant to White House consultant Charles W. Colson. Other more tenuous links have been developed between the arrested suspects and elements of the Republican Party.

Mr. John Mitchell, the former Attorney General who is heading the committee for Mr. Nixon's re-election, has stoutly denied any knowledge of the affair as has the Chairman of the Republican National Committee, Senator Dole, as well as Mr. Ziegler. So life has imitated art up to a point; the "force" has been "caught"; "the Secretary" has "disavowed any knowledge" of its actions. What remains now to be seen—what is, in short, the crucial question in a time of waning confidence in the processes of government—is whether a Republican administration can bring itself to use every means at its command to prosecute perpetrators of the Watergate raid. From the sound of it, there would seem to be an abundance of evidence in the captured equipment and freshly-minted currency. It ought not to be left to the Democrats to dig into *Mission Incredible* by pressing a civil suit. In short, this particular tape ought not to be allowed to self-destruct.

Orlando Sentinel

Orlando, Fla., June 25, 1972

THE ZEALOTS, from whom the modern word is derived, were fanatics who opposed King Herod at the time of Christ. They'd do anything to further their cause or discredit that of others.

Although the Zealots supposedly disappeared from history in the 70 A.D. revolt that destroyed Jerusalem, we're not so sure five of them didn't reappear in Washington June 17 of this year. The men charged with burglarizing and trying to plant microphones in Democratic National Headquarters certainly resemble the Zealots of old to whom any means to an end was acceptable.

☆ ☆ ☆

NO HIGH Republican official has been implicated in the incident but it is sure to be at least a mild embarrassment to President Nixon because James W. McCord, the chief security officer of the Republican party and of the President's reelection campaign, was one of the men arrested inside rival party offices.

We're confident the President knew nothing of the spying and we hope responsible officials will investigate on their own, get at the bottom of it and act to insure against further acts of childish political espionage.

The Democrats, taking the part of another early sect, the Martyrs, are playing it to the hilt. Party chairman Lawrence F. O'Brien has brought a $1 million damage action against Mr. Nixon's campaign committee, claiming their civil rights were violated.

☆ ☆ ☆

A WASHINGTON electronics expert says meanwhile that the "bugging" equipment taken in evidence is sadly out of date, would have been easily detected, and that the whole affair was the work of clumsy amateurs.

The Bugging Burglary of 1972 will get some mileage but not as a spy thriller. Who could keep a straight face?

GAO ASKS REPUBLICAN FUND PROBE; LINKS TO BREAK-IN INVESTIGATED

The Congressional auditing agency, the General Accounting Office (GAO), reported Aug. 26 that it had found "apparent and possible" violations of the Federal Election Campaign Act by the Finance Committee to Re-elect the President. The GAO's findings, involving amounts up to $350,000, were referred to the Justice Department.

The GAO cited failure to keep adequate records concerning: (a) a $25,000 contribution made to the Republicans by Minnesota businessman Dwayne O. Andreas through Kenneth H. Dahlberg, chairman of the Minnesota re-election committee for Nixon, (b) $89,000 from four checks drawn on a Mexican bank and (c) the balance of some $350,000 in cash deposited May 25 to a media affiliate of the Nixon committee. Funds from the Dahlberg check and the Mexican check had turned up in possession of Bernard L. Barker, one of five persons siezed in the attempted raid on Democratic national headquarters.

A delay in the scheduled release of the GAO report Aug. 23 drew complaints from McGovern's campaign chairman, Lawrence F. O'Brien, and Rep. Wright Patman (D, Tex.) whose Banking and Currency Committee was also investigating the break-in at the Democrats' offices in the Watergate buildings. After the report was released, Patman complained about reversion of the case to the Justice Department. A "strongly partisan attorney general," he said, was being asked "to prosecute wrongdoings of the political party which boosted him to such a high place in government."

The Finance Committee to Re-elect the President called the GAO report "inaccurate" Aug. 26. Maurice Stans, chairman of the committee, said Aug. 27 the report contained "serious misrepresentations" and demanded that the GAO audit Democratic fund-raising records. Democratic nominee George Mc-Govern said Aug. 28 "we'll welcome the GAO or any other investigator who wants to look at our files." McGovern called upon the President to reveal the sources of $10 million in campaign funds collected before the new disclosure law went into effect.

At his news conference Aug. 29, President Nixon said technical violations of the new campaign law apparently had occurred "on both sides." He disclosed that his own staff had conducted an investigation of the Watergate affair and he could "categorically" state that the probe "indicates that no one on the White House staff, no one in this Administration, presently employed, was involved in this very bizarre incident."

(After a U.S. District Court judge had rejected a Republican request to postpone a $1 million civil suit filed by O'Brien against the re-election committee, O'Brien revealed Aug. 15 that his attorney would begin taking depositions from persons connected with the case, including Stans and John N. Mitchell, Nixon's former campaign manager.)

St. Louis Globe-Democrat
St. Louis, Mo., August 17, 1972

Sen. George McGovern, who once gave the impression that he would try to win the White House on his own merit, now appears bent on getting there by tearing down President Nixon with undocumented charges and innuendos.

This is certainly a low road but McGovern doesn't seem to mind taking it.

His latest unsubstantiated smear against Mr. Nixon is a charge that the President is "at least indirectly" responsible for the June 17 break-in at the Democratic National headquarters in Washington.

As usual, he offered no proof of the accusation.

In these circumstances most fair-minded Americans will recognize that McGovern, in desperation, has resorted to the basest kind of campaign—attacking the character and integrity of Mr. Nixon without justification.

The net result will be that McGovern, not the President, will suffer. Senator McGovern's credibility gap, which widened as he continually changed his positions on issues, will widen still further.

If McGovern keeps this up a lot of Americans will believe that he is just plain McNasty.

THE LINCOLN STAR
Lincoln, Neb., August 19, 1972

Until the matter is settled in court, and maybe not even then, people will not know how direct are the ties between the men caught snooping in Democratic National Committee headquarters and President Nixon himself.

But that will not stop the Democrats from capitalizing on the abundance of signs that point to the intruders as agents in the pay of the Committee to Re-elect the President.

The Democrats have filed suit and the issue is pending in court. In the meantime, new evidence against the President's campaign team is claimed and Nixon is being charged with at least indirect responsibility for the incident.

Former Democratic Party Chairman Lawrence O'Brien contends that new evidence shows his national committee offices were "bugged" for some time before June 17, the date the five men were caught inside the offices by Washington police. O'Brien says he plans to take depositions on the matter from a number of men prominently tied to the re-election campaign. And on the campaign trial, or the fist time, Sen. George McGovern charged that President Nixon was "at least indirectly" responsible for the break-in.

From the other side, Nixon, former campaign chief John Mitchell and other GOP officials have denied knowledge of the break-in. But the Republicans have also asked that the trial of the lawsuit be put off until after the election in November. And the evidence that has surfaced thus far is damaging. One of the men arrested was a paid employe of the Committee to Re-elect the President. A $25,000 campaign check has been traced to the bank account of another of the arrested men. Just on the surface, there are some very serious questions the President's campaign chiefs need to answer:

Is the bugging incident really serious? Is it a legitimate campaign issue? George McGovern seems to think so. He said the incident "ought to disturb every American, because if the leadership of the President's campaign will snoop and invade and wire-tap on the Democratic National Committee, what reason is there to believe it won't do that to the rest of us?" McGovern may be pressing it, but he has a point.

The Nixon campaign can't be allowed to sweep this incident under the rug. It has some explaining to do for its own good. We would hope that the President or his chief lieutenants wouldn't stoop to anything like political espionage. It would reflect badly on his high office and provide another reason to distrust public officials.

THE SACRAMENTO BEE
Sacramento, Calif., August 21, 1972

Clark MacGregor, the President's campaign manager, and President Richard Nixon himself, should come down from Olympus and tell the people what they know — or do not know — about the June 17 raid on the Democratic headquarters in the Washington, DC, Watergate Apartments. The bizarre affair, known in high political circles as the Watergate Caper, is no joke.

Curiously, a $25,000 check to the Nixon campaign was traced to the bank account of Bernard L. Barker, alias Frank Carter, who was one of five men arrested at 2:30 a.m. in the headquarters of the Democratic National Committee.

And the Washington Star reported another $89,-000 was channeled to Barker through the Committee to Re-elect the President.

Until the President, Republican campaign treasurer Maurice Stans and MacGregor are willing to talk about the raid on the Democratic headquarters they inevitably leave the suggestion there is Republican involvement.

At the time of the break-in, John Mitchell, then Nixon's campaign chairman, denied any GOP complicity.

When the new Republican chairman, MacGregor, was asked by reporters about the campaign contribution winding up in the bank account of one of those caught in flagrante in the headquarters of the Democrats, MacGregor invoked "legal rights" as the basis for not responding. This leaves unfulfilled the party's moral obligation to truth.

As the story of the Watergate Caper unfolds it is clear more than indignant denials and pious statements are needed. The people have a right to know, for the Watergate incident is an ugly one and is an unsettling influence upon the confidence of the people in the political processes.

Above all others, President Nixon should demand prompt and honest disclosure for the benefit of the public and so should his campaign manager.

Rocky Mountain News
Denver, Colo., August 18, 1972

ONE MORNING IN JUNE, police arrested five men inside the offices of the Democratic National Committee in Washington, D.C. The offices were in the Watergate apartment complex, which otherwise largely is populated by higher-living people, many identified with the Nixon administration.

The five accused men had in hand assorted bugging devices and a wad of crisp new money. The purpose of the trespass still is unknown, but the characters who thought up this caper hardly qualify as gents of great common sense. It was a stupid stunt, whatever the motive.

Naturally, the Democrats are trying to make this into a cosmic campaign issue and to this end Lawrence F. O'Brien, Democratic chairman at the time, has filed a million-dollar damage suit against the Committee for the Re-election of the President, which previously had employed at least one of the suspects.

Meanwhile, a Justice Department lawyer has been representing a White House consultant, whose name has been involved. A Washington judge ruled the lawyer off the case because the FBI and other parts of the Justice Department are supposed to be investigating, along with a grand jury.

But the Justice Department, which can't seem to quit while it is ahead, has gone to a higher court to keep its lawyer in the case.

All along, the White House has taken an aloof attitude toward the whole prank, while Sen. George S. McGovern is out on the hustings trying to build a big bonfire out of it.

This is not the type of issue on which the country is likely to decide a presidential election—not at least unless it can be proven that some "higher-ups" the White House or on the President's campaign committee either condoned this ridiculous affair or dreamed it up.

But until the full story is cleared up, the Republicans are running the risk of looking more and more foolish. And if they persist in trying to smoke the whole thing over until after the election, they simply will be making themselves look guilty, as well as silly.

The Topeka Daily Capital
Topeka, Kans., August 18, 1972

When Washington police surprised those five men attempting to bug national Democratic headquarters in the Watergate Apartments, the incident was treated more like a scene from a Keystone Cops comedy than the serious campaign issue it fast is becoming.

Readers were hard-pressed to imagine just what information could be gleaned by bugs from headquarters of any political party, Democratic or Republican, that would be worth such an effort and risk.

Who, persons asked laughingly, would anyone want to have advance information on the planks the Democratic platform will include, or how much the Democratic deficit is, or does McGovern really have a chance, or what new strategy will be used to defeat President Nixon for a second term.

Lawrence O'Brien, then Democratic national chairman, took it more seriously. He immediately filed a $1 million damage action against the Committee for the Re-election of President Nixon and the five men arrested. The court since has narrowed the case to O'Brien and the five men, saying the Democratic national committee and the Nixon re-election committee are unincorporated associations and do not have the status to sue and be sued.

Since O'Brien's action, sparks have been flying in all directions. Police and Federal Bureau of Investigation agents have sorted out aliases given by the five men, and have been linking them with former Nixon aides, past employment by the Central Intelligence Agency and Free Cuba agents. A grand jury also is investigating.

The Watergate Affair took on a distinct Republican flavor when $25,000 in political contributions to the Nixon campaign were converted into a cashier's check and deposited in the account in Miami of one of the buggers. Subsequent investigation shows that similar deposits of at least $114,000 have been placed in the same account.

While influential Republican leaders, including John Mitchell and Maurice Stans, both former cabinet members, deny any knowledge of the amateurish bugging attempt, they have a deep responsibility to find the truth and tell the people of the United States exactly what they find.

If they do not, and it is possible no one in the White House is privy to what really happened, they should understand the great urgency to clear the record. While they remain silent, a believable mixture of fact and fiction snowballs and worsens.

The truth is, the Watergate Affair isn't funny anymore. It is a deadly serious campaign issue that grows faster in silence than in honest disclosure.

The Evening Star
Washington, D.C., August 24, 1972

There is something disquieting about the decision of the General Accounting Office to delay issuance of its audit report on the finances of the Nixon re-election committee until Finance Director Maurice Stans and GOP bigwigs have a chance to examine and offer suggestions about the 8-page document.

The GAO, after all, works for the Congress of the United States and not for the executive branch of this or any administration. It may be true, as aides of Comptroller General Elmer Staats say, that it is standard operating procedure for the GAO to show investigative reports to the investigated agencies unless some member of Congress specifies that this not be done.

But the GAO is working with a new Federal Election Campaign Act that did not become effective until April 7 and, beyond this, the Committee for Re-election of the President is not an "agency" in the sense that the Pentagon or the Peace Corps is.

There is a strong instinct to suppose that Stans' phone calls to GAO officials an hour before scheduled release of the audit report caused Staats to delay public disclosure of a matter that is central to the Watergate bugging of the Democratic National Committee in which CRP people are suspect. If it is routine to submit audit reports to investigated agencies, why was the submission not made until after Stans had called GAO at least twice?

The GAO, like all investigative agencies, must be like Caesar's wife in irreproachability. We cannot take kindly to the spectacle of GAO officials sitting down with GOP campaign leaders in Miami Beach to edit, check, delete from or add to a report that should be based only on documents the committee is bound by law to have submitted long since.

We believe Stans has even more to explain now than he did before about how GOP campaign funds were used and now the GAO, a watchdog agency, has created the appearance of evil if not evil itself.

New York Post
New York, N.Y., August 28, 1972

At a time when President Nixon is being depicted as a political superman by many analysts of the 1972 campaign, the unsavory mess in Washington involving the Finance Committee to Reelect the President must be a deepening source of discomfort to the White House. Some members of the Nixon entourage must be wondering why it was necessary to get into so much trouble in a year when money is flowing so freely into the GOP treasury, and when euphoric commentators even question whether it is needed.

But what began as a seemingly minor unpleasantness is steadily assuming large dimensions, and the latest developments suggest that Mr. Nixon himself may not be able to remain aloof from the controversy, as he has tried to do so far. There is a potential storm rising that will require a good deal more effective response than the cry of "foul" recited yesterday by GOP Finance Chief — and former Commerce Secretary Maurice Stans, who had remained mute and inaccessible for so many days when the story began to unfold.

The Administration's initial belief that the silent treatment could effectively dispose of the matter seemingly ended when the General Accounting Office, a body noted for its political independence and technical competence, flatly declared on Saturday that Mr. Stans' committee had been guilty of numerous "apparent and possible violations" of the Federal Election Campaign Act. It said the alleged violations involved up to $350,000 in gifts to Mr. Nixon's campaign.

How much of this amount was directly related to subsidizing the bugging of Democratic headquarters remains to be established; plainly part of the fiscal hanky-panky was connected to that dreary invasion. But the questions emerging cover wide ground.

More than enough has already emerged to justify Democratic demands that Mr. Nixon name a special prosecutor to press the inquiry. Certainly these proposals are "political," in the sense that this is a campaign year and that the Democrats detect pay dirt in the saga. This is how democracy operates; one of the dividends of election seasons is that people learn things normally concealed by bipartisan arrangement.

The Administration can hardly expect to evoke public confidence in an investigation conducted by the present leadership of the Justice Dept. As Rep. Wright Patman (D-Tex.) has validly observed, it is absurd to entrust Attorney General Kleindienst with the prosecution of the same political forces to whom he is indebted for his appointment. One of the figures whose role warrants full scrutiny is Kleindienst's chief sponsor, John Mitchell.

We do not profess to know where all the trails will lead if a diligent inquiry is pursued by an unfettered prosecutor. But as long as Mr. Nixon resists that course, the suspicion that a massive protective maneuver is in progress will inevitably grow. For the logical public conclusion will be that he views political risks of full disclosure as graver than the hazard of flagrant coverups by an avowed "law-and-order" Administration.

The New York Times
New York, N.Y., August 28, 1972

The findings by the General Accounting Office that the Committee to Re-elect the President has committed "apparent and possible violations" of the Federal Election Campaign Act calls for an immediate, full-scale inquiry by investigators of unassailable credibility.

The issues are far more serious than even the substantial amounts of campaign contributions and expenditures which apparently changed hands without the required public disclosure. Some of these hidden resources seem to have found their way into the pockets of those shadowy figures who were arrested in June while breaking into the Democratic National Committee headquarters at the Watergate apartments. This suggests something more sinister than illegal efforts to protect the anonymity of bashful campaign contributors.

The list of unanswered questions grows longer every day. Elusive funds have been transferred from committee safes to banks in Miami and Mexico City. Some participants in these dubious events—including at least one former member of the White House political staff— have refused to answer questions or disappeared altogether. Former Commerce Secretary Maurice Stans, who now is the chief Republican money raiser, has not to date given full and satisfactory explanations concerning the source and disposition of some of these mysterious funds. Mr. Stans moreover had also directed the crash campaign to get a maximum of anonymous cash into the campaign coffers before the new public disclosure laws went into effect last April.

The risk incurred when those who seek favorable governmental rulings are also anonymous campaign contributors was once again underscored. A charter to open a suburban bank appears to have been expedited shortly after the applicant contributed $25,000 to the Republican campaign. And according to the Federal Bureau of Investigation, all or part of that contribution, which the donor had hoped would remain anonymous, seems to have found its way into the bank account of one of the planners of the Watergate political espionage.

The White House remains silent. The Justice Department promises only that the G.A.O. findings will be handled "routinely." Does this mean that the stable doors are to be locked after the elections have gone?

Responsibility to investigate cannot be left in the hands of the Administration's own officialdom. The G.A.O., as the Congressional watchdog, lacks subpoena power. The Committee to Re-elect the President—not surprisingly—"welcomes the opportunity" to deal with the Justice Department in these matters. Indeed, a spokesman for the committee expressed confidence that the Justice Department will find the alleged violations to be "nothing more than minor and technical." This is precisely why this investigation cannot be left to a department with strong political ties to the Administration and to the Nixon re-election committee.

What is involved in these tawdry proceedings is not an obscure political caper but the integrity of the election process and of government itself. The issues range from allegations of serious financial abuses to nothing less than political espionage. The charges implicate persons close to the White House.

This is why the President himself should act at once to appoint a special prosecutor of unquestioned political independence and judicial integrity. The American people have a right to demand all the facts and the fair and impartial prosecution of any violators of the laws.

LEDGER-STAR
Norfolk, Va., August 28, 1972

The mystery that continues to surround both the attempted bugging of the Democratic national headquarters and the misdirection of Republican campaign checks ought to be cleared up for the public with as much dispatch as possible.

The questions that the events, the charges and the counter-charges have raised are serious. A large amount of money is involved, and the channeling of funds, $114,000, into the bank account of one of the five men charged in the Democratic headquarters break-in obviously has worrisome implications.

The Democrats themselves have been airing the details almost daily, but they have done so in a plainly partisan way in an effort to make election campaign progress. They have not, however, offered much enlightenment along with their rhetoric.

On the other side, the Republicans, too, have been less than helpful. To a finding by the General Accounting Office of five "apparent" and four "possible" violations of election law by the Finance Committee for the Re-Election of the President in the handling of funds, the GOP has offered no clarifying response.

And the Watergate caper—as the headquarters break-in has come to be called—has long since changed in its implications from the almost ludicrous to the very ugly, with connections being made to the GOP campaign operation.

★ ★ ★ ★

There are public responsibilities here, one to bring out the facts with respect to the campaign funds —not only the apparently misdirected $114,000, but other "possible" and "apparent" violations cited by GAO—and another to establish just what connections did exist between the headquarters break-in and the Republican party.

The responsibility is a crucial one because for a long time there has seemed to be a growing public cynicism about politics and politicians. This is a trend that can only erode further the public's confidence in government.

Certainly, too, the questions that have been raised hang unhappily over the presidential campaign. So the Republicans not only owe a clear and complete explanation as a public responsibility; in a sense, they owe this to themselves as well.

The Evening Bulletin

Philadelphia, Pa., August 29, 1972

President Nixon can no longer remain silent on the reported misuse of campaign funds contributed to his re-election committee.

The report of the U.S. General Accounting Office, which answers to Congress, alleges that as much as $350,000 in campaign contributions may have gone unreported or been misused in a way that suggests outright violation of the new federal laws governing election campaign expenditures.

What started out as a relatively trivial or even comic incident with the apprehension of five men with electronic espionage gear at the Democratic national headquarters last June 17 has now ballooned into a potential scandal that could have impact on the presidential election.

The response — or nonresponse — of top Republican officials so far has been silence or countercharges that the Democrats are exploiting the incident for political purposes.

And so they are. But that doesn't disprove the GAO's finding that there may have been extensive misuse of campaign funds through "apparent and possible" violations in the new federal elections expenditures law.

GOP Finance Chairman Maurice Stans' defensive request that the GAO turn its attention to Democratic spending practices may have merit but right now it is not to the point. It is the Republicans and not the Democrats who are under the spotlight.

The affair has taken on a sinister air with the revelation that some $114,000 of the allegedly misused or unreported funds was deposited to the Miami bank account of a principal suspect in the June 17 break in. The collection and disposition of these monies remain a central mystery in the entire matter.

The incident has now reached the stage where it cannot help but reflect unfavorably on some key managers in the President's campaign organization and thus, indirectly at least, on the Administration itself.

No one would suggest that Mr. Nixon had knowledge of the shadowy transactions involving some of the funds of his reelection committee. But President Nixon does offer himself as a take-charge Chief Executive and as a man well in control of all situations. Thus he is certain to be judged in part by the way in which he reacts to the Watergate affair and to the other matters involving his reelection committee's funds.

Mr. Nixon should assert his leadership now.

He should assure the American people that a full, fair and fearless inquiry will be made into all of the circumstances of the entire matter.

He should assure the American people that it will not be handled as merely another routine matter in the Department of Justice or be allowed, perhaps, to wait until after the election for attention.

It is up to Mr. Nixon to take action. If he feels the inquiry can be handled within the executive department of the Federal Government he should so state and give assurance that he will be personally responsible for seeing that it is carried out. If Mr. Nixon feels that an outside inquiry is necessary he should get this under way at once.

There is far too much involved here for the White House even to appear to be sitting this one out.

HERALD-JOURNAL

Syracuse, N.Y., August 30, 1972

Sen. George S. McGovern, the Democratic presidential candidate, and nearly every member of his staff are demanding almost hourly that President Nixon reveal sources of campaign funds and explain how $114,000 of Republican campaign money apparently landed in the office of Bernard L. Baker, one of five men arrested in the Democratic National Committee Watergate offices in June.

Atty. Gen. Richard Kleindienst has said he expects a grand jury to report soon on the Watergate affair.

A grand jury investigation is the proper way to clear the air. It probably is too much to ask of the issue-starved McGovern and his staff that they await this report.

We also suggest that a grand jury with a special outside prosecutor look into the campaign fund charges from both political parties with orders to report their findings before Nov. 1.

Such an outsider could do much to silence the chatter about the Justice Department answering to a Republican President and the General Accounting Office answering to a Democratic Congress.

The Washington Post

Washington, D.C., August 29, 1972

Well, now that the General Accounting Office's elections office has issued its report, Maurice Stans has talked again. The GAO has given us a bit more clarity about the Watergate-Nixon campaign financing affair, but Mr. Stans has contributed—against his own staff's prediction that he would have a "logical" explanation—nothing but smog. As soon as the GAO report was released, Mr. Stans rushed into print claiming that the report was wrong and that its defects were the fault of the Democrats, going on to demand a full audit of the financing of the McGovern campaign. He also claimed that there have been no "purposeful" violations of the campaign financing act and that any violations are "purely minor and technical." There is not one whiff of explanation in all this and the argument is so contorted as well as so brazen in its assault on the public's capacity to reason that it makes the head spin. The Democrats are not the issue. Republican campaign financing is what is at issue.

So, since Mr. Stans would rather obfuscate than explain, let us just run lightly over the GAO report and some of the other major issues surrounding the Nixon campaign finances. First, there is the matter of several hundred thousand dollars—perhaps as much as $750,000—which was at least in part generated by a fund raising trip in which Mr. Stans participated and which was "laundered" in Mexico. That is, checks and stock certificates donated to the Nixon campaign were deposited in a Mexican bank account and then converted into dollar drafts so that the donors could retain anonymity. Then there is the confirmation of the fact that in addition to the $25,000 Nixon campaign check which ended up in the bank account of one of the men arrested at the Watergate, there was another $89,000 in Nixon funds which also landed in that

account—all of it "laundered" through Mexico. Then there is the matter of at least $350,000 which was just lying around in Mr. Stans' safe. Another highlight of the report is that the GAO asserts that the Nixon campaign money managers comingled personal and campaign funds.

Much can be made of all of this, but two points at least deserve particular attention. The first is that Mr. Stans and others have been trying to give the impression that no one high in the Nixon campaign organization had anything to do with the authorization or the financing of the Watergate caper. Yet, now the GAO tells us that the $114,000 (25 + 89) in the suspect's account came out of the funds Mr. Stans kept in his safe until May 25. It stretches credulity just a little to suggest that a fund so closely held by the financial chief of the campaign committee could be tapped for a sum as substantial as $114,000 without his authority and without his having some knowledge of the use to which the money was to be put.

And then, of course, no one knows just how much was originally in Mr. Stans' safe. All we know about that money is that it was deposited in a bank on May 25, 1972, with a notation on the deposit slip indicating that it had been, "cash on hand prior to April 4, 1972, from 1968 campaign." Yet, Mr. Stans told GAO investigators that it was not money from 1968, but rather that the money had been raised this year. We have no way of knowing which is true nor is there any way of knowing now how much was in Mr. Stans' safe originally, how much was taken out of the safe and spent or for what purposes such expenditures were made.

The Mexican laundry operation also reeks. Much has been made—appropriately, we think—of the fact that the Nixon campaign managers have re-

fused to disclose the names of the donors to the secret $10,000,000 fund raised by the campaign committee prior to April 7, the date on which the campaign financing law requiring disclosure of donors took effect. Until the GAO report, however, the lengths to which the campaign committee went in order to keep the sources of their funds secret was not clear. The disclosure of the convoluted Mexican transactions cannot help introducing questions about how the money was raised and what promises were made in order to secure those funds. The disclosure that Dwayne Andreas, the secret donor of the $25,000 that found its way to a Miami bank, received a federal bank charter in unseemly haste does nothing to relieve ever darkening suspicions.

So, there it is. The GAO has apparently done a competent job, but it admits that without subpoena power, there are "gaps" it cannot close. The rest of us can only wonder about those gaps and about what Mr. Kleindienst's Justice Department—from which we got the ITT case and the cover-up of Harry Steward's indiscretions as a U.S. attorney in San Diego—will do to restore public confidence in the electoral process in this election year. We have asked repeatedly that Mr. Stans speak out to clear this whole matter up. Apparently, he does not intend to do so. But the matter is far larger than Mr. Stans now. The questions are so numerous and so grave, that nothing less than a full disclosure by the President of all of the sources of his campaign funds and the appointment of a special investigatorial and prosecutorial team from outside the government would seem to be required to dispel the Republican-created sense that there is a great deal of dirty business in the effort to re-elect this particular President of the United States.

The Courier-Journal
Louisville, Ky., August 30, 1972

PRESIDENT NIXON'S Attorney General says that President Nixon's Justice Department should have exclusive control of the investigation into President Nixon's campaign committee's handling of President Nixon's secret campaign fund and the bugging or attempted bugging of the Democratic Party's headquarters by President Nixon's campaign workers.

And when the investigation is over, says Attorney General Richard Kleindienst, "no credible, fairminded person is going to be able to say that we whitewashed or dragged our feet on it."

Of course not.

How could any clear-headed citizen even entertain such a thought, after President Nixon has spoken out so forthrightly, has initiated such vigorous action to track down the spymaster of those five men caught skulking about the Watergate Hotel with wires and batteries and funny little microphones?

And Mr. Kleindienst—he who recently cited the thousands of illegal arrests in Washington on May Day 1971 as a laudable example of how Mr. Nixon has curbed "mob violence" around the country—who could be so cynical as to believe that anything less than a thirst for pure justice motivates his pursuit of Republican spies?

And Maurice Stans. Who could doubt that his refusal to talk about the Watergate caper is, indeed, motivated by what he says is deep concern for the civil rights of those whom a federal grand jury might indict? His fingering of Gordon Liddy as the owner of the last known hands to touch that mysterious $25,000 Nixon campaign check that came to rest in the bank account of one of the spies—who could construe that as an attempt to designate a scapegoat?

No, Mr. Stans' yearning for justice is at least as powerful as Mr. Kleindienst's After the General Accounting Office reported "apparent and possible violations" of the Federal Election Campaign Act by Mr Nixon's campaign committee, was it not Mr. Stans who immediately and forthrightly demanded a "full and complete audit" of Democratic Party finances, too? The public can only hope that Mr. Stans will follow up his call with a list of his specific complaints and an official request for a GAO investigation, lest his demand be mistaken for a smokescreen.

With the case of the Watergate bugging and the $10 million Republican slush fund firmly in the hands of Mr. Nixon, Mr. Kleindienst and Mr. Stans, the Democrats' demand for a "special prosecutor" is obviously, as Mr. Kleindienst put it, "political." And, of course, politics is the very last thing that should intrude into an attorney general's pursuit of his duty.

Indeed, the persons implicated in the bugging of the Democratic headquarters are, as Mr. Kleindienst said so beautifully, "entitled to all the protection of the law, like the Chicago Seven, Daniel Ellsberg and the Berrigans."

Ah, how Mr. Nixon's Justice Department protected them! If Mr. Kleindienst pursues the Republican spies half as vigorously as he hounded the critics of Mr. Nixon's war policies, his investigation will be a monument to Nixonian justice. And what will it matter if such thoroughness requires much time, and protection of the accused requires much silence, even into 1973? .

O Nixon! O Kleindienst! O Stans! How cozily the Republic rests in your hands.

THE ANN ARBOR NEWS
Ann Arbor, Mich., August 30, 1972

ATTY. GEN. Richard Kleindienst has promised the forthcoming investigation of the break-in at the Democratic National Committee will be the most extensive, thorough and comphrehensive "since the assassination of President Kennedy."

It is in all parties' interest that Kleindienst be held to that pledge. The Watergate c a p e r, as this break-in has come to be known, is beginning to smell. There is a lot of explaining to do.

At this point the Democrats are foolish to let the matter drop and give up a potentially damaging issue. For their part, the Republicans are foolish if they try to cover up the mess any longer.

If Maurice Stans, as chairman of the Committee to Re-Elect the President, has nothing to hide, he will cooperate with the Justice Department probe, and in the meantime document the flow of funds which has gone through his committee.

* * *

IN addition to the bugging incident at the Watergate, Stans has to answer for a General Accounting Office (GAO) r e p o r t which, after an audit of Stans' committee's b o o k s, concluded that there was an apparent or a possible violation of campaign finance laws.

Stans has dodged and ducked the issue, which unfortunately adds to the suspicion that plenty is amiss here. Stans has to explain two main questions and probably a host of sub-questions. They are:

The link between the Watergate Five and a large sum of money which passed through Stans' committee. More specifically, how did money supposedly intended for GOP campaign coffers get into the account of one of the Watergate Five?

GAO says $25,000 was contributed to Stans' committee after April 7 which makes that s u m subject to the 1971 campaign finance law. Stan says that sum was in the committee's hands before April 7.

Breaking and e n t e r i n g and eavesdropping a r e not matters lightly dismissed. This clearly is a cut or two above the cheap political party espionage that goes on all the time. When the trail leads so close to the White House as it apparently does here, t h e country needs to know what's going on.

That is why a prompt, thorough investigation is to be encouraged. If Kleindienst delivers on his promise, there won't be any charges of "coverup" after t h e probe is completed.

THE DAILY OKLAHOMAN
Oklahoma City, Okla.
August 29, 1972

ODORS of politics rise unmistakably from the charges and counter-charges over the handling of some $350,000 in campaign funds by the Committee to Re-elect the President.

The General Accounting Office, the auditing and investigating agency of Congress, issued a report alleging "apparent and possible violations" of the 1971 Federal Election Campaign Act. To put the whole affair in proper perspective, it should be kept in mind that the GAO is responsible solely to Congress, which is controlled by the Democratic majorities in the Senate and House.

The GAO referred the matter to the Department of Justice for possible further investigation. This puts the monkey squarely on the back of President Nixon's administration, since the head of the department, Atty. Gen. Richard G. Kleindienst, a Nixon appointee, is considered to be strongly partisan. O b v i o u s l y, it would suit the campaign strategy of the Democratic presidential nominee, Sen. George McGovern, for Kleindienst to neglect to follow up on the report so he could be accused of covering up for the administration.

For its part, the Committee to Re-elect the President, through its finance chairman, Maurice Stans, Nixon's former secretary of commerce, demanded that the GAO begin immediately an audit of the Democratic fund-raising records. He said the committee has "reason to believe" such as investigation would be "very revealing."

The McGovern campaign is also trying to make political hay with the "Watergate caper"—the June 17 arrest of five men armed with electronic gear inside the offices of the Democratic National Committee. Some of the "apparent violations" cited in the GAO report centered on a $25,000 contribution to the Nixon campaign. The money showed up in the bank account of one of the men arrested in the raid.

The GAO report did not make a connection between the "apparent violations" and the Watergate arrests. But Sargent Shriver, the Democratic vice presidential nominee, has been trying to make it singlehandedly. Recently he spoke of employees of the Committee to Re-elect the President being caught in Democratic headquarters, although the only actual link with the committee was a security coordinator who had been retained on a contract basis.

Lacking other issues with which their liberal candidate can score with the American electorate, the McGovern people hope to hurt the Nixon campaign by capitalizing on the Watergate incident. Interestingly, campaign contributions turned up by the investigation include $89,000 from four Texas Democrats and $25,000 from a Minnesota supporter of Hubert Humphrey. At this rate, McGovern may find out to his dismay just how many big Democartic contributors are shying away from his candidacy.

The Detroit News
Detroit, Mich., August 29, 1972

Although important, the questions raised about the handling of Republican and Democratic campaign finances are not and should not become the central issues of the 1972 presidential campaign.

Unfortunately, those questions of finance threaten to occupy the headlines while the real issues — the relative merits of the candidates, the total record of the administration and the alternatives offered by the Democrats — retire to the background.

Nothing, we suspect, would suit George McGovern's managers more. The Republicans should act promptly to blunt this diversion and restore the campaign to proper perspective.

Acting with ample justification and with the cooperation of the Republicans, the General Accounting Office conducted an audit of the books of the Committee for the Re-election of the President. In its report the GAO charged apparent or possible violations of the federal election campaign act.

Maurice Stans, chairman of the GOP fund-raising operation, now accuses McGovern campaign operatives of using the offices of sympathetic Democratic senators to exert undue p r e s s u r e on the GAO. Further, Stans demands a GAO probe of the finances of Democratic candidate George McGovern.

Such accusations and recriminations could easily occupy the remaining nine weeks of this campaign. To prevent that from happening, President Nixon should encourage a prompt and thorough investigation by the Justice Department and issue a crisp statement deploring any impropriety which may have occurred.

We share the curiosity of others regarding certain matters. For example, how did checks apparently i n t e n d e d for the GOP campaign fund get into the account of a man suspected in the break-in at Democratic headquarters? What does Stans know about McGovern finances which causes Stans to believe that "very revealing" discoveries will be made?

Let's have the answers, and let's have them soon, but let's not allow the questions or the answers to overshadow the more important business of this campaign year.

The national economy, Vietnam, isolationism, national security, radicalism versus moderation — those a r e t h e t o p i c s t h e candidates and their supporters should be discussing. On most of those issues, incidentally, George McGovern is on the hook; the Republicans are foolish if they let him off.

Chicago, Ill., August 30, 1972

SHOULD a special prosecutor be named to look into the attempted bugging of Democratic Party headquarters last June? Spokesmen for Sen. McGovern's organization have been demanding one, saying that it's absurd to entrust the inquiry to the administration's own Justice Department. Atty. Gen. Richard Kleindienst, however, has been just as emphatic on the other side, arguing that it would not only be unnecessary to pick a special prosecutor but downright impossible.

"There is just no way you could do it," Kleindienst said Monday. "It's not a matter of looking into the conduct of government officials, but alleged criminal conduct on the part of private individuals."

The statement may be true. It is possible, tho, to wonder how Kleindienst can be so sure of it. Evidently the most awkward question about the bugging incident—whether any government officials were involved in it—has already been answered to the satisfaction of the Justice Department, and the answer is "No." Which brings up the second question, "How do we know you're right?"

The Justice Department has been investigating the appalling Watergate incident, in which five men carrying spy equipment were found inside Democratic offices in Washington's Watergate Apartments complex. One of the five was later found to have, in his private bank account, $114,000 that originally had been contributed from various sources to Mr. Nixon's campaign fund. No one has yet explained what route the money took. Kleindienst promised that the Justice Department inquiry would be extensive and thorogoing, and we have no grounds for disbelieving the statement.

The fact remains that findings by the Republican-run Justice Department, even if they are the precise truth, are not likely to settle all doubts, and any doubts left over will be promptly seized on by the Democrats. The point of naming a special prosecutor is to put the inquiry clearly out of reach of partisan politics and make sure the findings are not affected one way or the other by party allegiances. That may or may not be done, but we do not think it's impossible.

THE DALLAS TIMES HERALD
Dallas, Tex., August 30, 1972

HAVING FINALLY realized that the Watergate bugging affair simply won't go away, the Nixon administration is now indicating that it will do a thorough investigation of the matter.

Atty. Gen. Richard G. Kleindienst has declared that the Justice Department is undertaking "the most extensive, thorough and comprehensive investigation since the assassination of President Kennedy."

It is indeed high time that this sordid affair were thoroughly probed, and the responsibility for its instigation determined without further questions. That, too, no m a t t e r where the responsibility may rest.

The fact of the matter is that the investigation promised by Kleindienst should have been under way long since. Instead, high Republican administration officials and former officials, along with the Nixon Re-election Committee, have sought to gloss over the matter, if not to ignore it entirely. This they have done seemingly with the illusory hope that interest in the bungled bugging of Democratic National Headquarters would die out.

But it won't die out, and it shouldn't until full and complete exposure is made.

There is the still unanswered question of a $25,000 campaign contribution check which once was in the hands of Maurice Stans, former secretary of Commerce and now treasurer of the Committee for the Re-election of the President. That check later found its way into the Florida bank account of Bernard L. Barker, one of the five suspects arrested in the Democratic headquarters break-in.

There is also the question of James W. McCord Jr., another of the five suspects. McCord, a former CIA employe, was retained in January by the Committee for the Re-election of the President and by the Republican National Committee to supervise internal security for them.

These as well as other aspects of the affair must be explained. As for the contention by prominent Democrats that the Justice Department cannot conduct a fair investigation, that is nonsense. The department can do so, and it must do so. If there is any indication that it is dissembling in that assignment, the President, who himself has remained silent too long on this matter, must step in and see to it that the investigation is thorough, complete and without prejudice.

It could have been the work of a bunch of zealots, but the real story must be uncovered— and soon.

SEVEN INDICTED IN WATERGATE RAID; TRIAL OF DEMO CIVIL SUIT DELAYED

Seven persons, including two former White House aides, were indicted by a District of Columbia federal grand jury Sept. 15 on charges of conspiring to break into the Democratic national headquarters in the Watergate building. The two former Nixon aides were: G. Gordon Liddy, a former presidential assistant on domestic affairs and, at the time of the raid June 17, counsel to the finance committee of the Committee to Re-elect the President; and E. Howard Hunt Jr., a former White House consultant and associate of Liddy. The other five indicted were those seized by police inside the Watergate office building during the raid. After the indictments were made public, a Justice Department spokesman said "we have absolutely no evidence to indicate that any others should be charged."

Lawrence F. O'Brien, who was Democratic national chairman at the time of the break-in, said Sept. 15 "we can only assume that the investigation will continue since the indictments handed down today reflect only the most narrow construction of the crime that was committed." The same day Democratic presidential nominee George McGovern called for "an impartial investigation conducted by somebody entirely outside the Department of Justice." In a statement Sept. 16, McGovern accused Nixon of ordering a "whitewash" and deplored the "questions left unanswered" by the grand jury, such as who had ordered and paid for the espionage attempt.

The trial of the civil suit brought by the Democrats against key officials of the Committee to Re-elect the President was delayed by U.S. Judge Charles R. Richey who said Sept. 21 "it will be impossible" to begin the trial before the Nov. 7 general election. Richey said he would extend his order barring depositions in the case until the persons under criminal indictment had been tried.

(Clark MacGregor, President Nixon's campaign director, had announced Sept. 13 that the Committee to Re-elect the President had filed a counter-suit in federal court seeking $2.5 million in damages from O'Brien. The suit accused O'Brien of having used the court "as a forum in which to publicize accusations against innocent persons which would be libelous if published elsewhere.")

THE CHRISTIAN SCIENCE MONITOR
Boston, Mass., September 16, 1972

The most suspicious thing about the whole Watergate affair is the effort of the Nixon administration to keep it under wraps until after election day.

When the Democrats brought a civil suit the Republicans moved for a postponement until after election day. When this failed they moved to have the case dismissed on technicalities.

Attorney General Richard Kleindienst promised "the most extensive, thorough, and comprehensive investigation since the assassination of President Kennedy." But he didn't say anything about when or how fast.

We can think of one legitimate argument against quick pursuit of the truth in this extraordinary matter. If any trial were under way now there would be daily news stories based on allegations and implications. The daily crop of headlines would help the Democrats and hurt the Republicans during the campaign. If it were discovered in the end that there had been nothing worse than excessive partisan zeal on the part of underlings it would then be too late to undo the unfair damage already done.

This is a point. But we think it overweighed by the appearance of an attempt to sweep it all under the rug.

If the Republicans were as innocent as they say they are they should seek the earliest and most complete vindication possible. The bald effort to avoid a speedy trial of the Watergate case compounds the bad appearance already produced by secrecy about that $10 million collected just before the new disclosure law went into effect.

Republicans are loud in their claims of innocence. If they are truly innocent they should not fear complete and full disclosure. Their failure to seek it puts them in an unfavorable light.

Honolulu Star-Bulletin
Honolulu, Hawaii, September 16, 1972

The Department of Justice will render an injustice to itself and to the people it serves if it moves with less than utmost speed and energy toward a solution of the bizarre Watergate affair.

Reports of a disposition within the department to let the case lie until after the November election are, if true, a reflection not only on the department but on the President himself. The Department of Justice is the chief law enforcement arm of the nation, and for it to refrain, deliberately, from imposing the law for purely political reasons cannot be condoned as anything less than scandalous.

The issue has become so obscured by political charges and counter-charges that its real nature is hard to see. Yet the facts are that (1) five men were caught redhanded "bugging" the Democratic party's national headquarters; (2) some of these men had close connections with the Republican party's Committee to Reelect the President; and (3) one of them, admitting his complicity in an interview with the New York Times, has inferentially accused others by saying he will never testify against them.

The President himself is the titular head of his party. He also, as President, is head of all the people of both parties. If the Republican party, or any of its offshoots, such as the Committee to Reelect the President, was involved in eavesdropping on the Democratic opposition, it should be revealed.

It simply is not good enough for the White House to remain silent and pretend it never happened. On the contrary, it is the responsibility of the White House, acting through the Justice Department, to find out what happened and, if such is indicated, to prosecute those involved, be they Republican or Democrat.

The News and Courier

Charleston, S.C., September 19, 1972

As might be expected, federal grand jury indictments in the Watergate caper won't satisfy George McGovern and his supporters. Nothing will do, it seems, but that top names in the Republican Party be linked by tangible evidence to the bugging operatives caught at Democratic headquarters.

By crying whitewash over the indictments, the Democrats are telling the public they have no intention of abandoning the Watergate affair. In fact, it appears they will continue to nurture it into the significant campaign issue they so desperately need.

For voters looking for excuses not to vote for Richard Nixon, the Democrats may be scoring points with their calculated effort to paint corruption all over the Nixon administration. Even staunch supporters of the President are considering these hearty hints of wrongdoing. Tip-offs on the Russian wheat deal, funny political money from Mexico and the Watergate affair itself suggest to the hesitant that the Nixon team is at least capable of wrongdoing.

It appears, however, that hanky-panky rhetoric spawned by the Democrats is merely affirming the public's already cynical view of national politics. Manipulation of campaign money like chess board pieces (sometimes under the board, too) and operations by party spies are no surprise. Many voters may have concluded by now that the idealistic McGovern legions would be up to the same tactics were they in charge.

As Democrats couch their prime campaign thrusts around negative issues, public opinion polls show Mr. Nixon's favor with voters holding steady or growing. Democrats in Congress apparently aren't banking on a big McGovern comeback, either. As a Page One story in The News and Courier Monday noted, many Democrats are eager to educate voters on ticket splitting procedures.

The cries from the McGovern camp, where "new politics" is supposed to be in vogue, are the old sounds of "outs" trying to get in. Having grown accustomed to it all, U. S. voters seem unmoved.

The Birmingham News

Birmingham, Ala., September 19, 1972

Whoever authorized the so-called Watergate Caper made a collossally damaging blunder and in time, presumably, wil have his hide nailed to the wall.

The incident of political esplonage was illegal, morally wrong and pragmatically stupid. The proof that it was stupid is that the culprits got caught—and now have been indicted—and getting caught is the worst blunder in that sort of dirty game.

Nevertheless, the Democrats have not been able to turn the campaign around on the single issue of bugging. The damaging attempt to gather Democratic secrets may have hurt the Republicans, but how much is hard to tell when the polls continue to show a 34 per cent gap between the President and his Democratic opponent.

Some observers say that even many traditionally Democratic voters shrug off The Caper, determined to cast a rare vote in the Republican column because of the vastly more important issues of substance in the campaign.

Perhaps the Democrats have hurt themselves somewhat in capitalizing on the embarrassment of the spying incident by being too gleeful in the first place that it happened and subsequently by being too shrill in day-after-day denunciations of the Republicans.

Certainly Democratic campaign leader Lawrence O'Brien went too far in accusing Republican campaigner Maurice Stans of a criminal act when no proof has been established that the charge is true.

Democrats, who have been critical enough of some Republicans for "rhetorical overkill" should themselves take a lesson.

When the offended party becomes so wild in its charges that its own credibility is rendered suspect, the average voter is tempted to dismiss the whole thing as another exercise in partianship. This is what seems to be happening in regard to the Watergate Caper.

In the final analysis, the election will be decided by the real issues. Those made apprehensive by the McGovern candidacy are not likely to vote for him because the Democratic headquarters was bugged, as reprehensible as that was.

The Virginian-Pilot

Norfolk, Va., September 18, 1972

On Friday a Federal grand jury returned indictments against seven men in the famous Watergate caper.

That is a beginning in getting to the truth of what appears to be a major political scandal. But it is only the beginning and the business is clouded with suspicions.

Indicted in Washington were the five men arrested on June 17 within the Democratic offices in the Watergate and two former White House aides, G. Gordon Liddy and E. Howard Hunt Jr., also implicated in the bugging of the Democrats' headquarters. The seven were charged variously with burglary, conspiracy, eavesdropping, and the possession of wiretaps.

The five men who were arrested in the Watergate are Bernard L. Barker, the alleged leader of the plot; James W. McCord Jr., who was on the payroll of the Committee for the Reelection of the President as security coordinator when he was caught by the police in the Watergate; Eugenio Martinez, Frank A. Sturgis, and Virgilio R. Gonzalez. All had been involved

with the CIA and Cuban exiles in the past.

Liddy was fired as counsel to the Committee for the Reelection of the President 11 days after the arrests for refusing to answer FBI questions. He had served as an aide to the Treasury and the White House prior to taking the campaign job. Hunt, who had been on the White House payroll as a consultant earlier this year, dropped out of sight for several weeks after the affair broke in June.

Both Hunt and Liddy are charged with entering the Democratic headquarters on June 17 "with the intent to steal property of another," although they were not arrested with the other suspects. They are also accused of renting rooms under false names at an adjoining motel and intercepting telephone conversations over a period of three weeks. They are believed to be the first White House aides ever indicted.

There is no question that the suspects were engaged in systematic surveillance of the Democrats, since they were caught in the act on June 17. Apparently the bugging had gone on for some time.

Who was behind the bugging in the Watergate? Who was paying the bills? Those are questions to be answered yet.

Friday's indictments do not touch upon the $114,000 in campaign funds that have been traced to Barker's bank in Miami. He is charged in Florida with fraudulently notarizing a $25,000 campaign check when he had difficulty in cashing it. (The donor was a Democrat who has since been awarded a bank charter.) Four other Republican checks, totaling $89,000, were routed through a Mexican bank to Barker's bank in Florida. The General Accounting Office has cited the Republicans for 11 "apparent violations" of the election laws in the handling of the $114,000 in campaign funds traced to Barker and the mysterious $350,000 in cash kept in the safe of Maurice Stans, the chief fund-raiser for the Republicans.

It appears that the burglary and bugging at the Watergate was financed from the Republican treasury. The links to the Committee for the Reelection of the President are suspicious.

Besides Messrs. Hunt, Liddy, and McCord, the chairman of the Committee for the Reelection of the President, former Attorney General John Mitchell, and the committee treasurer, Hugh W. Sloan Jr., both resigned after the arrests in June for "personal reasons." The current GOP line is that no one now on the payroll had anything to do with the Watergate.

While it is conceivable that the bugging was a cloak-and-dagger operation undertaken without the knowledge of GOP higher-ups, it requires the willing suspension of disbelief to stick to that view. The Nixon Administration—and especially the Justice Department under Mr. Mitchell and his successor, Attorney General Kleindienst—hasn't been scrupulous about civil liberties. It has been eager to snoop upon a variety of alleged conspirators, protesters, and simple wrongdoers.

The business at the Watergate smells to high heaven.

OREGON JOURNAL

Portland, Ore., September 22, 1972

So far, Democrats do not seem to be getting the political clout they expected from the Watergate bugging incident and the reason probably lies in the public attitude toward politics.

It has been shrugged off as just another case of political wickedness. The people have not been aroused to outrage by one group of politicians invading the offices of another group.

But breaking into private quarters and using the devious devices of electronic surveillance to desecrate another's privacy is fully worthy of outrage. Were something other than a political party involved, the public reaction might be quite different.

At least it is to be hoped that electronic snooping into private lives is not gaining the acceptance of apathetic acquiescence.

Perhaps if the Democrats would change their approach to the issue they might achieve more success. Perhaps they could paint the Nixon administration as providing the kind of climate that encourages Big Brother to break into private quarters and to bug private lives, and then to expand the incident beyond the crime in their own headquarters and picture it as a threat to the home and privacy of all citizens. Perhaps then they would get their point across.

But regardless of political mileage, the Watergate caper should help to stir public reaction against the threat of unjustified invasion of personal privacy via the sophisticated gadgets of modern technology.

Partisans of President Nixon as well as those of Sen. McGovern should sound the alarm against unwarranted electronic spying.

Watergate is not simply an evil perpetrated by one party on another. It is a case of breaking and bugging and no one knows how many cases of illegal bugging it may represent.

But the public attitude ought not be allowed to be interpreted as surrendering to or not caring about being spied upon—by government, by private agencies or by fellow citizens. With the wiretap granted certain legal standing, and applied far beyond the confines of the law, the only way to keep the bugs off will be for the people of this country to keep the heat on.

THE SUN

Baltimore, Md., September 22, 1972

With only six and a half weeks remaining until election day, it is becoming steadily more doubtful that voters will know the essential facts in the Watergate case before they enter the polling booths. This is deplorable, not because the Democrats say it is in their efforts to help Senator McGovern. It is deplorable because the standards of legal and political morality, as perceived by members of President Nixon's re-election team, have been brought into question—and left hanging. Criminal indictments have indeed been brought against five men arrested on the premises of the Democratic National Committee last June 17 and against two former White House aides accused of assisting their alleged attempt to bug and burglarize the Watergate offices of the enemy. But neither the Federal grand jury nor the General Accounting Office of Congress has dealt adequately with the broader questions: Who authorized this disgraceful episode and the free-wheeling use of GOP campaign funds so intimately connected with it?

The defendants named in the criminal indictment and the accompanying civil suit lodged by the Democratic National Committee have legal rights that, of course, must be protected. Justice cannot be dispensed to conform to political timetables. But this cannot excuse high Republican spokesmen in their blustering attempts to protect those with ultimate responsibility for the Watergate operation. Funds under the control of Maurice Stans, former Secretary of Commerce, were involved. Personnel answerable to John Mitchell, former Attorney General, figured in the case. Procedures in violation of the spirit and perhaps the letter of new campaign-financing laws apparently were condoned at high level. These are matters of serious import that should be clarified before November 7. They can hardly be considered "third rate" (to quote a White House spokesman) or political skullduggery dismissible as normal campaign background noise.

Arkansas Gazette.

Little Rock, Ark., September 20, 1972

THE NIXON GANG has the nerve of burglars, as it appears from one of the most direct evidential forms there is—arrest on the burgled premises—some of the members actually are. It would have afforded some slight degree of comic relief in a most unfunny business, indeed, if the Watergate Five (which turns out now to have been the Watergate Seven), before being flushed in the wee hours at Democratic National Headquarters, had been asked who was there and then had managed to respond weakly, "Nobody here but us chickens." As it was, there wasn't time even for that much after-the-fact subterfuge.

Yet there was Mr. Nixon himself, possibly the nerviest of the lot, saying in his first and last remarks on the case that none of the several accused men with close links to the Committee to Re-elect the President or to the White House itself was on either payroll "at the present time." This meant only that Gordon Liddy, counsel to the Committee and former White House aide, had been fired *after* he had been implicated in the Watergate scandal and had refused to answer such questions as the FBI was asking in the matter, and that the others, including, notably, the "chief of security" for the Committee, had severed for reasons of their own earlier, whether as a conscious prelude to the act of political espionage we may or may not ever be allowed to learn.

Mr. Nixon, delivering his defense and disclaimer, was as cool as he must have been on the famous occasion when he crawled through the transom at Duke to find out his test grades. He probably would have liked to lead the Watergate raid himself, and might have, had it not been for an exaggerated sense of the dignity of the office that he has come to honor only after being elected to it himself. The careful qualifier, "at the present time," apparently sailed over the heads of lot of Mr. Nixon's auditors at the August 29 news conference at San Clemente—or at least was taken at face value along with the rest of the statement, rather than being singled out for the attention it deserved—and that was supposed to put an end to the matter, which we now were supposed to believe was nothing more than a tempest in a teapot, really, much ado about nothing.

IT HAS REMAINED for Chairman Dole—who, if Nixon isn't the nerviest of the lot, surely must be—to seize upon the occasion of the formal federal indictments against the Watergate Seven to demand that the Democrats "apologize" to the Republicans for continuing to dwell on the subject. Not content with that, the chief highbinder of the GOP National Committee, demanded that the Democrats apologize to the *American people*. The Chairman stopped short of demanding that the Democrats apologize for having a national headquarters there to be broken into, pitifully financed though it may be in comparison with the operation run by Chairman Dole himself.

We suppose the Democrats could just have refrained from reporting the break-in, and thereby saved themselves from the necessity of apologizing for anything, but in that case, the Republicans might have accused them of failing to co-operate with the program by which (as is well known) the President has succeeded in sharply reducing the crime rate in the Federal District. "Might have," but we rather suspect wouldn't have, though the temptation to indulge in this final feat of nerviness no doubt would have been great. But since the Democrats *did* make the crime known—or, rather, since the non-partisan security guards they had retained for the purpose made the crime known, there was nothing to do but for the old piano player in the White House to play the thing down—"*Pianissimo,* everybody!" —for everyone else in the official Republican family to take his cue accordingly.

Thus, the Republicans have done everything they could to try to insure that the Democrats' civil suit over the Watergate goings-on is not brought to trial before the election. The federal criminal case, which we can be assured will not be brought to trial until after the election, Attorney General Kleindienst has represented as the fruit of one of the most thorough criminal investigations of modern times. We rather doubt this, but the air of finality with which Mr. Kleindienst has foreclosed on any further indictments certainly was about as an abrupt such cut-off as you are likely to see, anytime, anywhere.

THE LINCOLN STAR
Lincoln, Neb.
September 23, 1972

If it were possible, the best and cleanest way to resolve the disputes surrounding the bugging of Democratic National Headquarters and the campaign financing practices of both political parties would be to fully investigate the complaints now and have the courts dispose of the cases quickly so that the people would know before the election who the culprits are.

But we are backed up against the election time-wise and so the complaints are being swept under the rug — necessarily.

Complaining that this is "a time of very intense political activity," Attorney Gen. Richard Kleindienst indicated that the Justice Department would probably delay its investigation of campaign financing violations until "it's all over in November," so as to avoid a "whitewash " And a federal judge this week halted further proceedings in the civil suits stemming from the Watergate caper until the criminal trials are concluded — meaning, in effect, that legal conclusions will not be available for the voters' edification.

The establishing of guilt might have made a blockbuster impact redounding to the Democrats' favor. But time was on the Republicans' side, if they had anything to hide. Prosecutions which are rushed, like the judge said, are fair neither to the defendants nor the public.

What remains before the election, however, will not be particularly noble or edifying. Accusations and counter-accusations will fly, mingled with only a smattering of evidence and no proof.

That dispassionate investigation and review which is needed — if it can be had — cannot possibly come before the election, the investigators, judges and prosecutors say, because of the relentless turn of the calendar.

With respect to our system of justice, we wish it no other way. There is the gnawing feeling, however, that the President's campaign organization has gotten away with something through outrageous luck.

The Philadelphia Inquirer
Philadelphia, Pa., September 22, 1972

A law professor at George Washington University has asked the federal courts to appoint a special prosecutor to investigate the attempted bugging of Democratic national headquarters at the Watergate last June and the links of the suspects with the White House and the President's re-election campaign.

John F. Banzhaf 3d charges that former Democratic National Chairman Lawrence F. O'Brien, who along with other Democrats has been calling for an outside impartial investigation of this extraordinary affair, would rather have the political issue than the special prosecutor.

We do not know how successful Mr. Banzhaf's legal manuever is likely to be. Neither do we know whether he is right about Mr. O'Brien.

We do know that the Democrats are enjoying the discomfiture of the Republicans and making the most of it. We also know that the Republican administration has refused to appoint an outside investigator, and we doubt that the Republicans are working hand-in-glove with Mr. O'Brien and other Democrats.

Instead, the White House has conducted its own investigation and assures us that it has found no one now on the staff or now in the administration who was involved.

And the Justice Department—headed, of course, by a Republican Attorney General, Richard G. Kleindienst—has conducted its own investigation, resulting in the indictment of the five men who were captured inside the Democratic headquarters, plus two former White House aides.

A Justice Department spokesman also assures us that that wraps it up: "We have absolutely no evidence to indicate that others should be charged."

Having "absolutely no evidence" does not mean that it must exist, but neither does it mean that it has been sought assiduously. There are just too many unanswered questions in this bizarre business, beginning with the question of whether any administration can be relied upon to pursue an objective, thorough investigation of itself.

Without going into all the ramifications of the Watergate affair, certain facts have been confirmed. We know that Republican fund-raisers collected some $10 million from sources they will not reveal. We know that substantial sums were sent to Mexico, but not for the sunlight, and returned to Washington. We know that some of this money passed through the hands of GOP finance chairman Maurice H. Stans and somehow landed in the bank account of one of the men indicted, and we know that Mr. Stans' stories about how this happened have been self-contradictory and contradicted by others.

We also know that Mr. Stans had a safe stuffed with campaign funds amounting to about $300,000. It is now reported that three GOP campaign officials, all former White House aides (one of them indicted), tapped that cache for purposes unknown, and that records of who had access to Mr. Stans' safe and what they did with the money were destroyed after the Watergate break-in.

Now Vice President Spiro T. Agnew has advanced his "personal theory" that "Someone set up these people to have them get caught ... to embarrass the Republican Party."

That is a bit hard to accept. What we need are not such far-fetched personal theories but facts, and the best way to try to get them all is through an impartial investigation.

The TENNESSEAN
Nashville, Tenn., September 22, 1972

THE seven men who were indicted in the Watergate break-in of Democratic headquarters have pleaded innocent to the charges, which is what the administration has been pleading all along.

★ ★ ★

The Republicans have steadfastly denied that any men of "senior status" were involved in the case of political espionage, even though two former White House aides were indicted along with the five men arrested at the scene.

The great, unanswered question is who gave the five the "go-ahead" and provided the financing for the Watergate caper. Even campaign organizations rolling in money are not noted for dispensing large amounts of cash to underlings who can use it as they see fit.

It is obvious that Mr. Maurice Stans had a personal knowledge of the checks amounting to $89,000 which ended up in the bank account of one of the men indicted in the case. He first denied, both publicly and privately, that he knew anything about the money.

The funds in question came from Texas businessmen who funneled them through an intermediary in Mexico to keep it from being known.

Subsequent and detailed testimony by Mr. William Liedtke, a leading money raiser for Mr. Nixon in Texas, disclosed that he had Mr. Stans' approval to include the Mexican funds in a batch of cash, checks and securities in the amount of $700,000 that was transmitted to Mr. Stans on April 5.

It is, of course, illegal for foreign nationals to contribute money to U.S. political campaigns, even if they are acting as a middle man in simply transferring funds on. But the illegality of the situation apparently didn't impress Mr. Stans much—and still doesn't.

However, Mr. Liedtke's testimony did refresh Mr. Stans' memory a bit and he admitted that he was aware the money came from Mexico.

The next unanswered question is how the money that Mr. Stans knew about ended up in the bank account of Mr. Bernard Barker, one of those arrested in the Watergate case.

It is evident the Republicans hope—and it has so turned out—that the seven men indicted will not be brought to trial before the elections and that, in any case, they will refuse to implicate anyone else in the Watergate case.

★ ★ ★

Maybe the whole thing can be pushed out of the limelight long enough for the public to forget it temporarily, but it is doubtful. Behind the curtain the White House has drawn between itself and the indicted men is a smell of political corruption that rises to high heaven.

WINSTON-SALEM JOURNAL

Winston-Salem, N.C., September 23, 1972

TWO basic rights are brought into conflict by the decision of a federal judge to hold up the civil suits in the Watergate case until the criminal proceedings are out of the way.

One is a clear constitutional right of the seven men facing criminal prosecution for breaking into Democratic headquarters at the Watergate in Washington. These men have a right to a fair trial free from the prejudicial publicity that the civil proceedings might bring.

The conflicting right is the right of all American citizens to know the truth about a major issue in the presidential campaign before they vote on Nov. 7.

The issue is this: Were President Nixon and his two highest campaign managers, John Mitchell and Maurice Stans, ultimately responsible for the break-in, the bugging and the burglarizing of Democratic headquarters?

The answer to that question will not come out of the criminal prosecution. President Nixon's attorney general and the political appointee he has put in charge of the FBI have ruled out in advance any culpability by higher-ups. And the President himself has refused to permit a non-partisan investigation by a jurist or panel of unquestioned integrity.

The best chance, then, of getting at the whole truth lay until Friday in the civil proceedings initiated by the Democratic National Committee but now suspended by Judge Richey in Washington.

What we already know is disturbng

enough to warrant the most urgent investigation.

—Two of the seven men under indictment are former White House aides. Evidence presented to the grand jury put them in the Watergate on the night of the break-in.

—Two of seven held high positions in the Nixon re-election campaign. One of these two was caught redhanded in the Democratic offices.

—The leader of the break-in gang received at least $114,000 from the Nixon campaign treasury.

These and other known facts are enough to suggest that the nation is faced with one of the most alarming political scandals in its history. For if the party in power is going to use police state techniques against the opposition, the fabric of American democracy is in serious danger.

If Judge Richey's ruling stands, the only hope for the American voter to get closer to the whole truth before Nov. 7 will rest with the American press.

Despite all the efforts of the Nixon-Agnew administration to intimidate the press, the newspaper correspondents in Washington have been pursuing the case with their traditional diligence.

The reporters of the conservative Washington *Evening Star* and the liberal *Washington Post* in particular have been digging out the facts with admirable ingenuity and persistence.

Let us hope that they and their colleagues in Washington will succeed in bringing out the full dimensions of the Watergate scandal before Nov. 7.

Detroit Free Press

Detroit, Mich., September 22, 1972

VICE PRESIDENT Spiro Agnew's intimation that some mysterious person "set up" the Watergate incident to embarrass the Republican Party should cause President Nixon to immediately put all the forces at his command to seek out this individual.

For if such a phantom fixer does exist, he must possess genius and daring far beyond anyone presently in government or espionage in this country. The genius of such a man is surely a national asset which is far too valuable to go untapped. Consider, if you will, what this man (we will call him Mr. W.) had to accomplish.

First, he had to convince two former White House staffers and James W. McCord, then security director for the Committee for the Re-Election of the President, that it would somehow be to the advantage of the Republican Party for them to be caught red-handed bugging the offices of the Democratic National Committee. If he was able to accomplish this, as Mr. Agnew suggests, it was sheer genius.

How then would he assure Mr. McCord that he would be nabbed? Apparently by convincing him to hire as his accomplices Bernard Barker and Frank Sturgis, both of whom had roles in the Bay of Pigs invasion. "Ingenious!" Mr. McCord must have exclaimed. "From the people who brought us the Bay of Pigs, we cannot fail now to bring you Watergate."

And sure enough, the plans of Mr. W. came to magnificent fruition on June 17 at 2 a.m. in the Watergate Hotel in Washington. Following conspicuous trails of masking tape over locks and bolts to keep them open, police surprised the five intruders smack in the middle of the office of the Democratic headquarters tangled up in $30,000 worth of photographic equipment, electronic surveillance devices, burglar tools, walkie-talkies, chemical stunning devices, wire and other sundry incriminating evidence. The men were also wearing rubber surgical gloves in a clever attempt to hide their fingerprints.

The incredible Mr. W. is presumably a Democrat. But President Nixon should not let party partisanship interfere where the national welfare is concerned. A man who combines the talents of Metternich, James Bond and Henry Kissinger should not be allowed to remain in anonymity. He should be brought out to serve his country.

So we urge Mr. Agnew to come forward and identify Mr. W., or provide the FBI and the CIA with more information to help in their search. Mr. W. must be found!

ST. LOUIS POST-DISPATCH

St. Louis, Mo., September 25, 1972

After more than three months of evasive legal dancing by Republican officials, lawyers and the FBI, U.S. District Judge Charles R. Richey has announced that all proceedings in three civil suits filed in connection with the Watergate burglary and bugging case have been halted until after the election. Although the White House might like this stop-everything order to indicate that justice is on her pedestal and all's right with the world, the voters should not be satisfied with appearances.

Seven men, four of them directly connected with the White House and/or the Nixon campaign, have been indicted as a result of the midnight June 17 break-in of Democratic offices at the Watergate building. But the indictment falls far short of answering all of the disturbing questions that arise from this outrageous example of invasion of privacy and political espionage. Even if the criminal trial of the indicted seven should start before the election, which is unlikely, it does not promise to resolve the issue potentially most embarrassing to presidential candidate Nixon — how $114,000 of secret and apparently illegally diverted GOP campaign funds got into the hands of one of the indicted burglars.

The FBI, which is under the control of the Nixon Justice Department, did not investigate this aspect of the case. And Attorney General Kleindienst, the Nixon appointee who succeeded former Nixon campaign director John N. Mitchell, has said that the indicted seven can be tried at their "leisure." When former Democratic National Chairman Lawrence O'Brien tried to get at the root of the scandalous affair by filing a civil damage suit against the chief Nixon fund raiser, Maurice Stans (through whose hands the $114,000 had passed), Mr. Stans filed counter suits, which no doubt had the desired effect of obfuscating the issues. All the civil suits have now been postponed by Judge Richey, a Nixon appointee. Meanwhile Mr. Stans has put out a flurry of press releases but refuses to answer questions.

By causing or allowing the wheels of justice to be halted until after the election and by refusing to appoint a nonpartisan special prosecutor in this case, the Nixon Administration has cast serious doubt on the integrity of the law enforcement process. The voters have a right to hold it accountable for not honestly answering questions as to who ordered the espionage and why GOP campaign funds were behind it.

THE INDIANAPOLIS NEWS
Indianapolis, Ind.
September 27, 1972

While the courts of law will determine the individual guilt or innocence of the men indicted for breaking into Democratic headquarters at Washington's Watergate complex, the larger implications of the deed are obvious enough on the face of it.

One does not have to presume the truth of campaign suggestions that higher-ups in the administration knew a b o u t or encouraged the Watergate break-in to realize the episode is symptomatic of an unhealthy climate in the nation's capital. When t h i s many people with ties to the Committee for the Re-Election of the President and/or the official apparatus of government are involved in such an affair, full-scale investigation is obviously required.

We would add only that such scandalous goings-on are not distinctive of either party, and we recall that there were documented instances of bugging and break-in during preceding Democratic administrations as well. What we confront, all too obviously, is a growing atmosphere in w h i c h wiretaps, b u g s, and intrusions upon personal privacy are becoming standard operating procedure.

That anyone would think it advisable to bug the headquarters of the Democrats in this particular election year suggests just how standard the procedure is. Why anyone would want to engage in such a bugging operation, or what anyone could possibly derive from such an enterprise, is a mystery to us. By all accounts, the Republican national ticket is home-free in this election, and the idea that its interests could possibly be served by tapping "inside" data at t h e disorganized McGovern headquarters is faintly ludicrous.

Despite g e n e r a l distaste for such activities it a p p e a r s that Democratic efforts to t u r n the Watergate caper into a burning issue of the election have not succeeded. In the weeks that all this controversy has gone on, President Nixon's popularity ratings have continued to soar and McGovern's have continued to sink. This, too, fits past experience. We recall that in 1964 the national flap over the Jenkins c a s e and other skeletons in the Democratic closet did little or nothing to impair the image of President Johnson.

The truth seems to be that the public makes up its mind about political candidates on deeper, visceral questions, and that issues of scandal like Jenkins or Watergate can do little to deflect such massive tides of opinion.

The Washington Post
Times-Herald

Washington, D.C., September 25, 1972

There is something to be said for corruption. It stinks. No matter how many lids you try to put on it, the stench will out. And that is what is happening with respect to the financial manipulations and related espionage activities involved in the effort to re-elect Richard Nixon, despite the best efforts of the administration and the Nixon campaign committee to stuff more lids onto the mess.

Without being dreary about it, we know there was burglary at the Democratic Party's headquarters in the Watergate—breaking and entering for the purpose of committing a crime. We know there was bugging equipment on the premises for electronic eavesdropping. We know there was tapping of telephone lines. We know there was $700,000 stuffed into a suitcase and rushed to the Nixon campaign headquarters just before the deadline for reporting on campaign donations—and we know there was a shift in the position on milk price supports favoring dairy farmers just after receipt of some hefty contributions from associations of dairy farmers. We know there was a slush fund in Mr. Stans' safe. We know that some of the money intended for the President's campaign ended up in the bank account of one of the men arrested at the Democrats' headquarters. We know that some of the President's money was "laundered" by having checks from contributors deposited in a bank in Mexico from which nice, clean cash could then be withdrawn. We know there was a $10 million secret campaign fund and we know that one $25,000 donor got a federal bank charter a good deal faster than most people do. And we know, finally, that all this was done on behalf of the effort to re-elect the President of the United States.

But what do we hear from the President, his administration, and his high campaign advisers? First, we hear some scoffing from his campaign chief, Mr. John Mitchell . . . then a resignation . . . then, nothing. Next, from Mr. Maurice Stans, the financial chief of the Nixon campaign, we hear background promises of a perfectly "logical" explanation . . . and then silence except for vague denials when he was cornered in what Mike Wallace called the "dark reaches" of the convention hall in Miami Beach. In the civil suit brought by the Democrats, the Nixon committee and its representatives have done everything they could to make sure that the depositions being taken, which might shed some light on the whole affair, be sealed from public view and, indeed, be put off until after the election. In the criminal action, we are told that we can be told very little because of the administration's delicate sensibilities concerning the defendants civil liberties. This is the same administration which was perfectly prepared to try the brothers Berrigan in the newspapers before any grand jury was ever convened, and this is the same President who found Charles Manson guilty in advance of his trial and intervened to hold out the possibility of clemency for Lt. Calley while his case awaited review. And, now it turns out that the judge in the civil suit—a man who freely admits that he owes his position on the bench to the friendly intervention of the Vice President of the United States—has determined that the depositions cannot be taken until after the trial of the criminal action, an event which probably will not take place until after the election.

Meanwhile, the administration in whose behalf these various acts were being committed urges us to trust it and its investigations. We are assured that before his fairly precipitous departure, Mr. Mitchell conducted an investigation and that he found that everything was fine. Yet we are given no documentation. We are told that the White House counsel, Mr. John Dean, conducted an investigation in which he assured himself and the President that no one *presently employed* in the administration was involved in the burglaries and the electronic surveillance. But when asked about it on the Public Broadcasting network by Elizabeth Drew, Mr. John Ehrlichman of the White House conceded that Mr. Dean's investigation "didn't go beyond the government"—to the question of Mr. Mitchell's role, for example, or that of Mr. Stans. Mr. Ehrlichman said that the investigation was "satisfactory to us" but that it did not tell who ordered the surveillance and that even after the "satisfactory" investigation, Mr. Ehrlichman didn't know who ordered it.

And then, there is Mr. Kleindienst. He is fairly sure that the investigation into the matter by the FBI is the most thorough conducted since the investigation into the murder of President Kennedy. Yet, when queried by the same persistent Mrs. Drew about reports that important documents had been destroyed at the Nixon campaign committee just after news of the Watergate break-in, Mr. Kleindienst allowed as how he hadn't known of that. He also seemed vague about the connection of that matter with a criminal investigation until Mrs. Drew suggested that there might be an issue of obstructing justice.

And now comes Henry Peterson, head of the Justice Department's Criminal Division—in charge of the investigation—guessing that "the jail doors will close behind" the suspects before the real motivation for the Watergate break-in is ever discovered.

So, those are the investigations that are supposed to put our minds to rest.

And after that, there is the Republican rhetoric. Mr. MacGregor says that all of this will redound to the President's political credit. Mr. Mitchell, in one of his infrequent lapses into public utterance, has said that he doesn't see how this has hurt the President in the polls—as if it were merely a matter of public opinion rather than an issue that goes to the heart of the integrity of our electoral process and of our elected officials. And Mr. Agnew says in one breath that the Watergate burglary may just have been—yes—a frame-up by the Democrats to embarrass the Republicans and in the next that the Democrats are trying to make the wheat scandal into "another Watergate."

Well, if this whole thing is so good for the Republicans and if their investigations show them to be as clean as they say, why don't they tell us all? Who ordered the burglary? Who ordered the tapping? Who ordered the bugging? Who had control of Mr. Stans' safe? Who had access to it? Who were the contributors to the $10 million secret fund and what were they promised? What do the reports to Mr. Mitchell and the report to Mr. Dean really say? What is Mr. Stans' "logical explanation" of the hundreds of thousands of dollars of money laundered in a bank in Mexico? Were the secret fund books destroyed? And if so, who destroyed them?

Why don't they talk to us about these things instead of hurling around charges of "frame-up" without any supporting evidence? Until they do, the suspicion can only grow that their reason for keeping silent is that the whole thing stinks.

WATERGATE PROBE BARRED IN HOUSE; WIDE GOP SABOTAGE EFFORT REPORTED

The House Banking and Currency Committee Oct. 3 rejected a proposal to probe possible violations of banking laws in connection with the break-in at the Democratic headquarters in the Watergate office building and possible irregularities in Republican campaign financing. The vote was 20–15, with six of the panel's 22 Democrats voting with the majority. Chairman Wright Patman (D, Tex.), who offered the proposal, accused the White House after the vote of "engineering" the rejection of the probe, which was set under his proposal to subpoena some 40 individuals and organizations, including top Nixon campaign aides, for testimony.

Other major developments in the Watergate case:

■ L. Patrick Gray 3rd, acting director of the Federal Bureau of Investigation, Oct. 2 upheld the propriety of the Nixon Administration itself investigating the Watergate case even though it involved former Administration aides and a Republican committee. Gray said he had taken the case "under my own wing" and "there's not been one single bit of pressure put on me or any of my special agents" concerning the probe. Gray also discounted the possibility of presidential involvement in the incident. "It strains the credulity that the President of the United States—if he had a mind to—could have done a con job on the whole American people," he said.

■ Chief U.S. District Court Judge John J. Sirica issued a broad order prohibiting all law enforcement agencies, defendants, and witnesses, "including complaining witnesses and alleged victims . . . and all persons acting for or with them in connection with this case" from making extra-judicial public statements to anyone, "including the news media," concerning the Watergate case. Democratic presidential candidate George McGovern said Oct. 4 that he would not allow himself "to be muzzled or intimidated." Sirica eased the ban Oct. 6 by deleting the phrase referring to witnesses.

■ Alfred C. Baldwin 3rd, a former FBI agent, disclosed Oct 5 in the *Los Angeles Times* that he had monitored telephone and other conversations at the Watergate for three weeks while employed by the Committee to Re-elect the President. He said he had delivered the information he obtained to a Nixon campaign official who had not yet been indicted in the Watergate case.

■ President Nixon said at a news conference Oct. 5 that he would not comment on the Watergate case because grand jury indictments had been handed down and the case was before the courts.

■ *The Washington Post* reported Oct. 10 that the Watergate raid was but part of a larger espionage and sabotage effort against the Democrats on behalf of the Nixon re-election campaign. The paper quoted federal investigators as describing the operation as "unprecedented in scope and intensity." The story reported that a letter used in the New Hampshire primary against Sen. Edmund S. Muskie (D, Me.) was one such sabotage attempt. The letter, in which Muskie was accused of condoning the use of the epithet "Canucks" in reference to Americans with French-Canadian backgrounds, according to the story, was written by White House aide Ken W. Clawson. At the time it had been ascribed to a Paul Morrison of Deerfield Beach, Fla. Morrison had never been located.

ARKANSAS DEMOCRAT
Little Rock, Ark., October 7. 1972

Now we learn that a former FBI agent says he bugged the Democratic Headquarters at Watergate and delivered transcripts to Nixon campaign headquarters.

This adds to the already large accumulation of evidence that somebody in the Nixon campaign was employing illegal means of snooping on the Democrats. Additional evidence indicates that the snooping was ordered or at least condoned at high levels. Maurice Stans, former commerce secretary and campaign fund raiser, handled a check that went to one of the men charged with the bugging. And John Mitchell, former attorney general and later head of the Nixon campaign, reportedly controlled a secret intelligence fund, the records of which have been destroyed.

The matter has been confused considerably by political rhetoric. Some say for that reason it should wait until after the election. But the fact remains that it is a political issue. It involves very serious charges concerning one of the candidates, and the public deserves a full investigation, or at least an explanation by the Republican Party.

The charges filed against the five men who were arrested in the Watergate Offices and two other men serve more to prevent full disclosure than to bring it about. Standard prosecution procedure would have granted immunity to one of more of these alleged lower-echelon agents to acquire information about who ordered and paid for the operation. With all of them charged, none is obliged to do anything but plead his own case, which is pretty well sewed up by the fact that they were caught on the premises with bugging equipment. That is all the more reason to believe that the Nixon administration's Justice Department is not the proper agency to investigate charges against employes of the Nixon campaign for President. The FBI could be working just as well for a special prosecutor that has no connection with either party's presidential campaign.

Congress had an opening to break through the roadblocks to an investigation set up by Republicans. The House Banking Committee, under the leadership of Rep. Wright Patman, D-Tex., tried. But a committee hearing was voted down 20-15 Tuesday, when six Democrats joined the 14 Republicans on the committee in opposing it. This is a surprising and sad performance by a Congress that has been complaining about its loss of power to the executive branch. But mostly it is a blow to the chances of the public to learn more about what could be one of the most important issues in the election campaign.

The Republicans' refusal to discuss the matter and their actions to delay investigations until after the election increase the cynicism about government that permeates American society. And Congress' reluctance to do any more, in its haste to adjourn, doesn't help. We urge Patman to continue his efforts to bring about a congressional investigation. If he fails there, we wish him luck in his latest effort to get the General Accounting Office to make a study and make a preliminary report by October 26.

Los Angeles Times

Los Angeles, Calif., October 6, 1972

District Court Judge John J. Sirica has sought to prohibit further investigation of the Watergate electronic eavesdropping case with an order so sweeping that he has acknowledged it might affect discussion of the case by presidential candidates.

The order is a shocking abuse of judicial power, an obvious infringement of constitutional rights. And it is the more worrying because it has been taken on the initiative of one of those under indictment in the case with particular interest in suppressing information on the case prior to the election, because he was on the White House staff at the time of the eavesdropping. There simply is no evidence to support the premise of Judge Sirica that publicity makes impossible a fair trial. The whole history of judicial operation in an open and free society demonstrates the contrary, that the best assurance of a fair trial is freedom of information.

Neither President Nixon nor Sen. George McGovern was silenced by the judge, however.

Mr. Nixon reaffirmed at his press conference Thursday that he had known nothing of the case and that he was confident, from the thoroughness of the FBI investigation, that no one in his campaign organization was involved beyond those already among the seven indicted last month.

Senator McGovern said he would not be silenced in his discussion of the case. His fellow Democrat, Senate Majority Leader Mike Mansfield, expressed "grave doubts about the wisdom and the legality of the judge's dictum."

The campaign for silence is pervasive. A federal civil court action has been postponed on grounds it might jeopardize the criminal proceedings, and Congress gave the same reason for voting down an inquiry. If the public is to learn anything more before election day, it will be through the unlikely possibility of a speedy criminal trial, or through the press, or in the General Accounting Office study due Oct. 27.

The need for further investigation was made clearer than ever in the account of the bugging of Democratic National Committee Headquarters written for The Times by one of the participants, Alfred C. Baldwin III. His account suggested that not all of the Nixon headquarters staff involved in the eavesdropping are named in the indictment. His story makes it difficult to accept the insistence that no senior Republican campaign official was aware of this operation or in control of the large sums of money involved.

Secrecy and silence will not solve these mysteries.

The Cleveland Press

Cleveland, Ohio, October 4, 1972

There won't be any investigation of the Watergate caper or the "roaming check" story by the House Banking Committee, Chairman Wright Patman notwithstanding.

Soon after he heard that several checks headed for the Committee for the Re-election of the President had been wandering from Mexico to Florida and elsewhere, Patman saw a chance to investigate on the possibility that some banking laws had been violated.

The Watergate caper broke when five men were arrested last June and charged with breaking into Democratic National Headquarters. The suspects since have been indicted and accused, among other things, of bugging the Democratic offices.

Later there were charges that checks contributed to the Nixon committee for campaign expenses at one point had been in the hands of one of the men accused of the Watergate bust-in.

But the banking committee has voted down Patman's plan, 20 to 15. Fifteen of the no-probe votes came from Republicans, not surprisingly, on the theory that a congressional inquiry might prejudice the trial of the defendants in the Watergate caper.

That's possible, of course, but it is fair to wonder just how sympathetic the Republicans would have been for the rights of the defendants if the defendants had been Democrats.

However, six Democratic members of the committee voted against the investigation on this same principle — or perhaps they didn't think the investigation would learn much anyway, or because they didn't think it was much of a campaign issue.

Until the men indicted in the bugging go to trial, we are not apt to learn much more about the reasons for this caper. But meanwhile there is no excuse for the Committee for the Re-election of the President to remain mute about those itinerant checks.

THE LINCOLN STAR

Lincoln, Neb., October 5, 1972

By a vote of 20-15 Tuesday the House Banking Committee refused to investigate the financial aspects surrounding the June break-in of Democratic National headquarters by agents linked to the Committee to Re-elect the President. The vote apparently stifles the last opportunity Democrats hoped would result in public hearings on the Watergate incident before the election.

The 14 Republicans and six Democrats who formed the committee majority on the vote were in general agreement that a House investigation would mingle politics with justice and that it might prejudice the government's case against and/or violate the rights of those indicted in the break-in.

The 15 Democrats who sought the investigation predicted that public opinion would force a reversal of the committee action. And if it did, it would be for the good.

For one thing, the investigation, as proposed by Rep. Wright Patman, committee chairman, would be aimed at tracing the campaign contributions which allegedly financed the break-in to determine whether any U.S. banking laws had been violated and to see if political favoritism had any role in awarding of bank charters. That seems to be within the purview of a congressional committee.

For another, none of the seven men indicted in the Watergate caper was on the list of those to be subpoenaed by the committee if the investigation had come off. This would have diminished the possibility of prejudice for or against any of the defendants in the civil or criminal actions.

The committee's action amounts to an abdication of the responsibility it has to set the record straight.

Rep. Henry Reuss, who fought for the investigation, best summed it up. The committee, Reuss said, has a duty to "uncover skullduggery, whether by Republicans, Democrats or nonpartisans."

St. Petersburg Times

St. Petersburg, Fla., October 4, 1972

The indictment of seven men, including a recent $100-a-day White House consultant and two officials (now resigned) of the Committee for the Re-Election of the President, for burglarizing and bugging Democratic National Committee headquarters exposed the odor but not the substance of what is recognized in Washington as possibly the smelliest political scandal in our history.

Although the original arrests were made four months ago, trials of the accused men and of a related civil suit brought by the Democrats are not scheduled until after the November election.

EVEN THEN, prosecution by the Nixon Department of Justice is unlikely to provide answers to the larger questions: Who instigated the electronic surveillance of the opposition party's headquarters, who profited by it, and how and why was $114,000 in CRP campaign funds channeled by devious routes — most of it through Mexico City — into the Miami bank account of one of the self-admitted burglars.

For weeks top Democratic Party officials have brought quiet but intense pressure on Sen. Edward M. Kennedy, D-Mass., to take jurisdiction for the Senate Judiciary subcommittee which he heads, and to hold public hearings at which witnesses, including responsible officers of the CRP, could be examined under oath.

But Sen. Kennedy has "no plans" to pick up the political hot potato. Apparently, no other congressional committee is in a position to conduct an effective investigation.

THE HOUSE Banking Committee, which might have taken jurisdiction, voted 20-to-15 yesterday not to conduct an investigation, with six Democrats joining all 14 Republicans in opposition. The Justice Department had formally protested Chairman Wright Patman's plans to hold hearings and to subpoena top officials of the CRP and financial records relating to the questionable transfer of committee funds.

Meanwhile, the public is lulled into dismissing the whole affair as a "caper," the misleading headline term that the press has attached to it.

We believe, in this case, Sen. Kennedy should place the public's right to know ahead of any personal political considerations.

Wire-tapping and electronic bugging of political opponents is not a caper. It is deadly serious public business.

THE MIAMI NEWS
Miami, Fla., October 9, 1972

The President is having an uncommon amount of good fortune in avoiding a searching examination of the Watergate affair prior to the Nov. 7 election.

Even the court decisions concerning this incident are going the administration's way. In what surely must have been the broadest mandate of its kind ever issued, a federal district court judge in Washington ordered all persons involved in the case — defendants, attorneys, potential and actual witnesses and victims — not to discuss Watergate with anyone, in or out of court.

Had that order stood, it would have destroyed any hope the Democrats had of bringing more information into the public arena before the general election. Similarly, the House Banking Committee also contributed to suppressing the facts on Tuesday when it rejected a proposed investigation of the financial aspects of the break-in at the Democratic National Committee Headquarters last June.

The judge's order, an outrageous abuse of judicial authority, is aimed ostensibly at providing a fair trial for the defendants. Its effect, however, would be to shield public officials from potential embarrassment prior to the national election in November. This sort of maneuvering can only undermine the people's faltering faith in the political system.

"Potential victims" of the Watergate affair might well apply to George McGovern as one of the persons who has to keep silent about the incident. That point became moat when the judge modified the order along more reasonable lines. But the essential point remains the same.

The President and his top campaign officials are obviously nervous about the whole caper. But if the Committee to Re-Elect the President is as innocent as its top staffers claim, they should come clean with all the information they have and stop impeding other investigative efforts.

The Dispatch
Columbus, Ohio, October 6, 1972

MEMBERS of the House Banking Committee have rejected a proposal there be a full-scale congressional investigation of the so-called Watergate Caper, reasoning correctly that politics should stay out of the judicial process.

As one committeeman said, the question was whether "the political benefit which we hope to derive" from the probe would justify the risk of jeopardizing the government's case against the Watergate defendants.

SEVEN MEN already have been indicted by a federal grand jury for burglarizing and installing electronic listening devices in Democratic National Headquarters in Washington's Watergate building.

It must be recorded as a bizarre episode of the kind expected in a third-rate spy story.

CONGRESSIONAL probes have their place in this nation's legislative process.

But when an episode is in the process of working its way through judicial channels, a congressional probe, especially one born of partisan politics, would be not only counterproductive but jeopardize the trial of those defendants already indicted.

MORE importantly, the call for a congressional probe appears to be an act of desperation.

The general public has displayed little interest in the Watergate Caper and there is reasonable doubt whether even injection of entry of the United States Congress could kindle that interest.

THE STATES-ITEM
New Orleans, La., October 12, 1972

The Republican party has consistently engaged in unfair, if not illegal, tactics in its pursuit of a second term for President Nixon. We still do not know the full extent of the Nixon Administration's involvement in the Watergate bugging case, but it seems clear there was a connection.

The latest evidence of political foul play on the part of the Republican party and the White House is contained in the testimony of law enforcement sources quoted in the Washington Post.

The investigative findings of the Post are shocking. There is strong evidence, moreover, that direction for the jackboot campaign emanates from within the White House.

Investigators are quoted as saying that the Nixon Administration-run campaign to sabotage the Democratic cause included "following members of the Democratic candidates' families; forging letters and distributing them under the candidates' letterheads; leaking false and manufactured items to the press; throwing campaign schedules into disarray; seizing confidential files, and investigating the lives of dozens of Democratic campaign workers."

A prime operator in the low road campaign apparently is Ken W. Clawson, a White House aide. He first admitted fabricating a letter that damaged the presidential campaign of Sen. Edmund M. Muskie. Later he denied authorship. The letter, given wide distribution, accused Sen. Muskie of a racial slur against Americans of French-Canadian extraction.

Three attorneys in Tennessee, Iowa and Georgia were allegedly offered "big jobs" in government if they would act as undercover agents for the Nixon campaign and carry out various maneuvers to disrupt Democratic activities. They refused.

The purpose of a political campaign is to provide a forum for free discussion by candidates. Out of that discussion comes a decision by the voters. The Republican party apparently has determined to substitute strong-arm tactics and manipulation for free political discussion of the issues.

We agree with U.S. Rep. Wright Patman, chairman of the House Banking Committee, who concluded that "President Nixon is in control of his own campaign. He is responsible."

Omaha World-Herald
Omaha, Neb., October 6, 1972

Because six Democratic members of the House Banking Committee joined with the 14 Republican members, a proposed full-scale congressional investigation of the Watergate break-in will not take place.

Chairman Wright Patman said he wanted the inquiry because "harassment of opposition political parties through espionage and other means" has no place in American politics.

But harassment of defendants in a criminal case has no place in politics or congressional inquiry. It was on that ground that the committee majority voted down their chairman. The proposed investigation would violate the rights of those indicted in the break-in and bugging of Democratic headquarters.

"Politics should stay out of justice," said Rep. Frank J. Brasco, D-N.Y. A bipartisan majority of the committee agreed with him.

The Watergate affair is messy. Nothing in connection with it makes the Republican party look good. But Patman was out of bounds in trying to put a congressional spotlight on it when men were awaiting trial. His committee's decision was the right one.

The Courier-Journal
Louisville, Ky., October 11, 1972

DESPITE the Nixon administration's efforts to keep the voters benighted until after the election, the facts are beginning to emerge.

The bugging of Democratic Party headquarters in Washington's Watergate Hotel apparently wasn't just an isolated bizarre incident of a few zealots playing spy for their own pleasure or profit—as Attorney General Richard Kleindienst has encouraged the public to believe—but rather a part of a well financed, well planned, well executed campaign by the White House and President Nixon's re-election committee to sabotage the electoral process.

The story—gleaned by *The Washington Post* from FBI and Justice Department files and interviews with federal investigators and some of the people who have been investigated—reveals "Offensive Security" (the Nixon forces' euphemism for the campaign) to be the type of political subversion usually associated with totalitarian regimes.

John Mitchell, even while he carried the title of the nation's highest law enforcement officer, evidently held the key to a secret espionage and sabotage fund of $350,000 to $700,000 which was stashed in the office of Mr. Nixon's chief campaign fund-raiser, former Secretary of Commerce Maurice Stans.

Out of this fund were paid agents who reportedly spied, forged letters and impersonated campaign staff members of the stronger Democratic presidential candidates, in an effort to throw their campaigns into disarray, discredit them personally and divide their party. One of the apparent fruits of their efforts was the destruction of the candidacy of Senator Edmund Muskie, who was the early frontrunner for the nomination and considered by many to be the potential opponent most dangerous to Mr. Nixon's bid for re-election.

It's a sordid, frightening story, which the *Post* has pursued tenaciously in the highest tradition of investigative reporting, and in the face of government-created obstacles.

Mr. Kleindienst, for example, has insisted throughout recent months that the men indicted for the spying at the Watergate couldn't possibly go on trial before Election Day. And he has opposed Congressman Wright Patman's efforts to launch a congressional investigation of the matter on grounds that the rights of the defendants might be infringed. Yet, as Senator Sam Ervin has so beautifully phrased it, "Any lawyer who is qualified to try cases before a justice of the peace ought to be able to try five men caught red-handed in a burglary within 10 days. Certainly there must be someone in the Department or the U.S. attorney's office who can."

Certainly. But "qualified lawyers" also have reasons for wanting to delay trials sometimes, and they can find many ways to put off their cases until public interest in them has waned, or until a public decision which might be affected by a trial—such as an election—has been safely deposited in history.

On the other hand, it should be pointed out that Mr. Nixon's Justice Department simply can't devote its entire staff and energy to the Watergate espionage case. For there is, in addition, the question of the perjury possibly committed by Mr. Mitchell and others during Senate hearings concerning the confirmation of Mr. Kleindienst, Mr. Mitchell's successor as Attorney General.

Last June, the Senate Judiciary Committee sent its 1,751-page hearing record to the Justice Department for a written report within 30 days on whether contradictions in the testimony constituted perjury. What particularly bothered the senators was Mr. Mitchell's contradictory testimony concerning the Justice Department's settlement of several antitrust suits against ITT. Now that Mr. Mitchell's control of a political sabotage fund while Attorney General has been alleged, Senator Birch Bayh and others are also wondering about Mr. Mitchell's testimony last March 15 that he had not yet taken on any responsibilities in Mr. Nixon's re-election campaign.

But now, more than 60 days after the Justice Department was to have reported its findings to the Judiciary Committee, Department officials say the review is "nowhere near completion," because "there are lots of pages to read."

If the Justice Department lawyers had managed to read only 17 pages per day since they received the hearing record, they would have completed it by now.

It's obvious that the President and the Attorney General don't want the voters to know too much about these cases before they go to the polls November 7. It's obvious, too, that the law-enforcement arm of the national government—at least in its highest echelons—has been converted into the personal political tool of the President. Not only has it been used to unjustly harass the Berrigan brothers and others who have been openly and eloquently critical of the President's policies; it apparently has become a hotbed of conspiracy itself, supporting the efforts of the White House and Mr. Nixon's re-election committee to narrow the voters' options on November 7.

Senator Ervin, Senator Bayh, Congressman Patman and others on Capitol Hill who are now demanding congressional investigations into these and other apparent attempts by the administration to keep the public blinded until after Election Day must receive the encouragement and support of every American who is troubled by government-in-secret. Otherwise, we'll enter the voting booth blindfolded.

THE ATLANTA CONSTITUTION
Atlanta, Ga., October 12, 1972

There is a feeling abroad that people are just not interested in the famous Watergate Caper where James Bond Republican types allegedly broke into, bugged and tried to steal information from Democratic National Headquarters in Washington. Politicians snooping on politicians — it happens all the time. So what?

Well, it may happen all the time on a piddling level, but if the Watergate Caper turns out to be what it is beginning to look like — a major espionage operation by the political party in power against the political party seeking power — then we'd better call a halt.

The case is going to court, people have been indicted. The guys caught red-handed in flagrante delicto. But who sent those fellows over there? Who nodded his head and said, "Okay, fellows, go ahead — and remember, you're on your own"? John Mitchell, who was heading President Nixon's campaign until Martha said she was fed up with dirty politics? The President himself, who seemingly rises above that sort of thing? These are questions that pester some folks, and they have not been convincingly answered yet. At the President's last press conference he was asked bluntly why he didn't make "a clean breast" of it and explain the whole deal. Nixon, a lawyer by training, said the case was in the courts and it would be inappropriate to comment.

Suppose the President didn't know a thing about what his top political aides were doing? That would argue he's a bit out of touch politically, something he's never been accused of before. Suppose he did know? That would argue he's permitting an extremely dangerous new mode of political operation, one that smacks a bit too much of the totalitarian police state instead of a free and open democracy where people do their own thing without fear that the party in power has agents frowning over their shoulders.

The President was perfectly correct in withholding comment on a case pending in court. But maybe he might have ventured some remarks on his personal philosophy concerning this sort of thing, just some abstract principals or something like that to reassure the citizenry. However, he didn't see fit to do that.

Now the Washington Post says the FBI has determined that the Committee to Re-Elect the President used a secret espionage fund in efforts to sabotage the campaigns of every major Democratic candidate, concentrating on McGovern after he won the nomination. It said, further, that federal investigators have determined the committee's objectives included "following members of Democratic families and assembling dossiers on their personal lives, forging letters and distributing them under candidates' letterheads, leaking false and manufactured items to the press, throwing campaign issues into disarray, seizing confidential campaign files, and investigating the lives of dozens of Democratic campaign workers."

Them lying newspapers again? Maybe. These are charges, or reported charges, not proven facts. What we're saying is that they better not be, better never be, the facts of political life in this country. In fairness, we all should remember that there have been arrests, there have been charges, trials are scheduled, presumably it will all come out in the wash and maybe somebody's going to jail. That separates our system from those where the party in power is all powerful, from totalitarian states. Still, let's be sure we stop edging over in that direction.

The Des Moines Register
Des Moines, Iowa, October 11, 1972

In most election years, the Washington Post's report about an apparatus for carrying out political espionage and sabotage in behalf of Republican campaign efforts would be dismissed as so much politicking, attributable to Democratic sources.

According to the Post's account, at least 50 undercover agents were assigned to disrupt and spy on the Democratic campaign. The purported skulduggery includes forging letters, leaking false stories and fouling up Democratic campaign schedules.

But the Post story in this campaign cannot be dismissed, if only because Republican figures already have been implicated in an incident of political espionage more bizarre than anything alleged in the latest account. The bugging of Democratic national headquarters was a violation of federal law in addition to being a gross invasion of privacy and breach of accepted standards of political behavior.

The Post says the bugging incident was part and parcel of a larger espionage scheme conducted under a program of "offensive security" operated by the White House and the Committee to Re-elect the President. The Post claims the FBI investigation of the bugging affair uncovered the espionage apparatus, and it quoted information obtained by the FBI in its investigation.

The Washington Post story was labeled "fiction" and "a collection of absurdities" by a spokesman for the Nixon re-election committee. The public is left to guess and wonder. It will continue to be in the dark until Congress investigates and lays the facts on the table.

The alleged political espionage is said to have been financed by a secret political fund of $350,000 to $700,000. The existence of such a fund is a legitimate subject of congressional inquiry.

President Nixon declared last week that the FBI conducted an exhaustive investigation of the bugging of Democratic headquarters. He said the FBI assigned 133 agents to the case, followed 1,800 leads and conducted 1,500 interviews. The President said he "wanted to be sure that no member of the White House staff and no man or woman in a position of major responsibility in the Committee for Re-election had anything to do with this kind of reprehensible activity."

The President left the impression that he was reassured. He may be, but the public has no basis for reassurance. It is entitled to suspect the worst until it is given the full story.

THE SACRAMENTO BEE

Sacramento, Calif., October 15, 1972

The moral breakdown implicit in the Watergate bugging incident is frightening. The public as a whole seems somewhat indifferent about what should be treated far more seriously than a "caper." For Watergate can touch us all.

Evidence by FBI agents has established that the raid on Democratic National Committee headquarters and the electronic spying that went with it were part of a widespread campaign of snooping and political sabotage conducted on behalf of President Richard Nixon's re-election. The investigators pinned down, too, that these activities were directed by White House aides and the Committee for the Re-election of the President.

———

Nixon's press secretary, Ronald Ziegler, at one point dismissed the Watergate affair as "third-rate burglary." This soft, head-in-the-sand attitude is not shared by Chairman Wright Patman of the House Banking Committee. The feisty Texas Democrat called it "the most sordid political tactics ever employed by a major political party."

Many people are disturbed by the thought that if Watergate can be glossed over or covered up, it will invite police-state surveillance over public officials, political leaders, professional people and even the average citizen. Americans may not be aware of the extent to which governmental agencies and private companies now use computers and microfilm to collect, store and exchange sensitive information about the activities of private individuals. It is, alas, a documented fact.

If you think "it can't happen here," just go back a few months to the disclosure of Army spying on the lawful political activities of a wide range of groups, and incident reports on individual citizens. Protests and a lawsuit prompted the Army to announce it was abandoning the data bank — but turning over the data to the internal security division of the Justice Department.

Watergate should wake up Americans to the inherent threat to the precious fundamental right of privacy. Every aspect of the case demands the broadest possible airing and everyone connected with it should be brought to trial.

The New York Times

New York, N.Y., October 12, 1972

The Watergate affair has taken an astonishing and profoundly disturbing turn.

At first, it seemed that the men arrested for burglarizing and "bugging" the offices of the Democratic National Committee in the Watergate Building in Washington, D. C., were engaged in an ugly but isolated act of political espionage. But investigative reporting by The Washington Post and other newspapers has now uncovered a complex, far-reaching and sinister operation on the part of White House aides and the Nixon campaign organization. This operation involves sabotage, forgery, theft of confidential files, surveillance of Democratic candidates and their families and persistent efforts to lay the basis for possible blackmail and intimidation.

For more than a year, a secret fund existed in the Nixon headquarters which financed these "special activities" and to which only certain key officials had access. Many hundreds of thousands of dollars in cash flowed through this secret fund. Dozens of people, including numerous ex-F.B.I. and ex-C.I.A. agents, were employed in this clandestine work. High-ranking officials including some still employed at the White House and at the Committee to Re-elect the President received copies of the confidential reports prepared by these agents on the basis of their wiretapping and their surveillance of leading Democrats.

A notably dramatic episode involves a letter which surfaced in the New Hampshire primary last February. It stated that Senator Edmund S. Muskie, while campaigning in Florida, had made a derogatory reference to Americans of French-Canadian background. The letter never seemed plausible on its face but, played up by the scurrilous Manchester Union Leader, it weakened Mr. Muskie among French-Canadian voters in that city.

It is now asserted that this letter was forged by a White House staff member in a deliberate effort to weaken Mr. Muskie, then the front-running Democratic candidate. The staff man has denied the allegation, but Senator Muskie is surely right that this serious charge and the many others which have come to public knowledge in recent weeks demand a personal response by President Nixon. The veracity and integrity of the President's staff and campaign organization are at stake.

Much of the public has reportedly taken the attitude up to now that there is nothing particularly unusual in the Watergate affair. It cannot be reiterated too strongly that, on the contrary, such practices are unprecedented in American politics. No national party and no incumbent Administration has ever set out in this systematic fashion to invade the privacy, disrupt the activities, and discredit the leadership of the political opposition. These are ambitions and police-state tactics which have no place in a democracy.

THE MILWAUKEE JOURNAL

Milwaukee, Wis., October 14, 1972

Tales of skulduggery swirl ever more thickly around the Nixon administration. Yet, observers report, the public seems strangely unmoved.

Lack of exposure cannot be blamed. Many are aware of such damaging things as the ITT affair, which cast doubt on the enforcement of antitrust laws and left suspicion of influence peddling in high places; the milk case, which revealed linkage between dairy lobby donations to the Republican Party and higher milk price support; the Watergate bugging caper, with its ties to the Committee for the Re-election of the President (CREEP) and money contributed by secret Republican donors; the Russian wheat deal, with its indications of questionable ethical conduct by government officials and insider profiteering by large grain firms; and now the astonishing stories by the Washington Post, apparently based on leaked FBI information, showing widespread spying, sabotage and other sinister activity directed at the Democrats by members of the White House staff and CREEP.

If the public response is as limp as it seems, there probably are several explanations. The stories of scandal are complicated; pieces are difficult to fit together. Many of the worst charges have not been adequately proved, at least not yet — and with Congress hurrying to adjourn and wrongly willing to let the administration investigate itself, it seems that solid answers to allegations of guilt will be postponed until well after the election. It must also be noted that the president himself has not been tied to any particular misdeed, leaving people free to believe, or at least hope, that the presidency is clean even if there is some corruption in the ranks.

Perhaps the most important reason for lack of discernible public alarm is the general mood of the electorate. Apathy is the wrong word, because even the nation's rather comfortable majority seems concerned about many problems. But, as several voter surveys suggest, people are rather depressed and heavily inclined to caution and disbelief of politicians as a breed. Most voters are not thrilled by Nixon but neither are they ready to accept challenger George McGovern as, on the whole, a better alternative. They are wary of promises and of attempts by both sides in this election to claim purity for themselves while attributing only wickedness to the opposition. Many voters, in short, see things like the Watergate break-in as "politics as usual," as an example of the dishonesty that both political parties have practiced through the years.

Up to a point, of course, public skepticism is healthy. An easily bamboozled citizenry is no asset to a self-governing society. And surely both parties are capable of corruption. Yet there is danger in the mood today. One must wonder: As questions of misconduct in Washington pile up faster than answers, how long can a conscientious citizen react with a shrug instead of an outcry? At what point does sensible skepticism become useless cynicism — a mental swamp where moral indignation is smothered in the ooze?

AKRON BEACON JOURNAL
Akron, Ohio, October 12, 1972

In any normal presidential election year, the Watergate scandal would be a major campaign issue. The fact that revelations of political espionage and ordinary crime have hardly caused a ripple on the surface of public opinion is fresh proof, if any is needed, that 1972 is not a normal year.

The reasons why the public is apparently unmoved and indifferent to the Watergate affair are probably bound up with the complex and shifting allegiances of this campaign. The concern of many people has focused on the shaky credibility of Sen. McGovern; others focus on the President's foreign policy accomplishments; for others, the over-riding issue is the progress of the Paris talks.

The result has been that attention has been diverted from Watergate. And, this diversion of attention has been made easier by the fact that some elements of the story, as they have unfolded, have been so bizarre that they have the same kind of believability for the public as an episode in the adventures of Maxwell Smart.

The press itself is partly responsible for this because it has relied heavily on unnamed sources in the development of the story. Despite substantial investigative efforts, it has failed to pin down the allegations and the people involved.

★

But the Watergate affair is no ordinary piece of election-year skulduggery.

The real issue is the essential integrity of the whole American electoral process; the right of free people to be untrammeled in their political campaigns; the right to privacy and to freedom from electronic surveillance. It involves, in short, respect for the rights of others.

Failure to respect those rights is a corruption different in both degree and kind from that which involves the misuse of government funds and the buying and selling of influence by highly placed officials. It is, in fact, more serious because it reveals in those guilty of it an ethical and moral bankruptcy that goes to the heart of a free government.

If the Washington Post reporters are right, and if the unnamed and unidentified FBI sources are correctly quoted, then at least one segment of President Nixon's reelection team has displayed this kind of gross indifference to the principles of free and fair elections. The massive effort at political sabotage revealed through the Post should be repugnant to every American.

Under the circumstances, it is not sufficient that DeVan L. Shumway of the Committee for the Reelection of the President, dismiss the story as "not only a fiction but a collection of absurdities." With the loose ends of intrigue sticking out in every direction, it is no longer acceptable to shrug the matter off as being in the "hands of the authorities."

★

The degree to which people accept or reject charges of President Nixon's direct involvement in the affair is probably a matter of personal political belief. But, regardless of personal beliefs, the case has brought a bad odor directly to the White House door.

Nixon should no longer stand above the battle or decline to comment because of the legal rights of the seven men who have been indicted in the Watergate burglary.

He needs to make a definitive statement on the case. He needs to take a stand, and he needs to rid both his Administration and his reelection committee of everyone who had anything to do with it — no matter how highly placed they may be.

Such a stand is necessary to get the conduct of politics in 1972 out of the gutter. Without it, serious damage can be done not only to the already shaky credibility of all politicians, but to the system itself.

THE ROANOKE TIMES
Roanoke, Va., October 11, 1972

With all doors firmly closed to a pre-election probe of the Watergate bugging case, the public is left with what reporters can dig up. The Washington Post reports the Watergate spying was part of massive spying and espionage directed at possible Democratic nominees since 1971. To which a spokesman for The Committee to Re-elect the President replied: "The Post story is not only fiction but a collection of absurdities."

Well, the Post can be mistaken and it is hardly known as pro-Nixon but it isn't given to printing fiction. In the realm of absurdities, for instance, what can be more far-fetched than a man in Deerfield Beach, Fla. (never yet located) writing a letter embarrassing to Senator Muskie and having it published in the Manchester Union Leader in New Hampshire—two weeks before the primary? The spokesman for the committee would not discuss any specifics of the Post story.

The most appalling aspect of the Watergate and related smells is that the public reaction apparently is: So what? A large majority seems to be convinced that Senator McGovern is so incompetent it doesn't make any difference what Mr. Nixon's strategists and tacticians did or didn't do.

WORCESTER TELEGRAM.
Worcester, Mass., October 13, 1972

Something smells in the area of Washington, D.C., and it is up to President Nixon to get to the bottom of it.

If the FBI has actually linked the Watergate bugging incident directly to John Mitchell and Maurice Stans, as is being reported in news stories, and if Watergate was just one facet in a general campaign of political spying, faked phone calls, faked letters and undercover political sabotage, we are seeing something ugly and unprecedented in American political history.

The American people are traditionally tolerant of campaign shenanigans. Political candidates are usually not averse to taking the low road if it looks promising in terms of votes. This is taken for granted and therefore discounted.

But there are limits — limits set both by law and the American sense of fair play. And acceptable campaign practices in this country do not include burglary, telephone tapping, blackmail and faked letters and phone calls.

The Committee to Reelect the President has denied the charges. However, none of President Nixon's top campaign figures has been willing to testify or even to comment. At a news conference last week, White House Press Secretary Ronald L. Ziegler declined 29 times in a row to comment on the allegations.

The Watergate affair itself is in court, and is unlikely to be resolved before the election. But these new charges are highly disturbing in themselves. President Nixon owes it to himself to find out what has been and is being done in his name, and to straighten out whatever needs to be corrected.

And then he owes it to the American people to make a full disclosure before the election of what he finds out. Unlike the usual political volleys, these charges are too grave to be dismissed with a "no comment" and wave of the hand.

FIVE DEFENDANTS IN WATERGATE CASE PLEAD GUILTY AT CONSPIRACY TRIAL

Former White House consultant E. Howard Hunt Jr. pled guilty Jan. 11 to all six charges against him in the second day of the conspiracy trial of seven defendants charged in connection with the June 1972 break-in at Democratic National Headquarters in the Watergate complex in Washington. Hunt had offered the preceding day to plead guilty on three charges, but U.S. District Court Judge John J. Sirica refused the offer because of "the apparent strength of the government's case" and because of the public's right to be assured of "not only the substance of justice but also the appearance of justice." Hunt, freed on $100,000 bail pending sentence, told newsmen that to his knowledge no "higher-ups" in the government were involved in the affair and that he believed his activities were "in the best interest of my country." The six counts, carrying a maximum sentence of 35 years, included conspiracy, burglary and wiretapping.

Assistant U.S. Attorney Earl J. Silbert had depicted the Watergate incident in his Jan. 10 opening statement as part of a well-financed espionage program against the Democrats. Defense attorneys in their opening arguments had stressed the lack of "criminal intent" or "evil motive" in the defendants' actions.

On Jan. 15 Bernard L. Barker, Frank A. Sturgis, Eugenio Rolando Martinez and Virgilio R. Gonzalez, who were apprehended inside the Democratic offices, pled guilty to all charges. Sirica accepted the pleas and the trial was resumed for the remaining two defendants, James W. McCord Jr. and G. Gordon Liddy. (McCord had been security coordinator for the Committee to Re-elect the President at the time of his arrest. Liddy had been counsel to the committee's finance committee and was charged by the prosecution with being the head of Republican espionage operations.) McCord's attorney Gerald Alch told reporters Jan 16 that his client acted under "duress" after learning "potentially violent groups" supported the Democrats and may have "indicated" their plans to the Democrats. The defense would contend, he said, that "if one is under a reasonable apprehension . . . he is justified in breaking a law to avoid the greater harm, which in this case would be violence directed to Republican officials, including, but not limited to, the President."

Those pleading guilty denied pressure had been put on them or that they had been bribed by "higher-ups" to change their pleas. Gonzalez, Sturgis and Barker claimed that their participation in the Watergate affair was based on their desire to liberate Cuba from Communist control. Barker had said that he "cannot state" who supplied him with the $114,000 found in his possession.

The *New York Times* reported Jan. 15 that "great pressure" had been put on the four defendants to change their plea to guilty and avoid testifying. *Time* magazine reported Jan. 22 that the four had been offered long-term cash settlements for pleading guilty.

WINSTON-SALEM JOURNAL
Winston-Salem, N.C., January 7, 1973

WHATEVER the final verdict in the Watergate trial opening tomorrow, the issues raised by this case go far beyond the scope of the indictments of seven men.

Two of the seven are former White House aides, while the others have backgrounds resembling the fictional world of adventure and espionage. All are charged with conspiracy, burglary, intent to steal property, attempted wiretapping and eavesdropping on private conversations. And several of the men are charged with added, related acts.

But the issues in this trial will bear upon the integrity of the American political process itself.

When the Watergate break-in occurred last June 17, the case seemed remarkable only for the intruders' inept performance and their rather bizarre backgrounds. The matter became known as an "affair" or "bungled caper," and that was the image that has prevailed in the public's mind. During the election campaign, it was to the Nixon administration's advantage to perpetuate' this public impression, for thereby it obscured the seriousness of the case as it developed. The intruders were taken, as President Nixon described them, to be simply "overzealous people," who in the heat of election campaigns sometimes "do things that are wrong."

Subsequent investigations by the Washington Post and other publications, however, linked the seven intruders to the Committee to Re-Elect the President, and other members of the White House staff. There is enough solid evidence in these reports to push the Watergate trial well beyond a simple matter of burglary and wiretapping. For the men caught in the Watergate were carrying money contributed to the Republican party, and some $114,000 of GOP contributions had wound up in the bank account of one of the seven men.

Later reports told that this $114,000 was but part of a much larger secret fund that was to be used for spying upon and sabotaging the Democratic party. Various persons around the country swore they had been approached for such roles, and the man they identified as the recruiter is linked by phone company records to the President's appointments secretary.

These are but some of the elusive and disturbing aspects of the Watergate affair. Obviously it was more than a simple case of burglary and wiretapping. But exactly who else was involved, and was the break-in in fact ordered or directed by Republican officials, or others on the White House staff?

That is the larger question in this trial, and it must be answered in detail. If the Nixon administration has nothing to hide, its best strategy is to allow the trial to get into those questions.

The presiding judge has said that the purposes and men behind the break-in were proper questions for the prosecution to pursue. If the Watergate trial is to resolve any of these questions, that is exactly what the prosecution should do.

THE DAILY HERALD
Biloxi, Miss., January 14, 1973

The sordid details of the Watergate affair, gradually unravelling in the trials in Washington, are a distasteful indictment of the ethics of men surrounding President Nixon. We fail to see how Mr. Nixon, in the light of testimony thus far given, can continue to remain aloof and uninvolved.

E. Howard Hunt Jr., described as a former White House consultant, has acknowledged with a plea of guilty a series of serious charges. They involve burglary of the Democratic party headquarters in the Watergate Apartments, conspiracy, electronic bugging and wiretapping.

Robert B. Fletcher testified also that Hunt, a former CIA agent, was behind the scheme to employ a youth to infiltrate the campaign headquarters of Democrats Edmund S. Muskie and George S. McGovern to develop information on their campaigns and turn it over to Hunt.

Hunt is only one of seven on trial. We hope that further testimony will provide full disclosures of what happened to that information — how far up the line it went, how it was used, and by whom.

Hunt says he would be willing to testify that to the best of his knowledge no officials higher in the Administration were involved. It seems unlikely that the buck stopped with him. If any material of campaign value came through the sneaky manuevering, we believe Hunt would have wanted to pass it on to higher channels where it might be used.

Federal Judge John J. Sirica acted properly in refusing to accept from Hunt a guilty plea to a reduced number of charges. He appears to be insistent upon getting all details on the record where they be long.

We do not believe that the stupid affair was under Mr. Nixon's personal direction. But, like all candidates for high office, Mr. Nixon is responsible for those who labor politically for him.

By now, he should have made his own investigation. And he owes it to the voting public, Democrats and Republicans alike, to divorce himself from such associates and such tactics and to explain fully how and why the burglary at Watergate happened.

There is more to the matter than a mischievous caper by overly-motivated supporters. The integrity and the honor of Mr. Nixon's administration are at stake.

Newsday
Long Island, N.Y., January 16, 1973

On Friday, Newsday reported that four Watergate defendants were "being urged to cut their trial short and plead guilty by a group that promises to pay them $1,000 each for every month they spend in jail, plus a lump sum when they are released." All four have CIA backgrounds dating from the Cuban Bay of Pigs invasion. Sources said "friends from Miami" also linked to the abortive 1961 invasion made the offer, presumably to avoid a trial that might embarrass them.

Yesterday, the four *did* withdraw, joining former White House aide E. Howard Hunt in pleading guilty to conspiracy, burglary and bugging at the headquarters of the Democratic National Committee. Their reasons weren't spelled out. But whatever they were, it's going to be hard to erase the suspicion that a deal was made to hide those responsible for the Watergate scandal.

With only two defendants remaining, the trial—if it goes forward at all—is bound to be less illuminating than it might have been at first. There'll be fewer witnesses for questioning and fewer mysteries cleared up.

Will the public ever learn who ordered the operation and who bankrolled it? Were some defendants acting to head off a thaw with Cuba that they feared a Democratic administration might promote? Were they self-propelled zealots for President Nixon, or were they acting directly on orders from the White House or the Committee for the Reelection of the President? It's now been reported that the Nixon reelection committee cannot account for $900,000 in cash contributions. Is that what fueled the Watergate operation?

So far, neither the courts, nor the investigative agencies, nor the highest political leaders have done anything to clear up the mystery. That's bad enough. What's worse—because it's so subversive to the democratic process—is the cynical conclusion that Watergate was only a "caper" to be expected in the shoddy game of politics. If self-government is to have meaning, that perception must be changed.

Orlando Sentinel
Orlando, Fla., January 13, 1973

"WE HAVE met the enemy and he is us," said the comic strip character Pogo in what might be a summation of Republican party involvement in the Watergate bugging case.

It is ironic that the Nixon administration, which is commendably free of corruption after four years in office, finds its name blackened by a pulp-novel plot instigated by third-echelon GOP campaign zealots.

Still, the guilty plea of E. Howard Hunt Jr. to six counts related to political espionage at Democratic National Headquarters June 17 gives Watergate a new complexion.

※ ※ ※

THIS IS especially true now that the lawyer for five other defendants has announced a "Nuremberg defense" — that is to say, a contention his clients were following what they understood as military type orders which mitigated their individual responsibility.

The only fairly substantial Republican figure, besides Hunt, is G. Gordon Liddy, former counsel for the Committee for the Reelection of the President.

The other five caught at Watergate were Americans of Cuban extraction from Miami who had not previously figured in top-level politics.

The prosecutor, Assistant U.S. Atty. Earl J. Silbert, says that's all — there aren't any higher-ups involved unless some are implicated by testimony at the trial or before a continuing grand jury.

※ ※ ※

WHAT WE HAVE so far, then, is a stupid maneuver unworthy of a late-late television movie rerun.

But as silly as Watergate is, the incident is serious enough to cause concern and to suggest vigorous party action to plug campaign holes once the trial is ended, for Republican headquarters is clearly responsible for the loose handling of campaign funds that could let a Watergate happen.

Being the honorable man he is, and the pragmatist he is, Mr. Nixon is undoubtedly planning a move to tune the party machinery and see that he and other responsible Republicans aren't again embarrassed or the American people compromised.

※ ※ ※

THE PRESIDENT shouldn't be faulted for his reticence about making public statements deploring Watergate; remember the furor set off by his off-the-cuff mention of Manson's devil cult prior to the Manson family trial?

As shameful as Watergate is, the case has a hopeful and reassuring aspect: Nothing is being swept under the rug.

The government — that is, the prosecution — is not sparing the feelings of the government, meaning the Nixon administration.

And Federal District Judge John J. Sirica is faithfully following the role of the independent judiciary to keep defense and prosecution in line and assure the defendants a fair trail.

※ ※ ※

THE JUDGE has made it clear, moreover, that Hunt's guilty plea has earned him a date with the grand jury that indicted him in the first place.

The questions he is asked there will surely bring to the surface any names, dates and facts that might have been missed by the law.

The hopeful phoenix rising out of the Watergate ashes is that America's three-pronged system of government is working even when it deals with something that embarrasses those in power.

Could anybody imagine a Watergate trial in Moscow or Peking?

THE RICHMOND NEWS LEADER

Richmond, Va., January 10, 1973

When the Watergate Affair first broke into the headlines, Democratic cries of outrage tended to obscure what otherwise would have been a primary question about the incident: that is, why would any five men of normal intelligence bother to bug the headquarters of the Democratic National Committee? Only political babes-in-the-woods could have believed that the Watergate telephones — in the normal case of events — would offer up anything so damning as to be worth five men risking capture with their wiretaps down. So, a few commentators suggested, there existed, or the five men had strong reason to believe that there existed, some devastating piece of information that could be acquired only by listening to Democratic conversations.

With obligatory pooh-poohs, Democratic leaders denied such a possibility, and shifted the public's focus onto the White House, which the Democrats accused of launching the Watergate raid; the Democrats fervently urged that the White House be torn down brick by brick in order to arrive at the "truth." Once found, of course, that truth would show not just Republican complicity at the highest levels of government, but Republican cupidity and stupidity in intercepting worthless Democratic chit-chat over the telephone.

Well, in Washington the other day, members of the Democratic National Committee — with, for good measure, members of the Young Democratic Clubs of America — entered a motion at the Watergate trial that would prevent the disclosure of any illegally recorded conversations. According to the motion, such a disclosure would violate the privacy of the conversations' participants, and would be completely irrelevant to the trial itself. All of which is to say that if a man climbs Mount Everest to steal another man's strongbox, he should be convicted of robbery without anyone — including judge and jury — being allowed to see what the strongbox held that was so alluring to the thief.

Certainly the Committee members have a partial point: Wiretaps gather conversations between conspirators as easily as conversations between lovers using the same phone, and any existing tapes could prove embarrassing for the Democrats on several levels. But at least closed-court revelations are required for the judge and jury to reach valid decisions in the case, and the Democratic talk of the tapes' "irrelevance" is beside the point. If the Democratic higher-ups plan to play the same game that they have accused the White House of playing, then the Watergate Affair will remain a mystery forever, and the public will be left with nothing but speculation.

DAYTON DAILY NEWS

Dayton, Ohio, January 17, 1973

With the defendants tumbling over one another in their late rush to swear guilt, the chances have slimmed that the public will learn much from the Watergate bugging-burglary trial. The p o l i t i c a l process is being robbed by due process.

There remains the promise of a congressional investigation and, though it would be conducted by Democrats and thus discounted for partisanship, that pending inquiry takes on heightened importance with each new dropout among the trial's defendants.

Several questions remain unanswered. What, fully, were the puroposes of the sneak-by-night operation? Who ordered it, and how far up the chain of civil command did guilty knowledge extend? Where did the money come from and in what amounts?

Though the incident is receding in time, its stink has not abated. There are serious indications that the Committee To Re-elect the President — and with it, some top administration o f f i c i a l s — planned more than just the modern, electronic version of traditional political spying. The trade in turncoats and plants is, after all, as old as the traffic in votes.

Instead, Watergate and related operations run for the White House last year seem to have been meant not only to penetrate the opposition but to sink it with the kind of tactics that imperial nations — Soviet and western alike — use against bothersome, vulnerable governments, the techniques of disinformation, political sabotage and subordination.

If the point was, as it may have been, to make the political process a sham — for instance, to keep Democrats from being able to choose their strongest candidate — then something much worse than mere partisan games was involved. The intent then would have been domestic subversion, the willful blunting of the public will that, thanks to the vagaries of politics, is none too precise at its best.

It is not the courts' job to elicit information, except as that is needed to do justice. The indulgence of guilty pleas was in order, but that is pushing off on the Democrats a sterner obligation to conduct the coming hearings with political sobriety, fair-mindedness and meticulous procedural care. The issues are too important for the conclusions, whether of good or ill, to be tainted by inquisitional politics.

The New York Times

New York, N.Y., January 18, 1973

Chief Federal Judge John J. Sirica spoke for a host of incredulous observers at the Watergate trial when he told defendant Bernard Barker that he simply did not believe his story that $114,000 had arrived in unmarked envelopes from sources unknown. Since then the defense has moved from the incredible to the outrageous. It has presented the court with the extraordinary doctrine that anyone who, correctly or incorrectly, imagines himself or his friends to be in some sort of danger is thereby justified in breaking the law.

In enunciating this legal version of the protective-reaction strike, defense counsel Gerald Alch tried to cloak his clients' acts of political espionage in a mantle of patriotism. The violence which the defendants wanted to intercept, he said, would have been directed against "Republican officials, including but not limited to, the President."

Far from protecting high officials against violence, the validation of his thesis would constitute an open hunting license for every fanatic to take the law into his own hands. Guided only by hallucinations akin to the anti-Castro fanaticism that motivated the hirelings in the Watergate plot, any individuals or groups could feel free to take up arms or utilize any other repressive measures their paranoid suppositions dictated. Such a political law of the jungle might readily lead from protective espionage to defensive assassination.

The need becomes increasingly plain for extending the investigation beyond the case of the hirelings now on trial. The significant question in the unraveling of the Watergate scandal is less who carried out the orders than who issued them.

The courtroom scenario that has frustrated Judge Sirica's efforts to extract illuminating or even believable answers is all too transparent. The five defendants, who pleaded guilty to everything in order not to have to tell anything, acted in the tradition of an international espionage apparatus that considers caught agents expendable. That analogy is made stronger by indications that the invisible masters of the plot intend to compensate their exposed mercenaries for any temporary sacrifice of their freedom.

The guilty pleas entered by the five self-confessed political spies do not of themselves raise any legal barriers to their recall as witnesses in the trial of the two remaining defendants. It is doubtful, however, that their enforced testimony would serve any purpose in getting at those crucial questions that go beyond their personal law-breaking. The prosecution, after all, represents the Justice Department of the same Administration whose re-election the defendants sought to advance through their illegal activities.

A trial, in any event, is an inadequate instrument for probing all the ramifications of a political scandal in which no charges have been leveled against the string-pullers responsible for planning and financing the whole operation. Questions beyond the guilt of the defendants —assuming that the prosecution had much stomach to ask them—might indeed be difficult to sustain over objections by defense counsel.

That transfers to the Senate the task of getting to the bottom of this ominous affair after the present trial ends. The aim of its inquiry should be to bypass the cloak-and-dagger hallucinations of the hired spies and to identify the chain of command that issued the orders and provided the funds. The prior guilty pleas of the defendants in Judge Sirica's court would make it possible for the Senators to question them without the protective cover of self-incrimination.

Senator Sam J. Ervin has already asked the Justice Department and other agencies to safeguard "all pertinent public and nonpublic documents" bearing on the Watergate case. As one who long ago expressed serious concern over the erosion of civil liberties through growing resort to political espionage, Mr. Ervin can find in the Watergate scandal an opportunity for exposing to full public scrutiny a subversion of the political process that must not be allowed to happen again.

The Des Moines Register

Des Moines, Iowa, January 17, 1973

The Watergate bugging trial, which was expected to shed light on the case, is deepening the mystery instead. Not the least of the new questions raised by the trial is why five of the seven Watergate defendants suddenly elected to plead guilty.

Reports have circulated that four of the guilty pleas were prompted by promises of $1,000-a-month payments to families of each of the men. The source of funds to pay defense costs also is shrouded in mystery.

Federal Judge John Sirica has been doing his best to put the full story on the record, with limited success. When he tried repeatedly to get one of the defendants who pleaded guilty to reveal the source of the Watergate money, and the man expressed ignorance, the judge was limited to voicing disbelief.

The U.S. attorney handling the prosecution sketched the government's theory of the case in his opening statement to the jury. According to the prosecution, officials of the Committee for the Re-election of the President wanted information about planned demonstrations, attempts to disrupt the Republican national convention and such "intelligence" as whether a polluter had contributed to the campaign of Senator Edmund Muskie. The defendants were directed to gather the requested information, the jury was told, but they went far beyond this in their bugging of Democratic headquarters.

The government's view of the case may be accurate, but it also conveniently puts the committee that spearheaded the President's reelection in the best possible light. It portrays the former White House aides who initiated the intelligence operation as having a warranted interest in such matters as planned disruptive activity. It puts the blame for the illegal bugging and break-in solely on the defendants acting on their own.

The public can only speculate about the validity of the Justice Department's description of the case. Prior to the trial, federal sources had painted to the Washington Post a different picture of the extent of the involvement of White House aides in political espionage.

The guilty pleas, coupled with the belief that the Justice Department isn't eager to embarrass the administration, are likely to leave the public unsatisfied that the Watergate trial has revealed the full story. Senate Democrats responded last week by approving a resolution calling for a Senate investigation and naming Senator Sam Ervin (Dem., N.C.) to head it. We hope this will produce the full, fair and nonpartisan disclosure of facts the Watergate episode badly needs.

The Cincinnati Post

TIMES ⚊ STAR

Cincinnati, Ohio, January 27, 1973

The trial judge in the Watergate bugging case has earned the public's thanks by rejecting one of the most dangerous defense arguments to surface in years.

It came from James W. McCord Jr., former FBI agent and security chief of the Committee for the Re-election of the President, who, with six others, is charged with wiretapping the Democratic National Committee in the Watergate complex in Washington.

McCORD ARGUED that he acted under "duress" because he feared "radicals" would commit violence against Republican officials, including President Nixon. Thus, he continued, his role in the conspiracy, burglary and wiretapping at the Watergate, was not a crime.

To his credit, Chief Judge John J. Sirica of the U.S. District Court did not buy the McCord defense, which would be a precedent for anarchy and do-it-yourself vigilante actions on the political scene.

"All he had to do," said Judge Sirica, was pick up the telephone and call the head of the Secret Service, or the FBI or the chief of police and say 'now I'm head of security of the Committee to Re-elect the President. We have certain information that the President is in danger.'"

A Republican himself who previously was active in party politics, the judge added:

"The Republican National Committee is just another political organization. They don't have all the rights in the world to hire someone to go into the Democratic National Committee and bug that committee. What do you think they would say if the Democrats did it to them? They wouldn't like it, would they?"

In the smelly Watergate case, Judge Sirica has been a breath of fresh air. He not only rules with common sense but expresses himself in plain English. (Listening to a defendant claim not to know who had sent him cash to pay for the bugging, he said, "I'm sorry but I don't believe you.") If he's not careful, Judge Sirica will restore respect for the law.

The Evening Star

The Washington News DAILY

Washington, D.C., January 17, 1973

As the trial of the Watergate Seven moves on, the whole picture of bumbling political intrigue grows sillier and sorrier. Along with the fervor and naivete of the Cuban trio, who do seem to have undertaken their part in the bugging of Democratic headquarters in a spirit of revulsion against hard times in Castro's Cuba, there is mounting evidence of the kind of skulduggery and coverup that has, down through history, given politics a bad name.

The willingness — eagerness is a better word — of the defendants to plead guilty suggests that there's a lot to hide and that somebody is making it worthwhile for these people to keep it hidden. How far up the Republican hierarchy does involvement and responsibility go?

It may take a Senate investigation to bring out all the facts. If that's what it takes, we should have one. While everybody knows dirty fighting goes on in politics, everybody knows with even more certainty that it shouldn't. When it's discovered, the full range of public sanctions and censures is in order.

Perhaps even with a Senate investigation, the whole story would not come out. Many things are done with the implied consent of the powerful that would never come to pass if anybody had to give direct orders for them or even to know for sure what was happening.

Was Hamlet's mother in on the murder that gave her a new husband? It's that sort of problem.

But perhaps the most dangerous aspect of the case is the moral confusion stirred up around it by the administration's enemies. It's well to remember what the Watergate malfeasances, no matter how bad they turn out to be, are not.

There are disingenuously scandalized Nixon-haters who act as though using Big Brother techniques to spy out Democratic campaign strategies was a combination of high treason, grand larceny, and genocide. It's not.

It's dirty pool, to be deplored, punished, and avoided by one and all in the future. But it's important to distinguish it from the other undesirable things politicos have been known to do, such as grinding the faces of the poor to enrich themselves, building personal power through terrorism and widespread curtailment of citizen liberties, and disrupting the social order to push an ideology.

The message of the Watergate affair is the old one that eternal vigilance is the price of practically everything. Especially clean politics.

St. Petersburg Times

St. Petersburg, Fla., January 17, 1973

Three newsgathering organizations — Time, columnist Jack Anderson and The New York Times in a story by Pulitzer-prize-winner Seymour Hersh — working independently, have reported extreme pressures put on Watergate defendants to get them to plead guilty.

Those pressures went beyond persuasion. These three sources say the men's families were to receive $1,000 a month while the men were in prison and more money upon their release.

THE FACT THAT five of the seven defendants have now pleaded guilty lends credence to these reports.

Regardless of motive, it would appear that the four Miamians who have just changed their pleas to guilty are not only taking the rap for their own misdeeds but for the masterminds behind the political espionage.

The Miamians have contended they were motivated by patriotism, that they believed McGovern would take a softer line toward Castro which was abhorrent to them. Yet neither McGovern's campaign pronouncements nor any hard evidence yet made public supports their fear.

Certainly if there were the most fragile evidence on which the men could have been depicted as defenders of the U.S. against a Communist plot, a full court hearing would have been welcomed.

IT LOOKS as if the Miamians not only are being exploited now but that their Cuban chauvinism was exploited to induce them to do the dirty work for the Committee to Re-Elect the President in the first place.

Wrongdoing tends to beget more wrongdoing. Watergate is not yet history but a current, continuing conspiracy.

THE TENNESSEAN
Nashville, Tenn., January 27, 1973

PERHAPS most Americans would consider themselves too sophisticated to be shocked by disclosures about the tactics of a political party. But almost every day the Watergate bugging trial in Washington turns up some new fact which must be shocking—and saddening—even to hardened observers of the American political scene.

Mr. Jeb Magruder, who was deputy director of the committee to re-elect President Nixon last fall, testified Tuesday that he authorized $250,000 to run an intelligence network to gather information about radical groups and potential violence he claimed these groups were planning.

Mr. Magruder said he designated Mr. G. Gordon Liddy, a former White House aide, to run the spying operation in December 1971. Mr Liddy is on trial for conspiracy, burglary, bugging and wiretapping in connection with the breakin at Democratic headquarters last June.

Mr. Hugh W. Sloan Jr., Mr. Nixon's campaign treasurer, testified that he gave the money for Mr. Liddy's operation on Mr. Magruder's orders. He also testified that $199,000 in payments to Mr. Liddy were approved by former Atty. Gen. John W. Mitchell, who resigned as Mr. Nixon's campaign director July 1, and former Commerce Secretary Maurice Stans. This was the first time these two administration stalwarts had been linked to the spy funds in sworn testimony.

Mr. Magruder testified that Mr. Nixon ordered the site of last summer's GOP convention switched from San Diego to Miami Beach as a result of information obtained by Mr. Liddy about the number of antiwar demonstrators expected at San Diego.

Apparently this was an attempt to justify the Nixon administration's spying operation as a legitimate security action. But this will be hard to do. The antiwar demonstrators could go to Miami Beach as well as San Diego, and many did, in fact, show up at the new convention site. Besides, it seems many people are under the impression the site was changed because it was disclosed that the International Telephone & Telegraph Co. which had received a favorable decision by the Nixon administration in an antitrust suit, had put up money to help pay for the convention in San Diego.

In an unusual courtroom scene Wednesday, the judge in the case—U.S. District Judge John J. Sirica, who described himself as a Republican — denounced the bugging while the jury was out and accused one of the defendants, Mr. James W. McCord Jr., of taking the law into his own hands by breaking into Democratic headquarters. Mr. McCord had sought to establish as his defense the claim that he broke into the headquarters to protect President Nixon by obtaining information about radical groups who might harm the President.

Judge Sirica denied the defense permission to present a "defense of duress" before the jury. "It doesn't take a whole lot of common sense to come to the conclusion if this kind of defense were presented to the jury—well, I just think it would be rediculous, frankly, speaking bluntly," the judge said.

Regardless of how the administration may try to put a respectable face on its activities, the Watergate bugging is being exposed as an attempt by the party in power to use the resources of government to spy upon and harass the other party. The bugging was financed by presidential campaign funds and was approved by those in high position in the White House if not by the President himself.

Such tactics are foreign to the give and take of American political battles. If they are shocking and offensive to a federal judge who has the opportunity to hear evidence of all kinds of maliciousness and debasement in his courtroom, how much more shocking they must be to the average citizen who would like to believe there is some measure of decency left in the political process.

The Administration's actions in the Watergate case should be deplored by all who treasure a political atmosphere free of the suggestion of bugging and snooping and the use of government power to intimidate citizens and influence elections.

New York Post
New York, N.Y., January 26, 1973

There has been many a legal proceeding in which the court tried the case without a jury, but the Watergate trial presents some unusually distinctive features; the presiding judge has often been obliged to go ahead in the virtual absence of the prosecutor.

More specifically, the government is not conspicuously trying—either legally or in terms of exertion—and U. S. District Court Chief Judge Sirica has had to take over direct examination of witnesses. This week, he elicited the admission from one of them that a fat bundle of cash, some $200,000, was turned over to one of the remaining defendants in the political espionage case after former Attorney General Mitchell and former Secretary of Commerce Stans had given their consent.

Testimony on the point by these two figures is not in prospect at the trial; the prosecution has failed to subpena either of them, another instance of the desultory fashion in which the Dept. of Justice is proceeding, in contrast with the painstaking, scrupulously professional administration of the trial by Judge Sirica—a Republican appointed by President Eisenhower.

Both the President and the current Attorney General have gone to some lengths to describe the breadth of the government's Watergate investigation. Perhaps Congress should subpena the records and files; it is obvious that the prosecutors have little or no use for them in their flabby conduct of this politically explosive case.

ARKANSAS DEMOCRAT
Little Rock, Ark., January 20, 1973

It turns out that the defense in the Watergate bugging trial will follow the example of the Department of Defense. The bugging will be called "protective reaction."

Well, the exact words won't be used, but the implication is the same. One of the lawyers is claiming that his client was in the Democratic Party headquarters with bugging equipment because he suspected that President Nixon might be harmed by people in the headquarters. The "protective reaction" bombing raids in Vietnam, likewise, are based on suspicion that the bombees might perpetrate some outrage.

Apparently, there will be no attempt by the lawyers in the Watergate case to deny that bugging was attempted. That, of course, would be kind of silly, since the defendents were caught red-handed. And now 5 of the original Watergate 7 have pleaded guilty. The remaining defendants, in fact, tried to get a mistrial declared, because four of the guilty pleas came after the trial had started. The mistrial motion was denied.

The guilty pleas raise a serious question. Did someone pay the men to plead guilty so there would be no testimony in their cases? Such testimony could be embarrassing to the higher-ups who provided the money for the bugging activities. When they were asked if they had been paid, the four told the judge they hadn't. They also said they didn't know who was providing the money and giving the orders. Naturally, they would answer that way to both questions. But even the judge, Federal Judge John Sirica, said he didn't believe the last answer.

Some details still might come out in the testimony concerning the two remaining defendants, Gordon Liddy, former counsel for the Finance Committee for the Re-election of the President, and James W. McCord, Jr., the committee's security chief.

We must hope so. Bugging, carried on by government or private agents, is a serious invasion of privacy that cannot be taken lightly. The people who ordered the Watergate activities should be exposed as a deterrent to future attempts by them or others. If the trial does not ferret out the planners, Congress is obligated to carry out its own investigation. So we are pleased to note that Sen. Sam Ervin, D-N. C., will head such a study — after the trial, of course.

The "protective reaction" defense is an attempt to divert attention from the real issue. It is akin to another subterfuge used by government agencies to justify bugging and wiretapping of citizens, called "domestic security." The fear is raised that "some groups" plan violence. Then anyone can be spied on under the possibility that he might be a member of those "groups." Including members of the Democratic Party. If the Republicans happen to be in power.

LIDDY & McCORD FOUND GUILTY; SENATE INVESTIGATION BEGINS

Former Republican campaign officials G. Gordon Liddy and James W. McCord Jr. were convicted by a D.C. district court Jan. 30 of conspiracy, burglary, wiretapping and bugging in connection with the break-in at Democratic national headquarters at the Watergate complex in Washington in June 1972. Five other defendants in the case had pled guilty to all counts earlier in the trial.

Several times during the trial Judge John J. Sirica had interrupted examination of witnesses by both the defense and prosecution to conduct the questioning himself. He said Jan. 22 that neither side was developing "all the facts." It was under probing by Sirica that Hugh W. Sloan, former treasurer of the Nixon re-election finance committee, disclosed Jan. 23 that $199,000 in campaign funds had been paid to Liddy for an unspecified use after verification from former Attorney General John Mitchell, also a former Nixon campaign manager, and former Commerce Secretary Maurice Stans, Nixon's chief fund raiser.

On Feb. 1 a preliminary report by a Senate subcommittee stated that the federal government had failed to conduct a substantial investigation of political espionage during the 1972 election. Sen. Edward M. Kennedy (D, Mass.) said his panel had found evidence that "strongly indicates that a wide range of espionage and sabotage activities did occur" during the recent campaign and "neither the federal criminal investigation nor the White House administrative inquiry included any substantial investigation of the alleged sabotage and espionage operations apart from those surrounding the Watergate episode itself."

On Feb. 7 the Senate voted 70–0 to establish a seven-member select committee—four Democrats and three Republicans—to probe all aspects of the Watergate bugging case and other reported political espionage against the Democrats in the 1972 presidential election campaign. Sen. Sam J. Ervin Jr. was named chairman of the special panel Feb. 8. Judge Sirica had said Feb. 2 he hoped the Senate committee was granted power "by a broad enough resolution to get to the bottom of what happened in this case."

The Birmingham News
Birmingham, Ala., February 2, 1973·

The Watergate trial from start to finish was anticlimactic, a routine and lacklustre process that failed to answer questions the Democrats had wanted answered.

When at the beginning the defendants one by one pleaded guilty, it seemed for a time there would be no trial at all. But the guilty pleas stopped after the fifth of the seven admitted his guilt. Two were formally tried — G. Gordon Liddy and James W. McCord Jr.

Now the jury has wrapped up the case with a verdict arrived at in the minimum possible time of 90 minutes: Both guilty on all counts.

The espionage incident was embarrassing to the Republicans, but not embarrassing enough to cost President Nixon the election, although the Democrats tried their level best to wring the incident dry politically.

And even with the trial over, there is more to come as the Democrats crank up Senate investigative hearings under the leadership of Sen. Sam Ervin Jr., D-N.C.

Unless the Senate hearings turn up something truly explosive, however, the impact on the public is likely to be no more than that produced by Democratic campaign denunciations of GOP espionage or by the trial itself.

Somehow, the Watergate affair just didn't catch on as a political issue. The public has simply shrugged its shoulders and fixed its attention on other matters.

Clearly the intelligence arm of the Committee to Reelect the President got out of hand. It used tactics which were unlawful and unethical.

But how does the misdeed rank with other national problems? Is it as important as rising living costs? Ending the war in Vietnam? Government overspending? Crime? Drug traffic? Pollution? The public doesn't seem to think so.

No one condones the methods used by the Watergate Seven. But the trial's over and unfortunately the public seems ready to forget the entire episode.

THE LOUISVILLE TIMES
Louisville, Ky., February 1, 1973

Surely the jury's verdict of guilty was not the end of the affair in the Watergate case. If it should prove to be so, the case will have ended with neither a bang nor a whimper but a sigh of relief on the part of some and with elevated eyebrows on the faces of the multitude.

The jury's verdict of guilty against George Gordon Liddy and James W. McCord Jr. for their part in the spying on Democratic National Committee headquarters was hardly a surprise. In view of the testimony, any other conclusion would have been astonishing.

But the trial of Liddy and McCord (five others in the case already had pleaded guilty, four of them before the trial started) did not really answer the tough, intriguing questions. In fact, the conduct of the case was so cautious and discreet that even the trial judge, John J. Sirica, went out of his way to elicit information from the witnesses. He didn't get much, but his efforts may be used by defense counsel as a basis for seeking a reversal and a new trial.

The fact remains that with seven men found guilty or having admitted guilt, the public does not know what really motivated them, who inspired them, where the money that apparently was handed around casually came from, or how far up the Republican ladder the puppet strings extended. Intimations, suspicions, and half-concealed disclosures are available in abundance. Hard facts, however, are hard to find — that is, facts going beyond the men arrested.

Three possibilities for throwing a little more light on the affair remain. One is renewal of a grand jury investigation. Rather more promising is an expected congressional investigation to be headed by Sen. Sam Ervin, the North Carolina Democrat. That investigation could be highly enlightening. But its light will be shadowed inevitably by charges that it is politically motivated since Democrats will be in control. A third possibility lies in a civil suit the Democrats have brought against the Republicans.

Maybe out of all these things, some

so apathetic, so disinterested, so shrug-of-the-shoulders about the case.

The Watergate affair broke early last summer and was in the news constantly throughout the presidential campaign. But if it did anything to enhance the Democratic chances or hinder the Republicans, the November vote certainly did not show it. Moreover, we have been struck by how very few of the people who write letters to the editor on every subject under the sun have been inspired to express an opinion about Watergate. We are not suggesting that letters are the best method for testing the public pulse, but they do indicate what people are interested in. Apparently they are not interested in accusations of political espionage, perhaps feeling it is common practice. If that is so, it is not the least shocking aspect of the case questions will be answered.

But one question — and to us it is one of the most intriguing facets of the whole affair — will not be answered by any of these inquiries. It is why the American public has seemed

THE CHRISTIAN SCIENCE MONITOR

Boston, Mass., February 3, 1973

True, the Watergate affair has produced a trial. And out of it, two men were convicted on all counts, and now await sentencing, along with five others who earlier pleaded guilty on all counts, in the burglarizing and bugging of the national Democratic Party headquarters.

But it is not the charges, nor the limited testimony, nor the admissions of wrongdoing, nor the conviction and sentencing which make up the spirit and substance of justice. In a situation which involves the subversion of the American political system, and the participation in that subversion by unknown persons in the highest places of power, justice demands full revelation of what went on. Of course, it demands that the perpetrators of the deed be apprehended and dealt with. But even more it requires exposure of those who instigated and paid for the silence of the wrongdoers.

We do know that the two convicted men, and their five associates who pleaded guilty, were all employed by the Committee for the Re-election of the President. We do know, from testimony wrung out of a witness by Chief Judge John J. Sirica of Washington's U.S. District Court, that two of President Nixon's former Cabinet members had personally approved disbursement of $199,000 in Nixon campaign funds to one of the defendants to carry out the espionage.

But we know very little more than this. We are concerned at widely reported stories that these seven men have been offered considerable sums in terms of monthly payments during their jail terms, plus lump sums at the end of confinement. But we are not told who is the source of these funds, nor why this source is willing to continue to pay for an illegal act of political espionage which was, in fact miserably bungled.

And we are uncomfortably aware that all during this bizarre trial, in which Judge Sirica did his best to break through the witnesses' silence, the White House managed to time its headline-making announcements in such a way as to drive the few newsworthy developments in the trial from top news display.

If the American public is to have its confidence restored in the judicial system, if the blindness of Justice to power and person is to be made truly believable, the Watergate case must not be considered closed by the events of the last couple of weeks in the U.S. District Court.

The matter now rightly falls into the hands of Congress. There the Senate's respected Sam J. Ervin Jr., a constitutional lawyer and former prosecutor, has the duty and power to subpoena witnesses who can answer the questions that Judge Sirica could not get answers to. The facts must be pursued and all those connected with the case must be brought into the open. This pursuit must not be a personal nor a partisan exercise, but a fair and honest effort to bring out the truth. .

The American political system must be freed from the dark shadow that this sad and shabby affair has cast over it.

The Miami Herald

Miami. Fla., February 1, 1973

ADD one more mystery to the Watergate case: how, after 16 days of trial and a clean sweep of guilty verdicts, could so many questions remain unanswered?

Recall the men involved: an ex-FBI man and attorney serving as counsel for the Committee to Re-Elect the President; several ex-CIA men; a former White House consultant; a security chief for the Committee to Re-Elect the President.

These men revolved around the centers of power in Washington, and in some cases were satellite powers themselves. Going into the trial, the questions did not center on their guilt — they were caught in the act — but on their motive. That must remain a central question.

Who paid them to break into Democratic Party headquarters at the Watergate apartments, and to penetrate private party communications?

We marvel at the prosecutor who summed up his attack by saying confidently that no higher placed Republican officials were involved — only the seven men caught. Chief Judge John Sirica was moved to comment that the question of higher involvement had not been settled.

That same prosecutor repeatedly failed to ask tough questions of the witnesses that observers felt might relate to the question of whether there had been higher involvement. Twice, Judge Sirica sent the jury out of the room and asked some of those questions himself.

It was a trial of unasked as well as unanswered questions, of bad memories, of ludicrous excuses, of patriotic posturing at once pathetic and dangerous.

Presented with such a picture, who can blame the public if it suspects coverup? In a nation already torn by doubts, already questioning its institutions, already dismayed by revelations of the dirty underside of politics, this case deepens the malaise.

Up to this point, the Watergate case adds to the doubts and the dismay. Representative government itself is under attack in the issues of Watergate.

Two chances remain for a more persuasive conclusion: the U.S. Senate will hold hearings in pursuit of new information and a civil suit by the Democratic Party will attempt to fix liability.

For the sake of public confidence in government, we hope they will dispel the sense of unreality that lingers after the trial.

TULSA DAILY WORLD

Tulsa, Okla., February 8, 1973

WE DON'T hold much hope that the U.S. Senate investigation into the Watergate spying incident will be able to rise above partisan politics.

In theory Congressional bodies should be able to look into matters of importance and divorce them from partisanship. But as a practical matter that is about like asking a Senator to forget what State he comes from.

If anyone could conduct an impartial, objective inquiry into the bugging of Democratic National Committee headquarters, it would be Sen. SAM ERVIN JR. of North Carolina, who is scheduled to head the investigation. ERVIN, a Democrat, is highly respected in Congress as a man of fairness and integrity.

But it doesn't take an astute expert in politics to realize that some other Democrats are drooling at the chance to leap in and take a bite out of the NIXON Administration in the Watergate probe. Sen. BARRY GOLDWATER refers to "indications that a Democrat-controlled committee may set about conducting a fishing expedition designed to destroy the Republican Party."

Republicans have some partisan notions of their own. Senate GOP Leader HUGH SCOTT of Pennsylvania says he has "wholesale evidence of wiretapping" of his party in the 1968 campaign. And GOLDWATER wants the inquiry to be broadened to delve into alleged Democratic spying on his PRESIDENTIAL campaign in '64.

Obviously the Democrats aren't going to fall for those ideas. They figure they have the Republicans pinned down for 1972 misdeeds and they certainly don't want to go roaming around in other waters.

The upshot is that there will be so much babble and so many distractions in this inquiry that the public is likely to be turned off—refusing to buy any of it. That was a common reaction to the Watergate fuss during the '72 campaign, that it was a lot of politics and both parties probably were guilty of similar acts.

Whether that is true or not, it is a widely held view—and it makes ERVIN's job that much tougher. Like it or not, the Courts are a more believable forum than Congress for airing alleged criminal or immoral acts rooted in politics.

The New York Times

New York, N.Y., February 1, 1973

The conviction of two of the senior officials in President Nixon's campaign organization for criminal conspiracy, burglary and wiretapping of the Democratic National Committee's Watergate headquarters proves that this sinister operation was no trivial escapade by unimportant persons. It was part of a larger, far-flung, well-financed plan to use political espionage and sabotage techniques to disrupt and defeat the political opposition. The intrusion of these police-state methods into domestic politics is without precedent and deserves the most thoroughgoing exposure and condemnation.

The White House has dissembled again and again in a frantic effort to divert the searchlight of public suspicion from its own responsibility for this ugly business. But thanks to the courage and tenacity of Chief Judge John J. Sirica of the United States District Court who presided at the Watergate trial, the public now has on record sworn testimony that former Attorney General John N. Mitchell, the President's campaign manager, and former Secretary of Commerce Maurice H. Stans, his chief money-raiser, personally approved the disbursement of $199,000 to one of the convicted defendants to carry out this espionage. Judge Sirica elicited that testimony from Hugh W. Sloan Jr., the former treasurer of the Committee for the Re-election of the President, after the prosecutor in the case had unconscionably failed to do so.

Mr. Sloan also testified that one of the convicted defendants told him after the police made the Watergate arrests: "My boys got caught last night. I made a mistake by using somebody from here, which I told them I would never do."

That testimony was not contradicted, but neither did Mr. Sloan explain who was meant by "them." It is a fair deduction that senior White House aides as well as Herbert W. Kalmbach, the President's personal lawyer, not only had knowledge of this repulsive operation but also planned it, recruited agents for it, and received their reports.

Dwight L. Chapin, President Nixon's appointments secretary, has been forced to resign because he has been publicly identified as the White House contact for one of the agents. But no one who knows the amiable and loyal Mr. Chapin believes that this young man is more than the "fall guy" for others more senior than himself in the White House apparatus who are still in office.

"All the facts have not been developed by either side," Judge Sirica observed last week to the lawyers for the prosecution and the defense. The indictments were drawn as narrowly as possible, and the Justice Department has been less than ardent in exploring the case.

It is clearly the duty of the Senate to go forward with its inquiry and make an unremitting effort to identify all of the higher-ups and all of the ramifications of this ruthless conspiracy to subvert the normal exercise of political freedom.

New York, N.Y., February 3, 1973

In a letter printed on this page today, an official of the Committee for the Re-election of the President makes the valid point that testimony in the Watergate trial did not establish that former Attorney General John N. Mitchell, campaign chairman, and former Secretary of Commerce Maurice H. Stans, finance chairman, "personally approved" any specific espionage activity against the Democratic party. A reading of the actual transcript of the trial shows that the testimony of Hugh W. Sloan Jr., former treasurer of the committee, was less conclusive than had first appeared to us on the basis of news accounts. The Times regrets the erroneous statement in our editorial of Feb. 1.

During the trial, Jeb Stuart Magruder, who as deputy director of the committee was Mr. Mitchell's top assistant, testified that he had approved cash payments totaling $199,000 to G. Gordon Liddy, who used part of the money to finance the illegal espionage at the Watergate. Mr. Liddy has now been convicted for his part in the affair.

Mr. Sloan stated that as treasurer he had "no idea" for what purpose he had been authorized by Mr. Magruder to hand over the $199,000 to Mr. Liddy. And he added, under the judge's questioning, that he had verified with Mr. Stans, and through him, with Mr. Mitchell, that Mr. Magruder was indeed authorized to approve the payments to Mr. Liddy.

Chief Judge John J. Sirica of the United States District Court, who presided at the trial, has expressed "great doubt" that Mr. Sloan "told us the entire truth," as he reiterated yesterday. We also share the judge's hope that the Senate will bring out the facts the trial never produced—thus revealing how high inside the Administration the chain of responsibility for this sordid chapter in American political history really stretched.

The Boston Globe

Boston, Mass., February 1, 1973

The trial of the Watergate defendants, all of them employed by the Committee to Re-elect the President, is now ended. The two who were convicted on all counts in the burglarizing and bugging of Democratic Party headquarters during last year's presidential campaign (G. Gordon Liddy and James W. McCord Jr.) and the five who earlier had pleaded guilty to all counts (E. Howard Hunt Jr., Bernard L. Barker, Eugenio R. Martinez, Frank A. Sturgis and Virgilio R. Gonzales) presumably will be sentenced to long prison terms. The nation, which right along has tended to view the whole operation as a kind of college boy caper, analogous, say to a harmless panty raid, will be happy to call the book closed.

But the book is not closed. Or, at least, it should not be. From the very beginning the affair has been one of the most bizarre in modern American politics. The whole proceeding from indictment to jury verdict has been a shocking charade in which even Chief Judge John J. Sirica of Washington's US District Court was unable to wring from the defendants any shred of information identifying high White House personages without whose implication, Judge Sirica time and time again implied, the conspiracy could not have been financed or even tolerated.

"I'm sorry, but I do not believe you," the judge said bluntly at one point after defendant Barker had insisted that he had no way of knowing who sent him $177,000 in checks in a blank envelope to help finance the conspiracy. Judge Sirica thus joined newsmen and others who had sat through 16 days of testimony, marveling not at what was disclosed by 62 prosecution and defense witnesses but at what was concealed.

Prosecutor Earl J. Silbert has said he will ask the five defendants who pleaded guilty to appear before the Federal Grand Jury for further questioning on such matters as the exact amount of money that was available to them and its source. One figure that has been mentioned is $700,000, but the sum has been described as "a kind of office petty cash box" that was replenished, always by some mysterious benefactor, whenever it came near to being depleted. One wonders why the indictment against the seven was so neatly tailored in the first place that such matters could be and were sideslipped at the trial.

All of the witnesses had convenient losses of memory whenever Judge Sirica touched upon such sore spots as widely circulated news reports that the defendants have been promised large sums of money for every month they have to spend in prison, with another lump sum promised upon their release. And the White House sometimes released other news seemingly designed to drive Watergate from the headlines.

The day Mr. Hunt pleaded guilty, President Nixon announced the end of most wage and price controls. The day the other four pleaded guilty, Mr. Nixon announced the bombing halt. The day Judge Sirica voiced his suspicion that the "clandestine activities" were wider than had yet been explored, the White House announced that Mr. Nixon would make a TV speech on Vietnam. And yesterday, after the jury had found Mr. Liddy and Mr. McCord guilty, South Vietnamese President Thieu's planned visit to the United States was announced.

For all of the facts in this blatant perversion of the electoral process, the nation now must await the full scale investigation promised by the Senate's foremost constitutionalist and former prosecutor, Sen. Sam J. Ervin Jr. (D-N.C.).

Sen. Ervin will not be so chintzy as were Prosecutor Silbert and his superior, US Attorney Harold Titus, in issuing subpoenas to those who can answer some of the questions that Judge Sirica asked in vain of the only witnesses available to him in the curiously restricted trial that now has come to a preordained end.

The Washington Post

Washington, D.C., February 2, 1973

Well, the Watergate trial is over. Two defendants have been convicted and five others have pleaded guilty. We take no joy in those facts. Seven men's lives are to be changed and so are those of their families. And yet, for all that, there is an unsatisfactory sense that all that was rotten in Denmark is still largely in place. For, what is at issue in the whole Watergate-campaign espionage episode is not merely whether some men were or were not guilty of breaking and entering some offices in the Watergate complex, but rather how badly the electoral process has been mangled and abused, and by whom. The conclusion of the trial leaves much of that right where it was before court was convened.

There is now no longer any question about the fact that the Watergate operation and others directed at Sens. Muskie and McGovern were financed by Republican campaign money. Nor, despite vehement denials by top Republican campaign figures, is there any longer any question that there was a secret fund—nor any question that very large sums of unsupervised cash were floating around in the President's campaign. The questions remaining have to do with precisely how widespread the espionage activities were, exactly who directed and authorized them and how strong an effort those in authority made to get to the bottom of the whole affair once aspects of it had come to light.

Confirmation of some of the press reports (greeted at the time of publication by artful denials on the part of campaign officials) concerning the extent of the espionage operation has come in a letter reporting the preliminary findings of the Senate Judiciary Committee's subcommittee on Administrative Practice and Procedure. In that letter to Chairman Eastland, Sen. Kennedy reports that the committee's information "strongly indicates that a wide range of espionage and sabotage activities did occur during the recent presidential campaign." The Kennedy letter goes on to note close White House contacts of one of the "key participants" and also indicates that some of the financing was arranged "through a key Republican fund-raiser who is a close associate of President Nixon's." Finally the Kennedy report notes that neither the criminal investigation nor the administrative inquiry conducted in the White House "included any substantial investigation of the alleged sabotage and espionage operation" apart from those surrounding the Watergate incident.

But, even more than that still remains on the table. The trial brought out the fact that an amount close to a quarter of a million dollars was made available for the "intelligence operations." Even the operations scrutinized at the trial were something other than purely defensive intelligence gathering. Tom Gregory testified about how he attempted to penetrate the highest levels of the Muskie and the McGovern campaigns. And at whose authority was all of this financed? Judge Sirica elicited the fact that John N. Mitchell and Maurice Stans verified the authority of the deputy campaign director to disburse huge amounts of unaccounted cash for the intelligence operation.

Yet the trial leaves the impression that no one in authority knew how that quarter of a million dollars was spent, and to this day, the bulk of that money is unaccounted for. It leaves one a bit breathless to contemplate the expenditure of that kind of money with no one in a responsible position knowing what it was going for in the campaign of a President who prides himself on being an efficient administrator. That puzzle too is still on the table.

Thus, Judge Sirica's question about the authorization for the expenditure of the money and the purposes to which it was to be put are basic. Two of Mr. Nixon's closest advisers, a former Attorney General and a former Secretary of Commerce authorized the payments. But how much did they know? What did they think the money was buying and how did they think the information some of it had purchased had been acquired? Who else knew about this and how high in Mr. Nixon's councils were they? And, for that matter, are some of them still there?

These are important questions not simply because curious circumstances elicit large amounts of curiosity, but because the higher the authority for all of this dirty business and the broader its scope, the more the electoral process was mangled. And the questions are important because the integrity of the government and its investigative and reporting operations are very much on the line here too. Finally, it is important because it is necessary before the next election for the Congress and for the people to draw some lines between what is legitimate campaign conduct and what is criminal behavior and to decide what to do about huge amounts of cash sloshing around in presidential election campaigns.

The trial is over. But heavy questions still remain and a great many thoughtful people are ashamed by what we have learned. But it is even worse than that when one contemplates Sen. Mansfield's basic truth, "The question is not political, it is constitutional." Therein lies the essence and the importance of the task that congressional investigators will probably have to complete if the public is ever to be told the truth about this demeaning and destructive business.

ST. LOUIS POST-DISPATCH

St. Louis, Mo., February 3, 1973

As evidence of political espionage and sabotage began accumulating in the months preceding last November's election, it became apparent that the Watergate break-in represented only the most spectacular example of the dirty work that was being conducted on behalf of President Nixon's campaign. What was lacking then was the precise shape and magnitude of this effort to frustrate the process of orderly elections, and the identity of those responsible for the grand design. The Watergate trial is over now, its seven defendants all having pleaded or been found guilty, and the nation is no closer to this knowledge.

The trial itself, of course, of necessity was confined to the facts of the break-in and bugging of the Democratic National Committee offices. Still, a show of vigor by the prosecution would have been an encouraging indication that the Government was intent on getting to the bottom of the affair—and by extension could have been read as a sign that similarly intensive collateral efforts were under way regarding other acts of sabotage and spying. As it turned out, the prosecution declined to press witnesses on matters that might have been embarrassing to the Nixon re-election apparatus and it fell to U.S. District Judge John J. Sirica to do the most probing questioning, interrogations which almost always drew blanks.

We say "almost" because Judge Sirica did manage to establish a point of greater significance. Under questioning by the judge, Hugh W. Sloan Jr., former treasurer of the Finance Committee to Re-elect the President, admitted that the payment of $199,000 to one of the defendants had been "verified" with both former Commerce Secretary Stans and former Attorney General Mitchell, the two top figures in the re-election committee. The Government, however, did not think it worthwhile to ask either Messrs. Stans or Mitchell to testify.

Such an omission suggests a greater dedication to covering up the essential facts of the Watergate case—who ordered the job, who paid for it, who approved it—than in exposing them

But exposed they must be ultimately if the people are to have their confidence restored in the integrity of the electoral process. The grand jury that indicted the seven men is still impaneled and could be used to good effect, especially inasmuch as none of the Watergate defendants could now plead self-incrimination when asked sensitive questions.

Most certainly the lead provided by Mr. Sloan ought to be pursued by the Senate's investigation under the direction of Senator Ervin. Unlike the trial, however, Mr. Ervin's probe ought to cover far more ground. What role if any did White House insiders play in the dirty business? How extensive were the sabotage activities such as those allegedly carried out by Donald H. Segretti, a California lawyer? And what about all those fake letters and telephone calls which plagued Democratic presidential contenders?

After the Watergate trial, there is more need than ever for answers.

THE SUN

Baltimore, Md., February 1, 1973

The dismal performance of the prosecution in the Watergate trial shows quite clearly that federal attorneys employed by the Nixon administration are not about to seek out the whole truth in this shocking affair. If the American public is to learn the full extent of the Republican intelligence and espionage operation during the last election, it will have to hope that congressional investigators do a better job than the Justice Department. The Senate has gotten off to a promising start by entrusting its probe to Senator Sam Ervin, an intrepid and independent upholder of law. But in view of the politics and money and influence and flimflam involved in the Watergate case, it would be wise to withhold commendations until the results are in.

Senator Ervin has stated that when his hearings begin he will give some past and present top-echelon figures in the Nixon administration an opportunity to explain themselves. We await such testimony with interest since the prosecutors in the Watergate case took so narrow a view of their duties. We would like the former Secretary of Commerce, Maurice H. Stans, to tell the Senate why his Committee for the Re-election of the President found it necessary to finance activities out of a $350,-000 cash fund that could not be adequately audited. We would like to discover just what kind of intelligence operations Mr. Stans and John N. Mitchell, former attorney general, envisaged when they authorized large payments to the Watergate Seven. We would be intrigued if other witnesses were produced to show just how far the GOP intelligence network extended and just what kind of activities Republican leaders considered acceptable in their campaign against the Democrats.

The Nixon administration's explanation of this sad business is woefully unconvincing. It is not enough for the government (and its prosecutors) to try to prove that only the Watergate defendants were up to illegal dirty tricks. What is more important in determining the level of political morality in this country is what the GOP leadership considers legitimate dirty tricks. The infiltration of informers into rival organizations? The circulation of phony campaign literature to discredit opponents? The slapdash handling of money for unspoken purposes in defiance of statutory requirements?

Obviously Watergate is neither the first nor will it be the last scandal that reflects adversely on political behavior in this country. Both major parties, indeed all political parties, have always been plagued by operatives with a highly arrogant attitude toward the law. In all too many cases, this arrogance remains undetected and unpunished. While many questions have yet to be answered, this much can be said for the Watergate affair: It has served a purpose if it has made us more alert to the dangers of conduct that could undermine the integrity of our political system.

The Charlotte Observer

Charlotte, N.C., February 4, 1973

The Watergate trial has drawn to a close with guilt established in the cases of all seven defendants. But that hardly testifies to the prowess of the U.S. attorneys. The Nixon Administration's prosecution of its own campaign officials and workers proved to be an utter sham, a contemptible compromising of the integrity of the U.S. Department of Justice.

The prosecution seemed determined not to allow the court to arrive at the full truth in the case, a circumstance which moved U.S. District Judge John J. Sirica to protest not only during the trial but also after it was over. He noted that the prosecution declined to call several witnesses he had suggested and took depositions in private from such Nixon organization officials as Maurice Stans, thus preventing cross-examination of them.

During the trial the judge had found himself asking the tough questions which the "sweetheart" prosecution would not ask. And in the end he said that as a citizen and a judge he hopes a congressional investigation will get "to the bottom of what happened in this case."

At the outset of the trial it was reported that the Justice Department representatives were consulting with defense attorneys, a not-unusual practice, but one with ignoble implications in this case. Justice's attorneys apparently were indicating to the defense that they would do some trading, accepting guilty pleas on some of the charges and dropping others to avoid a trial.

The judge proved unwilling to go along with all this; for instance, he rejected White House consultant E. Howard Hunt's effort to escape further prosecution by pleading guilty to three of the six counts against him, and Hunt then pleaded guilty to all six counts. The judge was thus frustrated in one more effort to get to the facts. As one observer noted, it is difficult for a judge to halt defendants' desire to stampede to prison.

The Justice Department's prosecutors also made arguments at times that would have done credit to the defense. They argued at one point that a high-ranking Nixon organization official not on trial, Hugh W. Sloan Jr., "had no possible remote connection, direct or indirect, with the Watergate incident."

Yet Judge Sirica, who then summoned Sloan to answer questions without the presence of the jury, quickly had Sloan admitting that he turned over at least $199,000 to defendant Gordon Liddy, the boss of the break-in and bugging expedition at Democratic National Committee headquarters on June 17. And how did Sloan hand over that money from the Nixon campaign committee? Much of it was in $100 bills, contrary to the organization's usual practice of making disbursements by check.

Did Atty. Gen. Richard Kleindienst ever really bear down on this case? Clearly not. A former Nixon Administration official, Clark R. Mollenhoff, has written of that fact with disgust. He has noted in the publication Human Events that Kleindienst could have used federal immunity laws in the way it has used them against officials of organized crime to identify higher-ups in criminal activity. "It would appear from general observation that getting to the 'Mr. Big' in the Watergate affair is being blocked by the very type of 'conspiracy of silence' that has paved the way for organized crime to shield its bosses from the law," Mr. Mollenhoff wrote.

The prosecution never pressed on to find the "Mr. Bigs" in this crime. It was, after all, a case of the Nixon organization's prosecuting itself. So, left unanswered are questions about who really authorized the crime, as well as questions which have arisen since Watergate. For instance, who is providing the huge sums no doubt needed to pay the high-powered lawyers used by the defense? What of a report that the defendants going to jail will ultimately receive large sums of money for serving their time?

Sen. Sam Ervin's forthcoming inquiry into the Watergate case and related illegal activities by the Nixon organization will, we hope, bring answers to some of these questions. The senator can be of great service to the country in pressing for the truth.

As for the government's argument that only these seven defendants were responsible for Watergate, our view is expressed in the words Judge Sirica used when five defendants pleaded guilty and tried to take the whole matter upon themselves:

"I don't believe you."

THE CINCINNATI ENQUIRER

Cincinnati, Ohio, February 6, 1973

THE TRIAL THAT resulted in the burglary and conspiracy convictions of G. Gordon Liddy and James McCord Jr. in connection with the attempted bugging of the Democratic National Committee's offices in Washington's Watergate complex lasted 16 days, during which 60 witnesses were heard and more than 100 pieces of evidence presented. But the public now knows little more about the Watergate incident than it did before the trial began. In this respect, the outcome of the trial is as unsatisfactory as that in which James Earl Ray pleaded guilty of the 1968 slaying of civil-rights leader Martin Luther King Jr.

In cases of such national importance, it would appear that some mechanism should exist for the discovery of the truth, over and above the mere legalisms of an individual's guilt or innocence, either as an added function of the court or along the lines of the commission headed by former Chief Justice Earl Warren to investigate the assassination of President Kennedy in 1963.

Had Lee Harvey Oswald lived to stand trial for the shooting of President Kennedy, he, like Ray, might have pleaded guilty, leaving the underlying motivations and details open to public conjecture. Even with the well-documented findings of the Warren commission — which was composed of distinguished, irreproachable men — the conjectures about the Kennedy slaying have flourished. But these conjectures have, and rightly so, been dismissed as irresponsible.

Without the commission's work, however, the ravings of the extremists might have been taken seriously by a good many Americans.

To be sure, there are plans for Senate hearings about the Watergate affair, but those hearings are likely to be so partisan in nature as to lack credibility. Although five years after the fact is probably too long to get at the whole truth of Dr. King's murder, the time for appointment of a blue-ribbon panel to investigate the Watergate incident is now, when the matter is still fresh and when the rights of the defendants, now convicted, would no longer be jeopardized by its extralegal proceedings.

GRAY FACES SENATE OPPOSITION; TESTIMONY ON WATERGATE BARRED

The Senate Judiciary Committee held hearings in late February and March on the nomination of L. Patrick Gray 3rd, acting director of the Federal Bureau of Investigation, as permanent director. Among the important developments:

■ On Feb. 19 Sen. Robert C. Byrd (D, W. Va.) charged that Gray, a long time political associate of President Nixon, had been "openly partisan" during the 1972 presidential election.

■ Gray admitted Feb. 28 under Byrd's questioning that extensive records of the FBI probe of the Watergate affair had been supplied to the White House. Gray said John W. Dean 3rd, the presidential counsel conducting a separate White House inquiry into Watergate, had asked for and received all Watergate data beginning in August 1972. Gray also testified that Dean had been present when the FBI conducted investigative interviews with White House personnel.

■ Gray's involvement with Dean led to a unanimous committee vote March 13 to "invite" Dean to testify on the Gray nomination. The following day, Dean informed the committee that he would not appear to testify. Nixon had said a day earlier that members and former members of his personal staff normally would refuse to testify formally before Congressional committees.

■ Gray informed the committee March 20 that he was under new orders from Attorney General Richard Kleindienst not to discuss the Watergate case in the hearings. Gray's new orders forbade answering any questions that would reveal information from FBI files. Gray also said that the Administration had superseded his earlier offer to open the FBI's Watergate files to any senator who wished to examine them. As a result of an agreement worked out March 16 by Kleindienst, Sen. Sam J. Ervin (D, N.C.) and Sen. Howard Baker (R, Tenn.), chairman and vice chairman, respectively, of the select committee investigating the Watergate affair, Senate access to the files was restricted to Ervin and Baker and the chief counsels of the investigating panel.

■ Sen. Ervin said March 18 he would seek the arrest of any White House aide who refused to testify before his select committee.

■ Gray testified March 22 that Dean "probably" lied to FBI agents investigating Watergate when he allegedly denied knowledge of whether defendant E. Howard Hunt had an office at the White House.

■ Senate Republicans joined in the demand for full White House cooperation at Senate hearings on Gray and Watergate following disclosures March 26 that convicted Watergate defendant James W. McCord Jr. had told Senate probers that Dean and Jeb Stuart Magruder, former deputy director of Nixon's re-election committee, had prior knowledge of the Watergate spying operation.

The key question that must be addressed to any FBI director is whether he has kept intact the FBI's record for probity, particularly in matters involving political conflicts. That record was not perfect under J. Edgar Hoover but it was good, largely because of Mr. Hoover's toughness in the face of political pressures. Anyone who could do as well would give little cause for fear, though there would be much to fear if management of the national police agency should become politically partisan.

Mr. Gray came into the job with no police experience. He was a retired Naval officer practicing law in Connecticut. His main qualification had been a long-standing political association with Richard Nixon. At the Senate hearings he sounds like a man who wanted to take an independent line at the FBI but has not been entirely able to forget his old loyalties and associations.

If such a dichotomy existed, it got the acid test soon after Mr. Gray's appointment when the Watergate case broke. Since the GOP and White House were implicated in the break-in and bugging at the Democrats' Watergate headquarters in Washington, few cases could have been more political. Five men pleaded guilty and two others were convicted, and three of the seven worked either for the Nixon re-election committee or the White House. The FBI deserves substantial credit for the investigations leading to the case's outcome.

But the Senate testimony reveals that Mr. Gray buckled before the insistence of former Attorney General John N. Mitchell that the FBI could not question his wife, who had made some unguarded public comments about mysterious doings. And he acceded to a request from John W. Dean III, the President's counsel, for FBI investigative data on the Watergate caper. Mr. Hoover had made it a point never to give raw investigative data to anyone, the President included. The data that Mr. Dean got may or may not have been "raw" but it is said to have been voluminous. Moreover, Mr. Dean was allowed to sit in on some FBI interviews with White House employes.

Mr. Gray responded to Senate doubts about these procedures by saying that any Senator could look at the Watergate files as well. The case is "unique," he said, and does not set a precedent for release of FBI data. Further, he insisted that he hit the ceiling over some other White House requests and fully intends to keep the FBI out of politics.

The Senate is fully justified in giving a candidate for such a sensitive post its full-court press. While it may uncover further embarrassments, so far it has turned up nothing that would absolutely demand Mr. Gray's rejection. If confirmed as permanent director, he would be in a stronger position to keep the FBI "completely and absolutely non-political," as he vows.

Our general attitude is that the Senate ought to approve presidential appointments unless there is really damaging evidence against the nominee. But given Mr. Gray's less-than-impeccable performance, his origin in a political rather than law-enforcement background, and the sensitive nature of the post, it's easy to see why a skeptical Senator might take another view.

THE WALL STREET JOURNAL
New York, N.Y., March 8, 1973

L. Patrick Gray III has been getting what the FBI calls a "full court press," or an all-out grilling, from the Senate Judiciary Committee in preparation for a Senate vote on whether to confirm him as the FBI's permanent director.

In basketball, a full-court press can either break the opposing team's nerve or give it renewed determination. Mr. Gray is holding up reasonably well. He doesn't sound like the President's patsy, which is what some critics said he would be when President Nixon appointed him acting director 10 months ago. But the record of his stewardship is somewhat less impressive than his rhetoric.

The Charlotte Observer

Charlotte, N.C., March 9, 1973

Patrick Gray has been struggling to show some semblance of independence from the White House. But even as he has done so, his testimony before the Senate Judiciary Committee has crackled with good reasons why he should not be confirmed as director of the FBI.

Mr. Gray is a man with his eye on winning favor with his superiors. During nine months as acting director of the FBI, that has been too much of a concern with him. It shows. And it has shown again during the past three days in little things, as well as big things, that he has told the Senate committee.

Why did he give White House counsel John W. Dean III reports on FBI interviews with three Nixon campaign workers who were willing to talk privately to the FBI but anxious for their words not to get back to the Nixon organization? "He's a part of the chain of command in which I fit," said Mr. Gray.

Why did he stop answering questions about Watergate at one point? "I'm in enough trouble now," said Mr. Gray, apparently thinking of the White House.

Anxious To Please

Mr. Gray is making himself sound like a young corporate vice president who is anxious to please the management and who thinks it is quite daring to say or do anything not absolutely pleasing. That is not our idea of a man with enough substance to be director of the FBI.

It is difficult to imagine how a man could have been more completely responsive politically to the Nixon organization during only nine months at the FBI's helm.

—During the presidential campaign Mr. Gray ordered 21 FBI offices in 14 states to gather and report suggestions on how President Nixon might handle campaign issues having to do with criminal justice.

—He made speeches in Butte, Cleveland and Spokane that were obvious efforts on behalf of Mr. Nixon's candidacy. It has now been disclosed that a White House aide, in a memorandum, asked Mr. Gray to make the Cleveland appearance because Ohio was "vital" to Mr. Nixon's candidacy.

—Although the White House was involved in Watergate and related bizarre campaign activities, Mr. Gray gave the White House the FBI's investigative reports on Watergate.

— Mr. Gray apparently quickly yielded to Robert C. Mardian, a top Nixon campaign official, when Mr. Mardian said he should not answer FBI questions about Watergate because he had a lawyer-client relationship with principals in the Watergate case. (What principals — the seven convicted? When was Mr. Mardian an attorney for them? And why was he their lawyer if the seven were only unauthorized renegades, as the Nixon organization has contended?)

— Mr. Gray refused to allow FBI agents to interview Martha Mitchell when John Mitchell, who had headed the Nixon reelection effort, said he would not permit that. But, in testimony, Mr. Gray says he made that judgment without even knowing what the FBI wanted to learn from her. He acknowledged that it was "not customary" for a husband to be allowed to stand in the way in such cases.

— Time magazine reports that, until the Supreme Court stopped it, Mr. Gray was permitting the FBI — at the White House's request — to tap the telephones of newsmen and some White House officials in order to discover the source of news "leaks."

It is clear that Mr. Gray has been far more willing than J. Edgar Hoover ever was to bow to political demands and to questionable requests from White House aides. The FBI's reputation is suffering because of that. And it will suffer more if Mr. Gray wins Senate approval as director, only to be turned out the next time the Democrats are in power. For decades the FBI was regarded as being beyond the reach of political turnovers.

The Senate's Choice

We agree with Sen. Sam J. Ervin Jr. that the Judiciary Committee should insist upon having testimony on FBI-Watergate matters from Mr. Dean of the White House, even though President Nixon now has warned he would invoke "executive privilege" to prevent that. Mr. Nixon can do what he says. But if he does, the Senate should counter that interference by refusing to confirm Mr.

Sen. Robert C. Byrd, the conservative Democrat from West Virginia, has expressed it well:

"The Watergate cloud hangs over this nomination. Until we know in fact that the FBI did not act to protect higher-ups, we ought not to confirm."

St. Louis Globe-Democrat

St. Louis, Mo., March 15, 1973

The Senate Judiciary Committee's treatment of L. Patrick Gray III, President Nixon's nominee for permanent head of the FBI, is even worse than its browbeating of Richard Kleindienst when the latter was questioned by the committee prior to his confirmation as attorney general.

Democrats on the committee are using Gray as a hostage in their continuing battle with Mr. Nixon over the Watergate case. It has been almost impossible to determine whether this is a probe of Watergate or Gray's qualifications. So far nearly all the questioning has been aimed at White House aides who might have knowledge of the Watergate bugging.

Now the committee is threatening to oppose Gray's confirmation if the President refuses to allow his counsel, John Dean, to testify before the committee.

Democratic committee members are attempting to convey the impression that Gray acted improperly in turning over certain FBI reports to Dean during the Watergate investigation.

As far as can be determined, Gray was only cooperating with the White House in its own probe of Mr. Nixon's aides. Dean had been named by President Nixon to conduct the special White House probe. So why shouldn't he have sought, and been given, information the FBI had obtained in its probe?

It became obvious more than a week ago that Judiciary Committee Democrats were far more interested in trying to embarrass President Nixon than in evaluating the qualifications of Gray to head the FBI.

Gray has repeatedly offered to make the complete files of the FBI probe of Watergate available to committee members if they would promise not to make public statements that would affect the right to privacy of innocent parties in the reports.

The committee has refused to accept Gray's offer. Instead certain of its Democratic members continue to use Gray as a means of trying to get at Dean and other top aides of the President.

If the Judiciary Committee genuinely wants to evaluate the work of Gray and the FBI on Watergate, what better source material could it get than the complete files of the investigation?

The fact that the committee has not accepted Gray's offer indicates the Democratic majority has no stomach for such a direct approach.

If the primary intent of the Democrats on the committee is to investigate Watergate, let them say so openly—and then conduct a separate investigation of the case. To use Gray as a foil in this affair is shameful and even more malicious than the attempt the committee made to link Kleindienst to allegations (never proven) concerning International Telephone & Telegraph.

☆ ☆ ☆

Gray, a native St. Louisan, has an outstanding record. He served with honor as a Navy submarine captain. As a lawyer he rose to the No. 2 spot in the Justice Department. In our opinion he has performed admirably since being named acting head of the FBI and should prove to be a worthy successor to the late J. Edgar Hoover if he is confirmed.

The Judiciary Committee Democrats should stop using Gray as a whipping boy in their battle with the President and get down to the business of weighing Gray's ability to perform as permanent head of the FBI. The damage these Democrats are doing to the credibility of the Judiciary Committee is far greater than any punishment they can inflict on Mr. Nixon or his aides. In the meantime, they should get off Pat Gray's back and give him the fair hearing to which he is entitled.

THE COMMERCIAL APPEAL
Memphis, Tenn., March 15, 1973

PRESIDENT NIXON has the power to keep White House counsel John W. Dean III from testifying in Senate hearings on the nomination of L. Patrick Gray III to head the FBI. No question about it. The executive privilege applies. But the Senate and its Judiciary Committee have the power to reject Gray.

The question is which matters most to Nixon—having Pat Gray approved as FBI director, or keeping the Senate at arm's length from the White House?

The fact that Dean has now agreed to answer questions in writing is not likely to appease the Senate. A polished written response, undoubtedly cleared with the White House, probably would not be considered an acceptable substitute for the give and take of a hearing. Dean's offer may be an effort by the President to strike a compromise, but the senators appear more interested in substance than in form. Only very frank answers by Dean, written or spoken, apparently would suffice.

There are many ramifications to this confrontation. Partisan politics undoubtedly is involved. It is also an extension of the power struggle between Congress and the President resulting from Nixon's refusal to spend appropriated funds. The Watergate bugging case, still unresolved, is an element. There is the issue of the fitness and capability of Pat Gray for the job. And it goes beyond that to the question of what the nation wants the Federal Bureau of Investigation to be. If the FBI is to have the confidence of the public its integrity must be inviolate. Above all, it must be above the pressures of Washington politics. Its directorship, held only by the late J. Edgar Hoover until Gray was named acting director last May, is one of the most important appointments the President must send to the Senate for confirmation. And Hoover—whatever his faults in later years—is a hard man to follow. From its beginning in the early 1920s through its first 50 years of existence he gave the FBI the image of untouchable honesty.

THE SENATORS WHO want to know everything there is to know about Pat Gray are doing no more than their job demands. In any presidential appointment which requires the advice and consent of the Senate, there are hearings, and when it is a top post the investigating senators are expected to look into the qualifications of the appointee from every conceivable angle.

Any question which can be answered should be asked.

Senate Judicial Committee members have asked some pertinent questions which have not been fully answered. Among them is why presidential counsel Dean was present during FBI interrogations of White House personnel concerning the Watergate case. Also, why was Dean allowed to go over FBI raw material in the same matter? There is another question about the White House request for the FBI to gather data on various candidates in last November's elections, and the forced retirement of Thomas Bishop, an assistant FBI director who accepted blame for carrying out the White House assignment.

Pat Gray obviously cannot tell the Senate committee why the White House did these things.

And that leaves some people wondering whether Gray made his decisions in such matters free from political meddling, or whether he acquiesced to White House pressures because he wanted to please the President and get the coveted FBI job.

SENATE DEMOCRATS appear to be enjoying their power to make Nixon and his staff squirm. But they have every right to protest when the thorough kind of inquiry that is normally made in such an appointment is blocked off. It only makes the public wonder all the more what reason John Dean might have—aside from precedent—for not testifying.

President Nixon can win the executive privilege argument. But it may be a hollow victory if he has to sacrifice Pat Gray and embroil the FBI in controversy in so doing.

Los Angeles Times
Los Angeles, Calif., March 14, 1973

President Nixon has extended the doctrine of executive privilege to former members of his personal staff, a step that could and undoubtedly will be used to shield one or more past White House employes from questioning by a Senate committee about the Watergate bugging scandal. Some constitutional experts in and out of Congress have denounced this latest exercise of presidential power, but denunciations won't revoke it. Executive privilege, by custom, is what the President says it is. Mr. Nixon knows that as well as anyone else, and he seems confident that Congress will have to accept what he has done.

There is nothing explicitly in the law that gives a President authority to make active or former employes of the executive branch immune from congressional questioning. Rather the practice has been built on precedent, and the precedents have been validated by need and experience. What the principle comes down to is that communications within the executive branch must be protected as a matter of fairness and for the sake of efficiency. Without that privilege the policy-making process can be jeopardized.

The trouble is that, with his latest expansion of executive privilege, Mr. Nixon seems to have moved beyond essential protection of confidentiality in policy making to protection of possible wrongdoing, and the immunity shield was never intended to serve that purpose.

It is taken for granted in Washington that Mr. Nixon's action was prompted in good part by a desire to keep the special Senate committee from questioning his former appointments secretary, Dwight Chapin, about the Watergate scandal. Evidence already clearly points to some involvement by White House personnel in the effort to bug Democratic Party headquarters, and Chapin's name has come up as a link in the political espionage case. None of this has anything to do with policy making or the need for confidentiality in the conduct of executive branch business. It has to do with possible illegality.

Mr. Nixon has taken a valid doctrine and weakened its legitimacy by using it as a political tool. In choosing to prevent the appearance before a congressional committee of persons who may have knowledge of criminal activity, he has elevated an interest in avoiding political embarrassment above an interest in establishing the truth. That is not executive privilege; it is executive arrogance, and in the end it can only harm the Administration, and the doctrine of executive privilege as well.

The Charleston Gazette
Charleston, W.Va., March 14, 1973

West Virginia's Sen. Robert C. Byrd, the Democratic whip and a member of the committee examining Gray's credentials to be permanent director, summed up his opposition well when he said:

"Personally, I feel that Gray has been too politically active. In any other case such as that for a Cabinet post, it would not bother me too much. But I don't believe the head of the FBI should be a political person. The politicalization of the FBI is tantamount to setting up an American gestapo."

Placing a man of such inclinations in the position of FBI director would be particularly dangerous in view of presidential tendencies to head the Justice Department, of which the FBI is an arm, with political appointees. Under President Truman, J. Howard McGrath was moved from Democratic national chairman to attorney general. President Eisenhower appointed his campaign manager, Herbert Brownell, to that post. President Kennedy gave it to his brother Robert, his chief political adviser. President Nixon's first choice was his campaign manager, John N. Mitchell, and Mitchell's successor, Richard G. Kleindienst, has shown he's not above playing politics with justice. Indeed, over the last 25 years, only President Johnson to his credit gave professional attention to the office with his appointment of Ramsey Clark.

Certainly the Justice Department itself over the last four years has been deeply involved in politics, ever ready to protect the politically favored and to spy upon those looked upon as political enemies. To add to this an FBI director willing to play the political game — for the President, for the Congress, or for anyone—would be going too far.

Sen. Byrd has stated clearly that he will not vote for the confirmation of Gray. But we have not yet heard from West Virginia's senior senator, Jennings Randolph.

We're well aware of Sen. Randolph's long standing policy of voting to confirm presidential appointees on the ground that the president has the right and the responsibility to make such appointments. We appreciate Randolph's position up to a point — the point being that there is little reason for having the confirmation process if the Senate is to apply automatically the rubber stamp of approval, no matter who or what is involved.

Clearly, especially in the present situation, the new FBI director should be a man of impeccable qualifications who would be acceptable not only to President Nixon but to the next president if he be a Democrat. Otherwise we can expect to see a change of director with every new president — the politicizing of a federal agency whose independence should be kept sacred. Surely Sen. Randolph can perceive the dangers of Gray's confirmation.

To put it mildly, the Federal Bureau of Investigation has not been the same since L. Patrick Gray III took over as acting director 10 months ago.

From Gray's own testimony before the Senate Judiciary Committee, and from other evidence, one is led to the conclusion that the once-independent FBI has become immersed in politics and seems more interested in feeding information to the White House about the Watergate affair than in getting to the bottom of that shabby business.

It is hardly to be expected, for example, that the director of the FBI would trot off to Cleveland to make a political speech — as Gray did last year — at the request of a White House underling with the admonition that "Ohio is important to us." And it is hardly the measure of a non-political director to permit White House counsel John W. Dean III to sit in on all interviews with White House staffers, which Gray said he did against his better judgment because "if we want the interview, we take it the best way we can get it."

We do not think Gray is an evil man; indeed, he has made some admirable moves to update the bureau. But there is every reason to believe he is pliable, especially when the pressure of presidential politics is applied.

THE ANN ARBOR NEWS

Ann Arbor, Mich., March 11, 1973

L. PATRICK GRAY III suffers by comparison with his predecessor at the FBI (J. Edgar Hoover), as does nearly everyone who tries to fill a job formerly held by a household name.

The recognition factor hasn't been the only drawback to Gray, however. He does not have police experience for the job of director of the FBI. In a town where loyalty currently is held in the highest regard, Gray comes on as a loyalist of the first stripe.

It's obvious Gray wants to keep his job. As sincere and well-meaning as he has been, there's no way he was going to cross President Nixon or the White House staff last year.

At his confirmation hearings before the Senate Judiciary Committee, the political implications of Gary's speeches, his decisions concerning investigations of the Watergate bugging incident and charges of political espionage, the alleged electronic surveillance of newsmen by the government and the alleged leak of FBI documents all became subjects of intense questioning of the acting director.

Gray's speeches last year were not "designed, planned, written or intended" to be political; they merely expressed his "feeling about his country." That may be, but undoubtedly Gray wouldn't have jeopardized his standing as FBI chief in these speeches if it hadn't been for pressure from the White House.

*   *   *

GRAY stood up reasonably well under Watergate probing. His office worked hard in investigations which led to the case's outcome. But Gray also turned over to the White House upon request considerable data on the bugging incident.

At that point he apparently decided the matter was out of his hands: But he already had done something Mr. Hoover would never have done, i.e., turn over FBI investigative data. At his hearing, Gray presumed there was nothing irregular in the way that the White House handled the FBI reports. Hoover never gave any President or his staff the opportunity to use any such data to cover up or misuse in any way.

But if these examples of Gray's stewardship are grounds for criticism, they are hardly the stuff of rejection of his nomination. Here is a man worried about the credibility of the FBI, as he put it, and one who is determined to keep that organization out of partisan politics. He should be taken at his word.

As acting director, Gray has been under the gun to play the loyalist and not do or say anything which might tend to cut White House support from under him. As full time director, Gray would become the man he wants to be. In time, he would prove his intentions to keep the FBI "absolutely non-political." It may take a man with a political background to make a promise like that and go out of his way to make it stick, simply because he knows his every move will be watched for signs of favoritism.

The Detroit News

Detroit, Mich., March 15, 1973

Rarely has a committee of the U.S. Senate played a more brazen and ruthless game of politics than the Judiciary Committee is now playing with L. Patrick Gray III, President Nixon's nominee for the post of FBI director.

As acting head of the FBI, Gray has already demonstrated his ability to run the FBI in an effective and efficient manner. It is safe to say that if he were the appointee of a Democratic president, the Democrats on the Judiciary Committee would be singing his praises instead of trying to wash him down the political drain.

Ironically, Gray's nomination stands in jeopardy because he has displayed a wide measure of candor, the alleged lack of which drew so much criticism from liberals against the late J. Edgar Hoover. Hoover's detractors said he was too independent, too aloof, too reluctant to communicate desired information.

Even Sen. Edward Kennedy admits that in his dealings with the committee, Gray has been "responsive." Gray could merely have told the committee, with regard to the Watergate investigation: "This is a matter of highly confidential FBI information, and I cannot talk about it." Instead, he provided detailed information, some of which reflects none too well on people connected with the administration which nominated him.

As a reward for his patient and honest cooperation, Gray hears that he may not be confirmed unless President Nixon allows White House Counsel John W. Dean to testify about the Watergate investigation. Thus, some members of the Judiciary Committee hold Gray hostage in order to get the President to retreat on the issue of executive privilege.

This is politics at its shabbiest. Incidentally, President Nixon sought to avoid a political hassle over the FBI nomination when he appointed Gray last year as an acting, rather than permanent, official. That action assured the next president (It turned out to be Mr. Nixon, but could have been a Democrat, Sen. George McGovern) the opportunity to name his own director.

Such gestures mean nothing, however, to politicians with the smell of blood in their nostrils. Sen. John Tunney, for example, won't relent to the point of accepting an informal conference, rather than a formal committee hearing, with John Dean. The defeat of President Nixon on the issue of executive privilege must be abject and complete.

It is unfortunate that Gray may become a casualty in this conflict between Senate and President, but Mr. Nixon should stick by his guns. He should offer to let Dean talk with the committee under certain prearranged guidelines satisfactory to the White House, but should not retreat on the well-founded principle of executive privilege.

FORT WORTH STAR-TELEGRAM

Fort Worth, Tex., March 15, 1973

President Nixon and the Senate Judiciary Committee appear to be headed into an unpleasant situation if not an outright confrontation over Mr. Nixon's nomination of L. Patrick Gray as permanent director of the FBI.

Gray has been acting director of the bureau since the death of J. Edgar Hoover.

His nomination as permanent successor to Hoover presently is being scrutinized by the judiciary committee. Some members of the committee, at least, have expressed the view that they aren't getting enough factual information to enable them to make an intelligent decision on whether or not to confirm the president's appointment.

Specifically, committee members have voted to invite White House counsel John W. Dean III to appear before them for questioning about an investigation he conducted for the President of the bugging of Democratic headquarters at the Watergate complex in Washington last June.

President Nixon, invoking executive privilege, has said he will not allow Dean to appear before the Senate panel for questioning.

In his own testimony before the Senate committee, Mr. Gray has indicated he and Mr. Dean had extensive communication about the Watergate investigation and the FBI's role in it.

The Senators have heard in much detail Mr. Gray's version of the affair. Now they want Mr. Dean's version.

Sen. Robert Byrd, D-W. Va., a committee member and assistant Democratic leader of the Senate, said flatly that if Mr. Nixon is unwilling to let Dean appear then the President should withdraw Gray's nomination.

Mr. Nixon, in declining to allow Dean to appear, invoked the traditional "executive privilege" under which presidents prevent members of their staffs from making formal appearances before congressional committees.

The President did say, however, he would continue to "provide all necessary and relevant information through informal contacts between my present staff and committees of the Congress in ways which preserve intact the constitutional separation of the branches" of government.

Certainly, years of experience in use of the executive privilege have proven the value, and in some cases, the urgent necessity of the practice. Obviously, if he is to do an effective job, the president must be accorded the right to communicate privately with his advisors and staff members.

At the same time though, as with all rights and privileges, it is one that can be abused if not responsibly and judiciously used.

Because of the suspicions and doubts generated by the Watergate episode — and the FBI's role in investigating it — it seems entirely reasonable that the Senators are entitled to receive all factual and pertinent information about Mr. Gray's role in the affair.

Members of the Senate, like the President, have certain constitutional duties, and one of them is to pass judgment on and confirm appointments made by the president. It is difficult to imagine how they can discharge this duty in the public interest if they are denied information on which to base a decision.

In order to clear the air President Nixon ought to offer a compelling reason why Mr. Dean and other executive staff members with knowledge of the situation are not being allowed to appear before the committee or he ought to send them to testify.

That does not mean Mr. Nixon should surrender forever the executive privilege but rather that he should lend the full weight of his office to clarifying the situation with facts.

ST. LOUIS POST-DISPATCH
St. Louis, Mo., March 14, 1973

So many disturbing developments have emerged from the Senate Judiciary Committee's confirmation hearings on L. Patrick Gray III, President Nixon's nominee for director of the Federal Bureau of Investigation, that it may be well to take a moment to sort them out, for a number of issues not immediately related to Mr. Gray have evolved and threaten to overshadow the primary purpose of the hearings.

That purpose, of course, is for the committee to decide whether in its opinion Mr. Gray is qualified to be permanent FBI director. On his way to demonstrating—conclusively in our opinion—that he is not, Mr. Gray has made a number of significant revelations:

(1) That Mr. Nixon's personal attorney, Herbert Kalmbach, and his recently-resigned appointments secretary, Dwight L. Chapin, recruited and arranged payment of more than $30,000 in Republican campaign funds to Donald H. Segretti, who is alleged to have committed acts of political espionage for Mr. Nixon's campaign. This disclosure from the FBI's acting chief shows that the trail of dirty footprints left by political spies and saboteurs leads directly to the door of the Oval Office.

(2) That, at the request of a junior White House aid, Mr. Gray went to Cleveland and delivered a campaign speech for Mr. Nixon, an errand that indicates what a thoroughly partisan director he is likely to be if confirmed. It also indicates something else, namely, that the White House has no hesitation in using the FBI both as a resource and a commodity to further its own political fortunes. That is why it is so essential that the bureau's next director be a person of sufficient strength to resist attempts to involve it in partisan affairs.

(3) That Mr. Gray has allowed the integrity of the FBI to be thoroughly compromised. Not only did Mr. Gray allow the White House the unusual courtesy of having its special counsel, John W. Dean III, present during interviews with White House staff concerning the Watergate break-in, but he also sent Mr. Dean transcripts of interviews with Republican campaign workers who asked to be questioned by the FBI in private away from White House watchdogs.

Quite naturally, the last disclosure has made members of the committee curious as to the dealings that went on between Mr. Dean, who at the moment was supposed to be conducting the White House's official "investigation" of the Watergate burglary, and Mr. Gray. Even before the committee voted unanimously yesterday to ask Mr. Dean to testify before it, President Nixon was prompted to issue a statement that must be almost without parallel as an example of executive arrogance.

Mr. Nixon not only promised to invoke executive privilege to prevent Mr. Dean from testifying, but he said he would invoke it to keep Mr. Chapin from appearing as well on the ground that one does not even need to be employed by the White House to enjoy such protection. Under this theory, simply to have worked once for the President is sufficient to be granted everlasting immunity against congressional questioning.

The Senate cannot conceivably acquiesce in this preposterous doctrine and, well aware of this, Mr. Nixon has offered to make some executive branch officials available for interrogation on an informal basis so as to "preserve intact the constitutional separation of the branches of government." But unless the Senate is willing to accept crumbs from the President's table, such an offer plainly won't do. Both Messrs. Dean and Chapin have a good deal to say that is relevant to Mr. Gray's handling of the Watergate investigation, not to mention the White House's complicity in campaign dirty work. The committee should insist on hearing them even at the risk of a head-on confrontation with Mr. Nixon.

Mr. Gray's qualifications to be permanent director grow more slender with each new revelation of his subservience to the White House. But the Judiciary Committee should not even begin to act on his nomination until it has talked to Messrs. Dean and Chapin.

The Miami Herald
Miami, Fla., March 14, 1973

There is much less precedent — indeed, there is none the White House can cite — for muzzling ex-Presidential aides. Since the name of the game going on in the back room is Watergate, this principle would cover Dwight Chapin, former White House appointments secretary, who was caught with a finger in that mud pie.

The important thing, of course, is that neither the President nor the Congress should do violence to good, open government on the one hand or the separation of powers on the other.

What, for instance, is "necessary and relevant information," and who will define it? The presumption of authority rests with the President. He will need to use that authority thoughtfully not only to protect executive privilege but also to make certain that the public is kept informed on issues within the national interest.

Preserving the balance of powers is just as important. Congress on occasion has wanted to be king, too. The genius of the Republic and its living instrument of law, the Constitution, is that it has never yielded completely to either one.

AS he promised to do at recent press conferences, President Nixon has issued a policy statement on what is called executive privilege. In a few words, it is simply this:

All members and former members of his personal staff would decline to appear before committees of Congress upon formal demand.

However, the President will "provide all necessary and relevant information through informal contacts" between the White House and congressional committees "in ways which preserve intact the constitutional separation of the branches of government."

This seems altogether reasonable, for in part it has precedent. During the debate over the controversial Jay treaties in 1796 George Washington rejected the House's request for documents since the Senate, not the House, passed on treaties. "A just regard to the Constitution," said the Founding Father primly, "forbids a compliance with your request."

A Library of Congress study made last year shows that Mr. Nixon invoked executive privilege nine times (he says it's only three), President Johnson three times, and President Kennedy 13 times.

The New York Times
New York, N.Y., March 14, 1973

When President Washington first invoked the concept of executive privilege to protect the confidentiality of the diplomatic negotiations leading up to the Jay Treaty in 1796, a squalid political intrigue such as the Watergate affair was the furthest thing from his mind. When executive privilege is invoked in an apparent effort to cover up blatant political wrongdoing, the office of the Presidency is demeaned and this nation's constitutional practice is debased.

When President Nixon at a news conference on January 31 promised a precise statement concerning the use of executive privilege, he assured reporters: "The general attitude I have is to be as liberal as possible in terms of making people available to testify before Congress, and we are not going to use executive privilege as a shield for conversations that might be just embarrassing to us."

Now that the promised statement has been issued, it turns out to be vague rather than precise, restrictive rather than liberal in its effect, and designed to protect the President from grave political embarrassment rather than to assist him in the exercise of his proper official duties.

Executive privilege is comparable to the impoundment of funds. It is one of those Presidential powers which is implicit rather than spelled out in the Constitution. Its boundaries are inherently difficult to define. Presidents have traditionally used it sparingly, reserving it for a last line of defense when a Congressional committee has overreached itself. A decent respect for the comity that should prevail between equal branches of the Government has normally controlled its use.

Unfortunately, as in the impoundment controversy, President Nixon now seeks to exploit the necessary vagueness in this constitutional domain and to nail down as unchallengeable authority what is more wisely left flexible and loose.

Even worse, he is trying to extend the coverage of this doctrine in two significant ways. First, he would include not only members of the White House staff but also former members. No time limit is set on their alleged immunity from Congressional cross-examination. Secondly, he claims for Cabinet members who hold dual appointments as "Presidential counselors" the privilege of refusing to testify on that portion of their work which involves their White House duties.

These ambitious claims of a right to secrecy are novel and specious. Once individuals cease to be members of the White House staff, they cannot carry with them into private life the privilege of routinely "declining a request for a formal appearance before a committee of the Congress." Contrary to the President's statement, this is not a "well-established precedent." It is wholly unfounded.

Similarly, a Cabinet officer has always been regarded in normal constitutional practice as responsible not only for administering his own department but also for advising the President on broad issues of public policy. It is specious to assert that simply because the President has conferred on some of his Cabinet members the additional rank of "Presidential counselor" that he also confers on them some special added immunity. The duties of Cabinet members and Presidential counselors are so intertwined that any distinction in the degree of confidentiality and trust between the two positions can only be arbitrary and artificial.

*   *   *

The saddest aspect of this latest institutional wrangle between the President and the Congress is that Mr. Nixon is asserting such arrogant claims in so unworthy an affair. It is impossible to avoid the suspicion that the President is trying to cover up White House involvement in the ugly campaign of political sabotage and espionage which climaxed in the Watergate raid.

The assertion that executive privilege protects former Presidential aides, for example, looks very much like an effort to protect Dwight Chapin, the former Presidential appointments secretary, and perhaps former Attorney General John Mitchell and former Secretary of Commerce Maurice Stans from Congressional interrogation concerning their responsibility for the Watergate episode and related activities.

Chicago, Ill., March 20, 1973

WORCESTER TELEGRAM.

Worcester, Mass., March 20, 1973

President Nixon's suggestion that the Supreme Court should make a "definitive decision" on the question of executive privilege is a clever political ploy. There is not much chance that the Supreme Court wants to get involved in the sort of political crossfire now going on between the President and the Congress.

President Nixon likes to put the dispute on the lofty level of high constitutional issues. And, indeed, executive privilege does have important constitutional implications. Presidents as far back as George Washington have refused to allow Congress to get its hands on delicate information dealing with important domestic and foreign policies.

But Nixon's concern is not with matters of state policy. He is fighting a congressional attempt to pry into the open some sordid political dealings connected with his own re-election campaign. The Watergate Affair is the most dramatic of these episodes, but there are others that, if let out, would not add to the luster of the President's party.

We can hardly blame the President for wanting to keep these things under the rug. It might be awkward in the extreme if the roles played by some of his highest confidantes were exposed.

But Nixon is making a mistake if he thinks the American people are going to buy his talk about constitutional issues. The issue here is not the interest of the country, but the interest of the Administration that happens to be in the White House.

The Courier-Journal

Louisville, Ky., March 21, 1973

PRESIDENT NIXON'S arguments for invoking executive privilege may very well protect White House counsel John Dean from having to testify in the Senate inquiry into the FBI's role in the Watergate inquiry. But the over-all effect on presidential credibility of that political espionage "caper" continues to be the best argument for both the White House and the Committee to Re-Elect the President to make full disclosures of their shady-looking roles in last year's election.

Instead, Mr. Nixon appears willing to sacrifice FBI chief L. Patrick Gray III, while blaming senators for making the FBI directorship "hostage" to a political inquiry on the Watergate crimes. And the Attorney General has ordered Mr. Gray to withdraw what seemed at the time a good-faith, belief-inspiring offer to open an FBI file for senators' eyes only — in a manner that reminded Mr. Nixon himself (as he told the nation last week in his news conference) of J. Edgar Hoover's tactic in the late 1940s of showing "raw" FBI documents to then-decidedly-junior Congressman Nixon.

Now, listening to the President's justifications, one has the sense of panic hiding behind seeming candor—the same intuition that Mr. Nixon told biographer Earl Mazo he had felt on the opening day of the Hiss inquiry.

What's curious is that the President wavers between having one case for executive privilege and having three or four. The person who gives a bundle of reasons for his action may be found to have no single, legitimate reason. Is it (1) the argument that the President's aides must remain anonymous, or (2) the sanctuary of lawyer and client confidentiality, or (3) the assertion that the White House has told Congress all it needs to know, or will do so, in writing, on its own terms.

Without cross-examination

The first argument for executive privilege might, in itself, be good enough to maintain Mr. Nixon's case, as it happens. Who can say what the Supreme Court would decide in this field of constitutional law? There are few cases. More often than not, Congress has conceded to the Chief Executive his right to employ assistants with that "passion for anonymity" FDR sought as a touchstone of faithful service. However the second argument he advanced has put the President on dangerous ground. If Mr. Dean cannot testify because of the confidential lawyer-client relationship, then is one expected to believe that the entire White House staff employs Mr. Dean out of choice? That the "house lawyer" for the presidential mansion moonlights by caring for a staff that instinctively turns to him when in trouble? As for the third item in Mr. Nixon's brief, Senator Sam Ervin disposed of it by noting that it's "impossible to cross-examine a written answer." If the dealings between Congress and the White House counsel are to be in writing, and restricted, as the President said, to "pertinent" questions on the FBI and Watergate, then the Senate might as well close up its investigatory shop. Mr. Dean could define the issues, re-phrase the question and veer off on a self-serving course of his own choosing.

It could be, as the Republican members of the Judiciary Committee are arguing, that there's less to the Gray-Watergate-Dean matter than meets the eye. The same committee agreed last year to question Peter Flanigan on his dealings with Attorney General Kleindienst, despite White House bluster about executive privilege. It could also be that President Nixon has been ill-served by Cabinet cronies and by a presidential aide, Mr. Dean, who meddled in an FBI investigation, leaked the FBI's secret files to Republican Party leaders — not in government service — and recommended officials who recruited others for espionage and sabotage of the rival political party.

If Mr. Dean were to appear before the Judiciary Committee, and refuse to say anything, he would not compromise Mr. Gray's testimony — which, as Senator Bayh has noted, was frank and full, even if a little demeaning of the FBI as an institution. If Mr. Dean were to stand in contempt of Congress for that act, then the President could get the Supreme Court ruling he appears to want.

But the President shouldn't at the same time tell the people how open and forthcoming his administration is. The case is too intricate to be very good. Behind all this is a lawyer (and, as he reminds us now and then, Mr. Nixon *is* a lawyer) who isn't willing to reveal all he knows.

Chicago, Ill., March 20, 1973

IN SEVERAL recent pronouncements, President Nixon has been making clear—almost too clear—his own theory of government. In outline it seems to be this: It is wrong for Congress to challenge the President's powers, including his power to override Congress' wishes when he sees fit. This authority of the President is "clearly established"; the powers claimed by Congress, on the other hand, are flimsy excuses for spending too much money and interfering with the Chief Executive. When the President's authority is at stake, the "separation of powers" doctrine is sacred; when Congress invokes the same doctrine, it's just being obstructionist.

We believe these arguments are invalid, but that's not quite the point. Whether or not Mr. Nixon literally believes them, he clearly believes he can make them stick, with or without help from the courts. And if he succeeds, the theoretical rights or wrongs of his case won't matter. Nixon may singlehandedly redefine the Constitution to suit himself, not because he has proved his point but simply because he has the horses.

This Nixon doctrine, if we may call it that, has been spelled out most clearly in the debates over impounding funds voted by Congress and over withholding information or witnesses that Congress requires. The most startling recent example has come in the argument over confirming L. Patrick Gray III, the President's choice for permanent FBI director. The weight of testimony before the Senate Judiciary Committee has shown, in our view, that Gray would be an unwise choice—that he has been subservient to political needs and has allowed the FBI to be used to protect administration interests in the Watergate burglary-bugging scandal, and that the bureau under him would be in grave danger of becoming a political arm of the administration in power.

Mr. Nixon's chief efforts, however, have been aimed at preventing the committee from digging too deeply into that Watergate case and Gray's connections with it. He has not only invoked the doctrine of "executive privilege" to keep any of his aides from testifying, but has unilaterally broadened it to cover former aides and anyone he may designate as a "Presidential counselor."

It is quite true that precedents for most or all of these actions could be found. Again, that is not quite the point. There has always been a tug-of-war between the President and Congress over their respective power; sometimes one side has won, sometimes the other. There is disputed ground here, and should be. The new element is that Mr. Nixon has turned the tug-of-war into a crucial win-or-lose battle over principle. He is not merely trying to win one particular dispute, but all future disputes on the same ground. And Congress has no choice but to resist this attempt with all its power. That it intends to do so is strongly suggested by Sen. Sam Ervin's proposal that White House aides who refuse to testify before the Select Committee be arrested and, if necessary, jailed.

We regret this deeply. The borderline between Presidential and congressional powers should be left somewhat fluid; there should be an area that allows for different circumstances, where specific conflicts can be settled without nailing down a permanent new relationship. But Mr. Nixon seems to have ruled that out. He has staked out a permanent claim to what has always been no-man's-land between the White House and Capitol Hill. He wants it all, and clearly believes he can get it. And right now, we have no grounds for certainty that he can't.

TULSA DAILY WORLD

Tulsa, Okla., March 21, 1973

THE SIGNALS have been changed, and now FBI files will not be made available to all U.S. Senators. That's the word from L. PATRICK GRAY, Acting Director of the Bureau, whose nomination to become permanent Director lies perilously before the Senate Judiciary Committee.

Several days ago GRAY responded to insistent and unfriendly questioning about the FBI's role in the Watergate bugging case by saying all Senators could see the files for themselves. (Fortunately, hardly any of them has taken him up on his offer.)

Now the Acting Director says he has new orders from Attorney Gen. RICHARD KLEINDIENST and the offer is withdrawn. Only the Chairman, ranking minority member, chief counsel and minority counsel of the Committee may see the files.

Critics of GRAY and the FBI may pounce on this backdown and say it is proof that there is something wrong; why else would the files be kept from all Senators? And why will GRAY no longer answer any and all questions involving the substance of the FBI's investigation at the Watergate hotel complex?

We see it differently. The offer never should have been made in the first place. FBI files were never intended to be put on mass display, even before members of Congress. To do less than require strict secrecy would reduce the Bureau's ability to investigate effectively. Witnesses will not cooperate if they can't be sure their information will be held in confidence.

The limited exposure of raw files to key Senate Committee personnel will suffice. If there is any reason to examine the information gathered by the FBI, the group specified by GRAY should be enough to get all the necessary facts. And no precedent of open-arms welcome to secret files will stand. That is all to the good.

THE ATLANTA CONSTITUTION

Atlanta, Ga., March 20, 1973

The doctrine of executive privilege is sound. The confidential exchanges between members of the President's staff should not be the subject of congressional inquiries. President Nixon has stretched that doctrine to cover the political shenanigans of his staff in the Watergate bugging case, and it will not stretch that far. Sen. Sam Ervin of North Carolina is making good sense in saying he will pursue the matter.

President Nixon suggested that the question go to the third great branch of the federal government, the Supreme Court. The President added, "We think that the Supreme Court will uphold, as it always usually has, the great constitutional principle of separation of powers rather than to uphold the Senate."

Ervin takes the position that Nixon has gone too far. He wants the Senate to adopt a resolution "declaring that the man is in contempt of the Senate and request a prosecution" if a White House aide refuses to testify in the Watergate case.

The man in question is John W. Dean III, the President's counsel and the man who got all the data on the Watergate case from the Federal Bureau of Investigation. The Senate wants to ask him if he gave the FBI information to the Committee to Reelect the President. The question ought to be answered for the good of the political health of this nation.

Ervin's threat to have the Senate's sergeant-at-arms arrest Dean if he ignores the subpoena is drastic. It indicates just how seriously the Senate is taking this clash. The President's refusal to allow Dean to testify also is an earnest expression of his feelings.

The strategy may be to tie the case up in court for two or three years. The White House may hope that the public has forgotten in that time. That is an old, and successful, political strategy.

It should not succeed in this case. This is not a question of privileged communication within the White House. This is a case of the White House trying to keep from answering questions about political maneuverings last summer. Executive privilege does not stretch that far.

Orlando Sentinel

Orlando, Fla., March 21, 1973

THE SENATE Judiciary Committee is jousting with President Nixon over whether White House lawyer John W. Dean 3rd should be required to testify in the confirmation hearing of L. Patrick Gray 3rd.

It's a silly hassle over the long established principle of executive privilege.

Some of the senators are challenging Gray's fitness to be permanent director of the Federal Bureau of Investigation because of reports he handled the Watergate wiretap investigation as a Republican partisan rather than as a disinterested cop.

The senators can inquire all they want into Gray's background, and they're entitled to their opinions of his fitness, but executive privilege goes back to the roots of the republic.

If the President can't call in trusted people for advice, and protect them against political fishing expeditions from outside, he would soon be a lonely, isolated, badly informed and ineffective leader.

For nobody would want to give him the time of day.

The principle isn't too far removed from the privilege a news reporter should have in protecting the identity of his confidential news sources.

MR. NIXON makes a good point when he tells the senators there are two prospects for testimony who aren't shielded — GOP fund raiser Maurice Stans and former Atty. Gen. John Mitchell. They could probably tell as much or more about Watergate than Dean.

The likely reason a big thing is made of Dean's refusal to testify is that the FBI has become a revered American institution, ranking with the flag, motherhood and apple pie. People forget that the FBI is, after all, a part of the executive branch of government which Mr. Nixon heads.

Orlando, Fla., March 23, 1973

IT'S A SIGHT to sadden Americans — the director designate of the Federal Bureau of Investigation wasting days answering questions in a senatorial inquisition involving the bogus issue of executive privilege.

A gaggle of liberal senators, including the sly Chappaquiddick swimmer Edward M. Kennedy, have put a price tag on the confirmation of L. Patrick Gray 3rd as permanent FBI chief.

They'll say yes to Gray only if President Nixon violates his stated principles and lets White House lawyer John W. Dean 3rd answer a Senate Judiciary Committee subpoena.

MR. NIXON takes the position that the president must be free to draw on the advice of trusted aides who cannot then be subject to the untender mercies of partisan politicians armed with subpoenas.

To do so would weaken the chief executive and dry up his sources of counsel.

But Sen. Kennedy has discovered a new platform and he's using it for all it's worth to cast aspersions on the President by suggesting something is being hidden from public view.

✿ ✿ ✿

TRYING TO FORCE Dean to testify against his own wishes and the convictions of the President should be seen for what it is, a shabby partisan political trick.

The FBI is an investigative arm of the government headed by the President, and it would be strange indeed if the President didn't have full access to FBI reports.

Kennedy and his cohorts are saying in effect that there's something wrong when an employe, namely Patrick Gray, turns over to his boss, namely Richard Nixon, the facts of an investigation.

Nonsense. As far as we're concerned the Watergate case has been more effectively cleared up than the saga of Chappaquiddick.

The Burlington Free Press

Burlington, Vt., March 22, 1973

THE ACTING DIRECTOR of the Federal Bureau of Investigation, L. Patrick Gray, has been ordered by the Attorney General not to divulge to a Senate committee any more information from the raw files of the FBI. Senator Birch Bayh, Democrat of Indiana, responded with the utterly asinine remark that the Nixon Administration is "muzzling" Gray and attempting a "cover-up" of the Watergate caper.

Well, it all depends on whose ox is gored. Gray had been giving the Senate Judiciary Committee, controlled by the opposition Democrats, all sorts of information from the FBI raw (un-evaluated) files, and the names of many people were being tossed about. This same sort of thing happened two decades ago when the tables were somewhat turned. Remember the rampage of Senator Joseph R. McCarthy of Wisconsin, who attempted (unsuccessfully, thank heavens) to elicit information from FBI files to support his charges of Communist activity in the State Department and other places?

We remember the situation well. As students at American University in Washington at the time, we closely followed the McCarthy campaign of slander and libel and worse, and it was truly frightening. The so-called "intellectuals" were outraged by this trampling on individual rights, and properly so, but where are these "intellectuals" today? Or is it permissible to indulge in anti-personnel fishing expeditions and character assassination when the victims are of another political persuasion?

If "McCarthyism" was wrong for the Republicans two decades ago — and in our view it was terribly wrong — then it is just as wrong for the Democrats today. And we are dismayed by the silence of the "intellectual" community — a silence which can only be described as intellectual prostitution of the worst sort. — F.B.S.

THE ROANOKE TIMES

Roanoke, Va., March 22, 1973

Several days ago the editors of The Roanoke Times received a letter from L. Patrick Gray III, acting director of the Federal Bureau of Investigation. The letter thanked the newspaper for its editorial, published Feb. 23, praising Mr. Gray's tenure at the FBI and supporting his appointment as permanent director.

The letter was reminiscent of the ways of J. Edgar Hoover. Over the years, the late director of the FBI never failed to write appreciatively to editors of any publication that ran an article or comment praising Mr. Hoover's agency. Mr. Gray, like his legendary predecessor, recognizes the value of good public relations; and he has, as we observed earlier, done a lot as acting director to clear out cobwebs that accumulated during Mr. Hoover's later years.

Unfortunately, it has become evident in recent weeks that Mr. Gray does not also recognize, as did Mr. Hoover, the immense value to the bureau of remaining totally above politics. If he does recognize it, perhaps he simply has not been allowed to follow the rigid standard of independence J. Edgar Hoover set down for himself and the bureau back in the 1920s. Since Pat Gray's ascendancy to the Hoover chair, the White House has proceeded on the assumption that the FBI was just another functionary, an agency that could be commanded to jump to White House whim.

Thus, it had Mr. Gray make thinly veiled political speeches for President Nixon's re-election; it asked the FBI to feed to campaign officials any political tidbits that might be useful; it stationed its man to look over the FBI's shoulder while the Watergate bugging case was being investigated, and even insisted the director violate confidences for the White House's benefit.

Through all this, Mr. Gray was anxious to please. He went along with what was wanted of him and the bureau. He bowed and scraped when a former Attorney General declined to have his wife interviewed. He went on an "assumption of regularity" about what people in the White House were doing regarding the Watergate investigation.

He was even eager to please the Senate, which must confirm him, but there his effort boomeranged. He told the senators incriminating things about people like Herbert Kalmbach, the President's personal lawyer, and the White House—acting through the Justice Department—told him to shut up. Since then, Mr. Gray has been a courteous clam. All sensitive questions will be handled higher up.

It is impossible to imagine J. Edgar Hoover or his beloved FBI in such a situation. Mr. Gray remains a decent, well-meaning and capable man who has instituted some needed procedural reforms at the bureau. But he is not his own man; he is Mr. Nixon's, for that is what the White House insists on. It is a bad precedent for the FBI, and as the man who embodies that unhealthy change, L. Patrick Gray III should be rejected by the Senate as permanent FBI director.

The Washington Post

Washington, D.C., March 26, 1973

Senator Sam Ervin sounded very resolute, although a bit overdramatic, a week ago Sunday when he declared that he would ask the Senate to order the arrest of any White House aide who refuses to testify before the select committee probing the Watergate case and related political espionage. Most of Senator Ervin's colleagues on the special panel, Republicans as well as Democrats, seem equally determined not to be put off by President Nixon's sweeping claims of executive privilege as a shield for any and all activities by present and former members of his staff. The Senate's attitude is encouraging, because the list of questions for Mr. Nixon's aides, especially presidential counsel John W. Dean III, is getting longer every day.

Lawyers love precedent, and some instructive precedents can be found in the record of a tilt over executive privilege 11 months ago, during the Senate Judiciary Committee's hearings on the ITT affair and the nomination of Richard G. Kleindienst to be Attorney General. Then, as now, the names of presidential aides kept coming up in other people's testimony. Then, as now, Senator Ervin and others demanded that White House personnel appear; the list last year included Peter Flanigan, William Timmons and John Ehrlichman. Then, too, executive privilege was invoked, not by Mr. Nixon himself but by Mr. Dean in a letter to the committee chairman. But after several days of maneuvering, a compromise of sorts was reached. Mr. Flanigan agreed to testify—provided the questioning would be confined to four specified points. He did appear, but the most interesting matters proved to be beyond the boundaries agreed upon, and very little was learned.

After this experience, Senator Ervin and his colleagues seem to have recognized the folly of any concessions which enable the White House to get off the hook by sending up a witness but holding back the facts. There is a second lesson, too; as lawyers might expect, it appears in a footnote of sorts, a letter written by Mr. Dean to an interested citizen who had happened to inquire about the scope of the executive privilege which the White House had claimed. In this letter, written on the day Mr. Flanigan testified—and reprinted For the Record on the opposite page today—Mr. Dean cited the Flanigan appearance, along with "precedent and tradition," as evidence that no recent president, including President Nixon, "has ever claimed a 'blanket immunity' that would prevent his assistants from testifying before the Congress on any subject."

What makes this letter worth recalling is the fact that, in his efforts to keep Mr. Dean and others from Senate interrogation, President Nixon has not only claimed such a "blanket immunity" this month, but has tried to legitimize that novel doctrine by reference to traditions which, according to his own counsel, did not exist 11 months ago. There is no better evidence of the slippery, spurious nature of Mr. Nixon's current claim. There is no better illustration of the ways in which principles can be bent, twisted and stretched to suit the immediate needs of politics, especially the politics of self-defense.

Mr. Nixon has tried mightily to portray the approaching confrontation with Senator Ervin's select committee as a kind of constitutional high noon. In fact it is a political showdown between lawmen with questions to ask, and administration men desperately intent on suppressing the answers. Mr. Nixon's stance is not only bad law; it is increasingly bad politics as well. The course of wisdom and prudence would be to dispatch Mr. Dean and his present and former associates to testify right now. If the White House fails to set the wisdom of volunteering, Senator Ervin and his colleagues should be a lot more steadfast and persistent than they were in the Flanigan case in pressing their insistence that White House aides appear to testify on matters which in no way could compromise their confidential relationship with the President. After all, have we not been told repeatedly that Mr. Nixon has had no hand in the matters which come under the general heading of "Watergate"?

The Evening Star
and
The WASHINGTON DAILY News

Washington, D.C., March 26, 1973

Public indignation over the Watergate scandal has been slow in building. Despite the gradual accumulation of evidence over many months pointing to the complicity in the conspiracy of a number of people inside the Nixon administration there has been a general tendency to minimize the implications. For most people, it has seemed incredible that anyone of authority in the President's entourage could have been involved in an operation as crude, shabby and downright stupid as an espionage ring against the Democrats.

The White House, needless to say, has encouraged this feeing of incredulity. Every implication of complicity of persons within the administration has been promptly and categorically denied. White House officials whose testimony in the case has been sought have been sequestered behind an impenetrable shield of executive privilege. Administration spokesmen have volunteered nothing whatever about the results of their own investigation of the conspiracy. The trial of the seven Watergate defendants — five of whom pleaded guilty on all counts — revealed little in the way of additional information about the case.

Little, that is, until last Friday when Chief U.S. District Court Judge John J. Sirica made public the contents of a letter from convicted Watergate defendant James W. McCord Jr. With that letter, the conspiracy of silence surrounding the Watergate affair has come to an abrupt end. It now appears that the carefully-covered beans are going to be spilled all over the place and the resulting mess promises to be appalling.

Among other things, McCord has charged that:

● There was political pressure applied to the defendants to plead guilty and remain silent.

● Perjury occurred during the trial in matters highly material to the very structure, orientation and impact of the government's case.

● Others involved in the Watergate operation were not identified during the trial when they could have been by those testifying.

McCord also wrote that "several members of my family have expressed fear for my life." While he did not entirely share their concern, "I do believe that retaliatory measures will be taken against me, my family, and my friends" should he disclose the facts in the matter. McCord asked to talk privately with Judge Sirica, "since I cannot feel confidence in talking with an FBI agent, in testifying before a grand jury whose U.S. attorneys work for the Department of Justice, or in talking with other government representatives. . "

Taken together, these various charges constitute the most devastating indictment against the government's handling of a criminal case that we can recall. To the extent that they can be substantiated, they cast the gravest doubt on the validity of the trial of the Watergate seven, the investigation of the case by the FBI and the administration, and the continuing protestations of the President that "the White House has nothing to hide."

Quite surely, whatever has been hidden up until now will not be hidden much longer. Given the testimony of McCord and possibly other members of the Watergate band, the whole sordid mess is now certain to be exposed at last, either by Judge Sirica, or by a federal grand jury which reopens its investigation of the case today or by the Senate select committee which will begin its inquiry into the Watergate affair and related political espionage in May. As Sen. Bob Packwood (R-Ore.) has observed, things have reached the point "where either the information will be bludgeoned and dragged out day by day, or it's going to be voluntarily given."

We fervently hope, in the interests of public confidence in our political institutions, that it is voluntarily given. In the face of these most serious allegations against the executive branch, the President's continuing refusal to cooperate actively in clearing up the charges is entirely indefensible. He, above everyone else, should have taken the lead from the beginning in getting the truth in this business out in the open. Any further delay will expose himself and his administration to irreparable injury.

Los Angeles Times

Los Angeles, Calif., March 23, 1973

L. Patrick Gray is not qualified to be the director of the FBI. Indeed, as the record developed by the Senate Judiciary Committee so clearly shows, he has not been qualified to be the acting director of the FBI. He has repeatedly demonstrated an inability to differentiate between what constitutes proper responsibility to his superiors and what constitutes improper interference by those superiors in the independent investigative activities of the bureau. What it comes down to is that he has not known how to say no when he should have, and that failure is his undoing.

Blame it on Gray's inexperience as a custodian of power, blame it more on excessive loyalty to his superiors, blame it most of all on the too-evident manipulation of Gray by persons close to President Nixon. In the end, the result is the same. Gray has been compromised and, worse, has allowed the FBI's integrity to be eroded.

It should not have happened. With another man it might not have happened, though almost certainly the effort would have been made, because the political and personal stakes are high. For it is evident beyond any cavil now that there are persons high in the Nixon Administration who are trying above all else to protect the White House from the spreading taint of the Watergate bugging scandal. It is evident that the FBI did not pursue the investigation as vigorously as it should have. It is evident that Gray was a convenient, probably willing, though not necessarily fully understanding tool in that circumstance.

The sad thing in human terms is that, having let himself be compromised, Gray now finds that he is considered expendable. Mr. Nixon, whatever his press secretary says, seems ready to let the Gray nomination be rejected rather than allow the Senate Judiciary Committee to have full access to those of his aides who have information on the Watergate mess, or full access to the FBI files on the mess. So Gray becomes the fall guy, the loyalist who now finds fidelity carried to the point of self-sacrifice.

He is no villain, only an ambitious man whose judgment failed him. He very much wanted to be nominated by the President as permanent director of the FBI; what he seems to have forgotten is that confirmation must follow nomination, and that to win approval his behavior must satisfy not only the President but the Senate. So he did what the White House asked in the Watergate affair, and won his reward. Then he had to explain to the Judiciary Committee just why he carried his cooperativeness to such lengths, and that explanation has helped seal his fate.

To a considerable extent, the subject of the Senate's confirmation hearings on Gray has become of secondary importance. Gray's long-standing political ties to Mr. Nixon have all along raised the most serious doubts about his suitability as FBI director, and the Senate hearings rather quickly verified those doubts. It is the way in which the hearings have done so that has been significant—what has been indicated about the extent of White House personnel involvement in the Watergate scandal, and the lengths to which this Administration is prepared to go to protect itself from further polical embarrassment.

The manipulation of the FBI by White House officials says something about their attitude regarding the bureau. It makes all the more important the role of Congress in seeing to it that the next man Mr. Nixon nominates has the stature and courage to assure the integrity and independence of the bureau.

This will not be easy for the President to do. He must now know, if he did not before, that grave suspicion attaches to some close to him. It will be the responsibility of any head of the FBI to uncover violations of federal law, and there is no executive privilege that shields the criminal.

Oakland Tribune

Oakland, Calif., March 29, 1973

The full-scale Senate investigation of the Watergate affair has yet to be publicly launched, but already enough startling events and disclosures have surged into the public view to create a crisis of confidence that probably only the President himself can resolve.

Ironically, two men highly trusted by the Nixon administration have played critical roles in bringing the issues into early focus. This fact in itself puts added pressure on Mr. Nixon to take forthright action to dispel the present confusion and direct contradictions in the "facts" now emerging on last summer's breaking and entering, spying and perhaps even sabotage aimed at the Democratic National Committee.

L. Patrick Gray, testifying before the Senate Judiciary Committee regarding his appointment as permanent FBI director, brought presidential counsel John Dean directly into the Watergate matter with the statement that he had turned over FBI reports on the subject to Dean. The latter was investigating the possibility of involvement by White House staffers in the political espionage episode.

James W. McCord, the ex-CIA, ex-FBI agent who was sufficiently trusted by the Administration to be named to the sensitive post of security director of the Committee to Re-elect the President, later assured the chief counsel for the special Senate committee that Dean had known of the Watergate break-in before it happened.

If that charge is true, then Dean was in the uncomfortable position of investigating himself.

Gray also told the Committee that Dean "probably lied" to FBI investigators when questioned about E. Howard Hunt, another White House staffer deeply incriminated in the Watergate case.

Dean doesn't want to talk about these matters to either Senate committee involved and prefers instead to issue denials through the White House press secretary and to promise written answers to written committee questions.

Regardless of the real or alleged executive privilege precedents (uncovered, presumably, by Counsel John Dean) that Mr. Nixon would use to defend his refusal to let Dean personally testify, this is a very special situation requiring very special action.

The McCord and Gray statements have carried the issue far beyond the level of letter writing. Any exchanges of correspondence would now seem wholly inadequate to resolve the doubts and inconsistencies already established.

The issue is of such transcending importance, interest and concern to virtually every American that continued White House refusal to permit Dean to testify brings the inescapable public conclusion that Mr. Nixon is protecting or hiding something he does not want made public under any circumstances. Whether that's true or not, it's what people increasingly are beginning to believe.

If Dean didn't know anything about the Watergate spy plans, then he has nothing to hide and should feel free to testify only on that subject before the special Senate committee. If he did have some advance knowledge, then there is no purpose in the President protecting such a highly placed official who did not act at once to halt such grossly improper activities, or at least to inform the President, who would presumably have ordered it stopped.

Thus Mr. Nixon's options are simple: Let Dean talk or fire him. His present position is untenable.

THE RICHMOND NEWS LEADER

Richmond, Va., March 27, 1973

Although it once evoked mild mirth around Washington, the Watergate Affair has become unfunny in recent days, and may yet displace "Teapot Dome" in the annals of government scandal. At the least, the Watergate tar brush will sweep the American political canvas for quite a while before finding its way to the turpentine.

The Watergate mess has gone out of control: What started as slightly amusing anti-Castro hanky-panky has turned into Republican-directed political espionage that encompasses the question of presidential prerogative and the appointment of a new FBI director. From small bananas have mighty trees grown, and the credibility of the Nixon Administration is rapidly being put up for grabs, as speculation outruns truth in a race to unlock Watergate's mysteries.

The finish line, however, seems to be coming closer: When he appeared for sentencing, one of the convicted Watergate defendants, James McCord, advised the presiding judge that there had been more to the operation than had met the court's eye. McCord spoke of "perjury" and "political pressures," and he promised to fill ears of his own choosing with all the details that had been skipped during the Watergate trial. McCord apparently is making good on his word, and reports from Washington indicate that McCord not only is naming names to special Senate investigators, but also is un-naming some names that have been wrongly linked to Watergate in the press.

McCord might merely be spinning tales to put off his appointment in prison; if so, he will be found out quickly and made to suffer for his charade. But if he is telling the truth — and he probably is — then even now some unknown gentlemen are booking flights to Mexico, while others probably are enlisting their lawyers. Indeed, the Watergate mess may be resolved by a McCord Effect, as the first defendant-domino pushes over one accomplice, then another, then another still. Let us hope so, for the Watergate Affair is well past the point of being a lifeless lump under the rug. Watergate is fully alive and has consumed the rug. Unless it is met head-on, one day it could consume the house as well.

The New York Times

New York, N.Y., March 20, 1973

A growing number of Republican Senators no longer share the Administration's apparent hope that public apathy will allow President Nixon to ride out the Watergate storm by pretending that the affair does not really concern him. No amount of public apathy could justify Mr. Nixon's posture of disengagement; but the Administration can no longer claim that only the news media are interested in the Watergate "caper."

It has long since become evident that the Watergate scandal was no "caper." After hearing the testimony by James W. McCord Jr., Senator Marlow W. Cook, Republican of Kentucky, said he now believed that some of the Administration's "underlings" had "really thought that it might be necessary to rig a Federal election."

Tampering with the election process of the United States is no laughing matter. However, Senator Cook may be in error when he suggests that the effort to rig the election was masterminded at the "underling" level.

Underlings were caught in the act of political espionage. Underlings were brought to trial. Underlings apparently were persuaded, like good spies, to remain silent and take the rap—until Mr. McCord broke ranks. But the evidence is now overwhelming that the underlings were not just a gang of overzealous Nixon supporters acting on their own. The very term—underlings—implies that these men acted under instructions from more powerful quarters. It is perfectly clear that their money and their orders came from command posts very close to the center of the Administration.

*   *   *

John W. Dean 3d, the President's legal counsel, has been charged by L. Patrick Gray, the acting director of the F.B.I., of lying when he denied knowing that E. Howard Hunt, one of the convicted Watergate conspirators, had operated from an office inside the White House. Yet the same Mr. Dean still heads the "investigation" of the Watergate affair ordered by the President. The same Mr. Dean also took to himself the right to sit in on the F.B.I. interrogation of witnesses to the Watergate case. And the same Mr. Dean continues to enjoy the President's personal protection, labeled "executive privilege," that keeps him immune from Senatorial questioning.

The President's personal lawyer, Herbert W. Kalmbach, has told the F.B.I. that he paid substantial amounts of money to Donald Segretti, another "underling" alleged to have been involved in the political espionage. Mr. Segretti, in turn, came recommended from inside the White House by Dwight L. Chapin, then the President's appointments secretary.

The money allocated to these extraordinary activities that were characterized by Senator Cook as efforts to "rig" the election came out of accounts, safes and suitcases under the direct jurisdiction of the two top campaign managers, John N. Mitchell and Maurice Stans, both former Cabinet officers and the President's close personal and political associates.

*   *   *

Thus the web of the conspiracy was evidently spun by men who were the President's surrogates. The fact that it has not been charged that the President had personal knowledge of these crimes, plotted and committed in the cause of his re-election, is no longer particularly relevant. They were plotted and financed at a level of power for which the President must assume personal responsibility.

It would be a high watermark of hypocrisy for Mr. Nixon, who has made himself a spokesman for "law and order," to pretend that lawlessness within the high ranks of his Administration is of no direct concern to him personally as well as to the Office of the President.

Senate Republican Leader Hugh Scott, one of Mr. Nixon's loyal supporters, yesterday expressed his concern over these "developments which taint the political process." Senator Charles Mathias Jr., Republican of Maryland, demands a restoration of confidence. When those who have undermined that confidence are so close to the Presidency, it is clearly up to the President to take personal charge of the process of full disclosure. Nothing less can re-establish faith in the Administration and in the integrity of Government.

SENATORS HEAR McCORD IN SECRET; MITCHELL, DEAN LINKED TO CASE

News leaks concerning the testimony March 28 of convicted Watergate defendant James W. McCord Jr. before a secret session of the Senate Select Committee investigating the case linked high White House aides to the break-in at the Democratic national headquarters in June 1972. There were widespread reports that McCord had related, as uncorroborated hearsay from the Watergate co-conspirators, that former Attorney General John N. Mitchell had approved the espionage activity and was "overall boss" of the group conducting it and that John W. Dean 3rd, counsel to the President, had attended a planning meeting with two of the men later convicted as conspirators and had reported back that the operation had been approved. McCord also reportedly linked President Nixon's chief of staff H. R. Haldeman and former special counsel to the President Charles W. Colson to the plot. All the officials mentioned by McCord had denied such involvement.

Among other Watergate developments in late March and early April:

■ Sen. Lowell P. Weicker Jr. (R, Conn.), a member of the Select Senate Committee investigating the affair, said at a news conference March 29 that the leaked items covered only about "one-tenth" of the information provided by McCord to the committee. Weicker said April 1 that Haldeman should "step forward and explain" what he knew about the operation of the Committee to Re-elect the President. He said April 3 that Haldeman should resign on the ground he "clearly" had "to accept responsibility" for political espionage and sabotage conducted on behalf of the Nixon re-election campaign.

■ White House Press Secretary Ron Ziegler said March 30 that "no one in the White House had any involvement or prior knowledge" of the Watergate "event." To "dispel the myth . . . that we seek to cover up," Ziegler said, Nixon was ordering White House staff members to testify, if called, before the Watergate grand jury and was willing to negotiate with the Select Senate Committee some informal procedure whereby staff members could provide testimony about Watergate.

■ Committee Chairman Sam Ervin (D, N. C.) rejected the White House overture for informal testimony April 2, declaring White House staff members could not be excused from providing sworn testimony in public. Nixon's use of executive privilege in this instance, Sen. Ervin said, was "a terrible disservice to the high office of the presidency." The doctrine could not be applied to illegal or unethical activity, he said.

■ Convicted Watergate conspirator G. Gordon Liddy was sentenced April 3 to an additional jail term for contempt of court for refusing to answer questions about the case before a federal grand jury after being guaranteed immunity from further prosecution.

■ McCord was reported April 9 to have told the federal grand jury investigating the case that cash payments had been paid to defendants in the criminal case for their silence and pressure applied for guilty pleas.

■ The *Washington Post* reported April 12 that McCord had testified before the grand jury that Liddy had told him that transcripts of wire-tapped conversations of Democratic officials had been hand-carried to Mitchell. Mitchell denied the charge.

The Dallas Morning News
Dallas, Tex., April 3, 1973

WATERGATE II has already turned into a political show trial in the U.S. Senate instead of a trial of the facts in federal court. There may be some new indictments now that convicted Watergater James W. McCord has started talking—but by then everything will have been tried in the newspapers.

It stood to reason that the senators on the special Watergate investigating committee couldn't keep secret what McCord told them. They leaked his testimony as fast as he gave it. The federal grand jury, convened at the same time as the committee, is getting the scraps.

WHY U.S. JUDGE John Sirica sent McCord to tell his tale of perjured Watergate witnesses and involvement of higher-ups to the senators instead of the grand jury only the judge knows. But the judge was also bound to know that the atmosphere of the committee, loaded as it is with Democrats, isn't one of neutral inquiry—it is that of a bloodhunt.

In such hearings, innuendo may pass for fact; rumor for reason. No indictments are presented, no witnesses made to face one another. All questioning is admissible, moreover —and "the jury" of senators will keep up a gabbling chorus about the meaning of it all.

By itself, McCord's testimony means nothing. Some of the names he gave the committee were merely hearsay—but they are being bandied everywhere in what used to be called McCarthy fashion. What credibility can the committee expect to command with its absence of due process and inability to keep anything secret?

McCORD will have to sing before the grand jury, too—the same one that indicted him earlier. He admits now that he lied to the jurors; so indictments will not issue on his word alone—and there will likely be, White House aides, people he has named to testifying there, too.

It is well that they do so—well that Nixon has agreed to let them testify if subpoenaed. It is understandable that he refused to send his men to make sport for the Democratic investigators on the committee, but a grand jury is a grand jury.

The Watergate chips should indeed be allowed to fall where they may, but too many have already fallen outside the paths of due process —the grand jury and the courtroom. By the time any further indictments issue—if they do issue—the damage done by the shenanigans of the investigative committee may already be total.

Politics and justice don't march in double harness, as the judge should have known when he sent McCord to tell all and kick off the Senate show trial.

THE DENVER POST
Denver, Colo., April 1, 1973

A WEEK AFTER President Nixon's re-election last November, The Denver Post called upon him "to take his own strong steps to root out—even to the very doors of his office—any and all persons whose presence brings the slightest taint of wrongdoing to his administration."

At that time, we were convinced we had supported an honest man for re-election to the presidency. We believed it likely that the charges of corruption in high places, aired during the campaign, were mostly the product of political animus.

LIKE MOST AMERICANS, we were greatly impressed by the skill with which President Nixon had managed our withdrawal from Vietnam, and diplomatic relations with Communist China, Russia and North Vietnam.

But we feared that the President's leadership at home would be compromised unless he moved energetically to disprove the charges of corruption raised against various levels of his administration—including persons in the White House itself.

After all, there were two very serious general charges tarnishing the good name of the Nixon administration in November: 1) that administration members had engaged in corrupt and downright criminal behavior; and 2) that the administration had used the power of the White House and cabinet-level agencies to cover up this corruption.

IN SOME RESPECTS, we regard the second charge as more damaging to the reputation, not only of the Nixon administration but of the whole federal government, than the first. And we felt it imperative that the Nixon administration open up the records, expose all the questioned dealings to full public inspection and either prove it had nothing to hide or else bring any wrongdoers to full and exact justice.

Nothing of this sort has happened yet. And nearly five months passed before the President began, late last week, to talk as if he might begin to do soon what a decent respect for public opinion should have required of him last November.

In the intervening months the charges of scandal have multiplied and widened—and involved persons ever closer to the President himself. Perjury has been alleged in the Watergate federal district court trial, and the integrity of the FBI investigative process in that case has been impugned—not to mention the integrity of John Dean, the presidential aide who meddled in that FBI investigation.

And as of this writing, the President had not yet opened the records, had not yet cooperated in turning the full light of publicity on the various affairs and those involved.

Instead he had kept quiet, refused to let Dean and other aides testify before Senate investigators, and triggered a campaign of abuse against the newspapers and reporters who have done the most to investigate the Watergate.

IN SUM, ALTHOUGH HE has said—through an intermediary, not directly—that the White House has nothing to hide, he most certainly has not proved it. He has, in fact, acted like a man trying to hide whatever can be hidden.

So we are disturbed, and we have to wonder. We are no longer willing to accept on faith that this is a basically honest administration. We wonder when the President will drive out those who are tarnishing his administration.

And what we are wondering, many another American who supported President Nixon for re-election must be wondering too.

Only last Friday did the first signs of cooperation emerge from the White House — and those very small and vague signs. A presidential spokesman said the White House, while still unwilling to let staff members such as Dean testify under oath before an open congressional hearing, would be willing to work out some compromise- perhaps an appearance before an informal, closed committee hearing.

The spokesman added that if a grand jury called any White House staff member to testify, the President would require him to do so. This is not much of a concession. The President does not have the power to keep a White House staffer from answering a grand jury summons.

So what the President is offering is too little, and rather late. At the very least, he should order his aides to cooperate fully in any and all investigations of the scandals now imputed to them. And let any guilty heads roll where they may.

The good of the nation requires no less.

The Washington Post
Washington, D.C., April 4, 1973

As more and more allegations come tumbling out, some more substantial than others, it becomes increasingly difficult to keep track of that cluster of episodes and issues that are generally lumped under the heading of The Watergate. The heart of the matter is all the more easily lost sight of when the argument turns on such questions as the precise role of this or that White House aide or former Cabinet member in the sleazier aspects of the campaign for the re-election of the President. For all of these questions tend to lead us away from the central fact, no longer susceptible to serious challenge: that both the integrity and the future quality of the political process in this country have been called profoundly into question by the behavior in the 1972 presidential campaign of that mysterious institution known cryptically as the Committee for the Re-Election of the President.

The authority for that last statement does not rest on speculations about who told what to whom—on the second-hand reports of what Mr. G. Gordon Liddy, for example, might have told Mr. James McCord about the role of Mr. Nixon's closest advisers in the Watergate and related matters, or on the question of where former Attorney General John Mitchell fits into it all. We await with interest the clarification of these things, by further court proceedings or by the Ervin committee's public hearings. But we believe that the central point can be clearly perceived right now. It is that a group of people acting on behalf of, and indeed in the name of the President of the United States, subverted the political process in this country in the last election in a way which has no parallel in any presidential election in this country that we have ever heard about.

We know this because seven men have been convicted or have pled guilty to breaking and entering at the Democratic Party headquarters and to bugging the place and tapping the telephones. We know this because the President's own choice to head the FBI, Mr. L. Patrick Gray, has testified under oath that he was told by the President's personal lawyer, Mr. Herbert Kalmbach, that he—Mr. Kalmbach—paid a political operative, Donald Segretti, to do things which have been independently and abundantly characterized as political sabotage and espionage, and that he paid this money on instructions from the President's appointments secretary, Mr. Dwight Chapin. And we know this because we know that large amounts of unreported cash often delivered in suitcases or briefcases and in the form of $100 bills, were poured into the President's re-election campaign; this comes to us from a sworn deposition in an SEC suit against a man named Robert Vesco and in reports from the General Accounting Office.

There is much more—and much more than enough to make it clear that there was skulduggery and corruption in the last campaign that far transcends any particular incident, such as the Watergate burglary, and far transcends the norm in American politics. Writing on the opposite page today, Mr. Joseph Alsop would have us believe that the uproar over The Watergate derives from the fervent efforts of "key people in the newspaper and television communities" to "cripple the President politically." This, as Mr. Alsop might say, is the silliest sort of twaddle. Much of the uproar we hear nowadays on this subject is coming from Republican Senators and conservative commentators who have not in the past shown much inclination to do the President in. Mr. Alsop further bids us to find comfort and a better perspective in an examination of the political peccadillos of past Presidents, and this, as he would say, is the purest poppycock. For one thing, as Mr. Alsop concedes, what has been done in this instance "was far more ambitiously organized, and it was immeasurably sillier and more ill-judged."

That is an exceedingly generous way to view burglary and other improprieties and illegalities on behalf of the re-election of a President, but never mind. Let us assume, for the moment, that poor judgment, immeasurably greater than anything we have seen in such matters in the past, is the worst charge to be made against the President and his immediate advisers; surely this is something the public has a right to know about. And much more important, leaving aside whatever further violations of the law may be involved, this is also plainly something for which the President ought to be held accountable and responsible.

According to the word of his own attorney, orders to pay Mr. Segretti came right out of the White House. The men captured or implicated in the Watergate burglary came right out of Mr. Nixon's campaign committee, which was in turn created and, from all accounts, effectively controlled by the White House. Two of the most prominent figures in this committee, its director, John Mitchell and its finance chief Maurice Stans, came out of the President's cabinet. Mr. Mitchell's successor, Clark MacGregor, came out of the White House, as did such prominent figures as Jeb Magruder, G. Gordon Liddy and Howard Hunt. Whatever technical basis there may be for Mr. Ronald Ziegler's sweeping denial of a "White House" connection, as such, it defies common sense to believe that hundreds of thousands of dollars of campaign money were passed to Mr. Liddy without somebody in authority knowing about it—somebody who thought he was doing what the President wanted done. Are we to believe, as Mr. Ziegler suggests, that the Watergate Seven were an entirely autonomous unit, working, let us say, on a masters degree in American politics, when they decided to conduct intelligence operations against the Democrats? Didn't somebody in charge get the results of this intelligence gathering? Wouldn't that somebody have wanted to know how it was collected?

What, in short, do these people take us for, with their glib disavowals, their contempt for any inquiry, their concealments and evasions and dissembling about matters of plain fact? That is what is so ridiculous about the thesis that the outcry over the Watergate is some effort to "cripple the President politically." For if anybody is crippling anybody in this matter it is Mr. Nixon, by the very nature of his reaction to the outcry, who is crippling himself. If he has "nothing to hide," as he instructed Senator Scott to inform us, he could have whisked the Watergate out of the public mind in a matter of a few days, by simply telling us what it was all about and taking whatever remedial measures that might be appropriate. And he could probably do so now, by sending his men up to testify before the Ervin Committee with no holds barred—if he has nothing to hide.

The Salt Lake Tribune
Salt Lake City, Utah, April 3, 1973

The Watergate affair from its inception has to be marked down as one of the more stupid political exercises of the century. The person who proposed the clandestine operation of bugging the Democratic National Committee's headquarters demonstrated an amazing lack of foresight and perception.

From the moment Mr. Nixon announced he intended to seek a second term the outcome of the election was never in doubt. It didn't matter what poll was consulted, Mr. Nixon was going to win. The only question was by how much.

Because victory was in the bag, there was no reason, none whatsoever, for the Republicans to tackle the risks inherent in burglarizing the Democrats' headquarters. Increasing the chuckle-headedness of the whole affair is the fact that the Republicans have access to many talented investigators and other information gatherers. These people, by simply keeping their ears and eyes open, could have learned with virtual certainty how the Democrats planned to push forward the upcoming presidential campaign.

In short, there was no reason to stoop to the reprehensible low of burglarizing offices in Washington's Watergate complex.

As if the image of his administration hasn't been battered enough, President Nixon has chosen a course that, if persisted in, will only further discredit his years in the White House. This is a shame, because his administration has much to its credit.

It is with great reluctance that Mr. Nixon has finally allowed members of the White House staff to appear before the Senate committee investigating the Watergate mess. But the presidential aides may appear only on an informal basis, they may not testify under oath. This arrangement is totally unsatisfactory to Sen. Sam J. Ervin Jr., D-N.C., the chairman of the investigating committee.

Sen. Ervin has said he will issue "engraved invitations," then formal subpoenas and if those methods fail to produce the desired witnesses he will have the Senate arrest the reluctant White House staff member.

So far, Mr. Nixon's handling of the Watergate affair has unjustifiably blackened the eye of the FBI and tarnished markedly the accomplishments of his administration, including the easing of tensions with Russia and China and the ending of the Vietnam war. Whether the image will persist in history can't be determined at the moment, but Mr. Nixon runs the very real risk of having his administration remembered almost exclusively for the Watergate episode.

If Mr. Nixon doesn't want this to be his place in history he should instruct his White House staff people to tell the truth, the whole truth and nothing but the truth. Otherwise Teapot Dome and Watergate will, unless moderating influences prevail, enjoy a certain synonymity in the lexicon of American scandals. But, by allowing his aides to sit on the witness chair, the President will effectively patch the cloak of integrity about his administration that has been severly torn.

The Philadelphia Inquirer
Philadelphia, Pa., April 2, 1973

We are accustomed to preserving the bulk of the space in these columns for persuasions, arguments and observations of our own, for we believe that an independent newspaper has a duty to speak with its own independent voice.

Today, however, in contemplation of the growing aura of scandal about the Watergate case and the involvement in it of men close to President Nixon, we call attention to excerpts from an important speech by Mr. Nixon himself.

"My fellow Americans:

"I come before you. . . as a man whose honesty and integrity have been questioned. The usual political thing to do when charges are made against you is to either ignore them or to deny them without giving details.

"I believe we've had enough of that in the United States. . . To me the office of the Vice-Presidency of the United States is a great office, and I feel that the people have got to have confidence in the integrity of the men who run for that office and who might obtain it.

"I have a theory, too, that the best and only answer to a smear or to an honest misunderstanding of the facts is to tell the truth. . .

"I want the American people to know all the facts and I'm not afraid of having independent people go in and check the facts. . .

"Until the facts are in, there is a doubt that will be raised. . . Because, folks, remember, a man that's to be President of the United States, a man that's to be Vice President of the United States must have the confidence of all the people. And that's why I'm doing what I'm doing. . .

"Why do I feel so deeply? Why do I feel that in spite of the smears, the misunderstandings, the necessities for a man to come up here and bare his soul as I have? Why is it necessary for me to continue the fight?

"And I want to tell you why. Because you see, I love my country. And I think my country is in danger. . .

"You say, 'Why do I think it's in danger?' and I say look at the record. . . Take the problem of corruption. You've read about the mess in Washington. . .

"But just let me say this last word. Regardless of what happens, I'm going to continue this fight. I'm going to campaign up and down America until we drive the crooks. . . and those that defend them out of Washington."

These words were part of a nationwide broadcast on Sept. 23, 1952, when Mr. Nixon was candidate for Vice President.

We believe they have even more pertinence today than they did then. And although we applaud the announcement by the White House Friday that the Presidential aides connected with the Watergate matter will be allowed to appear before a Federal grand jury, we cannot accept that slight relaxation of Mr. Nixon's defensiveness as having much promise of allowing "the American people to know all the facts."

Twenty years ago, Mr. Nixon called for that, and we believe he owes no less today. Testimony before the grand jury is secret; the grand jury is largely under the influence of Mr. Nixon's own Justice Department, an office which has shown little zeal and fewer results in clearing up the case — even during the prosecution of the indicted Watergate burglars.

The ugly facts about the Watergate have grown disastrously beyond the point at which the President can "ignore them or . . . deny them without giving details," which has been the administration's posture thus far. The necessity for disclosure has gone far beyond the dubious convenience of executive privilege.

Mr. Nixon can redeem his administration's reputation only by ordering all present and past members of his staff to give full and public testimony, under cross examination, on all aspects of the case before the special Senate committee that is now investigating the matter.

The Morning Star
Rockford, Ill., April 2, 1973

In these days of high meat prices, crime in the streets and spring training, Watergate and the names that accompany it tend to be shrugged off as "just politics."

If most Americans don't know a G. Gordon Liddy from an L. Patrick Gray, they don't seem to mind. After all, wasn't the GOP bugging of Democratic headquarters in Washington's Watergate offices merely some of the inter-party intrigue that accompanies every election?

Unfortunately, Watergate isn't that simple. As information unravels thread by thread, Watergate is becoming more and more a case of high level government dishonesty.

Already, Senate investigators have learned enough to know that some top level officials have to be lying, and others, including President Nixon, are being less than candid.

For example, L. Patrick Gray III, still supposedly Nixon's choice to head the FBI, has admitted that presidential counsel John W. Dean III lied to FBI agents about the Watergate case. Dean denies he lied. Who's telling the truth and who isn't?

Convicted Watergate conspirator James M. McCord Jr. says former Atty. Gen. John Mitchell had a hand in the bugging. Mitchell denies it. Again, who's telling the truth and who isn't?

Meanwhile, the President, claiming executive privilege, refuses to allow his staff, including Dean, to testify before the Senate.

Why is the President of the United States stretching executive privilege to keep his staff from revealing, under oath, what they know about Watergate?

We can only join in the Senate committee's conclusion — that the truth would hurt too much. Apparently the imbecilic bugging of a Democratic office reached so far into the White House inner circle that it struck some sensitive, high-level nerves.

Now, its repercussions are hitting nerves elsewhere. Republican congressmen are complaining that Watergate is spreading distrust which could hurt their political chances in 1974. They want Nixon to let the truth out.

Clearly, it is the President's choice. Only he can give the word which will prompt his staff to testify.

We believe he should give the word immediately. By keeping Watergate secrets hidden behind White House walls, Nixon risks the sacrifice of innocent Republicans and the further erosion of public confidence in government.

The Burlington Free Press
Burlington, Vt., April 4, 1973

THE PUBLIC REMAINS largely apathetic about the Watergate caper. Some of the "molders of opinion" in Washington and New York cannot understand why. Perhaps we can enlighten them.

In the first place, it is a fact that political espionage and sabotage have been practiced routinely in this country for a good many years, on behalf of Republicans and Democrats and others. The distinction this time around is that the culprits were caught in the act. The dirty deed itself is hardly sensational, except perhaps to someone who is extraordinarily naive or remarkably ignorant.

In the second place, the opposition party (the one which lost the big election in a big way) is the majority in Congress and therefore controls the investigative machinery of Congress. Otherwise, there would be no fancy investigation with the television lights and all the rest. This is no reflection on the Democrats; the same thing would occur with the Republicans if the roles were reversed — as they have been in the past and well might be in the future.

In the third place, certain people can never forgive President Nixon for (1) successfully concluding the war in Vietnam and (2) winning reelection in a landslide of historic proportions. So if the Nixon-haters cannot embarrass the President on substantive things, perhaps the Watergate caper can raise a little dust.

In the fourth place, it should be remembered that this bugging episode in no way affected the outcome of the 1972 Presidential election — Nixon did, after all, carry 49 states. If Congressmen, or anybody else, were really interested in probing the subversion of a Presidential election, the best opportunity presented itself in 1960. Even Tom Wicker of the New York Times, one of the nation's leading liberal apologists, acknowledges that nobody ever will know who really won the 1960 Presidential election because of the "lost" and destroyed ballots in Illinois, Texas and Missouri which barely tipped that election to the Democratic candidate. And guess who rejected an official investigation of that scandal on the basis it would create a constitutional crisis? Richard Nixon.

Finally, it is somewhat difficult for the public to become aroused over a case of political espionage and sabotage when the "molders of opinion" who hoot and holler about it are the same people who moralistically excuse the distribution of classified government documents by a thief named Daniel Ellsberg. Now really, folks, bugging a political party is hardly as "subversive" as the stealing of classified government documents.

Now we should make it unmistakably clear that in no way do we condone the Watergate caper. But we can see it for what it is — a botched job of routine political undercover activity, no more and no less. A bit sad, perhaps, but we're only telling it the way it is. — F.B.S.

THE SUN
Baltimore, Md., April 1, 1973

President Nixon is duty bound to eliminate the "conflict of loyalties" in the Watergate case that Senator Mathias sees as a threat to government, law, politics and, yes, the Republican party. As memorably defined by Mr. Mathias, such a conflict exists when those in public office give "a greater loyalty to some lesser interest than the Constitution." The lesser interest in the Watergate case is the protection of top White House advisers whose complicity in the bugging of Democratic headquarters is increasingly suspected. The greater interest is the maintenance of public trust in our system, a trust that depends on the integrity of those in leadership positions.

Mr. Nixon may have had good reason to question the motives of hostile Democrats who have long been urging him to abandon the coverup in the Watergate affair. But he would be well-advised to heed the outcry for candor from Republicans who have been disturbed not only by recent revelations, but by the silence at 1600 Pennsylvania avenue. The roster of GOP senators who have spoken out now spans the party spectrum from Oregon's maverick Bob Packwood ("the most odious issue since the Teapot Dome") to New Hampshire's ruggedly regular Norris Cotton ("there's nothing that could be brought out that would be as detrimental as letting this thing go on"). Even Mr. Nixon's hand-picked party chairman, George Bush, described Watergate as a "grubby" business that will be detrimental to the Republican party if it is not cleared up promptly.

In this, the deepest ethical crisis of his administration, Mr. Nixon should learn from the Sherman Adams affair during his vice presidency. Governor Adams, it will be recalled, was easily the most powerful man in the Eisenhower White House from 1952 to 1958. The trusted lieutenant of a President who disliked politics and was afflicted by heart trouble, Mr. Adams had more authority than all the tough operators of the Nixon inner clique, combined. When he was found to have obtained government favors for an industrialist who gave him a vicuna coat, Mr. Eisenhower tried to keep him on, plaintively saying: "I need him." But as the 1958 elections approached and Republicans became uneasy, even Sherman Adams had to go.

It is hard to conceive of Mr. Nixon's needing any of his top aides in the sense that Mr. Eisenhower needed Mr. Adams. Yet our present President, in a scandal that reaches much deeper than vicuna venality, has seen fit to give his loyalty to the "lesser interest"—to the protection of his underlings lest their misdeeds splatter his record. The Watergate affair, because of this self-defeating approach by the President, has now gone well beyond the question of who in the White House knew what, when about the Watergate break-in. While these are the questions on which the firing or punishment of individuals must rest, we prefer to concentrate on loyalty to the Constitution—on the need to retain public faith in our government.

To this end, Mr. Nixon has a presidential responsibility to come clean on Watergate. He should disclose everything he has come to learn about the case, instruct his aides to co-operate fully with Senate investigators and, if need be, throw his support to a special inquiry chaired by the likes of former Senator John J. Williams (R., Del.).

Heads may roll; deceptions and wrongdoing may be exposed; the administration may have to endure humiliations. Yet the alternative—the prospect of four more years of suspicion and scandal—is even worse for those who worry about government, law, politics and, yes, the Republican party. Senator Mathias has stated that the way to restore confidence in our society "is for everyone who shares the privilege of leadership to obey the law and to meet the small questions and the great issues with equal courage." Watergate encompasses the smallest of questions and the greatest of issues. It is time for President Nixon to face both, with equal courage.

Los Angeles Times
Los Angeles, Calif., April 4, 1973

Presidential Press Secretary Ronald Ziegler has once again said that the White House intends to cooperate with the Senate committee investigation of the Watergate scandal, but its view of cooperation is not the same as the committee's. The White House still wants to set conditions on the testimony of presidential aides. Sen. Sam J. Ervin Jr. (D-N.C.), who is chairing the investigation, will have none of that. He insists that when the time comes for present and former presidential aides to testify, they must do so just like plain folks, not in any private or circumscribed way, but under oath, on the record, and for all the world to see.

The point Ervin is making has become central to the Watergate investigation. He is saying emphatically that people in the White House who know something about the political espionage effort involved in the Watergate case are not immune from examination by the Senate committee. What is under investigation is a crime, perhaps more than one crime, and the privilege that is supposed to protect communications about government business between the President and his subordinates does not apply here. The point is inarguable in either logic or law. No wonder that Mr. Nixon has called Ervin a great constitutional lawyer.

What adds weight to Ervin's stand is that a number of people whom the President has been trying to shield with his extension of the executive-privilege doctrine have been implicated by one of the convicted Watergate conspirators as participants in the hatching of the crime. Ziegler is upset about the way that has been made known, and has accused the committee of permitting irresponsible leaks of secret testimony. The complaint misses a key point. James McCord, the conspirator who has been talking to the committee in closed session, soon will be doing so in open session, and presumably he will say the same things in public that he has been saying in private. What will be the White House line then?

The people implicated by McCord have a right to respond and rebut. More than that, they have an obligation to do so, and Ervin intends to see that they meet that obligation. He and his committee want to get at the whole truth in the Watergate mess, and that requires obtaining information from a number of Mr. Nixon's past and present associates, without dictated restrictions on who can be talked to, or what can be said, or where. Ervin is firm on that and, though a lot more argument may be heard, it is a good bet that he has already had the last word.

Newsday

Long Island, N.Y., April 4, 1973

By every indication, events are maneuvering President Nixon and the Senate into a historic contest of wills over the Watergate investigation. The impending clash threatens political and constitutional fallout far more destructive than the Watergate scandal itself. In a way it brings to mind the Dreyfus case. That was an accidental miscarriage of justice which rocked the French nation to its very roots at the turn of the century. It happened primarily because the authorities proved powerless to reverse course after covering up a relatively minor scandal. In the end the Dreyfus affair became a lasting chapter in world history. Must Watergate?

In our opinion there's still a reasonable way to avoid constitutional chaos—a path that requires no real retreat on executive privilege and no surrender of the Senate's investigative powers.

At bottom the issue has been the Senate investigating committee's desire to interview John W. Dean III, counsel to the President. Dean's title means simply that he is the President's in-house lawyer. Watergate complicated his status, however, for he apparently carried out administrative and political functions over and above the traditional role of a counsel.

So, wittingly or unwittingly, Dean became a party to the controversy rather than merely the President's legal adviser in responding to it. One can argue whether it was appropriate to involve the presidential counsel in Watergate, but there's no argument that Dean's special political responsibilities diminished his capacity to serve as an attorney in the same proceeding.

For this entirely professional reason we urge that Dean withdraw at once as the President's lawyer, at least in the Watergate case. His doing so would enable the President to appoint a special counsel from outside—someone totally uninvolved, uncommitted, untouched by the present controversy—and the new man could re-evaluate the situation and advise Nixon accordingly.

The same act of voluntary withdrawal would free Dean to testify on his administrative and political actions in the Watergate case without diminishing executive privilege one whit. He could, quite appropriately, refuse to testify about any legal advice he had given the President on Watergate or any other executive business.

Dean's withdrawal would not of itself suggest guilt or complicity in the scandal. Lawyers and law firms routinely disqualify themselves when any past or pending affiliation gives the slightest appearance of conflict.

In suggesting a new tack on the investigation, we don't intend in any way to condone further cover-up at the White House or encourage any backing-down at the Senate. For the sake of public trust in government, Watergate *must* be fumigated no matter how high the involvement reaches. And with that in mind we also commend to Mr. Nixon the legal thinking of a former presidential special counsel, Theodore Sorensen.

Attorney Sorensen (a Democrat and also a member of one of Manhattan's most affluent law firms) reasoned in the New York Times yesterday that Dean's refusal to testify on grounds of executive privilege automatically signifies "regardless of the rationale offered . . . that the Watergate affair in fact involved presidential policy, presidential discussions or presidential orders for which Mr. Nixon himself rather than his aides should be held responsible."

So for legalistic reasons as well as the need to restore public trust in the White House, President Nixon should alter course on Watergate and wherever else there's the slightest suspicion of special deals and cover-ups in his administration.

The News and Courier

Charleston, S.C., April 6, 1973

As the fingers of Watergate guilt point ever closer at the White House, Congressmen of both parties are reported to be alarmed at what might happen if President Nixon were to be personally involved. Some are said to be whispering censure, or even impeachment. Friendly critics are blaming the President for failure to handle the scandal more quickly. They say he should have exposed the truth and let heads roll.

What if among the heads were to be his own?

Lacking inside knowledge, we can only speculate from a distance about the Watergate bugging and the ensuing investigation of the trail of political espionage.

Skulduggery is nothing new in politics. Kevin Phillips, a syndicated columnist whose articles appear locally in the Charleston Evening Post, performed a useful service April 4 in reviewing the stolen ballots that helped elect three Democratic Presidents: Harry S. Truman, John F. Kennedy and Lyndon B. Johnson.

In the 1960 election, Kennedy defeated Nixon by 110,000 votes.

Fraud in Illinois, Texas and Missouri was more than enough to make the difference. The New York Herald Tribune printed a post-election series documenting the thefts until, Mr. Phillips said, it was requested to stop by the defeated candidate himself. Mr. Nixon did not want to see the presidency dragged through the courts in election fraud cases.

Whether Mr. Nixon knew about the spying on Democrats in the Watergate office, or even personally engineered it, The News and Courier cannot say. The intrusion was illegal and unethical. The theft of votes for three other Presidents was even more reprehensible.

Compared to the life-and-death matters entrusted to the office of the President, the Watergate case pales into triviality. The office itself is more important than the transient incumbent. Congressmen yelling for blood are right, therefore, to turn back before laying hands on the man in the oval office over campaign chicanery. They can leave to history whether this President deserved the nickname Tricky Dick.

The Detroit News

Detroit, Mich., April 6, 1973

Since both Democrats and Republicans have been playing politics with the Watergate bugging incident, The News has been recommending all along that the investigation be left in the hands of a federal grand jury and that a special Senate committee bow out, at least until the jury completes its work.

Now there is new evidence that the members of the committee, Republican as well as Democrat, are more interested in headlines than in arriving at the truth about who was responsible for the Watergate affair.

Sen. Lowell B. Weicker, R-Conn., a member of the committee, hinted darkly the other day that H.R. Haldeman, one of President Nixon's top White House aides, "probably" knew a unit in Mr. Nixon's campaign committee was set up to carry out disruption and surveillance of Democratic presidential candidates.

When Weicker followed up with a demand that Haldeman testify before the committee and still later called on Haldeman to resign his White House post, it appeared that matters were nearing a showdown. The presumption was that Weicker was basing his allegations on testimony given in secret before the committee by Watergate conspirator James W. McCord Jr.

Then the committee chairman, Sen. Sam J. Ervin, D-N.C., and the vice-chairman, Sen. Howard H. Baker Jr., R-Tenn., pulled the rug out from under Weicker. They issued a statement saying, "In the interests of fairness and justice, the committee wishes to state publicly it has received no evidence of any nature linking Mr. Haldeman with any illegal activities in connection with the presidential campaign of 1972." Weicker, obviously unhappy, responded with a terse: "I concur with the statement."

As to what motivated Weicher's original attack on Haldeman, nobody knows for certain but we've got an idea about it. As a man with only two years of service in the Senate and little seniority, Weicher attracted unexpected and unusual attention with his first, rather tentative statement. When that happened, he got carried away and began believing his own publicity.

If that is an accurate scenario, it wouldn't be the first time a senator became more interested in getting headlines than in getting at the truth. Which explains our doubts about the value of a political investigation of a political affair.

But that's not much consolation to those whose reputations already have been smeared by the irresponsible comments of such men as Sen. Weicher.

THE SAGINAW NEWS
Saginaw, Mich., April 4, 1973

Regardless of what anybody may say, the fundamental issue at stake in the Watergate bugging affair is getting to the truth—or as close as it may ever be possible to get to it. This is more important than protecting reputations or advancing political self-interest.

It would appear, however, that before the investigation into Watergate can advance that far another question must be resolved. How far can a President stretch the doctrine of executive privilege to shield those close to him or formerly close to him from appearing under oath before a select committee of the U.S. Senate instituted for the purpose of probing the breadth and depth of an act of political espionage?

The fundamental issue is not being served by the refusal of President Nixon to allow White House staff aides to appear before the committee under those conditions.

Neither is it being served well by Republican Sen. Lowell P. Weicker of Connecticut. As a member of that committee Sen. Weicker, while he may be making good headlines, is jeopardizing the committee's effectiveness. At the minimum he is jeopardizing his own role on the it. This he is doing by divulging almost daily bits and pieces of second hand and as yet unsubstantiated information handed to the committee by those now doing a lot of talking.

Right now the one man who is on the proper course is that bulldog of Constitutional law, Sen. Sam J. Ervin, D-N.C.

It is he who heads the select committee and it is he, more than any other man on Capitol Hill, who is determined to get the White House to see this investigation in its proper Constitutional context.

It may seem to many to be less than charitable on Sen. Ervin's part that he has spurned Mr. Nixon's offer to permit his aides to appear informally and behind closed doors before the committee he chairs.

We don't think so Moreover, Sen. Ervin, who once served on the North Carolina State Supreme Court, is now willing to take the President to the mat over the issue of executive privilege. Ervin may not win this fight, but Mr. Nixon has put down the challenge and we're glad that a man of his expertise in Constitutional law has picked it up.

"Executive privilege," said Sen. Ervin last week, "is intended to enable a President to keep secrets, confidential communications between him and his aides, which occur in the course of an effort to assist the President to execute in a lawful manner his constitutional or statutory duties. I'm satisfied that executive privilege does not cover wrong doing."

Sen. Ervin's interpretation makes sense. Certainly the select committee looking into the Watergate spy affair is looking into an act of wrong-doing. That is already a matter of court record.

In matters of this kind Sen. Ervin can see no reason to draw a distinction between those ensconced in high level government positions and any other citizen. "We're not dealing with royalty or nobility here," says Sen. Ervin. We agree. And being the tenacious fighter that he is, he will go the subpoena route if he has to force this question to a test.

It may be that some members of Sen. Ervin's committee believe his efforts too slow. Slow they may be, but if the select committee is ever to have a fair chance to pin down the facts of who was and who was not involved in Watergate, it must be free to call whom it pleases for testimony under oath—and in open session.

The facts cry out for establishment. The shadow of Watergate lengthens. It has extended far beyond the original seven conspirators. Enough names have already been dragged into this mess. The truth is the only way alleged connections may be determined or innocence of any wrong doing established. Simply to say this was a stupid trick does not suffice at this stage of developments.

THE COMMERCIAL APPEAL
Memphis, Tenn., April 4, 1973

PRESIDENT NIXON seems to be feeling the pressure for a full explanation about the Watergate bugging incident. At first, invoking executive privilege, he told his White House aides not to testify before the Senate Judiciary Committee hearings on his nomination of L. Patrick Gray III to head the FBI. Then he allowed his counsel, John W. Dean, to offer to answer committee questions in writing. Last week it was suggested the President might let some of his aides talk privately and informally with the Senate's special Watergate investigation committee, whose chairman is Senator Sam Ervin (D-N.C.).

Senator Ervin has rejected all attempts by the administration to bargain for something less than a thorough and open probe. He has even vowed to seek the arrests of aides who don't respond to subpenas to testify.

The President would do well to let his aides appear before Ervin's committee. The bugging and raid on the Democratic National Committee headquarters and subsequent events related to the investigation have cast the White House in a very poor light. More high-ranking administration officials are being implicated all the time. The White House's image was especially damaged by the charge of James W. McCord Jr., chief of security for the President's re-election campaign last year, that political pressure was applied to defendants in the Watergate case to plead guilty and keep silent.

QUESTIONS have been raised in the minds of Republicans as well as Democrats, Nixon backers as well as Nixon opponents, concerning the role of the administration in the Watergate affair. The questions form a wall of doubt around the presidency, itself. And certainly H. R. Haldeman, presidential assistant, is in a position of shaky credibility.

Unless the President helps the Senate committee uncover the facts, the innuendoes and rumors about payoffs and coverups and manipulations at the highest level of the administration will leave a stain on his party and his personal record. He owes the people of the United States an honest and honorable accounting.

The Hartford Courant
Hartford, Conn., April 5, 1973

We have been asked why we have not commented on the Watergate incident which is now threatening to becloud what seems to us to be far more legitimate and important issues in Washington. The answer is a very simple one: We know no more than do our readers about the facts in the case and we think that to speculate beyond those facts at this time is unfair, unjust and would be a disservice to our readers.

As we said when the abysmally stupid attempt to bug the McGovern headquarters was discovered in Washington last summer the case called for Congressional investigation as well as criminal prosecution. When the trial ended, after four of the six who were apprehended pleaded guilty and the other two were found guilty, we repeated that Congress could not escape its responsibility for a full airing of the case.

The Senate has charged a committee of eminent senators, incuding our own Lowell P. Weicker, Jr., to investigate fully what has every appearance of being a scandalous mess. In one way or another, some of the supposedly secret allegations that have been made to the committee have leaked.

One of the most serious of the leaks, that alleging that a presidential aide had been linked by evidence with "illegal activities in connection with the 1972", has been forcefully denied in a committee statement with which Senator Weicker specifically concurred.

We have no idea where the Senate committee's investigations will lead it. We have no reason, at this point, to doubt the repeated assurance of the President's spokesman, Mr. Ziegler, that "the White House intends to cooperate" with the select committee headed by Senator Ervin. We have no illusions that this is the best of all possible worlds, but we must refuse at this point to comment when any conclusion can rest only on the known guilt of the six Watergate burglars and what the White House has called the tidal wave of hearsay evidence. We are confident the whole picture will be brought out. But we do not intend to speculate on what is, at best, hearsay evidence that would be inadmissable in any court of the land.

THE INDIANAPOLIS STAR
Indianapolis, Ind., April 9, 1973

The Watergate affair was undoubtedly a depth of foolishness in political skirmishing as well as a crime, and there can be no excusing either the participants or anyone involved in underwriting such a misadventure.

It is going to take the equivalent of a great purifying winds and torrents of clean water to flush away the effluvium.

It it is within the power of the administration to cleanse the Watergate stables, the sooner it is done the better. For there is much urgent business on the agenda and the Watergate mess, lying there like a pile of banana peels on a workshop floor, does not promise to make the job any easier.

One observation about the Watergate fiasco may be in order. Much of the "indignation" voiced over Watergate among left-liberal circles has a somewhat hollow ring.

For many of the same characters who claim to be "outraged" by the Watergate incident were, not many months ago, waving Viet Cong flags, collecting blood for North Vietnam and consorting with every type of radical busy bad-mouthing the United States and giving plentiful aid and comfort to Hanoi.

The morality exhibited by these chaps is, to say the very least, flexible. And it is hard to escape the feeling that if the Watergate conspirators were Communists, radicals and liberals would be staging mass protests all over America — in fact, all over the world—calling them "political prisoners" and demanding that they be freed.

THE MILWAUKEE JOURNAL
Milwaukee, Wis., April 3, 1973

The White House, all along, has attempted to brazen out the Watergate scandal and put it to sleep before it infects the whole administration. That's a lost cause; the mess won't wash. Instead of lying down quietly, Watergate is now well on the way to striking home. It has gone too far to be turned back now by mere pious denials and arrogant cover-ups.

The essential quest is to learn which Republican bigwigs, how high up in President Nixon's official family — whether with or without his own foreknowledge—conceived and financed a criminal conspiracy against the Democratic Party last summer. The plot surfaced when a seven man gang, including some with White House and Nixon campaign ties, were nabbed in the act of burglarizing and bugging Democratic National Headquarters in Washington's Watergate complex.

The seven have been convicted, but they were small potatoes. Who put them up to it and promised to protect them? Who pressured five of them to plead guilty and not pass the blame in self-defense? Who knew about the plot beforehand? Who put the campaign funds into it?

* * *

The continued search for these vital answers has raised other messy national issues. It has fouled up Nixon's nomination of his henchman L. Patrick Gray to be permanent director of the FBI, since the FBI's own integrity has been compromised. It is leading to a thunderous showdown over Nixon's abuse of "executive privilege"—extending the White House rule of secrecy even to a purely criminal investigation, unrelated to national policy making.

This has imperiled — in many minds already destroyed — the credibility of the Nixon administration itself. More and more by the week, it is appearing unprincipled, unscrupulous. The seasoned Washington journalist Joseph Kraft recently termed the Watergate affair "a political bomb that could blow the Nixon administration apart."

Not least alarming to the American public should be Nixon's attempt, now clearly shown up, to "politicize" the FBI through Gray, to turn the nation's powerful police arm into a submissive tool of the White House for partisan political purposes. Among other indications of this, Acting Director Gray let the president's chief counsel John Dean, with obviously chilling effect, sit in on FBI interviews about Watergate with White House aides. As one comfort at least, the Gray nomination is apparently a dead duck in the Senate.

* * *

It is not unusual for administrations to be embarrassed by misdeeds of persons close to the president, with or without his condonation. What counts is how a president responds. For months, Nixon has taken the role of Warren G. Harding, who responded with an excess of loyalty when cronies betrayed his trust. Nixon has obstructed investigation, withheld information from Congress, expressed undimmed faith in the purity of everyone associated with him.

But the bipartisan pressure is becoming too great. The president now at least indicates that his aides will be ready to testify before a federal grand jury and that some compromise is possible regarding appearances before congressional investigators. This is the direction in which Nixon must move in full good faith, otherwise the drizzle now spattering mud on the White House roof will soon become a deluge.

THE ROANOKE TIMES
Roanoke, Va., April 8, 1973

President Nixon's obstinacy in the Watergate affair is a reminder that in politics, as in physics, some rules seem to be unalterable. For instance, for every action there is an equal but opposite reaction. Mr. Nixon, still riding the waves of a powerful victory in the polls last November, seems to think he can do no wrong. That was what President Franklin D. Roosevelt thought after his amazing election victory in 1936.

Well, FDR was wrong. Even though he won every state but two in defeating Alfred M. Landon, he could not pack the Supreme Court, he could not purge his opponents from the Democratic party. FDR's supreme over-confidence after 1936 gave him trouble thereafter. That could well be Mr. Nixon's lot. Had Mr. Nixon acted swiftly when the Watergate buggers were first exposed last year, he would have suffered little harm. Every President has been surrounded by little men whose self-importance has been inflated. But Mr. Nixon was misled by the fact that he had a patsy for a political opponent—U.S. Sen. George McGovern, D-S.D. As long as Mr. McGovern was the alternative for president, Mr. Nixon could do no wrong.

George McGovern has fast receded from the national political scene. The American people can now look at the Watergate bugging, and the mysterious financing of Mr. Nixon's campaign, free of that distraction. They can also be puzzled by Mr. Nixon's determination to keep as much hidden as possible.

The President is headed for a fall. He could still recoup much, but not all, by a display of forthrightness. The dismal course, however, seems to be set. To leave by the same door as the entrance, there appear to be laws in politics as in physics. That may be one of the beauties of the American political system: You can't get by with everything forever.

The New York Times

New York, N.Y., April 8, 1973

Watergate, the office-and-apartment complex in Washington in which the Democratic National Committee formerly had its headquarters, has become the shorthand symbol for a year-long campaign of espionage and sabotage conducted on behalf of the Nixon Administration in 1971-72. The scope, complexity, and duration of those clandestine activities reach far beyond the single episode of breaking into the Watergate office for which seven men have been convicted.

It is now known, for example, that these men also had instructions to tap the telephones in the campaign offices of Senator McGovern and to "bug" the offices and hotel rooms used by leading Democrats at their party's national convention in Miami Beach. During the Presidential primaries, Senator Muskie, then the Democratic front-runner, was the victim of a sustained campaign of sabotage.

Some of those activities may be legal if reprehensible while others are illegal. The task of the select Senate Committee chaired by Senator Ervin of North Carolina, is to uncover the whole tangled story and ascertain who was ultimately responsible. As Senator Weicker, Connecticut Republican and a member of the Ervin committee, has repeatedly and properly emphasized: "It is not just Watergate. It's whether or not we as Americans are going to accept a new standard for our Presidential elections."

As in any Congressional investigation of possible wrongdoing, the public has to rely in considerable part on the character and competence of the chairman, the members of the committee, and the chief counsel. In the present instance, the public is fortunate. Senator Ervin is a former judge respected for his knowledge of the law. His chief counsel is also professionally well regarded. This is not a committee likely to act in the reckless style of the late Joseph R. McCarthy or J. Parnell Thomas.

Yet when sensational charges are made about powerful persons in secret committee hearings, they are bound to become public knowledge with the inevitable risk that the charges may be garbled or exaggerated or, at the very least, made public prematurely before evidence has been developed to substantiate them. That has occurred in the case of H. R. Haldeman, the President's chief of staff, and the committee has quite properly issued a statement that "as of this time it has received no evidence of any nature linking Mr. Haldeman with any illegal acts."

That statement does not exonerate Mr. Haldeman. It merely explains the status of the committee's investigation at this time. Still on the record and uncontradicted is the testimony before the Senate Judiciary Committee of L. Patrick Gray 3d, acting director of the Federal Bureau of Investigation, that Dwight Chapin, formerly the President's appointments secretary, directed Herbert Kalmbach, the President's personal attorney, to pay $30,000 to $40,000 to a political saboteur in California. It is doubtful that Mr. Chapin, a protégé and subordinate of Mr. Haldeman, would have undertaken an activity of this kind on his own authority.

Senator Weicker has pointed out that Mr. Haldeman staffed the Committee to Re-elect the President with White House aides. In calling for Mr. Haldeman to resign, Senator Weicker may well be right in his analysis of where the lines of responsibility ultimately run in this matter. Nevertheless, he has muddied the waters because his personal expression of opinion is naturally identified, though incorrectly, with the judgment of the whole committee. A judgment on Mr. Haldeman's role, if any, has to await completion of the hearings.

President Nixon has tried to enlarge the confusion by attacking the committee through statements of his White House press spokesman. As Senator Ervin has observed, "the President is conducting himself in such a way as to reasonably engender in the minds of people the belief he is afraid of the truth."

Unless President Nixon withdraws his sweeping and largely unwarranted claims of executive privilege and orders his aides to testify, that reasonable belief can only grow stronger in the mind of the public.

TULSA DAILY WORLD

Tulsa, Okla., April 10, 1973

THE CONTINUING ferment in the Watergate bugging is providing a textbook case of facts versus innuendo and rumor.

The latest instance is offered by the NEW YORK TIMES, which says the singing member of the Watergate cast, JAMES W. McCORD JR., has told a Federal Grand Jury he *believes* a lawyer for PRESIDENT NIXON'S re-election committee used money and pressure to keep other defendants silent after their arrest.

McCORD has been giving "secret" testimony—leaking all over the place —to a Senate investigating committee. He has refused to comment on the TIMES story.

But the newspaper quoted its unnamed sources as saying McCORD's testimony was based essentially on *hearsay . . .* mainly on remarks he said were made to him by the now deceased wife of one of the other Watergate defendants.

At the same time, NEWSWEEK Magazine says it has learned from an *unstated source* that McCORD is prepared to tell a news conference that *he had been told* JOHN N. MITCHELL ordered the June 17 Watergate raid after seeing some photographs of documents at the Democratic National Committee Headquarters.

MITCHELL denies again and again any part in the Watergate incident. Other denials are coming as fast as the spring-blooming rumors get into print.

So what is the public to believe? The Watergate case is undergoing exhaustive inquiry, not only from Senate investigators but by the Grand Jury. There is no reason to believe the facts will not be brought out—as they should be.

But what we are getting now is a spate of undocumented, second or third-hand reports, gossip and predictions with a great capacity to smear individuals who are named.

Only last week one of these reports, said to have come from Senate committee sources (again unnamed), implied that PRESIDENTIAL Assistant H. R. HALDEMAN was involved in the break-in and bugging of the Democratic Headquarters. Republican Sen. LOWELL P. WEICKER JR. of Connecticut leaped in with a sophomoric call for HALDEMAN to resign.

This instance was so unfair that the Chairman and Vice Chairman of the Senate committee felt compelled to issue a joint statement that they had no evidence linking HALDEMAN with illegal activities.

The facts on Watergate need to be explored and exposed. But the public should beware of unsubstantiated rumors and intimations. And we have to add—the press should be careful about circulating them.

Chicago today American

Chicago, Ill., April 12, 1973

ATTY. GEN. Richard Kleindienst has given the clearest statement so far of the Nixon administration's views on "executive privilege" — the doctrine that says Presidents don't have to tell Congress everything they're doing or thinking. As explained by Kleindienst, the Nixon version is that this President doesn't have to tell Congress anything at all. If Congress disagrees with that, said the attorney general, it can always cut off funds for the executive branch or maybe impeach the President—suggestions of such bland, cynical impudence that even Kliendienst must have had some trouble keeping a straight face while making them.

Testifying Tuesday before a joint session of three Senate subcommittees, the attorney general asserted that Congress had no power to order any employe of the executive branch to testify before a congressional committee if the President barred such testimony. This claim is simply stupefying. At one move, it would expand the "privilege" doctrine to cover some 2.5 million persons and give President Nixon, in effect, unappealable power to decide what executive dealings Congress might or might not inquire about.

This radical claim resembles the usual idea of executive privilege about as much as Godzilla resembles a garter snake. The traditional comity between Congress and the White House does allow the President privacy in his own councils; of course he must be able to discuss policy choices with his advisers without having to let Congress in on the discussions. But an attempt to stretch this protection into a blanket covering the entire army of executive payrollers seems like a bad joke. It is either that, or a direct, unabashed move toward giving the United States a secret government and a powerless Congress.

Can this really be what Mr. Nixon has in mind? Apparently it can. Along with this fantastic assertion of power, his administration has submitted to Congress an Official Secrets Act that seems quite frankly designed to prevent the American people from finding out what their government is up to. This effort, part of a Justice Department bill revising the federal criminal code, would impose severe penalties—up to seven years' imprisonment and a $50,000 fine—for violating governmental secrecy.

The penalties would apply to government employes who gave out the wrong kind of information and to newsmen who published it. The gag would cover all classified information regardless of whether the classification made sense—the effect being to make a powerful censor out of every burocrat with a stamp pad. If it were passed, Congress and the press would be virtually powerless to investigate executive dealings in any field, from scandals of the Watergate type to foreign policy. And that, evidently, is just the way Mr. Nixon wants it.

These proposals are a burlesque of law and responsible government. They seem to us the kind of proposals made by persons who genuinely do not understand what is meant by such concepts as separation of powers or constitutional checks and balances; who speak of them the way a tone-deaf person sings — confidently, but all wrong.

It is deeply regrettable that Mr. Nixon and his top echelon are tone-deaf as regards the Constitution, but of course their disability cannot be allowed to endanger the nation's freedom. Congress will have to make up for their deficiency by knocking down these poisonous proposals and any others like them.

HERALD-JOURNAL
Syracuse, N.Y., April 15, 1973

Richard G. Kleindienst, the U.S. attorney general, advised three Senate subcommittees meeting in joint session that a president could order anyone working for the executive branch to take the Fifth Amendment when summoned by Congress.

A president wouldn't gag his subordinates 99 per cent of the time, Kleindienst said, and in this context he was talking about his boss, President Nixon.

Kleindienst's reasoning escapes us.

He seemed to say that everyone on the payroll of the executive departments from the commander of the Joint Chiefs of Staff to a clerk in the Denver office of the Department of Interior could be ordered to clam up when subpoenaed to talk to a congressional committee.

His reasoning rested more on the notion that the President is boss and, by golly, all others starting with the vice president had better hop to when the President barks an order.

Such off-the-cuff opinion strikes us as the kind of reasoning that serves neither the President nor the Congress.

It's probably true, in fact. There aren't many J. Edgar Hoovers in government today. And that's what Kleindienst should have told the committee. The boss bosses.

Beyond reality there's also custom, law and the Constitution to be drawn upon in making a reasoned response to the committee's question which, in our mind, went beyond the imposition of executive privilege, limiting the testimony of those presidential aides who serve the President directly.

The question was:

How far can Congress go to obtain information?

Kleindienst failed to respond with an educated answer.

When he's asked a similar question by the President, we're hopeful he will take advantage of hindsight and present a more responsible response.

Detroit Free Press
Detroit, Mich., April 13, 1973

ATTORNEY GENERAL Richard Kleindienst's definition of executive privilege covers a lot of ground; in fact it covers the globe and extends to more than one percent of the American public. A definition that broad can be dangerous.

The Constitution makes no mention of the privilege, although few would argue that it is sometimes necessary and that it might be implied in what Kleindienst calls "the sacred doctrine of separation of powers."

But the privilege was originally intended to protect the President from having to testify before Congress. As government grew, it was expanded to cover those who advised the President in his role as President.

Kleindienst, and we would assume Mr. Nixon, has expanded "executive privilege" to cover all of the 2.5 million employes of the executive branch, many of whom have never seen the President, most of whom have never talked to him, and only a handful of whom have ever advised him about anything.

The attorney general, speaking in Detroit after the Senate appearance in which he expanded the doctrine, backed off a bit. "Executive privilege applies to a specific person when he has intimate contact with the President," he said. Unfortunately, he did not say it did not apply to other cases.

Mr. Nixon has shown a penchant for secrecy and surprises. Under his interpretation of "executive privilege," it could well become impossible for Congress or anyone else to discover what the executive branch of government is up to. What was intended as a courtesy to the President could become a blanket "top secret" stamp over the execution of decisions.

Kleindienst

At the very center of the executive privilege controversy is John W. Dean III, legal counsel to the President. In some instances, Mr. Dean may be covered by executive privilege in the traditional sense. But what Congress wants to find out about is not Dean's legal advice to Mr. Nixon in his role as President; Congress wants to learn about a crime—the breaking and entering and bugging of Democratic headquarters at the Watergate.

Dean directed the official White House investigation of Watergate, and therefore must know something about it. Congress, and the American people, have every right to find out just what that is. Surely strong law-and-order men like Messrs. Nixon and Kleindienst cannot be serious in asserting that knowledge of criminal activity is covered by "executive privilege."

Mr. Kleindienst said that criminal matters, such as the Watergate investigation, were "uniquely the province of the judiciary."

Fine, but prosecution and grand jury investigation in the judicial process are hampered by the fact that they are controlled by the executive branch. It was no secret in the Watergate trials that federal District Judge John Sirica, a Republican, was upset by the prosecutors' lack of enthusiasm.

The administration seems intent on kicking sand in Congress' face. Mr. Kleindienst has in effect dared Congress to do anything about any assumption of powers Mr. Nixon may care to make.

That is the danger. As Sen. J. William Fulbright said, if senators did not act after hearing the attorney general, "then they deserve the contempt the White House obviously has for them."

The administration's apparent attempt to protect somebody from criminal prosecution for Watergate may rouse Congress. And in its arrogance of power, the executive branch may lose some of the powers and privileges it needs to operate.

ST. LOUIS POST-DISPATCH
St. Louis, Mo., April 15, 1973

Ever since five burglars, men paid and directed by the Nixon re-election apparatus, were arrested inside the Democratic National Headquarters last June, the Administration has consistently attempted to divert public attention from the true significance of the crime. In its latest maneuver, the White House is trying to portray the Watergate affair, which is now a shorthand term for political espionage and sabotage, as a constitutional struggle between a prying, witchhunting Congress and an executive branch that is properly insisting on preserving the integrity of its doctrine of special privilege.

Nothing could be farther from the truth. To prevent his aids, who in sworn testimony have been implicated in the break-in, from being questioned by Senator Ervin's investigative committee, President Nixon has stretched executive privilege to the frightening extent of stating that any past or present White House employe need not testify. Attorney General Kleindienst, going even farther, says executive privilege covers all 2,500,000 executive branch employes and calls the doctrine "sacred"—although it is not mentioned in either Holy Scripture or the Constitution.

Executive privilege has one, and only one, legitimate use, and that is to protect White House aids from having to disclose to Congress their confidential advice to the President, advice on which policy matters are decided. To invoke privilege in the Watergate case can only suggest that Mr. Nixon was confidentially advised about the crime and that he may have formulated policies on the basis of that information. To invoke privilege, in short, is for the President to implicate himself in the crime.

What should be clear to even the most obtuse member of Mr. Nixon's palace guard by now is that the stench from Watergate will not be blown away by fanciful explanations or attempts to shift the emphasis from a palpable crime, for which seven men already have been convicted, to a debate on an abstract issue of dubious constitutional legitimacy. As Senator Goldwater, perhaps the most consistently conservative senior Republican says, Watergate is "beginning to smell like Teapot Dome . . . Let's get rid of the smell."

More than enough has been adduced to show conclusively that a massive, lavishly-financed effort existed to rig the last election against the Democrats. The rigging process included the use of illegally collected funds, burglary, wiretapping, sabotage, misuse of the Federal Bureau of Investigation and, most cynically, the recruitment of college students for dirty work on the pretext that they would be doing field work in political science. It is immaterial that these tactics were used by Republicans against Democrats. The point is that they represented a wholly reprehensible departure from traditional American electoral politics, and until every aspect of the Watergate mess is fully exposed and those responsible held accountable, the specter of this scandal will hang over elections for years to come.

Fortunately, the public is well aware of what is happening—despite the White House's efforts to keep things under cover. A poll by the Wall Street Journal shows that 91 per cent of the American people know about "the Watergate affair," nearly 40 per cent believe that top Nixon advisers such as H. R Haldeman and former Attorney General Mitchell knew of Watergate in advance, 60 per cent want investigations to continue and 50 per cent believe the incident has "seriously reduced" trust and confidence in political affairs.

The longer the White House plays its game, the more people will become convinced that Mr. Nixon has something to hide, and the greater the poisonous effect that Watergate will have on the people's faith in democracy.

GRAY ASKS NIXON TO WITHDRAW HIS NOMINATION AS FBI CHIEF

The nomination of L. Patrick Gray 3rd to become director of the Federal Bureau of Investigation was withdrawn April 5. Gray disclosed he had asked President Nixon to withdraw his nomination, and a spokesman at the Western White House at San Clemente, Calif. said the President had "regretfully agreed." Gray had been acting FBI director since the death of J. Edgar Hoover in May 1972.

The nomination had become enmeshed in the Watergate political espionage controversy. The Senate Judiciary Committee, in its hearings on Gray's confirmation, had explored the connection between Gray and John W. Dean 3rd, counsel to the President, who had been linked to the Watergate defendants. After Dean's refusal to testify, the committee sought to broaden the inquiry and delay decision on the nomination. The panel held a surprise session April 5 to consider a motion to kill the nomination by indefinitely postponing confirmation, but adjourned without taking action. A few hours later, Gray announced his withdrawal, saying the FBI should have "permanent leadership at the earliest possible time."

The President's announcement observed that, "in view of the action of the Senate Judiciary Committee" it was "obvious that Mr. Gray's nomination will not be confirmed by the Senate." Therefore it was being withdrawn, he said, "in fairness to Mr. Gray, and out of my overriding concern for the effective conduct of the vitally important business of the FBI." The President referred to Dean's controversial role in his statement. Because he asked Dean to conduct a thorough investigation of "alleged involvement in the Watergate episode," he said, Gray was asked to make FBI reports available to Dean and "his compliance with this completely proper and necessary request . . . exposed Mr. Gray to totally unfair innuendo and suspicion and thereby seriously tarnished his fine record as acting director and promising future at the bureau."

DAYTON DAILY NEWS
Dayton, Ohio, April 8, 1973

President Nixon typically hymned Acting FBI Director Patrick Gray toward oblivion, as he has others of his failed nominees, with a denunciation of the senators who were repelled by the proposition to confirm. The President said Mr. Gray was a victim of "totally unfair innuendo and suspicion."

Like blazes he was. Mr. Gray was a victim of his and the President's acts, as forthrightly (to give Mr. Gray his due) testified to by the acting FBI director in his hearings before a Senate committee. The fact is that Mr. Gray at the President's behest, unable to resist invitations to impropriety, used the FBI as a partisan political agency.

Whatever his failings — and they were several in his later years —, the late and so-far-only FBI Director J. Edgar Hoover kept the bureau out of politics, a bedrock integrity the public interest demands. Mr. Gray, however, stumped for Mr. Nixon's re-election, used FBI agents as campaign researchers and played ball with White House staff members assigned to damage-limiting the Watergate crimes.

Those are not matters of innuendo and suspicion. Mr. Gray swore to them. Like depressingly many of Mr. Nixon's nominees for the judiciary, Mr. Gray turned out to be a man habituated to the short-term rewards of acquiecence.

President Nixon can do better by the FBI now that he has had his way with Mr. Gray and has got him out of the way. He can look beyond his anteroom of political hacks for a person of irreductible integrity, one with germane qualifications and with some appreciation of the necessary subtleties of modern law enforcement. The Senate would be charmed.

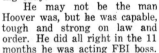

New York, N.Y., April 7, 1973

Three liberal Senators, Birch Bayh (D-Ind.), John Tunney (D-Calif.) and Teddy Kennedy, must be hugging themselves with glee now that L. Patrick Gray 3d has been forced to withdraw from nomination as head of the FBI.

L. Patrick Gray

What a sorry scene it was! All those guys had been riding former FBI chief J. Edgar Hoover unmercifully for years. Then when Gray came along they kept comparing him unfavorably to Hoover, practically making a hero out of their former prey—while attacking Gray.

He may not be the man Hoover was, but he was capable, tough and strong on law and order. He did all right in the 11 months he was acting FBI boss.

He moved younger men up the ladder, hired women agents and relaxed some of Hoover's rigid rules.

The FBI as an institution has come through all the hearings unscathed and with continued public confidence. That is a tribute to Gray's ability and leadership.

The big mistake Gray made was in acting too eager for the job. He talked too much and too rashly to the Senate Judiciary Committee, and he never should have shown those raw FBI files to Presidential counsel John Dean. Dean should never have asked for them. He needed only a summary. For that mistake President Nixon should censure Dean.

Any nominee to head the FBI was likely to be attacked as political in the wake of the Presidential election, even if he wore wings and had a halo. That's why it might be a good idea to stagger the director's term by making it 7, 9, or 11 years to keep it out of Presidential year political vendettas.

The President should act quickly on a successor. The man should be experienced, non-political and respected. Then if those high binder Senators will hang up their political bullwhips for a while and vote his confirmation, the FBI can get on with the important work it has to do for the country.

THE ARIZONA REPUBLIC
Phoenix, Ariz., April 8, 1973

The Eastern establishment has made Pat Gray walk the plank.

At Gray's r e q u e s t, President Nixon has withdrawn his appointment as director of the Federal Bureau of Investigation.

Of course, all's fair in politics. But abrasive, repetitive attacks on Nixon a p p o i n t e e s, the use of smear and innuendo to force the rejection of his nominees — these tactics can only increase the difficulty every president has in getting good men to accept high position in the federal government.

One charge against Gray was that he had shown a congressional committee some raw files containing material collected by the FBI. Oddly enough, Gray's predecessor, J. Edgar Hoover, was frequently condemned because he would not s h o w congressional committees the files they wanted to see.

Another charge against Gray was that he indicated some support for President Nixon. Again it is odd to note that the charge was brought largely by those who criticized Hoover for being too independent.

Pat Gray's full name is L. Patrick Gray III. He follows the path of G. Harrold Carswell and Clement F. Haynsworth Jr., both of whom were Nixon nominees for the S u p r e m e Court, in being forced to bow out.

It would be facetious to say all three appointments were scuttled because they put the initial at the beginning of their names instead of in the middle, or because they remembered their ancestors with designations at the end of their names.

But that would be just about as good an excuse as any given by the senators who fought these appointments.

The real reason is politics.

The Detroit News

Detroit, Mich., April 9, 1973

Now that Senate Democrats have succeeded in torpedoing the nomination of L. Patrick Gray III to be director of the FBI, the question is whether any other nominee will be able to win confirmation.

Having had their taste of blood, the Democrats are unlikely to pay much attention to Gray's parting comment that "the FBI, a great and unique American institution of vital service to the president and the American people, is entitled to permanent leadership at the earliest possible time."

What sank Gray's hopes were his admissions to the Senate Judiciary Committee that he had given White House counsel John W. Dean III access to raw FBI files on the Watergate investigation and had made pro-Nixon comments in at least one speech during the 1972 presidential campaign.

The major criticism centered on the Watergate investigation which the Democrats are still pursuing, in large part for political advantage. Yet on this issue it appears Gray merely obeyed the order of the President himself, as transmitted through his counsel, Dean.

Yet what is any future nominee to reply, when he is asked whether he will obey the orders of the President and the attorney general, his bosses, and whether he will provide them with information they request? Presumably, if he replies affirmatively, he will be denied confirmation just as Gray was.

That being the case, Gray possibly could stay on as acting FBI director for the last 45 months of Mr. Nixon's term because it is unlikely Mr. Nixon will nominate anyone who would announce in advance he wouldn't obey the President.

Whether matters will reach such ridiculous heights is problematical, however. Gray, after all, is the victim of the confrontation between the President and the Democratic Congress over the Watergate case and the broader issue of the executive privilege claimed by Mr. Nixon for his administrative aides.

As The News has said before, the White House staff has bungled the handling of the Watergate case and thus in part is responsible for the fate that befell L. Patrick Gray, who was torpedoed by the Democrats, not because he lied but because he told the truth as he knew it.

Ironically, it was the Republicans who back in 1968 persuaded Congress to make appointment of future FBI directors subject to Senate confirmation in order to protect the post from politics. What has happened is just the opposite. The FBI has been thrust deep into politics with the help of those who claimed they wanted to save it from that fate.

The Standard-Times

New Bedford, Mass., April 9, 1973

And so L. Patrick Gray 3d is out as a candidate for permanent head of the FBI, thanks largely to a political power play, his own candor and perhaps a touch of naivete.

Certainly, Gray made mistakes since he took over as acting director after J. Edgar Hoover's death almost a year ago.

He really should have known better than to go off making partisan political speeches on President Nixon's behalf. And Gray's handling of some aspects of the Watergate bugging investigation left something to be desired.

His giving FBI reports to White House counsel John Dean 3d, who has been accused of involvement in the Watergate affair, seems particularly naive . . . but perhaps only through hindsight.

The fact remains Gray was caught in a political tug-of-war between the President who nominated him and the Senate, who had to confirm him.

Since President Nixon has refused to let aides such as Dean testify, Gray was the only man the Senate Judiciary Committee could use to reopen Watergate and reopen it they did — with a vengeance.

Gray was frank — painfully frank in his replies to the committee's days of interrogation and this undoubtedly led to his downfall. Because he answered questions so honestly — and revealingly — the White House turned cool on his nomination and withdrew its support . . . all the while voicing its wholehearted endorsement.

It's ironic that some of the same senators decrying Gray's "involvement" are the same senators who so bemoaned J. Edgar Hoover's aloofness from everyone.

The most important thing now is to find a permanent FBI head, one in whom the Congress, the President — and the country — can have complete confidence.

The Washington Post

Washington, D.C., April 11, 1973

Having spearheaded the effort to turn back President Nixon's nomination of L. Patrick Gray III to be director of the FBI, Sen. Robert Byrd (D-W. Va.) has turned his attention to quite serious issues of the governance of the bureau which flow both from J. Edgar Hoover's 48-year tenure in the director's chair and from the Gray hearings. Senator Byrd has introduced a bill which he hopes will improve the bureau and take it out of politics. The central purposes of the bill are to take the bureau out of the Department of Justice and make it an independent agency and to limit the director's term in office to seven years. Sen. Henry Jackson (D-Wash.) is introducing a bill which would give the director a 15-year term with no possibility of reappointment and require that the nominee have at least 10 years experience in the FBI.

There can be little doubt that the issues which these two measures seek to address are extraordinarily important. The dangers of politicizing the FBI or even giving the appearance of doing so have been graphically demonstrated in the last few weeks. It is not simply the distribution of John Ehrlichman's request for information which would be useful in the campaign to FBI field offices last year or even the appearance that Mr. Gray acted at least like a quasi surrogate for the President in the campaign. Those things are bad enough. More to the point is the nightmarish position of a few employees of the Committee for the Re-election of the President who, wanting to discuss matters involved in an FBI investigation freely and out of the presence of their superiors, arrange to do so and then find that their information has made a full circuit right back to the people whose intervention they sought to avoid in the first place. Finally, of course, there is the sad story of Mr. Hoover's ossifying political views and concurrently ossifying control over the FBI in his later years.

Although these two bills attack very real problems, we are not, at least at this juncture, persuaded that the remedies proposed are either appropriate or wise. The establishment of the bureau as an independent agency, while attractive at first blush, might create more problems than it solves. In a very real and substantial sense, the FBI serves as the investigative arm of the federal criminal process. As such, it is imperative that it have the closest and most cooperative relationship with the lawyers who are trying to develop cases and who ultimately will have to try them. During the last years of Mr. Hoover's tenure, that relationship was either nonexistent or constricted and carried out with the greatest difficulty by lawyers within the Justice Department for, although Mr. Hoover was nominally the Attorney General's subordinate, he and the bureau were in a very real sense independent. Sen. Byrd's bill would simply perpetuate that problem.

We have already addressed the fixed term proposals in this space. Sen. Jackson's 15-year idea with the requirement that candidates be drawn from people who had put in at least 10 years in the bureau seems to us unduly restrictive of the President's freedom to choose the best person available, no matter what he or she might be engaged in at the time of the vacancy. Moreover, the trouble with a fixed term, whether it be 7 years or 15 or something in between, is that it would prevent the President from firing a person who had turned out to be his or some past President's mistake. Despite the perils of politicization, we think the system can be made to work if the President and his Attorney General are convinced that the Congress actually wants and is prepared to work to achieve a truly non-political and highly professional FBI.

And that, it seems to us, is the healthiest aspect of the Byrd and the Jackson proposals. For Sen. Byrd said some very important things when discussing his reasons for introducing his bill. He said that there was a real need to take a careful look at the FBI after Mr. Hoover's long rule, that he did not want the directorship to become a patronage plum and, most importantly, that he considered his bill a stimulus to congressional oversight and study of this whole matter. That last is the nub of it. If Congress can mount serious and sustained oversight on the problems of the governance of the bureau, all of these problems will be manageable. If it cannot, no gimmicks like fixed terms for the director will work. In providing a stimulus to active congressional participation in the management of the FBI, Sen. Byrd and Sen. Jackson have performed a useful public service.

AKRON BEACON JOURNAL

Akron, Ohio, April 9, 1973

The long battle over Senate confirmation of L. Patrick Gray III as head of the Federal Bureau of Investigation has served at least two useful purposes.

First, of course, was the removal of Gray himself from consideration for the post. It had gradually become unmistakably clear that his confirmation should be refused or he should be withdrawn as a nominee.

Second, it opened for healthy and useful congressional debate the whole question of what the FBI ought and ought not to be.

★

Nothing emerged in the confirmation hearings to suggest that Gray is in any way less than a decent and honorable man. But there was much to indicate that he lacks the sturdy independence of character needed in an FBI chief to keep the agency from becoming a political tool of the party controlling the White House.

His background is political, lacking anything to suggest special competence to manage the nation's foremost investigative and law enforcement agency. And somehow he seemed to want the job so much that he was altogether too eager to p l e a s e all through whom he might get it — ironically, the administration and his Senate questioners alike.

The resulting picture was one of too-great pliability, and therefore too much likelihood of subservience to the political purposes of the administration, for the good of the FBI.

It is good, then, that the President finally decided it was hopeless to go on trying for Gray's confirmation, and withdrew the nomination.

More fundamental than the question of Gray's suitability for a role made peculiarly difficult by the curious and special history of the FBI under the long and feisty domination of J. Edgar Hoover is that of the FBI's proper role.

The bill offered by Senate Majority Whip Robert Byrd (D-W. Va.) to make the agency independent of the attorney general and to limit the director's term to seven years does not, as Byrd himself granted, settle the question of what the FBI ought and ought not to be.

But it is, Byrd argues, a good starting point for a thoroughgoing discussion of the FBI's role.

Few in this country want to see the FBI become a sort of superpowerful political police, serving White House notions of what is at any given moment politically useful.

Because the agency is unavoidably a part of the executive branch machinery in government, it is not easy to blueprint some sure way to prevent this. And it is unlikely that Congress can come up with any absolutely foolproof way to do it.

But at least the Gray hearings, the Watergate matter, and the suggestions from Sens. Byrd, Henry Jackson (D-Wash.) and others are helping to bring forth some things the bureau should not be and not do.

Exhaustive public discussion of the whole problem can, it seems to us, do much both to suggest action Congress can take to keep the FBI out of politics and to help restore once-great public confidence in the agency as "the untouchables," in a political sense as well as in every other.

The Houston Post

Houston, Tex., April 13, 1973

The withdrawal by L. Patrick Gray of his nomination for the office of FBI director has evoked a number of new ideas in Congress on the directorship.

The FBI was established in 1908 by the attorney general. The directorship was shaped by the only FBI director in history — J. Edgar Hoover. But, by his longevity, Hoover revealed the potential danger of making this a lifetime appointment.

Patrick Gray had been an excellent administrator in the Department of Health, Education and Welfare under Secretary Robert Finch. As acting director of the FBI, he stirred the predictable mixture of admiration and ire that comes from a change of management. Gradually it became apparent that the directorship itself would change if L. Patrick Gray held the post. Unlike Hoover, Gray was frankly partisan, and he suggested that the FBI director should resign every four years to enable each newly elected president to name his own. This would have removed the FBI director from his peak of non-political justice and made him a member of the presidential team.

The Senate committee hearings on Gray's nomination would have been a harsh experience for any man, but they revealed qualities in Gray that made him seem not well suited for the appointment: A volubility that bordered on the indiscreet, and a seeming belief that his first loyalty was to the White House rather than to the nation. Though he has proved capable in many ways, Gray might have diminished the directorship of the FBI.

With his withdrawal, a fresh spate of suggestions began to flow from Congress: That future FBI directors should have at least 10 years experience in the bureau; that the term should be for seven years or for 15 years; that the FBI should be taken out of the Justice Department and made an independent agency.

Now is the time for all fresh ideas to be explored and discussed thoroughly. The nation has never before had this opportunity and must make the most of it.

To make the FBI an independent agency does not recommend itself to those experienced in the ways of Washington. The FBI would become subject to incredible congressional pressures.

But it is essential that the term be limited and that the director remain nonpartisan. The governors of the Federal Reserve Board, for instance, serve 14-year terms on presidential appointment with Senate approval, and William McChesney Martin showed a true greatness of political integrity and of unyielding courage while chairman of that board. The comptroller general and the deputy comptroller are appointed for 15-year terms, and Federal Communications Commission members serve in staggered terms of seven years each.

Before President Nixon nominates another candidate, the White House and the Congress should work together in a bipartisan task of redefining the FBI directorship. If the executive and legislative can agree on the office, it should be easier for them to agree on a candidate for the office.

The Wichita Eagle

Wichita, Kans., April 9, 1973

And so L. Patrick Gray isn't going to become director of the F.B.I. It's probably just as well.

It seems doubtful that the country would be comfortable with him in that position, at least for a long time to come, because of the many doubts raised in the Watergate investigation and the intensely partisan feelings that cropped up in the Senate's questioning of him after the president submitted his nomination.

It must be said in Gray's behalf, however, that he served well during his time as acting director. He has succeeded in breaking down some of the rigidities that grew up in the Bureau under the lengthy tenure of J. Edgar Hoover, and the heads of a Senate that deeply resents his refusal to make appeared to be badly in need of the knocking.

The whole incident must be seen as a setback for Nixon at the hands of a Senate that deeply resents his refusal to make available the pertinent details of the Watergate incident.

Actually it is doubtful that Gray, himself, had any other connection with that affair than to provide files to White House aides as ordered, and the reluctance of the judiciary committee to confirm his nomination is less a criticism of Gray's personal qualifications and integrity than a slap at the President himself.

Now that Gray has asked his nomination be withdrawn and the President has acceded, the first order of business must be to get on with finding a satisfactory director.

Americans will hope that Mr. Nixon comes forward shortly with the nomination of someone who cannot be faulted in any way, and whose experience is such as to fit him for the job as the nation's No. 1 policeman.

St. Louis Globe-Democrat
St. Louis, Mo., April 7, 1973

L. Patrick Gray III should have been confirmed as director of the FBI. He would have been a worthy successor to the late J. Edgar Hoover.

He simply was a victim of the deadly cross-fire between the Senate Judiciary Committee and the White House.

Certain members of the committee charged Gray had made a grave error by showing FBI reports on the Watergate investigation to John W. Dean III, counsel to the President.

The point that was not emphasized during the lengthy hearings is that Dean also was investigating the possible role of White House staff members in the Watergate incident. There was every good reason why Gray should provide Dean, as the representative of the President, reports on the FBI findings to aid Dean in his investigation.

President Nixon also failed to back up Gray as might have been expected. In our opinion, Mr. Nixon should have ordered every member of his staff to cooperate fully with the Judiciary Committee rather than try to claim executive privilege. Since none of Mr. Nixon's policies were involved in this issue, there was no valid case for executive privilege.

If full cooperation had been given to the committee, we are confident that Gray would have been confirmed because the compete picture would have shown he (1) was guilty of no wrongdoing in the Watergate probe; (2) conducted a thorough investigation, (3) is well qualified for the post of FBI director.

It is tragic that a man who has served his country with distinction as a submarine captain and as acting director of the FBI should be used for bayonet practice in the battle between the Judiciary Committee and the White House.

The nation is the loser as well as Gray in this sordid affair. He deserves high praise for his conduct before the committee and his courage under the most difficult and unfair circumstances.

The Pittsburgh Press
Pittsburgh, Pa., April 8, 1973

With the Gray nomination wisely withdrawn, President Nixon now has the opportunity to appoint an FBI director with qualifications the U. S. Senate cannot question.

This means nominating a man who is neither a close friend nor a political ally of the President. He should be a strong administrator with a keen knowledge of the law.

The nomination of acting Director L. Patrick Gray III was in trouble from the start because Mr. Gray, for all his energy and candor, was a Nixon crony and political partisan.

In the Watergate investigation last summer, he chose to turn over confidential Watergate files to White House lawyer John W. Dean III on the questionable theory that because Mr. Dean was the President's man he had a right to such information.

★　★　★

Unwittingly or not, Mr. Gray made a series of what sounded like pro-Nixon speeches last summer and fall, and FBI agents (mistakenly, the White House says) were asked to gather background material for the presidential campaign.

It should have been no surprise, then, that the more the Watergate case began to unravel, the slimmer were Mr. Gary's chances of being confirmed by a Democratic-controlled Senate.

His request that the President withdraw his name was the only sensible course Mr. Gray could take. Even if he had been confirmed, his credibility — and the credibility of the FBI — would have been damaged.

Speculation now is that Mr. Nixon will act promptly, perhaps within a day or two, to submit a new nominee in Mr. Gray's place. Certainly a long delay would be unwarranted.

For the FBI has been operating without a permanent director since last May. That's long enough for any organization — and particularly for an organization that depends on leadership and esprit de corps.

It isn't necessary for the President to pick a police chief, or a prosecuting attorney, or a judge or even an old FBI hand for the job.

What matters most is that the President nominate the best man available.

Chicago Tribune
Chicago, Ill., April 9, 1973

Seven men have pleaded or been found guilty of complicity in the Watergate affair; but the first to be formally penalized for it, ironically, is the acting head of the FBI, L. Patrick Gray III, who had nothing to do with the ill-fated invasion of Democratic headquarters.

At Mr. Gray's request, President Nixon has withdrawn his nomination as director of the FBI.

Mr. Gray found himself in the impossible position of having tried to investigate a crime which his bosses in the White House did not want investigated, at least not too thoroly, and of then trying to explain his actions to a Senate committee which was ostensibly considering his confirmation but seemed really more interested in tying the White House to Watergate.

From the moment he found himself in this arena, Mr. Gray was almost a sure loser. If he had sung [or rather kept quiet] to the White House tune, he would have queered himself with the senators. If he had sung the song the senators wanted to hear, he would have angered the White House and the job he sought wouldn't have been worth much to him. As matters turned out, he offended both sides, and under the circumstances this is probably to his credit.

Mr. Nixon blames Mr. Gray's troubles on his compliance with a White House request for secret FBI reports on the Watergate investigation. "This completely proper and necessary request," the President said Thursday, "exposed Mr. Gray to totally unfair innuendo and suspicion and thereby seriously tarnished his fine record."

Since the request for the reports was from John Dean, the Presidential assistant who has himself been named as a participant in the planning of Watergate, the propriety and necessity of the request come out somewhat blurry. But no matter how you look at it, Mr. Gray's real problems stem not from unfair innuendoes by the senators or the public, but from the White House itself.

If the White House was right in asking for the secret data, and it is hard to deny it that right, then it was wrong in not cooperating with the investigation. If Mr. Gray was right in everything he did, then it was cowardly of the White House to abandon him just because he was having trouble with the senators. If the suspicions aroused by Mr. Gray's action or inaction were unfair, the White House could have cleared him by seeing that all the facts were made public.

The longer the uncertainties persist, the more suspicions are going to be aroused and the more people may be spattered unfairly with the Watergate mud. Federal Judge John J. Sirica has shown a commendable determination to get to the bottom of the whole thing, and he deserves the cooperation of everyone, including the President.

The Seattle Times
Seattle, Wash., April 11, 1973

FOUR years before the death of J. Edgar Hoover, it was apparent on Capitol Hill that choosing a successor to that living legend would be a matter of considerably more importance, interest and controversy than most cabinet appointments. So Congress in 1968 passed a law requiring that nominees for director of the Federal Bureau of Investigation be subject to Senate confirmation.

L. Patrick Gray became the first such to be put through the confirmation wringer. Gray got caught up in the Watergate whirlpool and became a victim both of his own controversial actions and a power struggle between the White House and Congress. His nomination has been withdrawn.

Whatever one's view on the Watergate controversy or on any other aspect of the running political duel between the Republican President and the Democratic majority in Congress, the Gray hearings served a useful purpose, it seems to us, in pointing up the need to remove the post of F. B. I. director as far as possible from politics.

President Nixon's next nominee should be a figure with a strong law-enforcement or, preferably, legal background but without a marked partisan political identity.

Beyond this, Congress should give careful consideration to two new bills aimed at further isolating the F. B. I. from politics.

One, by Senator Byrd of West Virginia, would divorce the F. B. I. from the Justice Department, creating an independent agency administered by a director serving a fixed term.

The other, by Senator Jackson, would provide for a 15-year term for the director and require "extensive professional experience," including at least 10 years with the F. B. I.

Recent Presidents, including Mr. Nixon and John F. Kennedy, have placed their top political advisers in the attorney generalship.

The existing chain of command did not give the F. B. I. a political tinge during Hoover's time because his long tenure and great stature enabled him to stake out a position of independence. The same conditions might not apply in the future.

Here is an issue that should command congressional attention beyond the matter of confirming or rejecting the next nominee to walk in Hoover's giant footsteps.

NEW DISCLOSURES FOLLOW NIXON REVERSAL

A series of important disclosures relating to complicity by present and former White House officials in the Watergate affair were made following President Nixon's April 17 announcement that there had been "major developments" from a "new inquiry" he had initiated into Watergate, which would be "improper" to discuss at the present time. The President said he had also agreed on ground rules to permit testimony by his aides before a Senate committee investigating Watergate that would "totally preserve the doctrine of separation of powers." "They provide," he said, that a witness could first appear at a secret session of the committee, "if appropriate," and that executive privilege was "expressly reserved and may be asserted" during the testimony. He said White House staff members "will appear voluntarily when requested" and "will testify under oath and they will answer fully all proper questions." The following day committee chairman Sen. Sam Ervin (D, N.C.) said that the panel would be the final judge whether a witness could refuse to answer its questions. White House Press Secretary Ronald Ziegler explained that the President's previous statements denying Watergate involvement by White House officials were now "inoperative," since they were based on "investigations prior to the developments announced today."

In the days that followed, there were these major developments in the Watergate case:

■ On April 19 the *Washington Post* reported that Jeb Stuart Magruder, an aide to former Attorney General John Mitchell after the latter resigned to head the Nixon re-election campaign, told federal prosecutors April 14 that he and Mitchell, presidential counsel John Dean 3rd and convicted Watergate defendant G. Gordon Liddy had planned and approved the Watergate wiretapping at a meeting in the attorney general's office in February 1972. Magruder was said to have told the prosecutors that Mitchell and Dean later arranged to buy the silence of the seven convicted Watergate conspirators.

■ On April 19 Attorney General Richard Kleindienst removed himself from the Watergate case after having been "advised ... of information which related to persons with whom I have had a close ... relationship."

■ On April 19 Dean issued a statement that he would not "become a scapegoat in the Watergate case." Newspaper accounts, based on information from Dean's associates, reported Dean was prepared to implicate people "above and below" if he was singled out for prosecution.

■ On April 20 Mitchell told reporters after testifying before the federal grand jury investigating Watergate that he had "heard discussions" of the Watergate operation but had never approved them.

■ The *Washington Post* April 23 quoted high Administration sources as reporting that the President had been warned "as early as last December" that members of his staff, specifically including Mitchell and Dean, were involved in Watergate but that Nixon had wanted evidence before taking any action.

■ According to leaked testimony from the grand jury investigating Watergate, convicted conspirator James McCord testified that Dean had warned that the Watergate operation would have to be undertaken in such a way that Mitchell could deny it at a future date. Columnist Jack Anderson, who had used copies of grand jury transcripts in reporting on the case since April 16, agreed April 25 to stop publishing the excerpts.

■ On April 27 L. Patrick Gray 3rd announced his resignation as acting director of the Federal Bureau of Investigation. Environmental Protection Agency Administrator William D. Ruckelshaus was named later that day as his temporary successor. Gray said he was resigning, effective immediately, "as a consequence" of reports he had burned files removed from the office safe of E. Howard Hunt Jr., a confessed Watergate conspirator who had worked as a White House consultant. The New York *Daily News* and the *New York Times* had reported hours earlier that Gray had been handed the files in June 1972 by Dean and presidential assistant John Ehrlichman and had been told by Dean that they "should never see the light of day."

In the midst of the mounting criticism of the Administration's handling of the affair, President Nixon was spending a secluded 5-day working Easter vacation in Florida and the Bahamas.

THE ROANOKE TIMES
Roanoke, Va., April 19, 1973

Pressed from all sides—hardest, perhaps, from within his own party—for some meaningful response to the Watergate charges, President Nixon has at last changed position. His promise that White House aides will give sworn, public testimony before a Senate investigative committee is a major concession toward bringing out the long-concealed truth about that seamy affair.

Mr. Nixon has acted none too soon. All his words and actions, and those of his spokesmen, up until Tuesday had been calculated to minimize the affair, to deny any part had been taken by administration officials, to ward off public questioning of White House aides. As evidence mounted that higher-ups had been involved, suspicions grew that the administration had something to hide.

The President is admitting nothing for now, but his cryptic announcement about a new White House investigation and his reference to "major developments" in the case put him on the right side at last. He is no longer defending, covering up, defying; rather, he is willing to cooperate with others in finding the facts and is pledging that any who are implicated will be properly dealt with.

Too bad it took so long; by nature, Mr. Nixon would rather fight than switch, and his dogged stand on the Watergate matter had threatened to do lasting damage to his presidential image and to the Republican party. He is not a last-ditch man, however; he knows when the time has come to change position, and how to put the best face upon it. His statement Tuesday did not clear up the Watergate fog, but it came as a refreshing breeze from a different quarter.

THE STATES-ITEM

New Orleans, La., April 19, 1973

President Nixon has refused to level with the American people about the involvement of the White House in the reprehensible Watergate political espionage affair. Now he would have us believe that he has seized the initiative in an effort to get at the truth.

It is much too late for empty theatrics.

The truth is going to be told despite the Nixon Administration's 10-month campaign to suppress it. Mr. Nixon obviously understands this and has now attempted to soften the blow.

Sworn testimony before the Senate's special Watergate investigating committee and before a federal grand jury has made it impossible for Mr. Nixon to pawn off any longer the fantasy that his administration was not involved in the Watergate Democratic headquarters break-in, or the months of espionage aimed at disrupting the Democratic party's presidential campaign effort.

The pressure has now moved the President to say that he began conducting his own investigation during the latter part of March and that "there have been major developments in the case concerning which it would be improper to be more specific now, except to say that real progress has been made in finding the truth."

If "real progress has been made in finding the truth" it is in spite of the roadblocks thrown up by the Nixon Administration.

Mr. Nixon trundled the first barrier into place on Aug. 29 of last year in commenting on the whitewash non - investigation conducted by presidential counsel John W. Dean III:

"I can say categorically that his investigation indicates that no one in the White House staff, no one in this administration, presently employed, was involved in this very bizarre incident."

Contempt for history

The administration line was repeated many times during the ensuing months by persons in and close to the White House.

Much too late, Mr. Nixon has changed his mind. He is now ready to say that no individual holding a position of major importance in the administration should be given immunity from prosecution.

And, with a measured contempt for the history of the Watergate crimes, the President adds, "I condemn any attempt to cover up in this case, no matter who is involved."

It is the Nixon Administration that has attempted to hide the truth from the American people.

The new search for truth comes only after certain hired operatives of the Republican party's Committee to Re-elect the President have decided to tell what they know of the Watergate affair.

A tortuous process

Mr. Nixon has also relented in his determination that White House aides shall not give sworn testimony before the Senate investigative committee headed by Sen. Sam Ervin of North Carolina. They will now be allowed to answer "all proper questions."

Again, it should be pointed out that the decision is not entirely magnanimous or laudatory on the part of the President. The guidelines for testimony are those of the Senate committee. Sen. Ervin, it turns out, wrote them.

Getting at the truth in the very serious Watergate matter has been a long, tortuous process. It should not have been that way. The Nixon Administration should have agreed to cooperate 10 months ago, as it has been forced to cooperate now.

The Birmingham News

Birmingham, Ala., April 19, 1973

The Watergate espionage episode, as bad as it was, does not merit the long, drawn-out belaboring of every detail Senate Democrats are making of it.

Last summer the public was apathetic about the issue during the presidential campaign. It would probably be accurate to say that the average American now simply is sick and tired of reading and hearing about it month after month.

Sen. Sam Ervin, D-S.C., is in charge of the Watergate sideshow, which so far has produced a lot of rhetoric beneficial to the Democrats and a lot of unsubstantiated "leaks" to the press.

The "leaks" have consisted of wild charges based on hearsay of the variety made famous by the late Sen. Joseph McCarthy. That the Senate Democrats persist in this form of partisan witch-hunting is almost as reprehensible as the shenanigans for which the Committee to Re-elect the President was responsible last summer.

It is not as if the nation depends on the Senate investigation for justice to be done. Concurrently, a federal grand jury has been holding hearings also. And, equally reprehensible, testimony supposedly made in the secrecy of the grand jury room has been piped to the press and aired daily in the news pages.

Civil libertarians once set up a clamor over the rights of Black Panther defendants, saying they couldn't get a fair trial in America. It's getting to the point where the same should be said for accused members of the administration.

To refresh memories, it should be pointed out that the principals in the Watergate affair already have been brought to justice. G. Gordon Liddy and James W. McCord Jr. were convicted Jan. 30 of conspiracy, second-degree burglary, attempted wire-tapping and attempted bugging. In the same trial, five others earlier had pleaded guilty —Bernard L. Barker, Frank A. Sturgis, Eugenio, Rolando Martinez, Virgilio R. Gonzales and E. Howard Hunt Jr.

As for any possible link with higher-ups in the administration, the grand jury is quite capable of getting to the truth.

Another point should be made about the Democratically controlled Congress' sense of outraged justice: That outrage through the years has been selectively applied.

Remember the Bobby Baker scandal? Baker was then-Sen. Lyndon Johnson's protege. But did Congress investigate the connection between Johnson and the wrong doing? No.

Then there was the undeniable vote swindle in the 1960 election in Illinois and Texas that allowed John F. Kennedy narrowly to win the presidency. The stealing of an election, an act which changed the history of the nation, is certainly more shocking and of far greater consequence than the Watergate bugging case. But did Congress form a committee to investigate the fraud? No.

There are a lot of skeletons in the Democratic closet that the majority party is content to let lie. For this reason, the public cannot be blamed for being cynical about the Watergate case. A common attitude is, "So what? The Republicans just got caught."

The courts are the place to settle such matters and the congressional Democrats could have stayed out of this affair with no harm done.

Meanwhile, Congress is getting very little of its own work done. Only 13 bills have become law since the 93rd Congress convened Jan. 3. Four of them resolutions such as one designating "National Employ the Older Worker Week." Most major legislation still is in committee.

Even worse, the Democrats risk a boomerang of their drawn-out Watergate inquisition. The cardinal political sin is to bore the public. And the Democrats are getting dangerously close to provoking one vast public yawn.

ST. LOUIS POST-DISPATCH
St. Louis, Mo., April 19, 1973

As with any pronouncement that comes from this Administration, the thing to do with President Nixon's statement Tuesday on the Watergate case is to ask one's self, what is new and significant, what only appears new but in truth is meaningless and what, finally, is nothing but a restatement of the status quo? Mr. Nixon's remarks are replete with examples of all three categories; and Press Secretary Ziegler's elaboration of them reveals that the White House is still unprepared to yield an inch—an inch toward the truth, that is—on the matter of political espionage and sabotage without a grudging fight.

In his statement, Mr. Nixon made two concessions that may be considered to fall within Category A—something new. He has admitted White House complicity in Watergate by raising the question of a "person in the executive branch" being indicted by a grand jury. It is impossible to imagine that Mr. Nixon has not been given foreknowledge of one or more impending indictments. Still, the statement demolishes 10 months of steady White House denials of any involvement in Watergate.

The other concession is Mr. Nixon's agreement that White House officials may testify under oath before Senator Ervin's Watergate investigation committee. Hitherto, Mr. Nixon has claimed executive privilege protects his aids from such appearances, although the assertion itself was a damaging one: it suggested the President had received confidential information about political dirty work from his lieutenants. Now, in ordering his aids to testify, Mr. Nixon says that he "condemn(s) any attempts to cover up in this case, no matter who is involved." A welcome statement, significant, however, only because it has been so long resisted.

In Category B, that of the apparently new, we find Mr. Nixon saying that if members of the executive branch are convicted, they will be dismissed. That is not only proper but practical; one can scarcely imagine White House work being efficiently conducted behind federal prison bars.

Mr. Nixon also says that a new investigation was begun "as a result of serious charges which came to my attention" on March 21. Those charges were made by convicted Watergate defendant James McCord in a letter to a federal judge stating that former Attorney General Mitchell, presidential counselor Dean and Jeb Stuart Magruder, deputy head of the Nixon re-election committee, had prior knowledge of the Watergate mission. Since the White House has had steady access to Federal Bureau of Investigation records it seems unlikely that Mr. McCord said anything Mr. Nixon had not already known or suspected.

As to the status quo, Category C, Mr. Nixon, despite his total surrender to Mr. Ervin in this case, is standing firmly on his interpretation of executive privilege. He has not taken back his assertion that any executive branch employe, past or present, could be granted this immunity; worse, he failed to take the opportunity to repudiate the preposterous doctrine put forward in the name of the Administration by Attorney General Kleindienst—that s u c h privilege covers all 2,500,000 executive employes. Still, if he ever intends to reassert these claims he would be advised to wait a long time; Congress won this round, hands down.

Despite his statement that "real progress has been made toward the truth," the facts indicate that the White House is progressing just as slowly as possible. If the President's knowledge of White House involvement in Watergate, why wait for an indictment to act? Why continue in Government service someone the President knows or strongly suspects to have attempted to rig an election?

Mr. Ziegler's remark that "The President's statement today is the operative statement" ought not to be glossed over. It suggests that words—statements by the President—are like automobiles and toasters that wear out with time and become no longer "operative." Like used cars, used statements can be traded in for operative new ones. Mr. Ervin's committee and the grand jury, therefore, must keep conscientiously to their work to get to the bottom of the Watergate mess, for who knows when Mr. Nixon's most recent words, such as they are, will no longer be operative?

Detroit Free Press
Detroit, Mich., April 19, 1973

IF PRESIDENT NIXON thinks he deserves a pat on the back for his about-face on the Watergate, he is wrong. At best, he is simply going to do what he plainly should have done 10 months ago.

But his retreat from his previous hard-line position on executive privilege is welcome, as is his promise of complete co-operation in the investigation of the break-in and bugging of the Democratic national headquarters last June. He has promised complete co-operation before, though, and we will have to wait and see if he means it this time.

In fact, Mr. Nixon's lack of co-operation has perhaps drawn more attention toward the White House than it may deserve. While the President sat on the lid making statements against covering things up, all White House aides were under public suspicion.

By allowing his aides to testify before both Congress and the Watergate grand jury, Mr. Nixon can get out whatever bad eggs he may have in his administration. Those aides not involved in the Watergate episode should welcome the opportunity to testify.

There is considerable evidence that the President did not change his tune voluntarily. He might have carried on the fight with congressional Democrats indefinitely, but he was getting considerable flak from Republican members. And there were indications that campaign money, from contributors overwhelmed by the stench from Watergate, was drying up.

No matter how firmly the President now acts, he cannot escape his ducking and dodging of the past 10 months. No matter how sincere his present attitude may be, he is going to have to face the fact that it appears Barry Goldwater and Lowell Weicker, among others, had more to do with his change of heart than any desire for the truth.

We hope the President is sincere, now that he has recognized that Watergate is not going to go away. And, for that reason, Mr. Nixon has much to gain and little to lose by opening up the White House to inquiry.

Even specific charges against top aides would be less damaging to Mr. Nixon's place in the history books than the general taint of the Watergate mess, which has already led to comparisons between the present administration and that of Warren G. Harding.

But if the President is going to get rid of the taint, he will have to take the lid off, not just raise it slightly. He cannot offer the Senate and the American people a "sacrificial lamb," a single aide designated to take the blame.

There may be only one aide who was involved—or there may be none, for that matter—but there are several who must be investigated before what Sen. Goldwater called the "smell" of Watergate will go away.

Mr. Nixon's "couldn't care less" attitude toward the whole affair was inexcusable, and his turnabout came 10 months late. But it is not too late; there is still time to reach the facts in the case.

As Sen. Weicker said of the Watergate, "Believe me, we're going to have that story." We must.

Arkansas Gazette.

Little Rock, Ark., April 21, 1973

RICHARD Nixon has all the survival and restorative capacity of one of those cirrhotic livers that the liver men have all but unanimously written off — along with its owner — but that somehow proves to have had one more fling in it yet.

It is for this reason — and because of the well-known Nixon Luck — that many serious students of Nixon and Nixonism still are predicting that at some point when the Watergate mess is at its worst (it doesn't, in truth, have much farther to go), Nixon somehow will be able to turn it to his credit account, after all. One flick of the cape and — presto! — ain't nobody here but us Easter Bunnies.

We, however, just do not see how he can bring it off this time. If there is any logic left in the country — and we think there is — there is no way we can see that he can win this one.

There is, we believe, revolving, compounded perjury in this business at the very least, and, in one form or another, the issue is going to be heard about and talked about for quite some time to come.

More and more people each day are being obliged to decide for themselves either that (1) Mr. Nixon is complicit himself, to some degree or other and in one way or another, or (2) that the reputation for detecting the misdeeds of others on which he built a whole career is pretty much a phony. No Sherlock Holmes, he, applying former Pulaski County Judge Arch Campbell's ear lobe test or its equivalent during the screening of the men who were to become his very closest hand-picked associates!

On this point, as we have already suggested, all the "kooks" by whom Mrs. Martha Mitchell says Mr. Nixon is almost exclusively surrounded were chosen by Mr. Nixon himself for their special talents, which, though quite special indeed, nonetheless are held in common by all of them, including, most notably, Mr. Nixon himself. In brief, Mr. Nixon, in our judgment, did not make any mistake in choosing the kind of pack he wanted to run with him.

As to the other point — the central question of whether Mr. Nixon is himself personally complicit in the matter, and if so, *how* complicit, we have no choice but to say that, yes, he is, and, as to the matter of how complicit, our answer must necessarily, be "very."

Nearest the mark, we shouldn't be surprised is a theory expressed by (among others), Kermit Bensing, a "man on the street" from deep in the heart of Nixon Country, in Stow, O. Bensing was one of a number of people from typically strong Nixon precincts who were interviewed before the election last fall and then re-interviewed in light of the more recent Watergate unfoldings by Haynes Johnson and Jules Witcover for distribution nationally through the Los Angeles Times-Washington Post News service. The revised Johnson-Witcover report showed a marked degree of disenchantment with the reality of the

Nixon second term and for a variety of reasons, but Bensing himself is still inclined to be "for" his man in spite of all. But. The big "but" is the Watergate scandal, and here is what Bensing believes was Nixon's role in it:

"I think he probably told his head honcho. 'Look, do whatever is necessary, but don't tell me about it. So if it ever comes out I can truthfully say I don't know about it'."

That sounds about right. It has the right ring of Nixon.

★ ★ ★

AT THE PRESENT the Watergate case is proceeding along three broad fronts: (1) The new criminal indictments that administration themselves concede are imminent. (2) The congressional investigation with full power of subpoena being conducted by Senator Sam J. Ervin of North Carolina, whose reputation as a

bird-dog, unlike Nixon's, is unblemished. (3) The action for civil damages that the impoverished Democrats still are refusing to settle out of court in spite of the Republicans' offer of a cash settlement out of some of the leftover money that wasn't spent on the Watergate bugging.

Alger Hiss — it naturally will not be remembered — was never convicted of "treason." He was convicted for perjury in a federal proceeding resulting from an action for civil damages. Wouldn't it be ironic if we should be brought full circle and see Nixon's head finally spiked on a White House fence post because of one or more perjury convictions arising out of the Watergate conspiracy, most especially if the convictions should come in a federal court action for civil damages.

Rocky Mountain News

Denver, Colo., April 22, 1973

READERS WHO DISLIKE the sight of inky wretches patting their own trade on the back are advised to look away now.

Why? Because the theme of this little sermon is that this country's much-maligned press was honest and right about the Watergate scandal, while the White House was deceitful and wrong.

From the start, the White House tried to pass off Watergate as a bad joke in no way involving the President's men. White House press secretary Ronald Ziegler called it "a third-rate burglary attempt" and warned the media not to "try to stretch this beyond what it is."

To their credit, many reporters went "beyond" what Ziegler and company wanted them to believe. Witness the present parade of a former attorney general, counsels and other White House potentates before the grand jury.

The Washington Post, a newspaper with which we often disagree, did a particularly noteworthy job. Its reporters covered Watergate clues with persistence and initiative.

Credit is also due U.S. District Judge John J. Sirica (a Republican, by the way), who would not let the seven convicted Watergate conspirators remain silent and take brief (and well-paid?) jail terms.

By threatening to send them away forever, Sirica got one of the burglary crew, the wiretapper McCord, to talk, and the sordid attempt at cover-up began to come apart.

Sen. Sam J. Ervin Jr., D-N.C., head of the special investigating committee, also worked for justice by not letting President Nixon wrap the doctrine of "executive privilege" around a clutch of present and former aides who look worse all the time.

Nevertheless, we believe that without hard-nosed reporting and digging by the media, the higher-ups involved with Watergate and related political espionage and sabotage would have got away with it.

The Des Moines Register

Des Moines, Iowa, April 24, 1973

Atty. Gen. Richard Kleindienst has taken himself out of further involvement in the Watergate case because of "close and professional relationships" with new suspects in the case. Kleindienst's show of propriety comes too late to do him much good.

The attorney general was No. 2 man in the Justice Department at the time John Mitchell headed the department. When Mitchell left to run the Committee for Re-election of the President, Kleindienst replaced him. Though the committee was deeply implicated from the outset in the Watergate scandal, Kleindienst did nothing to assure independent investigation or prosecution or take himself out of the case.

The presiding judge was so appalled at the prosecution of the first seven Watergate defendants that he openly rebuked the government for its part in helping keep the full story hidden. Klein-

dienst sat idly by while the FBI conducted a gingerly probe of White House ties to the case, and while the agency failed to pursue the source of Watergate financing. When L. Patrick Gray began divulging politically embarrassing details about Watergate at his confirmation hearing, Kleindienst promptly muzzled him.

The attorney general performed throughout the Watergate case as a political functionary rather than as the nation's chief law enforcement officer dedicated to the even-handed administration of justice. President Nixon appointed Kleindienst knowing full well that he was a partisan politician first and foremost. One of the tragedies of the Watergate case is how Kleindienst was unable to rise above his assigned political role and do his sworn duty as the chief law enforcement officer of the country.

The New York Times

New York, N.Y., April 22, 1973

On this 100th anniversary of the publication of their novel, "The Gilded Age," Mark Twain and Charles Dudley Warner could find much familiar material in the America of today. Once again, White House aides, former Cabinet members and other Presidential appointees are parading in and out of grand jury rooms and Congressional hearings as major scandals erupt. A century ago it was Credit Mobilier, the whisky ring, railroad stock frauds and "burn this letter!" Today it is Watergate, the wheat windfall, the milk scandal, the fixing of antitrust suits and the shredding of documents.

Both parties are besmirched. In Illinois, a Federal judge who formerly served as Governor is sentenced to prison for bribe-taking, while other prominent Democrats are under indictment. In New Jersey, leading figures in both parties are convicted of systematic graft in the letting of public contracts.

Once again, there are scandals in business as well as in politics. It is a time of shoddy practices and compromised standards, of rampant cynicism and a get-rich-quick psychology, of sleazy political methods and an anything-goes popular culture.

The motives and ideas of President Grant, who presided over that first gilded age, are still elusive to historians. President Nixon, after nearly three decades in public life, is equally enigmatic. But what matters is less Mr. Nixon's psychology than the record.

* * *

The record suggests that Mr. Nixon has been the last rather than the first to try to establish the truth about the Watergate affair and the campaign of espionage and sabotage which it brought to a climax. In his press conferences and repeatedly through his White House press spokesman, the President has denied, dismissed and ridiculed these charges and cast aspersions on the press for inquiring into them. Only after participants in this squalid operation began to testify against one another to the grand jury and further criminal indictments became likely did Mr. Nixon last week belatedly intervene.

President Nixon's obstructionist tactics in the Watergate case are similar to those he has followed with greater success in the wheat scandal, the milk scandal and the I.T.T. antitrust settlement. There is still doubt that the public has learned all the truth about the Agriculture Department's dealings with the large grain companies that made huge profits out of last year's Russian wheat sale. The public has never had an explanation from President Nixon of why an increase in Federal milk prices was ordered only after the dairymen began making large contributions to his political campaign chest.

If Mr. Nixon felt any indignation about I.T.T.'s campaign of influence and pressure on White House and Justice Department officials prior to gaining its favorable antitrust settlement, he has never articulated it. Former Secretary of Commerce Maurice Stans, as the campaign finance chairman of Mr. Nixon's re-election committee, conducted a relentless and partially secret hunt for money, accepted and kept huge sums in cash contrary to any sound or defensible practice, and is still trying to keep hidden as much of his operation as he can. Instead of trying to clean up a distressing situation, President Nixon still displays confidence in Mr. Stans.

This is not the kind of leadership the country has a right to expect from its President. Instead of the "open administration" pledged by Mr. Nixon in 1968, the nation has had a succession of big deals followed by big cover-ups.

The President's responsibility is inescapable even if his motives are sometimes inexplicable. Mr. Nixon either had personal knowledge of the deeds that have been done in his name or, if he was ignorant of them, as seems more likely, he has been deficient in his judgment of men and he has established incompetent and undependable arrangements for keeping himself informed about the work of his subordinates.

More than a few firings or a few artfully worded statements are needed to clear up this situation. There is need for the President, in choosing a new Attorney General, a new Director of the Federal Bureau of Investigation and a new White House counsel, to go beyond the circle of his acquaintances and choose men of genuine distinction and demonstrated experience in whom the public can have confidence. Even more, there has to be a Presidential recognition that long-established standards of probity, propriety, fair dealing and sound constitutional practice have to be observed and enforced from the top downward. And surely it is not too much to believe that the President henceforth can see to it that his Administration no longer contributes to the active debasement of those standards.

The TENNESSEAN

Nashville, Tenn., April 24, 1973

AS MORE and more details pile up in the Watergate scandal, White House credibility continues to erode, and Mr. Nixon has little choice but to make public the "major developments" in the case that he said his own investigation had uncovered.

* * *

Until last Tuesday, when the President made a statement on the case, the White House and Nixon campaign workers had steadfastly declined to come to grips with allegations. The usual thrust of their remarks was that the press was trying to make a mountain of a molehill.

President Nixon's first personal statement on the case came last Aug. 29. After telling newsmen that Mr. John W. Dean III, his special counsel, had conducted an independent investigation, he said, "I can say categorically that his (Dean's) investigation indicates that no one in the White House staff, no one is this administration, presently employed, was involved in this very bizarre incident . . ."

In the briefing that followed Mr. Nixon's statement of April 17, White House press secretary Ronald L. Ziegler called previous statements from the White House "inoperative." He said, "The President's statement today is the operative statement."

That is a fascinating concept of presidential and White House staff statements: that they are "operative" until such time as events make them "inoperative."

Mr. Nixon's operative statement disclosed that he reviewed the situation of the Watergate with an assistant attorney general instead of his chief law enforcement officer, Attorney General Richard Kleindienst. His operative statement also constituted a vote of no-confidence in Mr. Dean, the in-house counsel.

Thus the President let it appear that Mr. Dean didn't perform his investigatory duties properly, and therefore it became necessary for him to begin his own investigation.

As a result of this, the impression was, he had acquired evidence that might well lead to indictments of someone in his administration.

Who the someone might be was left in mystery, and the impact of this was to leave a cloud hanging over everybody.

Still another impression that has been left—whether by intent or by accident—is that Mr. Nixon is now acting from information he could not have obtained earlier.

* * *

It stretches credulity to be asked to believe that the President of the United States doesn't know what his staff is doing, much less what his re-election committee was doing. In a televised interview on Jan. 4, 1971, Mr. Nixon said: "When I am a candidate, I run the campaign." That certainly has been borne out in previous campaigns.

If the assumption is valid that the President knew nothing of the Watergate and the accompanying campaign of political sabotage directed at the Democrats, but now knows of major information, he doesn't need to wait for indictments to make it public. He can simply lay it on the line and let the whole world see.

Winnipeg Free Press

Winnipeg, Man., April 24, 1973

Opponents of President Nixon are determined to wreck the president's long-term ambition. Rather than having his niche in history as the president who ended America's involvement in Vietnam, established links with China and endeavored to find a modus vivendi with the Soviet Union, Mr. Nixon is to be marked as "The Man of Watergate." It is a questionable enterprise and, judging from recent precedents, one might doubt that it will succeed.

It will be recalled, for instance, that President Eisenhower was reluctant to drive in the inaugural parade side by side with President Truman, whom he considered the epitome of corruption in high places. Even Adlai Stevenson, who campaigned as the Democratic presidential candidate to succeed Mr. Truman, promised that he would "clean up the mess in Washington." Who today remembers those "cronies" — a term stamped on the Truman era by the president's enemies? Viewed from historical perspective, Mr. Truman appears as a shrewd politician whose achievements — in saving Berlin from Stalin's clutches and in preventing totalitarian communism from encroaching further upon Europe — have by far overshadowed the minor peccadilloes that from this distance appear quite insignificant.

We remember Dwight Eisenhower as an able war commander, a president who fearlessly enforced desegregation and who presided over a country that, at home and abroad, was largely at peace. Yet he too had troubles with his own "cronies," only they were no longer cronies but respectable Republican governors who somehow lost their bearings in the White House maze. Sherman Adams of vicuna coat fame wrote a thick book about it but today only a specialist will recall Mr. Adams' name; and how many know what a vicuna coat is, or even can spell the word?

Yet at one time the word was as much on everybody's lips as is Watergate today. Instead of Democratic cronies with refrigerators and Republican governors in vicuna coats we now have up-to-date electronic gadgetry. But the basic motives of the accused and the accusers have not changed. Once one had to bribe a hotel porter and a chambermaid to be allowed to peer through keyholes. Today one plants an electronic device — a far costlier procedure, no doubt — and it's called progress.

It was undeniably an egregious blunder to bug the Democratic campaign headquarters, particularly when there was so little doubt about President Nixon's re-election. It was both foolish and unethical, but in this scientific age electronic ethics have become regrettably blurred. We are so proud of our inventiveness, of what the device can do, that we have stopped questioning the ethics of employing such clever devices. In a society in which, according to the 1967 findings of the President's Commission on Law Enforcement, 58 per cent of all urban white males are arrested at some time in their lives (the figure for non-white males is 90 per cent) and where the FBI computer receives daily 29,000 sets of fingerprints that are stored and made freely available to whoever asks for them, the implanting of a bugging device in a political opponent's headquarters was probably considered by those who conceived it, smart rather than criminal.

Perhaps it did require this minor earthquake to wake up American public opinion and make it aware of the direction society has been taking. Nor is it a bad thing to bring forcibly home to all concerned — and this includes every politician and every bureaucrat — that eavesdropping is something that just is not done. However, having said all this one cannot but feel that the Watergate affair has been blown out of proportion, and that those who have called the present ballyhoo McCarthyism-in-reverse are not entirely wrong.

This is not a matter over which the U.S. should be tearing itself to pieces, and a concerned neighbor cannot but believe that there are far more serious problems, at home and abroad, that require urgent attention of the Nixon administration. The Democratic opposition has been whipping up the Watergate scandal for all it is worth in the hope of reversing the people's verdict of last November. The Democrats should think again. They might yet inherit the shambles.

The Providence Journal

Providence, R.I., April 24, 1973

It is not enough to deplore the moral overtones of the Watergate mess as it hits the daily headlines. Prudent concern for tomorrow demands thoughtful consideration of its future political importance.

The affair must necessarily have longrange effects on national and international problems. We can only guess at these effects until all the facts have been fully publicized and dealt with. But we already can begin to map out the direction in which its forward shadows are falling.

President Nixon's closest aides in the White House have been shown to have had knowledge of the plot. The very admission by John Mitchell that he knew of the plot, even though he claims to have resisted it, inevitably brings suspicion that the plot had to be known by the President himself. The public will be hard put to believe that as a close friend and advisor, Mr. Mitchell would have done other than to warn Mr. Nixon of the plot and the dangers it presented to the Presidency.

Thus, already the integrity and credibility of the President has been thrown sharply in doubt. With the loss of credibility comes weakening of authority and leadership. This is already evident in the fact that Mr. Nixon has been thrown from the strong offensive stance of his first four years in office to a defensive position. He is on the defensive in the Watergate issue. He is on the defensive in Southeast Asia. He is on the defensive at home, where the inflation rate has hit a record high.

A President on the defensive lacks flexibility of action and the range of options that a President in an offensive position has at his command. Take, for example, the war in Indochina. Instead of being wrapped up as a veritable "peace with honor," fighting has continued between North and South Vietnamese in South Vietnam. American bombers continue to pound Cambodia, where the ground fighting has intensified since the signing of the ceasefire. In Laos, the government is tottering. But the President is preoccupied with Watergate. He is in a poor position to take any decisive, carefully planned steps in an unpopular war which is anyway supposed to be over. Yet there is talk in Washington of a possible resumption of bombing of Hanoi; and the minesweeping operation in Haiphong Harbor already has been curtailed.

Meanwhile, other national and world problems are on the back burner: trade negotiations with Europe and Japan; monetary talks with America's trading partners; the SALT talks; mutual balanced force reduction negotiations in Europe; the energy crisis.

With Mr. Nixon on the defensive, a power vacuum appears in Washington. Into that political vacuum, new forces begin to intrude. A Democratic Party, revitalized at least for the moment by Republican misfortunes, has begun to shake off the shock brought on by November's disastrous defeat. It still lacks a leader — George McGovern is gone with the wind, Hubert Humphrey is old hat, and Edward Kennedy is not ready to stack Chappaquiddick up against Watergate — but the Democrats sense that Mr. Nixon's New Republican Majority may go over the dam with Watergate.

Further, the Congress, which has been champing for a second chance to exercise the constitutional powers it long ago shunted off to the White House, is already in the process of regrouping strength. The President may not be able to resist these efforts if the Watergate results show him or his trusted aides to have misused the powers of his office.

We see, in these ways, the working of new forces that will shape not only the remainder of Mr. Nixon's second and last term, but the face of domestic politics for years to come. We can only hope that the Watergate does not impair the President's ability to act decisively and constructively in the many areas in which he has started promising overtures to world peace and progress.

THE CHRISTIAN SCIENCE MONITOR
Boston, Mass., April 26, 1973

Watergate has long since become a political disaster for Richard Nixon and the Republican Party. It is now a constitutional crisis calling for drastic remedial measures. The issue is the capacity of the incumbent President to govern effectively during the remainder of his term of office. That capacity must be restored. There is no other practical way out of the crisis. The question is whether Mr. Nixon himself is yet ready to take the steps which he must take to restore the institution of the presidency to effectiveness.

To rescue the institution itself justice must be done, and seen to be done. This is a case where the housecleaning must be thorough, quick, and evident to all skeptics. Leaving the management of the housecleaning in the hands of anyone connected with the White House itself will not be good enough. There is a cloud of suspicion over everyone in the administration who has anything to do with domestic politics. That cloud can be lifted only if the housecleaning is put in the hands of someone free of all personal connections with the White House, with the defendants in the case and even with the high command of the Republican Party.

As we are writing the prosecution is under Henry F. Petersen, Assistant Attorney General in charge of the Criminal Division of the Department of Justice. The burden fell on him when Attorney General Richard Kleindienst disqualified himself on grounds of "personal and professional relationships" with persons involved in the case.

We have not the slightest reason to doubt Mr. Petersen's probity. But he has served under Mr. Kleindienst and he is a long time personal friend of the lawyer now acting on behalf of John Mitchell. That is too close a relationship to a main character in the case. Mr. Mitchell was Mr. Nixon's Attorney General during most of the first term. He resigned to run the re-election campaign. He repeatedly asserted that he had never heard of the Watergate business until the arrests at the Democratic National Committee Headquarters. Yet, before a grand jury he has now confessed that the break-in and bugging operation were discussed in his presence at least three times prior to the burglary. He stands guilty on his own testimony of concealing the truth and thus of helping to try to conceal information about a criminal act.

Many eminent lawyers are doubtful as to whether Mr. Nixon has yet sufficiently divested himself of control over the investigation to allow it to rise above suspicion. When he changed course and announced "major new developments" in the case he also expressed "my view that no individual holding, in the past or at present, a position of major importance in the administration should be given immunity from prosecution." According to some lawyers this has the legal effect of discouraging defendants from talking.

Sooner or later the whole truth in this most unseemly and sordid affair is coming out. The question now is whether it will be dragged out by bits and pieces through the Senate committee hearing process and in various lawsuits, with the administration holding back at every turn and doing its best to limit the disclosures. If it comes that way it will continue to do harm to Mr. Nixon's capacity to serve out his term effectively. The other way is for him to do what must be done to raise the official government prosecution above suspicion.

The reason to put it above suspicion is, in our opinion, of first importance. As many have already pointed out, the criminal actions and, even more seriously, the long devious effort to conceal them, would, in a parliamentary democracy have already forced the resignation of the Prime Minister and Cabinet. In the United States the presidency is for a four-year term. Mr. Nixon has just been re-elected by an enormous majority, the second largest in the history of the country. There is no evidence that even an important minority want anything other than a chance to regain confidence in the man they elected less than six months ago. No responsible figure is calling for his resignation. All are calling for a quick, thorough, and credible housecleaning. Hence we urge Mr. Nixon to put the prosecution of the case in the hands of a person who is so free of White House connections that the results will be believable.

But one more thing is needed to restore the prestige and authority of the man elected last November to the presidency. There has been a tone about the White House which was detectable during the first term, but has become strident since election day. It is a tone of self-righteousness bordering often on arrogance. It has raised a formidable barrier between the White House and the Congress.

It has come out over foreign policy—the assertion of presidential power to bomb at will regardless of how contrary the sentiment might be in the Congress. It has come out in assertion of executive privilege — the alleged (now abandoned) claim of the White House to have the power to blanket the entire federal establishment under executive privilege. It has come out a thousand times in the cold contempt of White House staff men toward those who disagree, including even high Republicans from Capitol Hill. It has come out above all, in the attitude toward Watergate — a bland assumption that whatever they do is right and moral and permissible.

Watergate will be purged and Mr. Nixon will be restored to the confidence of the country if and when the purging has been thorough, quick, and above suspicion and also when the White House itself acts with humility. Mr. Nixon must in the future be seen to consult the leaders of the Congress with respect, not give them orders in a manner too reminiscent of some imperial court.

The American people want, and need, a restoration to them of the ability to believe in the integrity and decency of the man they have chosen to be their President. But they also want a president, not a king-emperor.

Mr. Nixon can give them what they want and need. We urge him to do it — just as fast as possible.

THE RICHMOND NEWS LEADER
Richmond, Va., April 26, 1973

Watergate promises to linger for months, but some tentative conclusions may be drawn now:

Conservatives and pro-Nixon moderates stunningly misjudged the extent of Nixon administration involvement in the Watergate fiasco. Two primary assumptions led Nixon supporters astray: (1) that no one closely connected to the President would be so criminally stupid as to take part in the Watergate operation; (2) that the nation's heavily anti-Nixon press was incapable of producing more fact than fiction. Both assumptions were reasonable, but neither proved accurate.

Because of their abiding detestation of Mr. Nixon, certain leftists in the media have consistently opted for a presumption of guilt in evaluating the President's motives and actions. If he bombed, it was often described as genocide—not an attempt to end the war. If he said an unkind word about the press, it was described as repression—not an appeal for fair treatment. If he asked the FBI or the Justice Department to investigate a bomb-lobbing radical, it was incipient gestapo-ism—not an attempt to have a criminal locked up. There has been a consistent imputation of deliberate evil on a grand scale, no matter how scanty the corroborative evidence. So it was not surprising that these same reporters assumed that Watergate was a White House-level conspiracy that demanded further investigation.

For the wrong reasons the leftist press made evidently correct assumptions about Watergate. They lucked out, and therein lies one of the unnoticed tragedies of this tawdry affair. Watergate constitutes the single vindication of leftist assumption relating to the Nixon administration. Yet henceforward Watergate will overshadow the countless reportorial excesses of the past. In their zeal for Mr. Nixon's neck, even now they are going beyond the limits of journalistic propriety. Last Thursday, for example, *The Washington Post* ran a double-decker banner headline across the top of page 1: "Mitchell, Dean Approved Watergate, Payoffs, Magruder Reportedly Says." Neither Mitchell nor Dean had been—or has been—indicted or tried or convicted for any crime.

How far the anti-Nixonite press will go in the future depends on the President. He alone can salvage both the potential of his second term and the dignity of the presidency itself. If he does not—in the military term—"seize the initiative," then Watergate may become his Waterloo, for nothing he does in the remaining years of his presidency will be free of the innuendo-encrusted sniping engendered by the spectacle of his staff stumbling across the front pages of the daily newspaper. Now-or-never situations seldom arise in politics, but the President surely confronts one today. His supporters must be reassured. His enemies must be sidetracked. His nation must know that it is guided by leadership above reproach. Failure could well force the President to a political Elba from which he could never return.

Chicago today American

Chicago, Ill., April 26, 1973

THE ORIGINAL Watergate scandal by now has so many descendants that it would take a genealogist to trace them all. And yet they all seem to have a strong family resemblance and a common ancestor.

The burglary-bugging of Democratic headquarters, the crummy little plots to sabotage the campaigns of Democratic hopefuls, the elaborate attempts to cover up traces and fool investigators, the slick ways of getting around laws on political contributions, the scornful denials of reports either known or strongly suspected to be true—every one of these acts reflects the same origin: A mistrust of everything but power.

These things could not have been done by officials who respected the law, or who regarded ethics as more important than their own purposes. They could only be the acts of fearful, insecure men who do not trust the electoral process, who doubt the good sense of the American voter, and who feel compelled to rig the system for greater safety. And to judge from the statements of some, they are also men who are genuinely unable to see anything wrong with these tactics — who are honestly unaware that there's anything more to the American political system than acquiring and using power by any means that seem likely to succeed.

We are thinking of some offhand comments made Tuesday by John N. Mitchell, the former attorney general and manager of President Nixon's reelection campaign, who had just testified before a New York grand jury on a suspect campaign contribution of $250,000. Told by a telephone interviewer that he might be indicted in connection with the Watergate breakin, Mitchell said, "My conscience is clear," and added: "When you've done what you've done for the interest of your country . . ."

Mitchell referred to some former associates in the reelection campaign as "those weak little characters running for cover."— evidently meaning those who had agreed to tell investigators what they knew, rather than keeping quiet and taking the consequences. Speaking of the factional quarrels now breaking out among the Nixon team, he commented: "Their loyalty should be to the President."

Whether or not Mitchell in fact had anything to do with the Watergate plot, those few phrases sum up a great deal about what might be called the Watergate mentality. It is the belief that anything goes, if it's for "the interest of the country." Loyalty is to the President, not to the nation. Telling the secrets of the in-group is "weak," siding with the law against the team is "running for cover."

Men who think this way are not necessarily evil. On the contrary, we are sure most of those involved acted from a sincere conviction that what they were doing was "best for the country." But we are seeing more and more clearly where that conviction leads. It produces a powerful, secretive inner ring of officials who have convinced themselves that they know better than the people; who think they are entitled to decide what purposes are more important than truth or legality or good faith. Can there be any belief more hostile to every ideal of American government?

For nearly 200 years, we have staked the life of this republic on trust—primarily, trust between the people and their government. Without it, there is nothing left but power, whether it's the brutal, undisguised power of the police state or the power to manipulate and deceive and doctor facts. Those responsible for the Watergate, it seems, either do not understand that choice, or they understand it and are willing to sacrifice trust for power.

In either case they have failed totally. The men who wanted to take no chances on the people, who tried to insure and increase Mr. Nixon's power at all costs, instead have left him gravely weakened at home and abroad.

The trust that is the real strength of the Presidency has been eroded to the point of collapse. The only way for Mr. Nixon to restore it, in our view, is to reject and condemn the manipulators and everything they stand for. And to mean it.

Chicago Daily Defender

Chicago, Ill., April 25, 1973

At long last, the Watergate tempest is subsiding, leaving in its wake ruined reputation of scores of faithfuls to the Nixon Administration who had pursued with exceptional vigor the pernicious philosophy of all means, fair or foul, to achieve a political goal--win an election.

The atmosphere for so frightful a concept was created by Mr. Nixon himself who was afraid of being drummed out of the White House as his predecessor, President Johnson, was by the militant opponents of the Vietnam war.

One by one, the perpetrators of the sinister acts committed at the Democratic headquarters at the Watergate Apartment-hotel, are being exposed and forced to confess their sins. What is yet evading public grasp is the extent of Mr. Nixon's personal involvement in the scandal. He created the climate of fear and suspicion in which those close to him felt that they could use any means to assure his reelection.

In the light of the facts that have unfolded thus far, it is difficult to see how Mr. Nixon could have been totally unaware of what was being concocted in his behalf. It is not at all fallacious to suppose that he gave the go ahead signal with the stern admonition not to bring his identity into focus of the clandestine operation.

Anyhow, the Watergate bugging beclouds the future of the Republican Party. It is the biggest scandal since the Teapot Dome under the Harding Administration. Republicans, from here onward, will not have an easy time winning any election of local or national consequence.

The Boston Globe

Boston, Mass., April 27, 1973

The nation waits, thus far in vain, for President Nixon to take the firm action that reason dictates in the Watergate and other scandals that are breaking in and around the White House.

Mr. Nixon does not yet seem to appreciate either the enormity of the scandals or the unalterable fact that he himself has to assume the responsibility for them. If he did not know what was going on under his own roof, then he must assume responsibility for White House operations so slipshod as to tax the imagination.

Such surrogates as Henry Kissinger have been sent to the fore by the President to warn against "an orgy of recrimination" and "guilt by association" to plead for "compassion" for the accused.

Americans will have compassion in abundance for those who are worthy of it. But compassion is not the point. The point is that the nation waits for the President to proceed energetically, as he has not yet done, to demonstrate that an Administration, which rose to power on its frequent proclamations that it stood for law and order, is not itself shot through with the lawless and disorderly.

When Mr. Nixon, a few days ago, could no longer ignore the scandal, could no longer let his press secretary, Ron Ziegler, try to pass it off as an aberration of a venal press, he summoned the television cameras to the White House for a news conference which lasted about six minutes. He read a prepared statement and disappeared again, permitting no questions.

The first disposition was to applaud the President for his forthright declaration that no immunity should be granted any past or present members of his entourage by the grand jury. Only later did it come to be generally recognized that, whatever the President's intent, the denial of immunity to grand jury witnesses was the best possible way of assuring that no witness, fearful of incriminating himself, would incriminate anyone else, either, if he could help it. Denying immunity might hamper the grand jury's inquiry into who did what.

Mr. Nixon's designation of Assistant Attorney General Henry F. Petersen as the chief prosecutor in the case, after Attorney General Richard G. Kleindienst had backed away from it on the ground that former Attorney General John N. Mitchell and others who are accusing each other are friends and former associates, likewise was at first accepted as a token of the President's determination to get at the whole truth. Mr. Petersen, in charge of the Criminal Division of the Department of Justice, would normally be the man for the job. But even with his integrity accepted as a fact, the investigation he is pursuing comes down to a case of the Administration investigating itself.

We have been through this nonsense already, with the President first stating that an investigation conducted by his White House counsel, John W. Dean 3rd, had exonerated everybody in the White House, past or present, Mr. Dean included. But Mr. Dean is himself now one of the accused, and there is some question as to whether the facts in the investigation he says he conducted were communicated by him to the President, as the President says they were, or to the President's chief of staff, H. R. Haldeman, who denies everything and has disappeared from the view of White House reporters.

From the moment the Watergate scandal first broke, this newspaper pointed out that it is absurd for the Administration to investigate itself. The demand for the appointment of a prosecutor wholly independent of the Administration and all its parts, a man of national repute, unquestioned integrity and nothing to fear or hide, is now being heard in all quarters as the Watergate scandal drags on and on, very clearly threatening to drag the President, if not the Presidency, down with all of those who now are so freely accusing each other. In his own best interest and in the interest of assuring the nation that great wrongs will be put to right, we strongly urge Mr. Nixon to appoint such a man without any more delay.

Total frankness and all of the humility a proud man can muster are what the circumstances demand of Mr. Nixon.

The President, just as does the country itself, needs to accept the fact of his and our own dark side, and to accept the moral responsibility for presiding over it. What made Watergate so awful was the cover-up, emanating from an inability to admit there had been wrongdoing.

President Kennedy accepted the final responsibility, and the blame, for the Bay of Pigs fiasco—and that ended the matter as an issue. Today, once again, the White House ought to act with some humility, not in any groveling way but in a grown-up manner. Confession of final responsibility is good not only for the soul, but for the nation as well.

The San Diego Union

San Diego, Calif., April 28, 1973

If all of the words written and spoken about the Watergate scandal were put end to end they undoubtedly would reach three times around the moon—with enough left over to flood the basement of the Library of Congress.

For all of that, we wonder if there is a single American who fully understands what actually transpired during bugging of the Democratic national headquarters about a year ago or the motives behind the felony. Nor, despite the field day that resourceful reporters are having, has the outpouring of words added much more than confusion to a complex situation.

Most current judgments about Watergate appear to be drawn from the urgency, volume and tone of the media revelations rather than from their unimpeachable content. Generally, the tone is apocalyptic.

It is time, we think, to step back from the forest to see its entirety, to strive for a realistic assessment. The analysis should begin, we believe, with a statement that can be accepted by everyone: The Watergate affair represented deplorable political immorality that has no place at all in the American system of self governance, most particularly no place in the lives of important political appointees.

Secondly, we believe all responsible persons can agree that the welter of innuendo and confusion over Watergate and its implications has reached the point where it will require all the prestige and credibility of the President's office to reassure Americans that their nation is not bursting its seams with corruption. The time is here, we believe for Mr. Nixon to give us that reassurance.

When all of these things are said, there still remains the apprehension as to what long-term effect Watergate will have upon us as a nation, both at home and in our dealings abroad. For all its seriousness, we believe there is reason to hope that the ultimate effect will not be great.

Abroad, our affairs, as well as those of all other nations, are guided by self interest. Bugging by a political party would hardly raise an eyebrow in France or Italy, for example. Neither would such political aberrations have much influence on the finance ministers of the industrial nations engaged in monetary matters.

At home, we believe that the current tempo of self-condemnation about Watergate is a testimonial to American morality instead of the opposite. To those who are worried about what Watergate will do to sagging public confidence in government, we might point out that it is the American political process that has been responsible for bringing this incredible political shenanigan to light—the courts, the legislative bodies and an observant press. In this regard, and to those who rank Watergate at the head of American problems, we might point out the matter is out in the public arena where it belongs — and it will be corrected.

Many negative things can, should and will be said about Watergate.

In the constructive sense, however, it is timely to reflect that the uproar about the bugging is another example of the American system of checks and balances at work—in all of its splendor as well as in some of its excesses.

The Washington Post

Washington, D.C., April 29, 1973

In a much more precise meaning of the term than Ronald Ziegler had in mind when he sought to nullify his past statements on the Watergate affair a short while back, the government of the United States is rapidly becoming inoperative. We mean no little joke, no sardonic play on words. For if anything has become clear in the onrush of disclosures and events over the past 72 hours, it is that the persons charged with ultimate responsibility for directing this nation's executive branch affairs have become crippled and immobilized and unable fully to carry out their duties. That is because the President is caught in a monstrous web of administration malpractice and corruption and deceit. And what is even more disturbing than the shattering drama being played out in full sight of us all is the fact that evidently Mr. Nixon still has not decided to take those steps which are essential to restoring the dignity of his office and the capacity of his administration to fulfill its constitutional obligations.

The first of these steps is to guarantee that the nation's system of criminal justice, so gravely and thoughtlessly maimed by the cover-ups and complicities of the past 10 months, is finally permitted to work its will without obstruction where criminal actions on the part of Mr. Nixon's colleagues and subordinates are concerned. Work —*really work*. That, as we have said before, means a prosecution which ensures that the guilty will be brought to book and—equally important—that the innocent will be cleared. Can anyone any longer doubt that justice in these crucial respects and the public's faith in it will only have been served when the President takes steps to remove the prosecution from the guidance of those who have (1) had various degrees of responsibility for the failures of investigation so far and (2) stood in close personal and professional relationships to the men under investigation?

On Thursday the prestigious Association of the Bar of the City of New York asked Mr. Nixon to remove the criminal investigation from the jurisdiction of Assistant Attorney General Henry Petersen and to appoint a special prosecutor in his place. We also renew our plea that he do so. Surely the revelations late last week that the acting director of the FBI, Mr. L. Patrick Gray III, had himself been compromised by the drive to destroy evidence in the case, should reinforce the argument for removing the criminal prosecutions from the hands of those accountable for what has gone on so far.

To our way of thinking, a presidential move to assure strict and fair prosecution of crimes is, however, despite its importance, only a first step. It is required to get at one kind of truth, but inadequate to get at another. That other truth is not reducible to a list of which administration or party functionaries or bigwigs violated which criminal statutes at what time. It is the truth about the men who, whether or not they committed actual crimes, systematically and grossly betrayed their unsuspecting political constituency, the public at large, the institutions and values that are most important to this country and the faith so universally held that direction of the executive branch of government presupposes certain basic decencies in the men and women who are in charge. How grotesque it is that we have been reduced to speculating as to whether our national administration owes us confidence that its appointees and aides will not commit criminal acts. Is that not selling out pretty cheap? Are we not entitled as well to knowledge that these people who have been given such a large public trust will observe the basic decencies we require of a 7-year-old child? Or are lying and cheating all right— so long as no actual criminal statute has been broken?

Mr. Nixon got advice from Senator Stennis the other day that can be badly construed, when the Mississippi senator counseled him to "tough it out." And the President's own record of commentary on a variety of ordeals he has gone through in the past unfortunately suggests a propensity to do just that—to "tough it out," which is to say, to resist a change of course and wait for public attention to be distracted or for the political storm to blow over. He has also taken pride, in both the near and distant past, in what he evidently regards as the repeated vindication of this tactic—especially as it has run counter to much of the advice he has received from others. We would argue, however, that this particular "crisis" is different in both degree and kind from those others which Mr Nixon has written and spoken about. For

(continued on next page)

(continued from preceding page)

"toughing it out" in this case can only mean failing to terminate the services of those men around him who have so thoroughly abused their power and so shockingly betrayed the good faith of those who put them in office. And failing to get such people out of office in turn can only mean that the larger and more damaging truth of the matter has been missed—namely, that this array of official, tax supported abuse and deception and contempt for the public and its rights and its self-respect represents a whole approach to governing that is and must remain intolerable to the American people

It is hard, of course, to put a precise measure upon public trust, to separate it out from subjective judgments having to do with likings or dislikings, support or non-support. What is beyond question, however, is that the President's standing in the country has already slipped severely as a consequence of "Watergate." A Lou Harris poll published in this newspaper today attests undeniably to that. And it cannot be said, as often as some partisans of the President may argue it, that this is a partisan matter: the outcry from Senator Goldwater and Senator Dole and Republican Party Chairman Bush suggests that, if anything, dismay and disenchantment is running deepest among Republicans in general; and among those congressmen who must stand for re-election in particular.

In short, the "Watergate" and its attendant crimes cannot damage the presidency nearly as much as the President can if he finally fails to address the problems in a manner that can convince people that he is, first of all, not a part of it, and second, that he is prepared to assume his proper responsibility for setting things right. Putting it another way, Mr. Nixon will be gambling recklessly with that incalculable but essential ingredient—call it public trust or respect or confidence. For without it as George Will points out in an article elsewhere on this page today, he risks being reduced to a condition of holding power without authority.

It is not difficult ot add up the potential cost of this gamble. One need only examine what is at play. We are not among those who believe that corruption in the government is in itself a crippling liability for a President in his dealings with foreign friends or adversaries—who among them could cast the first stone? But it is almost an axiom that an American president who is incapable of exercising authority at home—incapable of dealing convincingly with domestic crises—is unlikely to cut a very impressive figure around the world. From this generality one can proceed, by way of illustration, to specifics, what does it profit Dr. Kissinger, for instance, to launch a "historic" initiative in our dealings with Europe and Japan, if the President is so politically weakened at home that he cannot deliver the international trade legislation which is the vital substance of the Kissinger initiative? How persuasive can Mr. Nixon be in his carrot-and-stick maneuverings with Hanoi in pursuit of a Vietnam cease-fire if he is under attack and on the defensive in his own country? A Congress or a people aroused and alienated on one issue can usually be counted on to move onto the offensive all along the front. The list of urgent business runs on and on. Soaring prices; impending and potentially inflationary wage settlements; the gasoline shortage that looms this summer; scores of unfilled, high and middle level government positions; a backlog of unsent messages to Congress; a full schedule of visitations by foreign leaders; critical negotiations on arms control and European security—all these are matters commanding presidential time and energy, as well as authority, and all would be placed at risk by trying to temporize, by "toughing it out" in the conventional sense on the Watergate scandals.

Surely everyone, the President included, must acknowledge that much more than one man's political survival is at issue. What is at issue is the survival of effective government. We believe that "toughing it out" in the best sense means, first, recognizing this fact and, second, acting upon the obligation it imposes. That obligation mean accepting personal responsibility for what has been done — or countenanced — by those he put in office. And it means ridding his administration of all those, whether guilty or not of outright crimes, who have had a hand in the degradation of our institutions of government and our processes of law enforcement. Neither the Congress nor the public can any longer be expected to place its faith in programs and policies and actions fashioned and executed by the same cast of characters—with the same cast of mind—that brought forever into our language that cryptic and odious catch-word, "Watergate."

WORCESTER TELEGRAM.

Worcester, Mass., April 29, 1973

Some of the recent news stories on the spreading Watergate scandal suggest that the government of the United States is close to chaos or collapse as an effective institution.

Columnists Evans and Novak recently warned that, if President Nixon does not act soon, "the poison now permeating the White House will spread and threaten the entire executive branch with neurotic civil war and eventual stalemate."

Without in any way discounting the seriousness of the squalid Watergate affair, we think it worthwhile to note some distinctions between the Nixon administration and the government of the United States.

Few would care to dispute the thesis that the Nixon administration has been crippled by the Watergate affair revelations. Its middle echelon of political operatives has been exposed as cynical, ruthless and willing to break the law. Some of its top people are facing grand jury investigations that may result in criminal indictments. President Nixon himself will probably wear the Watergate, like an albatross, for the rest of his life and beyond, in the history books.

The credibility of his administration will never be the same.

This is indeed a grievous state of affairs for those who put their trust in Richard Nixon and the Republican party. Beyond that, it is a shock for all decent Americans to think that the White House could be so prostituted.

But there is another side to the Watergate affair, and one that is most encouraging. It shows the government of the United States, in the last analysis, as a government of laws and not of men.

Rather than revealing the decay of the basic institutions of U.S. government, Watergate is proving that those institutions are as sturdy as ever — more sturdy, in fact, than many believed. Men in the supreme circles of executive power are discovering that they are not immune to the processes of the law. The former attorney general of the United States is having his day before the grand jury and may have his day in court. The executive branch of government — which many feared had become predominant over the other branches — is being brought to heel by the legislative and the judiciary with the help of the news media.

Looking ahead, it is possible to see considerable benefits deriving from the Watergate affair. It seems likely that there will be a revision in the campaign fund-raising and spending laws at last. There will be stricter prohibitions on such things as electronic surveillance, faked documents, disruptive tactics at campaign rallies and the like.

It will be surprising to us if future political campaigns are not somewhat cleaner than the 1972 confrontation. We find it hard to believe that there will be such large bundles of cash collected and concealed, and such blatant payoffs as those made by the Committee to Re-elect the President. As has been said, the actual bugging of the Democratic party headquarters was only the tip of the iceberg in a nasty political campaign.

A few years ago, during the height of radical unrest in this country, many militants condemned "the system" for being ineffective. As we see it, Watergate proves that the system works. Slowly, spasmodically, uncertainly, at times, perhaps. But it works. There is a limit on what is allowed even the most powerful people in the country.

And that is something to be thankful for. Ask anyone who ever lived under a system that has no checks and balances on power.

THE SACRAMENTO BEE
Sacramento, Calif., April 27, 1973

Pulitzer prize-winning columnist Jack Anderson showed good judgment and a sense of responsibility in agreeing he will no longer quote secret Grand Jury testimony on the Watergate case in his nationally syndicated columns.

It is the constitutional right of the press to publish any and all news generated by the White House, the Congress or the courts. Court rules or federal rules of criminal procedure do not supersede the Constitution.

However, Anderson quite properly took into consideration the United States attorneys' pleas that the prosecution was having trouble getting witnesses to testify because the witnesses said they were afraid anything they said could end up in Anderson's columns.

As Anderson said in agreeing to voluntarily turn over his copies of secret testimony to Chief US District Judge John J. Sirica: "We are working for the same purposes, to get to the bottom of Watergate."

In reporting and investigating the Watergate matter Anderson, whose columns appear in The Bee, has done this nation a valuable service. White House sources told Anderson one factor which persuaded the President to throw open the Watergate investigation was Anderson's access to the Grand Jury testimony.

Because of the dogged investigation by Anderson and the thorough reporting job done by the Washington Post, the disquieting significance of the Watergate bugging and burglary was brought home to the public, instead of being dismissed as a "third-rate burglary," as a White House press secretary termed it.

It is good for this country to have gadflies like Anderson in Washington. In the long run his unstinting devotion to the people's right to know may serve to keep the government officials more honest than they might be otherwise.

Pittsburgh Post-Gazette
Pittsburgh, Pa., April 27, 1973

THE STORY, uncovered by The Washington Post, about an alleged campaign of grand-scale deception by Richard Nixon's re-election committee last May comes at the worst possible time for the beleaguered President and his White House staff. The almost hourly revelations and accusations concerning the White House's involvement in the Watergate scandal are increasingly taking their toll in eroding the people's confidence in their government.

Mr. Ziegler

But The Post's report about a supposed effort by Mr. Nixon's campaign committee to fake the public's response to the mining of North Vietnamese harbors verges on the incredible.

* * *

That Mr. Nixon's committee would pay for telegrams to be sent to the White House in support of the mining and for the placing of a deceptive and possibly illegal advertisement in the May 17 New York Times smacks of the kind of banana republic political tactics which most citizens of the United States cannot readily believe of their own government.

According to The Post, a re-election committee official said that the grand deception included "petition drives, organizing rallies, bringing people in buses to Washington, organizing calls to the White House, getting voters to call their congressmen." The purpose? "We felt (the decision to mine Haiphong harbor) could make or break the President," the unnamed official said.

White House Press Secretary Ron Ziegler told the nation on May 10 that telegrams, letters and phone calls were running 5 or 6 to 1 in support of Mr. Nixon's action and cited them as indicating "substantial support" in Congress and among voters for the mining, said The Post story.

It also reported that a former Nixon campaign official said that the Committee to Re-elect the President was "totally mobilized for the biggest piece of deception—we never do anything honestly. Imagine, the President sending himself telegrams, patting himself on the back."

The apparent involvement of two convicted Watergate conspirators, Bernard Barker and Frank Sturgis, in the campaign to fake support for Mr. Nixon's mining decision adds a cinematic gangland twist to a barely credible plot.

On top of all that, the ad in The Times, says The Post story, was signed by people passing themselves off as representing citizens' support for Mr. Nixon's harbor-mining decision.

The most damning piece of evidence apparently is the reported admission by an executive of the group handling the Nixon committee's advertising that the ad was paid for with 44 one-hundred dollar bills sent from the President's re-election committee in Washington.

* * *

That the Watergate crimes seemingly were perpetrated in adherence to the re-election committee's and White House staff's apparent belief that victory in the presidential election was worth any cost is unfortunately consonant, moreover, with the reported fake-support campaign in May.

What defies our understanding of logic, finally, is how any of Mr. Nixon's advisers could have believed that such criminal deception could justify the risk of dishonoring the very office which they fought so hard to win.

The Miami Herald
Miami, Fla., April 26, 1973

MAY 1972 was the time when the Nixon administration evened it up with the lying media — the newspapers, the TV, the radio — all the print and talk people who thought the war in Vietnam was unwise and who thought the people thought so, too.

On May 8 President Nixon announced he had ordered the mining of Haiphong harbor and six other North Vietnamese ports. On May 9 it was done.

Next day, May 10, White House Press Secretary Ronald Ziegler announced that telegrams, letters and phone calls were running 5 or 6 to 1 supporting the Presidential action. A $4,400 signed ad denouncing that newspaper appeared in The New York Times May 17.

Over the next two weeks busloads of approving citizens descended on Washington. There were pro-Nixon rallies in several cities, including Miami. Petitions were circulated. People telegraphed their congressmen. A Harris Poll showed that 59 per cent of Americans approved the war action.

But this was no spontaneous, popular reaction. It was organized, set up, staged, rigged, manipulated by a quasi-governmental organization, the Committee for the Reelection of the President (CREP), perhaps the most fateful albatross ever to light on the White House.

CREP has spilled its guts to the press it once denounced as biased and out of touch with the thinking of the people. One former campaign official told The Washington Post that the organization was "totally mobilized for the biggest piece of deception — we never do anything honestly. Imagine, the President sending himself telegrams, patting himself on the back."

There is nothing wrong in urging citizens to become articulate on government or any of its issues. This is done every day, and if it is done honestly it is wholesome.

The involvement of the government itself in such an exercise, however, is quite another matter. It smacks almost of Herr Dr Goebbels, promoting the Fuehrer Prinzip through his Reichministry of Propaganda and Enlightenment.

The technique may well call in question other evidences of spontaneity in public reaction to government doings. What are we left to believe?

Of all the revelations of the weeks past this is the most disappointing, the most disheartening.

Other governments have maintained corps of publicity men grinding out releases designed to place the boss in the best light.

But to put words in the mouths of people with money — surely some of it tax money — is the ultimate desecration of free, untrammeled speech. It is the greening of American public opinion, and in sadness we deplore it.

NIXON ADDRESSES NATION AS 4 AIDES RESIGN

White House chief of staff H. R. Haldeman, domestic affairs adviser John D. Ehrlichman, Attorney General Richard G. Kleindienst and presidential counsel John W. Dean 3rd resigned from the Nixon Administration April 30 as a consequence of the widening Watergate affair. The resignations were discussed in an evening nationwide television address by President Nixon. Nixon stressed that he meant "to leave no implication whatever of personal wrongdoing" on the part of Haldeman and Ehrlichman. The action was taken, he said, to restore public confidence in the integrity of his office. Alluding to Kleindienst, Nixon said the .latter had "no personal. involvement whatever" in the Watergate affair, but because he had "close personal and professional" associations with some of those who were implicated, both men felt it necessary to name a new attorney general. Defense Secretary Elliot L. Richardson was named to the post and given "absolute authority" to make all decisions bearing upon the prosecution of the Watergate case and related matters including that of naming a special supervising prosecutor. The President announced Dean's resignation without amplification.

The President said he would do "everything in my power" to insure that the Watergate conspirators were "brought to justice" and to see that such abuses were "purged from the political processes." He continued, "... the easiest course would be for me to blame those to whom I delegated the responsibility to run the campaign. But that would be a cowardly thing to do... In any organization the man at the top must bear the responsibility ... I accept it."

Nixon said the Watergate affair had taken "far too much" of his time since March and that he would turn his full attention" once again to the larger duties of the office." During the speech, Nixon paid tribute to the press for bringing "the facts to light." Following the address, Nixon told reporters "we have had our differences in the past, and I hope you will give me hell every time you think I'm wrong." On May 1 the White House formally apologized to the *Washington Post* for its denunciations of the paper's coverage of Watergate. (Six days later the *Post* was awarded a Pulitzer Prize for distinguished public service in journalism for its investigation of the Watergate case.)

During early May, there were these developments in the Watergate case:

■On May 1 the F.B.I. put agents in the White House to guard the files of Haldeman, Ehrlichman and Dean.

■The Senate May 1 passed a resolution calling upon the President to appoint a special Watergate prosecutor from outside the executive branch, subject to Senate confirmation.

■The *New York Times* reported May 2 statements from "government investigators" that they had evidence that high White House officials and Republican campaign officials including Haldeman, Ehrlichman, former Attorney General John N. Mitchell, Administration aides Dean, Jeb Stuart Magruder and Frederick C. LaRue conspired to obstruct the federal investigation of Watergate. The conspiracy was said to have involved payments to the Watergate defendants, promises of executive clemency, and public denials of any knowledge of the case by those involved.

■ Based on a preliminary examination of grand jury evidence, federal investigators reportedly believed H. R. Haldeman to have been the coordinator of extensive political sabotage and espionage beginning in early 1971 and continuing throughout the 1972 presidential campaign in an effort to assure the nomination of Sen. George McGovern (D, S.D.) as the Democratic contender for the presidency and to deny the nomination to the man considered Nixon's strongest potential opponent—Sen. Edward S. Muskie (D, Me.).

■The Administration offered a more detailed version of its position on executive privilege May 3. It stated that "Past and present members of the President's staff questioned by the F.B.I., the Ervin (Senate select) committee or a grand jury would invoke the privilege only in connection with conversations with the President, conversations among themselves—involving communications with the President—and as to presidential papers."

■The White House May 7 repeated its denial of presidential involvement in the Watergate affair or the alleged coverup. The denial followed reports in *Newsweek* magazine that Dean was prepared to give testimony implicating President Nixon in the attempted coverup.

■Elliot Richardson announced May 7 he would appoint, if confirmed by the Senate as attorney general, a special Watergate prosecutor. At the confirmation hearings May 9, Richardson said he would retain the "ultimate responsibility" for the Watergate investigation and prosecution and would make the final decision on granting immunity to witnesses. The likelihood that he would overrule the special prosecutor was "very remote," he said.

■On May 8 the Senate committee received from the White House a set of guidelines for testimony by Nixon aides at the hearings. The White House no longer advised Watergate prosecutors to withhold immunity from current or former Nixon aides.

■On May 10 Dean charged there was "an ongoing effort to limit or prevent my testifying fully and freely" concerning Watergate.

Amidst the new Watergate revelations, President Nixon's ratings in public opinion polls continued to drop.

Chicago Tribune

Chicago, Ill., May 1, 1973

The Watergate dam burst yesterday, and four top administration officials were swept out of office in the biggest White House purge in memory. Resignations came from the President's two top assistants, H. R. Haldeman and John Ehrlichman; White House Counsel John Dean, and Atty.-Gen. Richard Kleindienst. These followed close after the resignations of the acting director of the FBI, L. Patrick Gray, and Jeb Stuart Magruder, a former White House aide and campaign committee official.

In a television speech last night which was reminiscent of his Checkers apology of 1952, the President took upon himself the blame which he could not escape anyway, and sought to drown his Watergate sorrows in a recitation of the other and more important problems of his administration.

Despite the havoc, there is a sense of relief. Relief that something is at last being done; relief that in large measure the suspense is over, along with the sickening pretenses and the all-too-obvious concealment that have marked the investigation so far. And relief, too, that Mr. Nixon still seems to be holding his footing and to be in some measure of control.

The necessary investigation should now be able to proceed with the cooperation of the main actors. Mr. Kleindienst stepped aside in order to insure that the Justice Department's role will be as disinterested as possible, even tho he is personally untainted by Watergate. Elliot Richardson, a lawyer who has earned the respect of Democrats as well as Republicans, has been moved from the Pentagon to the Justice Department to handle the investigation. As Mr. Nixon said, Mr. Richardson is a man of unimpeachable integrity.

But to say that Mr. Nixon is still in control is not to say that he will step out of the floodwaters unsplattered by mud. Neither the resignations nor the speech answer any of the many questions that have been asked. If Mr. Haldeman or Mr. Ehrlichman, whom Mr. Nixon called his "closest friends and most trusted assistants," prove to be involved in the Watergate deception, it will be bad enough. If John Mitchell, his former attorney-general and campaign chairman, proves involved, it will be worse.

Even under the best conditions, Mr. Nixon's assumption of responsibility was redundant. The men involved were his appointees, or appointees of his appointees; and if a President as politically astute as Mr. Nixon is deceived by his appointees, one may suspect that in some measure at least he wanted to be deceived by them.

Mr. Nixon's responsibility, even if indirect, has led to reminders that if we were a parliamentary democracy, the whole government might have been swept out of office with yesterday's deluge. And it has led even to talk of impeachment.

Here too, we feel a sense of relief. Granted that Watergate is a political and moral disaster whose dimensions are still undefined. Granted that it has badly and perhaps irreparably damaged the Nixon administration's image. But would Britain have been better off if the Tory government had fallen with John Profumo's confession of sexual adventures and lying [as it almost did]? And would the United States be better off if the sins of a relative handful were to evict a government consisting largely of experienced and capable men, and to thrust the infinitely more important problems of the country into the hands of inexperienced men? Mr. Nixon was reelected primarly on the basis of his position on the war, on relations with the Soviet Union and China, on matters of inflation and crime. Would we be better off turning all these matters over to a new administration because of Watergate?

Hardly. To this extent Mr. Nixon was right last night. Much as we may lament Watergate and much as it may reflect on the White House, we are better off trying to weather the storm in our present ship than allowing it to be sunk and looking for a new one.

ST. LOUIS POST-DISPATCH
St. Louis, Mo., May 1, 1973

President Nixon last night attempted the not unsizable trick of accepting the responsibility for the Watergate scandal while disassociating himself from any of the blame. He was "appalled" to learn of the break-in while recuperating from the rigors of foreign diplomacy last June, was too absorbed with the high matters of the presidency to give the affair much concern during the campaign and even now, the subject having "claimed far too much of my own time and attention," must turn away toward the "vital work" of building a lasting peace. So he has handed the entire scandal over to his Attorney General-designate Elliot Richardson, which is scarcely acceptable.

The degree to which Mr. Nixon indeed has been "appalled" by Watergate may be judged in part by the descriptions of the crime and accounts of it which those speaking in his behalf have given: "third-rate burglary," "a collection of lies," "shabby journalism." These phrases have become the trail markers along the path the White House palace guard fought as it grudgingly gave ground and finally yesterday surrendered.

It would be erroneous as well as premature to say that as of this moment the Watergate scandal has destroyed the presidency of Mr. Nixon. But the affair, and all of its ramifications, have inflicted upon this President political damage such as none of his predecessors ever bore. It is damage that must be probed relentlessly and it is damage that in the end may even prove fatal. For its own sake, that is a risk the nation must be prepared to take. The United States can survive a ruined presidency, but it cannot endure as a democracy if some citizens and not others are placed above the law.

The resignations of three of Mr. Nixon's closest associates — White House chief of staff Haldeman, domestic policy adviser Ehrlichman and Attorney General Kleindienst — and the firing of presidential counsel John W. Dean III have confirmed what has been evident for so long, namely, that if not directly guilty of attempting to sabotage a presidential election, those who have sat at the right hand of Mr. Nixon were implicated in or compromised by the crime. The degree of their involvement was not minor. It was of such magnitude that Mr. Nixon could no longer afford to keep them.

Had Watergate occurred in any other Western democracy — say or Great Britain — the government would have fallen long ago. Much of the success of the American democracy is due to its stability, and that, in turn rests on the fact that the people's mandate of a national election cannot easily be withdrawn. But that is also why the possibility exists here to a greater degree than elsewhere that a President or advisers who are cloaked with presidential power may abuse the democratic process without paying an immediate penalty. The only protection against this abuse, as the nation has now seen to its shock, is vigilance, and that is why every piece of dirty work conducted in the name of Mr. Nixon's re-election campaign must be subjected to swift, sure justice.

Thus it is imperative that a special independent prosecutor of unimpeachable integrity be appointed immediately to take complete charge of the Watergate investigation. There are several ways such a prosecutor might be selected; but there could hardly be a worse way than to leave it to Mr. Richardson. Congress would be fully justified in immediately approving legislation to create a respected panel composed of members of Government and representatives of the bar and law schools to select the special prosecutor.

The qualifications of Mr. Richardson, now Defense Secretary, for Attorney General will be reviewed in due time by the Senate, but he clearly is unsuitable as the chief investigator of the massive campaign of political espionage and sabotage that took place last year. In his various previous Administration positions, Mr. Richardson has demonstrated a singular talent for aligning himself—with appropriate shifts as the tune changes—with whatever position the White House dictates.

Furthermore, as a loyal member of the Administration, Mr. Richardson can scarcely be expected to conduct a tough, impartial investigation of a trail that already winds about the White House like a series of soiled carpet runners and that may, in fact, lead into the Oval Office itself. In his letter of resignation, Mr. Kleindienst referred to the case as a "tragedy." That word implies a bit more than just the conviction of a few burglars and their chiefs and the involvement in the crime of some junior White House staff members.

Mr. Nixon said that it would be "unfair and unfounded" to regard the resignations as evidence of wrongdoing. Strictly speaking, that is so; resignations by and of themselves are of no evidentiary value. But the pregnant suggestion in Mr. Kleindienst's letter that he had learned that "persons with whom I had had close personal and professional association would be involved" in illegal activities suggests that there may well be evidence to come.

The press has not been shabby; it has been doing its job by reporting facts. The courts, especially that of the courageous Judge Sirica, are doing theirs. With its special Senate investigating commitee, Congress has not been derelict. These efforts must continue; but they must be occompanied by the appointment of an independent prosecutor if the public is to be confident that the White House is not standing in the way of a thorough accounting for the Watergate scandal.

ARKANSAS DEMOCRAT

Little Rock, Ark., May 1, 1973

President Nixon came down from his mountain retreat after deliberating alone all weekend and his yellow tablets were filled.

First, there were the announcements of the firings and resignations, including two of his "closest friends," H. R. Haldeman and John Ehrlichman.

Then there was the 20-minute TV speech, his lips drawn tight, his usual confidence missing. He had even counted the days he had left in the White House — 1,361. He evoked a lot of homilies — "two wrongs don't make a right" — and he signed off with a Presidential blessing. To shore him up, he surrounded himself with a family portrait and a bust of Lincoln.

But even though he was too long getting around to it, he did the right thing Monday in sending four men packing. One was John Dean III, a White House lawyer who appears to be directly connected to the actual misdeeds. Haldeman and Ehrlichman had to go because they were the President's closest aides and administrators, who are culpable either for not knowing about the bugging or for knowing and not stopping it. The fourth man, Attorney General Richard Kleindienst, stands for law and order, and plainly there wasn't much of that going on in Mr. Nixon's councils. Despite their oozy letters of resignation and Mr. Nixon's praise of them on TV, it's our hunch that, like Dean, Haldeman, Ehrlichman and Kleindienst had to be told to resign. They don't appear to be men who would surrender power voluntarily.

The President also was right in making the point that Watergate proves that the American political system does work, instead of the reverse, which is what some critics are saying. He did this by crediting the grand jury, the federal prosecutors, "a vigorous free press" and a "courageous judge," U.S. Dist. Judge John Sirica, a Republican appointee who felt from the start that higher-ups were being protected and pushed on until one of the burglars started singing.

And, last, the President was right in appointing Elliot Richardson as attorney general. He is a respected public servant, and this fact combined with his authority to appoint outside prosecutors will satisfy the public of the fairness of investigation and prosecution the Justice Department will now conduct.

We hope he gets at it right away because there has been a lot of nonsense said and written about Watergate. The President indulged in some last night when he said new rules ought to be adopted to keep things like this from happening in political campaigns. Well, we already have rules against burglary and wiretapping; what we need are people working in campaigns who will observe them. Then there are the writers and commentators who insist on calling this the worst political scandal in this century. No one knows yet, of course, but it's highly doubtful if anything is going to equal the scandals of the Harding administration, which included some of the nation's oil barons and three cabinet members.

Watergate has hurt, but not to that degree. For the system to work, Americans have to trust the President and they want to — especially one who has always observed those middle-class values most of us think important. Last night, although shaken, he did it again. He removed himself from bad company, he accepted the responsibility (but not the blame) for what has happened and he promised that all lawbreakers would be found and punished. That will be good enough for everyone but those people who have always believed Mr. Nixon kicked dogs, and they will never be satisfied with anything he does.

TWIN CITY SENTINEL

Winston-Salem, N.C., May 1, 1973

President Nixon's address to the nation on Monday night turned out to be a plea to the American people for a silent vote of confidence.

In effect he asked to be freed from suspicion and further accountability for the Watergate crimes so he might be able to cope with the heavy tasks that confront him both abroad and at home.

It was an uncomfortable moment — uncomfortable for the President and uncomfortable for his audience. No American who respects the presidency and cherishes its traditions could have relished that moment any more than Mr. Nixon. But the list of Watergate crimes — proved or alleged — had become so long and so heinous that Mr. Nixon could no longer remain silent.

That list now includes burglary, wiretapping, bugging, perjury, subornation of perjury, bribery of witnesses, acceptance of illegal campaign contributions, failure to report campaign contributions, illegal spending of campaign funds, failure to report campaign disbursements, destruction of evidence and conspiracy by the President's closest advisers and campaign managers to set all of these illegal activities in motion and then cover them up.

In these circumstances, the President, with his special sources of knowledge, might have been expected to shed some light on the whole deplorable affair.

But he revealed nothing — absolutely nothing. Actually, he added only a little more bafflement to an already baffling situation.

—Thus he said he accepted responsibility for the Watergate crimes — but he put the blame on his subordinates.

—He said he was "appalled" when he first heard about the break-in and bugging at Democratic headquarters last June 17. But if he was really appalled, the record does not bear him out. Two days after the arrest his press secretary was authorized to belittle the crime as a "third-rate burglary attempt." And Mr. Nixon himself subsequently talked about it as only "a bizarre incident" and condoned the action of "overzealous people in campaigns who do things that are wrong."

—He gently praised the press for bringing the wrong-doing to light. But for 10 months all of the power of the White House had been used to discredit what the press was reporting.

—He defended the integrity of the American system. But it was not the integrity of the system but the integrity of Richard Nixon that was in question.

—And he maintained that until only a month ago he believed in the innocence of those around him in the White House and his campaign organization. But can anyone readily believe that his closest friend and adviser, John Mitchell, never told him about those meetings at which Mitchell now admits the Watergate bugging was discussed? . . . Or that his personal lawyer, Herbert Kalmbach, and appointments secretary, Dwight Chapin, never told him that they were doling out money for acts of political sabotage . . . Or that his finance chairman Maurice Stans, and his former finance committee treasurer Hugh Sloan, never let him know that they were passing out hundreds of thousands of dollars in greenbacks for the benefit of the Watergate 7 both before and after the seven were convicted . . . Or that his trusted chief of staff, H. R. Haldeman, and chief assistant for domestic affairs, John D. Erlichman, never passed along to him the reports they are alleged to have received on the whole range of shady activities?

To believe all this is to indict Mr. Nixon for absolute incompetence as an administrator. Indeed, if all this free-wheeling activity was actually going on in his official family, we can only be thankful that one of his enterprising subordinates never pushed the button that might have started a nuclear war while the trusting President was looking elsewhere.

So what will happen now?

In moments like these we must trust the deep, instinctive wisdom of the American people.

Will the American people, like the people of the fairy-tale country, decline to admit even to themselves that the emperor has no clothes?

Will they decide to suspend judgment so the presidency may retain something of its historical aura and so Mr. Nixon may carry on for the next three and a half years?

Or will they insist on a full accounting and an appropriate penalty?

The choice is not easy. For that choice involves an office even more than it involves a man. And the preservation of the authority and credibility of that office must now be the concern of us all.

The News American

Baltimore, Md., May 2, 1973

WHAT HAD to be done and said by President Nixon in the Watergate scandal has finally been done and said. Key government figures were swept out of office in a dramatic shakeup. Promises were made to the American people that "the whole truth" will be uncovered; assurance given that confidence in their leadership need not have been shaken.

It remains to be seen if the public will accept the presidential performance as adequate. On the negative side is the fact that the shakeup, however dramatic involved only one man who was actually fired. And the President's speech, despite its emotional affirmation of highest ideals, came both with obvious regret that there was no alternative and with a seeming insensibility to the sweeping importance of a truly historic disgrace.

The President's response to the challenge of Watergate, in sum, was the bare minimum of what he had to do and say. Even so, with the single exception noted, all the men who lost their jobs are departing with the President's effusive thanks — and primarily because their usefulness has been destroyed. As for himself, having spoken, Mr. Nixon henceforth intends to devote himself to what he regards as more vital matters of state.

There is much more the President could have done and said. He could, for one example, have appointed an unimpeachable outside special prosecutor to explore all ramifications of Watergate instead of leaving that option open to his own new choice for attorney general, Elliot L. Richardson. He could have done or said something specifically about the wholesale abuse of his campaign funds, and how great chunks of it were obtained.

Instead, while deploring all that has happened, the President chose to declare that both major political parties are guilty of Watergate-type activity. This is quite untrue. Never in American political history has there been anything to approach this scandal, either in its extent or in the depth of official contempt for all manner of laws.

On the plus side of the President's response was proper acceptance of ultimate blame for what happened. His excuse that he had been kept uninformed by zealous close aides who thought they were acting in his best interests can also be accepted, at least in part, in view of the extraordinary isolation he had constructed for himself.

Despite that isolation it is difficult to believe that somehow the President could smell no White House entanglement in Watergate until last month. Even more difficult to understand is why he didn't personally take some corrective action right after Republican agents were arrested during their break-in of Democratic headquarters last June, even though the White House itself may not have been involved. His party was.

We have strongly supported President Nixon in most undertakings of his administration. We will continue to give him such support, whenever merited, but we retain grave reservations about his handling of the Watergate scandal and his personal patch-up job.

Watergate is not going to go away, and may even get worse as time goes on. We regret the President did what he had to do and say at such a very late date. We regret he didn't do and say more.

Especially do we regret the damage to public confidence in its leadership which today — from any viewpoint — still remains seriously diminished.

The Virginian-Pilot

Norfolk, Va., May 2, 1973

President Nixon's desire to make the 1,361 days remaining to his Administration "great days for America" surely is as sincere as it is understandable. The Nation, and much of the world, shares it. But Mr. Nixon's preoccupation with it Monday night seemed to be diversionary.

For the President, who spoke from the wreckage of his personal and political staff, poked but lightly into the scandal of Watergate. He first learned of the break-in at Democratic headquarters on June 17, the day it occurred, "while I was in Florida trying to get a few days' rest after my visit to Moscow." He immediately ordered an investigation.

Mr. Nixon deserves to be believed there. Contrary to his political style, he said, he had left the direction of his campaign for re-election to a committee headed by John Mitchell, newly resigned as Attorney General. He was busy with affairs of state. And anyway, it was clear that the Democratic nominee, who was almost certain to be George McGovern, could hardly hope to win.

But between June 17 and March 21, when he "personally assumed the responsibility for coordinating intensive new inquiries into the matter," Mr. Nixon remained unsuspecting. As the investigations multiplied, he asked repeatedly whether anyone in the Administration was involved in the wrongdoing and he was assured repeatedly that no one was.

"Because of the continuing reassurances — because I believed the reports I was getting, because I had faith in the persons from whom I was getting them — I discounted the stories in the press that appeared to implicate members of my Administration or other officials of the campaign committee," the President reassured us.

But it is not a very reassuring story. For the actions of the Administration between last June and March of this year are consistent with the attempt to cover up Watergate, and inconsistent with the diligent pursuit of the truth. Those actions include the continuing denial and disparagement of the incriminating stories until it was no longer possible to deny them. They include the attempt to claim executive privilege to prevent the aides of the President from testifying about Watergate. The actions of the Administration appear, far more seriously, to have included the obstruction of justice by the Attorney General of the United States and the director of the Federal Bureau of Investigation. It is even reported that the convicted conspirators were bribed to keep quiet, using funds from a safe within the White House.

The best interpretation that can be put upon the evidence in the public record is that the President of the United States was deceived by the men that he most trusted, that he was gulled by the men he had placed in positions of great power and public trust. They defiled not only the President's trust, but the public trust.

Mr. Nixon isn't foolish and he isn't naive. To accept the story that Mr. Nixon, ostrichlike, was unaware of the implications of Watergate for many months requires the willing suspension of disbelief. Many will be willing to believe Mr. Nixon because they want to believe the President of the United States, want to believe in both the man and the office.

Others won't. The man, if not the office, is badly damaged by Watergate. But barring his impeachment, resignation, or some tragedy, Mr. Nixon remains the only President that the country has for the next three and a half years. Mr. Nixon and the Nation must salvage what he — and we — can from the balance of his term.

That can only be done if the inquiry into Watergate is now pressed vigorously, as Mr. Nixon and Elliot Richardson, who is to be the Administration's clean-up man, promise that it will. Mr. Richardson would be wise to name an outside prosecutor as the first step to restoring the integrity of the White House. Both the big fish and the small fry in Watergate must be brought to justice as quickly as possible. The cash flow of the several secret funds must be traced, and made public, to restore the integrity of our political process.

Mr. Nixon says that he wants the days left to him in the White House "to be the best days in America's history." The country will not fail him in his high purposes if he doesn't fail us. But for Mr. Nixon there can be no escaping history's hard judgment on Watergate.

The New York Times

New York, N.Y., May 2, 1973

The Watergate scandal has become a crisis of Presidential authority. In his address to the nation Monday evening, President Nixon tried but failed to resolve that crisis. The whole trend of future events remains in doubt.

Although he has dismissed three of his senior aides and formally accepted responsibility for whatever misdeeds may have been committed without his knowledge, Mr. Nixon basically has conceded nothing except what events have wrenched from him. In making those minimum moves, he has at the same time played down the seriousness of the scandals and tried to blur responsibility for them.

He praised H. R. Haldeman and John D. Ehrlichman, who resigned under pressure, as "two of the finest public servants it has been my privilege to know," adding: "I greatly regret their departure."

The President then offered this appalling excuse: "I know that it can be very easy under the intensive pressures of a campaign for even well-intentioned people to fall into shady tactics, to rationalize this on the grounds that what is at stake is of such importance to the nation that the end justifies the means. And both of our great parties have been guilty of such tactics."

But these excuses and words of praise come after Mr. Ehrlichman had already told the Federal Bureau of Investigation that it was he who assigned two of the men later convicted in the Watergate trial to investigate Daniel Ellsberg. When he learned that they had burglarized the files of Mr. Ellsberg's psychiatrist, Mr. Ehrlichman, although he is a member of the bar, took no action. He merely told them not to do it again.

That took place not during the heat of a hard-fought political campaign but in September, 1971. Mr. Ehrlichman's complacent acceptance of such criminal behavior is on a par with former Attorney General Mitchell's participation without public disclosure, much less denunciation, in conferences early in 1972 to discuss the illegal "bugging" of the offices of the Democratic National Committee. Mr. Nixon may find it easy to understand such attitudes on the part of high officials. Most citizens do not.

Even more dismaying is the planned obstruction of justice in the Watergate case by senior Administration officials, as reported in the news columns of this newspaper today. When an atmosphere of criminality prevails in the highest levels of the Administration, it is impossible to know what other public business may be tainted with fraud.

Under these circumstances, Mr. Nixon cannot plausibly say that in some vague way both parties and all of America are to blame. He cannot assert that Watergate "has claimed far too much of my time and my attention" and that he now intends to busy himself with other matters. He cannot play a game of musical chairs inside his Administration and declare that moving about a few insiders is sufficient to restore public confidence. Such acts and attitudes are an affront to the public.

The full facts on this monstrous interference with the political process are unlikely ever to come out until prosecution is removed from control by this Administration. The Senate has pointed the way by approving a resolution offered by Senator Percy, Republican of Illinois, calling for nomination of a distinguished special prosecutor from outside the executive branch and for his confirmation by the Senate. Representative John Anderson, Republican of Illinois, has introduced a similar resolution in the House, which also deserves prompt approval. It is significant and encouraging that members of the President's own party in Congress have taken the lead in urging this essential action.

Finally, however, the ball returns to President Nixon. It is up to him to recognize that, important as are international negotiations, inflation and other public problems, what matters now is the breakdown of public confidence in his Administration. He cannot cope with specific problems on a business-as-usual basis as if Watergate were a minor diversion. It was neither a caper nor an isolated event; it was proof that something is radically wrong in the central relationships of this Administration. Mr. Nixon's task is to focus on repairing confidence by developing new relationships with his staff and Cabinet, with Congress and with the people. Nothing else can be accomplished until the President begins to put those relationships on the right basis—the basis of candor, lawfulness, mutual respect and sound constitutional practice in the conduct of the public's business.

The Courier-Journal

Louisville, Ky., May 2, 1973

AS ONE of the last citizens of America to concede that Watergate was more than a "third-rate burglary attempt," Mr. Nixon has finally acted decisively to halt the erosion of public confidence in his integrity. Whether he can repair what has been damaged, however, will depend on much more than the ouster of four key aides, protestations of personal shock and assertions that "there can be no white-wash at the White House."

The start is encouraging, in some ways. The President assumes responsibility for what has happened, if not the blame. He has offered at least a momentary olive branch to Congress and the press, whose own integrity he has been so busily attacking. He has moved to start restoring the stature of the Justice Department and the FBI, which he has so thoroughly politicized. He has restated his April 17 demand that all the facts about Watergate and its associated crimes be brought out. And, perhaps most important of all, he has pledged to work "toward a new set of standards, new rules and procedures, to ensure that future elections will be as nearly free of such abuses as they possibly can be made."

But "how could it have happened? Who is to blame?" Nowhere in the President's speech did one hear any hint that the "people whose zeal exceeded their judgment" might have had too faithfully reflected the atmosphere — "anything is fair in politics" — which has followed Mr. Nixon through his 27 years in and out of government. Nowhere was there mention of John Mitchell, his closest political associate who now admits he discussed (but says he repeatedly vetoed) the Watergate affair, but who we are supposed to believe never mentioned the matter to the President. Individuals, if they are found guilty, will be punished and their kinds of abuses "purged from our political processes in the years to come." But what of the kind of cynical manipulation of the electorate, so revealingly described in Joe McGinnis' book, The Selling of the President—1968, which was engineered by Mr. Nixon himself in every one of his campaigns?

What justification is it, indeed, to talk of two wrongs not making a right, and to misleadingly stress that both major political parties have been guilty of assorted abuses of the electoral process? Perhaps no laws can ever rid government entirely of influence-peddling, personal profiteering and "dirty tricks" at election time. But can anyone remember a previous instance of corruption in Washington in which the goal was not private gain but to perpetuate power?

Unless proven otherwise, no one wants to believe that the President himself knew in advance of the Watergate bugging and break-in. Yet if he now says he was "appalled" to read of it, why was his press secretary for months to characterize the incident as a piddling crime? His two closest associates, Mr. Haldeman and Mr. Ehrlichman, have "resigned" to protect the institution of the presidency, and Mr. Nixon still wants to "leave no implication whatever of personal wrongdoing on their part." That is quite proper, given his new dedication to individual rights and the integrity of the judicial process. But was it only Mr. Dean who lied to him when the President asked whether the news reports were true? It's hard to believe that for 10 months the No. 2 and No. 3 men in the White House—men who could not offer the excuse of being diverted by the urgency of foreign affairs—could also have believed that Watergate and the rest was simply much ado about nothing.

It's hard not to believe, in fact, that what actually prodded Mr. Nixon himself into action, first in his April 17 statement and now in his televised address, was public opinion polls and spreading political anguish, not new-found facts or a sudden surge of conscience. But this, too, may become clearer as the investigation continues.

This is the President who talks of electoral reform, yet fought against tightening of campaign spending rules; who speaks of judicial integrity yet tried to name second-raters to the Supreme Court; who deplores divisiveness yet cruelly used the law-and-order and busing issues as wedges to split the electorate; who hails individual liberties but has used grand juries as political weapons.

This is the President whose drive for one-man rule, defiance of Congress and contempt for law have amounted to calculated assault on the constitutional system of checks and balances; a man who began his second term with talk of going forward together and peace with honor, only to intensify hostilities toward the House, Senate and Cambodia; who cautions that what may be the worst case of corruption in government since the founding of the Republic not distract us from foreign affairs and the other "vital work before us."

The President has provided that his new Attorney General may appoint a special prosecutor if he prefers—and this Mr. Richardson should do immediately. Mr. Richardson seems to have the kind of moral scruples that will be useful in restoring integrity to a Justice Department left in shreds by Mr. Mitchell and Richard Kleindienst. But the public has just endured a prolonged period of watching the administration investigate itself; and this simply won't do any longer. Moreover, Mr. Richardson would be bound by the President's injunction against granting immunity to any witness—a procedure which might be the price of getting John Dean to testify to all that he seems to know.

But the greatest challenge in rebuilding public confidence in the highest office in the land falls to Mr. Nixon himself. As he sat Monday evening with a bust of Lincoln to one side, a viewer could not help wondering again why it is that today's President continually voices so many of the same ideals of peace, generosity, decency and human dignity, while acting simultaneously to undermine them.

Even the usually sympathetic Wall Street Journal could comment two weeks before Mr. Nixon's re-election last November, in an analysis of the gap between presidential moralizing and performance: "The image has not been one of an administration intent on preserving and restoring traditional virtues, but of one practicing a rootless pragmatism that moves whichever way the political pressures push."

The President may be ready now to emerge from the insulation that has cut him off from direct access to the people and the rest of government. He may be ready now to try to be a leader of all of the people, a man remembered as a unifier and not a divider, a man of principle and not solely of pragmatism, of honesty and not deception. But President Nixon's first attorney general, John Mitchell, once advised reporters to judge the administration not by its words but by its deeds. That part, except for the limited ouster of mostly faceless men announced Monday, is still to come.

THE CHRISTIAN SCIENCE MONITOR
Boston, Mass., May 3, 1973

To understand what President Nixon has done in his dramatic reorganization of the White House staff one must start with the fact that there are two separate and distinct parts to this story. The issues and the people involved are different in the two parts. The first involves Watergate, the other is the relationship between White House and Congress.

By firing his chief legal counsel, John Dean, and by substituting Elliot Richardson for Richard Kleindienst at the Department of Justice Mr. Nixon has recognized that wrong things were done in the Watergate affair and that the White House must be purged of the wrong. He has promised that it will be.

By accepting the resignation of his two closest and most trusted aides, H. R. Haldeman and John Ehrlichman, he is not only dealing with the Watergate taint in the public mind but also making concessions to the principle that Congress is a separate but coequal branch of the government and that it cannot be treated as it has been treated by his White House since his re-election of last November.

One measure of the weights of the two separate issues is that it was not the Dean and Kleindienst departures which brought the loudest applause from Capitol Hill, but news of the departure of Haldeman and Ehrlichman. And those who cheered loudest were the Republicans.

Mr. Kleindienst had to go because, as he stated, recent disclosures had shown "that persons with whom I had had close personal and professional associations could be involved in conduct violative of the laws of the United States."

Mr. Haldeman and Mr. Ehrlichman had to go—not only because of possible involvement in Watergate but because they symbolized an attitude at the postelection White House which had come to seem intolerable on Capitol Hill.

Rightly or wrongly, in the eyes of Congress these two devoted and long-term aides to the President represented the most extreme assertion of presidential authority and presidential privilege in American constitutional history. The men of the Congress, Republicans and Democrats alike, identified them with the assertion of the presidential right to wage war, to abolish branches of government, to spend or refuse to spend — without the advice and the consent of the Congress.

Whether they themselves were rightly identified with these attitudes or were only the faithful executors of Mr. Nixon's views is beside the point. The men of the Congress saw the two as the personification of the White House attitudes and positions that have alienated Congress and opened a gulf between Mr. Nixon and his own party.

Involved in the new Washington equation may be an implicit promise that in the future the leaders of the Congress (and of the Republican Party on Capitol Hill) will have easier access to the President, will be more seriously heard, and in all major issues will be consulted. The Congress is insisting on a return to the days when the United States was governed by a process of consensus between executive and legislative branches of government.

Mr. Nixon can be expected in the future to lean more heavily on people like Mr. Richardson who have accepted and survived the ordeal by ballot box. Congress is distrustful of anyone at the White House who has come in to power from outside of the political world.

This complex of new arrangements in Washington is a minimum withdrawal by the President from two untenable positions — minimizing Watergate and exaggerating executive authority. It can open the way to a revival of an effective working relationship between President and Congress — if Congress remains satisfied.

THE BILLINGS GAZETTE
Billings, Mont., May 3, 1973

The nation was treated to an unpleasant performance Monday night of an unforgiving man asking the nation for understanding that he so seldom gives others.

The very thought of a United States president having to appear before the people who gave him such a mandate to admit he had been duped, shown bad judgment in the selection of his cohorts and been too busy to watch the store does not make a strong case for credibility in his actions.

What he told us was that his first team was a bunch of bums that he had to give the gate over Watergate. Dress it in any other words you wish, wrap it in the robes of the exalted office of the presidency, that's what the man said.

Oh, he made his excuses that he had been busy. That phase of his explanation went along quite well until he used the round-heeled phrase "peace with honor" that has such a hollow ring.

He even paid lip service to the diligent men who nailed his first team's hide to the wall—the gentlemen of the press.

This late-in-the-game accolade to the men his first team has reviled so long is mindful of a coach who has been soundly trounced congratulating his opponent in tones that are better interpreted as "wait'll next time."

And they'll be waiting for next time because actions of his administration and first team to date are those which spawn suspicion, not forgiveness.

President Nixon will be around for three plus more years. Whether he is kicked around by the press will depend upon his deeds.

St. Louis Globe-Democrat
St. Louis, Mo., May 5, 1973

As the incredible misdeeds committed under the banner of the Committee for the Re-election of the President continue to surface, perhaps the most shocked Americans of all are members of the regular national Republican Party organization.

Both Sen. Robert J. Dole, former chairman of the Republican National Committee, and George Bush, the present chairman of the GOP Committee, have gone to great lengths to point out the regular Republican organization was completely separate from the Committee for the Re-election of the President and had no part in the reported illegal and unethical activities of the latter.

Furthermore, both have charged that the Committee for the Re-election of the President was superimposed on the regular organization and took most of the campaign contributions and used them exclusively for the President's re-election. The regular GOP organization was left out in the cold.

As a result, GOP candidates from the local level, state level and congressional level found they had very little campaign money behind them. Most of it had been siphoned off by the Committee for the Re-election of the President.

Many observers believe that this inequitable distribution of GOP funds had a direct relationship to the election results that gave the President a landslide majority and the GOP candidates in Congress a virtual stalemate. Local Republican candidates also are still bitter at the lack of help from the President's election committee.

In retrospect, it is clear that one of the main reasons the Committee for the Re-election of the President fell into disrepute and scandal was the fact that it was run and staffed by too many men who were either political amateurs or "Madison Avenue" types who became intoxicated with their own power. They failed precisely because they were not professional politicians.

The typical professional politician, profaned as he may be, is far too intelligent and experienced to contemplate the use of illegal and unethical means to gain his ends. He relies on his skills and hard work to get his people elected. may be, is far too intelligent and experienced to contemplate the use of illegal and unethical means to gain his ends. He relies on his skills and hard work to get his people elected.

This is why the "pros" in the national Republican Party are so angry and disillusioned. They are getting an undeserved "fall out" from stupid, Mad Hatter activities of the Committee for the Re-election of the President.

The Watergate scandal appears to be the almost exclusive property of the Committee for the Re-election of the President. It should not be visited upon the regular Republican organization. It is hoped that this dismal affair will make certain that no attempt will ever again be made to superimpose a committee of amateurs, wiretappers, break-in artists, disrupters and wheeler-dealers upon the respected and competent national Republican Party.

Amsterdam News

New York, N.Y., May 5, 1973

In his half-hearted attempt to rescue the White House from the slur of Watergate, President Nixon has destroyed the little confidence in the White House that America still had.

Mr. Nixon went on network television to announce his acceptance of the blame for Watergate in an attempt to get public sympathy. What he accomplished, instead was to further insult the nation's intelligence, with his claims of ignorance of the bugging incident.

We don't believe that Nixon didn't know. But, if his statements **are** true, then the situation calls for a careful reevaluation of the judgment of this country's Chief Executive. If his staff operates in secret and is not accountable to the Chief, then the entire nation is in danger and serious steps must be taken to correct this.

Nixon's acceptance of the resignations of MacGruder, Gray, Kleindienst, Dean, Haldeman and Ehrlichman are supposed to prove that he is cleaning up the White House. But, his subsequent appointments further indicate that this shakeup has not brought fresh, objective leadership to the White House. The replacements, Elliot Richardson, William Ruckelshaus and Leonard Garment, are party regulars with good records, but whose chief qualification is their loyalty to the President.

We don't want unswerving, misguided loyalty to the President — we demand government officials who act in a responsible and ethical manner, even when those assets conflict with the will of the President.

If these traits are not the major qualifying factors for important governmental posts, then we need to do something about the man who's changing the rules and creating a mess like Watergate at the seat of the government.

Congressman Charles B. Rangel has called for impeachment of Nixon, on the grounds that his official conduct leaves much to be desired. We concur with Rangel.

The President has abused his office to the point where we must consider him totally lacking in judgment, discretion, morals and responsibility. If his staff is not accountable to him, and he is not accountable to the nation, the government has reached the point of anarchy.

There has already been a mutiny of sorts in the White House and the seed of this rebellion manifested itself over the years, as the same men responsible for Watergate struck out against the mandates of the Constitution.

These Watergate scoundrels are the very persons responsible for the destructive social policies that ignore the needs of urban America and deny justice, liberty and opportunity to the poor and the Black.

As they leave their offices, we want to be assured that these repressive, discriminatory attitudes leave with them. Nixon's new appointees do not provide us with that assurance and so, he should go, right along with the scapegoats who are being made to carry the burden and the shame of the President's guilt.

WORCESTER TELEGRAM.

Worcester, Mass., May 6, 1973

According to reports from Washington, there is renewed and widespread discussion of an ominous topic: impeachment.

Impeachment and conviction is the only way a president of the United States can be removed from office. It has been tried only once, when it failed by one vote. President Andrew Johnson was impeached by the House of Representatives in 1868, but the Senate failed to convict him.

Speculation about impeachment of President Nixon rests on the possibility that he may be implicated so deeply in the Watergate scandal as to make it clear that he conspired to break the law. In that case, Sen. Barry Goldwater said in his blunt way, "I think the impeachment would certainly come."

If it came to that, impeachment would be a possibility, although not a certainty by any means. William F. Buckley Jr. argues that even if President Nixon is "guilty of a misprision of felony," he should not be impeached, but censured by Congress. Buckley feels that an impeachment would wreak such damage on the government and the nation that it should be avoided at practically any cost.

But Arthur Schlesinger Jr., a person who harbors an intense dislike for Nixon and all his works, argues for impeachment and gives the impression he can hardly wait for the day it comes. "Should this complicity be proven, Congress will have to bite the bullet and move toward impeachment. There is no halfway house."

This is exciting stuff; there is something in human nature attracted to disasters. It is linked to the secret satisfaction most of us feel when bad luck befalls someone wealthier, stronger or more favorably situated than we are.

But it is also dangerous talk. An impeachment of the President would shake the republic to its roots. It would weaken us badly both at home and abroad. Buckley's instincts are sound.

Before this sort of thing gets out of hand, we will do well to remember that it is grossly premature. Those who dislike and distrust Nixon may be convinced that he was one of the Watergate plotters. However, it is equally plausible that he and his campaign staff had an understanding that he was to be told nothing about the dirty tricks used in the campaign. If that turns out to be the fact, it will not reflect well on Nixon. However, it will be a long way from the grounds for impeachment set forth in the Constitution — "Treason, Bribery, or other High Crimes and Misdemeanors."

What is at stake is more than the President — more than Richard Nixon. It is the presidency itself. And the presidency is the driving force of our system of government. This is no time to let feelings of partisan revenge against Nixon sway the judgment.

We thought Sen. George McGovern put it well in his talk to the American Society of Newspaper Editors last week.

"These are difficult days for President Nixon," said McGovern. "He is the elected leader of the nation, and he is struggling to restore his leadership. We must help him, for the sake of the office he holds . . . I take no satisfaction from this sad affair. Indeed since the election I have repeatedly refused to respond to press inquiries about Watergate. And I take no joy today in the President's difficulties. With him, I hope they will be resolved soon so that he and we can fight out the future on other, better issues."

Post-Tribune

Gary, Ind., May 5, 1973

Permit us to disassociate ourselves from the mounting number who insist on finding the Watergate mess as bad as the Teapot Dome scandals of the 1920s. It's bad, but it's not that bad.

What Teapot Dome involved was permission of cronies of Cabinet members and others in high authority to exploit for personal and corporate profit a national oil reserve previously set aside for defense purposes. It wound up with one member of the Warren G. Harding cabinet in prison for taking bribes and others in considerable disgrace.

While the evident, but as yet not wholly disclosed, high level cover-up efforts and double dealing in the Watergate case are more than reprehensible, the central act itself did not involve any effort to mulct the government of money while at the same time potentially weakening national security.

Certainly breaking and entering is no more excusable for the advancement of a presidential campaign than for any other purpose. Likewise, invasion of privacy (of which most politicians expect comparatively little) is a violation of individual rights.

Nevertheless, we still refuse to put Watergate on a par with Teapot Dome.

Once that's been said, however, we still think Watergate is bad and all efforts should continue to get to the bottom of it as impartially as possible.

The Des Moines Register

Des Moines, Iowa, May 8, 1973

The President's new policy on "executive privilege" calls for present and past presidential aides to testify fully about Watergate except "in connection with conversations with the President, conversations among themselves [involving communication with the President] and as to presidential papers." The White House said the policy on executive privilege "shouldn't be interpreted as a mandate or order or prohibition" against testimony by witnesses.

We don't know what that White House interpretation means, but the approval given to invoking executive privilege to shield conversations with the President has an ominous ring. It seems to clear the way for John Mitchell, John Erlichman, H.R. Haldeman and others to refuse to tell grand jurors, the FBI and Senate investigators about the extent of possible presidential involvement in Watergate.

A cloak of confidentiality around the conversations between the President and his aides may be justified ordinarily. But Watergate is no ordinary case. Wrongdoing extending into the uppermost reaches of government has been alleged. Despite the President's disclaimer of personal involvement in the Watergate break-in and cover-up, substantial numbers of Americans suspect the President either knew about the bugging in advance or participated in hiding the facts.

This is an extraordinary situation that requires full disclosure of everything connected with Watergate, including the part played by the President.

We are surprised that the President would seek to bar testimony dealing with his role in Watergate. The President told a nationwide television audience last week that he knew nothing about the break-in in advance and that his aides gave him false assurances about White House involvement. The President ought to be eager to provide documentation and testimony that would support his assertions.

The administration has advanced a variety of untenable positions on executive privilege. It first asserted that no present or former White House aides could be questioned under oath. Then it extended the privilege to include all 2,500,000 employes in the executive branch. The latest stand represents a narrowing of the circumstances under which the privilege could be invoked, but it is broad enough so that it could prevent the full story from being revealed.

The administration's fluctuating positions on executive privilege give the impression of being based on expediency rather than principles of government. When the administration sought to keep John Dean from being questioned under oath, it constructed an executive privilege policy that effectively protected him. Now it seems to be trying to protect the President.

Talk of impeachment has begun filling the air. The best antidote to that talk is total disclosure that convinces Americans the President has told them the truth, the whole truth and nothing but the truth.

The Chattanooga Times

Chattanooga, Tenn., May 8, 1973

Three former White House aides are closely involved in the maneuvering now going on within the Justice Department which is attempting to unravel the Watergate affair. But the trio is divided, with H. R. Haldeman and John Ehrlichman on one side and former White House counsel John Dean 3d on the other.

But the first two have a powerful ally: President Nixon, whose contempt for Mr. Dean is fairly obvious.

The key to the situation lies in the President's April 17 statement in which he decreed that "no individual holding a position of major importance in the Administration should be given immunity." Many lawyers have criticized this action as "sheathing" a major weapon used by prosecutors as a means of not prosecuting a secondary figure so that the case against a major one can be vastly strengthened.

Mr. Dean, logically enough, is unwilling to disclose the evidence in his possession unless given immunity in return. Considering the fact that he had access to all the initial FBI reports on the matter, it is presumed that the information is impressive.

We wonder if Mr. Nixon's low regard for his former counsel is based on recognition that, since Mr. Dean is considered likely to receive immunity, the possibility exists that Messrs. Haldeman and Ehrlichman, whom the President lauded so effusively, face indictment?

THE TENNESSEAN

Nashville, Tenn., May 8, 1973

IN RESPONSE to increasing pressure, Mr. Elliot Richardson, the attorney general-designate, has announced he will name a special prosecutor to investigate Watergate. Even so, there seem to be conditions attached.

Mr. Richardson said his choice would not be anyone associated with any involved, or suspected of involvement in the Watergate. That is not quite good enough. Too, Mr. Richardson said he would not relinquish final authority in the case, although the special prosecutor would have "ultimate accountability" to the American public. That is ambiguous.

★ ★ ★

Although Mr. Richardson indicated he was willing to let the Senate approve his choice, leaving that selection to him in the first place is not the way it should have been done.

Any special prosecutor should not only be outside government, but not linked in any way to anybody in the administration. Preferably he would not even be associated with the Republican or the Democratic parties. He should certainly not be an old school chum of Mr. Richardson—or anyone else in the administration.

In the second place, Mr. Richardson ought to be asked to clarify in detail what he means by saying he would retain final authority in the case. That could be stretched to include almost any and everything, from which leads to pursue to which witnesses to omit.

If Mr. Richardson intends to be the grey eminence behind a special prosecutor, then there can be no overwhelming feeling of confidence that the investigation of the Watergate will be complete or that the "whole truth" will come out, no matter who is involved.

No matter what can be said about Mr. Richardson's capability or integrity, that fact remains that in his various positions within the administration, he has been a loyal member of the "team" and has been noticeably responsive to the way the wind blows from the White House.

It can be said that a large number of ordinary American citizens are quite anxious to believe that the Watergate didn't reach as far as the presidency itself. Almost certainly Mr. Richardson can be counted among them, along with other members and former members of the administration.

One of the strangest expressions of this came the other day from former Defense Secretary Melvin Laird, who told reporters that he is certain Mr. Nixon was not involved in Watergate, but if it proved otherwise, he would not want the truth to come out because of the damage to the authority of the President.

That is no odder as a statement of public morality than others which have come from administration stalwarts. But it illustrates the problem of Mr. Richardson and the Justice Department in letting the chips fall where they may in the Watergate case.

★ ★ ★

If the American public loses complete faith in the integrity of the presidency, the authority of that office must indeed suffer disastrously. But the point made the other day by the St. Louis Post-Dispatch is nevertheless valid: "The United States can survive a ruined presidency, but it cannot endure as a democracy if some citizens and not others are placed above the law."

THE DAILY OKLAHOMAN
Oklahoma City, Okla., May 9, 1973

WATERGATE is said to differ from the usual governmental scandal in that it didn't proceed from personal avarice but had as its purpose the subversion of the political system.

Nothing in the incredible tale suggests that the conspirators were motivated by personal greed. Their obsessive purpose was to make certain that President Nixon won re-election last year over any Democratic candidate who might oppose him. The millions of dollars available in secret campaign funds were to be used for this purpose only by the Committee to Re-elect the President.

On this simple premise, an elaborate structure of conspiratorial theory is being erected to show that the perpetrators had as their purpose nothing less than the subversion of the political process. Exactly what is meant isn't clearly explained. Presumably, the conspiracy is viewed as an attempt to deprive the people of their rightful presidential choice.

A defect of this theory is that it gives Watergate an importance it didn't have when the people were in the process of making up their minds about the presidency. The vast majority of the voters were completely unaware of Watergate a year ago, and it isn't apparent how they could be influenced unduly by something about which they knew nothing at the time.

The Nixon committee's so-called department of dirty tricks was busily engaged in all manner of juvenile idiocies, of course, but the central question is whether its activities were crucial to the political process or merely peripheral. All the evidence suggests they were peripheral.

An example is the committee's supposed role in helping Sen. George McGovern win the Democratic nomination. The theory is that the Republican conspirators regarded McGovern as the weakest Democratic possibility and were intent on sabotaging the candidacy of Sen. Edmund Muskie, D-Maine, the early front-runner.

Mysterious telephone calls, missing papers, and unsigned scandal sheets are among the merry pranks ascribed to the department of dirty tricks in its effort to sidetrack the Muskie candidacy.

This sort of thing is not uncommon in politics. Unsigned circulars containing politically damaging canards turn up routinely in Oklahoma election campaigns. They aren't even seen by most voters, and many voters who do see them are not influenced in the slightest. If the political system could be subverted so easily, it would have vanished long ago.

The truth is that Watergate didn't have the slightest bearing on either the Democratic convention or the November election. Muskie eliminated himself when he broke down and wept in the course of a diatribe delivered Feb. 26, 1972, against William Loeb, publisher of the Manchester, N.H., Union Leader, in front of the newspaper's office. The performance was that of a man too unstable emotionally to be entrusted with the heavy responsibilities of the presidency.

But Muskie couldn't have won the nomination anyway. The Democratic party's revised rules for delegate selection played squarely into McGovern's hands. He had been the original chairman of the Commission on Party Structure and Delegate Selection which the Democratic National Committee had appointed in 1969 to come up with new rules. Thus equipped, his tightly organized young supporters were able to control the precinct caucuses and later the convention at Miami Beach.

Watergate may be the most widely publicized governmental scandal since Teapot Dome, but it wasn't a significant factor in the outcome of the 1972 election. Therefore, it couldn't have subverted the political system.

The Washington Post
Washington, D.C., May 8, 1973

"Whatever may appear to have been the case before—whatever improper activities may yet be discovered in connection with this whole sordid affair—I want the American people, I want you to know beyond the shadow of a doubt that during my terms as President justice will be pursued fairly, fully and impartially, no matter who is involved. This office is a sacred trust and I am determined to be worthy of that trust." *President Nixon, in his television address, April 30, 1973.*

These were the words with which the President sought last week to assure us that at last he had fully comprehended the magnitude and the seriousness of the Watergate affair. All of us wanted to believe him and hoped that the new phase would bring us all the facts and restore, in large measure, the credibility of the presidency. In the week that has passed since Mr. Nixon's speech, that hope has been put to a terrible test.

Consider, for example, the case of Egil Krogh, former assistant to John D. Ehrlichman on the White House staff and now Undersecretary of Transportation—on leave. When the Ellsberg case revelations on the ransacking of a Los Angeles psychiatrist's files began turning heat on the White House, Mr. Krogh apparently decided to make some kind of a confession of his role in the thing, which he subsequently did. But, while he was considering his course of action, his associates tell us, he was subject to intense pressure from the White House not to do so. We know, at least, that freshly-minted guidelines on executive privilege were rushed to him before he sent his confessional affidavit by mail and by official channel to Judge W. Matt Byrne in Los Angeles.

Or, consider the new guidelines themselves. When compared with the two most recent Nixon administration versions of the doctrine—the Dean and Kleindienst doctrines—the new version seemed, at first blush to be more reasonable. But, when compared with the Eisenhower version of the privileges—followed by Presidents Kennedy and Johnson—the new Nixon claim is extraordinarily broad. Consider only two points. First, under the Eisenhower view, only the President could assert the privilege or direct his subordinates to do so. The new guidelines permit present and former White House aides to determine for themselves when and where to invoke the privilege or direct his subordinates to do so. The new cluded within the scope of the Nixon guidelines and presidential papers are defined to cover anything generated in the White House and anything written outside the building, but directed to it. That is a far broader assertion than any President before Mr. Nixon ever made.

Then take the President's statement that he would not want any of his former aides or associates to be accorded the privilege of immunity from prosecution. Again, the first look is deceiving. There is John W. Dean, III hanging out there in limbo with a number of interesting documents in his bank deposit box and some interesting stories to tell. Ordinarily, prosecutors would leap at the prospect of such a productive witness and a grant of immunity would be made to aid the prosecution as was the case with Alfred Baldwin, the wiretap monitor, in the first Watergate trial. But, this time, Mr. Dean is having to beg for word of immunity from somewhere out there, so he can come in and tell one of the most interesting stories in the whole affair.

And, there is Donald Segretti, the alleged saboteur and reported recruiter of as many as 50 accomplices, being indicted quickly in Florida for the relatively minor offense of making up and causing to be issued a phony letter in the Florida Democratic primary. What stories Mr. Segretti could probably tell to Sen. Ervin's select committee—if only he were unfettered by his indictment. Now, he can appropriately claim that he can't talk about the whole affair because he faces prosecution. So, suddenly, only a week after the President's speech, it looks like cover-up as usual.

But all is not necessarily lost, for us or for the President. The last clear chance, as the lawyers say, is the matter of the Special Prosecutor. Mr. Nixon announced that his new attorney general would have authority to appoint a "special supervising prosecutor" if he deemed it necessary. Though the President could have easily have done it himself, if he really wanted it done, the timing and the handling of the special prosecutor's appointment and role could still make the difference for the President in terms of the faith that he supposedly hopes can be restored.

Unfortunately, however, Mr. Richardson has apparently decided to name the special prosecutor only *after* his own nomination as Attorney General is confirmed by the Senate. If the Judiciary committee buys that, it is buying a prosecutor in a poke.

There are at least three conditions which are required to make the prosecutor fully credible. The first is that his selection itself be made under a process at least once removed from the administration—by a group of past or present leaders of the bar, for example, or by some other body of distinguished jurists or experts on the law with no partisan connections. Second, the special prosecutor should be confirmed by the Senate or at least approved by the Judiciary Committee. Third, he should be chosen immediately—for each day's delay means that the investigation is proceeding under the direction of the same unwonderful people who brought us the shockingly unsatisfactory first Watergate investigation. Finally, he should be given the broadest possible independent authority with regard to the scope of his activities and picking of personnel.

Given the history of this affair—which the President has appropriately dubbed "sordid"—and given at least the appearance of things proceeding almost entirely as usual since the President's speech, it is imperative that the administration take this last opportunity to regain the faith of the public in its willingness and capacity to run an honest government. Anything less than a readiness to permit the sort of investigation the President has himself promised us can only be read as an admission on his part of foreknowledge and complicity not only in the crimes and improprieties that have been committed in his name but in the still continuing effort to stall and evade, and cover up.

THE WALL STREET JOURNAL.

New York, N.Y., May 9, 1973

Now that Mr. Haldeman and Mr. Ehrlichman have been cut down by Watergate, an inexorable momentum carries us to the question of Mr. Nixon himself. It is a moment to recognize that toppling the most exalted White House aide is one thing, and toppling a President quite another.

That is not to suggest that presidential wrongdoing ought to be beyond remedy, or that the nation ought to take an ostrich-like posture toward the possibility of direct presidential involvement in the Watergate bugging and the subsequent cover-up. But it would be wise to think for a moment about where the momentum is taking us, and especially about the standards of prudence, judgment, and evidence that should govern what is potentially so momentous a journey.

It is of course hard to maintain an attitude of care and reasonable detachment as the passing days pile one disgusting disclosure upon another. The circle of apparent complicity in the Watergate case and related crimes and improprieties spreads ever wider, embracing a dozen or so White House aides, officials of the Justice Department, the head of the FBI, a high official of the CIA who is now Marine Corps commandant, the President's personal lawyer. It is only natural to expect the disclosures to continue, and to assume that in the end they will prove the worst.

In the face of this it is understandably difficult but doubly important to remember that when you damage the President you also risk damaging the nation. Some may scoff at this point, but it was remembered by Mr. Nixon in the hour of his 1960 defeat (see alongside), and it no doubt also accounts for the statesmanship with which Senators Kennedy and McGovern, among others, have treated the present controversy. The point is that while the President must take the responsibility for crippling himself already, anyone else who would aggravate the wound had better know precisely what he is doing.

We are already seeing the epitome of the danger in loose talk of impeachment among the public and a few of the dizzier types on Capitol Hill. Impeachment is the gravest possible constitutional action, a last resort when there is no other way to salvage the system itself. A House committee must study the possible charges, the House must vote by a majority to impeach and the Senate must hold a trial requiring a two-thirds majority to convict. The unsuccessful impeachment of President Andrew Johnson took three months from the time of the House vote to final disposition. Given the domestic and international trouble that could arise, that is a long time to have a paralyzed President.

The worst outcome of the Watergate episode we can conceive is an impeachment effort that does not succeed, that leaves half of the nation feeling the President can get away with crime and the other half feeling he was the victim of an overreaching and politically motivated assault by his long-standing enemies. If a time for impeachment does arise it will be obvious to nearly everyone; we can imagine Senator Goldwater in the forefront of the effort. In the meantime, the talk of impeachment from Bella Abzug, who was taking out impeachment ads when Watergate was only a collection of buildings, only cheapens the constitutional instrument, making it more difficult and less effective to use if the time does arrive.

The least bad outcome, by contrast, would be that as the full facts come out they show that the President had no direct involvement but was misled by his aides. This would not remove his responsibility, of course, but the mistake would be of a sort that a newly reelected President should have full opportunity to set right. It disturbs us to meet and read a few whose tones of glee suggest they would be disappointed by such an anticlimax. It disturbs us only slightly less to meet and read a great many who cannot resist leaping to conclusions that also tend to preclude this least unhappy outcome.

The latter attitude we can at least understand, for there is a highly plausible line of conjecture pointing toward presidential involvement if not in the original bugging at least in the subsequent cover-up. It is hard to believe that his most loyal aides would not take the full story to him; it is hard to believe that someone in politics as long as Mr. Nixon would fail to press for a full answer when Washington was abuzz with scandal; and so on.

But there is an opposite line of conjecture that cannot be dismissed as implausible. Mr. Nixon has made himself probably the most isolated President in history. He delegated huge amounts of authority to his palace guard. He has lost no love on the press and would see no reason to believe it instead of his own staff. A staff of tough guys might conclude it was protecting the President by keeping him ignorant of wrongdoing.

Amid these conjectures about presidential involvement, the only direct evidence to emerge so far is scarcely worthy of the name. John Dean's revelations, for example, that the President told him he was doing a "good job," are consistent with either line of conjecture. Their importance lies strictly in the further conjecture that Mr. Dean will have more to come later, specifically in documents he has put in a safe deposit box now under trusteeship of the Watergate judge. But his obvious interest in tantalizing federal prosecutors into granting immunity in return for testimony leaves us wanting to see the documents before we judge the case.

Where it will all end we certainly would not predict. Given the implausibilities that have emerged so far we are prepared to believe anything. But we are going to believe nothing on the basis of conjecture. The episode is far too important to the future of the Republic to make judgments on any but the soundest and most careful basis. And it seems to us that if a President is not entitled to ask for the assumption of innocence we routinely grant to accused murderers and rapists, he is at least entitled to ask us to suspend judgment until a solid fact or two has emerged.

Miami, Fla., May 10, 1973

The irony of Vice President Spiro Agnew's latest blast at the press is inescapable. Mr. Agnew said he applauds the press for uncovering Watergate, but he cannot applaud its techniques.

Well, no one has accused the press of breaking and entering, illegal wiretapping or conspiring to frustrate the due process of law. This is an inappropriate time for anyone in the Nixon administration to criticize "techniques."

We are more respectful of the alarm sounded by Sen. William Proxmire, an administration critic who thinks the press may be convicting the President on the basis of hearsay and unsubstantiated charges.

The newsmen aren't charging Mr. Nixon with anything. They are passing along charges leveled by other involved persons. Where those involved persons have an obvious ax to grind, the newsmen are reporting that fact as well.

With new revelations breaking almost daily, and with the original Watergate caper spawning five or six related scandals, one need not be a Chicken Little to believe the sky is falling. To that extent we can understand Sen. Proxmire's concern.

Nevertheless we are confident the reading public can distinguish between suspicion and proof, between indictments and self-serving accusations.

We suppose Vice President Agnew, Sen. Proxmire and much of the public would feel more secure if the press stuck closely to established information channels and official statements.

The trouble is that established channels have been subverting the electoral, judicial and news gathering processes and official statements have proved to be mistaken, lying, or "inoperative." So the press has been left to its own "techniques," which are fairly innocent when compared with those of the administration.

As for Sen. Proxmire's main concern, we cannot think of anyone in a better position to defend his own good name than the President of the United States. He has at his disposal a corps of counselors, the entire Justice Department and more undercover agents than anyone knows.

If he really intends to get to the bottom of the matter, as he has promised, he should be confident the truth will out.

Detroit Free Press
Detroit, Mich., May 10, 1973

AS A SIMPLE statement of principle —that President Nixon is entitled to the same presumption of innocence as anyone else—Sen. William Proxmire repeated a truism that was probably in need of repeating.

But when he compared the role of the press in the Watergate story to the tactics of the late Sen. Joe McCarthy, Sen. Proxmire was about as wrong as McCarthy was.

The senator, a strong opponent of the President on most issues, took particular exception to reports that John Dean, fired on April 30 as White House counsel, is said to have told grand jury investigators that Mr. Nixon was linked to the White House cover-ups. This he called "McCarthyistic destruction" of the President that represented "the press at its worst."

True that testimony before a grand jury is supposed to be secret, and true also that Dean's credibility leaves much to be desired. But it was not the press that leaked Dean's testimony any more than it was the press that leaked his testimony before a secret Senate hearing.

It is also true that the grand jury is not an adversary procedure. Only one side of the story is told. And when a grand jury returns a true bill, the accused is still entitled to the presumption of innocence until he is found guilty in a court of law.

But where Sen. Proxmire wanders afield is in comparing the investigative reporting of the press to the wild assaults made by McCarthy 20 years ago.

In spite of the administration's attacks on the Washington Post last fall and through the winter, everything it reported about Watergate has turned out, in the long run, to be true. Mr. Nixon, Mr. Agnew and Ron Ziegler, the White House press spokesman, have all apologized in public.

Not a single charge that Joe McCarthy made — and he made thousands — turned out to be true. McCarthy had no evidence at all. Ben Bradlee, executive editor of the Post, said that his paper did not run a Watergate story until it had been documented by at least three different sources.

We cite the Post because it took the lead in investigating the case, and every other part of the media either ignored the story, copied the Post or played catch-up. We know of no newspaper which has accused the President of knowing about Watergate before the event, though many have wondered how so astute and suspicious a politician could have been deceived by his closest friends for so long.

Sen. Proxmire is, of course, correct in citing the tendency, in the last six weeks especially, on the part of the press to turn leaks into headlines. We accept the rebuke. But we also suggest that had the President —he is where the buck stops—been more forthright with the people and more diligent in searching out the truth, there would have been no necessity to resort to secret sources and leaked, even if sworn, testimony.

It was not the press which caused Mr. Nixon's troubles. It was his campaign committee and his over-zealous aides, for whom he is ultimately responsible. He has our sympathy so long as he and his administration search diligently for the facts and prosecute relentlessly the wrongdoers. And he has our presumption of innocence in spite of Sen. Proxmire's opinion that Mr. Nixon was "involved in Watergate up to his ears."

We shall try to do as the senator says, not as he does.

TULSA DAILY WORLD
Tulsa, Okla., May 10, 1973

A FEW people in Washington and elsewhere have begun to be quoted saying impeachment proceedings should be either considered or brought against PRESIDENT NIXON as a result of the Watergate affair.

That is totally irresponsible talk at this point; not only fundamentally unfair in prejudging some kind of guilt by MR. NIXON but also dangerous to the institution of the PRESIDENCY.

The Watergate whirlpool is swirling so swiftly now that it threatens to create an atmosphere approaching hysteria, particularly in Washington and in some segments of the press. It is a time for restraint, for protecting personal reputations and our political process itself, rather than for seeing how much damage can be done.

We do not minimize the sins and crimes that have gone into the Watergate episode nor the coverup that has followed. Every person guilty of wrongdoing should be exposed and made to pay a fitting penalty for whatever he has done. The entire sequence of events, for all its bizarre improbability, is so grave that it must be treated with utmost seriousness.

But to talk loosely of trying to impeach the PRESIDENT assumes far more than anyone knows. The presumption of innocence in the absence of proof to the contrary has not been changed in this country, even though at times it looks rather shaky. No evidence or proof has been offered for the notion that MR. NIXON was or is a part of the Watergate conspiracy; surely the CHIEF EXECUTIVE of the land deserves better than to bear guilt by association.

Impeachment is a subject to be mentioned in hushed tones, to be reserved for specific crimes against the Republic. It is not to be discussed lightly as if it were petty larceny.

Fortunately, we do not believe many Americans are taking the impeachment talk seriously. The trouble is that it may spread, leaping from one person to another in the excitement of a major scandal, until it takes on an air of validity.

The only way to prevent that is to see it for what it is now, before it becomes credible.

Impeachment is not an impossible turn in this crazy pattern of surprises. But let us keep it out of sight, out of hearing and out of mind unless some facts come forth that would seem to support it. Does the PRESIDENCY—our highest office—deserve less than that?

The Charlotte Observer
Charlotte, N.C., May 11, 1973

President Nixon seems to be well on the way toward making another bad mistake in the Watergate matter. The Administration is hardening its insistence that it must be in charge of the Watergate investigation if a special prosecutor is appointed. That insistence could sink the nomination of Elliot Richardson for attorney general.

Mr. Richardson said Wednesday he could see no reason to become attorney general unless he has full responsibility for the Watergate investigation. If he does not, he said, he might as well remain as secretary of defense.

It was an extraordinary position for him to take, and it seems evident that he would not have taken it unless he and the President had agreed to fight to the last against appointment of a fully independent special prosecutor.

The response from some members of the Judiciary Committee indicated that Mr. Richardson is risking rejection by the committee and the Senate — a rejection that would be another serious blow to the Administration.

Mr. Richardson indicated he is willing to name a special investigator—prosecutor for the Watergate matter but that he, as attorney general, must have "ultimate responsibility." Sen. Sam J. Ervin, among others on the committee, said that would prevent the investigator from having "sufficient independence."

We hope Sen. Ervin and others will hold to this position and that, if necessary, the nomination of Mr. Richardson will be rejected if that is necessary to assure a thoroughly independent Watergate prosecutor. The time has long since passed when the Administration itself can be entrusted with direction of this inquiry.

It is exceedingly presumptuous, in fact, for Mr. Richardson to stake off such a position. It is as if the Justice Department, which he presumably had been appointed to clean up, had never been tainted and as if no question remained about the Administration's integrity. Mr. Richardson wants, in effect, a Senate vote of confidence in the Administration's intention and capacity to be absolutely impartial in an investigation of itself.

Other evidence of President Nixon's hardening of that line is evident in a move among some Senate Republicans to take a position similar to Mr. Richardson's. Sen. Robert Taft. Jr. of Ohio has joined the White House effort, offering a resolution that calls for a special prosecutor accountable to and under the direction of the attorney general. That is in contrast to a resolution proposed earlier by Republican Sen. Charles Percy of Illinois to empower a special prosecutor who would be outside the control of the Administration, a proposal that is said to have infuriated President Nixon.

The Administration's insistence upon controlling the investigation is certainly audacious under the circumstances. It smacks of the same kind of arrogance and bad judgment that already have badly damaged public confidence in the Administration.

THE RICHMOND NEWS LEADER
Richmond, Va., May 11, 1973

To read of national and international events these days is by and large to read of Watergate, of Watergate-related matters, and of reaction to Watergate. Each day the newspapers carry accounts of still more examples of unrelenting imbecility in the court of King Richard. The chief courtiers have now left. Some have been indicted; others are expected to be. And one wonders: Is it not time that we drew back from this Watergate thing, and left it to the courts? Is it not time that we asked the drivers of that vehicle of righteousness, the Washington press, to take their foot off the gas?

Perhaps the true meaning of Watergate was contained in two votes in Congress yesterday. The Senate curbed President Nixon's power to impound funds. The House, in an unprecedented action, rejected additional spending authority for American bombing in Cambodia. Those votes suggest that possibly because of Watergate, the President is losing respect — and consequent influence — with the legislators on Capitol Hill. Yet if he cannot prevail in such important matters as the economy and Southeast Asia, then surely grim days are ahead.

Thankfully, even such a vigorous opponent of Mr. Nixon as Senator William Proxmire has called on the press to lay off the President. For Senator Proxmire evidently understands the danger to the nation if Mr. Nixon is so crippled by Watergate that he is rendered incapable of governing. The present infirmity of the President must not be allowed to become incapacity.

But the anti-Nixonites in Washington persist. Indeed, there is good reason to believe that The Washington Post saw from the beginning that in Watergate it had an issue that could wholly discredit the President of the United States. Writes Aaron Latham in the current issue of New York magazine, "Everyone at The Post knew that if the paper was wrong about Watergate, then Nixon was right about American journalism." The Post happened to be right about Watergate. And now, even though they have been wrong about so much that Richard Nixon has done, the anti-Nixonites are smugly citing Watergate as vindication of their entire case against him.

If Latham is correct, we may have here an ends-means situation. The "end" of the anti-Nixonites is to prove that Mr. Nixon was wrong about Vietnam, wrong about the economy, wrong about law and order, wrong about everything from busing to welfare reform to the SST. To that end, the anti-Nixonites are using rumor, innuendo, and gossip about Watergate to verify everything bad about Mr. Nixon that they want to believe — and that they want the public to believe. If they can unmask his administration as a fraud and hopelessly corrupt, then they can discredit the entire Nixon philosophy of what is good for the United States and the Western world.

Clearly those around the President at the time of Watergate were guilty of an excess of zeal in their efforts to re-elect their President. Today we face an excess of zeal in the press. Now that they have ripped open the White House cocoon, those in the press who detest Mr. Nixon and his philosophy are determined to show us that Watergate was not simply a temporary aberration. To them, Watergate proves the validity of all their accumulated resentments and discontents about the Nixon philosophy and the Nixon administration. And they are determined to take that administration from the high hopes that it nourished in November, to squalid destruction. It is crucial for the nation and for the Free World that they not be allowed to succeed.

THE SPRINGFIELD UNION
Springfield, Mass., May 14, 1973

The entire question of whether Elliot Richardson is to be confirmed by the Senate as attorney general boils down to a matter of trust. And that would apply to any individual, in or out of the GOP, in or out of the government, in or out of the public eye.

Richardson, while publicly accorded the respect of questioners at the Senate Judiciary Hearing on his confirmation, may not win approval. There is some opposition because the "appearance" of his ties to the administration would impair confidence in the "ultimate responsibility" he would take for the Watergate investigation and prosecution.

The nominee himself said that if the senators did not trust him to act properly they should not vote to confirm him. And in that case it is not likely they would confirm him.

Would the Senate then withhold confirmation of any nominee for attorney general until they found one who would be willing to compromise the meaning of the job for the sake of being approved? That would be an intrusion on the separation of legislative and judicial powers.

Some senators contend the special prosecutor should be fully independent. In that case, who should have the task of naming a supreme arbiter, responsible to nobody for what he decides?

As Sen. Hugh Scott, R-Pa., commented, "What we are trying to do is show the American system can work…You've got to trust the system at some point or abolish it."

St. Petersburg Times
St. Petersburg, Fla., May 14, 1973

When President Nixon on April 30 fed his staff to the sharks and promised to get to the bottom of the Watergate scandal, there was reason to hope that he meant it.

NOW, WITH the Senate's Watergate inquiry set to start Thursday, it appears he still thinks vital facts can be kept from the people, the Congress, the FBI and the courts.

All he has to do, Mr. Nixon seems to believe, is draw the cloak of "executive privilege" across disclosures that might damage him.

In his address to the nation accepting "responsibility" (but not blame) for last year's orgy of political sabotage, burglary, espionage and eavesdropping, Mr. Nixon said he had ordered "all persons in government" to cooperate in official inquiries into the matter.

LATER HE issued "guidelines" for testimony by members and former members of the White House staff — the persons in government most likely to be in position to tell the whole story.

We now have had a look at those guidelines, covering testimony before any grand jury, the FBI and Sen. Sam Ervin's investigating committee. They deal with the claim of executive privilege.

Executive privilege is a concept dating back to George Washington for shielding from congressional scrutiny the innermost thoughts and private talks of the president.

IT EXISTS neither in Constitution nor law. But it is grounded in precedent and when reasonably applied is recognized as valid by Congress. It never has been held to cover withholding of information on crime.

At first glance, it appeared Mr. Nixon wanted the doctrine reasonably applied in this case. He instructed his aides and ex-aides to invoke executive privilege as rarely as possible.

Specifically he said they should invoke it "only" in connection with their talks with the President, their talks with each other involving their talks with the President, and their knowledge of documents produced or received by the White House.

Let's see, now. That leaves all those Watergate experts perfectly free to tell all they know — about the Washington weather, the New York Mets, recent family visits to Disney World, and many other such matters.

Fortunately, not all Mr. Nixon's ex-helpers — of whom there seem to be more every day — seem inclined to abide by any such ridiculous order. Mostly they appear either fed to the teeth, or scared, and they are singing all over Washington.

SO WE BELIEVE Sen. Ervin and his fellow investigators will get to the bottom of the Watergate mess, no matter how high they have to go to get there.

It's just too bad they won't have Mr. Nixon's cooperation. Some Americans are sure to wonder if the President, himself, still has something to hide.

The Burlington Free Press
Burlington, Vt., May 15, 1973

WE ARE APPALLED by the sewer of hatred which the anti-Nixon crowd is spewing over this land. The Watergate case itself is nowhere near as poisonous to our national life as is this irrational spasm of hatred.

Many of the persons promoting this hatred describe themselves as civil libertarians. Yet they loudly proclaim that President Nixon is guilty until proven innocent. Some libertarians!

We have the spectacle of Daniel Ellsberg, the admitted Pentagon papers thief, grandly proclaiming that he will sue President Nixon for deprivation of liberties. Next we expect to read that Ellsberg will sue God for something, anything, which will help to satisfy a massive ego.

There are columnists like Nicholas von Hoffman and Art Buchwald (both employed by the Washington Post) who possess such fertile imaginations that they can think of nothing else to write about except Watergate, week after week after week.

All sorts of other intellectual punks are suggesting that the President should be impeached. These are the same people who looked down their long noses in contempt at the "Impeach Earl Warren" campaign a few years ago. Yesterday we received a letter from an outfit by the name of Concerned Citizens Committee demanding President Nixon's impeachment; such a suggestion can be described — most charitably — as being sick.

And we are told, believe it or not, that there is a constitutional crisis in this country because of the Watergate case. Our reaction to that in a word: Bull!

A great many things are happening in this world and in this nation of far, far greater significance than the Watergate case. Yesterday and today, for example, the first space station in history was scheduled to be launched and established. But the Nixon-haters are not impressed by such triumphs of the human spirit and intelligence.

No, they are having too much fun trying to tear down the man who brought the troops home from Vietnam, the man who opened communications with China for the first time in two decades, the man who is striving so valiantly to return some of the power of government to the folks back home, the man who unquestionably has accomplished more that is good and substantial for the peoples of this world — against overwhelming odds — than any other leader in memory.

* * *

THE PUBLIC IS not so stupid as the Nixon-haters would like to believe. There is going to be a severe backlash against the sordid press McCarthyism and intellectual punksterism which sought so mindlessly to tear down a great President, a great office, and a great nation. When that day comes we will feel pity for these haters, and a bit more compassion than they appeared capable of extending to others.

We admire the President greatly, we are absolutely convinced that his accomplishments will be written large on the pages of history when Watergate will merit only a footnote, and we extend to the President an apology on behalf of those relatively few Vermonters whose hateful jealousy clouded their minds and hearts to truth and justice and understanding.

PORTLAND EVENING EXPRESS
Portland, Me., May 12, 1973

It is good to see that the inquiry that Sen. Sam Ervin's subcommittee will start off next week will not confine itself to the Watergate burglary alone, but investigate every phase of the 1972 presidential election campaign, even if it leads to the President himself.

The President has laid down some rules which say that members of the White House staff ought to claim "executive privilege" when the questions involve "conversations with the President, conversations among themselves involving communication with the President, and as to presidential papers."

This is just not going to work, because there is no constitutional support for "executive privilege", while from this point on Mr. Nixon simply cannot isolate himself from a scandal that has already touched two former cabinet members and the two most powerful members of his staff.

Apart from this, there are two broad lines of inquiry the panel should pursue, one of which will lead to legislative recommendations.

Sen. Ervin will probe zealously into the Watergate break-in, and especially the person or persons who gave the orders as a part of Nixon's grand re-election strategy.

Equally important, it must examine the financial resources and those who provided them, in this most costly political campaign ever. And when the job has been done, as well as the subcommittee can do it, since many of the records have been destroyed, Sen. Ervin's group must recommend laws that will prevent wealthy individuals and great corporations from trying to buy influence at election time.

Common Cause lawyers have been examining Republican campaign fund records for months, since they have a disclosure suit underway in federal courts. On the basis of depositions taken from former Sec. of Commerce Maurice Stans and others, (just indicted with former Att. Gen. John Mitchell), it is estimated that Nixon's "department of dirty tricks" had around $900,000 available, and that the total amount of money secretly contributed to the GOP treasury was in excess of $22 million.

This is an enormous amount of money, and we are entitled to assume that much of it was contributed in the expectation of some sort of return. Certainly the dairy industry did — it kicked in over $300,000 and right away the Agriculture Department boosted the basic price for milk. For the milk men it was a very profitable deal. The GOP Finance Committee said it had $10.2 millions "in hand" in cash prior to the April 7, 1972 law that compelled disclosure of campaign gifts and who made them. But Common Cause is convinced that the actual amount raised prior to April 7 was $22 millions, which means that there is almost $12 millions more unreported as receipts and unidentified by donor.

Lord Acton once said that "power corrupts, and absolute power corrupts absolutely." And in politics, as elsewhere, money is power. Moreover, it is power that the Nixon Administration sought, and until Watergate broke, the administration was well on its way to centralizing vast authority over the government and over the people of this country in the White House.

It is this prospect, now fortunately torpedoed, that frightens so many students of contemporary politics and government. On the basis of what Sen. Ervin reports, Congress must make it impossible for so much money on the 1972 scale to be poured into a campaign, to go unreported but contributed in a manner to encourage corruption. Watergate is pure corruption in the sense that it reflected an intensive drive for power, to be achieved without regard for either ethics or morality or the law of the land.

The Birmingham News
Birmingham, Ala., May 15, 1973

The Washington Post has won the 1973 Pulitzer Prize for meritorious public service because of its persistent reporting of the Watergate case.

President Nixon himself has acknowledged that a "vigilant press" played a part in the refusal of the political system to accept a covering up of the many ramifications of the bugging operation.

At the same time, however, it should be recognized that much of the reporting of the Watergate case has been based on unidentified sources. While the preponderance of the facts brought out in the press reports may finally be proved through the judicial process, nevertheless a potential for error and false accusations is a danger of relying on this journalistic approach.

In one recent report, for instance, former White House counsel John W. Dean III is said to have told someone that President Nixon knew of the coverup of the Watergate affair inside the White House.

Sen. William Proxmire, hardly predictable as an ally of the President, has chastized the press for printing "disputed, unproven secret charges" against Mr Nixon.

Proxmire said, "The present, runaway tendency to rush into headlines with disputed, unproven, secret charges against the President is the press at its worst.

"As the senator who succeeded Joe McCarthy in the United States Senate, I find this kind of persecution and condemnation without trial McCarthyism at its worst."

Proxmire referred specifically to the report concerning Dean and the President. He said such reporting was "grossly unfair" to Mr. Nixon.

We agree. The press has a responsibility to print the facts, but it also has a responsibility to itself, its readers and to the institution of the presidency to guard against printing innuendo and rumor as hard news.

While it is true that, according to one poll, half the subjects interviewed believe the President took part in a cover-up of the incident, responsible journalists should resist whatever temptation they may have to try the President or any other individual in the media.

No doubt many journalists feel they are absolutely right to air any shred of third-hand "evidence" they can uncover about the case. But then, Sen. Joe McCarthy also may have felt he was absolutely right. This does not change the historical fact that McCarthy participated in the creation of a climate which was marked by a singular disregard for individual civil liberties.

Mr. Nixon must accept the responsibility for his own credibility having been severely damaged because of Watergate. But this does not mean that he now should be fair game for every rumor the Washington press corps can generate. And Sen. Proxmire is to be commended for pointing out that fact.

PENTAGON PAPERS CASE DISMISSED FOR 'IMPROPER GOVERNMENT CONDUCT'

Government charges of espionage, theft and conspiracy against Daniel Ellsberg and Anthony J. Russo in the Pentagon Papers case were dismissed by Judge William R. Byrne in Los Angeles May 11 because of "improper government conduct." Judge Byrne said his ruling, which precluded a retrial, was based on: (1) the government's inability to produce the records of wiretaps made on telephone conversations involving Ellsburg during 1967 and 1970, evidence of which was disclosed May 9 in a memorandum from acting FBI director William Ruckelshaus to Byrne; (2) evidence that a break-in had taken place at the office of Ellsberg's former psychiatrist by a special White House unit, whose other activities might never be known, operating independently of the FBI and with the apparent unlawful assistance of the CIA ; and (3) government delays in producing exculpatory evidence it possessed, which, Byrne said, had compromised the defendant's right to a speedy trial.

Earlier on May 2, Byrne had ordered both sides in the case to present arguments for and against dismissal and mistrial. This followed a defense motion May 1 that had asked for immediate dismissal of all charges because of the disclosure that presidential assistant for domestic affairs John D. Ehrlichman had, at the President's request, ordered a secret White House investigation of the Pentagon Papers case which led to the break-in at Ellsberg's psychiatrist's office by convicted Watergate conspirators G. Gordon Liddy and E. Howard Hunt. [see below] Ehrlichman reportedly told the FBI that he was not told of the break-in until after the incident occurred. He said he did "not agree with this method of investigation" and when he learned of it, he cautioned Liddy and Hunt "not to do this again."

The trial was further complicated when Byrne disclosed May 2 that Ehrlichman had twice approached him during the trial about a possible appointment as FBI director. Defense attorneys attacked the White House's "impropriety" in the timing of the offer. Attorney Leornard Weinglass said that if a member of the defense had made such an offer to the judge, "we would all be in jail." Byrne May 4 rejected a defense motion for dismissal on these grounds.

CIA director James R. Schlesinger admitted in testimony before a Senate panel May 9 that the agency had been "insufficiently cautious" in providing false identification papers, disguises, a tape recorder and a miniature camera for use by Hunt and Liddy in the raid on the psychiatrist's office. (The 1947 statute creating the agency forbids it from performing any law enforcement or internal security functions.) Schlesinger's admission followed testimony by Hunt May 2 before the Watergate grand jury that he and Liddy had been hired by White House aides Egil Krogh Jr. and David Young to investigate leaks of the Pentagon Papers outside the usual channels of investigation. Former deputy CIA director Robert E. Cushman Jr. testified May 11 he had given CIA assistance to Hunt following a request for such aid by Ehrlichman. Cushman said he was not told of the specific use to which the equipment provided was to be put.

(Ruckelshaus announced May 14 the discovery of the missing wiretap records in a safe in Ehrlichman's White House office.)

HERALD-JOURNAL
Syracuse, N.Y., May 3, 1973

In a federal district court in Los Angeles, Judge Matthew W. Byrne handed a two-page document to Leonard Boudin, the defense lawyer for Daniel Ellsberg, a defendant in the theft of the "Pentagon papers."

Judge Byrne said:

"I call your attention to the last paragraph on the first page of this document. Tell Mr. Ellsberg I want him to read it, too."

The report, based on an interview with John D. Ehrlichman, former aide to President Nixon, read in part:

"Mr. Ehrlichman, the just-resigned presidential aide knew that Liddy and Hunt had conducted investigations in the Washington, D.C., area and during inquiries were going to the West Coast to follow up on leads.

"There was information available that Ellsberg had emotional and moral problems and Liddy and Hunt sought to determine the full facts relating to these conduct traits.

"Hunt endeavored, to prepare a 'psychiatric profile' relating to Ellsberg. The efforts of Liddy and Hunt were directed toward an 'indepth investigation of Ellsberg to determine his habits, mental attitudes, motives, etc.' "

The quotes within quotes encase Ehrlichman's direct words.

G. Gordon Liddy and E. Howard Hunt Jr. are under sentence for bugging and breaking into the Watergate headquarters of the Democratic party.

Ehrlichman told the FBI agents he had initiated the inquiry during 1971 at President Nixon's suggestion, that he had given the assignment to Liddy and Hunt, that he had not known they had broken into the office of Ellsberg's psychiatrist until afterward, that he had told them "not to do this again."

But last month, Erlichman met with Judge Byrne at the western White House (reportedly to discuss the possibility that Byrne might be appointed head of the FBI).

Considering the burglary, defense attorneys must assume that Ehrlichman and Byrne might have talked, perhaps they did talk, about the trial.

Who is to believe otherwise, even a jurist of Byrne's upstanding reputation?

Defense attorneys for Ellsberg and his partner immediately asked Judge Byrne to throw the case out of court.

They had good reason.

The tactics smack of Germany's gestapo.

And of stupidity.

Chicago Sun-Times

Chicago, Ill., May 3, 1973

The text of a Federal Bureau of Investigation interview with John D. Ehrlichman, formerly one of President Nixon's two most intimate and trusted advisers, clearly reveals a complacent and unpardonable acceptance of a criminal act. If the FBI report is accurate and complete, Ehrlichman may also be guilty of misprision of a felony, withholding evidence, obstruction of justice and criminal conspiracy.

Ehrlichman told the FBI that, pursuant to a directive from Mr. Nixon, he organized a 1971 inquiry into the Pentagon papers case and that he enlisted the services of two men later convicted in the Watergate bugging trial — E. Howard Hunt Jr. and G. Gordon Liddy. Hunt and Liddy apparently took it upon themselves to burglarize the office of a psychiatrist then treating a defendant in the Pentagon papers case, Daniel Ellsberg. The FBI report revealed that when he was told of the burglary, Ehrlichman said, mildly, that he "did not agree with this method of investigation" and that he merely told Hunt and Liddy "not to do this again." Nowhere in the FBI report is there any hint that Ehrlichman even considered reporting his knowledge of this felony to the appropriate authorities or even that he disciplined anyone. Clearly, Ehrlichman was so deeply trapped in the miasma of chicanery that he was paralyzed. He was committed to persons who, like himself, regarded themselves as part of an imperial regime, immune from both criminal laws and basic standards of human conduct.

This is the same man who, in resigning his White House job, told Mr. Nixon that "the appearance of honesty and integrity is every bit as important to such a position as the fact of one's honesty and integrity." This is the same man Mr. Nixon on Monday night called one of the "finest public servants it has been my privilege to know" and whom Mr. Nixon defended against any hint of wrongdoing and allowed to remain on the payroll.

There can be no confidence in any investigation of the Watergate scandal conducted by persons associated, however innocently, with this arrogant and institutionalized hypocrisy. The Senate has adopted a resolution calling for the appointment of a special, independent prosecutor. We repeat our endorsement of this appointment. The resolution has wide, bipartisan support, and if Mr. Nixon wants a showdown over this matter, he is entitled to one. In light of the threat posed by this historic scandal on the office of the Presidency, the appointment of a special prosecutor may be the only — not simply the best — course of action.

The Evening Star
The Washington Daily News

Washington, D.C., May 8, 1973

On and on come the ugly revelations, the almost daily disclosures of how this nation's political and judicial processes have been manipulated and corrupted. Now we learn that the Central Intelligence Agency shares heavily in the responsibility for the Ellsberg case, which if not directly related to Watergate nevertheless helped set the stage for it and is indisputably part of the same poisonous syndrome.

Start with the premise that, for its own purposes, the CIA had no interest in digging up damaging information on Daniel Ellsberg and his role in leaking the Pentagon papers in June, 1971. But the White House surely did. And someone at the White House, possibly John Ehrlichman, induced someone high at CIA, probably General Robert E. Cushman, to authorize the use of the agency's clandestine services in the burglary of the office of Ellsberg's psychiatrist. That happened in September, 1971, while Richard Helms was still head of CIA and two months before General Cushman left his post as deputy director of the agency to become commandant of the Marine Corps. Meanwhile, and just as disturbing, the head of CIA's psychological assessment unit was directed (by whom?) to cooperate with the White House in working up a psychological profile of Ellsberg.

At this point, the CIA-Ellsberg episode is subject to any number of interpretations. Loose threads and unanswered questions are everywhere. Yet even an interpretation most favorable to the agency leads to conclusions that are devastating.

The CIA, in brief, has been used and compromised and discredited in somewhat the same way that the FBI, under Patrick Gray, was used and compromised and discredited in the Watergate investigation. Perhaps it was the guiltier of the two. For the CIA lent its offices to the perpetration of a shoddy crime, to the trampling of civil liberties and to a domestic surveillance operation that by law it had no business conducting even indirectly.

It is difficult to believe that Helms, a canny and professional man, would have known all this beforehand and consented to such an improbable venture as the Hunt-Liddy burglary of the psychiatrist's office. Of course, anything is possible, as the nation has learned with relentless regularity the last few weeks.

General Cushman, even if his implication in the affair can be partially explained as unthinking, has a great deal to answer for. He is, to be sure, a distinguished military officer. He is also a longtime friend and supporter of the President's. Those two things need not have been incompatible. But in this case, apparently, they were. In the anything-goes pattern of Watergate, an otherwise decent man appears to have blocked off conscience and good judgment, and gone along with whatever the White House requested.

At first the Watergate scandal was said to be the work of a few ideological zealots. Lately, it has been fashionable to lay the blame on men close to the President with a superloyal, ad-agency turn of mind. But the web of Watergate-Ellsberg spreads much farther than that. In the FBI, in Justice, now in the CIA, it involves men and vital institutions the American public should have had every reason to trust, but now do not. Aside from the diminished stature of the presidency itself, that is what is hardest to take.

BUFFALO EVENING NEWS

Buffalo, N.Y., May 3, 1973

The wisdom of John Ehrlichman's resignation as a premier White House aide to President Nixon becomes plainer almost by the day.

Entirely aside from whatever role he may or may not have played in the scandalous Watergate affair last year, we now learn that Mr. Ehrlichman apparently went no farther than a gentle reprimand when confronted with other illegal activities by that dauntless duo of Watergate conspirators, E. Howard Hunt and G. Gordon Liddy, in 1971.

Allegations that Hunt and Liddy broke into the office of Daniel Ellsberg's psychiatrist, while carrying out an independent White House probe of how the Pentagon Papers leak developed, are appalling enough, if true. And certainly this unerringly foreshadowed the Watergate bugging-burglary in which the same two men were involved a few months later.

But at least as dismaying is the report to the FBI by Ehrlichman himself last week that, while he neither ordered nor approved of the break-in of the psychiatrist's office, he only told Hunt and Liddy, once he learned of it, not to do that again.

If Mr. Ehrlichman didn't report this alleged crime to the proper authorities promptly, and there is so far no evidence that he did, then certainly it reveals shockingly poor judgment on his part.

At the very least, once the break-in was known, Mr. Ehrlichman should have seen to it that these two men received no more assignments from the White House or GOP organizations.

Equally shocking, too, is the attitudes of mind which this earlier break-in and its apparent cover-up reveal.

There can only have been a certain arrogance here that "we" stand above the law that applies to others. That we're not accountable in the usual sense. Then, at least with Hunt and Liddy, there was in this earlier case as with Watergate a distorted presumption that their ends justified almost any means. Just get the job done—and anything goes.

Such indefensible attitudes lie at the root of the Watergate trouble. They represent the attitudes that must be exchanged for integrity, a high regard for civilized restraint and an abiding respect for law and accountability and the political and personal liberties of others, for the White House to regain the full confidence of the American people.

The Miami Herald

Miami, Fla., May 13, 1973

THE tortuous pursuit of truth in the Pentagon Papers case has come to a dead end in circumstances which, says the presiding judge, "offend a sense of justice."

These are the subdued words of U.S. District Judge W. Matt Byrne, who has dismissed all charges against Daniel Ellsberg and Anthony J. Russo Jr. for leaking purloined documents. All or nearly all of the information was stale news, and the Defense Department itself decided that in most instances the papers contained nothing harmful to national security.

The effect of collated publication, however, was to render the whole tissue of official untruths about the Vietnamese war and hasten U.S. withdrawal. For this, Ellsberg, Russo and some of the news media incurred a vendetta which has gone far beyond the limits of legality or propriety.

In declaring a mistrial and dismissing the indictments Judge Byrne described an "unprecedented series of actions" taken against Ellsberg by the White House, the Central Intelligence Agency (which is not supposed to spook domestically) and the FBI.

These included deceptions, burglary, destruction of documents and deliberate withholding of information from the court. In an incident which he did not mention, the judge himself must have been offended by a White House offer of the directorship of the FBI in midtrial, an act which in any other league would be ruled as plain, unvarnished bribery.

So, no one will ever know through a court of law whether Ellsberg and Russo are innocent or guilty. And since "there remain more questions and answers," the case is neither fish nor fowl but an ample application of good red herring.

We know of no precedent for executive skulduggery practiced in and against a court of justice — in this country, at any rate. Germany had its Reichstag fire and France its Captain Dreyfus. But for the cold impartiality of a neutral judge the United States might have had its Pentagon Papers case.

It is incredible in the aftermath to learn that President Nixon's new counsel chosen to deal with the Watergate affair was accused of suppressing information in the Ellsberg-Russo case and is known around Capitol Hill as "a coverup artist."

When will Mr. Nixon recognize the enormity of what has fallen upon his administration?

THE TENNESSEAN

Nashville, Tenn., May 3, 1973

THE WHITE House's role in burglarizing Mr. Daniel Ellsberg's psychiatric records and injecting itself into Mr. Ellsberg's trial on charges of stealing the Pentagon Papers is one of the most shocking aspects in the series of scandals now rocking the Nixon administration.

Mr. John D. Ehrlichman, who resigned as adviser to the President Monday, told the FBI last Friday that Mr. Nixon designated him in 1971 to make an independent investigation into the leak of the Pentagon Papers.

* * *

Mr. Ehrlichman said Gordon Liddy and Howard Hunt — later convicted in the Watergate break-in — were sent to make an "in-depth investigation of Ellsberg to determine his habits, mental attitudes, motives, etc." In the course of their investigation, Liddy and Hunt — who seem to have been the administration's steady break-in artists — broke into the office of Mr. Ellsberg's psychiatrist and rifled Mr. Ellsberg's medical records.

Mr. Ehrlichman told the FBI he did not know about the burglary until after it occurred and that when he heard about it he instructed Liddy and Hunt "not to do this again." But apparently Mr. Ehrlichman's warning was not taken seriously, for a few months later — as members of the Nixon re-election campaign team — these break-in experts were involved in the burglarizing of the Democratic campaign headquarters at the Watergate Apartments in Washington.

This is the gist of the burglarizing of Mr. Ellsberg's private medical records. But it is not the end of the story of the administration's apparent attempt to influence the outcome of the Ellsberg trial.

In the middle of the trial, on April 5, the presiding judge was called to the western White House at San Clemente by Mr. Ehrlichman for discussion of his possible appointment as head of the FBI. Judge Byrne himself confirmed this yesterday but, to his credit, rejected the offer of the FBI post until the trial was over. Judge Byrne also deserves great credit for seeing that the facts of the break-in at the psychiatrist's office were dug out and made public.

Mr. Ellsberg and his lawyers have interpreted the job offer to Judge Byrne as an attempt by the Nixon administration to influence the outcome of the trial and see that Mr. Ellsberg was convicted for embarrassing the administration by making public the Pentagon Papers. It is difficult to see how the situation can be interpreted in any other way.

The disclosures in the Watergate and Ellsberg cases all but destroys the Nixon administration's credibility as an administration concerned about law and order and justice. An administration that fails to prosecute break-ins and concealment of evidence by its members, which attempts to interfere with the processes of justice, and sees nothing wrong with spying on the personal records of private citizens it wants to see punished for political reasons, has no claim to being a defender of law and order.

Mr. Ehrlichman told his story to the FBI last Friday. Three days later he resigned as Mr. Nixon's aide. That night Mr. Nixon went on television and expressed confidence in Mr. Ehrlichman, saying there was no implication of wrongdoing on his aide's part.

It seems incredible that a President who heads the most extensive intelligence-gathering agencies in the world didn't know one of his top aides was spilling the beans about administration complicity in criminal activity.

* * *

But the alternative to this is to believe that President Nixon did know what Mr. Ehrlichman was saying and could see nothing wrong in what his aide had done — or failed to do to uphold the law.

In either case, the Nixon administration's pretensions of concern for law and order in the nation are revealed as a monumental hoax on the American people.

St. Louis Globe-Democrat

St. Louis, Mo., May 3, 1973

Resigned presidential aide John D. Ehrlichman is reported to have told the FBI that President Nixon in 1971 designated him to make an independent investigation of the Pentagon Papers case.

The President certainly had good reason to do this.

But from what Ehrlichman is quoted as having told the FBI, the former top aide apparently went off the deep end in carrying out Mr. Nixon's request.

The two men chosen by Ehrlichman to conduct the probe, G. Gordon Liddy and E. Howard Hunt, were said to have broken into the office of Daniel Ellsberg's psychiatrist looking for information about Ellsberg's "psychological profile."

Ehrlichman told the FBI that he didn't learn of the burglary until after it happened and then told Hunt and Liddy "not to do this again."

If this interview represents the facts in the case, Ehrlichman acted improperly in several of ways.

First, he obviously failed to define the limits of the investigation and failed to properly supervise the two men who later became key figures in the Watergate scandal.

Secondly, his "don't do it again" response upon learning of the break-in was totally inadequate. At that point he should have fired both Liddy and Hunt and preferred charges against them. Instead they apparently remained on the payroll and continued their nefarious work.

This provides a prime example of how power, if not properly harnessed, can be flagrantly abused. Liddy and Hunt apparently thought they were the CIA, the FBI and Ehrlichman's secret agents, all wrapped up into one.

The penalty for such arrogance and stupidity is, of course, enormous. Liddy and Hunt, caught on their mission into Watergate with five others, now have been convicted for that break-in. Their exploits and the failures of those who were supposed to be keeping an eye on these "investigators" have now come back to haunt and plague President Nixon.

THE  SUN

Baltimore. Md., May 9, 1973

The Washington Post

Washington, D.C., May 13, 1973

Given the facts that had been disclosed during the past two weeks. Judge W. Matthew Byrne Jr. had no choice but to dismiss charges against Daniel Ellsberg and Anthony Russo Jr. The government had so mangled the investigation into their conduct and the prosecution had been so confused by its own inability to find out what had happened that separating legitimate from illegitimate evidence had become well nigh impossible. That is unfortunate: the country and, for that matter, the defendants deserved better.

If Ellsberg and Russo were guilty of crimes, they ought to have been convicted and punished. If their acts did not constitute crimes—and whether they did or not is the principal legal question left unresolved—they ought to have been acquitted. As it stands, the fundamental issues raised by the Pentagon Papers affair are still unresolved. Does the disclosure of classified information to the American public violate existing laws? If it does, do the laws abridge the First Amendment?

These questions are unresolved not because of anything Mr. Ellsberg and Mr. Russo did but because of the zeal (to put it kindly), bad judgment (to carry kindness still further), and essential lawlessness (to be blunt about it) of various government officials. A doctor's office was burglarized in violation of the laws of California; the Central Intelligence Agency was ordered (or at least persuaded) to aid in a domestic investigation in violations of the laws of the United States; the trial judge was approached with a new job offer by the White House in violation of well-known standards of judicial ethics; facts were concealed from the judge (and apparently from the prosecutors); records were destroyed—and lies were told.

Once all of this began to become known in a sudden flood of information, the Ellsberg trial turned from the three-ring circus it had already been into a farce. The judge had the responsibility of rejecting any evidence procured by the government through illegal means. Yet the government prosecutors in the courtroom couldn't tell him (a) whether any of the known illegal activities engaged in by government had produced evidence; (b) whether other illegal activities might have occurred; or (c) why or how the records which might provide that information had disappeared. Yes—disappeared. The situation was described accurately by Judge Byrne this way: "Much information has been developed, but new information has produced new questions, and there remain more questions than answers."

The inability of the government to provide those answers sharply limited Judge Byrne's options and he chose the fairest one available. His decision represented neither the triumph of justice nor the vindication of Daniel Ellsberg. It was, however, a demonstration that the government and the government's agents cannot operate outside the law and expect to have their lawless activities condoned by the courts. That is a lesson—an old lesson straight out of the law books—and one the Nixon administration has never seemed to learn. The Ellsberg case was not the first, and it may well not be the last case, which this administration has thrown away because some of its highest officials saw nothing wrong in using whatever means were at hand—and never mind the law—for reaching whatever goal they chose to believe, in their own view of the "national interest," was more important.

The White House once again has denied that President Nixon was aware of the Watergate operation, that he participated in any coverup activities and that he ever authorized the offering of clemency to anyone in the case. We shall learn in the course of events, perhaps, whether or not these new denials hold up: whether or not it was mere partisan zeal on the part of subordinates that has undermined the very office of the presidency.

Let us turn for the moment, then, to the continued unfolding of developments in another, and simpler and plainer, and balder, question which in its formal fundamental aspects is more serious even than Watergate.

There are connections between Watergate and the Pentagon Papers case now on trial in Los Angeles, notably in the participation in both of the former White House thug-in-residence, E. Howard Hunt, who almost incredibly appears to have had the help of the Central Intelligence Agency with equipment to burglarize the office of Daniel Ellsberg's psychiatrist. But for all such interlockings, these are two separate matters, and in the terms noted above the White House role in the second is worse than in the first.

Whatever Mr. Nixon may or may not have known about Watergate, it is beyond the bounds of comprehension that he was unaware of the progress of the Pentagon Papers trial and that he was less than intensely interested in its course; as he still is, according to the report in the New York Times that at least twice in the past two weeks he has sought to prevent the release to the Los Angeles court of details of the Beverly Hills burglary—only to reverse himself both times on the advice of administration officials who felt the contemplated invocation of the national security to be inadequate. (The White House, as might be expected, has called this report "irresponsible.")

However that may be, Mr. Nixon's interest in the Pentagon Papers case is obviously direct, and fervent, and goes beyond any question of subordinate partisan zealotry.

It was expressed most blatantly in the presidential summoning of the judge in the case, W. Matthew Byrne, to San Clemente, to be offered the directorship of the FBI.

Granted that Mr. Nixon has in the past displayed a peculiar insensitivity to the integrity of the judicial process, and granted that perchance in this instance, in his concentration on finding a good man to head the FBI (Judge Byrne declined to discuss the offer while a trial was in progress), he failed to see how the incident might be interpreted, his action still was a direct interference in the affairs of the judiciary.

Watergate aside, this alone would be an ineradicable blot on his record in the presidency.

ST. LOUIS POST-DISPATCH

St. Louis, Mo., May 13, 1973

Government agents had engaged in so many forms of improper and illegal behavior in preparing and prosecuting charges against Daniel Ellsberg and Anthony Russo for releasing the Pentagon Papers that Judge Matt Byrne had little choice but to throw the case out of court, which he finally did on Friday. The latest disclosure to the effect that the FBI had illegally eavesdropped on Dr. Ellsberg's conversations was only one more example of official misconduct in a case that had already been tainted by a White House-authorized burglary of the office of one defendant's psychiatrist, by a White House approach to the judge about a high federal position while the Los Angeles trial was in progress and by repeated prosecution failures to reveal, as required by law, evidence that would have helped the defense.

Judge Byrne in effect has followed the dictum of Justice Holmes when he said it is better that a defendant go free than that the Government should stoop to ignoble conduct. In this case, however, the declaration of a mistrial and the dismissal of all charges against the defendants means more than that the Government has been roundly scolded for its unconscionable behavior; it also means that the defendants may not be prosecuted again on the same charges. Given the circumstances of the case, they were charges which should never have been brought to court.

By a novel linking of espionage, theft and conspiracy provisions from criminal statutes, the Government had sought to achieve a conviction for conduct which had never before been subject to criminal penalties. In copying and releasing to the press the Pentagon's secret history of the Vietnam war, Messrs. Ellsberg and Russo had only engaged on a larger scale in a kind of activity common among people in and out of government, none of whom had been prosecuted before. In the Pentagon Papers case, the Nixon Administration, with its extraordinary penchant for secrecy, had first attempted to enjoin newspapers from publishing the material and, failing in this, had gone after Dr. Ellsberg and Mr. Russo in a vindictive spirit that seemed to epitomize its hostility to anyone in the antiwar movement.

The irony of the legal actions against the release of the Pentagon Papers was that the publication of the secret history exposed the misrepresentations and deceit of previous administrations rather than the current one. Yet the litigation was in character for the Nixon Administration because it was used as a vehicle to try to shut off all leaks of classified material that might be embarrassing to the Government in the past and in the future. If the legal theories of the Ellsberg-Russo prosecution had succeeded, the Government might have been able to threaten anyone tempted to disclose even the most trivial classified information with criminal sanctions.

Evidence introduced at the Ellsberg-Russo trial indicated that the Pentagon Papers had been routinely classified, with little thought as to whether the material in them might have been helpful to an enemy. Indeed, a district judge in the injunction case against The New York Times had concluded that the Government had failed to prove its claim that the material would be harmful. In the Los Angeles trial, the prosecution's allegation that the Pentagon Papers had injured the national defense was even undermined by some of the Government's own witnesses. Much of the material had in fact been published before the Pentagon Papers leak, some of it undoubtedly via intended leaks from Government officials.

The dismissal of all charges against Dr. Ellsberg and Mr. Russo does not mean that the Government may not attempt to use the novel legal weapons of this case against future, different defendants. It does mean, however, that this questionable legal attack on access to information for the public, and by indirection on a free press, has been severely discredited.

THE STATES-ITEM
New Orleans, La., May 12, 1973

Revelations that the Central Intelligence Agency provided disguises and equipment used by a Nixon Administration operative in the break-in of Daniel Ellsberg's psychiatrist's office should be of great concern to the American people.

The information is particularly-alarming because the people probably know less about the operation of the CIA, and have less control over it, than any other agency of government.

It is for this reason that there is in the CIA the potential for the kind of "secret police" operation that we deplore in totalitarian nations.

The dangers and the power of such an agency were fully understood when it was established. That is why the 1947 law under which the CIA was organized specifically bars the CIA from conducting covert operations inside the United States.

The CIA was intended to be an independent arm of government. Certainly it was not meant to be used as a partisan political tool of the administration in power. That, however, was the way the agency was used in the Ellsberg case, and the direction came from an authority in the White House.

Specifically, according to memorandum submitted by the CIA in the Pentagon Papers trial of Mr. Ellsberg, the agency equipped E. Howard Hunt Jr. with false identification papers, disguises, business cards and recording equipment. Mr. Hunt was later convicted for the Watergate break-in.

When the CIA decided to stop cooperating with Mr. Hunt, Gen. Robert E. Cushman, then deputy director of the CIA and now commandant of the Marine Corps, called a so-far unnamed White House official to inform him of the decision.

It is frightening to speculate on the ultimate consequences of a shadowy organization such as the CIA used at cross purposes with the people it was established to protect.

THE RICHMOND NEWS LEADER
Richmond, Va., May 14, 1973

So instead of being convicted and sent off to cool his hot ideological theories in a federal penitentiary, Daniel Ellsberg is to become the newest patron saint of the New Left. The dismissal of charges against him will be translated into an exoneration of all the irresponsible things he has said and continues to say, such as: The White House uses "Mafia tactics;" President Nixon masterminded a "conspiracy to deprive us of our civil liberties;" and the "country is run by criminals." One need only contemplate those crackpot statements to confirm that Daniel Ellsberg is on an ideological trip.

Yet it cannot be denied that a seemingly endless string of governmental buffooneries is the fundamental reason that Daniel Ellsberg is not on his way to the federal penitentiary. Governmental wiretaps on Ellsberg's telephone, the undercover White House investigation of his activities, the ransacking of his psychiatrist's files — all those things served to lead the judge to the ineluctable conclusion that the government was not leveling with the court. And this is but the latest example — for whatever reason — of the evident inability of the federal government to lock up for long the darlings of the New Left. Perhaps this ruling will mark the expiration of the statute of limitations on the government's incompetences, stupidities, and deceptions in such prosecutions.

The skunking of the government, however, should not be permitted to undermine the essential validity of the charges against Ellsberg. The charges against Ellsberg were charges of espionage, conspiracy, and theft. The defense sought — successfully — to cloud the major point through extraneity. The major point is that Daniel Ellsberg stole classified government documents. At the very least, and notwithstanding his pretentious justifications, he is an admitted thief. Whether he is guilty of espionage is debateable. But for the sake of argument let us assume that Ellsberg was engaged in espionage; let us also assume that the Nixon administration was engaged in espionage, albeit of a different sort, to keep itself informed about what Ellsberg was up to. Surely the espionage of Ellsberg should not be defended while the espionage of the Nixon administration is condemned.

The prospect now is that Ellsberg will be trotted across the pages of *The New York Times*, and before college audiences, which will pay him assiduous court. In self-congratulatory tones, he will verbally bump and grind before the bulging eyes of the media — mouthing his tired old non-sequiturs. He will tell the public about all the fascists in the Nixon administration, and, sadly, the public will listen, because these days there is nothing quite so safe to fall upon as the Nixon administration. But before cynically concluding that the Nixon administration is vile and Ellsberg is pure, it is important to reflect on a crucial fact: Sympathy for what Ellsberg did is sufficiently widespread that a majority of the jurors in the Ellsberg case have said that on the substantive issues, they would have voted for. . .acquittal.

The Charleston Gazette
Charleston, W. Va., May 9, 1973

The legal justification for the use of CIA resources in connection with the burglary of Daniel Ellsberg's psychiatrist's office may or may not be found in the National Security Act of 1947.

The act, which established the CIA, specifically prohibits it from "police, subpoena, law-enforcement, or internal security" functions.

But it also authorizes the CIA to "protect intelligence sources and methods from unauthorized disclosure." It is this provision which justifies CIA cooperation in the burglary, some CIA officials say.

Others, however, are doubtful about the application of the provision, and so are we. The very terminology of the act, it seems to us, negates the authority for CIA participation in the affair.

If the language of the act specifies that CIA resources may be employed to prevent the disclosure of intelligence sources and methods, it takes an unusual interpretation to apply it to a case in which the government's own claim is that intelligence sources and methods already had been disclosed.

It is with this very offense that Ellsberg is charged. With a defendant already accused of betraying government secrets, it is difficult to accept a CIA contention that it helped in the burglary in order to prevent the betrayal of government secrets.

It seems more likely that CIA materials and CIA research were employed as part of a pattern of government harassment of dissenters. When Lyndon Johnson first felt the sting of dissent he began to marshal the forces of government against his critics. Mr. Nixon continued the practice in the same spirit of vengeance.

There is an encouraging prospect, however, in the effort to give legal status to the CIA's limited role in the burglary of the doctor's office. Before Watergate, legal justification for unusual governmental activity wasn't thought necessary.

When an assistant secretary of state was asked the legal grounds for the President's continued bombing of Cambodia, for instance, he arrogantly answered, "Mr. Nixon's landslide election of last fall."

Perhaps this kind of wickedly evasive answer no longer will be tolerated as a substitute for legal justification.

Long Island Press

New York, N.Y., May 13, 1973

The judge's decision to throw out the Pentagon Papers case against Dr. Daniel Ellsberg and Anthony Russo was a foregone conclusion.

The government clearly violated the defendants' rights in many ways. It withheld evidence, it authorized the invasion of Dr. Ellsberg's psychiatrist's office, it tapped telephone conversations, it offered the presiding judge the directorship of the FBI while the trial was in progress.

As Judge Matt Byrne said in declaring a mistrial and acting to prevent a retrial, "The conduct of the government has placed the case in such a posture that it precludes the fair, dispassionate resolution of these issues by a jury."

The judge deserves the gratitude of the defendants, but even more, of the American people. In refusing to discuss the FBI job offer made by John Ehrlichmann, the ousted presidential aide, he properly put the integrity of the judiciary above self. And in demanding the answers to the covert activities of the government, he exposed the shameful lengths to which the administration was willing to go in its efforts to get a conviction.

The only regrettable aspect is that the judge's action precluded a jury decision on the case itself, and the larger issue of government secrecy. Most of the jurors said after the charges had been dismissed that they were leaning toward acquittal of Dr. Ellsberg and Mr. Russo. It is easy to see why.

From the evidence we saw, there was no real reason for keeping the Pentagon Papers secret. Rather, it appeared to be another instance of government trying to hide its embarrassments from public view under the abused label of national security.

Because the jury could not rule on the merits, the government remains free to pursue its secretive policies. We hope, though, that the public exposure of the abuses of governmental secrecy will lead to reform — by the administration itself and by the Congress.

The Philadelphia Inquirer

Philadelphia, Pa., May 15, 1973

"Government agencies have taken an unprecedented series of actions against these defendants."

So declared Federal Judge William Matthew Byrne Jr. as he dismissed all charges against Dr. Daniel Ellsberg and Anthony J. Russo Jr., and so ended the Pentagon Papers trial, nearly two years after the defendants were indicted on charges of espionage, theft and conspiracy, for copying and revealing the classified Defense Department study of the origins of America's involvement in Vietnam.

The issues raised at the trial, however, are by no means resolved. In its bizarre denouement, the trial became inextricably linked to what we generally refer to as the Watergate affair, which perhaps ought better to be referred to as the Watergate attitude. Consider some of the "unprecedented" actions taken by men working for the U. S. Government as a result of which Judge Byrne threw out the case as hopelessly "tainted."

It has been disclosed that the Beverly Hills office of Dr. Ellsberg's psychiatrist had been broken into in an effort to obtain his "psychiatric profile," and that this burglary, about a year before the Watergate break-in at Democratic headquarters, had been committed by a team led by none other than G. Gordon Liddy Jr., and E. Howard Hunt Jr., convicted leaders of the Watergate conspiracy.

It has been disclosed that the Central Intelligence Agency supplied Hunt with disguises and other espionage equipment, notwithstanding the law forbidding the CIA to be involved in domestic undercover activities.

It has been disclosed that this was done on the request of John D. Ehrlich-man, Mr. Nixon's former domestic chief of staff, who himself has acknowledged that he learned of the Beverly Hills burglary but did not report it — he just told its perpetrators not to do it again.

It has been disclosed that even before Ellsberg revealed the Pentagon Papers, the FBI had been intercepting his phone conversations, but the records mysteriously vanished until, as Acting FBI Director William Ruckelhaus informed a news conference yesterday, they turned up in — of all places — a safe in Mr. Ehrlichman's White House office, along with 16 other files involving wiretaps of government officials and newsmen.

Judge Byrne himself has disclosed that, as the trial was coming to its end, Mr. Ehrlichman personally discussed with him the possibility of his becoming the next director of the FBI.

In the beginning, the government had brought the defendants before the bar of justice for allegedly violating "national security." In the end, it is the government itself which is found guilty of violating national security in the deepest sense, through an extraordinary pattern of interference by the executive branch into the processes of justice and individual rights.

The legal question of the government's right to withhold information as against the public's right to know have not been settled. But if the Pentagon Papers case has had any beneficial effect, it is in the demonstration of what the obsession with secrecy can lead to.

The Watergate attitude is that for the sake of "law and order" the government itself may break the law — that the end justifies the means. This is not the traditional American attitude toward the governance of a free society.

The Virginian-Pilot

Norfolk, Va., May 14, 1973

The Pentagon Papers trial turned into "Watergate West" in the last two weeks. The disclosures of the Government's gross misconduct in the prosecution of Daniel Ellsberg and Anthony Russo Jr. were so sensational that Judge W. Matt Byrne Jr. was compelled to free the defendants.

The "extraordinary series of disclosures regarding the conduct of several government agencies," to borrow Judge Byrne's quaint understatement, started with the burglary of the office of Dr. Ellsberg's psychiatrist by an espionage squad working under White House orders.

The Central Intelligence Agency had a hand in the operation — that is against the law, too. Not only was defendant Ellsberg the subject of systematic wiretapping, the evidence of the wiretaps was concealed from the court and from the defense, which is entitled to it legally. The Federal Bureau of Investigation seems to have de-

stroyed the record of the wiretaps, a fact that was revealed only last week. The Government had maintained for the past year that there were no wiretaps. And the action that most offends one's sense of justice and fair play was the arrant attempt to bribe Judge Byrne by dangling an offer of the directorship of the FBI before him during the progress of the trial. That happened in March, when the scandal was starting to smell strongly. Judge Byrne declined to discuss the job, quite properly. A flintier judge might have declared a mistrial right there.

"The bizarre events have incurably infected the prosecution of this case," Judge Byrne summed up. So saying, he declared a mistrial and dismissed the indictment against defendants Ellsberg and Russo for conspiracy, espionage, and theft. That is the end of the Pentagon Papers trial, with the question of the defendants' guilt in the papers' publication unresolved. Under the circumstances

most will be satisfied with the Scotch verdict.

The defendants, meanwhile, are threatening to sue Mr. Nixon and others for "conspiracy to deprive us of our civil liberties," which would be in keeping with the reversal of roles in trial.

If the American people hadn't been conditioned by now to the notion that agents acting for the President of the United States were involved in burglary, bugging, bribery, destruction of evidence, obstruction of justice, perjury, and anything else necessary to law 'n' order, Nixon style, the story would be unbelievable. As it is, it's just part of the larger story of Watergate, which has brought the indictment of former Attorney General John Mitchell, his replacement's resignation, the sacking of the acting director of the FBI, the besmirching of the FBI, the CIA, the Presidency, and dozens of individual reputations thus far. And who knows what's to come next?

NIXON CONCEDES AIDES' ROLE IN COVER-UP

President Nixon May 22 conceded the probable involvement of some of his closest aides in concealing some aspects of the Watergate affair and acknowledged that he had ordered limitations on the investigation because of national security considerations "of crucial importance" unrelated to Watergate. He reiterated, however, his own lack of prior knowledge of the burglary and the attempted cover-up while acknowledging that aides might have "gone beyond" his directives to protect "national security operations in order to cover up any involvement they or certain others might have had in Watergate."

In a summary accompanying his statement, Nixon made the following replies to specific allegations against White House activities:

"1) I had no prior knowledge of the Watergate operation; 2) I took no part in, nor was I aware of, any subsequent efforts that may have been made to cover up Watergate; 3) At no time did I authorize any offer of executive clemency of the Watergate defendants, nor did I know of any such offer; 4) I did not know, until the time of my own investigation, of any effort to provide the Watergate defendants with funds; 5) At no time did I attempt, or did I authorize others to attempt, to implicate the CIA in the Watergate matter; 6) It was not until the time of my own investigation that I learned of the break-in at the office of [Pentagon Papers case defendant Daniel] Ellsberg's psychiatrist, and I specifically authorized the furnishing of this information to Judge [William M.] Byrne. 7) I neither authorized nor encouraged subordinates to engage in illegal or improper campaign tactics." Nixon also declared his intention to remain in office, saying "I will not abandon my responsibilities. I will continue to do the job I was elected to do."

In his statement, Nixon sought to separate secret investigations begun earlier in his term from the Watergate case. He told of a "special program of wiretaps" set up in 1969 to prevent leaks of secret information important to his foreign policy initiatives. He said there were "fewer than 20 taps" and they were ended in February 1971. (The New York Times reported May 17 that Henry A. Kissinger, assistant to the President for national security affairs, personally provided the FBI with the names of a number of his aides on the National Security Council (NSC) whom he wanted wiretapped. Kissinger confirmed the report May 29.) The President said that in 1970 he was concerned about increasing political disruption connected with antiwar protests and decided a better intelligence operation was needed. He appointed the late FBI director J. Edgar Hoover to head a committee to prepare suggestions. On June 25, 1970, Nixon said, the committee recommended resumption of "certain intelligence operations that had been suspended in 1966," among them the "authorization for surreptitious entry—breaking and entering, in effect"—in specific situations related to national security. He said Hoover opposed the plan and it was never put into effect. "It was this unused plan and related documents that John Dean removed from the White House and placed in a safe deposit box," Nixon added.

Further efforts to improve intelligence operations were made in December 1970 with the formation of the Intelligence Evaluation Committee, for which he said he had authorized no illegal activity, nor did he have knowledge of any. After the New York Times began publishing the Pentagon Papers in June 1971, Nixon said, he approved the formation of a special investigations unit in the White House to "stop security leaks." The unit, known as the "plumbers," was directed by Egil Krogh Jr. and included convicted Watergate conspirators E. Howard Hunt and G. Gordon Liddy. Nixon recalled that he had impressed upon Krogh the importance of protecting the national security and said this might explain how "highly motivated individuals could have felt justified in engaging in specific activities" he would have disapproved had he known of them. "Consequently," Nixon said, "I must and do assume responsibility for such actions, despite the fact that I at no time approved or had knowledge of them."

Nixon said he had "wanted justice done in regard to Watergate" but he had not wanted the investigation to "impinge adversely upon the national security area." He noted that, shortly after the break-in, he was informed that the CIA might have been involved and that he instructed H. R. Haldeman, John Ehrlichman and Assistant Attorney General Henry E. Petersen to "insure that the investigation of the break-in not expose either an unrelated covert operation of the CIA or the activities of the White House investigations unit." The President reiterated that in the months following the Watergate incident, he was given repeated assurances that the White House staff had been cleared of involvement. But with hindsight, Nixon conceded, it was apparent that "I should have given more heed to the warning signals I received along the way ... and less to the reassurances."

President Nixon would not give oral or written testimony to the grand jury or the Senate select committee investigating the Watergate case, White House Press Secretary Ronald L. Ziegler said May 29. "It would be Constitutionally inappropriate," he said. "It would do violence to the separation of powers."

President Nixon May 24 affirmed the government's right to secrecy in national security matters and denounced "those who steal secrets and publish them in the newspapers," a reference to Daniel Ellsberg's release of the Pentagon Papers. The President's remarks came at a State Department gathering of 600 former prisoners of war.

The Evening Star and The Washington Daily News

Washington, D.C., May 22, 1973

In his long statement on Watergate released yesterday, President Nixon assures us that he had no prior knowledge of the bugging operation, that he took no part in—and indeed was unaware of—any cover-up, that he neither authorized nor knew of any offer of executive clemency to the conspirators, that he did not know until his own investigation revealed it of any effort to fund the Watergate defendants or to break into the office of Daniel Ellsberg's psychiatrist, that at no time did he attempt—nor did he authorize others to attempt — to implicate the Central Intelligence Agency, and that he neither authorized nor encouraged his subordinates to engage in illegal or improper campaign tactics.

Mr. Nixon would have us believe that, in actions he may have taken as regards Watergate, he was motivated by nothing but concern for the national security.

It may be so. But there are a few matters which still confuse us and upon which we would welcome further presidential elucidation. For example, Mr. Nixon admits that the White House Special Investigations Unit ("The Plumbers") was set up in June, 1971, with his approval. He describes it as "a small group" under John Ehrlichman, consisting of Egil Krogh, David Young, E. Howard Hunt and G Gordon Liddy, a unit known only to "a very few persons at the White House."

Mr. Nixon says the task of The Plumbers was two-fold: to stop security leaks and to "investigate other sensitive security matters." We can understand the group's first function. But we find it a trifle hard to understand that, with a huge federal intelligence establishment at his beck and call, Mr. Nixon felt compelled to turn to this small group of buccaneers to undertake tasks of grave national security. Was the FBI really that useless? Could no one in the Secret Service be trusted? What about the National Security Agency, the CIA, the Department of Justice, the Treasury, the Defense Department? What qualities had Hunt and Liddy that were lacking in these great departments and agencies?

What were these "sensitive security matters" to which The Plumbers devoted themselves? Well, before their work "tapered off around the end of 1971," they investigated Ellsberg's "associates and motives." They traced down other national security leaks, including one having to do with the SALT talks. They were engaged in "compiling an accurate record of events related to the Vietnam War," which presumably is why they were rummaging through the State Department's files (no mention of forging telegrams, of course). For all this effort, it is difficult to see how The Plumbers could become privy to many legitimate state secrets.

Comes now the burglary and bugging of Democratic National Committee headquarters, "a complete surprise" to Mr. Nixon. His initial reaction is that the guilty should be brought to justice, but within a few days he is "advised" that there is "a possibility of CIA involvement." He

also is stricken with concern "that the Watergate investigation might well lead to an inquiry into the activities of the Special Investigations Unit itself."

When he is worried that the CIA may be involved, does Mr. Nixon ask Richard Helms, then director of the agency, if this is the case? He does not. He instructs Haldeman and Ehrlichman to see that Acting FBI Director L. Patrick Gray and the Deputy CIA director, General Vernon Walters, "coordinate" their activities so that nobody's covert operations are exposed. Why was Helms by-passed and then shipped off to Iran? We'd like to know. And when Walters told Gray that CIA had no operation which could be compromised by the FBI's investigation (in Mexico in this instance) and Gray told Mr. Nixon that on July 6, did not the President smell at least a small laundered mouse?

And why was Mr. Nixon so concerned about the inquiry leading to The Plumbers? National security matters, so he says. And that, presumably, is why he told Assistant Attorney General Petersen to treat his investigation of Watergate virtually as if it were only a common case of breaking and entering, and "to stay out of national security matters." But could the President not have realized that, no matter how pure his motives, instructions of that nature to Petersen could only result in so severely limiting the investigation as to make it virtually worthless? For by his own definition, anything and everything a White House-based group like The Plumbers did could have a national security construction placed on it.

Mr. Nixon declares in his statement that "it is not my intention to place a national security 'cover' on Watergate." We are relieved to hear that, because a close reading of his statement could lead someone who had not totally suspended his critical faculties to believe that that is precisely what Mr. Nixon is trying to do. We are equally relieved to hear that "executive privilege will not be invoked as to any testimony concerning possible criminal conduct or discussions of possible criminal conduct" when men like Haldeman, Ehrlichman and former attorney general John Mitchell testify under oath, and we trust that this will be the case concerning their conversations with the President.

In concluding his statement, Mr. Nixon declares that "as more information is developed, I have no doubt that more questions will be raised." In our view, Mr. Nixon's statement itself raises so many questions and provides so few credible answers that we are sure that he will soon once again find time from "his larger duties" to inform our doubts and dispel our fears.

THE SUN

Baltimore, Md., May 22, 1973

In the spring of 1969, certain senior officials in the White House and in other executive departments were alarmed at leaks to the press regarding sensitive foreign policy and defense matters. The Federal Bureau of Investigation was asked to investigate the leaks. Wiretaps were placed on the telephones of 13 high level government employees and four journalists. This was legal, and the White House would have been derelict in its duty not to take every legal step to find out which, if any, trusted employees were violating their trust.

Yet having said that, we also must say that this whole episode has a funny aroma. Something just isn't right. For one thing, Henry Kissinger, whose National Security Staff was suspected of including leakers, was unusually equivocal when asked to comment on the affair. He first indicated he wasn't aware of what was going on, then suggested he was aware, but only after the fact, when the official Justice Department version is that the White House asked for security checks in a way in which it could hardly have expected there to be no wiretapping. For another thing, the wiretaps went on much too long to have been only concerned with the specific information leaks given as excuses for the probe. One tap stayed on for

21 months. Only two stayed on for as short a period as one month.

That time frame means that literally thousands of private conversations were secretly monitored. The monitoring appears to have continued after suspicions about loyalty were laid to rest. Was whatever the White House looking for something that justified going on and on with the taps? Was it something that justified Dr. Kissinger's fumbling explanations? And was it suspicions not of disloyalty to country but just disloyalty to the White House that was really at issue?

The fact that these questions are now being asked in many quarters raises the worry that once more arrogance in the White House and a lack of a sense of proportion, have *damaged*, not bolstered, national security. For Henry Kissinger is more than an individual, he is an instrument of policy and almost an institution. If his reputation is harmed, the government's ability to conduct a foreign policy is, too. That is the last thing the government (and the nation) need at this time. The President's troubles with Congress, the pressure on the dollar, the potential for distasteful occurrences in Southeast Asia, the hair-trigger in the Middle East and the growing woes relative to foreign energy sources—the need for unencumbered foreign policy makers and advisers was never greater.

THE BLADE
Toledo, Ohio, May 20, 1973

LAST Nov. 3, in an editorial on this page in which The Blade endorsed Sen. George McGovern for president, we made these comments in reflecting on the Nixon administration:

► In domestic affairs, the Administration has used as its primary tool for governing what Adlai Stevenson III aptly describes as the "politics of wealth and stealth."

► Most Americans, including millions who will vote for Mr. Nixon, can only be appalled if they really stop and ponder what has been going on in the White House.

► The stench of corruption, of cynical abuse of power, of arrogant subverting of the political processes that are the marks of this Administration has never been more obnoxious than it is today.

► What is equally disturbing is that a President who promised an open administration has, in fact, turned his into one where secrecy and duplicity are the order of the day, where the most concerted effort in decades to intimidate the press is under way, and where a total lack of understanding of the Bill of Rights and the basic freedoms it was designed to protect is manifest in so many ways.

► Richard Nixon, in short, has failed as President to unite this nation, to move forward with broad social and economic reforms he held out, to calm the internal stresses that beset our society, or to inject any sense of rightful priorities or moral values into our national life.

We are aware that in many quarters those observations were discounted at the time as political hyperbole expressed in the course of urging support for the man who was running against Mr. Nixon. We submit now, however, that the incisiveness of those judgments stands out far more saliently today in the wake of the scandalous disclosures that have been brought to light so far in the Watergate mess.

We do not recite our comments of last election eve with any sense of gloating or out of any pretense at omniscience. No honest American of any political hue can take pride from the malodorous developments in which the Administration is now enmeshed. But weighed against the sordid facts of Watergate and last fall's gutter tactics employed to re-elect the President, our own verdict of last November that President Nixon was presiding over a tightly knit gang that condoned, encouraged, and perpetrated some of the rottenest activities that ever permeated the White House can only be viewed today as an understatement.

THERE have, of course, been scandals of all sorts in other administrations, but none of them can compare to Watergate and all of its evil ramifications.

The plain truth—and it is hard for many loyal Nixon supporters to accept it—is that the Nixon administration must now be regarded as the most corrupt in the history of this Republic.

Never has there been a national political scandal so insidious and all-encompassing in any administration as Watergate, tainting as it already has a dozen (at last count) key federal agencies, including the FBI, the CIA, the Justice Department, the Securities and Exchange Commission, and the White House itself.

Never has such a travesty against justice claimed as casualties so many in high offices and so close to the President; already, at least 25 men, including two attorney generals, one secretary of commerce, one acting FBI director, one SEC chairman, and three intimate presidential advisers have left

government service after their involvement in the tangled web of illegality that is Watergate was exposed to public gaze. More may well follow.

Never has such a complex and arrogant effort at sabotaging our political and electoral processes been plotted, undertaken, directed, and kept under cover in the inner reaches of the White House as the nefarious deeds of the Nixon staff and campaign committee—everything from illegal wiretapping, burglary, and forgery of documents to lying, bugging, and spreading phony letters, with the entire melange of impropriety and lawbreaking awash in that deluge of secret often illegally obtained funds sloshing from one end of the Nixon establishment to the other.

And never in our history has such a massive operation of deception and wrongdoing been launched so needlessly, so ridiculously, and so callously to insure the re-election of a candidate who was so clearly such a heavy favorite to win from the moment the two national tickets were set.

THE complete Watergate story has not yet run its course. But it is already apparent that the shocking activities indulged in at all levels of the White House were not intended—as was the case in previous great national scandals—to line anyone's pockets with money or to throw fortunes in natural resources to a favored few or to buy votes. The entire Watergate affair was planned and executed to achieve something those involved in it believed (and still do) was desirable and even necessary: the re-election of Richard Nixon and the destruc-

tion of any semblance of opposition to that goal.

And all of the damage that has been done to the office of the presidency, to this Administration, and to Mr. Nixon himself was made possible solely because he has from the start of his political career never been able to bring himself to function except through the shadowy manipulations of his closest henchmen whose overriding commitment was in terms of blind personal loyalty to him. That and — as we said last Nov. 3 — Mr. Nixon's inability to realize that even in politics there is a belt below which no decent man hits have been a self-destructing combination.

Mr. Nixon, as with most other presidents, no doubt longs to carve out a distinguished niche in history. He will not make it now, and he will not make it because he will forever be remembered not for what he has done or still may do but for the indelible stain the Watergate affair has etched on the annals of American politics and government. The Nixon administration will always be known for Watergate just as Warren Harding is remembered most for the shame of Teapot Dome and U.S. Grant — as president — for the scandals that rocked his administration.

The fall of Richard Milhous Nixon is not an edifying turn of events for any American to contemplate. But it has occurred, he in large part brought it upon himself, and the only question that remains unanswered is how much further Watergate will drag him down from the pinnacle he reached with his impressive victory last Nov. 7.

Detroit Free Press
Detroit, Mich., May 24, 1973

NATIONAL SECURITY is a good patriotic issue, one that everybody is for and the one President Nixon has chosen to cloud the real issue of his own questionable handling of the Watergate case.

Mr. Nixon's lengthy statement Tuesday in which he admitted for the first time that there was a high level cover-up of the break-in and bugging of Democratic national headquarters may well have been true—from his point of view.

But the President's point of view is now at least as questionable as his ability to choose honest aides.

And a platoon of plumbers, hopefully not from the White House, may be needed to plug the leaks in Mr. Nixon's statement. The President said, for example, that "Elements of the early post-Watergate reports led me to suspect, incorrectly, that the CIA had been in some way involved." If we believe that statement, and there is no reason we should not, then Mr. Nixon must explain why heads did not roll at the CIA, or at least why the suspected CIA involvement was not thoroughly investigated.

The CIA cannot, by law, involve itself in covert domestic activity. What could be more covert than a late-night burglary? What could be more domestic than the Washington, D.C., headquarters of the nation's majority political party?

Mr. Nixon also said he "specifically instructed Mr. Haldeman and Mr. Ehrlichman to insure that the FBI would not

carry its investigation into areas that might compromise these covert national security activities or those of the CIA."

Why the distrust of the FBI, whose agents have security clearance? Was the President really concerned about national security or did he fear that FBI agents would discover that the CIA was being used illegally for political purposes?

Secrecy is, of course, sometimes required for national security. No one doubts that. But it is too often used as a face-saving device. Make a mistake? Classify it top secret and nobody will ever know you made it.

The Pentagon Papers, cited in Mr. Nixon's statement as "a security leak of unprecedented proportions," did not hurt the United States, but they did embarrass some former government officials. Most of the information was already known.

Now, in the name of national security, Mr. Nixon admits wiretapping and says burglary ("surreptitious entry") would have been given official approval except for opposition by J. Edgar Hoover.

Unchecked, national security can obviously lead to police state tactics. The law, of course, provides a check, but some of Mr. Nixon's chosen henchmen considered themselves above the law.

So Mr. Nixon now says he thought he was covering up for illegal activities of the CIA and not illegal activities of his re-election committee. He has more explaining to do.

ST. LOUIS POST-DISPATCH

St. Louis, Mo., May 24, 1973

President Nixon's admission that he tried to frustrate certain aspects of the Watergate inquiry in the name of national security is a measure of the desperate state of his presidency. The admission was clearly prompted by an awareness of the contents of "classified" documents bearing on 1970 incidents that soon may surface in the investigation. The plea that these documents be kept secret, also in the name of national security, is not persuasive.

For national security was not involved in the matters at issue. What was involved was the Nixon Administration's credibility in the face of widespread protests over its unconstitutional conduct of the Vietnam War. The White House reaction, bred on fear and suspicion, generated a whole incredible apparatus directed toward protecting executive dominance of the Government.

What is one to think of a President who would initiate and approve a clearly illegal *domestic* intelligence program, such as Mr. Nixon admits was set up in 1970 but not implemented? Against the background of anti-Vietnam demonstrations the President met on June 5 with J. Edgar Hoover, FBI chief; Richard Helms, director of the CIA, and two others to discuss counter-measures. In connection with Mr. Helms, did Mr. Nixon not know that the CIA is forbidden by law to engage in internal security activities?

No matter, perhaps. The group's recommendations were adopted and the appropriate agencies notified on July 23. The approval authorized, as Mr. Nixon said, "surreptitious entry — breaking and entering, in effect — on specified categories of targets in specified situations related to national security." Mr. Hoover objected, and the plan was cancelled five days later. But in December of that year an "intelligence evaluation" committee was created; it also included the CIA.

Mr. Nixon did not spell out details of the 1970 plan, but he did say that the documents describing it are "extremely sensitive." It is these documents that John W. Dean III, discharged former presidential counsel, turned over to the custody of United States District Judge John Sirica, the Watergate judge. It is these documents that the President wants to conceal from public scrutiny. The inference is inescapable that the security involved is more likely that of Mr. Nixon than that of the nation.

In his Tuesday statement Mr. Nixon also addressed himself to the 1971 case of Daniel Ellsberg and the publication of the Pentagon Papers. He said "there was every reason to believe this was a security leak of unprecedented proportions," posing a "grave" threat to sensitive international negotiations then in progress. So he approved the establishment of a special White House investigations unit charged specifically by the President to "find out all it could about Mr. Ellsberg's associates and his motives." He denied he authorized unlawful activities (such as illegal wiretaps and the burglary of Mr. Ellsberg's psychiatrist's office). Again, national security was not involved in the Pentagon Papers; what was involved were historical details about the Government's irrational and irresponsible conduct of the Vietnam War.

What Mr. Nixon has done in his statement is give the country a frightening picture of a Chief Executive so dedicated to secrecy, in contravention of American traditions, as to establish clandestine personal investigative task forces to spy upon Administration critics. If he did not order these groups to commit illegal acts, he created the climate in which his lieutenants understood that the end justifies the means. This sort of thing is the hallmark of totalitarian societies; it has no place in the United States.

Mr. Nixon's statement gives added reason why Congress and a special prosecutor must get to the bottom of the mess. Many questions remain unanswered, as the President acknowledges. Could he not arrange a forum, such as an unlimited press conference, to answer questions? He will need to take heroic measures to restore a semblance of his lost prestige.

Mr. Nixon has obviously given serious thought to whether he should resign, else he would not have specifically stated that he intends to continue in his job. This decision is subject to change, for if his position erodes to the point at which he cannot govern he will have no option. The nation's welfare must be his first priority.

HERALD EXAMINER

Los Angeles, Calif., May 24, 1973

President Nixon's strong, comprehensive statement on the Watergate case clearly shows that the President himself was not involved in the sordid mess or in the subsequent attempts at coverup.

The statement is particularly welcome at this time when the nation is caught in a whirlpool of rumors, innuendoes and unsubstantiated charges which threatened to pull to the unjustified conclusion that Nixon is politically corrupt.

As in the days of lynchings, many self-styled zealots had heard enough allegations, gossip and hearsay to convince them to string up the President.

Nixon has freed his aides to testify openly, without recourse to executive privilege, about any conversations they may have had with him concerning the Watergate affair.

In his statement, Nixon explained the necessity of protecting the secrecy of domestic intelligence operations run by both the CIA and the White House and to keep them separate from Watergate. "I sought to prevent the exposure of these covert national security activities, while encouraging those conducting the investigation to pursue their inquiry into Watergate itself," Nixon said.

There were several leaks within the Administration that threatened national security — leaks to the press about U.S.-Soviet arms limitations, a wave of campus unrest and widespread bombings and other guerrilla style political activism in 1970, and Daniel Ellsberg's leak to the press in mid-1971 of the Pentagon Papers dealing with the Vietnam war.

The President did the right thing in seeking to find the source of the leaks.

Statements to date indicate that the President was persistently, flagrantly and arrogantly lied to about the Watergate scandal, by men to whom he had given total confidence. But that is a matter for the courts to decide.

It is now time to free the President's hands to get on with the nation's work.

The Oregonian

Portland, Ore., May 24, 1973

President Richard M. Nixon's restatement of his lack of knowledge of and lack of vigilance to prevent the Watergate break-in and other 1972 campaign misdeeds is essentially a plea for understanding and reservation of judgment pending final disclosures in the Senate hearing and the courts.

The government of the United States has not, as some have asserted, come to a grinding halt because of Watergate. But it is not functioning as it needs to function either in Congress or the executive branch in a period of major stresses at home and abroad. The President's baring of his personal recollection of events, including denial of direct involvement and his betrayal not by his enemies but by his overzealous, overloyal and most trusted aides, should go some distance toward restoring the faith of the millions who voted for him. The President is prepared to make additional comments as the Senate hearing brings out more conflicting testimony. A major press conference may be expected soon.

This newspaper, for one, is willing to give the President of the United States the benefit of every doubt that his conduct was proper until or, unless there is convincing evidence to the contrary. So are most members of Congress. The stakes are too high to do otherwise.

The President's two long statements Tuesday provided in detail the directives he gave for the safeguarding of national security and accused confidential aides, now resigned or fired, of going beyond those directives in the break-in and bugging of Democratic National Committee headquarters and in other political and nonsecurity fields. His denials of personal involvement included prior knowledge of Watergate, of efforts to cover up that and other scandals, of offers of executive clemency to buy guilty pleas and silence of Watergate defendants, of the raising of money for these defendants, of trying to implicate the CIA in political surveillance, of the break-in of the office of the psychiatrist for Daniel Ellsberg, who leaked the Pentagon Papers to the press and Congress, and other illegal and unethical acts.

"None of these took place with my specific approval or knowledge," the President stated. "To the extent that I may in any way have contributed to the climate in which they took place, I did not intend to; to the extent that I failed to prevent them, I should have been more vigilant."

It may be said that Mr. Nixon could have strengthened his position against the onslaught of revelations of skulduggery had he included more details in his statement of April 30. But the Watergate expose is a growing scandal. The President confessed that, even at this late date, "My own information on these matters is fragmentary, and to some extent contradictory." Any man bearing the awesome responsibilities of the presidency must rely on his own staff and the heads of departments and agencies for truthful and complete information. Mr. Nixon's explanation clearly admits that he was not getting it through the chain of command.

The President has pledged complete support of the Watergate investigations and denial of the refuge of "executive privilege" to members of his staff in testimony or defense. He said he would not, by resignation, "abandon my responsibilities. I will continue to do the job I was elected to do." That decision merits support of the American people, whatever they may think of Richard M. Nixon. Presidents and their aides and cabinets come and go but the presidency is transcendent.

THE WALL STREET JOURNAL.

New York, N.Y., May 24, 1973

President Nixon's latest statement on Watergate offers a plausible and even persuasive explanation of events leading up to the break-in and bugging. His explanation of events after the bugging is far less persuasive, and most of all it's a pity the same statement was not made long ago. Coming as it does it reinforces an impression of Greek tragedy, with the President carried by the Fates and the nation dragged along.

We find it absolutely fascinating, in fact, to read of how the Watergate conspirators were first hired to plug the leaks that led to the Pentagon Papers and other disclosures of classified information. And how once started, this rather seamy business became steadily more so, escalating first into illegality in the name of national security, then into illegality in the name of partisan politics.

It in no way excuses any of the offenses, or ignores that those in charge of enforcing laws have a special responsibility to observe them, to note that in this chain of events the Watergate conspirators were neither the only ones nor the first ones to conclude that their purposes were more important than the law. It is a lesson in how much the law depends on a climate of civility, on a consensus that certain offenses are unthinkable, that erodes when the nation becomes politically polarized.

A certain teleology is evident in the sequence leading to the bugging, and one suspects something similar prevailed after the arrests as well. But the President was far less detailed and specific in describing how the cover-up came about, though he was more willing than before to admit personal failing, as opposed to mere institutional responsibility. But this admission was wrung out under tremendous pressure, and after one supposedly final explanation. The context can only add to the impression that the President is acting like a man with something to hide.

Now, even if Mr. Nixon has been intent on preventing the full truth from coming out, we do not find it impossible that he has been hiding something other than his personal involvement. Motives of national security and personal loyalty could also work to create the same impression. Further and most important, we do not think judgments should be made on the basis of implications or likelihoods. The matter is too crucial to the nation to be judged on anything but the soundest basis in fact.

The nation's stake in all this involves those same questions of civility and polarization that helped give birth to the mess in the first place. We fear that the President's most outspoken critics are again misreading the nation, as they have so often in the past. The polls show that the public believes the President is implicated. They do not show that the public yet is persuaded the President should therefore be deposed. Least of all do they show that the public believes the reins of national leadership should be turned over to the political forces the President so convincingly defeated in the 1972 election.

Yet something of a reversal of the presidential election seems to be taking place, most spectacularly in the intervention of Daniel Ellsberg to cause a one-day delay in the confirmation of Elliot Richardson as Attorney General. Mr. Ellsberg had no little to do with the events at hand, and was far from completely vindicated when he proved more clever than the Watergate conspirators in having charges dismissed. And if the verdict of the American people in 1972 meant anything at all it meant the rejection of Mr. Ellsberg's view of American society and American institutions. Yet for a moment he seemed to have more clout with the Senate Judiciary Committee than the President did.

The danger here is not that the Ellsbergs of the nation are going to take over the government. Conservatives and Republicans will survive Watergate, just as liberals and Democrats survived Chappaquiddick. Presidents may come and even go, but the character of the American people and American institutions will endure. The danger, rather, is that all the old battles will have to be refought, that the lessons of the 1972 elections will have to be relearned, with all the pain and turmoil that implies.

That is the significance of Watergate. That is why the President's critics should operate only on the soundest basis in fact; only in that way can they hope to achieve any degree of national consensus. The same need for consensus ought to be taken more seriously by the President himself. His statement Tuesday, cloaked as it was in terms of not telling the whole story because of ongoing court actions, was only the barest start toward dispelling doubt and clarifying national opinion.

With Mr. Nixon's reelection and his Vietnam settlement, it appeared that his patience and perseverance would at last lead us out of the agonies of the 1960s. Now it seems that one gratuitous lapse will thrust us back into the heat of them. That is the path the Greek tragedy is on, and we can only hope that the President and Congress can somehow wrench control away from impersonal destiny, that responsible leaders can yet make themselves masters of the nation's fate.

ALBUQUERQUE JOURNAL

Albuquerque, N.M., May 24, 1973

President Nixon's latest statement on the Watergate affair stretches the credibility of the nation's chief executive rather than relieving the anxiety of the American public.

It is totally inconceivable that the President, no matter what the circumstances, would approve "surreptitious entry — breaking and entry in effect," even in "National Security" matters. Yet that is exactly what President Nixon — himself a lawyer and by virtue of both his vocation and his office pledged to uphold the law of the land under all conditions — admitted.

The fact the 1970 plan was terminated after five days does not alter the fact the President tentatively approved the commission of felonies rather than resorting to the time-honored — and legal — method of obtaining court warrants to accomplish the same ends.

In view of the tenseness of the times — rioting, violence, campus unrest, bombings — the President may well have felt compelled to act to avert total anarchy. But illegal acts do not justify the means, no matter how noble the intent.

Even now the President's political paranoia is evident in his efforts to disguise the activities of the former Intelligence Evaluation Committee and a Special Investigations Unit — the "plumbers," some of whom became directly involved in the Watergate break-in — under the blanket of national security. It stretches credulity to believe a domestic spying plan — unused at that — could compromise national security.

The plan for "surreptitious entry" no doubt will be publicized despite the President's efforts to keep it under wraps. Former White House Counsel John Dean has made certain a copy of the document was made available to the court hearing the Watergate case. The court in turn has made the paper available to Congress.

The President no doubt recognizes the vast difference between national security and political embarassment. Naturally he would like to avoid the latter and protect the former.

The President's statement leaves the distinct impression it was tailored to fit hindsight based upon revelations in both court and Senate committee hearings.

To quote the President, "It is clear that unethical as well as illegal activities took place in the course of the campaign." And those activities, no doubt, were encouraged by the President himself, albeit unintentionally.

The political abuse which Watergate reflected leaves no room for equivocation by the President. The sooner the matter is settled the better, but it will drag on for months and months if the President does not go much farther with his explanation than he has thus far.

St. Petersburg Times

St Petersburg, Fla., May 23, 1973

To the sickening revelations of White House involvement in the Watergate felony and cover-up, President Nixon's bombshell admission that his orders, in fact, started the cover-up leaves the nation stunned.

No belated claim of protecting national security, no feeble excuse of not knowing what subordinates were doing can now undo the damage done to public confidence in Mr. Nixon's ability to govern this country.

FOR A DECADE, the blanket of "a threat to national security" has been draped over every dubious government activity from the Vietnam War through the Pentagon Papers prosecution to Watergate itself. Americans have heard that song before, so many times they have no reason to accept it this time.

Moreover, it is only now — after Senate investigators have learned from James McCord and John Caulfield of wiretapping foreign embassies in Washington — that Mr. Nixon contends some undefined security matter involving foreign countries is at stake — a crucial point which, if true, should have been mentioned in the President's previous Watergate statements. His effort, aimed at blocking release of papers held by his fired staff lawyer John Dean, should not be permitted to succeed.

Dean's papers should be revealed; the Senate hearings should press on; an independent prosecutor should investigate. There can be no trust that the full story of the sordid episode has been aired until Mr. Nixon's technique of obscuring facts by hiding behind this transparent screen of "giving the facts" is punctured.

AT THE very least, Mr. Nixon has convicted himself of an incredible incapacity in office. To claim he didn't know about or authorize illegal acts, but to admit such acts were carried out in pursuance of his orders, is for the President to confess he was not in proper charge of his job.

Take his account of the break-in at the office of a psychiatrist who had treated Daniel Ellsberg. Ellsberg had made public the Pentagon Papers. Rather than leave his prosecution up to the FBI, Mr. Nixon set up his own private force to plug security leaks.

HE ORDERED this unit to "find out all it could about Ellsberg's associates and his motives." His order did not cover burglary, the President said.

"However," he added, "because of the emphasis I put on the crucial importance of protecting the national security, I can understand how highly motivated individuals could have felt justified in engaging in specific activities that I would have disapproved had they been brought to my attention."

No doubt. Especially in view of the fact that a year earlier, according to the President's belated account, he had sought to set up a super-security unit with powers, among others, to commit burglary. That one was too much even for J. Edgar Hoover, who blocked it.

HOOVER vetoed this unprecedented plan for domestic infiltration by the CIA, NSA, FBI and Treasury and Justice departments. But the dwarf version of this strangling vine came to flower with burglaries, wiretaps, other illegalities and at least in its seed with Mr. Nixon's admitted approval. These were works of the White House "plumbers."

An extraordinary insensitivity to basic constitutional ideals permeates this admission. It is not dissipated by Mr. Nixon's invocation of a "threat so grave as to require extraordinary actions." He leaves the unshakeable impression that the larger espionage effort — illegal on its face for the CIA — would have proceeded but for the objections of Hoover. It is more than probable that the abandoned plan created the climate in which the second White House security unit thrived.

Once a President foresakes the Constitution, it is easy for others to do the same. In all this talk of defending the national security, it should be remembered that the political espionage was conducted primarily against Democratic candidates for the presidency.

IN MANY ways, the content and the timing of Mr. Nixon's statement raised more questions than they settled. How was it possible that the President of the U.S. was misled into believing that the CIA was involved in the Watergate break-in? Why did Mr. Nixon not reveal until now his order that led to the coverup?

The question inevitably nagging millions of Americans today is whether Mr. Nixon now has compromised himself to the extent he should resign. We think it is too early to answer that question. We hope thoughtful people of all political persuasions will ponder what comes next with prayerful concern for the country's best interests.

"THE PROPER forum for settling these matters is in the courts," Mr. Nixon said. That is not quite correct. There is more need than ever for the Senate investigating committee to get to the bottom of this scandal.

"I should have been more vigilant," the President said. He certainly should have. He should have been more vigilant in protecting the Justice Department, the FBI, the CIA and the Securities and Exchange Commission from political manipulation. He should have been more vigilant in supervising his own White House staff. He should have been more vigilant in preventing a widespread conspiracy to undermine the national election. He should have been more vigilant in preventing the admittedly illegal activities that marred his campaign finance operations. He should have been more vigilant in preventing the cover-up of the Watergate crimes. He should have been more vigilant in protecting the principles of the Constitution. Finally, he should have been far more vigilant in informing the American people of these high crimes and misdemeanors — which he should have done long before sworn testimony in the Senate placed his back to the wall.

For the sake of our country, we hope Mr. Nixon can restore the authority and the credibility of his government.

But we are not reassured by either the content or the timing of yesterday's statement.

The Boston Globe

Boston, Mass., May 27, 1973

In his May 22 acknowledgement of "unethical as well as illegal activities" in his re-election campaign, President Nixon touched briefly on the possibility that he himself "may have contributed to the climate in which they took place."

He denied any such intent. But the truth is that Mr. Nixon did indeed create the climate. It is a climate of fear, hyperbole, innuendo and coercion on which he has thrived politically for almost three decades.

In the beginning, it was the fear of communism that was implanted with carefully-worded suggestions that all of his political opponents were so tainted. In his presidency, the steady drumfire has been that the national security somehow is in grave jeopardy and can be restored only if Mr. Nixon and the men around him are permitted the freest possible exercise of the presidential will.

Thus, the end of national security was served in the 1968 campaign's aftermath, as Mr. Nixon saw it, through the means of "authorization for surreptitiuos entry — breaking and entering, in effect — on specified categories of targets."

It is served by supplying tools, plans, and leadership to dissident groups, as most recently, in the case of the Camden, N.J., war protesters and others before that.

It is served, at least as Mr. Nixon sees it, by bombing Cambodia, and, conversely, it was "threatened" by dissenters during Mr. Nixon's four years of war in Vietnam.

It is served, or so we are told, by the illegal impoundment of funds authorized by Congress for specific purposes. Is it then served or threatened by the constant denigration of Congress as "irresponsible" when it asserts its own constitutional will?

The climate the President has created is one in which civil rights go down the drain one after another, all somehow in the interest of national security — preventive detention, no-knock raids on private homes in the dead of night, sweep-street arrests, the bugging of private telephones, the misuse of grand juries to entrap dissenters, the suppression of evidence that might acquit in criminal cases. The nation is asked to suffer all of these invasions of traditional freedoms guaranteed by the Bill of Rights lest the nation teeter on its foundations. Security is "threatened" by those who protest these lawless invasions.

The unwary could be led to believe that the Bill of Rights is itself a threat to the national security.

In his Watergate statement last week, Mr. Nixon referred to "national security" 24 times. And where he did not see the "national security" endangered, it was "internal security" or "domestic security" that somehow was at the brink despite the vigilance of intelligence and secret police agencies which the President himself listed in another part of his statement — the FBI, the CIA, the National Security Agency, the Secret Service, intelligence agencies of the Defense Department (and other departments the President did not list) as well as the Intelligence Evaluation Committee in the White House.

National security has become a code word. A President can invoke it at will, without either explanation or consultation.

One wonders, however, how the national security could really be threatened were a national election permitted to run its unimpeded course. By exposing the unlawful impediments?

The security of the nation can of course be imperiled. The bombs that fell on Pearl Harbor are proof enough. But how secure is a nation which becomes either inured to or bored by the repeated cry of "wolf?" How secure is it when "the national security" is invoked to permit or to conceal the lawless acts of those sworn to enforce the laws?

San Francisco Chronicle

San Francisco, Calif., May 28, 1973

TODAY, MEMORIAL DAY, has been set aside to honor men who died in battle to defend this nation and its ideals, and to remind the living that much blood has been spent in the preservation of national security—genuine national security, and not the flimsy ersatz that has been evoked to defend and excuse government excesses which the Watergate affair and the Pentagon Papers trial have exposed.

In those episodes, it is increasingly apparent, the compelling concern was less for the protection of true national security than for the protection of secrecy in government. Gross proliferation of such concern, noted in the capital in recent years, displayed itself in the President's remarks to returned prisoners of war last week.

Without secrecy in negotiations with North Vietnam, he said "You men would still be in Hanoi rather than in Washington today." He added: "I think it is time in this country to stop making national heroes out of those who steal secrets and publish them in the newspapers"—a curious comment about the Ellsberg trial in which there were, in our opinion, no heroes except Judge Byrne, but a covey of villains, all government-connected.

★ ★ ★

SECRECY IN NEGOTIATIONS with foreign nations is, of course essential, and almost nobody disputes it. What is now bitterly complained of is secrecy which withholds information that Congress and the people ought to have. Such information was contained in the Pentagon Papers and its early disclosure might well have abridged the dismal history of the American presence in Vietnam to a point where no POWs would have been in Hanoi and a prodigious expenditure of blood and national treasure could have been avoided.

Yet if the President's comments are read aright, secrecy will remain for the time at least a national policy. He has flatly called for "a new sense of dedication of everybody in the bureaucracy, that, if a document is classified, keep it classified."

★ ★ ★

THIS IS A SHARP TURN from his attitude of last year, when an executive order was put forth to remedy the system under which classification runs wild. Furthermore, the turn comes at the precise time when a bipartisan congressional committee, following a two-year study, has called for a statutory system to replace the executive-order formula.

The committee reported that the President's 1972 order has been sterile in operation, that hundreds of millions of overclassified documents have accumulated, that their handling, guarding and storage are costing more than $100 million a year. The committee suggests that the Freedom of Information Act be amended to permit a system that would limit classification of papers under strict guidelines, that would give defense and foreign-policy secrets due protection and which would "let Congress and the people know how the affairs of their government are being conducted."

THIS APPEARS TO BE one route toward ending the so-called "lust for secrecy" which bred Watergate and sullied the Pentagon Papers trial — a kind of secrecy common to despotic, dictatorial governments but foreign to the democratic government that the founding fathers blueprinted in the Constitution.

THE DALLAS TIMES HERALD

Dallas, Tex., May 31, 1973

NOW, IN THE latest of the headline blasts at the White House, comes the charge from the usual "sources close to the Watergate investigation," that the government has used secret agents to spy on American radicals.

Question:

So what's wrong with that? Is it totally wrong for the U.S. government to establish certain surveillance over dangerous internal threats? Are we supposed to ignore revolutionary radicals who throw real bombs, kill people and destroy property?

To leave the impresssion with the American public that a huge, evil Gestapo was planned for the United States is carrying this uncontrolled Watergate fever a bit too far. This is not a nation of dictators and thugs putting the screws on the people; running us indoors in fear behind shuttered windows and wondering when the midnight knock on the door will come. That belongs to someone else.

In fact, the Watergate headline hunters of the East should soon come to realize that the rest of the country is weary of the whole thing as a daily fare. It wants to go on to other things — like where are they going to get a tank full of fuel for their car for the family vacation.

This latest story primly reports that the late J. Edgar Hoover vetoed the White House plan for spying on domestic radical groups, but that it was later implemented through an interdepartmental undercover team. Understandably, Mr. Hoover balked at the plan for a new security arm because of his intense pride in his FBI.

It is irony, indeed, when the same elements who fought to shove Hoover out of office now put the white hat on him for opposing this dastardly scheme.

Does anyone recall, in this current sweep of political hysteria aimed at the presidency, that a group called The Weathermen had a game plan to bomb postoffices, banks, public buildings, college science laboratories, etc.? And that they actually pulled off some bombings?

Does anyone recall that the feared violent wing of the Students for a Democratic Society (SDS) planned mad disruption? That it was driven underground and that FBI, and other agents, still seek some of them after raw acts of violence that killed the innocent and did untold property damage?

To call domestic protective measures "a cover for secret police operations" in this pell-mell rush for more Watergate lineage, is putting things out of focus.

Watergate conspirators, whoever they may be, should be handled by grand juries and courts. But to keep traveling these anonymous by-roads through hearsay and supposition is damaging this country.

DAILY NEWS

New York, N.Y., May 24, 1973

President Nixon

The statement made on Tuesday by President Richard M. Nixon on the Watergate scandal was the fullest he has yet put out on that sordid affair. But it stops short of answering all the questions buzzing around in the public's mind.

While steadfastly denying any connection with the Watergate bugging or the subsequent coverup attempt, Mr. Nixon conceded he acted to limit the probe —though only to the extent of trying to keep the bug-chasers from accidentally kicking the lid off national security operations.

The line-drawing, however, was not done by the President; he had trusted agents H. R. Haldeman, John Ehrlichman and John Dean carry his wishes to investigators. Although Mr. Nixon didn't say it in so many words, this is where the trouble began. It seems the emissaries abused his trust and misused their authority to cut off valid lines of inquiry into the Watergate doings.

The Chief Executive presented his Watergate rundown in the context of security problems his administration faced and measures taken to solve them.

Faced with the constant seepage of important documents and vital diplomatic secrets that plagued him, Mr. Nixon would have been remiss in not making a major effort to plug the leaks. The attempt to do so led to formation of—

THE 'PLUMBERS GROUP'

—headed by G. Gordon Liddy and E. Howard Hunt Jr. For various reasons—press of international affairs, the Nixon style of operations, the President's implicit faith in his underlings—supervision of this shoofly squad was placed in the hands of Ehrlichman & Co.

It was, we believe, a mistake on the President's part to let total control over such a sensitive undertaking pass into the hands of subordinates.

The President's disclosures about how the plumber crew came into being and how its activities were run make his actions immediately following the Watergate break-in baffling.

Within days, Liddy and Hunt were fingered as the chief Waterbuggers. Since their earlier work for his office had brought the two into close association with Haldeman, Ehrlichman and Dean, Mr. Nixon's failure to sense the—

POTENTIAL DANGER

—to the White House—and act accordingly—has still not been properly explained.

Common prudence would dictate that the three men be given no duties connected with the Watergate investigation.

Instead, he vested them with authority and assigned them to chores intimately involved with every detail of the probe.

Although Mr. Nixon's statement leaves many gaps and comes many months late in the game, it does clear the air somewhat. We hope it will also serve his other purpose of preventing legitimate intelligence and security activities from becoming entangled in the Watergate mess.

One Senate panel already has procured copies of a top secret internal security plan devised—but never carried out —in 1970 from the files of ousted White House aide Dean.

It's something to be handled with the utmost care, as should any other highly sensitive data that Watergate probers may stumble across accidentally in the course of their work. And speaking further about Watergate, the—

U.S. SENATE

—yesterday confirmed with a rush President Nixon's nomination of Elliot Richardson as Attorney General.

Richardson and his choice as special prosecutor, Archibald Cox, can now begin in earnest to see that all the material evidence about Watergate is unearthed, that indictments are obtained where warranted, and that the guilty —whoever they may be—are punished.

THE INDIANAPOLIS STAR

Indianapolis, Ind., May 28, 1973

Should counterespionage operations in behalf of national security be made illegal in the United States? Is national security obsolete?

Should the President be permitted to hold meetings of the National Security Council in secret? If he finds that secret details of such meetings are being "leaked" does he have the right to find out who is at fault?

Should he be allowed to assign investigators to uncover disloyal individuals in security-sensitive positions? Should he be allowed to use special procedures to catch spies and traitors in the executive branch?

Or should he be hamstrung by rules while the cheaters are not?

The inference to be drawn from some of the left-liberal interpretations of the current uproar in Washington is that the President should not be permitted to do anything except stand still and be undermined — even if he discovers his staff is honeycombed with "leakers" and that secret agents of the "Third World" are stealing confidential government documents by the bushel.

It is true that civil liberties should not be violated by government operatives in the name of security. But it is equally true that national security should not be destroyed in the name of civil liberties by individuals and groups that pay only lip-service to freedom while they are busy trying to subvert the nation that is the anchor and bastion of freedom in the world.

Complex legal and moral problems must be met and dealt with capably if United States national security is to be defended well.

Internal security is an especially complicated and delicate matter.

Seizure of the United States through a coup d'etat by alien forces bent on establishing a totalitarian dictatorship may seem unlikely, but it is not impossible. The apparatus exists and it would take only the wave of a successful tyrant's hand to set it in motion.

In the last decade one American president has been assassinated by a leftist defector to the Soviet Union and a presidential candidate has been slain by a "Third World" fanatic. The deadly potentiality of revolutionaries inside the USA is not fiction. It is bloody historic fact.

The wind from the left these days leaves no doubt as to radical views on U.S. security. Leftists want it demolished. They would turn every secret-document department of the U.S. government into a free public gallery and every parcel of classified information into a free grab bag. It is not inconceivable that they would demand that National Security Council meetings be t e l e v i s e d and bounced via satellite to Moscow and Peking.

After a generation of boring by leftist termites the U.S. internal security system is riddled. Systematic sabotage has made it leaky as a sieve, as weak as rotten wood which if leaned on is almost certain to collapse.

Men around the President sought to construct an alternate system almost overnight. Their structure, a jerry-built, ad hoc apparatus, was a spectacular and costly failure.

But its failure, as gaudy as it has been and as joyously exploited by partisan politicians and left-leaning media, does not signify the end of the necessity for effective, foolproof security in the highest and most sensitive echelons of U.S. government, no matter how tough the problem of making security mechanisms work and reconciling them with the demands of constitutional liberties.

In a hostile world, confronted by powerful, ruthless and dangerous adversaries, the United States of America cannot hope to conduct the most crucial affairs of government naked and unarmed, inside a goldfish bowl—and survive.

TULSA DAILY WORLD

Tulsa, Okla., May 28, 1973

PRESIDENT NIXON may be having his troubles with some parts of his public, particularly those who feel he is implicated in the Watergate coverup. But he still appears to be ace-high with one group—the former prisoners of war in Vietnam.

Last week he entertained about 600 ex-POWs plus members of their families at a White House dinner, and reports of the affair indicate it was a mutual love affair. The PRESIDENT paid high tribute to the guests and they responded by showing their appreciation for what he has done for them. At one point they gave him a standing ovation.

This group, of course, did not include all the former POWs who returned home after MR. NIXON and HENRY KISSINGER worked out a plan for their release. No doubt there are some who do not share the admiration for the PRESIDENT shown by those who attended the White House celebration. Some have made no secret of their disaffection.

But certainly nobody has better reason to be grateful to MR. NIXON than these men who became pawns in the Vietnam war and could have been held in prison indefinitely. And there is every reason to believe that the big majority of them do have strong favorable feelings toward the PRESIDENT who engineered their freedom.

For his part, MR. NIXON is drawn by his nature to these men who represent one of his signal accomplishments of the past year. They justify his insistence on "peace with honor" and his continuing stress on "national security." They are his answer to all the doves and critics who put so much pressure on him to end the war immediately, at almost any cost.

Finally, the ex-POWs are close to his heart because most of them hold the same old-fashioned view of patriotism as MR. NIXON does. In a day when many Americans are cynical about America The Beautiful or turned off by the love-the-country theme, these newly returned Americans are unabashed flagwavers — kindred souls to the NIXON philosophy.

Some suggestion is heard that the PRESIDENT is using the former prisoners for political purposes. Perhaps he does reap some such benefit by playing up to them, but it seems more likely his reason is simply that he feels at home with them—he and they think alike and understand each other. It's a true mutual admiration society—and what's wrong with that?

New York Post

New York, N.Y., May 26, 1973

There were too many moments when President Nixon's Washington receptions for the returned PWs sounded like a rally of a Watergate Defense Committee. Although Mr. Nixon never explicitly mentioned the subject, he clearly and crudely seized the occasion as a theme for political counter-attack against rising opposition and disaffection at home.

This was hardly the first time he has sought time to mute great national issues by exploiting popular sympathy for the PWs. In the present setting, the effort was peculiarly graceless and frequently grim.

Thus, initially greeting his guests on Tuesday afternoon, he unleashed an angry attack on "those who steal secrets and publish them in newspapers." His words were obviously intended to suggest that all those associated with the Watergate scandal were acting in self-defense against enemies of the republic.

In fact, if Mr. Nixon's account of his own role in the scandal is to be believed, his basic troubles have stemmed from an obsession with secrecy among his top aides; they rarely told him (according to his recital earlier in the week) what was going on in the top levels of his own government and re-election campaign.

There is, indeed, a very real secrecy issue. It is Mr. Nixon's continuing conviction that massive government suppression is a valid weapon in a free society—not to withhold vital military information from adversaries but from the American people. What other rationale could possibly have justified his concern about early disclosure of the bombings of Cambodia? How else can he explain the blanket of suppression over the recent weeks of bombing there? Does anyone seriously contend that the men and women being bombed might not have guessed where the planes came from until the news found its way into the U. S. press?

Mr. Nixon stressed the necessity and value of secrecy in preparing his diplomatic talks with Moscow and Peking. But that is not what the true argument is about. It is about the infinite number of situations—both domestic and foreign—in which his Administration has denied or distorted truth about events because it feared the test of public debate. It is about his compulsion to confuse his political safety with national security.

"It's not that we're trying to keep something from the people that they should know, or from the press that they should print," Mr. Nixon said.

But that is exactly what has been done, time and again, by men in his regime who believed they always knew best how much—or how little—of the truth should be revealed.

Democracy admittedly lives under certain risks that totalitarian societies are spared. But Mr. Nixon's present predicament is perhaps the strongest proof that a clandestine Administration plants the seeds of its own disaster.

The New York Times

New York, N.Y., May 27, 1973

In a lengthy public statement and again in a speech to former prisoners of war, President Nixon has retreated into a fortress called "national security" as his ultimate defense shelter against the storms of Watergate. The tapping of telephones, the illegal break-ins and burglaries, the creation of a secret police staff operating outside the supervision of Congress or any duly authorized Federal agency, the collection and disbursal of huge sums of cash for undercover activities, and the obstruction of an F.B.I. investigation are all justified because foreign agents and domestic radicals threatened the security of the nation. It is an extraordinary argument which has enjoyed repeated use in recent decades. It is time that argument received careful examination.

What is first of all apparent is that this concern with national security is far out of proportion to any real danger. Secrecy becomes synonymous with security and then becomes an end in itself. Few citizens dispute that military plans are necessarily secret and that certain discussions by a President and his advisers concerning relations with foreign countries are best kept confidential. But the crucial element in whether diplomatic negotiations succeed or fail is how the parties appraise the objective realities of their own situation. No position paper or secret conversation is going to affect decisively how another nation perceives its interests.

As the inner history of the Nixon Administration becomes better known because of the Watergate revelations, it is astonishing to learn how concern with imagined dangers to national security persisted in the absence of evidence. Thus, Mr. Nixon and his associates took office in 1969 with the uneasy conviction that there were financial and espionage links between Black Panthers, student radicals and other dissenters in this country and hostile foreign governments. The Central Intelligence Agency was ordered to investigate such possible relationships. According to reports last week, the C.I.A. not once but twice submitted lengthy reports showing that no evidence supported these suspicions.

* * *

Instead of being reassured, President Nixon turned to the Federal Bureau of Investigation and agreed to the opening of F.B.I. offices in twenty foreign countries, duplicating the C.I.A.'s work but still finding no evidence. Not satisfied, the President approved a far-reaching plan in 1970 to mount a campaign of spying, wiretapping and burglaries against domestic radicals.

When J. Edgar Hoover of the F.B.I. refused to carry out the plan unless he received the President's written authorization, Mr. Nixon rescinded the plan. He next turned to a "special investigative unit" set up in the White House without public knowledge but paid for by public funds to do undercover work. It is this unit which burglarized the files of Daniel Ellsberg's psychiatrist.

If fears about national security were excessive to begin with and persisted in defiance of the evidence, the efforts to validate those suspicions first paralleled and then fused with sleazy undercover work by the Administration against its political opponents. Thus, from the spring of 1969, John D. Ehrlichman, one of the President's senior aides, had two former New York policemen on his staff—one on the public payroll and one on the payroll of Mr. Nixon's private attorney—to gather incriminating or embarrassing information about leading figures in the Democratic party. As the 1972 campaign approached, these ex-policemen were joined in their political undercover work by members of that "special investigative unit" which had been protecting the national security by plugging "leaks" to newspapers and shadowing radicals and peace movement leaders.

* * *

The final irony is that when the bungled burglary at the Watergate endangered the secrecy of these multiple operations, President Nixon and his aides did not hesitate to involve and compromise the F.B.I. and the C.I.A.—the two principal legal agencies established to protect national security—in order to cover their own tracks.

At last Thursday's hearing of the Ervin committee, Senator Herman Talmadge of Georgia asked Bernard L. Barker, one of the convicted Watergate burglars: "How did you think you could liberate Cuba by participating in a burglary in Washington, D. C.?"

A similar question might be asked of President Nixon and his senior White House aides: "How did you think you could make the United States more secure against its foreign enemies by adopting here at home the police state methods of those enemies?"

The only valid answer—but one not found in Mr. Nixon's statements and speeches of recent weeks—is that security is found elsewhere than in private detectives and wiretaps or in ever deeper secrecy. Those are the methods and the favored atmosphere of tyrants who fear the truth and fear their own citizens.

Free men and women find true security in the justice of their laws, in the subordination of police power to an independent judiciary, in the honesty and candor of their elected and appointed public servants, and finally in the freely offered devotion of each citizen to the republic. Total security is the fantasy of a child. Free nations live by the vigorous self-confidence of men and women who understand their own interests and ideals and are prepared to defend them. There is no other security.

Des Moines Tribune

Des Moines, Iowa, May 31, 1973

The White House has announced that President Nixon will refuse to answer questions of Watergate investigators, judicial and legislative. The closed-mouth policy applies to sworn testimony, informal statements and written responses to written questions.

The President is invoking a double standard in connection with probes of the Watergate scandal. He declared on Apr. 18, "All members of the White House staff will appear voluntarily when requested by the (Ervin) committee. They will testify under oath and they will answer fully all proper questions. . . . The judicial process is moving ahead as it should; and I shall aid it in all appropriate ways. . . . All government employes and especially White House staff employes are expected to fully cooperate in this matter."

The President thus wants everyone else in government to submit to questioning about Watergate, but he refuses to do so himself.

The President evidently intends to reveal his version of events as he has in the past, through broadcasts and issued statements. The President's efforts to date have failed to satisfy the public that it has been told the full story. The inability to question the President has left unanswered questions and lingering suspicion. Polls following the President's statements denying involvement in wrongdoing show a majority of Americans believe he was involved in the attempted Watergate cover-up.

The President claims that responding to questions about Watergate from probers "would do violence to the separation of powers." There may be a question whether a President can be compelled to answer questions from representatives of the legislative or judicial branches of government. But there is no issue of separation of powers involved in responding to questions of newsmen. The President's statements about Watergate thus far have been of a self-serving nature, without opportunity to pin him down or obtain clarification.

An effort to force the President to testify might do "violence" to the separation of powers, as the President claims, but there is no constitutional bar to the President volunteering the information he has. Under the circumstances, he ought to be eager to share his knowledge about Watergate with congressional committees, the courts and the public.

The invoking of "separation of powers" to block testimony is reminiscent of the invoking of "executive privilege" to prevent John Dean, then White House counsel, from being questioned under oath. The use of an ill-defined constitutional technicality to maintain a cloak of secrecy around White House involvement in Watergate provoked widespread public suspicion that the White House had something to hide. The suspicion subsequently proved justified.

The President is courting the same suspicion with his separation of powers argument. Until the President is willing to impose on himself the same obligation to give testimony he has imposed on others, that suspicion will not go away.

ERVIN COMMITTEE HEARINGS BEGIN; NIXON AIDES SOUGHT CIA HELP

The Senate Select Committee on Presidential Campaign Activities opened hearings May 17 into the Watergate scandal and related charges of wrongdoing during the 1972 presidential campaign. In his opening remarks, committee chairman Sen. Sam J. Ervin Jr. (D, N.C.) declared that an "atmosphere of the utmost gravity" demanded a "probe into assertions that the very [political] system itself has been subverted and its foundations shaken." Ervin said the hearing's purpose was not "prosecutorial or judicial but rather investigative and informative." The hearings, broadcast nationwide on television and radio, began with detailed questioning of witnesses on the Watergate burglary itself; alleged attempts at a cover-up by White House officials; and charges of a widespread plot of political espionage and sabotage initiated and operated by officials of the Committee to Re-Elect the President and the White House.

Convicted Watergate conspirator James W. McCord Jr. told the committee May 18 that former White House aide John J. Caulfield had offered him executive clemency in the name of President Nixon in return for his silence. Caulfield, who resigned his post May 13 following allegations of such an offer, testified May 22 that former White House counsel John W. Dean 3rd had ordered him to offer clemency. A bitter controversy arose over McCord's contention that his former attorney, Gerald Alch, had suggested basing his defense on CIA involvement. Alch took the stand May 23 to deny the allegations and suggest that McCord had participated in an anti-Administration vendetta. Watergate conspirator Bernard Barker told the committee May 24 he broke into the Democratic National Committee headquarters in search of evidence that the Democrats were receiving financial support from the Castro regime in Cuba.

According to testimony presented before the Senate Armed Services Committee, high Administration officials, including former presidential advisers H. R. Haldeman, John D. Ehrlichman and John Dean sought to involve the CIA in the Watergate affair. In releasing a summary of testimony by deputy director of the CIA, Lt. Gen. Vernon A. Walters, committee chairman Sen. Stuart Symington (D, Mo.) May 15 reported: (1) Dean had asked Walters 10 days after the Watergate break-in if the CIA could provide bail or pay the salaries of the men apprehended there Walters refused, declaring he would rather resign than implicate the agency in such a scheme). (2) As recently as January or February, Dean sought to obtain CIA assistance in retrieving from the FBI "some materials" obtained from the CIA for use in the break-in at the office of Pentagon Papers defendant Daniel Ellsberg's psychiatrist. (3) Haldeman and Ehrlichman intervened in an attempt to get the CIA to press the FBI to limit or call off its investigation in 1972 into Nixon campaign funds that had been routed —or "laundered" to prevent tracing—through a Mexican bank and, at one point, through several of the Watergate defendants. The CIA's approach to the FBI was to have been made on the ground that national security was involved and pursuit of the probe would jeopardize certain CIA activities in Mexico. (4) Direct entanglement was avoided when then CIA director Richard M. Helms, informed FBI acting director L. Patrick Gray 3rd that CIA activity was not in jeopardy by the FBI. Helms, currently ambassador to Iran, confirmed Walters story May 16.

ARKANSAS DEMOCRAT
Little Rock, Ark., May 20, 1973

On February 7 when the Senate decided to conduct an investigation into Watergate and appointed a committee, it seemed like a good idea. Today, after the first two days of televised hearings, we are not so sure.

Although many persons had their suspicions that there was more to it than a clumsy burglary by overzealous political activists, that was all we knew for certain then. The seven burglars had been indicted and convicted. U.S. Dist. Judge John Sirica, after bawling out the Justice Department for not being more aggressive in its questioning, looked with favor on the Senate committee's upcoming investigation, saying that it could maybe turn up further details.

But on February 28, L. Patrick Gray, trying to be confirmed as head of the FBI, told a Senate committee that White House Chief Counsel John Dean had lied to the FBI when questioned about Watergate. A few days later, one of the Watergate Seven sent word to Judge Sirica that he wanted to tell all. Nothing has been the same since. Eleven members of the Nixon administration have resigned or been fired, two ex-cabinet members have been indicted, vital agencies of our government have been tainted and the President has had to defend himself publicly.

"We are in a national crisis," wrote Erwin Canham, editor of the Christian Science Monitor. And a "national crisis" is not something that can be taken care of by a televised investigation. Sen. Howard Baker, R-Tenn., vice chairman of the committee, is defensive, calling it a "fact-finding" exercise and urging, "Let's just wait and see how it works."

Well, we've had an example. All day Friday, James McCord, one of the burglars, spit out names, hearsay and startling stories. No one who heard the testimony — despite the proper legal disclaimers that were made regularly by Chairman Sam Ervin — could help but believe that the administration offered McCord executive clemency if he would keep quiet and go to jail and that if he didn't he might be killed. In other words, the President of the United States made McCord one of those offers he couldn't refuse.

Four weeks of that and the next step will be not impeachment but internment. Innocent (until proven otherwise, remember) people will be hurt in these non-adversary hearings. Also, as the Justice Department has pointed out, the guilty are liable to go free because of them. Prosecutors say it will be hard, maybe impossible to convict anyone who testifies on TV before he is tried.

Vice President Agnew has said that Senate investigations are "not a forum that produces enlightenment" but "a forum that produces emotion, and we don't need that right now in this matter." We agree. A brutal war has created bitter divisions in this country, and watching our leaders and our institutions of government torn apart could create more antagonism than we can bear right now.

We are by no means suggesting a coverup. Judge Sircia has recalled the grand jury, all but one of the Watergate Seven are now singing and on Friday, a highly-respected Democrat, Archibald Cox, was named as an independent Watergate prosecutor. It is people who are guilty, not the agencies of our government. Let's find them and punish them — but in court, not on television.

Long Island Press

New York, N.Y., May 21, 1973

Public hearings in the Senate on the Watergate scandal constitute the most important official inquiry into high-level corruption in the nation's history. From these hearings may flow fundamental changes in our political system.

Yet when the television networks devoted more than five hours to live coverage of the first day's testimony, station-switchboards were busy with angry phone calls from viewers. They found more drama in game shows and soap operas the televised hearing had preempted. Complaints are still being received, as the hearings continue.

This should come as no great surprise, sad to say. For months, newspapers have been confronted with similar complaints from readers who say we are devoting too much space to Watergate.

But responsible newspapers are convinced that this unfortunate attitude by no means represents the sentiments of the great majority of Americans. These papers continue to cover Watergate as it should be covered — completely, impartially, sparing no one. That's what a free press is all about.

So hang in there, TV networks. Watergate is a sickness, but not a cancer, and can be cured with a heavy dose of public exposure. Televising the hearings, of course, is an important way of helping people find the truth, bitter as it may be.

If this means that some people must do without their favorite game shows and soap operas for a while, that's a small price to pay for saving the Republic.

Maine Sunday Telegram

Portland, Me., May 20, 1973

"Play it cool on Watergate!" That is the advice we give ourselves — and others, when asked about the Watergate mess these days.

We are as badly rocked as the next fellow by the revelations which are being uncovered daily.

But we sense a real danger too in the mounting loose talk of "impeaching" the President; in the babbling of Congressmen before reporters and TV-cameras demanding that Nixon and Agnew resign and so forth. This is a time to curb and not cut-loose with wild talk, exaggerations and innuendos.

The issue merits more gravity and less emotion.

For impeachment is the ultimate remedy under our Constitution. It should be approached with the utmost caution. And its consequences could be devastating to the nation at home, shattering to the nation in the world, and leave an indelible national wound, perhaps a permanently crippling wound upon our body politic.

Talk of impeaching the President of the United States is wildly irresponsible on the evidence now known. It should be stopped.

Yet what is known so far about Watergate demands massive surgery to cut out the cancer at the center. And so far Nixon has done only some trimming at the edges. Painful to him as was the dismissal of Haldeman and Ehrlichman and Kleindienst and Dean, and the departure of other officials in his administration and the indictment of Mitchell and Stans, the self-surgery must go deeper. So far, Nixon has merely reshuffled familiar faces in his top echelon. John Connally, James Schlesinger, Elliott Richardson, General Haig may be the finest of men, but each is a Nixon man, beholden to the President in the past, beholden now and perhaps beholden in the future.

What the nation needs to see is an accession of independence from outside the White House circle, not a reshuffle of familiar faces, however reputable.

Most Americans want to see justice meted out swiftly to those who have committed crimes in this whole shoddy business. This is why we wish the nasty business could get into the courts of law quickly.

Instead of this, the public is deluged daily by leaks; leaks from grand jury hearings, which are supposed to be secret; leaks from investigations by Senate staff, which are supposed to be private; leaks from resigned officials out to save their own necks; leaks from would-be witnesses who have not yet testified.

One reason these leaks are treated with more credulity than mistrust is because government officials have for so long apparently tried so hard to cover-up the truth. From the President on down, the Administration is now paying the penalty for this stupidity. Too many people are too ready to believe almost anything bad said about the Nixon Administration now.

This is injustice at its worst. This is McCarthyism all over again, in reverse. This undermining of all confidence in the White House can grow into a grave and present danger to the conduct of necessary government in America.

There is only one cure. And that is the prompt process of law. But the Senate hearings in front of TV cameras are happening before the due process of law really begins. This makes it doubly necessary for senators participating in those hearings to prevent them from becoming a grandstand for backstairs gossip, for accusations based upon hearsay, for innuendos and half-truths and, most of all, those messy charges levelled at others that are made for the self-seeking purpose of saving the witness's own neck. Considering the subject under Senate inquiry and the witnesses being called, it will be nigh impossible to keep partisan political grandstanding out of the limelight.

For these reasons, we urge the quickest possible full investigation of Watergate by the Special Prosecutor in whom the nation can place full confidence. The President must join forces quickly with the Congress on this. For at this stage, the burden is on Mr. Nixon to prove that he had no part in and no foreknowledge of the very dirty games that were played in his name.

It is not fair and it most certainly is not just that any man, let alone the President of the United States, should be judged guilty in the court of public opinion until he is proved innocent. It should be the other way around. But it is not. This is why speed is essential. Before this Watergate infection on the body politic spreads further, it must be lanced in the open, for all to see.

Meanwhile let us all remember that the final verdict is far from in. Let us therefore suspend judgment. Let us remember that 'indictment' is only the first step toward a trial, and not a verdict of guilt. Let us weigh with care the reliability and the accuracy of leaks which often come from self-serving sources on both sides.

In short, let us play it cool on Watergate. Zealots on one side of the Watergate fence have sullied the nation too much already. Let us not double their misplaced sense of right and wrong by over-zealousness on the other side too.

THE INDIANAPOLIS STAR
Indianapolis, Ind., May 20, 1973

Many overwrought commentators are still bathing the Watergate affair in the language of Goetterdaemmerung or Apocalypse.

They are saying such things as that it "struck at the very root of American democracy" and that the investigation, which for the moment has supplanted soap opera as the television entertainment offered to stay-at-homes and tired housewives, is "the most important thing in the politics of this century."

They are saying that it will radically alter the American system of government.

Much of what they are saying is such obvious nonsense that it deserves no more than passing comment.

If Watergate is a threat to the national existence it is such only to the extent that left-liberal commentators on a binge of joy disguised as moral outrage — ideologues who have always hated President Richard M. Nixon anyway — are capable of spreading panic. There are ample signs that their capability of doing so, like their capacity for unbiased analysis of news events, is sharply limited.

If Watergate results ultimately in effective reforms in campaign financing, at least that much good will emerge from the turbulence.

But there is among some an overriding hope, which liberal commentators are taking no pains whatever to conceal, that Watergate somehow means a repudiation of principles of moderation in the Federal government. There is no justification for this feeling. It is merely wishful thinking on the part of left-liberals who are trying to transform Watergate by means of shouting and hocus-pocus into a massive mandate for their own bankrupt policies.

With this in mind, let us stress some of the things that Watergate does not mean.

It does not mean the majority of Americans have been converted into enthusiastic supporters of deficit spending, higher taxes, continued inflation and other fiscally unsound and damaging policies for the perpetuation of w h i c h liberals were battling fang-and-claw with President Nixon when the latest wave of Watergate broke.

It does not mean the majority want more and bigger welfare programs, fatter and more arrogant bureaucracies or further intrusions and controls by the government in Washington.

It does not mean most Americans are anxious to dismantle their missile defense system and the armed forces and pursue a policy of retreat and defeat when confronted by Communist pressures, threats, blackmail and aggression.

It does not mean that most Americans are suddenly eager to surrender their personal freedoms and individual decision-making power to a Socialistic supergovernment run by a left-liberal-radical oligarchy with the advice and consent of the Eastern liberal press and the television networks.

The hyperbolic interpretations being placed on the Watergate affair by biased pundits no doubt will continue, and the public no doubt will continue to take them with a grain of salt. But those are things that Watergate doesn't really mean, and all the haranguing of all of the one-sided commentators in the country will not change that one whit.

THE PLAIN DEALER
Cleveland, Ohio, May 22, 1973

All right, goes the argument now, call off the dogs.

Suspend the Ervin committee's Watergate hearings. Stop the reportorial digging.

Let the federal grand jury assemble the facts, indict the possibly guilty and relieve the probably innocent — without further damage to reputations and American institutions.

The argument has some merit. Ordinarily, this procedure would be taken for granted. But this is not an ordinary situation. It is one which presents an uncommon set of circumstances demanding new judgments.

Much about Watergate is still unknown or unproved. But it is possible to reach the judgment that Watergate is at least a massive conspiracy in which persons in one branch of the federal government — the executive — attempted to subvert the machinery of government to gain domination over the other branches and the electoral process.

In its complexity and ambition the conspiracy forbids comparison with scandals of previous administrations. Those who still think of Watergate in terms of an isolated bugging simply have lost track of what is happening.

But who is to investigate such a situation? Who is to see that the guilty are punished? More important, who is to tell the people what is going on in Washington?

Normally the information would come from the process of criminal investigation by the Justice Department, indictment by a grand jury, and prosecution. But in this case the threads of conspiracy have been sewn through many executive agencies and across many levels, from the White House down. There are too many threads and they involve too many vital personal and political interests to expect the Justice Department — an executive department — to pull them out and hold them to light.

But a federal grand jury depends for its deliberations on facts brought by the Justice Department and its investigators. So a grand jury would produce nothing that this federal department fails, for whatever reason, to produce.

The truth of this is obvious from what actually occurred. Watergate first became public knowledge last June. A grand jury looked into it. Seven men were convicted. But by far the greater part of what Americans now know about the situation was then still hidden. It came finally to light because of a federal judge's persistence, some reporters' enterprise — and the threat of the Senate investigation.

The grand jury continues its investigation. Good. But given the peculiar circumstances of this case, the grand jury's sources almost certainly would dry up without the continuing pressure of public exposure by the news media and Sen. Ervin's committee. The executive branch itself needs these external pressures as a sick man needs medicine or surgery to regain his strength and confidence.

We do not regard lightly two dangers in the Senate investigation: the danger to reputations and the danger to the effectiveness of subsequent prosecutions.

But in the long run Senate hearings that carry this search far enough are likely to rehabilitate some reputations already damaged by the crossfire of Watergate participants.

As for future prosecutions:

• To repeat, there is reason to believe that the grand jury would run short of evidence without these other pressures.

• Anyway, the nation's primary concern in this matter must be to determine exactly what happened and why, and to see that it never happens again — not to jail a satisfactory number of miscreants.

Which brings up one last point. Given a conspiracy of this size, the executive branch cannot effectively investigate — especially considering the strategic positions of some conspirators and the feeling among many of them that they were acting in the nation's best interests. But with the present machinery — the appearance of an investigation by an executive department — Congress and the federal judiciary were handcuffed for many months. Thus, the check-and-balance system stumbled, and the nation suffered.

A new instrumentality is needed, a new way for the other branches to oversee and guarantee the investigation of possible misconduct in the huge executive establishment. We called months ago for appointment of an independent investigator such as Archibald Cox is reputed to be. Next time—if there is one—there should be statutory provision for a free hand to be brought in immediately.

THE BLADE

Toledo, Ohio, May 26, 1973

THE unfolding of the Watergate scandal has yielded an abundance of exposures on how able and willing the Nixon White House was to use and abuse its power in the achievement of its ends. Now, in what seems almost like a mere footnote in the appalling scope of the whole sordid story, the testimony of Richard Helms has provided a significant glimpse into the means of dealing with resistance to that power and obstacles to those ends.

Mr. Helms told the Senate Foreign Relations Committee that he did not really want to step down from the directorship of the Central Intelligence Agency early this year. Indeed, he said he would have preferred to stay on in the job specifically because he believed he could be more successful than any newcomer in fending off attempts to involve the CIA in the Watergate cover-up. Instead, Mr. Helms was sent off to become ambassador to Iran, an assignment that he told the committee he neither sought nor particularly wanted.

That version of the CIA change of command stands in sharp contrast to the cover story provided for the announcement of his resignation last winter. The White House said then that Mr. Helms wanted to abide by a CIA policy of retirement at age 60. And the President's press secretary talked to newsmen of Mr. Nixon's praise for the outgoing director's dedicated service and the total satisfaction of the White House with his performance.

Nevertheless, it now turns out that Mr. Helms had in fact been repeatedly instrumental in resisting efforts from the Executive Mansion to ensnarl the CIA in the Watergate web. As far back as last June 23—six days after the arrest of five burglars in Democratic headquarters — presidential chief of staff H. R. Haldeman was asking Mr. Helms' deputy to discourage an FBI investigation into at least one aspect of the nefarious affair. And Mr. Helms in turn—although pointedly bypassed in the contact between the White House and his agency—instructed his aid not to comply lest the CIA risk being besmirched and finished "as an American institution."

That may sound strange, perhaps even laughable, to those citizens in whose view the intelligence agency already was tainted with sinister repute. But Mr. Helms was legally, morally, responsibly, and pragmatically right, of course—and it is another of Watergate's many ironies that the CIA appears to stand as one of the few agencies of the U.S. Government able to keep itself relatively clean and aloof from the corrupting pressures of the White House. And, by peculiar coincidence, after thus standing his ground against the schemes of that crew, Mr. Helms found himself summarily exiled to a distant outpost where, it apparently was thought, he could no longer get in the way.

THE RICHMOND NEWS LEADER

Richmond, Va., May 25, 1973

It used to be that an individual would be praised by most Americans if he undertook any task — even a clandestine task — in the interest of national security. But among the many things that the Watergate affair has shown, it has shown that we might as well start writing epitaphs for such individuals. The god of national pride, upon whom they relied so long, evidently has withdrawn.

Last week James McCord said that he agreed to particiapte in the Watergate break-in because of national security considerations; his statement was ignored by the Senators, who were more interested in determining why he didn't think it peculiar that he was paid in $100 bills. Three days ago President Nixon issued an extraordinary deposition in which he outlined several convincing national security reasons behind his authorization of super-secret investigative procedures that now are under attack. His deposition fell on deaf ears. Last night he told more than 500 returned POWs: "It is time to quit making national heroes out of those who steal national secrets and publish them in the newspapers." The POWs cheered in approval, but most of the POWs were not in America when many of our honored national principles — particularly the principle of national security — were washed away.

And yesterday the nation heard the testimony of Bernard Barker. A Cuban freedom-fighter born of American parents, he said he saw nothing wrong in attempting to learn — via the Watergate break-in — whether the Democrats were using cash from Castro; he added that he sees nothing wrong with it now. He is not a suave man; not brilliant. He was an easy polemical mark for Senators who get their kicks bumping and grinding for national TV. In response to his answers, snickers rippled through the hearing room.

His pride battered, he concluded his testimony with a statement both courageous and piteous. He said that the men who participated in the Watergate break-in did so out of love for their country — out of profound devotion to the good things that it represents. It did not matter whether what they were doing was wrong before the law; they were operating in obedience to a higher law, a law that told them that America was in trouble and possibly was threatened by persons who wanted to take it down the same road that Castro took Cuba more than a decade ago. Call that obedience patriotism.

Few in the media who will comment on what he said will call it patriotism. Many of them justify their own uselessness to their monstrous egos by assuming that their country is not worth their energies. So they will mock Bernard Barker, who resolutely believes that his country needs the energy of everyone. And to the conservatives who may side with Barker, they will raise the obvious rhetorical question: How can you justify what Bernard Barker was trying to do, if in the effort he had to break the law? The obvious reply is that sometimes the ends do justify the means. The commentators in the media know that. They know it, because most of them supported Martin Luther King, who — like Barker — broke the law for his beliefs.

So one of the critical consequences of Watergate is beginning to be seen. By putting the national spotlight on certain procedures used to guarantee national security, those who disdain the importance of national security are having their day. We send people like Bernard Barker, a patriot, to the federal penitentiary. Weep for Bernard Barker: His patriotism is a crime. Those in the hearing room snickered at what he said yesterday. And because of those snickers, the commissars in the Kremlin surely are beside themselves with joy tonight.

The Des Moines Register

Des Moines, Iowa, May 25, 1973

John Caulfield, a former White House aide, has admitted that as a White House emissary he urged James McCord to plead guilty and remain silent about Watergate in return for aid to his family, eventual rehabilitation and a promise of executive clemency. Caulfield thus confirmed in essential detail McCord's shocking account of White House participation in an effort to buy silence and obstruct justice.

McCord's story about the CIA, however, was denied totally by his former attorney, Gordon Alch.

One of the more significant aspects of McCord's account is his description of White House efforts to blame the Watergate break-in on the Central Intelligence Agency (CIA). According to McCord, this angered him and he threatened that "every tree in the forest will fall" if the efforts persisted.

McCord's testimony contrasts sharply with the President's latest statement on the Watergate issue. According to the President, he "instructed Mr. Haldeman and Mr. Ehrlichman to ensure that the investigation of the break-in not expose either an unrelated covert operation of the CIA or the activities of the White House investigations unit." Any successful effort to fix the blame for Watergate on the CIA would have had just the opposite effect. Instead of deflecting attention from the CIA, the move would have made it all but certain that a searching public inquiry would be undertaken of the intelligence agency.

This is but one of many contradictions and loose ends that remain to be resolved and tied down by the Ervin committee. Meanwhile, Americans have reason to be grateful to McCord for his rejection of the White House overtures and for his eventual decision to contact the judge presiding at the Watergate trial and tell his story.

The story is painful for Americans to hear, but it is far less painful than if those responsible in the White House had succeeded in their scheme to subvert justice.

AKRON BEACON JOURNAL
Akron, Ohio, May 22, 1973

There has been much talk in recent days of possible damage to the fair trial rights of potential "Watergate" defendants through the investigative efforts of the Senate Select Committee on Presidential Campaign Activities.

And it does seem obvious that the committee's interrogation of witnesses, spread to all the nation on television, would make it very difficult to find opinionless jurors to try defendants whose activities were ruthlessly explored there.

Further, the President, both directly and through his press secretary, Ronald Ziegler, has given the American public to understand t h a t his silence on precisely what he knows grows out of a respect for the fair-trial rights of some who may be accused on crime in the case.

★

In other and less momentous cases, we would be inclined to real concern over such possible damage from the hearings, and to full respect for the President's expressed point of view.

But in this case too much is at stake. We are driven, instead, to the view expressed the other day by Sen. Sam Ervin, the North Carolina Democrat who is chairman of the investigating committee.

It is more important, he said in substance, that the American public get at the facts here than that any of those who took part in this sordid mess be punished for their possible crimes.

All of those who may be incriminated in the hearings should have ample opportunity, there and elsewhere, to defend themselves at the bar of public opinion. All that is lost by making formal fair trial impossible is the public's right to hold them legally accountable and to punish them with fines or prison terms.

By comparison with the real issues involved here, this seems a small loss.

★

It seems to us, too, that the President could perform a vital service to the nation if he could persuade himself that in this matter the importance of his own candor far overshadows possible punishment of any of his erring subordinates.

As Sen. Ervin has emphasized and re-emphasized, absolutely nothing in the Senate hearings thus far, or elsewhere on the formal public record, has connected the President himself with any of the buggings or other campaign malpractices under examination — except by forms of several-hand hearsay that wouldn't stand up for a minute in a court of law.

And yet, when polls show some 60 pct. of the American public unable to believe that the President can have remained ignorant of the cover-up efforts that followed the Watergate arrests last June, it is clear that it is in a real sense the President himself who is on trial in the hearings.

And what is at stake here is far greater than the right of Richard Nixon or any other citizen to "fair trial" in the unsual legal sense.

President Nixon, as the unseen defendant, faces no real risk of property or liberty at this bar — the kinds of risk against which the Constitution is intended to protect the citizen. Instead the question is far more important and less personal: his fitness for the highest position of trust in the nation's government.

In settling this question, lost prosecutions of subordinates become trivial.

To restore the faith of Americans in their highest officer, two things, it seems to us, become essential:

That the Senate's investigation be pursued without stint until it is obvious to Americans that it has uncovered every shred of available truth here.

And that the President himself — willingly, voluntarily and without further appearance of only responding defensively and grudgingly to pressure — tell Americans exactly what he knew and did not know, and what he has since discovered.

We continue to find it hard to believe that the President of the United States can have been personally and knowingly involved in the sordid business exposed in the hearings.

But only full exposure through the investigations, on the one hand, and full candor by the President himself — without concern for whatever punishment might be lost for subordinates — can clear the air and take the presidency out of its present paralysis.

THE TENNESSEAN
Nashville, Tenn., May 20, 1973

SEN. Herman Talmadge is right about the need for the Senate Watergate investigating committee to get on with the questioning of high-ranking former Nixon aides and not spend so much time on the small fry.

★ ★ ★

The plan favored by Chairman Sam Ervin and other committee members of bringing the hearings along gradually and building the evidence from the ground up is interesting. But such a leisurely pace may work against the committee's purpose, for it is proving to be too slow in developing testimony from those in position to know the full details about the White House's involvement in the scandal.

The danger in delaying the testimony of those who have first hand knowledge is that some of them may be indicted in the courts before they can testify. In that case some may decide it would be in their best interests to keep silent and their knowledge about Watergate could be permanently lost to the public.

For example, Mr. John Dean III, former White House counsel, is reputed to have information about an administration coverup of the Watergate facts and about an alleged White House offer of clemency to some if they would plead guilty and keep quiet.

But the administration, which claims it is cooperating fully in the Watergate investigation, is refusing to cooperate in granting Mr. Dean immunity from prosecution for what he tells the committee.

The Justice Department wants to go ahead with indictment and prosecution of Mr. Dean for crimes he may have committeed in connection with Watergate. But Mr. Dean says if he is indicted he'll probably never testify before the committee. The committee may run into similar difficulties with its most important witnesses if it delays too long and lets the prosecution get ahead of the Senate probe.

It is more important that the American people know the full extent of the corruption of the nation's political process during this administration than it is that a few minor figures be convicted and sent to prison. But it is clear that the administration — while claiming it is trying to help uncover the facts — is still doing what it can to keep the facts from coming out. The administration plainly doesn't want Mr. Dean on the Senate committee's witness stand.

Sen. Howard Baker, R-Tenn., member of the committee, says Senator Talmadge's prodding may result in calling the principal witnesses sooner than planned—probably by the end of June. Late June is better than late July or August, but it still may not be in time to obtain testimony uncomplicated by the involvements of criminal prosecution.

★ ★ ★

It is essential for the Ervin committee to get the most important Watergate witnesses on the stand as soon as it can—before ways are found to keep them quiet.

RICHARDSON IS CONFIRMED BY SENATE AFTER NAMING COX SPECIAL PROSECUTOR

Attorney General-designate Elliot L. Richardson May 18 appointed Harvard Law School professor Archibald Cox special prosecutor for the Watergate case. Cox, 61, a Democrat, had served as solicitor general in the Kennedy and Johnson Administrations. Richardson said he had not consulted the White House prior to the selection. He said he would submit the appointment to the Senate for confirmation, although that was not mandatory. Cox would be able to select his own staff, Richardson said, or use the staff currently investigating Watergate. The resources of the entire Justice Department, including the Federal Bureau of Investigation, would be available to Cox. Richardson said he would have no control over the investigation "for all practical day-to-day purposes." He would make no effort to keep tabs on the special prosecutor, he said, and Cox "will determine to what extent he will keep me informed" and the "occasions on which to consult me." Cox told reporters at Harvard May 18 he considered his main job as prosecutor was to "restore confidence in the honor, integrity and decency of government." He said he had "not the slightest doubt I will be independent." Cox was nominated for the post after it had been refused by two other candidates, U.S. Judge Harold J. Tyler Jr. and lawyer Warren M. Christopher.

The question of the special prosecutor's independence from Richardson was the dominant topic at the Senate Judiciary Committee's hearings on Richardson's nomination. Richardson May 17 sent the committee his guidelines for the role of the prosecutor. Among them: the prosecutor would serve within the Justice Department and would have "full" authority for the probe and prosecution of Watergate and for decisions on executive privilege or immunity. Richardson's nomination was unanimously approved by the committee May 23. He was confirmed as by the full Senate later in the day by an 82–3 vote and sworn in May 25.

Cox had appeared before the Senate Judiciary Committee May 21 to pledge that he would not "shield anybody and [did not] intend to be intimidated by anybody" in conducting a thorough and independent investigation of the Watergate affair. Asked how he would react to a possible request by President Nixon to provide the White House with progress reports of his investigation, Cox replied: "I would feel I would have the absolute right, if I felt it were against the interests of the investigation, to refuse. I would feel I had no official or legal duty to him. It would seem to me, I can't help remarking, an extraordinary request." Regarding the guidelines drawn up by Richardson insulating the special prosecutor's investigation from Administration pressure, Cox said: "It seems to me the only authority he [Richardson] has retained is to give me hell if I don't do the job, and I think he ought to keep that authority."

Evident committee satisfaction with Cox' testimony played a major part in the Senate's decision to confirm Richardson's nomination. After being assured by Cox that he would follow the "trail of federal crime ... wherever that trail may lead," key Committee member Sen. Robert C. Byrd (D, W. Va.) announced he would support the Richardson nomination, "albeit reluctantly."

DESERET NEWS
Salt Lake City, Utah, May 21, 1973

Now that Harvard law professor Archibald G. Cox has accepted the job of special prosecutor for the Watergate case, he should be freed from any political influence in his efforts to get at the facts.

Only in that manner can the public be assured that there will be no new cover-up attempt to hide the facts or to mitigate their importance.

One could feel more certain that is the course the investigation would follow if Attorney-General designate Elliot Richardson were not insisting on retaining "ultimate power of removal over the special prosecutor," as Richardson put it.

What Richardson means by those words should be thoroughly aired during Senate confirmation hearings which begin today. Would Cox be removed, for example, if the investigation began to implicate the President? Will Cox be his own man in developing his method and scope of inquiry, in interpreting the results, and other matters?

Richardson has said that Cox would have "full authority" in the investigation, and Cox has confirmed that it will be up to him whether he keeps Richardson briefed. That's an encouraging sign, but should be pinned down more firmly.

Another is the Richardson-Cox relationship of past years as student and teacher. Cox was one of Richardson's professors at Harvard Law School, and the implied message is one of continuing cordial relationships. That may or may not prove to be the case.

What is most hopeful about Cox's selection is the high regard in which he is held by many Senate members, and the perspective he has on his responsibilities.

"It's an enormously important job," Cox told the press after his selection. "It is essential to restore a sense of honor, of integrity, of confidence in our government. The only way to do it is through an investigation of the failures. It is an awesome task."

That it is. Not only must the guilty be brought to justice under careful application of the law, but the reputations of the innocent must be preserved. And it is already apparent from the Senate hearings into the case that guilt and innocence come in a wide variety of colors. Even the innocent are being tarnished by the black deeds of others.

Cox thinks the job can be done in 18 months. He may be on the optimistic side. The Teapot Dome scandals which resulted from the Harding administration took a special prosecutor six years to unravel.

Out of all this must come a new respect for the law — and that will be Prof. Cox' utmost charge. If the public feels the case is being handled judiciously and expeditiously, it can have a great healing effect in restoring public confidence in government integrity.

No wonder Cox labeled it "an awesome task."

THE DALLAS TIMES HERALD

Dallas, Tex., May 22, 1973

THE NIXON administration, it seems to us, has bent over backwards to establish that prosecution of the Watergate case won't be rigged.

As special prosecutor, Atty. Gen.-designate Elliot Richardson has named his old law professor, former U.S. Solicitor Gen. Archibald Cox.

Cox is a liberal, a Democrat, and an experienced courtroom practitioner. Accordingly, he ought to be acceptable to the Democrats. He has no national credentials which make him instantly acceptable to the general public, but the same would probably have been true of anyone Richardson appointed. It may be that Cox will prove a suitable choice.

Now that Cox has been selected, one hopes leading Senate Democrats will cease worrying themselves over the liberty of action he is to possess. Richardson has been criticized for not freeing the special prosecutor's hands altogether. "Ultimate power of removal over the special prosecutor," the attorney general-designate has declared, must rest with himself. As indeed it has to, unless it is proposed that Richardson create a Frankenstein's monster, then turn him loose to do what he will. That would be more latitude than even the President posesses.

Surely it is enough that Richardson pledges to Cox "the greatest degree of independence that is consistent with the attorney general's statutory accountability for all matters falling within the jurisdiction of the Department of Justice," and that Cox professes himself satisfied with that pledge.

Certain Democratic misgivings to the contrary, the administration is not going to be prosecuting itself. Archibald Cox will be doing that — and with spirit and resolution, unless we miss our guess.

Chicago Tribune

Chicago, Ill., May 21, 1973

The Senate hearings on Elliot Richardson's appointment as attorney general are to resume today. They will no doubt go a good deal more smoothly now that Mr. Richardson has announced his intention to name Archibald Cox, a Democrat, as special prosecutor in the Watergate affair.

It will be hard for even the strongest Nixon critic to object to the appointment. Indeed there is little in history to compare with the action of a Republican administration, up to its neck in an unsavory scandal, entrusting its reputation to a former Democratic solicitor general—and, what's more, a man appointed to that office by John F. Kennedy after he defeated Nixon in the bitter campaign of 1960.

So what began as a question whether a Nixon administration appointee could avoid pressure to soft pedal the investigation now becomes a question whether a Democratic prosecutor can avoid the temptation to make political capital by "getting" the Nixon administration.

This is a serious question which the senators must examine carefully. But while we have differed with Mr. Cox at times, we know of no reason to question his integrity or his desire to do a fair job. Clearly Mr. Richardson has confidence in him. Both went to Harvard, both taught there, both have been members of the Harvard Board of Overseers, and both worked for the same Boston law firm. Whatever may be said against the "old school tie" approach to public life, this job calls for somebody whom both Mr. Richardson and the administration's critics can trust, and Mr. Cox seems to fit the bill. He lacks trial experience, but can overcome this by naming a man with such experience as his deputy.

Mr. Cox says he is satisfied that he will have the necessary independence; Mr. Richardson meanwhile insists that he will bear the final responsibility for Mr. Cox's actions. Despite this apparent incompatibility, the two men seem to have agreed on their relationship. If a difference does develop, it is sure to be aired in public and any final decision will have to be justified to the public—or the investigation will lose its credibility and fail in its purpose.

Mr. Cox's experience in labor relations has equipped him to face sticky questions, and he will have plenty of them. One is what to do if the trail should lead beyond the President's advisers and to the President himself. We agree with those legal experts who say he should turn any such information over to the House of Representatives, which is the only body constitutionally empowered to act against the President.

As for granting immunity, he should do so as sparingly as possible, if at all.

Finally, there's the matter of time. Mr. Cox predicts that the job will take at least a year. Teapot Dome dragged on for five years. Watergate already has escalated into a much worse scandal than if the White House had come clean right away. Unlike the case with Teapot Dome, the administration involved now is still in office and will be at a disadvantage as long as any doubts remain. It is therefore in the interests of both the administration and the country to get the job done as quickly as possible, consistent with thoroness and fairness.

The Boston Globe

Boston, Mass., May 25, 1973

There have been two main streams from which the truth, the whole truth and nothing but the truth could be ascertained for the people of this coutnry about Watergate and all its ramifications. One, now flowing daily over nationwide television, was and is the hearings of the Senate committee headed by Sen. Sam Ervin (D-N C.). It has been doing a most commendable job.

The other stream has been legal and criminal proceedings in court, in some of which former high officials and others have been indicted and in which no less than eight grand juries have been involved. But this stream for weeks has been blocked by a logjam after the resignation of Atty. Gen. Richard Kleindienst and debate over President Nixon's appointment of Elliot L. Richardson to succeed him and direct the overall supervision of the Watergate cases.

That logjam has now been broken up, and fortuitously so, with the Senate's resounding 82-to-3 vote to confirm his appointment, and with the assurance that Prof. Archibald N. Cox of Harvard Law School will have a free rein as Mr. Richardson's special Watergate prosecutor.

It should be said at this point that the press, including The Globe, has overreacted, in its treatment of news stories, columns and editorials, by over-estimating the trouble in which Mr. Richardson found himself. The reason for this was not any naivete, but rather the full knowledge of past attempts by others to cover up the facts and of the danger of future attempts. Still and all, there was overreaction.

But now it is at an end. We believe both Mr. Richardson and Mr. Cox are superbly qualified to take charge of the legal proceedings in the case and to detect any further cover-up by anyone. And Mr. Cox, himself a former US Solicitor General, has brought with him two able legal aides from Cambridge, Harvard Law Profs. Philip B. Heymann and James Vorenberg.

For Mr. Richardson the Senate vote was a tremendous tribute, not merely because the vote was so overwhelming but because he is the only high official in a very long time to have received from the Senate three confirmations of appointment to Cabinet Office.

He has doubtless learned much in his sometimes tortuous passage from Undersecretary of State first to Health, Education and Welfare, then Defense and now to the Justice Department. It is an exceptional experience. During it he has often deserved high praise, but on several occasions—most notably on busing and the bombing of Cambodia — has merited criticism for what we regard as compromising on matters of principle.

It must be quite a change now for this frank admirer and follower of President Nixon for the last four years to be so suddenly cast in the role of the only reliable, "clean" high official the Nixon Administration could find to see that justice is done. By confirming him the Senate has given him a mandate to investigate thoroughly the Administration and the last campaign of his political hero. That is quite a turn of the tables.

In this task, doubtless he will know better, even if tempted, than to exert any undue influence — or even the appearance of it — upon Mr. Cox, his former law teacher. He owes Mr. Cox a great debt for assuring his confirmation, and moreover Cox's own record proves him to be honest, fair, conservative, and in political debt to no one.

Mr. Richardson and all others may be sure that even the most subtle pressure upon Cox would result in a reaction that would send Mr. Richardson back to private life for good. And we think Mr. Richardson and, by now, the rest of the Administration are smart enough to know this.

In naming Mr. Cox, Richardson has done what he does best — attracting good men to help him. If he convinces the public that he let an honest job be done, his political future is bright. And there are two possibilities here.

If he restores credibility to President Nixon, the Republicans will know how to reward him in 1976. Calvin Coolidge got to the White House on much less — his statement as governor during the Boston police strike that "There is no right to strike against the public safety by anybody, anywhere, any time."

If on the other hand Mr. Richardson's prosecution leads to discrediting Mr. Nixon permanently, or even to his resignation, Richardson would still come through untarnished, and the only such in town. He might have troubles in reaching the Presidency—perhaps from Vice President Agnew or John Connally, or perhaps from a certain woodenness in televised speech, or from the kind of wobbling on principles that he has already shown. But he would still be "Mr. Clean."

And that is saying a lot.

Elliot Richardson's public record shows that he thrives on challenges. He should meet his latest and biggest one with relish, not forgetting the "back-of-the-hand" he received from Messrs. Haldeman and Ehrlichman when they referred to him as the "professor who didn't know anything about politics."

He is now, apart from the President, the biggest Administration man in Washington.

For the sake of the nation and its spirit and self-confidence, we extend to Elliot Richardson and his Democratic professor-prosecutor the very best wishes as they try to show that the American system of government, though beset by grave crisis, can really work.

The Evening Gazette

Worcester, Mass., May 22, 1973

The United States Senate would do well to accept Archibald Cox as special prosecutor for the Watergate scandal and quit the semantic dueling game with Elliot L. Richardson.

Richardson's confirmation as new broom in the Justice Department probably hinges on the definition of acceptable ground rules for a further judicial probe of Watergate.

The ability of a Nixon appointee such as Richardson to bear final responsibility for an all-out investigation has been legitimately questioned.

As one politician put the problem: "I believe that Richardson would follow the trail all the way to the President's door, if necessary. But if the trail doesn't lead that far, will the people believe the attorney general when he says so?"

Or as conservative Sen. Robert Byrd, D-W. Va., said: "I just wish he (Richardson) would disqualify himself. It makes no difference how pure he is. The result is that this investigation, in the minds of many, will still be impure...but he seems unwilling to go that absolute last mile."

The last mile, in the eye of the critics, would be for Richardson to remove himself from any role in the investigation.

But could he, or any attorney general, do that?

As the nation's highest law enforcement officer, the attorney general must bear the final, ultimate authority for the manner in which the federal code is upheld. That he must also be the appointee of the incumbent president is an inevitability of our system.

So it would seem that if Congress wishes to remove the Justice Department from prosecution of the Watergate case, new laws will be required. That course of action is possible, but has not been a significant part of the debate thus far.

Richardson, on the other hand, has gone about as far as he can go to assure the freedom and independence of the special prosecutor without abandoning his own Constitutional prerogatives.

By choosing Cox, Richardson has neutralized any aspersions of political prejudice. Cox is an outspoken Democrat who served as solicitor general under Presidents Kennedy and Johnson. He supported George McGovern for president and has been critical of President Nixon's stewardship.

On the legal side, Cox brings a distinguished career as an expert on labor law at Harvard. He has arbitrated disputes as diverse and complex as a Worcester teacher contract and the Columbia University disruptions of 1968.

Richardson himself has granted Cox "full independence and complete authority" in the Watergate case. The mandate even allows the special prosecutor to determine whether and to what extent he will consult with the attorney general.

Perhaps the best guarantee of all is Cox's character. Most observers agree that he would blow the whistle loudly if any attempts were made to interfere with his work.

At this point, the Senate confirmation of Richardson and tacit approval of Cox would help the nation down the last mile of the Watergate journey. Beyond lies the hope of a renewed faith that justice will be done at highest levels of government.

THE SAGINAW NEWS

Saginaw, Mich., May 27, 1973

The Senate's virtually unanimous confirmation of Elliot L. Richardson to be the new U.S. attorney general carries with it much greater signficance than Mr. Richardson's elevation to the nation's top law enforcement officer. It opens the way for the one probe of the Watergate break-in and related abuses of the political process that can establish the facts and pin down the abusers—for with Richardson comes Archibald Cox, distinguished professor of law at Harvard, the man designated to do just that.

And now that the confirmation of one gives the green light to the other, it is absolutely essential that Archibald Cox get on with his work as soon as possible. This man faces an enormous task. He bears a heavy responsibility. In effect the nation has reposed its trust in him to untangle Watergate and associated events bearing the marks of scandal and come up with the facts and the names.

This is not something that can be accomplished in a matter of weeks but more likely over a period of months. Yet the sooner the job can be completed, formal indictments issued and the accused brought to trial, the sooner the truth will be known, justice can be served and this nation can once again pull its frazzled nerves together — hopefully with some renewed confidence in government.

Still, it can be said that Professor Cox enters the picture under most unusual circumstances.

First he had to satisfy Elliot Richardson that he was a man capable of doing the job. Then he had to be willing to accept the assignment after others had turned it down. Then he had to satisfy the Senate. And finally Mr. Richardson had to satisfy the Senate Judiciary Committee that if it was to be Richardson in as attorney general and Cox in as the government's chief prosecutor, there had to be maximum assurances that Cox would operate with a free and independent hand.

Thus there was quite a straining process before everything fell into place—and on the latter insistence of the Senate about a free and independent hand, Mr. Richardson did have to give some ground, considerable ground, in fact, from the way he had originally perceived the working relationship between himself and the designated investigator.

Hence one of the most unusual attorney general confirmations in history in which the nation's top legal investigator has agreed to yield up normal powers to the man he named to work for him.

In all probability, under normal conditions there would have been no such delay in confirming Mr. Richardson, a man considered of impeccable character in Washington and one already previously confirmed to two other Cabinet level posts. But these are not normal times around the nation's capital and the Senate insisted on full satisfaction in this situation.

As a result, Cox commences his long and arduous probe about as clean and free-handed as it is possible to be.

He has been given the authority to hire his own staff under guidelines mutually agreed to by Richardson, himself and the Senate Judiciary Committee. He is empowered to conduct grand jury proceedings, initiate prosecutions, and decide whether to seek immunity for witnesses. He will have full access to documentary evidence from any source. He can make use of whatever it is he wishes to make use of that has been turned up in various hearings conducted by congressional committees.

In short, Mr. Cox' authority is virtually unlimited. He is free to roam where he wishes, summon who he wants and investigate unfettered by any restraints placed upon him by Attorney General Richardson.

Thus Cox becomes the investigator, Mr. Richardson the recipient of his findings.

"I will not countermand or interfere with the special prosecutor's decisions or actions," Richardson has told the Senate Judiciary Committee.

Cox has said that he is completely satisfied that this arrangement gives him all of the freedom he needs and that he will follow the probe wherever it leads. Eighty-two members of the Senate of 85 voting are also satisfied that the federal government is now properly geared to investigate Watergate objectively.

It is now up to Archibald Cox, the law professor summoned by a former law student, to press forward with vigor. He has the authority. He has the independence. He has the legal skill. He has the power to bring order out of chaos and to see that justice is served. That makes him not only an important man but a man to be feared by those who have anything to fear.

Arkansas Gazette.

Little Rock, Ark., May 30, 1973

Barely had the Senate confirmed Elliot Richardson as Attorney General — against the better judgment, surely, of many of the members —than there was Richard Nixon into the breach, trying to exploit for all it was worth the latest opening the Congress had given him, pretty much out of the goodness of its heart.

Nixon himself, *in person*, showed up for the swearing in ceremony at the White House, described by the news services as "unusually elaborate" for such an occasion, all things considered. A gallery claque had been provided, made up not just of the appointee's personal family, but of some of the other interchangeable parts of the Nixon machine, including some like Richardson's predecessor as A-G — Richard G. Kleindienst — who we suppose figured to benefit retroactively by a kind of rub-off from Richardson's image as one of the administration's "clean" guys. (Richardson's clean-ness, to us, is a relative thing, for the rub-off works both ways; in fine, we do not see how anyone could stay on in this administration, however innocent or wrongdoing himself, without feeling just a little sullied by the exposure.)

Nixon's news photographs are beginning to look more and more bizarre, and this time (Friday) he appeared to have been made up to look like the late Bela Lugosi playing the late Count Dracula of Transylvania. (Our advice to all those "dogs" Mr. Nixon says keep showing up for White House parties is to not allow their host any affectionate nips on the neck.)

The President did not stay for the swearing in of Archibald Cox, as the choice of Nixon's choice (Richardson) to be the independent prosecutor who supposedly will pursue the Watergate thread all the way back to daylight. Instead, Mr. Nixon had to whip off, first, to Key Biscayne, and thence to Grand Cay and the island retreat of Robert H. Abplanalp, the "Angel of San Clemente" (or, at least, the financial angel of Mr. Nixon's "other" second White House there.) The haste of the President's departure, one judges, is a fair gauge of his concern that Archibald Cox will really get at the truth in the Watergate affair.

Mr. Nixon did not leave, however, until after he had ostentatiously announced that Mr. Richardson, as Attorney General, would continue to sit on the National Security Council, as he had been entitled by right to do in the last musical chair he had occupied, which was that of Secretary of Defense.

This little reward to the Democrats in Congress without whose votes Richardson could not have been confirmed was supposed to undergird the propaganda note Nixon lately has fallen back upon with regard to the Watergate and everything else, the fanciful — not to say, mendacious — notion that any threat to the re-election of himself as President or the election of anyone he may choose as his intended successor must be, perforce, a threat to the security of the Republic. Richardson, beaming, took it all in.

The new Attorney General's own contribution to the great occasion was curious enough, we thought, when read against Mr. Nixon's transparent National Security Council gambit of the same day, and, more particularly, when read against Mr. Nixon's intemperate remarks at his big POW party the day before, when he implied that he would have Daniel Ellsberg's psychiatrist's office ransacked again, if it came to that, and the evidence of wiretaps placed on Ellsberg illegally concealed by the Justice Department again, all in the name, again of "the National security."

What Elliot Richardson said was that as Attorney General, he would put "the individual" first and "the truth" second: "The first of these demands fairness; the second demands fearlessness. I will endeavor to be faithful to it." No, Mr. Attorney General, the truth has to come first, always, and if it is really *the* truth, the rights of the individual will take care of themselves.

It is hard not to regard the inversion here as a play on *another* of the administration's lately-developed theme, a belated concern for the rights of the individual that surfaced only after its own people started getting caught out and that still does not — as we have seen — extend to anyone whom the Chief Magistrate chooses to regard as a threat to his feeling of "security."

HERALD EXAMINER

Los Angeles, Calif., May 22, 1973

The designation of Harvard law professor Archibald Cox as special Watergate prosecutor could constitute a major step toward cleaning up the mess and restoring public confidence in the integrity of its national leadership.

As the nations's Solicitor General under Presidents Kennedy and Johnson, and as chairman of the Wage Stabilization Board under President Truman, he understands Washington power politics as well as he knows law and official responsibility.

Although a Democrat, Prof. Cox has a reputation for political independence. Colleagues and former associates alike describe him as a hard-nosed man of the highest competence whose objectivity is impervious to stress.

Far too much time has been lost already in getting an impartial special prosecutor of outstanding ability to insure full disclosures and justice in the Watergate case. Senate confirmation action on Cox should be concluded as quickly as possible so he can get on with that kind of total cleanup.

BUFFALO EVENING NEWS

Buffalo, N.Y., May 21, 1973

Archibald Cox — Democrat, former top government lawyer and Harvard law professor — impresses us as an excellent choice for special prosecutor in the Watergate scandals that have rocked the Nixon administration to its foundations. He is a better choice, in fact, than any of the less well-known names bandied about earlier.

His selection by U. S. Atty. Gen.-designate Elliot Richardson, along with the guidelines that both men have agreed to concerning how the assignment will be handled, should reassure the public that a rigorously independent investigation is in the making. They also, in our view, merit prompt confirmation by the Senate.

The political loyalties of Mr. Cox, a Democrat who worked in the presidential campaign of John Kennedy against Mr. Nixon in 1960 and who voted for Sen. George McGovern in last fall's presidential election, obviously do not lie with the Republican President.

As U. S. solicitor general under Presidents Kennedy and Johnson, a job that involved arguing the government's case before the Supreme Court, Mr. Cox had extensive legal experience at the highest levels in Washington. As a professor at Harvard, he knows the perspectives and breadth of the law as a scholar. Among other personal qualities, Mr. Cox is regarded by those who know him as learned, unflappable, stubborn, "friendly but not warm," self-confident and perhaps even arrogant. Whatever else that implies, it suggests a tough-minded independence of judgment. As for his courage, his willingness to undertake such a demanding assignment speaks for itself.

Beyond this, the guidelines to which Mr. Richardson stands publicly committed seem certain to magnify and strengthen Mr. Cox's independence. He is to have a free hand in choosing his staff. He would decide questions of immunity for witnesses and whether to challenge assertions of executive privilege. He would be free to handle relations with congressional committees and to decide on indictments and prosecutions. Mr. Cox said any evidence implicating the President "would be reported" and that he will from time to time "make public such statements or reports" as he deems appropriate.

Mr. Richardson, correctly we believe, will retain the ultimate authority to dismiss the special prosecutor, but here again he is publicly pledged to do so only for "extraordinary improprieties." Mr. Cox's ultimate power, by the same token, lies in his right to resign at any time he feels he cannot conduct the investigation as he sees fit.

It is important at the outset for the Senate, which must confirm the attorney general and will have the opportunity to approve the special prosecutor, to be satisfied with them and with the ground rules for this investigation. We hope that can be achieved promptly, so that the process of unearthing the full truth about Watergate, and bringing those responsible for it to justice, can proceed fairly and vigorously as soon as possible

TESTIMONY RESUMES AS COX REQUEST IS DENIED

The Senate Watergate committee rejected June 5 a request from special prosecutor Archibald Cox to delay its public hearings until further resolution of the "enormously complex" federal case. In requesting the delay in a letter to the committee June 4, Cox had argued that "the continuation of hearings at this time would create grave danger that the full facts about the Watergate case and related matters will never come to light and that many of those who are guilty of serious wrong-doing will never be brought to justice." He was not suggesting that the hearings be called off, Cox said, but that he be given time—one to three months—"to assess this enormously complex case and to advise the select committee about the consequences of the appearance of particular witnesses at televised hearings." He was of the opinion that public hearings prior to further development of the federal probe would impede the probe and "increase the risk" that major guilty parties, "quite possibly all" of them, would go unpunished.

Chairman Sam J. Ervin Jr. (D, N.C.) said the committee voted unanimously to continue the hearings in light of three considerations: (1) the panel was authorized by the Senate to conduct the probe and had no authority to postpone it; (2) the committee did not agree that the courts would "permit guilty parties to go unwhipped of justice" because of the hearings; and (3) there was more likelihood of a "fair trial in an atmosphere of judicial calm" after the hearings than before its probe was done. The government had been investigating the case for almost a year, he pointed out, while Watergate cast a "dark cloud" over the nation and the "government has come to a virtual standstill."

The Ervin committee also rejected June 5 proposals from Sens. Herman E. Talmadge (D, Ga.) and Edward J. Gurney (R, Fla.) to speed up the hearings and immediately call high-level witnesses to determine as soon as possible President Nixon's role in the Watergate affair.

Former Republican Finance Committee Chairman Maurice H. Stans testified before the committee June 12-13. Under pointed questioning from committee chairman Ervin and other senators, Stans denied any knowledge of or involvement in the Watergate break-in attempt or subsequent cover-up. Stans, whose appeal to delay his testimony was denied by the committee, claimed he had been entirely isolated from policy decisions regarding use of the money he had collected for the Nixon campaign.

Jeb Stuart Magruder, former deputy director of the Committee to Re-elect the President, told the Watergate committee June 14 that he, campaign director John H. Mitchell and other high White House and campaign officials had authorized the wiretapping of the Democratic National Committee headquarters at the Watergate building as part of a "broad intelligence-gathering" scheme. When their agents were arrested at the Watergate, Magruder said the same Nixon aides decided immediately and without debate to fabricate a cover-up story in order to protect Nixon's re-election chances. Magruder admitted he had perjured himself numerous times by denying involvement in the break-in attempt and provided the committee with its only first-hand account linking former Attorney General Mitchell to the plot. Magruder also named former White House chief of staff H. R. Haldeman and former Nixon counsel John W. Dean 3rd as parties to the cover-up conspiracy. Magruder said he believed Nixon was unaware of the wiretap operations and cover-up attempt. Magruder also claimed that Stans had been told of the cover-up about the funds.

Chief Judge John J. Sirica of the U.S. district court in Washington had granted Dean and Magruder immunity June 12 for their testimony before the Senate committee. He also had rejected a request from Watergate special prosecutor Archibald Cox to bar television and radio coverage of their testimony. The immunity grant meant that prosecution would have to be based on evidence gathered independent of the Senate testimony. In another ruling June 12, Sirica denied a grant of immunity for Dean before the grand jury. He ordered Dean to "appear before the grand jury immediately following court proceedings this morning."

ALBUQUERQUE JOURNAL

Albuquerque, N.M., June 2, 1973

Once more the White House has repudiated its own commitments by issuing directives to Attorney General Elliot Richardson and his impartial Watergate prosecutor, Archibald Cox, pertaining to a news leak.

This intervention strongly implies the administration's unwillingness to respect the mandate that Cox be permitted to perform his duties with complete independence from White House pressures.

But the White House action is disturbing in these additional aspects:

— It indicates that the administration is continuing along an established course of obstructing the gathering and publication of newsworthy data.

— It betrays a persistence on the part of the administration to intervene in the judicial processes of government. The latest act of White House arrogance only amplifies earlier efforts to limit testimony and prosecutions in the Watergate trials and President Nixon's own extraordinary communications with U.S. District Judge William M. Byrne Jr. while the Pentagon Papers trial was in progress.

The administration's recent efforts to draw broad lines delineating the realms of the executive, legislative and judicial branches of government is not without merit, but its sincerity is open to question when it deliberately stretches, bends and extends the lines drawn around its own realm.

THE CHRISTIAN SCIENCE MONITOR
Boston, Mass., June 14, 1973

The Senate Watergate hearings will continue to be offered to the American public over color television in spite of Vice-President Spiro Agnew's objections. This is both a mixed blessing and also as it should be.

It should be because Federal Judge John J. Sirica declined to ban television from the hearings on the soundest of legal and constitutional grounds. "The court," he said, "could not go beyond administering its own affairs and attempt to regulate proceedings before a coordinate branch of government."

It is a mixed blessing because there are two sides to the question of getting information to the public by way of television. Mr. Agnew was being excessively pessimistic about the televised hearings when he said they would cause "a swelling flood of prejudicial publicity" which would make it "virtually impossible" to find an impartial jury in Watergate cases. We have more confidence than he in the capacity of American jurors to watch television without being unduly or unfairly influenced. But television is no more perfect as a channel of information to the public than any other. It does have enormous impact. And there is an element of theater in it which can and sometimes does work against judiciousness.

Mr. Agnew's desire for a ban on television coverage of the Watergate hearings is politically understandable. Much that is being said there is not favorable to the administration. Judging from some of his past speeches he would like to convert television from critic into handmaiden.

Thanks to Judge Sirica American television is not to be put into the handmaidenly position. It will continue its imperfect coverage of the action on the Senate committee stage which will not always be judicial and may sometimes unfairly impugn the reputation of some possible future defendant in a criminal case.

But the greater good is the presentation of as much information as possible to the public over whatever channel is available. And those who would protect the present administration in this case by keeping television out of the Senate hearings must remember that there might at some future day be a different political party in office. Any benefit which is claimed today for the present White House would work to the advantage of a future incumbent of another party. Would Mr. Agnew want to exclude television from Senate hearings if those on the witness stand were all Democrats?

Judge Sirica deserves commendation for his ability to keep his eye fixed firmly on the law and the facts. He was being asked to bar television from the Senate

hearings on the ground that it might damage future prosecutions to be brought by the office of the special prosecutor in the Watergate cases. But as yet, Judge Sirica noted, "there are no indictments, no defendants and no trials." The court, he said, "cannot act on suppositions." "The matter is simply not ripe for judicial action."

The problem of television and the hearings has been stated as a choice between getting the truth into the open by the hearings or the culprits behind bars by legal proceedings. We doubt that they are mutually exclusive. We are confident that Special Prosecutor Archibald Cox will find it possible to prosecute effectively no matter what happens in the Senate committee. Meanwhile it is right and proper that Judge Sirica decide the matter of television on legal, not on philosophical, grounds.

THE KNICKERBOCKER NEWS
··· UNION-STAR ···
Albany, N.Y., June 6, 1973

The dispute between Archibald Cox, special Watergate prosecutor, and Senator Sam J. Ervin Jr. over whether Senator Ervin's committee should postpone its Watergate inquiry boils down to a single question:

Do the American people want more to know just what has been going on in Washington or do they want legal guilt determined and someone sent to jail.

The first of those two choices must take precedence. The Senate inquiry should continue without delay.

Mr. Cox, in his careful legal fashion, makes a considerable case for delay. He doesn't want possible prosecutions imperiled by disclosure before the Senate. And, quite rightfully, he raises the question that innocent persons might be injured by the public hearings. His argument that the public hearings would impede his investigation cannot be taken as bearing great weight.

What is essential in these Watergate proceedings is that the truth be ferreted out and that not only illegal acts be uncovered but also those that skirted the edge of legality while being unethical, immoral or simply stupid. Conviction in the courts is of lesser concern. Continuation of the Senate hearings is the proper way to bring out the entire story.

Are the innocent endangered by the Senate inquiry? If a Joe McCarthy were presiding, the answer would have to be yes. But Senator Ervin is taking great care to distinguish between evidence and hearsay, he is being meticulous in preventing the hearings from becoming a witch hunt, he is a man of probity. There is little danger to the innocent from the manner in which the hearings are being conducted.

Mr. Cox, in asking delay, acted in good conscience, most certainly, and followed the dictates of his legal training. In this instance, however, public display of the facts through Senate proceedings is the swifter and surer road to justice.

The Courier-Journal
Louisville, Ky., June 6, 1973

SPECIAL PROSECUTOR Archibald Cox put as well as anyone could the case for postponing the Senate's Watergate investigating committee hearings while he pursues the more traditional paths of judicial inquiry. But Committee Chairman Sam Ervin was more persuasive in arguing that the greater public good lies in "the right of the people of the United States to learn, as speedily as possible," how high and how wide the evils of Watergate ran.

The key point was acknowledged by Mr. Cox himself, in his concession that "There is more to this question than whether one or two people go to jail. Confidence in our institutions is at stake." This confidence would not necessarily be restored if a year or two from now—after Mr. Cox and his investigators have pursued the various threads of Watergate through the labyrinth of the judicial process—various people are brought to trial and convicted.

It may well be that the Ervin committee's televised hearings will, as Mr. Cox cautions, prejudice by pre-trial publicity or grants of immunity the chances for full prosecution of the guilty. But it is equally true that his own investigation could be derailed by the willingness of some defendants—as in the Watergate burglary trial which was "saved" only by the curiosity and toughness of Judge Sirica—to plead guilty and never say a word that would implicate others or bring out more of the truth.

So anyone with a feel for the traditional processes of law will welcome Mr. Cox' statement, which puts so well the various arguments for letting due process run its course. But the arguments on the other side, as marshaled by Senator Ervin and others, are stronger because they run deeper.

The importance of the My Lai investigation, for example, was not that it resulted in the conviction of a young platoon leader for atrocities in wartime. It was in the clear finding—to the satisfaction of the public if not to courts bound by all the strictures of the laws of evidence—that although Lieutenant Calley may not have been following direct orders, he was doing what many of his colleagues also assumed to be desired by their superiors all the way to the top.

The lasting importance of the Nuremberg and Eichmann trials was not that victorious nations executed or imprisoned high-ranking Nazis for crimes against mankind, since what these men had done was behind them. It was that the world became aware of the point at which obedience to orders becomes a denial of higher and universal laws of civilized behavior.

The importance of the televised Army-McCarthy hearings was not that the Senator's case was shown to be so flimsy or that he was later censured by colleagues. It was that the people finally grasped the essence of a kind of tyranny, rooted in public fear, that was as evil as anything it purported to expose.

Similarly, the lasting importance of the Watergate hearings is not whether they result in convictions. It's in what we learn, as a nation, about how to minimize the chances that such perversions of leadership can happen again.

Boston Herald American

Combining the best features of the Herald Traveler and Record American

Boston, Mass., June 10, 1973

The two extraordinary requests made this week by Special Prosecutor Archibald Cox—first that the Senate postpone its investigation of the Watergate mess, second that parts of the inquiry should be closed to the press and the public if it can't be postponed—were entirely out of order. And fortunately, both requests were promptly and flatly denied.

Though we can appreciate and sympathize with Mr. Cox's concern for the rights of the Watergate defendants and the danger that some of the guilty could go scot free as a result of pre-trial publicity stemming from the Senate probe, these problems cannot be allowed to thwart a full and completely open search for the truth. That objective still must receive the greatest priority.

The Senate's investigation to date, however, is hardly moving toward that objective with the despatch and sense of direction that is obviously essential to such an enterprise. In fact, the probe so far has been painfully slow and ponderous, moving at a snail's pace, questioning witnesses who for the most part played relatively minor roles in the scandal and dwelling to a large degree on matters which are tedious and trivial.

Unless it calls the major witnesses soon and begins to zero in on the single, overriding issue of the entire Watergate mess—determining who was really behind the whole business and whether or not or to what extent President Nixon may have been implicated—the Senate is likely to bore the nation to death and might just as well postpone its hearings.

For the unhurried pace of the investigation so far and its failure to focus on the central issue, as our columnist William S. White remarked the other day, is the equivalent of the Chinese water-torture treatment "which is falling drop by agonizingly slow drop upon the capital's morale."

What is worse still, the longer this agony continues, the longer the President and the rest of the government will be hobbled in trying to carry out the necessary functions of running the nation and attending to the urgent business that lies ahead.

We're not suggesting that the complete Watergate mystery can be solved overnight, nor that the Senate should proceed with its probe with undue haste. But it is not unreasonable to submit that that the investigation should now begin to focus on the main issue and call the principal witnesses as quickly as possible.

After all, it is not the Senate's duty to prosecute anyone. Nor is it required to follow the painstakingly slow judicial procedures which Archibald Cox must observe and which will obviously be necessary before the entire case is unraveled in the courts.

It is the Senate's job to determine as best it can where the major responsibility for the Watergate mess lies, and to provide the public with the answer to that question as soon as possible. That job can best be done by postponing the testimony of minor witnesses, eliminating much of the trivia and turning to the central issue and the principal witnesses without further delay.

HOUSTON CHRONICLE

Houston, Tex., June 13, 1973

It is wholly refreshing in these times to come upon an official who forthrightly says he has no power to do something. The country has been subjected to an endless spate of claims of power by this or that individual or body; it has almost seemed sinful to admit the lack of it.

Those who abhor the arrogance of power and power-seekers can take heart from U.S. District Judge John J. Sirica of Washington. Sirica candidly noted Tuesday that his court "lacks completely any power of intervention" when he was asked to restrict the Senate committee probing the Watergate affair to either closed sessions or no broadcast coverage when questioning potential defendants in criminal cases.

It is not necessary to agree or disagree with the effect of Sirica's ruling to admire the philosophy of a man who — in a power-grabbing world — grants there are things beyond his authority.

This is not the first time in the Watergate scandals when people have had reason to be appreciative of Judge Sirica. His skepticism and perseverance after justice in the original trial of those who actually broke into Democratic National Headquarters was a major factor in finally bringing the case into the open, breaking the wall of cover-up which had surrounded it.

Now that the Senate committee's right to proceed as it sees fit has been established, we trust it will act as befits anyone in authority, with responsibility, taking into consideration of its own accord the proper reservations which were expressed about the rights of those appearing before it.

St. Louis Globe-Democrat

St. Louis, Mo., June 2, 1973

Special Watergate Prosecutor Archibald Cox has asked the U.S. Senate Select Committee headed by Sen. Sam J. Ervin Jr. of North Carolina to stop all hearings on the grounds they are jeopardizing future trials.

If Ervin and other members of his committee seriously want to see justice done, they will grant Cox's request. Mr. Cox, who was solicitor general under President Kennedy, is very highly regarded in the legal profession. If he has concluded the Ervin Committee hearing may undermine future trials, that is more than sufficient grounds to cancel them.

Refusing Cox's request can only mean that the Senators on the Ervin Committee are more interested in staging a sideshow than in seeking successful prosecution of those allegedly involved.

☆ ☆ ☆

From what we have seen, it is evident that the committee, dominated by Democrats, has designed its proceedings so they can be stretched out interminably—perhaps six months or more. The intent appears to be to heap the maximum amount of horror and public indignation upon President Nixon and anyone allegedly involved.

In their anxiety to gain total revenge upon the President and former top aides whom they detest with a passion, certain Democrats appear willing to bombard the nation with an endless diet of rumor, hearsay and invective no matter what effect all of this may have on future trials.

But they misjudge the American people. The public already has indicated it is growing weary of the Ervin Committee's three-ring circus. Television networks are cutting back their coverage, as viewers demand a return of their regular shows.

This is not because those who watch television are unaware of the seriousness of the charges. And it isn't because they are not repelled by the alleged activities of agents and directors of the infamous Committee for the Re-election of the President. It is simply because they recognize that the committee hearings have been programmed to stretch out this nauseating business until the whole country is physically ill.

If the Ervin Committee had really wanted to get to the bottom of the Watergate affair, it would have held the introductory questioning to a minimum and then called Mr. Nixon's former top lieutenants—John Mitchell, Maurice Stans, H. R. Haldeman, John Ehrlichman and Charles Colson.

But, no, the committee apparently felt it had the duty to punish the public with every last lingering detail of the bugging fiasco and the unexpurgated accounts of James McCord, Bernard Barker and other "poor fish" caught in the enveloping web of Watergate.

☆ ☆ ☆

What committee members failed to see is that this Chinese water torture approach could jeopardize the investigation of the Special Prosecutor and at the same time bring about mass revulsion by Americans.

At this moment the nation is under a Watergate Pall. Congress itself is neglecting serious business as many of its members spend great amounts of time expressing righteous indignation about the sorry episode.

The best and the quickest way to conclude the Watergate investigation is to give Special Prosecutor Cox a clear field. This means that Senator Ervin and members of his committee will have to forego further hearings on Watergate.

This does not involve the question of the Senate committee's right to conduct hearings. If a majority of the committee decide to push ahead no matter what the consequences to Special Prosecutor Cox's probe, they probably can. But in the interest of justice and fairness, they should stop. We are certain this is the decision most Americans want.

The Topeka Daily Capital

Topeka, Kans., June 7, 1973

On the surface, it appears the Democrat-controlled U.S. Senate is at cross-purposes with itself. It wants prosecution of the guilty in the Watergate scandal, but it will not forgo the opportunity to make political hay of it.

On the one hand, the Seante created a Select Committee, chaired by Sen. Sam J. Ervin Jr., D-N.C., to investigate the Watergate affair and related incidents.

On the other, it demanded and won a voice in the naming of a special prosecutor to conduct an independent investigation of the Watergate caper and bring guilty persons to justice.

Senators approved wholeheartedly the appointment of Archibald Cox as a condition of confirmation of Elliot L. Richardson as attorney general. They contended at the time they wanted a special prosecutor who would be free of Nixon administration influence.

But now, when Cox wanted the senators to delay their investigation of Watergate for 90 days while he proceeded with his investigation, they turned him down out of hand. The Senate hearings are being telecast in their entirety, an opportunity for nation exposure senators find irresistible.

Cox expressed the fear that publicity generated by the Senate hearings could make it impossible for any defendant to get a fair trial and would destroy chances for convictions.

Senator Ervin replied quickly that the investigation had been going a year and that the Senate couldn't damage anything now because it would not impede the search for truth.

Ervin expressed concern, too, th   if he were to accede to Cox's request for the 90-day delay that there would be an additional delay of six months or more while trials proceeded.

Sen. Herman E. Talmadge, D-Ga., was blunt in his rebuff of Cox. He said that Cox had been an executive branch employe only seven days and he should get on with his own job and not try to advise the Senate of its responsibilities.

Cox's written request brought answers from the Democratic senators which showed conclusively they are more interested in piling up political points for themselves than in bringing the guilty into the open for prosecution.

Before Cox requested the delay by the Senate Select Committee, there had been expressions of concern over the Select Committee's authority to grant immunity to witnesses in selected situations in exchange for testimony.

By injudicious granting of immunity by the Senate committee, the kingpin of the Watergate burglary and bugging could slip through the fingers of the prosecutors. Cox added that all might go free under grants of immunity to some.

Were it not for the golden opportunity to get hours and hours of free national television time and exposure, the senators might have been more willing to leave the investigation to Cox, the man they accepted with full faith.

Perhaps if the TV networks would withdraw their cameras, the senators would get back to work on some projects much more urgent than the droning, repetitive questioning of witnesses to obtain answers which already are public knowledge.

Instead of an investigation, the Senate Select Committee is turning its inquiry into a political circus. What the people really want is a speedy conclusion to the whole mess.

THE WALL STREET JOURNAL.

New York, N.Y., June 14, 1973

Testimony by John W. Dean III before the Senate Watergate subcommittee, currently scheduled for next week, may well provide new shocks and carry the investigation into ever more dangerous waters.

Yet we can find little fault with Senator Ervin and members of his subcommittee for obtaining immunity for Mr. Dean and pressing on with the hearings over the objections of Special Prosecutor Cox. The committee chairman was right when he said it is more important for the American people to get the facts than to send a few people to jail; matters have gone too far for backtracking on that sound position now.

If what Mr. Dean has leaked is supportable, his testimony could be the ninth wave of the tide of doubt that has been threatening the President. According to Newsweek, Mr. Dean has told investigators among other things that the President was aware of a Watergate cover-up effort in the White House and that the White House pressured a federal judge into delaying some Watergate civil suit depositions until after last fall's election. Mr. Dean's leaks, of course, are to some degree suspect because he has used them to entice the subcommittee into granting him immunity.

That the President might suffer serious damage at the hands of a man whose credentials for a position of high responsibility were mediocre at best is another of the ironies of Watergate. John Dean had distinguished himself at practically nothing before being admitted to the White House inner sanctum of supposedly bright young men. Now, he could play a key role in a political climacteric, testifying to a pattern of official connivance and cover-up that cries out for reform. The attitudes and practices revealed by the Watergate hearings need not be the ambience in which the nation conducts its political affairs.

It would be unfair to the Nixon administration to ignore the groundwork previous administrations laid for what went on around the White House in the late '60s and early '70s. Bobby Kennedy was, after all, one of the early champions of wiretapping. And the cloak and dagger approach to government was in some vogue in the early '60s. It also bears repeating that hysteria and civil disorder had invaded the American political process during the first Nixon administration. The President, by ending the Vietnam involvement, played a leading role in calming the disorder.

But none of that justified official lawlessness. The President admitted in his May 22 statement that in July 1970 he approved the revival of "national security" operations that had been abandoned in 1966, including illegal breaking and entering by federal agents. He withdrew his approval five days later because of J. Edgar Hoover's objections, but later created a "special investigations unit" in the White House, operating under "extremely tight security rules." E. Howard Hunt and G. Gordon Liddy, of later Watergate fame, were part of that unit.

The President has admitted that he must take responsibility for the climate that developed out of these decisions even though he denies knowledge of specific illegal events. Out of that climate, if we can believe testimony so far, there developed a whole series of bizarre events involving White House aides.

White House attitudes towards Mr. Dean himself have been erratic. He was first endorsed and later fired by the President. His contention that he met with the President 30 to 40 times early this year to discuss Watergate was first scoffed at and then admitted.

By the end of next week, conceivably, the weight of allegations of mischief and wrong-doing in the White House made public in Senate hearings will be very heavy indeed. There may even be some sort of coherent pattern emerging that will serve the committee's goal of informing the American public on the total dimensions of the Watergate scandal.

The hearings won't, however, decide for the public the broader question of how much these were the standards of a single administration and how much they were political attitudes and practices developed over decades. They won't decide how much weight should be given to administration fears about the climate of anarchy and the tactics of political radicals. Members of the TV audience, as voters and citizens, will have to make up their separate minds on that.

Nor will the hearings necessarily chart a constructive course of reform. It can be guessed that there will be less public tolerance for official secrecy and executive privilege claims of future presidential administrations. We expect, and support, a further toughening of federal laws requiring disclosure of campaign contributions. Mr. Kristol, writing on this page today, predicts restrictions on campaign spending as well. We would hope for a clear delineation of federal investigatory powers, assignment of sole responsibility for security investigations to the FBI or some other accountable agency and a clear separation of the Attorney General's office from politics.

These are the minimum measures that the hearings suggest. There may be others, but they can wait until more evidence is weighed and the dangerous waters that the hearings are entering are further explored.

More heat is being applied to President Nixon to come out of his shell on Watergate and mend his ways in other respects by ranking members of his own party than by Democrats or the so-called liberal press.

In spite of repeated assurances by Sen. Hugh Scott and the vice president, Mr. Agnew, that Mr. Nixon is not for a moment allowing Watergate to interfere with his attention to other pressing business, leading lights of the Republican party are not assured. They are worried, and with good reason, about the spin-off effects Watergate may have across the broad spectrum of government and political operations.

They are worried about the President's future relationship with Congress.

They are worried about the sizable number of top, middle and third level executive and administrative agency jobs still vacant in the wake of an unprecedented number of resignations over the past year and in recent weeks.

They are worried about the effects of Watergate on the Republican party nationally. They are worried about improving their own communications with the White House in the future — assuming that Mr. Nixon manages to weather the grave political crisis with which he is confronted.

They are worried about all of these things to the point where the key ones who speak for the Nixon administration in Congress have carried their concerns directly to Mr. Nixon and spelled them out in language polite but exceedingly frank.

This happened in an eyeball-to-eyeball meeting Tuesday morning. The President's response was described as contrite and apolgetic for past policies. One gathers that Mr. Nixon at least listened well.

He reportedly promised that he would pay more attention in the future to the wishes of Congress. There will be established a much closer liaison with the men who carry the ball for him on Capitol Hill. No longer would they have to get around a palace guard to see him. And henceforward they will be given more time to study administration proposals. They will also be brought into much closer consultation on appointments rather than merely being handed them and told to promote them.

There can be little question that the President got an earful — not from political adversaries but from allies who have some grasp of the consequences and the potential consequences if matters, as they now stand, are not changed drastically.

From all appearances, however, Mr. Nixon's promises to do better by those on his own team, while

THE SAGINAW NEWS
Saginaw, Mich., June 8, 1973

gratifying to those who confronted him, does not ease all concern about the President's ability to govern effectively. These address themselves to the future. There is still the present and Watergate — a storm which has engulfed the White House — yet one which still finds the President sitting as a man on a raft attempting to ride it out.

It was Sen. Barry Goldwater, an elder statesman of the Republican party, who not many weeks ago flatly declared that Mr. Nixon had better do something and do it quick to set the record straight on this scandal.

Since that time Goldwater has gathered company. Similar appeals have come from a number of Republican members of Congress. This week the same was emphasized repeatedly by prominent Republican governors at the National Governors Conference in Nevada.

The clincher comes, though, when Michigan's Sen. Robert P. Griffin, whose loyalty to Mr. Nixon in the past compares favorably with that of the Scotts and Agnews, says that the President, at some time soon, must go before the Ervin committee or a full-blown press conference "and answer the tough questions."

This statement may seem rash to some. It may be viewed as ill-considered in the White House. Regardless, it points up the degree of concern which fellow Republicans feel toward the President's sit-tight stance on Watergate. That is becoming a growing chorus.

The messages to Mr. Nixon this week are clear. They read this way: You are in trouble with Congress. You need all of the friends you can get. You must take us into much closer confidence Ours is shaken. That of the people is shaken — not only over the office of the presidency or toward a single party, but toward the entire democratic system and its ability to resume normal functioning. You must come forward, let the people see you and answer some questions on Watergate. Ron Ziegler will no longer do, Mr. President — and neither will prepared press statements written by legal advisers.

These are the messages coming from erstwhile friends and allies, not critics. Apart from an abortive and ill-conceived attempt to pass censure resolutions at the governors' conference in Nevada, Democrats are not indulging in political overkill — and wisely we might add. A few old skirts of their own escaped laundering when laundering might also have been in order.

As for the press, it will simply have to live with and accept the

charge that it is stigmatizing the President by reporting the news.

For now the real heat on Mr. Nixon is coming from his own camp. It may, in way, be a case of chickens coming home to roost. It is, after all, a camp which hasn't quite got over the way it was disassociated from the 1972 GOP presidential election when amateurs took over the decision-making and largely forgot about the professional pols who were also seeking office.

The New York Times
New York, N.Y., June 13, 1973

The latest developments affecting the testimony ot John W. Dean 3d, former White House counsel, tend to dissipate the concern expressed by Vice President Agnew and others that the Senate Watergate hearings may seriously hamper the work of special prosecutor Archibald Cox.

Chief Judge John J. Sirica of the District of Columbia has granted the Senate committee's request for limited immunity for Mr. Dean. In a parallel action, however, Judge Sirica refused to cancel a subpoena ordering Mr. Dean to appear before a grand jury — without any grant of immunity against prosecution. Mr. Dean then exercised his constitutional right under the Fifth Amendment not to give incriminating evidence against himself before the grand jury.

Despite his refusal to provide information to the grand jurors, the prosecutors believe that this record of interrogation—taking place prior to his Senate appearance—will serve to demonstrate that their case against Mr. Dean is not based upon anything he divulges in his Senate testimony. At the same time the Senate's right to gather information for the purpose of eliciting all the facts needed to frame future legislation is not impeded. Having accepted the limited immunity which is the most the Senate could offer, Mr. Dean cannot now invoke his Fifth Amendment right in that proceeding. Were he to do so, he would be subject to imprisonment for contempt.

Other participants in the Watergate case have taken courses different from that of Mr. Dean. Jeb Stuart Magruder, who was deputy manager of the Nixon campaign, has reportedly accepted the prosecutors' offer to plead guilty to a single count in expectation of receiving a light sentence for his cooperation—the same deal that Mr. Dean rejected.

L. Patrick Gray 3d, former acting director of the Federal Bureau of Investigation; Herbert Kalmbach, formerly President Nixon's personal attorney, and John Caulfield, the former New York City policeman who performed undercover missions for the White House, have all chosen to cooperate with the prosecutors without obtaining immunity and without reaching a prior understanding about whether they may be indicted and, if so, on how many counts.

The so-called "transactional immunity" which Mr. Dean has been seeking from the prosecutors and which would give him total protection against possible indictment for any of his actions is usually forthcoming only when the testimony of a single participant is crucial to obtaining the conviction of other participants. In this instance the prosecutors have consistently maintained that Mr. Dean's cooperation in a future trial is not essential.

It is arguable that Mr. Dean is unfairly caught between the Senate committee's limited grant of immunity and the prosecutor's refusal to grant any immunity. But the legal situation as it has actually evolved renders implausible the assertion of Mr. Agnew that the Senate committee's hearings will frustrate the work of the grand juries and the courts and will produce "the spectacle of wrongdoers going scot-free."

TULSA DAILY WORLD

Tulsa, Okla., June 12, 1973

WHAT IS so special about JOHN W. DEAN, 3rd, the former White House Counsel, that he should be given immunity in the Watergate case?

Of all the persons involved in and around the Watergate bugging and cover-up, this lawyer fired by PRESIDENT NIXON is making the most determined effort to escape prosecution in exchange for telling what he knows.

Yesterday his attorney asked U.S. District Judge JOHN J. SIRICA either to cancel DEAN's appearance before the Federal Grand Jury in Washington or grant him immunity. The Senate Watergate investigating committee earlier asked SIRICA to give DEAN immunity for any testimony it receives from him.

DEAN has been trying for months to work out a deal with prosecutors for going before the Grand Jury, but he hasn't got what he wanted and now he has a subpoena requiring him to testify without immunity.

No one should be shocked by the idea of a witness being granted freedom from prosecution; it is a common practice in criminal cases—particularly when a relatively minor character can be persuaded to "sing" in order to convict an important one.

But with so many witnesses appearing in the Watergate case, and so many high-level figures involved, one wonders what DEAN could know that cannot be extracted from anyone else. There is also the question of how believable his testimony would be. Is it going to be his word against all the others'? Is he the man who is supposed to finger PRESIDENT NIXON—is that why he is considered such a key witness?

All this has not yet been made clear. but at least the Grand Jury prosecutors haven't found him indispensable enough to give him what he wants. Why should Judge SIRICA do more for him?

If DEAN has a big story to tell, he should be asked about it in the same way that other key witnesses are being questioned. If he fears self-incrimination he can take the FIFTH AMENDMENT just as they can. Does he deserve more than the others? We see no reason at this stage to make him an exception.

ST. LOUIS POST-DISPATCH

St. Louis, Mo., June 8, 1973

Special Watergate prosecutor Archibald Cox has now gone to court in an attempt to place certain, and we believe unacceptable, restrictions on the manner in which the Ervin select committee may receive testimony from two key witnesses. His reasons are essentially the same as those he advanced earlier in trying to persuade the committee to delay its sessions, namely, that public hearings may make successful prosecutions of those who are indicted impossible.

Mr. Cox has asked the court to put conditions upon the immunity it is expected to grant former Nixon deputy re-election campaign director Jeb Stuart Magruder and former White House counsel John W. Dean III. The prosecutor's first preference is that the testimony of these men be heard in executive session; his second is that radio and television coverage—but not that of newspapers—of these witnesses be prohibited. As an attempt to stifle publicity, the latter is a naive approach, for can there be any doubt that that which is published will not be picked up by television?

Immunity before the committee means only that the testimony of persons before the panel cannot be used as a basis for prosecution. As Senator Ervin has pointed out, federal prosecutors already have had more than a year to develop incriminating evidence from their own investigations. Unless they have botched things hopelessly, nothing said before the committee ought to seriously damage future prosecutions

Thus one conclusion that suggests itself is that Mr. Cox may well be unsure of the competence of the Government's investigation so far, and he has reasons for such doubts. Watergate trial judge John Sirica found the prosecutors' questions so inadequate that he was forced to interrogate the defendants himself. And as recent testimony by witnesses before the Ervin committee has shown, Government prosecutors were aware long ago of possible perjury and did little about it. The conduct of federal prosecutors, indeed, has become an element in the committee's examination of the case.

The Watergate investigation must proceed on two levels, one legal, the other political — that is, as the case relates to the conduct of the nations' political processes. And as the whole sordid Watergate scandal has demonstrated, the abuses of the political process must be made visible to the people. That is why the Ervin hearings cannot operate effectively behind the kind of curtain that Mr. Cox has suggested.

Chicago today American

Chicago, Ill., June 7, 1973

IT IS becoming harder, and may soon become impossible, for President Nixon to avoid doing what obviously needs to be done about the Watergate tangle; this is, hold a Presidential press conference. Mr. Nixon, in fact, is reported now to be considering several possible ways of conducting a limited press conference—some arrangement by which he would answer questions without facing an examination by the whole Washington press corps. Possibilities include an interview by one television commentator, or by the anchormen of the three major TV networks.

An interview in any format would be better than the present near-blackout at the White House, in which Mr. Nixon utters guarded comments thru official spokesmen but is not available for direct questioning. The idea, of course, would be a normal press conference [or what was considered normal under previous Presidents], and we hope Nixon decides on that at whatever risk he may think is involved. Nothing could do more to shore up respect for him personally and—depending on the answers—confidence in his administration.

Unfortunately, this seems about the least likely of the choices Nixon might make. Thruout the Watergate mess his record has been flawlessly consistent: He has given out only the minimum of information, or somewhat less than the minimum, and has done that only when it was absolutely necessary to say something.

If any conclusion can be drawn from Mr. Nixon's record, it is that he sees information as a weapon which will be used either by him or against him. He wants to be in control of information—to decide how much should be given out and when, which questions shall be answered and which ignored. Since the American press can never accept any such arrangement, Mr. Nixon has come to regard the press as hostile—a threat to "security"—and any face-to-face dealings with it as dangerous.

So it seems the wisest course is exactly the one the White House cannot accept. The instinct for secrecy that created the problem is also preventing a solution. We can only urge the President to decide that this crisis is unprecedented and calls for an unprecedented answer from him—complete frankness. A full-scale press conference may involve risks, but it also offers a great gain. Continued secrecy offers nothing but continued and deepening mistrust.

The Dallas Morning News

Dallas, Tex., June 13, 1973

The Cafe Society communicator, Earl Wilson, reported in his column the other day that, in headline language, "Saloon Set Bored With Watergate."

This is one instance in which the presumed leaders of fashion are lagging far behind the silent majority. If phone calls, letters from readers and back-fence conversations are any guide, the man in the street has been bored with Watergate for weeks now.

To a large degree this is due to media overkill. It is no great secret that Richard Nixon has never been a favorite of newsmen, particularly the newsmen who dominate the Eastern press and the national news agencies. Most of the big-name columnists and commentators who have led the outcry over Watergate are men who have a long history as Nixon-haters and they are recognized as such by readers.

And so, as the get-Nixon crowd warmed to its work, competing to see which columnist could view with the most alarm, which commentator could use the most outraged tones, the public was somewhat skeptical as to the detachment and objectivity these observers were bringing to the task. Performance of the press has borne out and reinforced such skepticism.

This has been true not only of the editorial and opinion side of the media but also of the news side, charged with the duty of unbiased reporting of the news.

It has long been clear that for some newsmen, any club will serve to beat Nixon. Watergate apparently was greeted by these journalists as the ultimate club, the one that would serve to destroy him.

The resultant excesses have instead served to undermine both public trust in the media's objectivity and its interest in the ongoing Watergate circus.

Chicago Tribune

Chicago, Ill., June 13, 1973

The Ervin committee yesterday rejected Maurice Stans' request for a postponement of his appearance in the Watergate hearings, just as it had earlier rejected Special Prosecutor Archibald Cox's request that the whole proceedings be delayed—or at least conducted in private. Both requests were based on the legitimate argument that the present televised hearings might interfere with a fair trial when and if the witnesses appear in court in connection with Watergate.

And yet the committee was right in rejecting the requests. The most eloquent criticism of the committee hearings has come from Britain—notably the London Times—and from Mr. Cox himself, who is a staunch admirer of the British system of justice. In one of the longest editorials it has ever printed, the Times described the publicity attending the hearings as "so prejudicial that it alone would seem to preclude the possibility of a fair trial for any accused, even including the President himself if there were impeachment proceedings."

There is much to admire about British justice, especially its speed and precision compared with our dilatory, meandering process which can be manipulated endlessly by clever defense lawyers. Perhaps if the courts functioned here as they do in Britain, we, too, could afford to abandon grand juries and muzzle the investigators. But they don't. The sad fact is that few of our scandals would ever have reached the surface if we had sat back and relied on "due process of law," British-style. Teapot Dome was aired in a Congressional hearing. The Watergate facts were dug up largely by the press. The Kerner and Barrett evidence was produced mainly before grand juries.

In Britain, the press is effectively prevented from undertaking "investigative reporting" as we know it. The courts treat as contempt the publication of anything which might be regarded as prejudicial. The British Press Council is ready to chastise any paper that oversteps the bounds of propriety. The only evidence that is likely to be produced is that gathered by the prosecution or the court.

The fact that political scandals are relatively rare in Britain [and, when they do occur, relatively frivolous] may be the result of Britain's system of justice or it may reflect the traditionally higher standards of public service in Britain. But whatever the reason for our poor showing, it is not going to be improved by calling off the dogs. The press and the legislatures and grand juries are likely to be essential to American justice for a long time to come.

Senators Ervin and Baker gave well reasoned arguments in favor of continuing with the hearings despite Mr. Stans' request. The hearings have been conducted with restraint. Incidentally, the London Times' "most damaging example" of prejudicial publicity arose not from the public hearings, but from secret testimony.

The committee hearings should continue because they remind us all that American office-holders are answerable not just to prosecutors and judges, but to the country as a whole. But to say this is not to say that the hearings should run wild. The senators must be judicious in their questioning and must do their best to see that those named have a chance to answer the charges made against them. We're thinking not so much of the President, who can get all the publicity he wants whenever he wants it, but of lesser men who may be innocent and yet may be unable to clear their names in court because of the difficulty of getting a fair trial.

Richmond Times-Dispatch

Richmond, Va., June 12, 1973

More and more people are suggesting that if President Nixon would only hold a press conference on the Watergate scandal, many of his troubles related to the affair would vanish. This implies that the President's remarks to a gathering of reporters would be more credible than the statements he already has issued on the matter.

Those who hold this point of view argue that by agreeing to submit to questions from newsmen, the President would show that he really has nothing to hide and that he is willing to promote full disclosure of the White House's role in the affair. Theoretically, this should contribute to the restoration of public confidence in the Nixon administration.

Conducted under proper procedures, a press conference might serve some constructive purposes. But the procedures that ordinarily govern presidential press conferences probably would not be desirable. With scores of reporters vying for the President's attention, the questions would lack continuity and depth and the answers, if Mr. Nixon wished to avoid the possibility that two or three newsmen would monopolize the conference, would have to be brief. A better approach would be for the President to meet with a small group of reporters on a pool basis, an arrangement that would permit both the questions and the answers to be thorough and precise.

Even under the best of conditions, however, a press conference on Watergate might be of only limited and temporary value. In his public statements on the affair, Mr. Nixon has insisted that he had no prior knowledge of the Watergate operation and that he was not personally involved in subsequent efforts to conceal the facts about it. It is unlikely that he would say anything substantially different from this at a press conference. On the contrary, he probably would be more adamant than ever in protesting his innocence.

This might strengthen the faith of his supporters, but it probably would not mollify his severest critics in the press and in Congress. Nothing will satisfy them except (a) a complete confession of guilt from Mr. Nixon or (b) proof of his innocence from *non-presidential sources*. His word, whether given in statements or press conferences, is not good enough for these people. Their suspicions will remain alive until those former presidential aides who have personal knowledge of the President's involvement or non-involvement in Watergate—John Mitchell, John Dean, John Ehrlichman and H. R. Haldeman—present public testimony that results in the President's exoneration.

So while a strong case can be made for a presidential press conference, it is possible to expect too much from one. The quickest and most effective way to resolve doubts about the President is to bring Mitchell, Dean, Ehrlichman and Haldeman before the Senate Watergate committee and let them tell their stories.

THE RICHMOND NEWS LEADER

Richmond, Va., June 14, 1973

Speaking for the CBS radio network, correspondent Dallas Townsend recently took umbrage with a *London Times* editorial that accused the American press, the Ervin Committee, and the Watergate grand jury of acting out "a Washington variant of lynch law." Not so, said Townsend, as he noted that the *Times* editorial "discredited. . . every institution that has had anything to do with bringing the scandal into the light of day. . ." But then Townsend sought to slough off the *Times'* charge that the Ervin Committee is obstructing justice by publicly prejudicing cases against potential defendants: "The fact is," said Townsend, "that justice, in this case, is not the overriding concern."

What is the "overriding concern"? According to Townsend, it "is one of high national issues, political as well as legal, one of ethics as of law. It is a case of a democracy being able to learn the scope of grave and dangerous flaws in its political system and thereby learn[ing] how to correct them." Up to a point, Townsend's opinion is justifiable: The government has failed to bring all the alleged Watergate participants to swift justice, and if, in order to know the full truth of Watergate, some of the guilty must have their cases so prejudiced as to escape justice, then that is the way the game must now be played.

But what Townsend ignores, and what the *Times* implies in its references to "lynch law," is the possible loss of justice for the *innocent* as well as the guilty. As an example, consider the performance before the Ervin Committee of former Secretary of Commerce Maurice Stans: In the face of an avalanche of innuendo in the press, Stans so plausibly professed his innocence that several Senators were visibly annoyed by their inability to nail his hide to the wall. Viewing the confrontation between Stans and the Ervin Committee, one could almost hear some of the Senators say in exasperated anger, "But you're supposed to be guilty!"

In a court of law, Stans' innocence would be assumed until he had been found guilty beyond reasonable doubt. Through a combination of grand jury leaks, press hearsay and speculation, and Ervin Committee publicity, Stans' innocence not only is not assumed — it is regarded as inconceivable. And that is why the *Times* spoke of "lynch law." So Dallas Townsend erred in completely dismissing justice as the "overriding issue." Perhaps the search for truth can override justice for the guilty. But the nation should not sanction any twisting of the truth that will render justice for the innocent consequently impossible. For in the long run, to do so would constitute a crime far worse than Watergate itself.

The Miami Herald

Miami, Fla., June 13, 1973

ON the popular theory, apparently, that the best defense is a good offense, the Nixon administration is striking back strenuously at Watergate, a symbol of the 1972 Presidential campaign. The object is the Ervin committee inquiry and the chosen instrument is Vice President Agnew.

The gist of the counterattack is that the Senate committee is engaging in a "gross perversion of justice" which may damage the innocent and "muddy the waters of justice beyond redemption" by trying the administration before "the court of public opinion instead of in established judicial processes."

Well, the argument is familiar, and it is credible to a degree. But as Mr. Agnew employs it with characteristic hyperbole, it is simply an act of self-pleading.

If the Ervin select committee hearings are perverting justice, then the whole Senate, which by unanimous vote instructed the committee to proceed, is guilty of a heinous act. And if the waters are turbid, surely the fault lies with the Nixon Justice Department: Watergate occurred just a few days short of one year ago; waters that do not run swiftly are likely to turn muddy.

Even so, we welcome the Vice President's stand. It lays things out. And one, and the most important, of these things is a need for a redress of the balance of power under the Constitution. The issue, in short, is between the Congress and the Executive.

Although a felony, Watergate as such was a caper as that sort of thing goes in politics. The perversion of justice is in the coverup, which instead laid bare an attempted seizure of power without example in American history.

CONSIDER some of the consequences:

Nearly 40 White House or other administration officials are implicated.

Two former Cabinet officers indicted in a related campaign activity; the heads of the FBI, CIA and Securities and Exchange Commission ousted or resigned; the Attorney General out, and his office implicated in the destruction of files.

Disclosure of a monstrous "security" scheme aimed at the civil rights of anybody and everybody, fortunately throttled by the late J. Edgar Hoover.

Meddling in a number of court cases, including the Ellsberg trial, allowing a number of accused to go free, and a job offer to a judge in the midst of a trial.

Revelation of widespread violations of the Corrupt Practices Act and its successor, the Campaign Spending Law.

Uncovering of a master burglary operation directed from within the White House, reaching into a number of cities, possibly including Miami.

Evidence of forgery of State Department cables and phony "public opinion" advertising in support of government policies.

THIS is only part of a growing list of events brought to light which have shaken public confidence in the conduct of the public's business. We say again that the administration has systematically underrated the seriousness of its predicament, as Vice President Agnew's words confirm.

Mr. Nixon has said time and again that his own office is innocent of any involvement, and we believe him. Thus it is to his advantage that the Ervin committee pursue the truth as such committees have done before in situations of national crisis, for if that course is abandoned or blocked the people will never know whom to believe.

As Mr. Justice Holmes once said, "When the ignorant are taught to doubt they do not know what they safely may believe," and that is the edge of chaos.

The Des Moines Register

Des Moines, Iowa, June 7, 1973

Robert Reisner, an aide to Jeb Magruder, deputy director of the Nixon campaign, gave the Ervin committee useful information Tuesday. Perhaps the most intriguing part of the testimony was his statement that no investigator had questioned him until he was contacted by an Ervin committee staff member on Mar. 30, 1973.

Magruder was an important witness at the trial of the men charged with the Watergate break-in. As Magruder's aide, Reisner kept a log of Magruder's activities, had contact with Watergate conspirator G. Gordon Liddy, distributed documents bearing on Watergate planning and played a part—apparently unwittingly—in disposing of incriminating papers showing a link between the Nixon re-election committee and the break-in.

Magruder testified at the trial that Liddy acted on his own, without committee approval, when he broke into Democratic national headquarters. This was the theory of the case adopted by Justice Department prosecutors and advanced to the jury at the trial of Liddy and others. Yet no one from the Federal Bureau of Investigation and none of the prosecutors bothered to question Reisner in advance of the trial.

Perhaps this reflects no more than sloppy investigative work by the FBI and the prosecutors. If so, it was sloppiness bordering on incompetence. It does not require hindsight to realize that the aide to a key re-election committee executive could have important information bearing on the responsibility of the committee for Watergate.

That a high-level effort was made to cover up and obstruct justice is clear. Unclear is the part played by the FBI and the Justice Department in the cover-up effort. The Ervin committee has an obligation to pursue the question of why the case put together by the Justice Department was so deficient that Federal Judge John Sirica scoffed at it.

The Cincinnati Post

TIMES ⋆ STAR

Cincinnati, Ohio, June 15, 1973

After months of leaks and secondhand reports, a central figure in the Watergate conspiracy has finally testified in public; and his story is appalling.

Jeb Stuart Magruder, who was deputy director of the Nixon campaign, now has told the Ervin committee that Watergate and worse crimes that thankfully were not committed were discussed in the presence of John N. Mitchell, then attorney general, and John W. Dean 3d, then White House counsel.

According to Magruder, he, convicted conspirator G. Gordon Liddy, Mitchell and Dean met to plan a massive campaign of espionage against the Democrats in, of all places, Mitchell's office in the Department of Justice.

Mitchell and Dean will get a chance to tell their own versions, and it is not fair to judge them on Magruder's testimony alone. But if he is telling the truth, it was more like a police state than a democracy for the Attorney General and the President's lawyer to hatch crimes against the political opposition.

Again according to Magruder, Liddy came up with a $1 million program that included kidnaping radicals and interning them in Mexico and tempting Democrats in convention at Miami with a yacht-full of call girls, the boat being "set up for sound and photographs."

If Liddy proposed anything like that to him, Mitchell served Nixon very badly. The Attorney General should have sent Liddy, along with his odd ideas, off to Antarctica to take charge of the penguin vote.

Instead, Mitchell is said to have sent Liddy "back to the drawing boards" for a cheaper and more realistic plan. Magruder said Mitchell, by then campaign manager, finally approved a $250,000 Liddy plan, without kidnapings or call girls but with Watergate.

Nowhere in Magruder's testimony did the law-and-order Attorney General express any qualms about crimes like conspiracy, subornation of perjury and obstruction of justice. If this is the case, no comment is necessary.

Other disturbing charges made by Magruder: The White House was kept informed about plans to bug the Democratic National Committee and got results of the tap; Magruder told White House chief of staff H. R. Haldeman all about the cover-up last January, but Nixon states he did not learn about it until two months later.

Obviously there is fertile ground for investigation in Magruder's confession. Pending that inquiry and without prejudging any guilt, we strongly feel that no future President should appoint his campaign manager or a party politician as Attorney General.

THE COMMERCIAL APPEAL

Memphis, Tenn., June 10, 1973

SLOWLY, DELIBERATELY, recognizing that he was going afield from the Watergate inquiry, Sen. Howard Baker asked the witness to explain how he could "abdicate your own conscience." The question was put to Herbert L. Porter, an aide in the Committee for the Re-Election of the President at the time of the Watergate bugging, a cog in the "dirty tricks" machinery, and now a self-confessed perjurer. But whether he meant to, Baker really was addressing this moral question to the nation.

And it would do all of us in America good to ponder the question.

BAKER ASKED Porter if he had not ever asked himself whether what he was doing was right. He had, said Porter. What did he do about it, then? Nothing. Why?

Porter's answer to that "why?" can be magnified a thousandfold to apply to an attitude which afflicts a vast part of our society. He was afraid of group pressure, he said. He feared he would be accused of not being a team player.

Before too many of us wag our heads and deplore the weakness of this individual we ought to practice a little self-examination.

That flimsy excuse of doing what we know is wrong or questionable because "everybody's doing it," because we fear being ostracized by the peer group, because we dare not appear different from the norm even if the standard of the moment may be immoral—that immature excuse is used too often by too many of us, young and old.

And why that is can be traced to a changing value system, an abandonment or at least distortion of a moral code that has served humankind for centuries. For some of us, it may be that the Ten Commandments have been forgotten. Replaced by what? By hucksterism. By pragmatism and materialism. By the idea that an end justifies the means. By the P. T. Barnum dictum that there's a sucker born every minute. By the depersonalized condition of man in a computerized society. And also by a political spoils system that has made corruption an everyday fact of life.

Whatever forces shaped the young political lackey who dreamed of a high government post are identical to those that lead young people to experiment in drugs, to cheat on school examinations, to consider shoplifting an innocent pastime and extramarital sex a contemporary life-style. They are the same pressures that lead businessmen to look for loopholes in the law, and employes to steal from the boss. Like they say, everybody's doing it.

It may be argued that Baker is going beyond the mandate of the Senate when, as vice chairman of the Watergate committee, he assumes a moral tone in confronting the witnesses. But thank goodness someone is, because we would never get this broadscale kind of deliberation on right and wrong through the courtroom prosecution of those accused in the planning, execution and cover-up of last June's Watergate incident. No trial could bring out the lessons being learned through the searching inquiry of the Senate hearings.

IT WOULD do no harm for each of us to put himself in the witness chair, to ask himself what he would have done under the same circumstances in which others found themselves in a phase of the presidential campaign which turned into a disaster.

Can each of us say for certain that he has the principles, the strength of character to have blown the whistle and called the law? Would we in another time and place and another set of circumstances have done right?

Let us hope that what we learn from these hearings can make us better, can prepare us to face similar tests of integrity.

But let us also rejoice that we live in a society which does dare to examine its faults. In the midst of this soul searching, The Christian Science Monitor said last week: "These are as glorious times to raise children, to work, to invent, and to enjoy life as ever before. That all mankind's venalities have not been overcome should not surprise us. The ferment of the times is the necessary sorting out of what is false from what is true."

HERALD-JOURNAL

Syracuse, N.Y., June 15, 1973

Are we to believe that Maurice Stans, finance chairman for President Nixon's re-election committee, really didn't know what he was doing in destroying records, showing who had contributed to the Committee to Re-Elect the President before April 7, 1972?

That he didn't know what he was doing, destroying records showing disbursement of $1.7 million of those funds on June 23, a few days after the Watergate break-in and arrests?

That isn't the way campaigning committees record their collections and expenditures according to our experience. Most are meticulous to a T in the keeping of records. They want to cite chapter and verse in response to any future mismanagement charges.

Stans by his testimony has put himself into a sorry spot. He was either blind and deaf deliberately or so guileless he lacked the perception expected of a person in that position. Obviously he was an extremely inept administrator.

Then the poor fellow asked the committee to "give me back by good name." Pathetic.

THE ATLANTA CONSTITUTION

Atlanta, Ga., June 9, 1973

Watergate is no laughing matter. Neither was the Great Depression. Neither were any of our major or minor wars. And yet, as always in time of great national stress or crisis, the wisecracks and gag lines are flying thick and fast. It is a characteristic of our people that, when the going gets rough, they try to ease the strain with a bit of humor. So it is with the Watergate mess. We'd even hazard the opinion that the whole Watergate affair might never have happened if there had been a little more humor and perspective among the buttoned-down, uptight types who engineered it.

You've probably heard some of the gags that are currently making the rounds. "Nixon's the One," a replay of last year's campaign button, but with a new meaning. Or the one about how top Nixon aides were competing last year for the honor of displaying the Number 2 or 3 license plates, and this year they are trying to avoid having to make the license plates. One wit has pointed out that the President had a "very serious staff infection," but he cured it by hiring a brand new staff, "all Kelly Girls." And then there is the political observer who was asked if he thought the President might end up in jail. "I don't know. But when I passed the penitentiary the other day I heard the band practicing 'Hail to the Chief.'"

"Being President means never having to say you are sorry," one comedian notes. Another quotes the President as saying "I need time to prove my innocence — I come here tonight to ask for a third term."

Philip Roth wrote a satire in book form in 1971 called "Our Gang." It seemed excessive and unfair at the time, but it has now been reissued in paperback in a special "Watergate Edition."

There is, no kidding, a Watergate Game on the market, something like Monopoly, where you start off in the White House and end up in jail.

Sick humor? Gallows humor? Maybe. A sense of humor implies a recognition of the incongruities, the ironies of life and politics. "My administration has taken crime out of the streets," one mimic quotes the President as saying, "and put it in the White House where I can keep an eye on it."

Even the Senate Watergate hearings have had their moments. When Mrs. Sally Harmony testified that she was involved in handling tickets or invitations to the inaugural, Sen. Talmadge grinned broadly: "The last one? Or the next one?"

Watergate is no laughing matter. We all know that. But Lord help us if we can't find the relief of a smile or a laugh even in the worst of circumstances.

Des Moines Tribune

Des Moines, Iowa, June 15, 1973

Maurice Stans, the Republican party's chief fund-raiser, seems not to have learned one of the more obvious lessons to be derived from the Watergate mess: the invitation to corruption implicit in secret political financing.

Stans and his fellow money-men raised millions of dollars, including large amounts of cash, with promises of confidentiality. In his appearance before the Ervin committee, Stans defended the practice as "legal" and done with the advice of counsel. He justified it as protecting the rights of donors to privacy.

At no time did Stans suggest in his testimony that even in retrospect it was a mistake to have deliberately hidden campaign financing facts from the public.

Stans defended his money-raising tactics in the face of incontrovertible evidence that the Watergate conspirators capitalized on the secrecy and lack of accountability to finance the break-in and cover-up. The secret money was an integral part of the Watergate corruption. Stans himself has been indicted for an alleged illegal conspiracy involving one secret donation.

The conflict between the right of donors to privacy and the right of the public to information was settled long ago by Congress in favor of disclosure. Both the Corrupt Practices Act of 1925 and the Federal Election Campaign Act of 1971 which replaced it show the importance placed by Congress on revealing campaign receipts and expenditures.

Stans and his colleagues seized on a technicality and raised the secret money in the period between the expiration of the old disclosure law and the effective date of the new one. This might have been "legal," but it was an evasion of the laws and the intent of Congress.

The wisdom of the preference by Congress for disclosure is borne out by the Watergate experience, which shows what unscrupulous men are tempted to do when they have access to money for which they do not have to account.

Hiding behind the "right of privacy" to justify the secret money-raising is disingenuous. If that right is of such overriding importance, why did the President sign the 1971 disclosure law? Stans would look a lot better if he candidly admitted that the decision to go after huge sums of unreported money was a mistake.

But Stans should not be made the scapegoat for the decision. President Nixon, for whom the money was raised, approved the money-raising scheme and defended it as legal. He declared last July, "I support the position that Mr. Stans has taken."

The President has assumed the responsibility for the Watergate cover-up without assuming the blame. The President deserves the responsibility and the blame for the money-raising tactics that contributed to Watergate.

The Evening Star and The Washington Daily News

Washington, D.C., June 15, 1973

Washington's criminals surely missed a bet in early April of last year. Had they familiarized themselves with the subtleties of campaign finance law, and had they positioned themselves outside the offices of the Finance Committee to Re-elect the President in the few days before April 7, they might have intercepted an astounding amount of money pouring through the front door.

Wasn't there a "mad rush," the former chairman of that committee, Maurice Stans, was asked, to contribute to the campaign before April 7? That was the effective date of the 1971 Federal Election Campaign Act, with its important requirement for disclosure of who gives what. Well, Stans told the Ervin committee, "mad rush" might be an unfair characterization. Wasn't there an avalanche of contributions in the few days before April 7? Oh sure, Stans conceded.

What Stans failed to mention was that all this had been pretty well stage-managed months earlier. The White House, along with elements of the Democratic-controlled Congress, had dallied for weeks over the final technicalities of the new law, so that its effective date was postponed from mid-January to April. On the presidential level, this worked largely in favor of the Republicans, who only had one candidate and who were in a very strong position to raise money.

What the Stans testimony did make clear, though, was that once they were in a position to expect large amounts of money, the White House and the campaign committee were not about to be satisfied with anything less than phenomenal amounts of money — as it turned out, more than $50 million. To Stans, a shrewd, professional political soldier, fell the job of raising the money. He did so, and he sounded rather proud of himself as he described the process.

He shouldn't be. Even granting that no fund-raising illegalities occurred, Stans and his associates, both before and after April 7, stayed barely on what Senator Ervin called "the windy side of the law." Asked about stricter disclosure provisions, or transactions in other than cash, Stans said he would welcome such changes, but only insofar as they would spare campaign fund-raisers embarrassing questions. He said he tried to abide by "the spirit and intent" of the election laws. It's fair to say he was relatively blind to such things.

Had the Republicans not been surfeited with riches, of course, Watergate still might have occurred. But maybe not. Certainly, all that money coming in eased the way for those who planned and carried out an array of dirty tricks. The Democrats were the victims, and in the end so were the President, his administration and all of us.

If anything redemptory comes out of Watergate, it will probably be a movement for campaign-financing reform going far beyond what the 1971 act was supposed to accomplish. Whoever puts his mind to such reform legislation would do well to nail Stans' testimony to the wall, ready for constant reference.

The Boston Globe

Boston, Mass., June 15, 1973

Jeb Stuart Magruder's sworn testimony at the Senate committee hearing into the Watergate and associated crimes and scandals was almost breath-taking. So far as he is concerned, the goose is cooked. He has nothing to hide. He admittedly perjured himself, and he does not now have any self-serving motive for doing so again. He almost certainly is headed for prison.

What devastatingly comes through his testimony is the insensitive casualness and the callousness with which he and the others he named planned the total sabotage of nothing less than a presidential election.

The crimes were all committed on the basis of "what was best for the President." And the cover-up was concealed from the President, at least as Mr. Magruder tells it, because disclosure to him somehow might result in public disclosure and public uproar, and the consequence of this would be that "the President would lose the election."

Never, so far as any historians disclosed, have so many crimes and dirty tricks been so casually devised as useful devices for a President's reelection. Burglary and wiretapping were not necessarily the worst of them. There were plans also to kidnap leaders of war protest groups and hold them in Mexico, not for national security reasons, Mr. Magruder gratuitously acknowledged, but to spare the President possible embarrassment. There were plans to employ agents provocateurs, which was indeed done, although Mr. Magruder did not testify that it was. There were plans to employ call girls on a wire-tapped yacht off Miami Beach to trap Democrats during their convention, faked telephone calls to try to trap Democrats in the kind of dirty tricks they themselves were perpetrating. There were the usual assortment of shredded records and covert phone calls from pay booths, the scurrying around for quick outs when it appeared the jig might be up.

It was not because any of the tricks was too scurrilous that some were discarded. It was because former Attorney General John N. Mitchell, as Mr. Magruder tells it, objected that the million dollar budget was too high.

Mr. Mitchell, who consistently has denied either complicity or knowledge, was only one of a whole slew of one-time big names in the Administration whom Mr. Magruder named as conspirators. Another, though equivocally, was former Secretary of Commerce Maurice Stans, who has sworn that he is innocent. Another is H. R. Haldeman. Mr. Magruder rattled off the names of a dozen others, excluding President Nixon himself, whom he still defends staunchly, though committee members expressed their own bafflement as to how the President could have known nothing when all around him his advisers and intimates knew (and were doing) so much.

Mr. Magruder has told as sordid a tale of a presidential campaign as long-time observers of the Washington scene have ever heard. The road will be a rocky one for other witnesses who will follow him. Mr. Magruder has supplied the abrasive against which the testimony of all others will have to be rubbed.

DEAN TIES NIXON TO COVER-UP IN TESTIMONY

Former presidential counsel John W. Dean 3rd appeared before the Senate Select Committee on Presidential Campaign Activities June 25–29 following a one-week postponement of the televised hearings during the visit of Soviet Communist Party Chairman Leonid Brezhnev to the U.S. Dean spent the entire session June 25 submitting 47 documents and reading a 245-page prepared account detailing his own involvement in the effort to cover up the Watergate conspiracy and relating how that effort spread among the White House staff, the Committee to Re-elect the President, the Justice Department and President Nixon.

While Dean's account was the first before the committee to directly accuse Nixon of involvement in the Watergate cover-up, Dean asserted that Nixon did not "realize or appreciate at any time the implications of his involvement." Dean said, however, that Nixon had permitted the cover-up to continue even after Dean had told him about some of the cover-up plans. Dean added that Nixon had discussed with him the possibility of executive clemency for some of the Watergate conspirators and "hush money" payments to maintain the cover-up. Dean's statement detailed the "excessive concern" in the White House for data on antiwar activists and other political opponents of the Administration. Dean suggested that this concern created the climate for the Watergate affair. Dean described his superiors in the White House—former presidential aides H. R. Haldeman and John D. Ehrlichman—as the principals in the efforts to conceal the ramifications of the Watergate break-in. But he also implicated others, including former Attorney General John N. Mitchell.

The subsequent questioning of Dean by committee members often centered on Dean's credibility against that of the White House, with Dean refusing to retreat from the allegations in his prepared account. Dean testified June 26 that Nixon had been "less than accurate" in the May 22 statement denying involvement in the Watergate affair, while a White House spokesman in San Clemente was saying that Nixon stood by the statement. Sen. Edward J. Gurney (R, Fla.) questioned Dean sharply June 27 on his own involvement in the Watergate cover-up and challenged Dean's accusations concerning Nixon's role as unsupported "impressions." Dean, however, maintained that his allegations were based on his recollections of fact.

The June 27 session was also highlighted by the release of the list of the Administration's political "enemies" and Dean's testimony that the White House had tried to "politicize" the Internal Revenue Service. The "Opponents List and Political Enemies Project" turned over to the Senate committee, Dean said, was compiled beginning in 1971 by various Administration officials and was frequently updated.

One of the documents, written by Dean Aug. 16, 1971, suggested ways in which "we can use the available federal machinery to screw our political enemies." Methods proposed included Administration manipulation of "grant availability, federal contracts, litigation, prosecution, etc." Although Dean later recommended that the Administration utilize Internal Revenue Service (IRS) audits to harass political enemies, other documents which were provided to the committee showed that the White House had been unable to win IRS cooperation.

Dean was confronted June 27–28 with a White House response to his charges in the form of a memorandum and questions submitted to the committee by special presidential counsel J. Fred Buzhardt Jr. The memo, read by Sen. Daniel K. Inouye (D, Hawaii), portrayed Dean as the "mastermind" of the cover-up and Mitchell as his "patron." Buzhardt's charges failed to shake Dean's insistence that he fell into an existing cover-up situation as a conduit between Haldeman and Ehrlichman and the campaign committee. In a statement released June 28, Buzhardt insisted that the memo "does not represent a White House position" and had not been reviewed by the President. Committee Chairman Sam J. Ervin Jr. (D, N.C.), backed by Sen. Howard H. Baker (R, Tenn.), suggested June 28 that the only adequate White House response to Dean's charges would be an appearance by Nixon before the committee. A presidential spokesman in San Clemente replied that Nixon remained opposed to answering a committee subpoena on the ground that it would be "constitutionally inappropriate" and said Nixon did not intend to appear voluntarily. (Near the end of the June 28 session, Sen. Lowell P. Weicker Jr. (R, Conn.) charged that Nixon supporters had tried to intimidate him after he had been named to the committee.)

The Senate Watergate hearings had been postponed after the committee had received the delay request from Senate party leaders, Sens. Mike Mansfield (D, Mont.) and Hugh Scott (R, Pa.). The two said in a letter that a delay of one week "would not jeopardize the hearings" but might give President Nixon and Brezhnev "the opportunity to reconcile differences, arrive at mutual agreements and, in the field of foreign policy, be able to achieve results which would be beneficial not only to our two countries but, hopefully, to all mankind." Ervin said he agreed to the request "with some degree of reluctance" but thought "there may be wisdom" in the postponement. Only Sen. Weicker voted against the postponement.

The Boston Globe

Boston, Mass., June 18, 1973

John W. Dean 3d, the fired counsel to President Nixon, is no choir boy. Certainly, apple-cheeked young innocence is not in any way reflected in his August 16, 1971, memorandum to the then Presidential aides H.R. Haldeman and John Ehrlichman:

"This memorandum addresses the matter of how we can maximize the fact of our incumbency in dealing with persons known to be active in their opposition to our Administration. Stated a bit more bluntly—how can we use the available Federal machinery to screw our political enemies.

There has been no testimony that Mr. Nixon saw the implications of this memorandum. But if it does nothing else, it at least makes it perfectly clear" that in some corners of Mr. Nixon's White House there was a veritable Mafia atmosphere in which no reward for friends was too generous and no punishment for "enemies" too brutal.

The conservative columnist, James J. Kilpatrick, an erstwhile Nixon supporter, has observed:

"The vise closes on Mr. Nixon. One jaw is labeled 'he knew,' the other, 'he did not know.' We are squeezed to an unhappy conclusion. If he knew, he was crooked; if he did not know, he was inept. If that is a fair metaphor, there is no way the President and his disappointed friends can wiggle out."

In our view, it is fair. We would add that ineptitude, though it may be disabling, is not a crime. As to Mr. Dean's charges that the President knew about and participated in the Watergate coverup and the crime of attempting to obstruct justice, it is noteworthy that Mr. Dean was shaken in no important respect in two days of cross examination. On the contrary, in most of his replies to the nine pages of questions prepared by White House counsel J. Fred Buzhardt, Mr. Dean added new details in support of charges against Mr. Nixon to which he had testified earlier.

As the record now stands, Mr. Dean repeatedly has said the President lies, and the White House has replied that it is Mr. Dean who not only lies but was himself one of the architects of the coverup. The Buzhardt questions, which were more in the nature of accusations, also quote former White House aide John Ehrlichman as stating that former Attorney General John Mitchell and Jeb S. Magruder, a deputy director of Mr. Nixon's re-election campaign, were participants in both planning the Watergate burglary and in ensuing coverup.

Thus, what Mr. Dean has called "the opening act in a great American tragedy" will become sharper (it hardly could become more tragic) when the testimony of Mr. Mitchell is rubbed against the testimony of Mr. Ehrlichman, who, in the Buzhardt questionnaire, has publicly accused Mr. Mitchell for the first time. They will appear after the Independence Day recess.

The one statement in the Buzhardt queries which no one can deny at this time is that "the political problem has been magnified a thousandfold because the truth is coming to light belatedly." This is indeed so. And the only way to get at the whole, clear and undeniable truth is to put all of the principals through the same grinding process to which Mr. Dean has been put.

The puzzle for all concerned, repeatedly expressed by committee members, is as to how and when the President himself can or will tell his side of this sorry mess, not through unsworn surrogates, such as Mr. Buzhardt, not through press releases, but in a forum where his credibility can be put to the same test as the credibility of other witnesses.

It would be unprecedented for a President of the United States to submit to cross-examination by a congressional committee. But the situation is already unprecedented. Mr. Nixon is fond of historic firsts. In this case, were he to abandon the protective shield of his office, he could establish a first that indeed would be historic. The White House has been too muddied for the President to stand on protocol or the separation of powers.

THE MILWAUKEE JOURNAL

Milwaukee, Wis., June 20, 1973

The week's postponement in the Senate Watergate Committee hearings seems justified in view of the summit talks between President Nixon and Soviet leader Leonid Brezhnev. While the delay may not strengthen Nixon's negotiating stance, it can be reasonably argued that holding the hearings on schedule — and airing testimony probably more wounding to presidential prestige than any so far — might have weakened him, or at least been a distraction.

Sen. Weicker (R-Conn.), the only one of seven committee members to vote against postponement, raised an interesting point when he noted that holding the hearings and the summit simultaneously "might give an idea to Brezhnev of the strength of our kind of government." Perhaps, but we are under no necessity to prove ourselves to the Soviet guest.

The major task of the committee is a timely, judicious and complete search for the truth concerning Watergate and associated foul play. To postpone the hearings for a few days will not impede this exploration. It only avoids igniting a side issue over propriety and further enhances the committee's commendable record of fair play.

The Montreal Star

Montreal. Que., June 22, 1973

ANY suggestions that the Senate Watergate probe was out to smear President Nixon, no matter what, should have been put to rest this week when the special committee investigating the scandal recessed during the Washington visit of Leonid Brezhney. This was done to avoid any embarrassment to the president—resulting from testimony by the committee's next scheduled witness, former White House counsel John Dean—and possibly impeding Mr. Nixon's discussions and negotiations with the Soviet party chief.

It was Senate majority leader Mike Mansfield who suggested a temporary halt to the hearings. Senator Ervin and his colleagues on the committee—who, for the most part, have handled the sessions with dignity and fairness—were quick to accept the recommendation.

That same sense of fairness was present, also, in the order by U.S. Judge John Sirica that federal prosecutors seal and deliver to the court prior to Mr. Dean's public appearance before the committee any evidence they might wish to present to the grand jury to support an indictment against the former White House aide. This would protect the immunity of Mr. Dean's testimony to the committee without precluding possible grand jury action based on separately gathered evidence.

By the time these various hearings are completed, the reputations of many individuals will have been seriously tarnished. But both the legislature and the judiciary are obviously making every effort to avoid a witch hunt and to accord to each witness as fair a hearing as possible.

DAILY NEWS

New York, N.Y., June 29, 1973

"What makes you think that your credibility is greater than that of the President, who denies what you have said?"

Sen. Herman Talmadge (D-Ga.) put that query to former White House counsel and star Watergate probe witness John W. Dean 3d on Tuesday. It sums up the dilemma facing the Senate committee and the nation at this stage of the spectacular public hearings.

John Dean

Dean has made many serious accusations about President Richard M. Nixon's alleged knowledge of and participation in the Watergate coverup.

But he has offered little if anything in the way of independent evidence to back his charges. Some of his most sensational "revelations" are based on surmise, assumption and conjecture—which only compound doubt and uncertainty.

The President continues to stand firmly—and silently —on his May 22 statement that he had no knowledge of the Watergate bugging and no hand in weaving the web of deception that followed.

We have no way of knowing how long Mr. Nixon intends to let matters rest there. We are sure, however, that prolonged silence would be unwise, as well as unhealthy for the nation.

Long shadows have fallen across the White House, and the American people are entitled to any first-hand information the President has that will help them arrive at the whole truth about Watergate.

In the strictly legal sense, Mr. Nixon has every right to keep quiet until his accusers have presented their full case. But this is hardly the occasion to stand on the niceties of due process—which in any event has been thoroughly trampled by the committee.

We think the time is ripe now for the President to present, in a form and forum of his choosing, a complete and detailed history of Watergate as it appeared through his eyes, laying out just what he learned—or was told— when, and from whom.

He should further disclose any notes, documents or records he has that will help clarify the whole mess.

Like it or not, this case has been thrown into the court of public opinion, and Mr. Nixon owes a full, frank accounting to that tribunal.

On the subject of Watergate, an—

UGLY SIDELIGHT

—surfaced on Wednesday when John Dean handed around a memo in which he had daintily suggested using the federal machinery, particularly the Internal Revenue Service, to "screw" certain opponents of the administration.

It's not clear whether Mrs. Dean's little boy John dreamed up this gem on his own or was carrying out someone else's warped ideas. Whatever the origin, the very suggestion of turning the tax-collecting apparatus to political use is sickening.

The fact that two IRS directors—to their eternal credit—refused to play that dirty game does not make it any less nauseating.

CHICAGO DAILY NEWS
Chicago, Ill., June 30, 1973

In watching the Watergate drama unfold, the public should remind itself from time to time that the Senate committee hearings, while immensely important and enlightening, are not judicial proceedings with their built-in disciplines and protections.

In listening to John W. Dean III, for example, it should be borne in mind that his testimony is as yet unsupported, in considerable part inferential or hearsay, and mostly elicited by politicians who themselves have a stake in the outcome.

As a matter of fact, in the Thursday session it was sometimes hard to determine whether Chairman Sam Ervin was the interrogator or the witness, so enthusiastically was he leading Dean along. At one time he quoted the Constitution to the effect that the President shall take care that the laws are faithfully executed, and demanded whether Dean knew anything Mr. Nixon did or said in the past year to see that the laws were faithfully executed in the Watergate matter. Dean said, quite properly, that that question asked for a conclusion he wasn't exactly in a position to make.

The North Carolina senator also went a bit off the deep end in trying to prod President Nixon into coming before the committee to testify. Like the old country lawyer he is, Ervin managed to suggest that it was the President's duty to appear without quite saying so. No, he said, he would not subpena the President (though he did not quite rule out the possibility). But, he asked rhetorically, "is there any way whatsoever to test the credibility of anybody when the credibility has to be judged merely on the basis of a written statement?"

The fact is that if Ervin were President he would undoubtedly take the same position Mr. Nixon has taken on that issue — and for the same reasons. The President is far more than an individual — he is a co-equal branch of government, subject to certain restraints and disciplines but not subject to the beck and call of a congressional committee. If this fact provides both a convenient refuge for a harrassed President and a source of frustration for the committee, that's the way it has to be. Ervin, of course, knows this, and is just trying to score his propaganda points. And that, too, is his right — but it is also the right and the duty of the public to keep the performance in perspective, and wait for all the evidence before reaching a conclusion.

THE DAILY OKLAHOMAN
Oklahoma City, Okla., June 29, 1973

WASHINGTON pundits caught up emotionally in the Watergate hysteria are not the most objective observers of the political climate in the rest of the country.

They suggest, for instance, that Sen. Edward J. Gurney, R-Fla., a member of the Senate select committee investigating the Watergate affair, may be scorching his own political goose by seeming to act as President Nixon's defender in the hearings. It is said that Gurney, skeptical of presidential guilt, has gone out on the limb for Nixon and thereby could be hurting his own chances for re-election next year. Of course, this could depend on the judgment the American people themselves finally make about the President after the whole story is told.

The assessment of Gurney's fortunes stems from his close questioning of John Dean III, the former presidential counsel who has emerged as the key accuser of Nixon. Gurney has earned himself a label of partisanship simply by striving to keep a semblance of balance in the flood of unsubstantiated charges and hearsay testimony laid before the committee. When he was named to the committee he said he wanted the inquiry to be as nonpartisan as possible but that "I certainly want to bring out every last piece of information."

Talk of Gurney hurting himself politically may be more valid in Washington than in Florida. Although the state is strongly Democratic, it returned a 72 per cent majority vote for Nixon last fall. The extent of the President's popularity decline because of Watergate is yet to be determined, either in Florida or in the rest of the United States.

Indeed, the long-range political effect of the supercharged Watergate investigation is difficult to predict. The more pessimistic Republicans might conclude their chances to retain the White House in the 1976 presidential election have been all but destroyed already. While Republican officials point out the party itself was not involved in the Watergate affair, it is certain that Democratic liberals, aided by some segments of the news media, will strive to keep Watergate before the public as long as possible.

That in itself could be self-defeating, however. There is evidence that a backlash against what the public sees as a Watergate overkill may be developing. Dean's most serious charges against the President so far are uncorroborated. Besides, he bears the onus of having become an administration turncoat. If the Dean story cannot be made to stick but if the committee persists in dragging it out, a backlash based on sympathy for the underdog, could redound to Nixon's favor. By 1976, moreover, there could be a new set of marbles and different players. Not only will the outcome depend on whom the Republicans nominate but also on whether the Democrats field another McGovern for the race.

Richmond Times-Dispatch
Richmond, Va., June 27, 1973

So now we have the portrait of President Nixon as painted by former White House counsel John W. Dean III. It is the portrait of a man who reportedly acquiesced in perjury, in the payment of "hush money" to the convicted Watergate burglars and in other sordid efforts to prevent the truth about the Watergate scandal from tainting the White House.

But the nation cannot hang this ugly portrait in its gallery of crooks without establishing its authenticity. It might well be a fake. In several important aspects, it differs sharply from Mr. Nixon's own self-portrait. It may differ significantly from the Nixon portraits yet to be unveiled by former White House aides H. R. Haldeman and John Ehrlichman and by former Attorney General John Mitchell. In short, Dean's reliability as a painter of presidential portraits is very much in doubt, and it would be unfair and possibly tragic to accept his rendering, without further ado, as the genuine Nixon.

— —

Dean has told the Senate Watergate committee that Mr. Nixon knew as long ago as September 15, 1972 of efforts to conceal the truth about the Watergate affair. On May 22 of this year, the President insisted that he neither participated in nor knew about "efforts that may have been made to cover up the Watergate."

President Nixon also denied, on that same day, that he authorized offers of executive clemency for Watergate defendants or that he knew of any "such offer." But according to Dean, Mr. Nixon referred to the matter of executive clemency at meetings on March 13 and April 15.

In his May statement, the President disclaimed any knowledge of efforts "to provide the Watergate defendants with funds" to keep them quiet, but Dean has told the committee that he informed Mr. Nixon of the payoffs at their March 13 meeting.

And at a meeting with the President on March 21, Dean confessed, he has testified, that he had assisted Jeb Stuart Magruder, deputy director of the Committee to Re-elect the President, in preparing the latter's "false story" for the Watergate grand jury.

— —

Thus, we have the President's word against the word of John Dean, and at this point the President's word is more credible than Dean's. The former counsel's accusations must be corroborated by future testimony for them to gain credence, for his actions as a participant in the Watergate cover-up and his performance as a witness have inspired questions about his veracity.

By his own admission, Dean, while still White House counsel, engaged in illegal and unethical acts. He helped concoct lies and participated in various schemes that resulted in the obstruction of justice. Are we now to assume that Dean has been transformed into a virtuous man of honor and truth? Perhaps. But once a man has been exposed as a weaver of lies, he cannot command trust simply by saying: "Believe me."

Dean's testimony to the Senate committee, true or false, has so far lacked the loud ring of sincerity. Unlike Magruder, who forthrightly admitted his errors and assumed complete responsibility for them, Dean has sought to convey the impression that he was a most reluctant participant in the Watergate cover-up, that he was pulled into it by forces over which he had no control. More than once he has told the committee that he "found" himself doing things he knew to be wrong, as if he were hypnotized. It is easy to get the impression from Dean's testimony that when he saw himself endangered by the collapse of the Watergate cover-up operation, he resolved to imperil as many other persons as possible, including the President.

Moreover, Dean has sought to exchange his testimony for immunity from prosecution. He has received immunity for whatever he says to the Senate committee, but he has not received immunity from prosecution by the Justice Department on the basis of evidence it obtains from other sources. Some people are convinced that Dean is trying to save himself by offering to serve as the agent for toppling the President of the United States.

— —

Dean's testimony, then, must be received with skepticism. The fact that this man has shown contempt for the truth before means that we cannot accept his word as gospel now. Certainly his testimony has raised damaging questions about Mr. Nixon that must be specifically answered. His statements cannot be dismissed casually as the fabrications of a desperate man trying to save himself. Considered with all other aspects of the Watergate case, Dean's testimony intensifies the suspicions of those who find it hard to believe that the President is totally innocent. But it would be wrong to assume, as some people may be tempted to do, that Dean is the only witness who matters and that his testimony constitutes the final, unassailable truth about Watergate.

The Washington Post
Times Herald

Washington, D.C., June 21, 1973

Monday the Senate Watergate committee will start taking public testimony from John Dean III, the former Counsel to the President and a man who has risen from obscurity to celebrity and, in some quarters, to infamy in a very short period of time. Prior to Mr. Nixon's misleading statement last August that John Dean had conducted a thorough Watergate-White House investigation under the President's own direction, it is probable that the public had not the smallest idea of who this young man was—and he was not widely known to the press corps either.

All that has changed. First there came the slow but steady trickle of disclosures: Mr. Dean may or may not have conducted a thorough investigation for Mr. Nixon, it was said (in fact, he conducted none at all), but he did turn out to be—one way and the other—involved in practically all the scandals that now go by the generic name of Watergate. Others might have picked and chosen, but evidently not Mr. Dean. His name turns up in connection with the Watergate espionage, the hush money fund-raising, ITT, the Daniel Ellsberg doctor's office burglary, the destruction of Howard Hunt's incriminating White House effects, the effort to subvert the CIA and the FBI, and the rest.

Things, as we all recall, weren't going terribly well for Mr. Dean at the White House this spring. To be sure, given the state of the White House this spring, that wasn't much of a distinction. What distinguished Mr. Dean's behavior was the fact that he plunged early and in a pretty headstrong way into the scapegoat politics that had begun to prevail, perceiving that in the game of musical chairs that had got underway, his chair—and his alone—seemed to keep disappearing. Mr. Dean went to the federal prosecutors. And he went public: he let it be known that he didn't intend to take all the heat or blame for assorted crimes and scandals that were closing in. He was fired by the President. He has since sought and received a grant of limited immunity for his Watergate testimony before the Ervin committee. And he has also since become the object of a merciless campaign to discredit the worth of his testimony.

To state the case modestly, it is not a pretty business, and no one should confuse John Dean with Emile Zola. But that hardly seems to us to be a clear and present danger at the moment. Rather, the danger seems to be that in a muddle of thought concerning the moral worth of Mr. Dean's motives and with a little "help" from those who stand to suffer most from his testimony, people may deny themselves the opportunity to hear this testimony in a dispassionate, discriminating way. *"Turncoat,"* Sen. Hugh Scott has said in disgust, for example, of Mr. Dean. *"Embezzler,"* he has added. So what else is new? To call a self-confessed criminal a criminal doesn't add a thing to our knowledge, and to denounce him as a "turncoat" carries at least a suggestion that he should have stayed faithful to the conspiracy that is now being broken open. It also carries another suggestion, namely, that Mr. Dean—who threatens to implicate the President—is somehow morally reprehensible in a way that the other "turncoats" and criminals who have been implicating each other are not.

The first thing to remember, we would suggest, is that renegades and lawbreakers who turn state's evidence, from Whittaker Chambers to Joe Valachi, were not meant to be loved but to be heard. Their circumstances put a premium on their telling the truth. Naturally, not all do so. But it is worth recalling in this particular affair that thus far, since his first venture to the pros-ecutors' office, Mr. Dean has in fact provided a wealth of previously unknown material that has checked out and that the White House has been obliged on a regular basis to revise and render inoperative its statements of the day or week before.

Judging from the interviews and depositions of many of those who, like Mr. Dean, are up to their eyebrows in Watergate trouble, you could get the impression that this admittedly inventive man was solely responsible for what went on across the board, managing to deceive all those who ranked him in the White House and to whom he reported, contriving to juggle the multidinous scandals on his own and issuing orders to half of Washington to misbehave itself—without a peep getting back to those in charge. That, of course, is the impression you are meant to get from the interviews and depositions in question. One year after the Watergate, however—a year of mind bending revelations—there are still a few things too preposterous to be believed. Not many, but a few—and among them is the proposition that John Dean, acting on his own, systematically and over a period of a couple of years, brought all these things about without the knowledge or understanding of the people he worked for and in whose behalf he was presumably doing them.

The element of knowledge—of knowing and not knowing—is important here, and it will be important to understand it in relation to Mr. Dean's testimony. What is it that people have in mind, or should have, when they wonder aloud whether the President "knew"? First, it should be recalled that we are no longer discussing a single burglary of the Democrats' Watergate headquarters when we confine the question to that particular episode; nor, when we discuss the June 17 Watergate burglary (in which the burglars were caught) are we even discussing the relevant one. The June 17 maraud, we now know, was a patch-up mission, very conceivably organized by Mr. Liddy without his superiors' specific knowledge and undertaken to repair and improve electronic snooping equipment that had been installed in a previous *successful* burglary in May. As a consequence of that previous burglary wiretap material had already been coming into the hands of Mr. Nixon's campaign officials. To the extent that it is still valid or even reasonable to limit one's inquiry about Watergate to the President's specific knowledge of the break-in and bugging of Democratic headquarters, the focus should therefore be shifted to his knowledge (or lack thereof) of the intelligence operation that culminated in the first, successful break-in in May.

The June break-in, which resulted in the arrests, is important in an entirely different way: it marks the onset of Phase II, a whole new and, in some ways, far more sinister series of crimes. That is, it marks the beginning of the cover-up. On that subject too, Mr. Dean is expected to have a great deal to say, and it is no secret that he is believed prepared to implicate Mr. Nixon directly in the effort to corrupt whatever judicial processes and government institutions were necessary for the purpose of hiding the truth. This will be dramatic and potentially explosive stuff. That is why we would urge a cold-eyed, dispassionate, discriminating look at Mr. Dean when he testifies. It is not impossible that he will be grinding some ax or that he will be indulging a vendetta. Neither is it impossible that he will be presenting a plausible and persuasive and truthful case. The only thing we know to be impossible is that Mr. Dean did *all* these things *from beginning to end* in total secrecy and on his own. Let us hear him out.

THE TENNESSEAN
Nashville, Tenn., June 29, 1973

THE White House is giving the impression of frantic confusion in its reaction to Mr. John W. Dean's testimony before the Ervin committee implicating President Nixon in the coverup of the Watergate scandal.

★ ★ ★

The White House fired off a memorandum to the committee Wednesday accusing Mr. Dean himself of being the "principal actor in the Watergate coverup" and blaming him for most of the evil consequences of the coverup.

The memorandum and the questions it contained for the committee to put to Mr. Dean were accepted by the committee as Mr. Nixon's considered answer to Mr. Dean's testimony of the last several days. Sen. Daniel K. Inouye, D-Hawaii, who read the memorandum and questions to the committee and Mr. Dean, even characterized the White House communication as a kind of cross-examination of Mr. Dean by the President.

But yesterday the White House issued another statement saying President Nixon was not involved in the compilation of the memorandum and that the memo should not be taken as the definitive White House position on the matter. Mr. Ronald Ziegler, White House press secretary, said it was incorrect to describe the memo as a substitute cross-examination by the President.

This raises the question of how the memorandum to the Ervin committee did originate and who it is at the White House accusing Mr. Dean of being the author of the coverup.

The memo was prepared and sent to the committee by Mr. J. Fred Buzhardt Jr., special counsel to the White House. But Mr. Buzhardt has been at the White House only since May 10 of this year. While the Watergate scandal was developing — and all during the time the coverup was being carried out from the executive offices in the White House — Mr. Buzhardt was working at the Pentagon across the Potomac River from the White House. So he is hardly in position to know first hand who authored the coverup and what part, if any, Mr. Dean had in it.

There are very few people at the White House now who were there when the Watergate coverup was being perpetrated. Mr. Ziegler was there then. But he admits he was so badly misled that he didn't even know a coverup was in effect, much less who its author might be. So Mr. Ziegler is not in position to accuse Mr. Dean of authoring the coverup.

Thus, it seems the memo accusing Mr. Dean just suddenly sprang to life in the inner recesses of the White House without any hint of its credibility or any trace of its origin. This is a sad way to answer charges as serious as those brought against Mr. Nixon.

★ ★ ★

Mr. Dean has given his testimony under oath and in full view of millions of Americans. His charges can be answered only in the same open way—and by the President himself. They cannot be successfully refuted by White House memos of vague authorship which the President is free to disavow the next day.

THE DALLAS TIMES HERALD
Dallas, Tex., June 27, 1973

PRESIDENT NIXON and his high command have been driven into a grave defensive position that now demands credible refutation—or ruinous consequences.

A 34-year-old ousted White House legal aide who vowed that he would not be the scapegoat of Watergate — John W. Dean III—has implicated the President, former Atty. Gen. John N. Mitchell, top White House hands John Ehrlichman and H. R. Haldeman and others in Senate select committee testimony.

No longer is Mr. Nixon on the edge of scandal. Dean, hoping that the President would be forgiven of his involvement because he didn't realize the full implications, put the President squarely in the middle of the coverup with droning, unemotional testimony that set off shock waves.

Dean says that President Nixon was aware of plans to spend upwards of $1 million to buy the silence of the convicted Watergate burglars. He says that he urged Mr. Nixon to halt the coverup maneuvering — to take the lead role himself in facing the truth.

He says that he advised the President that he (Dean), Ehrlichman and Haldeman were in an "indictable" position for obstructing justice.

Finally, he testified, he "hoped that going to the prosecutors (with his story) would not result in your impeachment." He said the President "jokingly" replied:

"I hope so also . . . "

Most of the conversations came in private meetings with the President; testimony that demands corroboration or denial.

Such is the serious spot in which President Nixon finds himself — along with Mitchell, Haldeman, Ehrlichman and others Dean has woven into his lengthy testimony.

The nation now has heard Dean. It has heard President Nixon in a nationally televised address. The two stories do not jibe. Dean spoke almost reluctantly in his opening day testimony concerning President Nixon's knowledge of Watergate coverup details. He seemed to want to assume a protective posture.

But pointed second-day interrogation by committee members and their counselors drew from Dean even more damaging assumptions. The matter now gets down to credibility. The nation, beset by other problems that are shaking confidence, needs direct communication from the President by press conference or nationwide statement.

It does not know what to believe. The growing gravity of Watergate is sinking in. The credibility of national leadership has been seriously challenged. It wants the truth.

The Evening Star
The Washington Daily News
Washington, D.C., June 26, 1973

The nation yesterday got its first long look at the man who probably represents the greatest single threat to President Nixon in the still unfolding saga of Watergate.

John Dean's testimony promised to be explosive. It was that, all right, despite the fact that bits and pieces of it had leaked out days and weeks before. The 34-year-old former counsel to the President had little to add on the subjects of the Watergate planning and similar espionage operations. But the scope and the detail of his six hours of testimony were relentless in describing the increasingly corrosive atmosphere in the White House as various presidential aides, and perhaps the President himself, tried every which way to cover up the scandal.

Can John Dean be believed? That remains the essential question. His motives and reputation, of course, have been attacked, with some success. By his own account, he is capable of a championship style of lying. But his chief accuser, the White House, has shown it is also capable of constant dodges and weaves as it tries to explain Watergate and then tries to explain prior "inoperative" Watergate explanations.

It comes down to a matter of backup evidence, and also of perception. The public at this point must rely on its perception of Dean, an undeniably central figure in the case. And we venture to say the public already has decided, by the sheer volume of his testimony, that it would be impossible for Dean to have made it all up. The public may well continue to suspend judgment on the President's role. But the Dean testimony will reinforce, as nothing else has done so conclusively, the picture of a tragically flawed administration, of an entire echelon of White House officials operating in a jungle of deception and Byzantine maneuvering.

Dean's allegations against the President stem almost wholly from direct sessions he had with Mr. Nixon. Taken as a whole, they are damaging to the President. They cannot—at least at this point—be called shattering.

For one thing, the Dean testimony on his meetings with Mr. Nixon was at points incomplete, or ambiguous, or downright puzzling — just as puzzling as the witness's opening, sweeping conclusion that the President was involved in the coverup but at no time realized "the implications of his involvement."

Alternately, the testimony invites the question of whether we have a President so obtuse or guileless that he couldn't understand what was going on around him for nearly a year, or a President so slick and clever, especially during his March-April meetings with Dean, that he was mainly concerned with setting his young counsel up for a fall.

Much will depend on careful analysis of the voluminous documentation Dean supplied the committee, and also on the caliber of the Senate committee's questioning of the witness. If, through hard evidence or testimony by other witnesses, Dean's most serious charges are corroborated, then Mr. Nixon is indeed in deep water. Of course, it could go all the other way, with Dean's major accusations blunted, or at least rendered inconclusive. In any case, this is a showdown week, one that may provide essential clues as to how the mess will end. That, in itself, would be something of a relief.

The Star-Ledger

Newark, N.J., June 29, 1973

The Senate Watergate hearing has taken a sharp new tack: The White House has gone on the offensive, hoping to batter and discredit the credibility of the President's former counsel, the still unflappable John W. Dean 3d.

The strategy appears to be carefully calculated. Mr. Dean has been the most damaging witness to date, his under-stated testimony has been fleshed out with documents, charts and transcripts. But it must be remembered, too, that thus far it is raw, unevaluated material that is yet to be corroborated.

It is testimony that, for the most part, would not have been permitted in a court of law, where rules of evidence are necessarily far more rigorous to protect those accused. But this does not detract from its importance in serving a useful public purpose in exposing the clandestine and criminal activities involved in this nefarious case.

And there should be a necessary point of reservation, too, in the fact that Mr. Dean himself was a principal in the bungling scheme of political deceit and the equally clumsy attempt to cover up the sordid affair.

* * *

ALL THIS should be kept carefully in mind in any premature attempt to make judgments on the Dean portrayal of a White House atmosphere permeated with mutual distrust, an abiding fear of political enemies that drove highly-placed men to arrogant abuses of power.

Mr. Dean's version, carefully inscribed in a 245-page statement, has now been put into the record, where it can either be picked apart for inconsistencies and inaccuracies or substantiated by other principals. That is yet to come.

If the former White House counsel is to be believed, then an assumption can be made that the President and his key advisers were so highly disturbed over the actions of militant elements and even those who opposed them politically that they resorted to what can best be described as police-state methods.

A long but well-executed cross-examination was conducted by Sen. Edward J. Gurney, a Republican member of the committee who is regarded as friendly by the White House. The thrust of this strategy was to discredit the Dean testimony and to cast doubts on the witness himself, making it clear that his actions were as culpable as those of his former associates, including the President, that he had involved in his previous testimony.

* * *

SEN. GURNEY was able to make some points, but it was apparent when the extensive examination of the witness had been completed that his main thesis remained unshaken except for some subtle shadings and variations in interpretations.

But this paled in comparison with the blistering charges contained in the White House memo, a document that branded Mr. Dean as the principal architect of the Watergate conspiracy, and casting former Attorney General John N. Mitchell into a similar role. It was clear that sides have now been chosen, and that Mr. Nixon's two top lieutenants, H.R. Haldeman and John D. Ehrlichman, would be isolated from the grubby machinations of Watergate — the planning and the cover-up.

For all of its sensational charges, however, the White House memorandum had some basic weaknesses that became glaringly apparent in the presentation by Sen. Daniel K. Inouye (D-Hawaii).

The White House statement was prepared by Mr. Dean's successor, J. Fred Buzhardt, and it revealed the lack of personal familiarity of its author with the events of Watergate as it transpired. Mr. Buzhardt was, in effect, a conduit who had to rely on other sources — including newspaper accounts — in attempt not only to discredit the witness but to enlarge the dimension of his role and to minimize the parts played by Messrs. Haldeman and Ehrlichman, the down-to-the-end loyal White House courtiers.

* * *

THE CHARGES were sensational and provocative in nature but they were gravely vitiated and weakened by repetitive references to their sources — Haldeman and Ehrlichman, who are no less impartial or unbiased principals than Dean himself.

Viewed in this perspective, the White House memorandum has no more — or any less — substantive quality than the Dean testimony and documentation. It does not enlighten or clarify the conflicting statements and recollections that have been entered on the hearing record thus far.

But what it does do, in a most disturbing manner, is to give further verification to a Presiden that was enmeshed in an unsettling pattern of trust and self-deception and shabby practices made Watergate the nightmarish reality that came — and remains, casting ominous, foreb shadows over the White House.

The Watergate hearings should serve a tharsis for this country's gravely damaged p institutions, a public purging that eventually restore credibility and confidence in gover and a sense of integrity in those who govern.

HERALD EXAMINER

Los Angeles , Calif., June 29, 1973

The Nixon-haters who placed their hopes on John Dean III to sink the President must have bitter tastes in their mouths today. In three days of hearings before the Senate Ervin Committee, Dean by his own words-sunk himself in the Watergate quagmire and revealed himself as a charlatan.

Under questioning by Sen. Edward J. Gurney, (R-Fla.) Dean conceded that he did not tell President Nixon directly about the Watergate involvement and coverup last Sept. 15. As if he were some kind of a mind-reader, Dean said he thought the President knew.

The infamous list of "enemies of the Administration", which has brought much clucking from the excitable left-leaning press, was revealed to be not particularly unusual, unprecedented or offensive. But Dean admitted he wanted to use the available federal machinery "to screw our political enemies" — a sinister suggestion that never was seriously considered.

The purpose of the list was very simple and straightforward: to keep the social office, the personnel office, the press office, the counsel's office and other offices in the White House apprised of people who had been particularly supportive of the President or people who had been particularly critical of the President. The information was primarily for consideration as names were proposed to White House social events or appointments to federal boards and commissions.

Then there is the matter of Star Witness Dean's taste in honeymoon — expensive, even in ultra inflationary times. He told the Senate Committee how he took $4,800 in Nixon campaign cash to pay for a lavish two-week honeymoon in Florida complete with servants dishing up the food. The money had been left in Dean's care by two White House officials, $15,200 cash he said was entrusted to him White House staffers Gordon St:chan and Richard Howard. But only took $4,800 for the honeymoon he was unable to take because the pressure of the Watergat coverup intervened.

Dean said he once replaced som of the cash, then withdrew it befo a second attempt at a honeymoon November. He said he eventually "began using the money for personal expenses." Dean said he comingled it with other funds.

"Do you know this is a crime, Mr. Dean?" said Sen. Gurney.

"I'm not aware what crime," Dean replied.

"Isn't it embezzlement?" countered Gurney.

"There was no intention on my part not to account for the full amount," replied Dean. "I knew at some point I would have to account for the $15,200."

And so it went. Dean has egg all over his embarrassed face.

There will be considerably more egg splattered and on the red faces of many Nixon enemies as the truth of Watergate is fully revealed.

THE WALL STREET JOURNAL
New York, N.Y., June 28, 1973

John Dean has performed exceedingly well in his first three days of Senate testimony. On the central point of whether the President was involved in the Watergate cover-up, Mr. Dean's allegations strike us as reasonably credible, pending a White House rebuttal.

Whatever anyone may conclude about Mr. Dean's character and motives—and Senator Gurney's questions about finances scored points against him on this issue—his account has an internal plausibility of its own. There are of course points we would like to see explored further, and some of the alleged presidential comments and actions remain ambiguous. But the account of an impression here, a presidential remark there, building into a pattern that spells involvement—this strikes us as precisely the way the real world would operate. By and large, the mass of detail and the lack of obvious inconsistencies weave Mr. Dean's story into a believable whole.

The only way to believe the President was not involved in the cover-up is to believe that Mr. Dean has contrived or maliciously distorted the parts of his testimony dealing with his conversations with Mr. Nixon. This is not entirely impossible, of course, for Mr. Dean has obvious interests of his own to protect. But it is difficult to believe that a contrivance could be skillful enough to produce the story Mr. Dean tells. People lie, but they do not ordinarily lie so well.

As regular readers of this column recognize, and as some of our letterwriters complain, we have consistently advocated caution in accusing the President of direct complicity in Watergate. The case, after all, concerns nothing less grave than the potential destruction of the third presidency in succession. Over the past decade, also, we have repeatedly seen "facts" instantly sweep the nation only to be later disproved. There is every reason to view charges against the President with the same skepticism and scrutiny his own statements have received.

In that spirit, we certainly do want to hear much more before reaching any firm conclusions, let alone advocating anything on the basis of them. Mr. Dean's testimony concerning the President is so far not corroborated. With the exception of Senator Gurney, committee members have not subjected it to close or skeptical questioning. Future witnesses will presumably dispute Mr. Dean. As further evidence is developed and the stories of further witnesses heard and judged, there will be plenty of time to make final judgments.

But it is not humanly possible, nor would it be responsible to keep a perfectly blank mind forever. It seems to us that Mr. Dean's account is quite enough for a prima facie case, to create the presumption of presidential involvement, to shift the burden of proof to the White House.

The tenor of the White House response to Mr. Dean, indeed, will go far toward making or breaking the case. We started to get the response at the end of the hearings yesterday, as Senator Inouye asked Mr. Dean for pointby-point commentary on a White House memo setting out a different theory of the case, painting Mr. Dean as the central figure in the cover-up.

An attack on Mr. Dean, though, will not be an effective reply to his account. Rather, the White House will have to come up with its own story, particularly of conversations between Mr. Dean and the President, that is as detailed, as consistent and as plausible as the one we have heard this week. Fabricating such an account would be a large and probably impossible order for the White House, while drawing up the truth is not so difficult. If the President is not guilty of involvement, his best tactic would be to get out everything—notes, minutes, presidential impressions, the tape-recording Mr. Dean suspects exists.

If the White House can come up with that kind of response, it will do much to neutralize the accusations of the last three days. But if the White House fails to produce its own solid account, that in itself will go far toward corroborating Mr. Dean.

THE RICHMOND NEWS LEADER
Richmond, Va., June 27, 1973

As former White House counsel John Dean continues to testify before the Ervin Committee, the central question in the Watergate case pivots. The question no longer is: Who was guilty?, but Who was innocent?

Dean's testimony implicates the President so deeply in the Watergate cover-up that obviously he or the President is lying. On May 22, President Nixon appeared on television and made the following statements:

(1) I had no prior knowledge of the Watergate operation.

(2) I took no part in, nor was I aware of, any subsequent efforts that may have been made to cover up Watergate.

(3) At no time did I authorize any offer of Executive clemency for the Watergate defendants, nor did I know of any such offer.

(4) I did not know, until the time of my own investigation, of any effort to provide the Watergate defendants with funds.

(5) At no time did I attempt, nor did I authorize others to attempt, to implicate the CIA in the Watergate matter.

(6) It was not until the time of my own investigation that I learned of the break-in at the office of Mr. Ellsberg's psychiatrist, and I specifically authorized the furnishing of this information to Judge Byrne.

(7) I neither authorized nor encouraged subordinates to engage in illegal or improper campaign tactics. . . .

Dean's testimony contradicts the President on points 2, 3, 4, and 6. But is Dean telling the truth? Everything in his testimony seems calculated to place Dean in the best light possible. *He* was the one who moderated some of the wilder plans for political espionage. *He* was the one who repeatedly warned the President of the dangers implicit in the Watergate cover-up. He is at once sanctimonious and clever, concerned and sly. He knows he faces criminal indictment and a possible jail term. His testimony ought to be received in that perspective. Others have admitted culpability and wrongdoing in the Watergate affair; Dean admits his mistakes in a "Yes, but. . . manner, attempting both to justify and exonerate his actions.

Yet so much of his testimony rings true that it fills in the pattern suggested by previous witnesses. The Watergate cover-up had become "a way of life" in the White House. The names fall from his lips in a roll-call of some of the highest White House and administration officials: Strachan, Petersen, Stans, Mitchell, Ehrlichman, Haldeman, Colson, Kalmbach, Magruder, Ziegler, Kleindienst. These are the men whom the President chose to insulate him from the exigencies of public life; they have been implicated by so many different witnesses that the President's judgment of integrity and character in the men he appoints stands seriously challenged.

Some of these men co-operated in the obstruction of justice. Others headed off a congressional investigation that might have broken the Watergate case wide open before election day. Others colluded in attempts to influence members of the Ervin Committee. Others perjured themselves. How could the President have erred so grievously in judging the men he chose as his closest associates? Even as he announced the resignations of Ehrlichman and Haldeman on April 30, the President still praised them as two of the finest public servants he had ever known. At that time, he must have known or have guessed that both were involved in the Watergate cover-up up to their eyeteeth.

The sad aspect of the Ervin Committee hearings comes from the nature of the hearings themselves. As Vice President Spiro Agnew has pointed out, "There is no absolute right of cross examination afforded the persons accused or named by a witness. . . . In the Senate hearing, the right of persons accused or named in testimony before the committee to be represented by counsel is severely abridged. . . . There is no firm guarantee of an opportunity for persons accused or named by a witness to rebut that testimony by calling other witnesses or introducing other evidence. . . . There is no guarantee of an opportunity for persons accused or named by a witness to introduce evidence which tends to impeach the accuser's credibility. . . ."

Thus, the President stands accused, on nationwide television, of malfeasance of office. Dean's portrayal of the President is of a man wise to the use — and abuse — of power, a man with a strong sense of survival by any means, a man obsessed by the need to be protected from dissent. Is this a faithful portrait of a man an overwhelming number of Americans trusted enough to re-elect to a second term as President? Dean says it is, but he may be overdrawing or misrepresenting facts.

His testimony under oath arouses the specter of President Nixon, with his back against the wall, asking the Ervin Committee for time to respond to Dean's charges on a point-by-point basis. As the damning web tangles more fatefully around the President, he must acknowledge that the extent of public trust in him has a breaking point, and opinion polls suggest that the breaking point may be imminent.

Chicago Tribune

Chicago, Ill., June 29, 1973

Back in college, as we recall, it took a B average or better to make the Dean's List. But different Deans have different kinds of lists, and the qualification for making John Dean's list, it seems, was to get a D average or worse in Popularity in the White House in 1971.

Certainly it is distressing to think that Big Brother, or even some Little Brother in the White House, has been keeping a list of "society's offenders who never will be missed," like the Lord High Executioner in "The Mikado." Moreover the list seems to have been drawn up quite haphazardly, by many people, on the basis of whims and pet peeves. We can think of eminently deserving names that are missing, and we find some unexpected ones on it. The excuses offered by the White House for maintaining the list are feeble, to say the least.

But what interests us at the moment is the reaction of those on the list. Not the fact that they consider themselves honored—that we can understand. After all, none of them seems to have suffered for being listed; most of them have made dislike of the Nixon administration their stock in trade; and they are clearly delighted with the many specific and serious charges that Mr. Dean has made against his former superiors at the White House, including the President. These charges demand a better reply than has yet been forthcoming.

What is more interesting is that even tho nearly all of those listed regard themselves as champions of liberalism and civil rights—especially the rights of defendants in court — not one of them to our knowledge has questioned whether the list is really pertinent to the Watergate investigation.

True, the Senate committee can argue that its scope is a broad one—"campaign practices"—but the legal charges that Special Prosecutor Archibald Cox is likely to bring to trial will be narrow ones dealing only with Watergate.

When Mr. Cox asked the Senate to postpone its investigation so as not to interfere with fair trials, we differed with him on the ground that it was important for the facts of Watergate to be exposed in as public a manner as possible. We still believe this. But we also urged the committee to be careful not to turn the hearings into a free-for-all which would make a fair trial difficult if not impossible. And in this respect, it looks as if Mr. Dean, in order to spread his immunity from prosecution as far as possible, and some of the committee members, in their eagerness to portray the White House in as bad a light as possible, are overdoing things.

THE WALL STREET JOURNAL.

New York, N.Y., July 2, 1973

Among the debris falling out of the White House at the Watergate hearings is the list of Nixon administration "enemies." It has set presumably serious people to talking of how close we have come to being a "police state."

Now, it is of course reprehensible that White House officials, allegedly including the President, should want to use the Internal Revenue Service and other government agencies to attack these enemies. And some of the results, as described by our John Pierson on this page today, are a telling commentary on White House pettiness. Still, fortunately, it takes more than bad intentions and cold shoulders to make a police state. Since it is not apparent that anything particularly important happened as a result of the list, we seem to have been saved by White House inefficiency.

Which is not surprising if you look at the list itself. Our first impression is to wonder why any Republican administration would need a list to remind itself that, say, Democratic presidential contenders are political enemies. But this mystery is cleared up when one reads the list to discover that Joe Namath is with the New York Giants and Hans Morgenthau is a former U.S. attorney in New York City. The media list includes Max Lerner, who must be the gentlest enemy anyone ever had, but omits Herblock, perhaps because he finally gave the President a shave.

After reading the list, we worry less about the danger that our governors are dictatorial than about the danger that our governors are silly. What a way for grown men to spend their time.

Those most frenetic about the disclosure, though, seem to us intent on matching the White House example in this respect. When they calm down, they ought to spend a little time reading The Federalist Papers, instructive for anyone but especially for someone who worries about police states. The way to avoid dictatorial governments, the readers would learn, is not to rely on governors not having evil intentions, but to structure institutions in such a way as to prevent governors from carrying out such intentions when they arise. Among the methods of doing this is something called checks and balances.

As to whether American institutions still function in the way the Founding Fathers intended, consider John Dean's testimony on how he went about getting a tax audit when suspicions arose about an enemy's financial affairs. In this police state, it seems, the counsel for the White House was afraid to call up the head of the IRS with such a request. But Mr. Dean knew someone who had friends in the IRS who could help. It turns out their help was coaching on how to phrase an anonymous letter giving the tax collectors a tip.

Or in other words, in trying to carry out a vendetta, the White House with all its pomp and glory is reduced to the same level as any other grubby infighter: sending an anonymous letter. Or to put a better face on it, to doing its civic duty in providing the IRS with the kind of information for which the laws provide an informer's reward.

Some police state.

Arkansas Gazette.

Little Rock, Ark., June 29, 1973

Senator Sam J. Ervin said of an honor roll of political "enemies" whom the Nixon administration set about to effectively destroy in August, 1971, that it appeared to him at first glance to be rather longer than would a comparable listing by name of the people who actually voted for George McGovern in 1972.

"Chuck" Colson — the White House utility infielder whose specialty as a starter was direction of the "Dirty Tricks Department" — has owned up to authorship of the list that appeared in memorandum form as part of the "John Dean Papers," which are now in the possession of the Ervin Committee.

Colson's only reaction to the disclosure was surprise — and not a little irritation — that anyone should be surprised at the existence of such a list of persons whom the Nixon administration, in the elegant drawing room language used in a memorandum on the subject proposed to "screw" for the sake of the higher national interest, the name of which of course is "Nixon." We are sure that Colson was surprised that anybody else should be surprised by the list, because he saw nothing wrong with it. We are sure that he saw nothing wrong with it, or, indeed, with any of the other scummy practices being revealed by the Watergate investigation, not even with those (if any there are) in which he did not actually have a hand.

The list itself is a mixed bag, and we are afraid that we were a little surprised at least by a few of the names appearing there, such as that of Joe Namath. We hang onto every pearl that drops from the lips of this multi-talented gridiron performer, but were never aware that his other off-field pursuits allowed much time for bad-mouthing Nixon.

We are surprised, too, that Senator J. W. Fulbright ranked only No. 2 (behind Senator Birch Bayh) in the order of precedence of the threat to the Nixon presidency supposedly posed by each of the listed names, though Fulbright himself, with that bland air of mild astonishment that he sometimes affects on such occasions, said he had no idea that the Nixon administration regarded him as any kind of enemy, though he supposed upon learning this that it all had something vaguely to do with the war.

As for the "media" folks, well . . . What some of the names appearing in this category shows is something that we have known all along, which is that Nixon does not expect or want "fairness" from the news media, but unanimous consent and approval.

For example, if Senator Fulbright was surprised by the inclusion of his name, how do you think "Scotty" Reston must feel? If the response is in character, the institutionalized New York Times pundit will be more hurt than angered. Reston has bent over backward to be "fair" to Nixon and Nixonism so many times that he could go on the boards as the Astonishing India Rubber Man. Yet this is how much appreciation and awareness he gets from Nixon, who we know is unable to appreciate the desperate effort that Reston has made to be "fair," the tortures he has submitted himself to, because Nixon does not himself know the meaning of "fairness."

Detroit Free Press
Detroit, Mich., June 30, 1973

EVERYONE KEEPS a list, written or mental, of people they don't like, and the White House is no exception. Most, however, refer to it in more earthy terms than "enemies list" used by the administration. As entertainer Bill Cosby noted, "Nixon was on my list long before I was on Nixon's list."

Most of the 173 people named on the enemies list supplied to the Senate Watergate Committee by former presidential counsel John Dean III felt more honored than outraged, although the list was pretty outrageous.

For example, there was that noted political commentator from Beaver Falls, Pa., Joe Namath, somewhat ignominiously traded by the White House from the New York Jets to the rival Giants. Who would have thought Broadway Joe could get away from booze, broads and knee surgeons long enough to become anyone's political enemy?

As befitting the lofty heights of the presidency, the list was bipartisan. It included Wally Hickel, a former Republican governor, Charles Goodell, a former Republican senator, and John Lindsay, a former Republican.

Paul Newman, who made a better Hud than did George Romney, thought he had won a Richard. "And I would like to thank John Mitchell, Jeb Magruder, John Dean

III and Maurice Stans for making this award possible."

The presidents of Yale and MIT were on the list, but not the president of Harvard. There would be gloom in the Square except Harvard's law school dean and three faculty members made it.

Ed Guthman made the list as managing editor of the Los Angeles Times, which prompted a New York Times staff writer to note:

"Alas, Mr. Guthman is not the managing editor, but the national editor, and the citation by itself does not make him eligible for promotion." It probably doesn't eliminate him from future consideration though, so no harm's done.

The list was remarkable both for those included and those excluded. Columnist Sydney Harris, who gives innocuous word tests, made it, but Herblock, who does scathing political cartoons, did not.

Barbra Streisand made it, but neither Shirley McLaine nor her brother, Warren Beatty, did.

Sen. Howard Baker, R-Tenn., reported that Watergate Committee Chairman Sam Ervin, D-N.C., leaned over as the list was made public and said, "I think I'm going to demand a recount. There are more enemies than we got votes."

The list was rather exclusive. It threatens to replace the Social Register in Washington.

THE KANSAS CITY STAR
Kansas City, Mo., June 19, 1973

A recent Gallup poll shows that 44 per cent of the people questioned—more than 4 out of 10—believe that newspapers, magazines, television and radio are paying too much attention to Watergate and related subjects. The poll isn't surprising and we would guess that it is accurate: A high percentage of the American people are tired of Watergate and wish it would go away for various reasons.

We cannot agree, however, that the press should reduce coverage or let the issues fade away no matter how unpopular the recital becomes. It is the obligation of the media to provide information to the people no matter how distasteful it might be. The First Amendment to the Constitution guaranteeing freedom of the press is not there by accident; a free press is an integral part of the system and the chief value of the media is not in the entertainment it furnishes but as a purveyor of information.

People who are disenchanted with Watergate can be divided into three broad categories:

The least important group comprises those who are unhappy if a soap opera is supplanted occasionally or who are not much interested in anything that doesn't concern movies, sports or TV personalities. These individuals take little, if any, interest in public affairs. If they vote, it almost always is an uninformed act. But they seldom vote, and democracy's loss is small.

A second group is composed of those who are very interested in government, but from a blindly partisan and very narrow view that often reflects a fundamental self-interest. They resent any unfavorable reporting on the President or his party as unpatriotic, if not disloyal. They consider it a personal attack upon themselves, so strongly do they identify. Right now these people are a certain type of Republican. If the occupant of the White House happened to be a Democrat, they would be a certain type of Democrat.

The third and probably biggest group tired of Watergate are concerned people who dread the implications of presidential involvement and would rather not think of this breakdown of a

system they revere and honor. It is frightening to imagine that a large majority might have been fooled in the campaign into voting for people who do not believe in the system at all. The alarm and uneasiness of this group is understandable. They wish it had never happened and want to act as if it didn't—somewhat in the manner of trying to ignore a doctor's bad report.

But why is full coverage of governmental failures important at all? For the answer, the essentials of representative government must be recalled. If such government is a pact between the rulers and the ruled, with the people claiming the right to change rulers, then the inviolability of the electoral system must be reasonably assured. The system is a peaceful means of change, of revolution. Rather than behead unsatisfactory Presidents, governors, mayors or representatives, we vote them out of office periodically and replace them with others.

The obvious key to representative government is the electoral system, and the essence of the electoral system must be a free choice arrived at through observation, information and the formation of clear opinion.

If one political group secures an unfair advantage over others, and if that advantage is secured by breaking the law, then it is best that the people know of it. If polls are rigged, if phony letters and telegrams are used to indicate support or disapproval or to disrupt a campaign, then the whole system is debased and the people are voting a lie.

Most important of all, if trusted institutions of government and sensitive offices—the Justice Department, the Federal Bureau of Investigation or the Central Intelligence Agency—are used to further the political cause of incumbents, then the basic concept of representative government is betrayed and an ugly corruption is being created.

All of which is why the American people do not dare to dismiss or ignore Watergate and its associated bad news—no matter how painful it becomes.

Los Angeles Times
Los Angeles, Calif., June 28, 1973

The list of White House "enemies," which John W. Dean III turned over to the Senate Watergate committee, makes a bizarrely disparate collection of names. Probably it marks the first time that Gov. George C. Wallace and Jane Fonda have found themselves in the same company. Included were senators and congressmen, newspapermen and Democratic political contributors.

Dean says the list was continually updated and embellished. It is not yet known what, if anything, was done with the list.

But it is known what was intended to be done with the list. White House memos proposed to use the power of the Internal Revenue Service to harass persons the White House thought of as enemies.

This plan was as shocking a proposal as we have encountered in the Watergate affair, for it was a proposal to use the great power of the government to intimidate citizens it considered unfriendly.

Most disturbing was the allegation by Dean that the White House arranged for the IRS to do a special audit on the tax returns of the Newsday editor in charge of an investigative series on the President's financial dealings with his friend, C. G. (Bebe) Rebozo. The editor, Robert Greene, confirmed that an audit had in fact been done and that no errors were found in his tax returns.

This charge requires the most thorough investigation. Required also is a thorough inquiry into whether any aspect of the plan proposed was put into effect. It is incumbent on the IRS to answer, and fast.

It will be most useful also to hear the results of the investigation ordered by Rep. Wilbur D. Mills (D-Ark.), chairman of the Joint Committee on Internal Revenue Taxation.

These memos illustrate again what had been glimpsed before the Watergate case broke, what has become glaringly obtrusive since then, that there were men in the Nixon Administration—and not just a few—who had absolutely no business being trusted with power, because they were simply incapable of understanding the necessary limits which law imposes on the exercise of power.

The list released by Dean was feverishly indiscriminating, a fact that speaks volumes about the cast of mind behind it. To Mr. Nixon's aides who compiled the list there seemed to be only "them" and "us," and that division having been settled, the next step, in the words of one of the memos accompanying the list, was simply to decide "how we can use the available federal machinery to screw our political enemies." The high-mindedness of that comment, the respect for due process and fair play it implies, pretty well sums things up.

What is one to make of the eager readiness of men in authority to exploit the police power of the state for petty and corrupt political purposes, a readiness that constituted a whole pattern of behavior? That is one question among the many that have emerged this week that the President has an obligation to respond to. His personal involvement in wrongdoing is for now an unproven allegation, but his overall responsibility for what has occurred in his Administration is a fact, and that fact must be addressed with greater candor and thoroughness than we have yet heard.

The Burlington Free Press

Burlington, Vt., June 28, 1973

AS THE WATERGATE circus continues in Washington this week, many observers are asking questions about the credibility of John Dean III, the fired White House counsel and principal accuser of President Nixon. Other observers are asking questions about the credibility of the President. And there are those observers, including ourselves, who feel compelled by the facts to question the credibility of a large portion of the nation's press.

A case in point: On Sunday President Nixon and Soviet leader Leonid Brezhnev completed a week of talks which produced agreements on a wide range of vital issues which directly affect the wellbeing of hundreds of millions of people for generations to come. On Monday the Ervin Committee heard the prepared testimony of Dean, one individual's version of the President's alleged involvement in a domestic political scandal.

The New York Times of Monday reported on the results of the Nixon-Brezhnev summit conference. The report on page one consisted of a five-column, three-line headline, two stories and two pictures. Two inside pages were devoted to the results of the week-long conference.

Then on Tuesday the Times reported on Dean's prepared testimony of the previous day. The report on page one consisted of a full banner, larger typeface, eight-column, three-line headline, four stories and two pictures. Five full inside pages and at least half of two other inside pages were devoted to the anti-Nixon testimony and its ramifications.

In other words, nearly three times as much coverage was accorded Dean's allegations as was given to the results of the summit conference. Yet the Times is always the first to heatedly deny there is any such thing as an anti-Nixon vendetta by the press.

Incredible. The facts are indisputable and they speak for themselves.

* * *

MEANWHILE, MANY readers will recall the coverage given Senator Goldwater several weeks ago when he was hammering away at the President to "come clean" on Watergate. One New York commentator, in fact, allowed as how he never doubted Goldwater's honesty and integrity even though he rarely agreed with the Senator's politics.

Well, last week, in Indianapolis, Goldwater delivered a speech in which he sharply ridiculed the attention given to the Watergate coverup, and compared this coverup with the one at Chappaquiddick. "If I had driven a woman off a bridge," he said, "I'd never hear the end of it."

Strange, but nowhere in the media have we found any mention whatever of Goldwater's Indianapolis speech, much less any commentary on it. And we read rather widely! This suggests, strongly, that personalities and ideology have a lot to do with coverage on sensitive political issues.

* * *

WE ARE NOT alone in questioning the credibility of a large portion of the nation's press.

The sharp criticism of the press role by the Times of London is well known. Less well known, perhaps, was the description of the Watergate coverage as a "personal witch-hunt" by the London Daily Mail. Similar sentiments have been expressed in print, here and abroad.

The credibility of the Watergate principals is an important question. But the credibility of the press is a vastly more important question at the moment. And it is a question which will be determined totally by the conduct of the press itself.

THE CHRISTIAN SCIENCE MONITOR

Boston, Mass., June 30, 1973

A rare salvo of applause interrupted the past week's Senate Watergate hearings. It responded to a burst of human fervor in keeping with American ideals. The episode echoed with the larger and potentially positive ramifications of Watergate worth considering as the nation turns from the Senate telethon for a while.

It was Republican Senator Weicker who got the applause. After a litany of the "proven or admitted" illegalities "accomplished by the executive branch of this government," he took a "partisan moment" to say:

"Republicans do not cover up. Republicans do not go ahead and threaten. Republicans do not go ahead and commit illegal acts. And God knows, Republicans don't view their fellow Americans as enemies to be harassed, but rather I can assure you that this Republican, and those that I serve with, look upon their fellow Americans as human beings to be loved and wanted."

✦ ✦ ✦

In effect, he was affirming that American party politics does not mean wrongdoing. His words recalled the earlier ones by Robert S. Strauss, chairman of the Democratic National Committee, who said of political espionage: "Everybody doesn't do it. Sound responsible professionals don't do it in the political process. Republicans don't do it, and the Democrats don't do it."

This is one point of Watergate — that it cannot be justified on the grounds that everybody does it. Nor can it be justified on the grounds that other individuals of whatever party have also done wrong in the past. Even allowing for an element of corruption in politics through the years, the emerging Watergate story suggests a kind and quantity of corruption of a new order of magnitude.

Which leads to the second point about Watergate — that as long as its memory lingers, any politician is going to think more than once before giving in to any temptation away from the proper standards of political behavior.

Chairman Ervin drove toward the definition of such standards when he cited the Constitution to Mr. Dean: " 'He' — that is the President — 'shall take care that the laws be faithfully executed.' Do you know anything that the President did or said . . . to perform his duty to see that the laws are faithfully executed in respect to what is called the Watergate affair?"

Mr. Dean replied to Senator Ervin that he had given the facts but declined to draw a conclusion on that question. It was a judicious reply. If only the President would come forward and say, "Yes, I did try to see the laws were faithfully executed, and here are the steps I took."

But whether or not a given man in the White House was faithful to that duty, Watergate reminds us that in a government of law it is not enough for responsible officials simply not to break the law. They must uphold the law, see that it is faithfully executed, establish by their attitudes and assumptions that this is what they expect of all those around them.

From all that has come out so far, it appears that Mr. Nixon has failed in this larger task of upholding the law, whatever his specific role in relation to the whole record of executive branch wrongs enunciated by Senator Weicker. There is hope in the fact that disclosure began before the White House went farther on the road being mapped in the Senate hearings. And the resulting ordeal for Mr. Nixon and those around him should at least have the effect of sensitizing those who follow to the vital necessity of maintaining the best tradition of American politics rather than any lesser standard.

Index

Index

This index includes references both to the news digest and the editorial section. Those index entries printed in a roman typeface refer to the news digest. They: (1) Describe the event; (2) Note the date of the event, e.g. 6-17-72; (3) Indicate the page, the marginal letter parallel to the item on the page, and the column in which the item appears in that order, e.g. 65D3. Index entries referring to editorials are printed in *italic type* after the news digest entries under the **boldface alphabetical headings.** Editorial entries refer only to the page number.